CONTEMPORARY WESTERN ARTISTS

PEGGY & HAROLD SAMUELS

BONANZA BOOKS
New York

Copyright © 1982 by Peggy and Harold Samuels.
All rights reserved.

This 1985 edition is published by Bonanza Books, distributed by Crown
Publishers, Inc., 225 Park Avenue South, New York, New York 10003, by
arrangement with Southwest Art, Inc., and Peggy and Harold Samuels.

Printed and bound in Italy

Library of Congress Cataloging in Publication Data
Samuels, Peggy.
  Contemporary Western artists.

1. Art, American—West (U.S.) 2. Art, Modern—20th century—West
(U.S.) 3. Artists—West (U.S.)—Biography. I. Samuels, Harold. II. Title.
N6525.S25 1985   709'.78 [B]   85-13963
ISBN 0-517-495946-9

ISBN: 0-517-459469
h g f e d c b

CONTENTS

PREFACE

This is a book that started out to be a biographical dictionary of today's leading artists of the American West and has ended as a celebration of the quality of the art. Although every imaginable kind of artistic training is represented, from study in Paris to no formal schooling of any sort, at least a hundred of these artists are demonstrably as talented as any other category of artists in the world.

Moreover, these Westerners are the most popular artists in the country today, and their work brings prices that are among the highest for living American artists of any persuasion, not only in gallery sales but in public auctions. The only thing these artists lack is recognition by their Eastern peers. They have not been elected to membership in the National Academy of Design despite their obvious eligibility.

The locus of this book is the West, which is really a state of mind expressive of the subject matter of the art rather than where the art was created or by whom. The time frame is today. Western artists who worked before 1950 are not here but are in our *Encyclopedia of Artists of the American West* published by Doubleday in 1976. Hard-edged cowboy art is included, whether of the earlier Remington/Russell era or of the contemporary cattle ranch, along with native Indian art, historical Western art, wildlife art, landscapes, regionalists, modernist art forms, and anything else that is at least nominally representational and Western and professional.

The book is composed of short biographies of the leading Western artists, along with photographs of them, examples of their signatures, and illustrations of their work in color. Presenting all of the information in one place gives viewers a peek at what type of person the artist is and what the work looks like, as well as providing reference data for libraries, galleries, and museums.

The artists in this book work full time at art, and they have met the requirements of listing in that they are members of an important association of Western artists like the Cowboy Artists of America, the National Academy of Western Art, or the Northwest Rendezvous Group, or, are represented by a major gallery, or, have been featured in *Artists of the Rockies, Art West,* or *Southwest Art* magazines through 1981. This is not a vanity press book. The credentials for admission are objective. No value judgment has been made as to inclusion or exclusion, and where possible, each biography has been presented in the words of the artist.

This is the first time that a biographical dictionary has been done for contemporary Western artists, despite the fact that the information has been needed for years. Sales of Western art are booming, not only among the affluent, but also among younger people who may start their collections with limited edition prints. Buyers need to have one place where they can look at an array of Western art, by the leading Western artists, to find the type of work that suits them.

In addition, the acquisition of Western art offers the potential for great monetary rewards. This book establishes the cast of characters for investment in contemporary Western art by providing a list of artists who can be assumed to be investment grade.

BASIC GUIDELINES FOR COLLECTING

The key to collecting Western art, whether for investment or for beauty, is to become a specialist in one aspect of the field, and the narrower that aspect is, the better. Concentrating on a speciality will generate a deeper expertise, allow prudent buying to begin sooner and result in a more satisfying, valuable, and exhibitable collection. The way to choose your specialty is to leaf through this book. Relax to what you see and try to reach out to the kind of artist, subject, style, or time period that is consonant with the kind of person you are.

You may, for example, want to interest yourself in one artist. This book will let you follow his career from its inception, to learn perhaps even in his words where he thinks he has been and where he is going. If you are involved in a particular place, in the Pacific Northwest or in Utah, or in Taos or in the Grand Canyon, the biographical data will tell you which artist works there. There are the artists of specific events, too, from Custer's Last Stand to the death of John Wayne. There are people painters who do Indian children, or Indian dancers, or Pueblo or Plains Indians, or early or modern cowboys, or prospectors, or cavalrymen, or farmers.

There are modernist painters who are uneasy about being in the same book with cowboy painters, and cowboy painters who accept all other painting styles as long as the artists themselves were once working cowboys. There are techniques like the 19th-century Hudson River School painters, or the photo-realists, or the pop artists, or the Impressionists. There are still life painters, landscape painters, portrait painters, and horse painters. There are sculptors of equally as many kinds, even including landscape sculptors, plus carvers, dyers, and collagists. There is literally no end to the possibilities for finding a specialization that will reflect your personal view and be tailored just for you.

The excuse of the uninformed collector who buys badly is generally something on the order of "I know what I like and that's what I buy." He fails to comprehend the second key to collecting Western art, that you should never buy any painting, print, or sculpture unless you know at least that the artist is a professional. You must avoid acquiring the works of students, amateurs, and Sunday painters. Works that are merely decorative will eventually have no more value than used furniture, and they will diminish your collection.

Some of the artists who are professionals can be identified by their listings in art reference books such as *Who's Who in American Art*, but acceptance into *Who's Who* is many times by chance and by choice rather than by talent. There is no defined objective standard for admission, and listing is generally the result of nominations by listees, not by selection. For that reason, an artist who is in *Who's Who* is a professional, but most of the finest Western artists are not included.

Substantially all of the leading Western artists are represented in this book, although a few are missing even here. Some could not be located and a few did not respond in time. When you are considering buying the work of an artist not listed here, you can judge the artist's professionalism by the same standards that were used in deciding which ones to include between the covers of this book, that is, by galleries, associations, and articles that have appeared in the leading Western art magazines.

If you ask the art expert what to buy, he will tell you to stick to quality, quality, quality. That is the third key, but unfortunately, the expert seldom explains what quality is. In buying Western art, quality means buying the best. There are a lot of bests that are involved, including the highest-priced best, the best at the time you

want to buy, the objective best, the expert best, the best by test, the artistic best, and so on; but, what you should be looking for is your personal best. Within your specialization and your budget, you have to weigh all of these other bests to pick the one piece that most suits your collecting pattern. Best is singular. Buy the one best piece that is available, rather than a group of pieces for the same price. Put all your eggs into the one-best basket.

The next consideration is the condition of the work of art itself, although condition generally relates to older art instead of contemporary work. The goal is to acquire the piece in "good" condition. This is not necessarily "good looking" condition, but original condition, the way the artist left it. Any alteration must have been performed in accordance with professional conservation practice and be documented by the conservator or the artist.

Authenticity is another problem that concerns older works of art rather than current pieces. Despite the fact that the work was done by a living artist, however, the collector might wish to write a letter to the artist, requesting authentication and enclosing a professionally taken photograph of the work that the artist can keep. The letter should be addressed through the artist's gallery to protect his privacy.

Condition and authenticity also relate to value. There is a decrease in value depending upon the degree and quality of any restoration, or upon whether there is any question at all as to authenticity. Ultimately, a damaged or impugned work may no longer have value as an investment, even though it may seem to be signed clearly and be in perfectly "good looking" condition.

Value is a result of appraisal, like the pre-sale estimates in an auction catalog or the evaluation needed to insure a painting or to settle an estate. These days, anyone can call himself an appraiser, from the framer or restorer who appraises high to justify his charges, to the antique dealer who knows a little about everything, or to a potential buyer who appraises low to reduce the price. Picking an appraiser is like picking a painter or a conservator. Get a listed professional who is familiar with the type of art you have, and do tell him the purpose of the evaluation.

Price is the appraisal put to proof. Price is what the work of art brings at an auction, for example, compared to the pre-sale estimate. At a gallery, price is the verification of the dealer's asking price that was based on his appraisal of what the market would bear. If you buy with "touch" and pick what is the best piece, the amount that you pay up to 150 percent of the value is not critical. Your best piece is unique, available just once in all likelihood, and you should not let it go for a modest difference in price that is still within your budget. The price will take care of itself, although you may have to wait a year or two to correct the overpayment.

How to buy is thus not much of a trick. What you buy takes precedence over the way that you do it, despite the cute buying tips that may be recommended to cover when you offer what, when you bid and how. There are only two usual places to purchase art, the private gallery and the public auction. Each has advantages and disadvantages.

The auction house once represented only the seller, who paid the entire commission on the sale price. The seller had the upper hand, participating in setting the pre-sale estimate and establishing the reserve. Today, the buyer generally pays half the commission, without having gained any advantage. He is forced to buy at auction because there is no other way to obtain the art that is knocked down. Buyer beware is the rule, but auctions are a necessary process.

At the end of this book, there is a list of the galleries and publishers that helped put the work together. To buy from a gallery, you must make the choice of a dealer carefully. You can expect that an established gallery will offer selected art with flexible purchasing arrangements. You can ask that a piece be held for you. You can request a search for a work that will meet your specifications, negotiate one-on-one, and obtain a detailed bill of sale guaranteeing signature and condition. You can even request exchange privileges or installment payments. None of these protective provisions is available at auction.

Selling may prove to be more difficult than buying. Many collectors who buy carefully get flustered when they sell. Some have had bad experiences with auctions, being turned away by indifference or by having reserves renegotiated just before sale time. Others are afraid to place art on consignment with galleries because they have heard stories about failure to make payment when due and about pieces shipped around the country from dealer to dealer. Selling is thus another ball game, but no collector truly understands art until he sells something. He should really try to find a personally acceptable selling route through established galleries or auction houses.

The function of this book, then, is to aid in the process of collecting art by providing information on the leading Western artists who are working today and on their styles and subjects. The field of contemporary Western art is constantly broadening. It is no longer just the Western artists working in the tradition of Remington and Russell, the ones whose authority is vested in their "having been thar" before 1950. It also goes beyond the wave of Eastern illustrators who migrated this way and took the center stage despite being criticized as ignorant of authentic Western practices and gear.

Instead, the core of Western artists is now the regionalists, the artists born or raised in the West who do the West because they live here. These are the ones who look up to Andrew Wyeth or Nikolai Fechin rather than to Remington or Russell, and who went to the Art Center College in Los Angeles rather than to the Art Students League in New York City. They live in the small towns in the Southwest, the Mountain States, and the Far West, although some do inhabit the art colonies like Santa Fe and Sedona.

As these Western regionalists take over, it will be seen that technically they are the equivalent in talent to the Eastern and Southern and Mid-Western regionalists who constitute the American Art establishment. Soon, they will be accepted by the Eastern museums and critics, elected to membership in the National Academy of Design, and assimilated into the American art world. Western sculptors have already taken the lead in this.

The frontier mentality of the Western artists and galleries will be dissipated, just as the geographic and economic Western frontier has gone. Even after Western artists have become national artists, however, what will still remain is the uniqueness of Western subject matter, the enduring Indians and cowboys and wildlife and terrain that are spread across the whole of this book.

Abbett, Robert K. Realist painter of outdoor and sporting scenes, born in Hammond, Indiana in 1926 and living in Oakdale Farm, Connecticut since 1970 and in Scottsdale, Arizona. "I learned quite quickly," he points out, "that I am not an artist who reconstructs historical scenes. I have to relate to things I can see and experience. My responsibility as an artist is to summon up feelings and experiences that have also happened to others. When they look at my paintings these sensations re-emerge and then my work has been done successfully.

"When I got out of the Navy, I decided to study art at the University of Missouri. After graduation, I got an agency job in Chicago and studied at the Chicago Academy's night school. Next I apprenticed at an illustration studio, a system beneficial to beginnners, like what vaudeville was to show business. I moved to New York in the early fifties and was a free lance illustrator until 1970. When we moved up to the Connecticut farm, I had to start painting it immediately, and began to sell through galleries. Secondly, I did 'Luke' the English setter as a commission, and that painting opened up whole new directions.

"The most important aspect of painting is something almost invisible called 'believability.' In addition to having all the elements correct, I want the subject to look so at home within its background that we as viewers are entrapped by the scene." Abbett's Arizona home is near where his grandfather taught school. He is listed in *Who's Who in American Art*, is a member of the Society of Illustrators and the Society of Animal Artists, has been written up in *Southwest Art* twice, *Artists of the Rockies*, and *Sports Afield*, and is represented by The May Gallery.

Abeita, Jim. Traditional painter of the Navajo people and the reservation landscape, born in Crownpoint, Arizona in 1947 and returned to Arizona in 1972. "I paint all that I see," he says, "all about my people, their way of life, their joys and sorrows. My art is 'You Alone,' to let the natural feelings flow. The subject matter and the drafting are not as important as the command to paint that is the motivating force.

"I started drawing on grocery sacks at the age of three, inspired by my uncle Joe Charlie who has been an influence on me throughout my life." Before Abeita could write his name, he was drawing objects that were familiar. While still in grade school, he would stand a horse against a flat rock and trace the horse's shadow on the rock, then fill in the details. In high school in Gallup, New Mexico, and Salt Lake City, he won student art honors and later attended the American Academy of Art in Chicago, comleting a two-year course in nine months.

In 1972 when he had been in Chicago for five years, he decided that he wanted to come home to the reservation for the uncomplicated ways. He had already painted the memories of his childhood in studies that he threw away and then was impressed when his wife fished them out of the garbage and sold them. The canvas is where he plays out his life of color and imagination. From the first minute he gets into a painting, he is "psyched up." It is fun when the "flow" is on, but after the painting is finished, he is through with it. "It has been done." Abeita has won major awards in Indian art shows and no longer enters many competitions. Written up in *Southwest Art*, July 1974, he is represented by Tanner's Indian Arts.

Jimmy Abeita, SERENE AUTUMN, oil, 24 x 36

Robert Abbett, WAITING AT HAWKEYE, oil, 27 x 40

Abram, Paul Jr. Realist painter and sculptor of the historic American West, born in Bloomington, Indiana in 1933 and living in Scottsdale, Arizona since 1975. "The American tradition," he believes, "owes the fur traders the recognition which has thus far gone to the cowboys. They broke the ground in civilizing America, and their efforts have long gone unnoticed. I'm doing my best to see that they get credit due."

The son of a landscape and floral painter, Abram says, "I had an interest in art since my early school years and entered into commercial art (lettering, sign work, window displays) during the first years after high school. In 1963, I moved to Houston where I worked as general manager of a billboard operation. During that time, I began to develop my talent as an artist in watercolor paintings and pencil drawings and had my work on display at a local gallery. As my skills improved, I began to focus more on my painting, until 1974 when I left my job and started painting exclusively.

"My work now includes watercolor, mixed media, and oil paintings, and I have just released my first bronze sculpture. Each picture begins as an idea sketched on paper, and I enjoy doing my own photography, staging difficult ideas through the use of models, authentic costumes, and weapons." His paintings have been featured on magazine covers such as *Western Horseman*. During 1981, he received gold awards for mixed media at the George Phippen Memorial Day show and for best show and best watercolor in the American Indian and Cowboy Artist show, and was elected a member of the AICA. He is represented by the Overland Trail Galleries and Newsom's Gallery.

Abril, Ben. Impressionist oil and watercolor painter of Los Angeles, born there in 1923 and living in La Canada, California. "People seem to relate to what I paint," he declares. "They will say, 'Hey, I've been there!' Or, 'I've seen that before.' And it's the color, too! They seem to like the color!" Abril explains that "I have always been fascinated by old buildings, the way the light plays on the forms, the patterns that sun and shadow throw on the textured walls."

Abril studied at Los Angeles' Art Center School, Glendale School of Art, Otis Art Institute, and Chouinard's School of Art following two years in England with the U.S. Air Force in World War II. He worked nights at the post office to be able to go to school and paint by day. For ten years, he was a color consultant to the County, and afterwards was a designer for motion pictures and television. When he first began to record the urban scene, "setting up for a day's painting was easier then. Just pick your curb or street corner! Not too much traffic to worry about. No great hordes of people, but still, enough of them to stop and watch an artist at work. Some days a passerby might ask, 'How much do you want for that picture?' I sold quite a few that way, for five or ten dollars apiece."

In 1969, the Los Angeles County History Museum bought 36 paintings from a retrospective exhibition. Abril's work is in 22 public collections, and he has had fifteen one-person shows. He is represented by Biltmore, attracting more than 600 people to an opening. He is listed in *Who's Who in America*, is a member of the National Watercolor Society, and was profiled in *Southwest Art*, September 1980.

Ben Abril, WILLOW SPRINGS, oil, 30 x 40

Paul Abram, SLATS & SKEETER, oil, 24 x 40

Acheff, William. Trompe l'œil oil painter of Indian artifacts, born in Anchorage, Alaska in 1947 and living in Taos, New Mexico since 1973. "I paint Indian objects," he says, "because I relate to them, maybe because I have some Indian blood and because I was close to my grandmother, but that's not the point. It's the ethnic quality of the artifacts. There's a purity in them. Nothing's manufactured by machine. There sits a pot. The whole mood of what went into making that pot is a story, and that's what I want to capture.

"I moved to California in the early 50s. Had taken numerous art classes in high school for the simple reason that I enjoyed art. Never had any intentions of going to art school even after the encouragement of my high school art teachers. Went to barber college in San Francisco in 1965. There I met artist Roberto Lupetti in the barber shop in 1968 and started taking art lessons from him in 1969, again for my enjoyment. After a month or so, he said he would like to train me on a more serious level because he felt I possessed the receptiveness and ability that he was looking for in a student.

"After six months of very regular training, five days a week and two days to cut hair, I would see him twice a month for the next two and a half years for his very enlightening criticism. Then I'd drive to Sausalito and sell a small canvas for $15 and feel just great. I moved to Taos out of curiosity at the Southwestern art movement and my first major show there in 1978 at Shriver Gallery was a complete sellout. In 1981, my Western Heritage Sale painting 'Yellow Rose of Texas' sold for $45,000 at auction." Acheff was written up in *Southwest Art*, February 1981.

William Acheff, TEWA SPIRIT, oil on linen, 38 x 30

AXEL AMUCHÁSTEGUI

Adams, Loren D. Representational oil painter of the Pacific Coast from Mexico to British Columbia, born in Linton, Indiana in 1945 and living in Vancouver, British Columbia, Canada. "When I was a child, my family was not well-to-do," he recalls, "but we were rich in music, art, and religion. I studied theology in college, intending to become a minister, and won awards for both paintings and the classical accordion. I preached and people responded, and yet the strongest response came through my paintings.

"In the late 1960s, I began to fall away from church doctrine at the same time that my painting began to move forward. I resigned as a hospital orderly the day after I sold my first painting, and three weeks later I was in a group showing. Within three months, I had an agent and two galleries. I paint because painting is what I do best and love the most and because through my art I reach an identity with others that I am unable to achieve myself.

"I know I could paint any number of subjects, but no other subject has the same impact on me that the sea does. I can remember as a small boy, standing for hours on the seashore—watching, feeling, hearing, imagining. As a man now, I do the same things for hours on end. The sea draws me and repels me, terrifies me and exhilarates me." He adds that "the transparent wave has become a fad in California. Someone is going to put out a $12.95 paint-by-number kit that shows how to paint that transparent wave, and then every seascape painter is going to have to start painting the sea again instead of lighted translucence with foam laced doilies." Written up in *Southwest Art*, June 1976 and April 1980, his publishers include American Masters Foundation and his galleries, Gainsborough and The Winters.

Amuchastegui, Axel. Realist painter of wildlife in South and North America and Africa in acrylic, born in Cordoba, Argentina in 1921 and living in Buenos Aires. "It is more usual," he states, "to paint that wonderful North American bird the Canada goose silhouetted against the sky in its characteristic V formation of spring or fall migration, but my choice was the nesting goose, influenced by my first meeting with the bird. It was in England where I met my Canada goose in a collection of exotic birds. The magnificence of the bird caused me to think of individual birds rather than the collective and anonymous V. Somehow the eggs became the symbol of determination to survive so I have tried to make the eggs throb with hidden life while the goose confronts us with dignity."

Because he wanted to be a pilot, Amuchastegui's (pronounced Ah-moo-chast-uh-gee with a hard "g") family sent him to the university to study aeronautical engineering. In the second year, he was taught watercolor technique to render aircraft sections, and that began his love affair with art. For the next few years, he worked at making landscape renderings from topographical measurements while the bird and animal drawings he did as a hobby were exhibited in the state gallery. A publisher who saw the drawings employed Amuchastegui as an illustrator, a job he held for 20 years while painting South American wildlife as a hobby.

When he decided to paint full time, he visited New York City with his paintings and his exhibition at Kennedy Galleries sold out. Three limited edition books of his birds and mammals of South America were published in London, and he is the author and illustrator of *Birds of the World*. His prints are published by Mill Pond Press.

Amundsen, Richard. Painter and sculptor of wildlife, born in the Sacramento Valley, California in 1928 and living in Bozeman, Montana. "Making paintings of birds, fish, and mammals requires constant study," he observes, "and in addition to my extensive library, I am an avid outdoorsman. Much of the accuracy in my paintings comes from personal experience through hunting, fishing, dog training, picture taking, and research trips."

Raised and educated in San Francisco, Amundsen "at an early age learned to see into, not look at, nature's wonders." His career began in San Francisco as an illustrator for an art service. In 1963, he decided to free lance, specializing in wildlife. While living in Seattle, he used a New York City agent to obtain commissions from major publishers like Golden Books and Random House, from *Field and Stream* (for 16 years), and from *Reader's Digest* and *Outdoor Life*. In addition, he has done Remington Arms wildlife calendars and Leanin' Tree Christmas cards.

As part of the transition to fine arts painter, Amundsen moved to Cody, Wyoming where Harold McCracken called him "tops in your field." He finally landed in Montana "near two of the best wildlife laboratories in the country, Yellowstone and Glacier National Parks." His commissioned painting of Theodore Roosevelt in the high country was presented to President Nixon, earning Amundsen the Presidential Seal. He has lectured on "animals in art" at the Buffalo Bill Historical Center, shown with the Northwest Rendezvous group, and won the National Wild Turkey Federation's 1978 stamp competition. Now also modeling bronze statuettes of wildlife, he exhibits at Trailside Galleries.

Richard Amundsen, HOMESTEAD ROAD, acrylic, 30 x 40

Axel Amuchastegui, NESTING CANADA GOOSE, acrylic, 31½ x 24

Loren D. Adams, FREEDOM SPIRIT, oil, 30 x 50

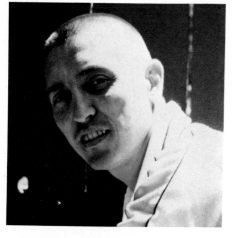

Anderson, Dennis P. Representational oil painter of wildlife, born in Everett, Washington in 1940 and living in Eldorado Springs, Missouri. "I'm really more of an impressionist now than a realist," he explains. "What interests me is the impression the animal makes on me rather than the reality, the reproduction of details, or the way other people might see him. I find I can achieve extraordinary results with my color effects.

"Animals have always captivated me. When I was a kid, I often sent off for them through the mail—rabbits, raccoons, foxes. I'd keep them around home, but they were more than pets. They were a source of art. Once I was old enough to get a drivers license, I was able to get back in the Cascades. In the off season, I'd go through the motions of a person with a gun, only I used a camera." Following high school, he worked for a veterinarian. "I took a class in commercial art and the instructor advised me that the best place for me was at art school, so I went."

After two years at Art Center School, his money ran out and he worked as a scientific illustrator and for a greeting card company until he left because "the company didn't feel that I should be doing outside work. I continued getting free-lance assignments, but the big problem was that I could never get any assignments for wildlife, so I just stopped and started painting wildlife the way I've always wanted to." He tries to keep "four or five paintings going at once. That way, you don't mind throwing one out if it isn't working right for you. If you only work on one, you get married to it." Written up in *Southwest Art*, April 1978, he is a member of the National Academy of Western Art and is represented by Wildlife World Art Museum and American Legacy Gallery.

Anderson, James P. Sculptor of marble figures including Western, born in Tulsa, Oklahoma in 1929 and living in Davenport, Iowa since 1979. "My work is not restricted to Western art," Anderson says, "or to any other style or period." At the beginning of his career, he sculpted realistic classical pieces that he kept to himself, as well as the modern pieces he exhibited: "I would lie like a dog trotting in the snow about my classical work. If anyone found out, I said I just did it for the money, but I can come out of the closet now."

A professor of art and a writer on art, Anderson received his BA from Eastern New Mexico University in 1954, his MA from Hardin-Simmons in 1960, and his Ed.D from Vanderbilt in 1965. He went to Italy in 1973 for the casting of his commissioned bronze statue of Benjamin Franklin. He returned to Italy in 1974 and since then "has selected marble as my medium because I love the beautiful Italian statuario and believe that impediment, labor, difficulty, and uniqueness constitute a higher nobility in art."

Despite the volume of Western subject matter that Anderson has modeled, he says that "to me there isn't any difference in doing Western subjects than any other. The artist does what he has the ability to do, the subjects that are meaningful and part of his experience, and he tries to be original in thought and composition. Some would argue that all the Western subjects have been done and that now the style is what is all important. I don't believe this for a moment." Public commissions and museum holdings are in Australia, Italy, Iowa, Arizona, California, Ohio, and Kentucky. Anderson is listed in *Who's Who in American Art* and is represented by Husberg Fine Arts Gallery.

Anderson, Troy. Traditional Cherokee painter of contemporary realism in acrylic, born in Siloam Springs, Arkansas in 1948 and living there in 1982. "When I was going to school," he recalls, "I took figure drawing. I told myself that when I got through with that, I would never do another face, body, or anything like that. Now, that's about what all my paintings have. I combine rich colors, strong patterns, and expressive figures to portray the great pride, emotion, spirit, and reverence for life that are inherent in the American Indian."

Raised in Arkansas and Oklahoma, Anderson earned a BS in art from West Texas State University and played football through 1969. For three years, he taught art and coached in Texas and Kansas schools, then returned to Arkansas where he worked for a canning company until 1979 when he established himself as a full-time artist. He had begun painting Indian subjects in 1973, but says that "art is just like any other business. You have to work up to a certain point before you can jump off. I had to build up my confidence and my clientele.

"The hard part is getting the basic colors on there. It takes time and it's monotonous. The fun part is when I can start putting value down and some detail. I hardly ever throw away a picture. If I get a splotch on it, I can make a tree out of it or a redbird. Sometimes an accident works out for the better. I just now feel like I'm getting into what is for me real good painting, but I'm still growing." Anderson is a member of the American Indian and Cowboy Artists, won its gold medal in 1981, and has also won prizes at Indian shows since 1978. His own studio sells his paintings and prints.

Troy Anderson, MOTHER OF CORN, acrylic/alpha mat, 20 x 16

James Anderson, THE ARMY SCOUT, marble, h 22, w 12, d 21½

Dennis Anderson, BULL OF THE WOODS, oil, 24 x 34

17

Andraud, Norma. Printmaker of embossed etchings of American Indian rituals and portraits, born in Phoenix, Arizona, in 1941 and living in Los Angeles, California, since 1970. "I'm very involved with circles," she stresses, "because I feel that a circle always leaves one in suspension. I believe that whatever you put out will come back. This is one way of expressing the central energy. The circle is very challenging. It looks simple but is extremely difficult to work with."

Raised in Phoenix, she recalls her fantasy of an Indian behind every boulder. At 16, she won a scholarship to the Traphagen School of Design where she studied until 1958, then became a free-lance illustrator in New York City's Greenwich Village. In 1966, she also studied at the Ecole des Beaux Arts in Paris, had shows at Paris galleries, and worked for *Women's Wear Daily* during a five-year stay abroad. After her move to California, she attended Santa Monica College.

Her choice of subject was not French but American Indian. "The Indian is very important to me," she points out. "I don't think it was a conscious choice that my subject matter is Indian. I feel very torn at times, as though I have a foot in the past. I have a very close rapport with my subject matter. Their color, beauty, and simplicity is my center of energy, my circle, my sun. Developing a drawing around the subject matter, I do a tremendous amount of research relating to family relationships, structure of buildings, patterns of rugs, and jewelry. I do at least 50 drawings for each work, continually changing shape and perspective. If I could, I would draw 24 hours a day."Written up in *Southwest Art*, July 1979, she is represented by Robert Andraud Inc.

Annesley, (Robert H.) Bob. Sculptor, painter, and printmaker of "the mysterious and legendary world of his Cherokee forefathers," born in Norman, Oklahoma, in 1943 and living in Houston, Texas, since 1966. "I'm more Irish than Cherokee, and I'm proud of both," he explains, "but for some reason, I've always been drawn to my Indian-ness. I've tried to live as close to the Indian way as possible, as much by choice as by blood.

"My father was of Cherokee-Irish descent from the east side of the Cookson Hills in Oklahoma. My Irish mother is descended from a Texas frontier ranching family. With all this Western heritage, I thought I would surely become an all-American cowboy, but after being stomped by the first bull I ever tried to ride, I decided to tell the story of these amazingly durable people through my art. I can't really remember when I wasn't involved in some form of artistic expression. I was drawing long before I knew what that word meant.

"I won my first national award in painting when I was only fourteen and had my first two-man show when I was eighteen. This encouraged me to continue my formal training in fine art at the University of Oklahoma and Oklahoma City University. I realized my dream of a full time career in fine art in 1973 and have received over fifty major awards since that time. I work in bronze sculpture, silverpoint and 24 karat goldpoint drawings, watercolors, and mixed-media paintings. In 1976, I became the first artist given a one-man retrospective by the Cherokee Nation." Written up in *Southwest Art*, June 1981, his prints are published by Annesley & Associates and his work is available through the Art Market and Indian Paintbrush Gallery.

Norma Andraud, EARTH TO CLAY, embossed etching with hand coloring, 22 x 30

Bob Annesley, bronze, "TSO BATSO"—TO THE ROCKS, h 12, w 13, d 10

Antis, Harry E. Realistic painter of North American big game, waterfowl, and upland game birds, born in Michigan in 1942 and living in Ann Arbor, Michigan. "As a teenager," he recalls, "I marveled at all the wildlife paintings that adorned the covers and pages of the sporting magazines and envisioned myself joining that gallant group of painters, such as greats John Clymer and Bob Kuhn. However, commerical art is where I got started after one year of formal art training at the Society of Arts & Crafts in Detroit, for as I soon learned, there was not a great demand at that time for wildlife painters.

"Starting out as an apprentice in an art studio and sticking to it, did wonders for me. As I worked up into the commercial illustration field over the next eight years, it disciplined and sharpened what artistic abilities I had and it paid the bills regularly. The one thing it didn't do, however, was to satisfy that still burning desire to paint the wildlife and wilderness world. Painting in the evenings and on weekends just didn't satisfy that desire. Finally, in 1970, I gave up on the commercial art field.

"Living and working as a wildlife artist is not just a profession, but rather a dedication. Birds and animals, mountains, forests and fields with all their wonder and excitement are a constant source of inspiration. By now, I have found it was all worth it. I have joined that august company of artists who have plied their trade of painting animals. In the last ten years, 35 different paintings have been reproduced in prints, all of which are sold out." A member of Wildlife Artists International, he is represented by Chrisman Wildlife Art and Trade Wind Galleries.

Armstrong, J. Chester. "Slightly stylized" realist sculptor of wildlife in wood, born in Berkeley, California, in 1948 and living in Sisters, Oregon. "The further we get from the forest floor," he believes, "the less human we become. As a humanist, I see man's fate tied to an ever-clearer understanding of himself-in-his-world. Fundamental to this understanding is an appreciation of the Earth and Earth-forms as the 'Mothering Power.' The North American Indian consciousness is a reflection of this attitude.

"As a kid, I grew up with wood-carvings—primitive masks, temple carvings, and divinity scenes. The other, outer world was represented there on the shelf to finger with wonder, and as a kid, I did. Those carvings possessed a simple power that was as close to a sense of reverence as any I had. At 21, I traveled to Central America in search of an ancestral culture living close to the land. Out of the corner of my eye an understanding grew.

"Starting again from the beginning, I moved to rural Vermont. I learned to be a tool user, pioneer style, and to work wood. It was a sense of wilderness that drew me back to the Pacific Northwest. I ended up living in the woods, time on my hands, trees all around, and a world waiting for some response. Wood is a resistive medium, like stone. Beginning from the first cut, all else follows. Chain saw bellowing, the raw round block yields to a line, lines take on the suggestion of form, and saw gives way to routers and chisels and sandpaper and the shape shows the nuances of life. I show my work personally on the Western art show circuit, have also shown in the Rendezvous and Ace Powell Galleries, and was featured in *Southwest Art*, April 1980. When the world chances to speak, I listen."

Arnett, Toni. Realistic oil painter of "still-lifes, street scenes and farm and ranch scenes," born in Dallas, Texas, in 1940 and living in Lubbock, Texas. "In my paintings," she says, "I try to capture the beauty of nature which I find in the effect of sunlight on different textures such as leaves, petals, and all foliage. I try to suspend my subject in an atmosphere. I want my flowers to seem like they are in a garden rather than cut or in a vase. My backgrounds are subtle. With strong contrasts in value and color, I push the subject forward so it is immediately accessible, almost to the touch. I try to portray a subject as more vivid and alive than it appears in nature.

"At ten, I moved with my family to the country where I spent much of my time either riding horses or drawing them. For my paintings of flowers, I would grind petals to make the various colors. A graduate of Texas Tech University in 1962, I only began painting formally in 1967 and studied privately. Today, my husband and I are managing a ranch, and I continue to select subjects from the rural experience, weathered chairs, patchwork quilts, antique lace, old utensils, to make the commonplace special.

"Each of my paintings is complete, the background is meticulously conceived and executed as the primary subject. I create the atmosphere in which the object exists by juxtaposing warm and cool colors and by carefully determining the direction of each brushstroke. Thus, the environment of a painting seems alive, filled with energy and movement, not flat or static. I exhibit regularly at the Driscol Gallery and participated in the 1981 show held in the Beijing Exhibition Center, China."

Harry Antis, HIGH COUNTRY BILLIES, oil/acrylic, 26 x 30

J. Chester Armstrong, A FLURRY OF WINGS AND TALONS, maple (one piece), h 3¾ ft, w 3 ft

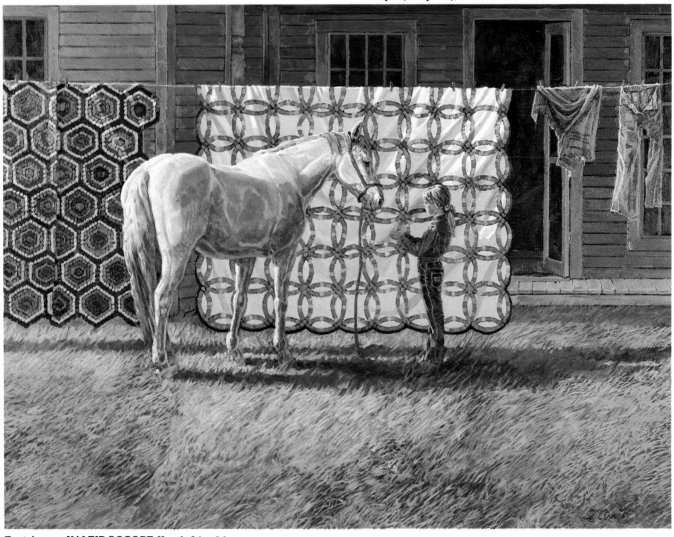

Toni Arnett, KALEIDOSCOPE II, oil, 24 x 36

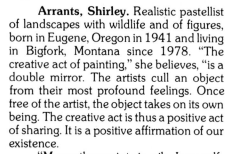

Arrants, Shirley. Realistic pastellist of landscapes with wildlife and of figures, born in Eugene, Oregon in 1941 and living in Bigfork, Montana since 1978. "The creative act of painting," she believes, "is a double mirror. The artists cull an object from their most profound feelings. Once free of the artist, the object takes on its own being. The creative act is thus a positive act of sharing. It is a positive affirmation of our existence.

"My mother paints in oils. I am self-educated in art since grade school. In high school in Kalispell, Montana, I was a first place winner in art competitions and I have recently taken a workshop under Ned Jacob. I paint in a realistic fashion, trying to illustrate, more dramatically, the colors and moods one misses in everyday life. I enjoy painting the Indian people because of their strong features, use of bold colors, and historical importance."

She asserts that she paints because "my soul tells me to." Her credo is to "absorb as much education as possible, but never relinquish your own approach toward the accomplishment of an artwork. Quality rather than quantity is important." She has been painting full time since 1978 and is listed in *American Artists of Renown*. She began exhibiting at invitational shows in 1977, was in four such shows in 1978, and by 1980 was best in show for painting in three shows and she won the purchase award in a fourth. She is a member of the American Artists of the Rockies and is represented by eight galleries including Trailside Galleries.

Asher, James. Representational painter, sculptor, and printmaker of the present Indian cultures of Arizona and New Mexico, born in Butler, Missouri, in 1944 and living in Scottsdale, Arizona, since 1974. "I try to create a romanticized version of *my* West," Asher comments, "not a historical version. The people and the situations I work with are those which I have personally witnessed in one way or another. Very seldom do I go back to a period prior to my own life span."

Born in farm country where his parents ran a store, Asher recalls that "we ate a lot of wild game that I caught, also plenty of fish." Elementary school was a one-room "superb place for a boy to be." He took art courses in high school, earned a science degree with a major in art from Central Missouri University, and then attended the Art Center School in Los Angeles where he felt closer to the illustration tenets of realism than to the fine arts' expressionism. He was employed as an art director in Los Angeles, was drawn to the subtleties of the Pueblo environment, and moved to the Southwest where he extended his scope to the Navajos.

He also travels to Mexico and the Mediterranean, feeling that "the more cultures of the world I come to know, the better able I will be to represent them in my art and the deeper my understanding of my own Southwest will be." In oil painting, he points out that he adds "glazes to certain features because of the brilliance they add to the color and because they suggest the appearance of true sunlight." At the "Preview '80" auction in Dallas, Asher's painting "Waiting by the Gate" sold for $10,000. He was featured in *Southwest Art*, October 1980, and exhibits at Trailside Galleries.

Asmar, Alice. Painter, printmaker, and weaver whose "work is a maximal expression of thoughts, feelings, and imagery, centering on the mysteries of being, with praises to God," born in Flint, Michigan about 1930 and living in Burbank, California. "I paint Indians," she notes, because "Indians are America's real ecologists. Seeing all animals as friends, they do not permit sport hunting. Respecting all phases of nature as gifts of the Great Spirit, they do not desecrate their environment."

Of Lebanese descent, she moved as a baby to Portland, Oregon. She started drawing and painting in early childhood, winning awards and recognition before the age of ten. After receiving her BA magna cum laude from Lewis and Clark College, she studied painting and sculpting at the University of Washington, earning a BFA in 1951. Employed briefly at Boeing Aircraft as a draftsman, she taught at Lewis and Clark College before winning a grant to the Ecole des Beaux Arts in Paris.

After studying and traveling through Europe and the Near East, she settled in southern California in the early 1960s, and from 1966 to the present has painted New Mexico themes of Indian ceremonials, Indian portraits, landscapes, and missions in a "highly personal style combining the intimacy of lines with fluid shapes which evoke a feeling of transparency and plastic rhythms, mysterious and very close to nature." Her work is in a large number of public collections and she has received many one-artist shows. Listed in *Who's Who in American Art*, she was featured in *Southwest Art* November 1978. Her graphics are distributed by Circle Art Corp., and she is represented by Palmcrest House Art and Investors Gallery Ltd.

Alice Asmar, ZIA CORN DANCERS—TURQUOISE CLAN, casein/Haruki, 32 x 20

Shirley Arrants, A LIGHT FROM THE WINDOW, pastel, 26 x 20

James Asher, CARMEN, oil/canvas, 30 x 36

C. ASPEVIG

Rogers Aston

W H Atkins

Aspevig, Clyde. Oil painter of the vanishing Montana countryside, born in Rudyard, Montana in 1951 and living in Ballantine, Montana since 1976. "The Montana terrain offers everything," Aspevig asserts, "from spectacular mountains to almost desert-like conditions. You'd have to be pretty picky to run out of things to paint here. I'm so thankful that I grew up in that area. It was so unspoiled and free. And my upbringing provided me with a strong moral foundation. Anyone who's lived in the country knows what I'm talking about. It's just the way things are."

Raised in a farming community on the Canadian border, Aspevig became adult at 12 when his father died. He left the farm to attend Eastern Montana College in Billings, dropped out to spend an isolated winter in the Bear Paw Mountains, then returned for a degree in art education "so I'd have a profession to fall back on." After one year of teaching in Sandy, Oregon, high school, he came back to Montana to paint full time. He works up to ten hours a day, blocking in a landscape in the field and finishing it in the studio. The Missouri and Yellowstone Rivers are favorite locales.

Aspevig believes that Montana is "one of the last pristine areas in the country," and now it is being strip mined. "We need to be very cautious about how we use our resources. Land like this is so fragile," he emphasizes, and he has donated prints to an environmental organization. His publisher is Salt Creek and he is a member of the Northwest Rendezvous Group. Featured in *Art West* July 1980 and *Art Business News* October 1981, he is represented by Trailside Galleries.

Aston, Rogers. Realistic sculptor of bronze statuettes of the Old West, born in Cedar Rapids, Iowa, in 1918 and living in Roswell, New Mexico. According to Aston, the painter "Peter Hurd once told me that 'an artist must see with the heart as well as the eye.' Good art is an expression more of the spirit than of the substance. I hope my bronzes will speak of respect for those who preceded us in the West."

Raised on a ranch, he rode on horseback to a one-room school. After military service, he has spent almost 40 years in oil exploration, including 21 years as manager of the historic John Chisum South Spring Ranch, south of Roswell. His personal American Indian and Western art collection is in the Roswell Museum. As a sculptor, he says that "I realize that I must observe with great accuracy as I work. I feel that I must be aware of not only the physical composition of my work but, equally, I must look for a spiritual quality.

"I have such a deep admiration for the hardy souls who carved a mighty nation out of a rough and unforgiving wilderness. I hope to catch the vitality and the dedication of the free spirits who made America. My interest is not limited to the Anglo, but extends to the Indian and the Spanish-American heritage that is so rich a part of our culture. My mind spins with figures just yearning to be reborn with dignity and character. It is a big dream, but for the first 52 years of my life, I bottled this spark inside and worked to give my family the material comforts. I now hope to devote much of my remaining life to trying to say in bronze what I feel inside." Aston is represented by Trailside Galleries.

Atkins, William H. Oil painter of the Upper East Verde River landscape near the foot of the Mogollon Rim in Arizona, born in Columbus, Mississippi, in 1926 and living in Payson, Arizona, since 1971. "Like a concert pianist, painting for a living means more than practicing on Sundays or weekends. It must be the most important activity of my life. Even family must come second. I have taught students who had enormous talent but who because of good looks or social status would never be able to devote their lives to art as a career.

"I have never wanted to be anything but an artist as long as I can remember," he adds. Bill Atkins came West in the 1940s to earn a degree in fine arts at the University of New Mexico with Randall Davey and later studied with O.E. Berninghaus and Ken Adams in Taos in 1950. His forte is the intimate, secluded, quiet spot. As a teacher, he "believes that students are a great source of inspiration for his art. It's as though the teacher were to take refresher courses himself. All artists would benefit from teaching, if only two hours a week."

On work habits, he points out that there are "artists who say that they work eight to five as they would in any other job. This is too long for inspirational achievement. For me, five hours of concentrated work per day is my limit as a steady diet. Most days I work less, but every day. There is a conversation that goes on between the artist and the canvas. I hear it distinctly when all is going well. If I work too long, the butterfly disappears from my shoulder." Atkins' "Amber Grove at Verde Glen" sold for $4,600 at *Preview '81*. He is represented by Trailside Galleries.

Rogers Aston, LOS CIBOLEROS, bronze, h 4", base 1½"

Clyde Aspevig, COTTONWOOD CREEK, oil, 24 x 30

Bill Atkins, EAST VERDE RIVER, view 4, oil, 30 x 48

Douglas Atwill

Keith W. Avery

Atwill, Douglas E. Contemporary acrylic painter of New Mexican landscapes, born in Pasadena, California, in 1933 and living in Santa Fe, New Mexico, since 1969. "I'm obviously interested in the design of my canvas," he points out, "rather than the emotion. I don't have a pre-conceived idea of a scene. My feelings don't vary that much from painting to painting, yet somewhere in every painting I get interested in the paint itself. The best of my paintings are those where at some point I left the motif and got into the paint."

A fifth generation Californian, he served in the Army in Europe, then attended the Universita per Stranieri in Perugia, Italy, for a year. After graduating from the University of Texas in 1961, he spent 1962 in further study there before working as an art director in Texas and Virginia. His first solo show was in 1963 in Arizona. In Santa Fe, he says that "I find myself more disciplined and doing more work than when I was in advertising. I hate to miss a day of painting." He calls himself gregarious and has his studio right in town.

He paints from 7 A.M. to 1 P.M. After that, he declares, "I build a house for myself and if someone buys it, that's okay. I get excited by first snows or a first sunny day. They have a fresh look. Although I do sketch with pen and ink, taking photographs is my preferred way of working. I compose with the lens, then I further refine the composition by matting the photographic print. Pattern is what I look for." He squeezes the acrylics onto paper plates that weigh several pounds before he throws them out, and completes about 100 paintings a year while "throwing out another 30." Written up in *American Artist*, January 1982, he exhibits in Munson and Dubose Galleries.

Avery, Keith. Traditional painter of cowboys and horses, born in Lansing, Michigan in 1921 and living in Roswell, New Mexico. One day when he was 30 and working as a ranch manager who painted on the kitchen table at night, Avery was "on a green horse looking down over a canyon edge, and I suddenly decided I had more to give than I was doing. I decided to go back to college and join the human race."

Raised in Michigan where his father was a photographer during the Depression, Avery met Wild West performers and artists who came to his home, thus launching the two directions of his life. He owned his first horse at eight and in the evenings would "sit in the corner and sketch" portraits. In high school, he won a scholarship to the Chicago Professional School of Art but couldn't afford to go. He broke horses and guided guests at a resort to pay for later studies at the School in 1940–41. His next job was as a director of visual education, and during World War II he did technical illustrating while in the Armed Forces.

After his discharge in 1946, he went back to training horses. He received his degree from New Mexico State University in 1955 and taught at a private school. In 1960, he started selling paintings for covers of *The Quarter Horse Journal* and *Western Horseman*, and in 20 years he has had 400 pieces published. His subjects are cowboys and horses because Frank Tenney Johnson once told him that "if you want to paint something, you've got to be it first." Avery says that "I've never met a stranger. I like people better than anything, although horses and cattle definitely rank second and third." He has shown with the Texas Cowboy Artists Association at The Galleries.

Douglas Atwill, ASPENS, SNOW, SUNLIGHT II, acrylic/canvas, 30 x 30

Keith Avery, HALFWAY TO HEAVEN, oil, 42 x 42

Axton, John. "Non-representational quality with an element of realism" painter of Indian subjects in acrylic or oil and printmaker, born in Princeton, Indiana, in 1947 and living in Albuquerque, New Mexico, since 1979. "Regardless of whether I have a subject in mind," he points out, "I lay in color at random, unmixed and direct from the tube. I work fast and instinctively. Almost always, I start with warm colors and work toward cool, going back and forth in layers."

Raised in Jacksonville, Illinois, he received an Associate of Arts degree from Southern Illinois University in 1967 and was employed by the Illinois State Museum at Dixon Mounds where he was uncomfortable because "it was violating sacred grounds." He painted and constructed collages in his spare time, selling at outdoor shows, and in 1970 started toward Phoenix. Passing through Taos, he says, "my ultimate goal was to be a painter and I knew I'd found a subject I'd never forget."

When Phoenix did not pan out, he located a job as a graphics designer in Denver and in 1976 became a full-time painter. "It comes to the point when, either you have to stop painting or you have to quit the job and paint. All you do is talk about when do you quit. I left my job and we ate pinto beans for two months." In two years, he was able to afford a new home. Very soon, he began printmaking, saying that "lithographs are a natural crossover for me after ten years of graphic design. I live in the West, and I'm dealing with Western subjects, but it is more important to me to be an artist than to focus on a single theme." Written up in *Artists of the Rockies, American Artist,* and *Art Voices/ South,* he is published by four printers and represented by Enthios and Marjorie Kauffman Galleries.

Joe, Eugene B. (signs Baatsoslanii), Navajo sand painter and watercolorist of traditional Navajo values, born in Shiprock, New Mexico in 1950, and still living there in 1982. According to Robert Redford, "it seems that we have lost our way. We have strayed from a finer, simpler direction. In times such as these, we look for some salvation, some real directions. I believe they are to be found in the work of Baatsoslanii. It is pure work. It represents a vision that contains great spirit."

Joe entered the Bureau of Indian Affairs boarding school when he was seven and was encouraged by his teachers to sketch. At home during the summers, he climbed trees to try to capture birds to use as models but had to settle for the feathers he began collecting. His grandfather then named him Baatsoslanii meaning Many Feathers. His father taught him technique, style, color, and the subjects for sand paintings during a six year apprenticeship in the traditional art. In 1972, Joe also enrolled in art classes in Shiprock.

As a contemporary painter, Joe does detailed character studies, landscapes, and the religion and legends of the Navajos, to preserve the culture of the people described by the older Navajos sitting at the trading post. Joe is also drawn to the Shiprock monolith. Using only sandstone, he finds natural colors ranging from warm ochre to red, gray, and even black, with turquoise providing the blue. He began winning awards in 1974, has been featured in *Artists of the Rockies,* winter 1975, and on television. He has exhibited and demonstrated in museums and galleries, and is represented by D'Oros Gallery.

Joe Baatsolani, THE GUARDIAN, sand painting, 24 x 18

John Axton, TAOS MOON (1982), lithograph, 22 x 30

WAYNE BAIZE ©

Baize, Wayne. Realist painter of today's working cowboy in mixed media, born in Stamford, Texas, in 1943 and living in Fort Davis, Texas. "Drawing was what I'd always liked to do," he points out. "I just didn't know you could make a living at it. My pencils caught on, then people started wanting color, but they weren't really satisfied with my oils. Drawing with colored pencils was a subtler statement that fit me better."

While in grade school in Stamford, he began private art lessons with a realist painter who had been influenced by Frank Tenney Johnson. He started in charcoal and progressed to oils in compositions that generally involved horses. When his family moved to Potosi and then Baird, he continued to take lessons from other artists and benefited from criticism by Tom Ryan. Meanwhile he farmed, ranched, and worked in a feed store. In Abilene, he worked in a Western clothing store that placed a table near the front door so he could draw when he was not selling boots.

His first gallery was in Stephenville where he also had his first one-person show at the Savings and Loan. As art sales increased, he took his table home and drew full time. He draws primarily from photographs of cowboys in the field, but changing and grouping the horses, cattle, and men to fit his design. In his pictures, "the cowboy is not boastfully striding the pages of history as the last of a dying breed, he is merely going to work." Baize's drawings have been on the cover of the *Quarter Horse Journal, The Hereford Journal,* and *The Cattleman,* and limited edition prints are published by Texas Art Press and the Frame House Gallery. Baize is represented by Texas Art Gallery, where a mixed media sold for $4,700 in *Preview '81.*

Baker, Joe. Pop art oil painter of the "punk" West, born in Davey, Oklahoma in 1946 and living in Phoenix, Arizona. "I find pigeonholing very restrictive," he points out. "I want to be an artist in a very simple way. Look, first I am an artist, and second, I have a Native American heritage. From my point of view, I don't see that it makes any difference. Who cares? I think people should lighten up on their attitudes to everything.

"My great-grandmother was a full Delaware, but she married a Swede. My father's family was English. My family lived in town and I spent a lot of time in imaginary worlds. I ran away from school all the time, and got my romanticized view of life in the West from watching rodeos. When I was in junior high, they let me take art in the high school. I also went to summer art camp. I wanted to be an artist so I could keep in touch with fantasy and play.

"After I received a BFA in graphics, I was drafted into the Air Force. Following that I worked for the Oklahoma Arts Council for two years. I then decided to get a graduate degree in painting and combined poetry with art in my thesis. I was two years a visiting artist at Oklahoma State University, driving 150 miles a day from Tulsa. I always thought that I would teach." But when art dealer Suzanne Brown saw his paintings on exhibition in California in 1980, she gave him a solo show in Scottsdale that sold out. "The fun," Baker emphasizes, "is on the canvas. My identity is inventing the characters, making them outrageous. My paintings are a way for me to do scenarios that I would enjoy, but I don't have to go that far, if I can paint them." He uses heart-shaped sunglasses as a motif and is represented by Suzanne Brown Gallery.

Baker, Lynn Elton. Painter and printmaker of the Southwest landscape and of artifacts, born in Siren, Wisconsin, in 1949 and living in Scottsdale, Arizona, since 1977. "The hills and rock formations of New Mexico and Arizona," he declares, "are like no other place I have ever been. Here the ancient culture of the Indian seems to me to have grown up from the very earth. The erosion of time which has tamed and flattened other parts of our globe seem here to be arrested by the very antiquity of the earth itself."

After graduating from the Jefferson School of Commercial Art in LaCrosse, Wisconsin, in 1969, Baker attended the Minneapolis College of Art and Design from 1970 to 1973 while employed as a printer in a graphic workshop. He graduated from the Tamarind Institute at the University of New Mexico in Albuquerque in 1974, was employed at the Institute as master printer-in-charge until 1977, and worked at Southwest Graphics Gallery as director until 1979 when he became a full-time artist. He believes that his "in depth understanding gives his original lithographs a distinct quality."

While "for his lithographs he often chooses cultural objects," his paintings are landscapes. According to Baker, "when I work in landscapes, my interest is not in great vistas but in the different components of the landscape as 'objects' upon the surface of the earth. The earth is like a continuum, and hills and great boulders are like monuments to the titanic forces that shaped them." He says that "he familiarizes himself with the landscape by walking, drawing, photographing and examining the rock formations for color, texture, and light reactions." He is represented by Gallery 3.

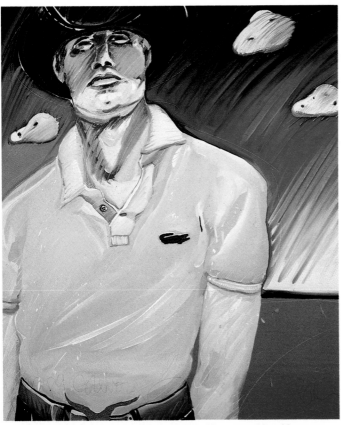

Joe Baker, PREPPY COWBOY (1981), oil/canvas, 49 x 42

Wayne Baize, GET ALONG LITTLE DOGEY, mixed media, 18 x 24

Lynn E. Baker, TAOS RUINS, monoprint, 20 x 30

Bales, Jean E. Contemporary painter in all media, sculptor, printmaker, and potter, born in Pawnee, Oklahoma, in 1946 and living in Washita, Oklahoma. "The question I'm asked most (not the most interesting) is, how long did it take you to do that painting? By the time I finish telling them my answer, I suspect they are sorry they asked. The question I hate the most and will not even comment on is, do you just paint or do you work for a living? That question always makes me want to blow a gizzard."

Educated in Chickasha public schools as a half Iowa Indian, she earned her BA in fine art from the Oklahoma College of Liberal Arts in 1969. By the time she was 27, she was named the Indian Artist of the Year, and she has now won more than a hundred awards and honors. "I work like crazy when I'm home," she observes, "and then go to my shows—talk, have a good time, and kick up my heels. I'm kind of a hermit. I have every day entirely to myself, so I can really get lost in my painting. I'm a day painter (I have to have natural light to work by). I spend at least eight hours a day in my studio.

"As an art group, Indian artists are expected to have stories behind each piece. Even galleries will write, wanting the legend for a certain piece. In my opinion, this sometimes stifles the creativity of the Indian artist. An artist has to keep striving. I have so many goals, sometimes when I accomplish one I sit down and wonder where I'm going next. It is not hard to do the same thing over and over but I feel my work has to continue to grow and change." Featured in *Southwest Art*, April 1981, she publishes her own hand-pulled prints and is represented by Tom Bahti Indian Arts and Whitney Gallery.

Balke, Don. Representational watercolorist and printmaker of North American animals and birds, born in Wyoming Township, Wisconsin, in 1932 and living in Nebo, North Carolina. "When I was a kid," he recalls, "we were poor dirt farmers. There were ten of us, and my folks would charge the groceries all winter and make up for it in the summer. We all worked hard, but I always found time to draw. I wasn't thinking about becoming an artist, but I drew anything I saw around me.

"All the time I was in the Army, I really didn't know what I wanted to do, but it was obvious I had to do something with my life. I knew I could draw well. Why not at least give it a try?" After studying at the Academy of Fine Arts in Chicago, he joined a studio there, then moved to Appleton, Wisconsin, where clients called on him to do "pigs and horses and cows—things like that—and I started looking at wildlife as something to do. I began painting wildlife and I couldn't turn it off."

In 1973, he left commercial art. "That first year, we won a blue ribbon from the Printing Industries of America, and we've won blue ribbons every year since." He recently completed a series of paintings of the animals and trees of the 50 states for philatelic covers, and in 1981 was painting the birds of the 50 states. As publisher of his own prints, he says that "collecting is fun and can be profitable, but I am always pleased when someone tells me his first reason for buying is he really likes the print." The 1981 resale value of his early prints increased from $6 to $55, from $50 to $275, $35 to $200 and so on. His distributor is Masterpiece Molding & Fine Art Co. Most paintings are done on commission.

Ballerna, Isabel. Collagist of American Indian figures "with a difference," born in Buenos Aires, Argentina, in 1941 and living in Cave Creek, Arizona. "Each piece is a very personal experience—a sincere expression of my innermost feelings," she declares. When asked how she could sell something so personal, she replies that "I have to admit that sometimes it is not easy, but then I have been fortunate. I consider my collectors as personal friends and I am honored that they have chosen my works to join their beautiful collections. I hope the collectors will consider me one of their friends since a part of me will be with them forever."

After she came to the United States, she studied at DeKalb College in Georgia and then at Atlanta College of Art. When she saw the Buffalo Bill Traveling Exhibition, she felt "there was something synonymous about the American Indian and the gaucho." Fascinated, she went West to study the Indian culture. She admires Indian craftsmanship and emphasizes that "collages we considered avant garde as an art form at one time were created by Indians so far ahead of our time."

She combines paper, embossing, pen and ink, paint, beads, and language, and says the response "is gratifying." She uses heavy rag paper that is embossed white on white to provide the basic design which is detailed in pen and ink, colored with paint, and embroidered with beads and feathers in Indian designs. Then the poetry that she writes in Spanish is added in a fine hand that may be worked into the design. Each "collage" is titled in a simulation of Indian thought. Written up in *Artists of the Rockies*, summer 1978, she has shown at Overland Trail and Sagebrush Galleries.

Jean E. Bales, HARVEST TIME, acrylic/Kinwashi
rice paper, dia 13

Don Balke, BALD EAGLE, watercolor, 27 x 35½

Isabel Ballerna, PERHAPS I GO ON EXISTING WHERE THE AIR MAKES YOU CRY, PERHAPS IF YOU LISTEN TO MY
UNTOUCHABLE SOUND, YOU'LL KNOW ME, embossing, pen & ink, hair bone pipes, Indian seed beads, antique sequins, 27 x 40

Bama

Bama, James E. "Very realistic" painter of contemporary Western portraits and still lifes in oil and watercolor, born in New York City in 1926 and living in Wapiti, Wyoming, since 1968. "I have always felt out of place with anecdotal paintings of historical scenes, roundups and brandings," he emphasizes. "I feel that my themes are universal. I would like to think that I am producing a body of work that makes a valid statement about life and the West today."

After he graduated from New York City's High School of Music and Arts, Bama served in the military and then attended the Art Students League for three years under the G.I. Bill. When he moved to Wyoming, he was a leading illustrator and for years he continued doing only commercial work because he "couldn't see" Western art. "As time passed, the local people began to interest me." He began painting his "childhood fantasies of the old Wild West," and in 1971 gave up illustration completely. "Convinced that I was being boxed in by subject matter," however, "I took my paintings back to the Coe Kerr Gallery in New York, hoping to gain acceptance as a 20th-century realist."

Bama photographs his subjects in black and white, enlarges them to 11 by 14 inch prints, and then makes an outline drawing on tracing paper. Light and color are determined on a series of small drawings. The large drawing is then shaded and transferred to a gessoed panel and painted. Bama says that "the photograph is just another tool and only as good as the painter who uses it." He has been featured in *Southwest Art, Art West,* and *Saturday Review,* is listed in *Who's Who in American Art,* and has declined membership in Western art groups. His publisher is Greenwich Workshop.

James Bama, SIOUX INDIAN WEARING RIBBON SHIRT (1976), oil, 23½ x 21½

Bannister

Bannister, Pati. "Poetic" painter of young female figures in various media, born in North London, England, in 1929 and living in Gulfport, Mississippi. "You'd think that only mothers should like my paintings," she says, "but men seem to like them just as well, and I'm very happy about that. Everybody sees something different in them. People see their own children—or something from their own childhood. I really don't know how to define my style. It's something of a landscape with figures.

"I can't remember a time when I didn't want to be an artist. When you grow up in an artist's family, you don't know anything else." During World War II, she was sent into the countryside to avoid German bombs. After the war, she attended the Slade Academy of Fine Arts in London. At thirteen, she illustrated books, and at seventeen did artwork for films. In 1952, she came to the United States as a governess and the following year became an airline stewardess. When she married, her husband did not know about her background as an artist. After he found out, they "plunged right in," starting with portraits and racetrack paintings and then moving into her present romantic style.

"My paintings usually include young women, lacy clothing, and spring flowers because this is what I like to paint. I love to sew and the clothes in the paintings are carefully thought out in pattern form. I'm just not interested in other themes. For one thing, I love painting lace and you can't put lace on little boys or put flowers in their hair. Once I get an idea, I see it in my mind's eye as a finished painting, completely in color." Written up in *Southwest Art*, April 1982, she is published by New Masters Publishing Company and is represented by Bill Cousins' Townhouse and Parkcrest Galleries.

Pati Bannister, MAIL ORDER BRIDES mixed media, 44 x 34

BILL BARBER U   CLIFF BARNES

Barber, William Harold. Realist painter and sculptor of the West of today and of the past, born in Glendale, California, in 1940 and living in Daniels, Utah, since 1967. According to Bill Barber, "while still in my teens, I felt some day I would be a writer and I knew I had to have experiences so I picked up with an old powder man from the Ohio mines who made me his partner in prospecting the Mojave. I would break horses in the Sierra country, fish, bum in Mexico, anything to fill my mind with material.

"Having been raised in a tough Mexican-American town, I was exposed to Spanish influences. As a boy, I worked at many odd jobs, woodcutting, farm work, illustrating, etc. After getting fed up with college and the abstract era, I worked for the post office as a money courier and began free lance illustrating but hated that confining feeling of doing what someone else wanted done. I moved to Utah and at the time I entered the field full time I was a packaging manager. A free man, I jumped in my old pickup and headed to the annual Death Valley Show.

"I don't think the West is so much a place as it is a way of thinking, the pride of rugged people against the elements in a harsh, unforgiving land. I love it—I've lived it. I've cooked on dried cow chips out of necessity, broke horses, been broke by horses, but I do not consider myself a cowboy. That title belongs to the men who make their living from working with cows on horseback. What I am trying to say is that I like any kind of adventure anywhere. I can look back and smile for I am of a fraternity called artists who share a secret of living." One of Barber's selling agents is Western Art Classics.

Barnes, Clifford V. Painter of "today's West," born in Bell, California in 1940 and living in Lake Arrowhead, California. "I travel everywhere in the United States," he comments. "I was especially drawn to the Indian reservations and the ceremonials, and I began painting them, particularly those of the Navajos. But the ghost towns, the old wagons and some of the 'old guys who could really tell a good story' also fascinated me ... and there I was, a painter of today's West."

After graduating from the Art Center School of Design in Los Angeles, where he studied drawing and illustration, Barnes served in the Army from 1963 to 1964. Stationed in Germany, he traveled through Europe as editor of the battalion paper. When he returned to California, he worked as an architectural illustrator until 1970, when he spent a year in Europe in a VW camper. Painting in Spain reawakened his interest in the history of the American West and the canvases he painted left him "excited and happy to see that not only was the response to my work rewarding, but also that I could from then on devote my time totally to painting."

"I paint primarily in oils," he adds, "either on canvas or on paper with conte. I like color and use it boldly and I enjoy broad strokes, highlighting with the palette knife whenever possible. I paint my subjects in a realistic way, but enjoy putting an Indian or a wagon against a more abstract background of color or in the form of an Indian rug design." He has won two gold medals at the show in Littleton, Colorado, is a member of the American Indian and Cowboy Artist Society, and is represented by Troy's Gallery.

Bill Barber, UTE SUCCESS, oil, 32 x 48

Cliff Barnes, ESCORT, oil, 20 x 40

BBBarrick

Ron Barsano

Barrick, Bill. Painter of the bygone rural Southwest, born near Abernathy, Texas, in 1945 and living near Austin since 1972. Barrick's treatment of past Southwestern farm life reflects his belief that agriculture deserves a more prominent place in history. "I disagree with the idea that the cowboy was the main instrument in the development of the West," he says. "I think the farmers did more than anyone. Painting the implements of yesterday's world is to capture the character of those who used them."

After growing up on a cotton farm on the plains, Barrick declared that "we didn't have art in the public schools. The fact that we didn't have it made it all the more appealing. Exposure found its way on the covers of the *Saturday Evening Post.*" When he enrolled in the art school at West Texas State University, he "went with the idea that I would come out a real weirdo, but instead I came out doing representational art." After graduation, he became a high school teacher and drove the school bus through the rural world he now paints.

"I'm familiar with life on the farm," he states, "and that's the kind of thing I depict. I paint things rather than ideas, and you don't have to guess what it's all about. I use a lot of acrylic glazes, much in the way watercolor is done." His paintings seldom have human figures because he prefers to let the viewer place himself in the frame. Austin Brown is his gallery and his printmaker. "Traditionally, only the upper classes could afford art," he declares, "but now everyone can." Barrick is a member of the Texas Association of Professional Artists. A third of his work is done on commission.

Barsano, Ron. Traditional Taos painter of figures and still-lifes, born in Chicago, Illinois, in 1945 and living in Taos, New Mexico, since 1970. "When I was a kid," he says, "an illustrator lived next door and I'd hang around and watch him by the hours. From there on in, it was just a matter of getting through grammar and high school. A mere legality and formality. As soon as I was free I headed for art school It was as simple as that."

At 17, Barsano fulfilled his dreams by entering the American Academy of Art in Chicago and studying under William Mosby. He received the Mosby Scholarship in 1966, graduated in 1967, spent two years in the Army, and moved to Taos in 1970 to paint. A quiet but outspoken man, he believes that "Taos light is as no other, except the south of France. I know of many cases where someone has looked at a painting and could tell immediately that it was done, not just in New Mexico, but in Taos."

He begins with a loose drawing and then lays in the lightest and darkest color values before adding the full color block-in for the finished effect. "I do this block-in carefully," he declares, "because I don't want to have to go back into the painting too much and risk losing that spontaneous feeling." Critics say that "he's not afraid to use brilliant color, but he uses it so skillfully that his paintings whisper. They never shout." After the paint is dry is "the time to put myself into it," he feels, because "an artist can affect a painting, the spirit it sends out, after the work is finished." A member of the Taos Six, Barsano is represented by Carlson-Black and Talisman Galleries.

Ron Barsano, LINDA HILL, oil, 30 x 34

Bill Barrick, MIDSUMMER, acrylic, 20 x 30

Robert Bateman.

Bateman, Robert McClellan. Realistic painter in acrylic of birds with "an abstract structure showing the total environment," born in Toronto, Ontario, Canada, in 1930 and living in Milton, Ontario. "I like to get out and sniff and smell around," he says. "I'm interested in what the other sides of things look like—the other side of the bird's wing that you can't see. And I don't want just any hillside. I want one where the wind blows across it in a certain way."

After having sketched since his youth, when he started his first bird list at 12 and wanted to be a wildlife researcher, Bateman earned his BA, with honors, in geography from the University of Toronto in 1954. He also took private art lessons for years, experimenting with Impressionism, Cubism and abstraction. He did summertime sketching in the Canadian North, hitchhiked through Europe, and in 1957 traveled around the world, filling books with wildlife drawings. In 1959, he became head of a high school art department, a position he held until 1976.

In 1963, Bateman went to Nigeria for two years on a teacher exchange program and began painting wildlife seriously. When he saw an Andrew Wyeth show in 1970, his personal style was resolved as "the rhythm of abstract patterns." By 1972, his work was included in the Bird Artists of the World Show in London. After other honors in 1974 and 1975, he quit teaching to paint full time. Featured in *Southwest Art* in September 1980, he is listed in *Who's Who in American Art* and is a member of the Society of Animal Artists and the Northwest Rendezvous Group. Published by Mill Pond Press, he is represented by Trailside Galleries where $5,500 was the listed price for a medium-size painting in 1981.

Robert Bateman, GRAY JAY, acrylic/masonite, 24 x 15¾

Baumann

PETER BEADLE

Beaugureau

Baumann, Stefan W. "Old Master" oil painter of the Western landscape, born in South Lake Tahoe, California, in 1962 and still living there. "I want to create paintings that have the quality and visual impact that classical music has for listening. Both are highly technical art forms, but I feel painting has greater longevity than music because the original work remains as the artist intended. Works of the great composers are interpreted by those performing the work and may not have the same feeling the composer would have given in performing."

At four, he began both classical piano studies and painting. It was assumed that he would pursue a career in music, but he was drawn to painting and at 12 went to Europe to study the landscapes of the Old Masters. He also studied in Mexico and Hawaii. According to *People* magazine, his paintings brought up to $12,000 each and he drove a Mercedes-Benz before he graduated from high school. He then attended Stanford University as an art history major, on grants, but his objective, he said, was "to learn, not to get a piece of paper.

"I relate to the grandeur of Nature," he adds, "and attempt to transfer this feeling to my work. Highly detailed, large paintings seem a more appropriate expression of the 'Grandscape' for me." Sponsored by M. Grumbacher, Inc., he has painted a "Pacific Ring of Fire" series that will be on postage stamps. One, from the series, "Mt. St. Helen," was painted with pigment that included the actual ash from the volcano. The painting appeared on the cover of *Southwest Art* January 1981, and a print of it hangs in President Reagan's ranch. Baumann's prints are published by his own company, and he is represented by Image West.

Beadle, Peter. Representational oil painter of the Western United States and Canada of today, born in Invercargill, New Zealand, in 1933 and still living there. "As an artist," he says, "my greatest desire is to achieve the state in which one transcends mind and thought and escapes the intellect, when the painting happens of itself. Awareness of the completed painting comes with a feeling of elation and joy. The painting is then a by-product of this state of being.

"I have painted professionally for fifteen years, and have painted and written three books for the New Zealand market. I am also the official artist for Air New Zealand, and have painted for the overseas embassies of the New Zealand government. Since childhood, I have always been drawn to the Rockies of America. My first view of them in 1978 was as though I had come home. Since then, I have traveled to the Western United States and Canada every year for two to three months. The peace and solitude found in the mountain and desert area gets close to a meditative silence.

"Meditation has helped my work dramatically. If an artist is stressed up, that stress will show in his style and subject, and his paintings will be a manifestation of his stress. The less stress an artist carries the more he can become one with his subject. His paintings then express this unity he has with his subject. Paintings are sometimes done within an hour or so, particularly if the deep state is achieved. Others take days or weeks. Often they become overworked and get thrown out. Working on location is a great joy, providing the elements don't hinder too much. My prints are available through Harrison Galleries and my paintings through Shriver Gallery and Biltmore Gallery."

Beaugureau, Francis H. Representational oil painter of horses, Indians, and the military of the Southwest, born in Chicago, Illinois, in 1920 and living in Tubac, Arizona. "About 1962," he explains, "it occurred to me that no painter had documented in a broad way the Indian War period in Arizona. After intensive studying, I presented my project to my first major client who commissioned me to execute 30 paintings of the subject. This was followed by four clients for whom I have continued to portray basically the same theme.

"When I was eight, my formal art training started in the Saturday classes at the Chicago Art Institute. In 1936, I enrolled at the Mizen Academy to get more training in draftsmanship and other fundamentals, and when I finished high school I attended full daytime classes. Indians and horses were always of tremendous interest to me. In 1938, I visited New Mexico and Arizona where I did landscape sketching and charcoal drawings of Indians who would accept candy in payment for posing. In 1939, I enlisted in the cavalry, later became a B-17 pilot.

"After leaving the service in 1946, I had a brief stint with a commercial art studio in Chicago and then entered portrait painting and watercolors. For two years, I was engaged by the Air Force, including going to Korea to depict the air war. In 1954, I moved to Arizona. Concerning my paintings, I attempt to vary the weather conditions, seasons, color ranges, and moods to avoid monotony. The painting technique is determined by the way I feel about the individual subject. I do not paint cowboys or ranch life because I know little about it, nor do I study works by other artists, to avoid being influenced. I am represented by Settlers West Galleries and O'Brien's Art Emporium."

Stefan W. Baumann, LOVERS' LEAP, oil/canvas, 40 x 50

Peter Beadle, TAOS PUEBLO, oil, 16 x 20

Francis Beaugureau, SNAKE DANCE ON SECOND MESA, oil/canvas, 26 x 40

Bedford, William J. Sculptor of bronze statuettes and statues of Indians and birds of prey, born in Orange, California, in 1948 and living in Laguna Beach, California. "My focus," he says, "is on the inner life of the Native American. I am searching to understand it, in the hope of learning how to apply his wisdom. The genocide of the Native Americans was not complete, and so now the white man can have another chance to learn how to live with nature. I believe this to be one of the tools that will work to better our lives, if we will use it.

"I began sculpting in 1969 and am entirely self-taught. My early work was welded metal sculpture. I evolved to jewelry when my need for greater detail began to show. This led me into my first experience with wax modeling and casting. Around 1973, I was approached by an art collector who recognized my potential and, for one and a half years supplied me with a salary, studio, and materials. This was my formal training, in my eyes, and during this time I began to apply my passion for philosophy in the conception and execution of my work. These years found me camping and hiking and sculpting the wildlife, especially the birds of prey.

"Around 1975, I began to cast my work in bronze. The heart and values of the Native Americans became my study and my expression, not as mythical heroes, but as people who live and as values which must survive. My work is about nature and how to live in an attitude of oneness with the environment and as a responsible part of our existence. I tell the story in native symbols. In sculpting the characters, I etch into them the emotions of their meanings." Written up in *Southwest Art* April 1978, Bedford is represented by Signature Galleries.

Beecham, Greg. Realist oil painter of wildlife, born in Goshen, New York, in 1954 and living in Renton, Washington, since 1978. "From childhood," he recalls, "I was influenced by wildlife because my dad is an artist, an avid hunter, and a fisherman. While I was still in grade school, I remember my dad would select a photograph of some animal and instruct me to look at it continually as I drew. I'd begin by observing the eye and drawing exactly what I saw, thus acquiring the power of observation and patience.

"While exploring the woods, I'd often have deer walk up to me while I didn't move a muscle. I remember going grouse hunting and standing motionless for two hours after spotting an eight point buck and a doe feeding in a field. When I graduated from high school in 1972, I joined the Navy as a boatswain's mate and then became a hospital corpsman. In 1975 I was discharged and went to Southern Oregon State College for art and geology. I left school in 1978 to study full time with my father and for three months we built on the earlier education.

"I moved to Washington in the fall of 1978 and have been painting full time ever since. My first show was a two-man show with my father in 1981. I study continually with my eyes. While driving my car, I look for patterns in the trees and landscape. I observe the way light plays on individual forms such as a leaf or the back of an animal and I also look for the way light, direct or indirect, affects a mass such as a forest, field, or mountain. Notwithstanding the importance of my work, the most vital thing in my life is my relationship with Jesus Christ." He is represented by The Western Flyway, Ltd. and Wild Wings Gallery, is published by Dallas Prints, and is in the American Western Collection catalog, 1981–82.

Beecham, Tom. Representational painter of Western, wildlife, and historical scenes, born on a cattle ranch and farm near Goodland, Kansas, in 1926 and living in Saugerties, New York. "My roots," he declares, "go back to the Western tall grass prairies and the Rocky Mountain high country. Around the turn of the century, my grandpa brought his family from Missouri in a covered wagon with seven children in the box. After he died, my grandmother took in boarders, men in their eighties and older who had seen the West in its wildest days.

"Our family moved to Colorado, on the western slope of the Rockies, when I was twelve. We hunted lions, mule deer, bobcat, sage grouse, quail, elk and bear, and we ran wild horses. I went to Grand Junction High School, graduated in 1944, and joined the Navy, serving in the South Pacific. In 1947, I was accepted at The St. Louis School of Fine Arts and chose to be an illustrator. During my last year, I simply did drybrush drawings of Western subjects.

"When I arrived in New York in 1951, I got my first job from a science fiction magazine, after wearing out a pretty good pair of shoes. I worked for about every publisher in the business and a large number of ad agencies. In 1973, I turned to gallery and commission painting, anything from Westerns and wildlife to portraits to anything else that comes my way. I love it. I like to paint and I am pretty good at it. It is knowledge of composition, the emotional excitement through design and symbolism, the rhythms that move within each painting, and the experience and love of the subjects that flow onto my canvases. Joining the Society of American Historical Artists just opens up broader horizons for me."

Greg Beecham, NOVEMBER HONKERS, oil/canvas, 19 x 25

Bill Bedford, WELCOME THE SPIRIT,
bronze with turquoise inlays, h 21, Edition 16

Tom Beecham, THE PATIENT ONE, oil/canvas, 22 x 36

Joe Beeler

Beeler, Joe Neil. Painter and sculptor of Western Americana, born in Joplin, Missouri, in 1931 and living in Sedona, Arizona. "Charles Russell has probably contributed more than any other artist to America's love and understanding of the Old West," Beeler believes. "He must be considered the Father of Cowboy Art, and he is the standard used by many to judge art and artists today. Any artist now painting the West feels that Russell and his contemporaries are a tough act to follow.

"Before I could read, I heard about the West from my grandparents," Beeler recalls. "They had experienced life on the frontier in Oregon and during the gold rush in California. My great-grandfather had fought in the Civil War, then gone to Texas as a cowhand." Beeler's father was part Cherokee, and "in the summer I wardanced in feathered costume as the other Indian youths did." He began art studies at Tulsa University, served in the Army for two years during the Korean War, and returned to Kansas State for his BFA. After a year at the Art Center School in Los Angeles, Beeler and his young family "moved into a small summer cabin in northeastern Oklahoma.

"In the late fifties, there were few western art collectors. We came very close to having to move to the city, but when all seemed lost some small commission would crop up. Things really began to pick up when the Gilcrease Museum gave me my first important one-man show in 1960, and soon rabbit and quail gave way to beefsteak at our dinner table." In 1965, Beeler helped found the Cowboy Artists of America, the group he says "has played a major role" in the popularization of cowboy art. The same year, his first bronze was cast. He has exhibited at Trailside Galleries.

Joe Beeler, THE BARRIER, oil, 30 x 48

Bill Bender

Cynthia Bennett

LENORE BÉRAN

Bender, Bill. Traditional painter of the West, "playing lights against darks" in oil and watercolor, born in El Segundo, California, in 1920 and living in Oro Grande, California. "It seems now-a-days," he observes, that "my own clientele keeps me busier'n a one eyed hound in a sausage factory and I'm geared to a frequency that doesn't cotton to all the glitter and back slapping of promotional art. Not a very exciting life, huh? Still, solitude and thinking time has been my one goal in life and art has been the vehicle for giving it to me, so I'm trotting through life a very contented hombre.

"School to me was a necessary evil, and from the first day I trotted in for my three Rs I was plumb certain that the only way to make a living was in the wide open spaces, astraddle an ol' pony an' drawing 30 a month as a cowboy." After he became a working cowboy, he moonlighted as a movie stuntman for $16 a day and entered rodeos where he "just rode for the hell of it on Fourth of July, Labor Day, or some other blow out. The money wasn't big, but it gave us a chance to head for town, whoop it up, and swap lies with old friends."

When he was "busted up," he turned to writing and illustrating stories during his recuperation. Advice from painter James Swinnerton was to "learn the subtle colors of the desert first" as a landscape painter "and then go back to painting horses later." In the course of years of struggling with color, Bender developed his own style, and only then did he return to horses, cattle, and cowboys. He was a civilian artist for the Air Force in 1963 and for the Navy in 1966. Listed in *Who's Who in American Art* and written up in Ainsworth and Hassrick, he doesn't choose to "show in galleries anymore."

Bennett, Cynthia. Abstract-realist painter of Arizona landscapes, particularly the Grand Canyon, in acrylic, born in Fostoria, Ohio, in 1943 and living in Sedona, Arizona, since 1976. "The city often lessens us with the unimportant, the unnecessary, the inane," she states. "The Grand Canyon has the effect of ridding people of pretensions and the clutter of citification. A Canyon trip helps to restore order and composition to our lives and feelings. We jettison the vapid and the stupid and are returned refreshed.

Raised in Scottsdale, Arizona, and Kailua, Hawaii, she "was interested in art as a kid. My mother was a Sunday painter." Being "crazy about San Francisco," she studied anthropology at the University of California at Berkeley and also took courses in art. On a horseback trip into Arizona, she visited the Navajo trading post at Tsegi Canyon, where she worked for five months, then moved to the Grand Canyon where she lived for ten years, doing black and white photography, designing postcards with ecological quotations, and making split-twig jewelry.

In 1976, she declares, "I moved to Sedona with the intent of painting." She took a clerking job to keep going and the next year had a show where all 12 paintings sold. Now, she paints the Grand Canyon almost all the time, saying that "I've drawn about 800 or 900 Grand Canyon scenes in 15 years. It will probably take the rest of my life to paint all the Canyon I have to paint." There are two groups of these hard-edged paintings, "Canon-Abeyance, with minimal abstractions, and Canon-Confluence, combining stasis with elements of naturalism." Most of her paintings are large because "sometimes size alone carries the message." She is represented by Elaine Horwitch Galleries.

Béran, Lenore. Impressionist oil painter and collagist of figures, born in Chicago, Illinois, in 1925 and living in North Hollywood, California. "People turn me on," she points out. "Models as people. I picked a model up once in Brooklyn Park and he played his flute while I painted. I like to paint people who come from a different background than my own. This eventually prompted me to paint Indians. These paintings I do for me, so what I have to say isn't a profound statement. Maybe it's just that all kinds of people are fantastic.

"I was trained and had worked in commercial art, primarily as a paste-up artist and illustrator. After the kids were big enough and I had a little bit of time, I could go to adult education classes once a week and paint a pretty little picture. And that was what I was doing, painting pretty little pictures, and I was selling them." In 1965, she entered a juried show, "and out of the 27 possible points, I got six. It was a bad painting—but a pretty picture," so she started studying privately "and things all came clear."

As advice to collectors, she says "a painting should do something for you, turn you on. I would not collect a painter. I would collect a piece that excites me. There are lots of pretty pictures that are bad paintings, and it is pulling a fast one on the public to sell celebrity art as good art. Red Skelton is pretty pictures, and I suppose when I'm very well known as an artist I'm going to get up on stage and tell jokes, sing, and dance. I am probably making my reputation with my collages, and I think of each piece of paper that I paste down as a brushful of paint." She is her own publisher for prints, and is represented by Shirley Meyers Gallery.

Lenore Beran, SONG TO MY PAST (1981), collage, 30 x 30

Cynthia Bennett, VERDE VALLEY SCHOOL, acrylic, 18 x 24

Bill Bender, SUNDAY AT THE ROCKIN' A, oil, 18 x 24

Ernest Berke

Berke, Ernest. Traditional painter and sculptor of the Old West in oil and bronze. born in New York City in 1921 and living in Scottsdale. Arizona. "As an artist of the Frontier West." he points out. "I use my era as a sounding board to reflect back for the onlooker not only what happened in those days of the Old West. but also as a commentary on what is happening in the very time. After all. environments and technologies change. but people do not. My work is about people and their relationships with their land. their animals. each other. and how these relationships have affected the philosophies and the prejudices and problems we face in today's society."

The son of Russian and Rumanian immigrants. the father an artisan in sheet metal and the mother a dressmaker. Berke left school to "roam the wooded areas" of the city park "and hunt rabbits and squirrels with my homemade arrows." He credits the lack of schooling for the "direction and the drive to work harder." During four years in the Army Air Corps. he discovered an aptitude for painting. and after his discharge he was employed as a commercial artist. first drawing animated films and then doing fashion art.

A co-worker got Berke started on Indian lore. and they would "spend most of their days talking about Indian laws. lives. wars. and religion." In 1957. he began doing small paintings and drawings of Indians and Western life. and he had his first show in Latendorf's Bookstore in New York City. The master Western illustrator Harold Von Schmidt put Berke on the right track technically. and in 1962 his Kennedy Galleries show in New York City sold out in two weeks. Next. Berke wrote and illustrated a well-received children's book on Indians. He also started sculpting. By 1980. he had issued 55 different bronzes. He was written up in *Southwest Art* March 1975. was the subject of the book *Ernest Berke* in 1980. and is represented by Overland Trail Galleries.

Ernest Berke, THE LAST STAGE, oil, 34 x 44

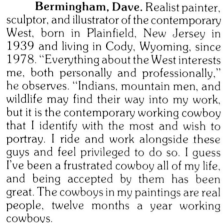

Dave Bermingham
NPA

Bermingham, Dave. Realist painter, sculptor, and illustrator of the contemporary West, born in Plainfield, New Jersey in 1939 and living in Cody, Wyoming, since 1978. "Everything about the West interests me, both personally and professionally," he observes. "Indians, mountain men, and wildlife may find their way into my work, but it is the contemporary working cowboy that I identify with the most and wish to portray. I ride and work alongside these guys and feel privileged to do so. I guess I've been a frustrated cowboy all of my life, and being accepted by them has been great. The cowboys in my paintings are real people, twelve months a year working cowboys.

"I was raised in New Jersey, but with a lifelong interest in the American West. I pursued a variety of careers, including professional auto racing and law enforcement before turning to commercial art and illustration. Mainly a self-taught artist, I worked as assistant to an East coast illustrator and in 1975 was elected to membership in the Society of Illustrators. On the advice of my friend and mentor, the noted Western illustrator Harold Von Schmidt, I moved to Cody to paint the West in the West.

"I suppose my style of painting falls somewhere between realism and impressionism, although I greatly admire several artists in the magic or photo-realism school. I like to push paint around, using detail only where necessary to convey my feeling for the subject. I try to gain the viewer's interest and have him share my feeling for the subject by the overall effect and design of my painting." Bermingham is a founding member of the NPA, the Northern Plains Artist Association. He is represented by Big Horn Gallery and Art Eclectic.

Berry, Libby. Realist oil painter of wildlife, particularly big game animals, born in New Haven, Connecticut in 1943 and living in Greenbank, Washington in 1977. While riding on a bus, she says, "it all clicked in my mind. As I gazed out the window, I saw colors I'd never seen before, and it was a visual symphony instead of unrelated separate notes. When the bus stopped near my home, I spilled my box of paints all over the floor in my haste to get off and run to tell my husband."

She had graduated from Marietta College in Ohio with an art degree in 1964, taught English and art to third graders, and did commercial art as a free lancer. When her husband found her in tears, he asked her, "If you could accomplish anything in life, what would it be?" She replied, "I'd like to be a great painter, like Leonardo," so he sent her to the Los Angeles Museum of Art to isolate a common denominator in the paintings. "Finally," she explains, "the secret dropped into place in my mind. The idea is to lay color on the canvas like a symphony, instead of in disconnected notes. I call the technique 'living oils.'"

That was in 1977. Now her oils are selling at prices up to $25,000, compared to a typical price of $18,500 for a canvas by Mark Tobey, dean of the Pacific Northwest fine artists. "I eat, sleep, and breathe the painting I'm working on," she states. "It's the last thing I see at night and the first thing in the morning. Sometimes I jump out of bed in the middle of the night and work on my painting." Her husband says that the last use of "living oil" was the Hudson River School at the turn of the century. Libby Berry has been commissioned to paint a series for the International Sheep Hunters Association, one a year for fifteen years. Her prints are published by Salt Creek Graphics.

Billis, Mitch. Traditional watercolorist of Western landscapes and wildlife, born in Ilion, New York, in 1937 and living in Boothbay Harbor, Maine. "Edna St. Vincent Millay once wrote a sonnet," he observes, "which begins, 'Still will I harvest beauty where it grows,' and that's what I want to reflect in my art. I want to go out and harvest the beauty where it exists, then share the feelings I have with the world."

When he graduated from high school, "science was the thing in the 1950s, and the best scholarship I could land, unfortunately, was to an engineering school." He earned a degree from Clarkston College, with honors, but "could not stand" professional engineering. He flew to Europe and began "bumming around, trying to see everything possible," then returned to school at the University of New Hampshire for his Master's in mathematics in 1962. After teaching at the university level, he received a Ph.D. in mathematics at the University of Utah in 1968 and was employed as a math professor at Montana State University in Bozeman.

In Montana, "I began to paint for the first time in my life," Billis states, "but I never took it seriously until 1973. That summer I attended two workshops and my life has never been the same since." In the summer of 1974, he went to Maine where he received private art instruction, and the following year became a full-time painter. "It was something I had to do. All the happiness afforded by any other work dissolved when weighed against painting." He was featured in *Southwest Art*, June 1978, is a founding member of the Northwest Rendezvous Group, and is represented by Trailside Galleries where a small watercolor was listed at $750 in 1981.

Mitch Billis, WINTER FEEDING, oil, 22 x 30

Libby Berry, THE BUCK STOPS HERE, oil/linen, 26 x 36

Dave Bermingham, GOOFIN', mixed media, 18 x 24

Billups, Elizabeth Jean. Representational painter of Western portraits and scenes, born in Manhattan Beach, California, in 1948 and living in Gardena, California. "Every artist has a 'style'," she points out, "a fingerprint of how they see and how they express it. Unlike many artists, I never know what my piece will look like—until it's done. I know a 'feeling' I want—but don't know the answers, until they are on the canvas or paper. The pieces that are very successful, I can seldom recall any stage they went through."

During her younger years, a Papago Indian girl lived with her family. Dancers from St. John's Indian School also stayed with them, and the regalia appeared in her early paintings. After private schooling, she studied fine art at El Camino Junior College in 1969, graduated from the Art Center College of Design in Los Angeles in 1972 with a BA in commercial art, and worked as an illustrator. Membership in the Society of Illustrators led to a commission from the Army to do a painting of Sacajawea for the Bicentennial. While in Montana for research, she was offered a solo show at the Historical Society in 1975.

"People inquire about the diverse forms my art takes," she observes. "I've never tried to be different. Whenever I work on a piece, I put my entire self into it, and this often exhausts me. Usually when I finish, I will 'escape' into something totally different. I turn to a model or a landscape. And at times my sense of 'surfaces' begins to fade and I turn to drawings. I fluctuate back and forth, to release exhaustion from one medium to another." A member of the Women Artists of the American West, she shows in Bob Higgins' Trails West and Grizzly Tree Galleries.

Billotta, Gloria Saaf. Representational oil painter of horses, western scenes, and Indian portraits, born in Chicago, in 1937 and living in Norco, California. "I found that in order to paint a horse well," she points out, "I had to learn to paint seascapes, landscapes, humans, and even roses! The conclusion was obvious to me— the secret was to learn to paint *everything* at least reasonably well. Then you may apply that experience to your own specialty. In the same way, I have found teaching others has expanded my art visualization.

"At ten, I won a children's scholarship to the Chicago Art Institute in a citywide competition, and after moving to California in 1948 I won a small scholarship to Otis Art Institute. I also studied privately, and in 1968 began selling my work and doing commissions. We were on a really tight budget, but I wanted a horse so badly that I took in ironing to pay the $25 a month board bill." She has showed horses, traveled throughout the Southwest, and attended rodeos.

"I sketch ideas as they come into my head. I may see a cowboy in a particularly interesting pose, or a clown coming to the rescue just at the right moment. If I don't have a sketch pad handy, I draw on just about anything—rodeo programs, envelopes, whatever. Then, if I get an idea for a painting and I need something special, I have the drawings to refresh my memory. My work is merely an extension of myself, a part of my personality that is so essential that it is completely natural to me. I can't help but see the beauty and magic in the world around me." The organizer of the Women Artists of the American West, she is represented by the Lost Dutchman and Sanders Galleries.

Blair, Robert H. Watercolorist of realistic historical scenes of mountain men and Indians, born in Bell, California, about 1937 and living in Mountain Ranch, California. "My works have run from abstract through rural to Western, but I finally settled into painting Western subjects, particularly the fur trade era. Most art has its roots in Europe, but Western art is uniquely American. After all, only in America were there ever cowboys, Indians, and mountain men."

Raised on a small farm near Whittier, Blair graduated from high school and entered the Chouinard Institute of Art in Los Angeles before attending the Art Center School of Design. When he left the Los Angeles area, it was to live and work on a ranch in the foothills of the Sierra Nevada. He has several horses, "just good old boys I keep around to live out their lives." There are also "a permanent tipi and a mountain man lean-to for photographic sessions" with models Blair outfits from his collection.

With his props, Blair "recreates 'possible' scenes of Western history, representative of unsung heroes whose names and deeds are neither recorded nor remembered." The background scenery is based on the Wyoming back-country and the characters are drawn from research into old manuscripts, but the scenes are recreated and not actual historical incidents. Blair calls himself "primarily self-taught" despite his schooling. And the works are "99 percent watercolors." Among his awards are the gold medal for watercolor at the 1979 Western Artists of America show. His gallery is Meiners.

Betty J. Billups, LAST OF THE MORE FORTUNATE,
mixed media, 20 x 20

Gloria Bilotta, THE HOMECOMING, oil, 20 x 24

Robert Blair, SUPPER ON THE GROS VENTRE, watercolor, 11 x 22

Buckeye Blake

George J. Bleich

Blake, (Jim) Buckeye. Traditional painter and sculptor of the old cowboy West, born in Fullerton, California, in 1946 and living in Augusta, Montana. "I find it very difficult," he observes, "to paint what everyone else is painting. It drives me crazy. I love the Western themes, but if I see another mountain man or a cowboy heelin' a calf for the branding fire—well, I hope it's reached its saturation point. I could make a million dollars painting fat little Indian children holding little bunny rabbits and looking sweet and helpless, but my heart just wouldn't be in it.

"My father rodeoed and we traveled quite a bit. We finally settled in Carson City, Nevada, on a ranch in 1956. My father built a rodeo arena and my mother painted murals in dance halls and became a portrait painter. I was always drawing and started winning school contests. I left high school in my junior year and went to work in Hollywood in some of the seedier studios making cartoons and back-drops, then came back to Nevada after a year as the Hollywood life was a little strange to me, to say the least.

"I would send in pictures to those art contests on the back of magazines and win a scholarship to some school some place. I figured if I could win enough of them, I could cash them in like Blue Chip stamps and pay for a year of art school, but that's not the way it worked. I started selling my work in galleries. Since moving to Montana in 1979, I made a series of decanters for a bottling company, and completed the large bronzes of the Charley Russell funeral procession and of a stagecoach with six running horses." His art may be seen in the Montana Gallery and Book Shoppe and at the Eagle Art Gallery.

Bleich, George. Traditional marine and landscape painter, born in Philadelphia, Pennsylvania, in 1936 and living in Carmel, California. "I try to paint to allow the eye to optically mix colors," he explains, "and create a certain vibrancy and life. I am interested in painting the atmosphere. I've never had any formal training, but I think that if you study the life of many painters you'll find that they had a feeling to express, something they wanted to say through their use of color, their brushstroke.

"My father was a Merchant Marine officer, lost at sea when I was six. At fifteen, I left home to become a professional seaman. I've always thought of the ocean as a male image, strong yet serene. I've had the reverse idea that the land was mother earth." Called the 'painter of the outdoors,' he began with marine scenes. During a visit to Europe, he turned to landscapes and when he returned home he painted on location in the Sierras and Yosemite. In 1979, he was artist in residence in Thomas Hill's Yosemite studio.

"I love panorama and grandeur," he declares. "I think part of the freshness of my paintings is due to my movement from mountain to seaside." His preoccupation is with lighting systems for viewing art. "My theory is," he stresses, that "if you can infuse a painting with color as it exists in nature, the work will respond to changes of artificial light the same as it does in nature. Many people are astonished to see how my paintings respond to variable lighting. Just think: If a painting is improperly lit, it may create an illusion entirely different from that intended by the artist." Written up in *Artists of the Rockies*, fall 1979, he is published by Art Frame Gallery, and is represented by his own gallery.

Buckeye Blake, THE MUSIC BOX, gouache, 22 x 16

George Bleich, SPRINGTIME AT YOSEMITE, acrylic, 60 x 36

Howard Bobbs

Bodelson

Joseph Bohler

Bobbs, Howard. Traditional painter and sculptor of diverse subjects including New Mexican scenes, born in Pennsylvania in 1910 and living in Santa Fe, New Mexico, since 1949. When he first saw Santa Fe, "after the chaos and confusion of New York and Chicago, I thought I had stumbled, quite by accident, on Paradise. It was rather like a small European village with its crudely constructed adobe buildings, the quaint flat roofs, the fantastic color everywhere, and the little old couples."

A sixth generation artist descended from Anton Wiertz in Brussels, Bobbs was raised in California and studied with his father at the Otis and Hollywood Art Institutes. He designed terrazzo floors in St. Louis for three years, lost his job in the Depression, and became a WPA supervisor teaching art in New York City while attending the Phoenix Art Institute, the National Academy of Design School, and the Art Students League. After trying Chicago, he found Santa Fe, a city that "is all changed now. Still, Santa Fe is the most desirable place to live that I can think of."

He spends at least two winter months in Carmel, California, and then heads for Hawaii for the rest of the winter. Mexico, France, England, Italy, and Scotland are other areas he has painted. One of his pet peeves is the self-appointed authority who "has been into art for at least a year" and wants to discuss the fine points of Bobbs' work. Another is the Eastern artist who moves to the Southwest, dons high heeled boots and a sombrero, and is transformed overnight into a cowboy artist. Written up in *Southwest Art*, September 1973 and April 1979, and in *Artists of the Rockies*, spring 1979, he is represented by his own Howard Bobbs Gallery.

Bodelson, Dan. Realist oil painter of the life and land of the Southwest, born in Minnesota in 1949 and living in Santa Fe, New Mexico, since 1973. "Painters of today that I especially admire," Bodelson states, "include James Reynolds, Tom Lovell, and Clark Hulings. All of them have a deep love for what they do and a craftsmanship that sets them apart from others. Their painting goes far beyond subject matter or style—they reach out to you—and this is what I want my work to do."

Raised in Boulder, Colorado, Bodelson graduated from high school in Santa Fe and went on to California College of Arts and Crafts in Oakland where he earned his BFA in 1972. He worked briefly as an illustrator in San Francisco and then returned to Santa Fe. He emphasizes that "living in Santa Fe is ideal. There is a tremendous energy and creativity flowing there. Some of the best living artists are here and are willing to give help and share their experiences when asked.

"I paint Westerns (past and present), animals, landscapes, damn near anything that I get excited about," he adds. "I try not to limit the flow of ideas, no matter what the subject matter, but I am a realist. I draw my ideas with pen or brush in oil on primed linen. Before the final painting is laid out, I do drawings and oil sketches when needed." *Business Week* on December 28, 1981 listed Bodelson "among those whose works are good bets" for investment. He began exhibiting as an illustrator in California in 1972 and was in invitational exhibitions by 1978, including Margaret Jamison Presents, Previews, and the Stamford Art Show. He is represented by Troy's Gallery, Texas Art Gallery, and Gaspard House.

Bohler, Joseph. Traditional painter of figures and landscapes in watercolor, pastel, and oil, born near Augusta, Montana, in 1940 and living in Monument, Colorado, since 1977. "You go to the mountain, become the mountain, and then you paint the mountain," he states. "I always try to go where I paint, and sketch and get a feel for the things I paint. I like to do trees a lot. You see lots of them in my landscapes. I make a lot of notes. It is my shorthand. You make your decisions with your little sketches."

Brought up on a remote cattle ranch, Bohler says that "I just think it makes a big difference, having been there." His only formal art training was a two year correspondence course. After serving in the Army for two years, he worked for a commercial art studio in Great Falls, Montana, for a year and for Hallmark in Kansas City, Missouri, for eight years. He painted for gallery exhibitions in his spare time. In 1972, he decided to paint full time, saying that otherwise "some day I would be sitting back there in my safe little place, saying to myself, 'could I really have done it?' "

Bohler notes that paintings "happen in my mind," and that his technique is "an economy of brushstrokes. Sometimes I don't even know I'm painting. I'm just describing what I see in my own way." He prefers to work outside, in natural light. "Many of the feels, smells, and moods of the outdoor life I knew as a boy come back to me now as I paint." After quickly becoming a member of the American Watercolor Society, he is also a founding member of the Northwest Rendezvous Group. Written up in *Art West, Artists of the Rockies*, and *Southwest Art*, he is represented by Trailside Galleries where a watercolor was priced at $3,000 in 1981.

Dan Bodelson, SUPPLY WAGON, oil, 24 x 36

Howard Bobbs, NEW MEXICO GOLD, oil, 18 x 24

Joe Bohler, SWALLOW CANYON, oil, 9 x 12

Truman Bolinger

Bolinger, Truman. Sculptor of bronze statuettes with multi-colored patinas, born in Sheridan, Wyoming, in 1944 and living in Scottsdale, Arizona. "Sculpture is competing with painting for the attention of the public," Bolinger says, "and the addition of color increases the realism and the drama. People who were once only interested in painting are now beginning to look at sculpture. They are interested in what their forefathers did. They are thinking more about what it took to make America what it is today.

"The West is bred in me," he declares. "that's where my heart lies." He grew up on his father's ranch near Ucross, Wyoming, and "never really thought about being an artist. I always thought I'd be a rancher." After a year at Sheridan College, he realized that he "had feelings about the West that could only be shared through art" so he transferred to the Colorado Institute of Art in Denver as a painter. His problem was color, and "all this frustration came to a head one day when I did a palette knife of a Western landscape. The instructor thought it was a seascape. I knew right then and there that I was in the wrong field." He switched to sculpting, "a natural art for me, as if I had done it before." Bolinger also studied at the Art Students League in New York City and began as a full-time sculptor in 1968.

He does not start with preliminary sketches for his models. "When I get an idea, I am excited about it. I don't want to mess around sketching on paper." He goes right to the wax. "There's not much detail at first but it's all I need. What I'm concerned with is the overall design—space and mass." Written up in *Artists of the Rockies*, summer 1976 and *Southwest Art*, October 1979, Bolinger is represented by The May Gallery.

Truman Bolinger, SETTLING OLD SCORES, bronze, h 32

Bongart, Sergei. Impressionist painter of California and Idaho in oil and acrylic,
born in Kiev, Russia, and living in Santa
Monica, California, and Rexburg, Idaho.
"When students ask how to paint flesh, or a
cucumber, I tell them it's a ridiculous question," he comments. "You paint the President of the United States and a cucumber
in exactly the same way. Look for the color
relationships, the right values, and arrive at
the right results. Tones and hues react on
one another just as much as notes interrelate to create certain harmonies."

A graduate of the Academy of Arts in
Kiev, Bongart had studied in Prague, Vienna, and Munich before coming to the U.S.
in 1948. He began as a portrait painter and
says that "there's no point in carefully
delineating all the features with charcoal.
You only need to put down a few basics
because you'll cover your layout anyway.
You must know drawing thoroughly and
this comes with endless practice in sketching.

"The whole process of painting is
really instant drawing. You draw with color,
and you must feel as you paint that your
medium can be molded freely like clay.
You must build form and modeling with
color, continually drawing with your brush.
To me, color is like music. It must sing.
Painting is not to tell a story, but a painting
should evoke a mood." Bongart is unique
in that he is a member of the National
Academy of Design. He is also a member of
the American Watercolor Society, England's
Royal Society of Arts, the National Academy
of Western Artists, and the Society of
Western Artists. He was featured in *Artists
of the Rockies*, summer 1978, and his
gallery is his own Sergei Bongart School of
Art.

Boomer, John. Traditional sculptor
of Indian figures in wood, stone, and bronze,
born in Chowchilla, California, in 1945
and living in Crystal, New Mexico, since
1972. His goal is "to get at the form, to
uncover that vision and release what is
waiting inside. The face is perhaps the
strongest force. This is my area for exploring
inner feelings. I never try to repeat a piece.
The natural shapes, colors, and grains of
wood are so different that they must be
considered on an individual basis."

His grandfather was a cabinetmaker
who treasured rare wood, so when Boomer
helped harvest lumber in northern California, he put aside the black walnut, even
though he had no immediate plan for it. He
was studying at California State University
at Chico where he received a degree in
psychology in 1968. To take time to resolve
his future, he obtained a job at the Rough
Rock Demonstration School on the Navajo
Reservation in Arizona, teaching elementary school.

When he married another teacher
who was a Navajo, she encouraged him to
follow his grandfather's feeling for wood
and become a sculptor. At the end of the
school term in 1972, they both quit their
jobs and with their savings moved to her
mother's ranch. For another year, Boomer
worked as a ranch hand for his board and
set up shop in an old hogan. Selling his
sculpture was difficult because each piece,
he says, was like a part of himself, but by
1975 he was an established professional.
His aim is "to grow more sensitive to the
spirit caught within" the wood, by "displaying the warm colors, bold forms, and
changing textures" that would otherwise
remain imprisoned. Written up in *Artists of
the Rockies*, summer 1976, Boomer maintains his own studio.

John Boomer, FIRST WOMAN (1979), walnut, h 17½

Sergei Bongart, LILACS, oil, 36 x 40

65

Stan Borack

James Boren 1982

Jodie Boren

Borack, Stan. Realistic oil painter of the Old West—Indians, troopers, cowboys, and mountain men, born in New York City in 1927 and living there since. "I've always loved a good Western movie," he comments. "That period was a classical era in American history with its unique clothing, colorful Indian costumes, and wagons. And, who doesn't like to look at a good horse in movement? When the Western art market took off, I got into it and left everything behind. I love what I'm doing."

After attending the High School of Music and Art, Borack served in the Navy in World War II and then enrolled in the Art Students League. A long career in illustration followed, with work for the magazines, advertising, movies, books, and records. In 1969, he began painting the West, and his studio is filled with costumes, gear, and texts on the West. "I think in pictures," he observes, "and I see them all the time. I'm always jotting them down, almost as a musician composes a score."

He begins a painting by selecting a landscape from photographs and letting the figures come to mind. The concept is roughed out on paper, and photographs provide the horses. After researching the costumes, he calls in the models and photographs them. The crucial stage is a six inch color sketch. Then the actual size drawing is done, fully detailed, and "it is only at this point that I begin to paint. After an eight hour day, I stop painting and study what I have done. I've been painting professionally for 30 years, and I never tire of the high that painting gives me." A member of the Society of Illustrators and written up in *Southwest Art*, January 1980, Borack is represented by Troy's Gallery.

Boren, James. Painter of the contemporary West in oils and watercolor, born in Waxahatchie, Texas, in 1921 and living in Clifton, Texas, since 1971. "An artist must have insight into his own feelings," Boren says, "the acumen to perceive subject matter as a vehicle for transmitting those emotions, and the talent to portray them through the medium of painting. What's really important is how you do it."

As a minister's son, Boren calls himself "a religious person." By the time he graduated from high school, he knew he wanted to be an illustrator but he quit Southwestern College to enlist in the Marines for World War II. After the war, he enrolled in the Kansas City Art Institute and in his second year transferred to fine arts. Boren earned his MFA in 1951 and taught art for two years at St. Mary's College where he says he would still be "if the pay had been good." With his savings, he traveled the Southwest and painted in Alaska until 1956 when he moved to Denver to work as a concept illustrator for the Martin Company. He began selling cowboy paintings in 1959.

In 1964 Boren was asked to become Art Director of the new Cowboy Hall of Fame in Oklahoma City "where I met all the great Western artists I'd only heard about." His exhibition at the Hall in 1969 sold 28 of 30 paintings: "I decided then it was time for me to be a full-time painter. I have been just that ever since." He was named Texas State Artist of the Year in 1976, and as a member of the Cowboy Artists of America he has won the gold medal in watercolor seven times. He has been featured in *Artists of the Rockies*, fall 1978, and *Southwest Art*, October 1981. His prints are published by Mill Pond Press and he has shown at the Texas Art Gallery.

Boren, Jodie. Representational painter of a "peaceful, tranquil" contemporary West in watercolor and oil, born in Sweetwater, Texas, in 1926 and living in Abilene, Texas, since 1956. "I paint about four watercolors to every oil," he explains. "It's pure expediency. I can satisfy three or four people with watercolors instead of only one with an oil. I paint over a hundred pictures a year to meet my commitments. What with travel and appearing at shows, watercolor is the only way I can do it.

"In his early years, Dad was a gospel preacher and we moved often. My childhood was spent in west Texas, the Rio Grande Valley, central Texas, and Oklahoma. Dad was chaplain for Camp Gruber in Muskogee when I finished high school and went into World War II. I saw about 20 months sea duty in the Pacific and was at the battle of Iwo Jima. Right after the war, my brother James was enrolled in the Kansas City Art Institute and so in 1946 I enrolled. When I finished in 1949, I went to work with Hallmark Cards for seven years. I left to come to Abilene where I hooked up with an advertising agency until 1971.

"I had begun making the transition to fine art in 1968 by working on weekends and evenings. I had been received so well that by 1971, I left the agency and have been making a very comfortable living ever since. I participate in six or eight shows each year and then usually have at least one one-man show. I do not belong to any group now. I am with Frame House Gallery for limited edition prints and with the Double T Ranch and the Corpus Christi Art Galleries." Featured in *Southwest Art*, October 1977, his 1982 Christmas card was Leanin' Tree's most popular of 160 designs, selling 200,000 units.

James Boren, RAINY DAY AT HILLSBORO, watercolor, 14½ x 21

Stan Borack, SHALLOW CROSSING, oil, 30 x 20

Jodie Boren, MAIN STREET—DODGE CITY, oil, 14 x 30

Nancy Boren *J. SHIRLY BOTHUM*

Boren, Nancy. Representational landscape painter of Texas, Wyoming, and Alaska in transparent watercolor, oil, gouache, and charcoal, born in Anchorage, Alaska, in 1955 and living in Clifton, Texas, since 1971. "I read and study other artists," she says, "such as Robert Henri, Edgar Whitney, Ned Jacob, Bob Lougheed, my father of course, John Singer Sargent, Fechin, Sir Russell Flint, Sorolla, Homer—the list goes on. I'm not trying to emulate any of them, but to understand their feel for capturing life, their ability to cut through the superfluous details to the heart of the matter."

Raised in Denver, Oklahoma City, and Clifton, she began painting in the studio of her father, James Boren, in 1965. During her grade school days, her father was always very good about letting her play around the studio while he was working. Sometimes, she'd set up a still life model in the corner and work on her own. By the time she went off to Abilene Christian University, she was firmly on the path toward a fine arts career. When she received her BFA cum laude in 1977, she moved back to Clifton and began painting full time.

The following year, she had her first shows, and by 1982, she was in the Western Heritage Show in Houston. She declares that "being a success in the art business takes inclination, knowledge, and a lot of practice. I try to keep pushing, keep working on figure drawing. I also enjoy painting landscapes and still lifes. I'm interested in many different things, which is good—you can always find something fresh to work on. I want people who look at my paintings to say, 'That girl really knows what she is about!' " She has exhibited at Troy's and Texas Art Galleries.

Bothum, J. Shirly. Sculptor of contemporary cowboy life, born on a Stafford County, Kansas, farm in 1938 and living near Clarkston, Washington. "I spent the first 30 years of my life wanting to be a cowboy and rancher," he says, "and now I want to spend the next 30 years recording that life in bronze. If I had time to do all my inspirations, I'd probably be the most prolific artist in the world."

When he was nine, Bothum's family moved to Oregon's Willamette Valley. After he graduated from high school, he worked as a cowboy for three years in eastern Oregon, then for another ten years in camps north to Washington. "I think it was 30 years before I ever rode a gentle horse," he declares, recalling "the excitement of riding the wild and spooky ones." He "stomped" horses for $50 a month, and from 1961 to 1967 rode in the Rodeo Cowboys Association Saddle Bronc Event. He also tried ranching and farming, and in the early 1970s began modeling in clay. When he enrolled in a sculpture class, however, "the instructor felt threatened by Bothum and asked that he not return." According to Bothum, "all that 'educated art professor' did was make me more determined to learn," so he taught himself out of books. He was encouraged to have his models cast, and people began buying them directly from him: "The first bronzes I had, I put in the back of the car and took off down the road."

Bothum works from live models of horses and cattle. "That's the reason I don't do nudes," he explains. "I don't have any nude models." Now a member of wildlife foundations, he is hailed for accuracy and invited to museum exhibitions. He is represented by Fowler's Gallery.

J. Shirly Bothum, WRANGLING THE WILD ONES, bronze, h 24, l 56

Nancy Boren, EARLY SNOW, watercolor, 13 x 18

Guy Botto

G. Boutwell

Parker Boyiddle

Botto, Guy. Representational painter of the Texas Hill Country in oil and acrylic, born in San Antonio, Texas, in 1920 and living in Harlingen, Texas, since 1977. "I don't try to do anything outstandingly dramatic," he explains. "For instance, you might have a cowboy and Indian scene. They're always coming to some point of action and you wonder if maybe the Indians are going to overcome the cowboys. That question mark is always on our wall, right? I like to tell the whole story, not leave them up in the air about what the painting means."

When he was nine, he received his first paints and studied privately. While he was in high school, he worked for a cartoonist in the evenings and after graduation was apprenticed to a watercolorist, but in 1944 he joined the Merchant Marine where he remained until 1951. His father had been in home construction and he entered the business, too, painting at night and in sidewalk shows on weekends. By 1969, his paintings were selling and in 1973, he became a full time artist.

To make out, he "had to have about a hundred paintings at cafes and beauty parlors. I would sell to the person who could afford a painting for maybe $25. Sometimes I would line up four or five paintings and paint them all at once. I had to do that to get by." Today, he paints mostly from photographs because "it's much easier that way. For some, I make sketches on location first, but after a while, you don't need that. You can just take a black and white photograph and paint whatever you want from it, but I make a complete drawing on tracing paper before I put it on canvas. I don't just start to paint." Written up in *Southwest Art*, January 1979, he is represented by Art Galleries at Bahia Mar Resort and by Thompson Gallery.

Boutwell, George. Realistic watercolorist of the central Texas farm country, born in East Hartford, Connecticut, in 1943 and living in Austin, Texas, since 1957. "The main reason I left commercial art," he says, "was the lack of recognition. There was something deep down inside of me that needed recognition. I was ashamed of that at first because no one in my family wanted to be in the spotlight. In commercial art, my work would be everywhere, but no one knew that. I finally made the decision to move into fine arts, and I've been happy with that.

"As a young boy," he recalls, "I traveled with my father all over the United States, finally settling in Austin. I've always been interested in art but, due to lack of money, I went to work after high school. I attended business school at night and studied drafting. After two years of doing technical illustration, I went to work for *Texas* as art director" and continued in commercial art before beginning to paint full time in 1973. "I never had a live instructor. I call my approach experimental watercolor because all the background masses are rendered loosely, wet-in-wet, and I work in detail with dry brush.

"I think that art for the average person," Boutwell continues, "has become a form of entertainment. In the old times there were no TVs or mass media. Paintings were historical records. Now we're entertainers and that's the reason for the huge public demand for art. Having been exposed to business has helped me a great deal." He sells his own paintings and publishes his own prints after polling the market. Boutwell has been featured in five national magazines and says he is "only breaking the surface of my technique."

Boyiddle, Parker. Delaware and Kiowa Indian painter in acrylic and watercolor and sculptor in metal, clay, and plastic, born in Chickasha, Oklahoma, in 1947 and living in Los Lunas, New Mexico. "The American Indian thought processes," he observes, "are akin to the Far Eastern train of thought. What I'm trying to convey is a general experience that many American Indians encounter when living a dual-cultural life. I idealize my ancestral past, and show our racial pride, humor, and the paradox of living in the space age.

"Since childhood, I wanted to be an artist. I attended school in Oklahoma City and Anadarko, then from 1964 to 1966 went to the Institute of American Indian Arts in Santa Fe, studying under Allan Houser and Fritz Scholder. I served in the Air Force from 1967 to 1971, and afterwards studied art at Pima College in Tucson in 1972 and 1973. Perhaps because of the early influences of my artistic development, I spent more than ten years perfecting my work and ideas before presenting the work to the public.

"In 1977, I started to exhibit my work publicly, receiving the Phippen Memorial award for sculpture, first prize in the Trail of Tears Art Show, and the Grand Prize at the American Indian and Cowboy Artists show. In 1978, I won the Grand Award at the Philbrook Art Exhibit, and in 1979 went with the American Indian Artist group to its exhibition in Paris. My professional affiliations include membership in the AICA, and in its 1980 show I was awarded first place for oil painting. I consider myself highly introspective, and don't want to come across as a case of the I-Me's. Marc Bahti publishes my prints, and I am represented by Tom Bahti Indian Art Shop and The Files' Gallery of Fine Arts."

Guy Botto, HILL COUNTRY BLUE BONNETS, acrylic, 22 x 28

Parker Boyiddle, SEEING THROUGH COYOTE'S EYES
acrylic, 24 x 30

George Boutwell, IN THE NICK OF TIME, watercolor, 18 x 30

Boyle

AMY BRACKENBURY

Boyle, Neil. Representational oil painter of the Old West, born in Fort Macleod, Alberta, Canada, about 1931 and living in Calabasas, California. When asked "Why do you like to paint saloons and whore houses," he replies, "I paint what I know!" When asked if he was ever a cowboy or whether he had lived on a ranch, he replies, "Absolutely not! Horses terrify me. You know, El Greco painted great crucifixions, but I don't think he ever attended one."

He was raised near the Blood and Piegan tribes of the Blackfoot Confederacy where his father was an honorary chief. "My mother," he recalls, "was the first to get the idea that I'd be an artist, but all kids have a charming way of drawing what they see. The only trouble is, they get past a certain age and it isn't charming anymore. Since I didn't quite make it through high school, I was just lucky my dad could afford to send me to Art Center. Even then, I didn't do too well. After a year or two of not knowing what I was doing, I got scared. I realized I'd actually have to make a living at illustration some day.

"Most of my free lancing was drawing a lot of round-bottomed animals for Walt Disney Studios. After awhile, the side stuff started paying more than the job, so I decided to quit and see what it was like out there." He says that "a painting is just an illustration with a frame around it. Pictures should tell stories. The feeling the individual viewer gets comes from the way he sees that event or person, not from me. Cowboy art is an escapist form, but there's a romance to it, as the past is depicted without flies or dust." Written up in *Southwest Art*, May 1979, Boyle is represented and published by Peppertree Fine Art, Inc.

Brackenbury Larsen, Amy. Representational painter of wildlife in acrylic, born in Fort Collins, Colorado, in 1953 and living in Livermore, Colorado, since 1975. "I try for a graphic, poster-like quality," she explains. "My main concern is the animal. The background is secondary, and I feel that the less background there is the better. I add as much detail as it takes to bring the animal to life, but not so much as to detail it to death. I admire Oriental art for its feeling for composition, negative space, and simplicity.

"I lived on the family ranch in the northern Colorado foothills until 1967 when I returned to Fort Collins to finish my schooling. In college, almost all my painting courses concentrated on abstract and nonobjective art and I still enjoy doing that type of painting for relaxation. While attending Colorado State University, I met my husband-to-be in a scientific illustration course, taught him to paint, and together we made enough money to live on, so he quit the Game and Fish Department and we were married.

"Painting wildlife lets me do what I like to do best—observe and be in close association with animals. I feel privileged to live where I do because of the great variety and abundance of wildlife that give me the opportunity to work from live models. I like the idea of Oriental screens where two or more paintings hang together as companion pieces, an idea that I've employed in many of my works. Gathering the source material and formulating the concept take a lot of time, and from when I sit down in front of a bare canvas till I lay down the last stroke can take anywhere from a week to a year. I am currently showing my work in Carson Gallery of Western American Art and in Gateway Art Galleries."

Amy Brackenbury, COTTON TAIL, acrylic, 24 x 34

Neil Boyle, GIVE THE LITTLE LADY A GREAT BIG HAND, oil, 30 x 40

GAROUTTE

Bernard Bradley
Sedona, Az.

Brackett, Don. Traditional and "abstract impressions of realism" painter of New Mexico landscapes in watercolor, born in Optima, Oklahoma, in 1932 and living in Placitas, New Mexico. "I prefer to paint the lovely villages and landscapes of the New Mexico that I have known all my life," he says. "I concentrate on New Mexico because it is a state that has character unequaled by any other. I often paint on location and find that watercolor best suits my purpose because it's a spontaneous medium that gives a fresh sparkle to the subject.

"My parents moved to Albuquerque in 1933 and I graduated from high school in 1951. During the Korean war, I joined the Marine Corps and served from 1952 to 1955, then attended the University of New Mexico until 1958, studying with Kenneth Adams. I later returned to the university from 1965 to 1967 for further watercolor classes with Ralph Lewis, and studied additionally with watercolorists Robert E. Wood and Millard Sheets of California, and Milford Zornes of Utah." Brackett's studio is at the foot of the Sandia Mountain.

Adobes and pueblos are typical Brackett subjects that he also paints in oil and acrylic. His work is in public collections in New Mexico and Texas and he has had ten one-person shows in the Southwest. He has received more than 70 national and regional awards, including a cash prize at the 1980 American Watercolor Society exhibition in New York City. Published by Starline Collector's Gallery, he is a member of the American and National Watercolor Societies. Along with his wife, Phyllis Garoutte he is represented by Golden Willow and Sussman Galleries.

Brackett, Phyllis Garoutte. Painter of florals and New Mexico landscapes, born in Freistatt, Missouri, in 1937 and living in Placitas, New Mexico. "Spiritual perception," she emphasizes, "this I'm striving to attain, to enlarge upon, to grow in, through my paintings. I love so much what Bach put on his manuscripts—'for the glory of God'—that is how I feel about my work and why I paint."

After high school, she enrolled in the Kansas City Art Institute and at 19 was employed in the art department of Hallmark Cards as a color plate artist. She "soon realized that commercial art was not what she wanted. The work was demanding and high pressure." In Socorro, New Mexico, in 1963, she studied watercolor at the New Mexico School of Mines, and after moving to Albuquerque in 1969, studied with Robert E. Wood in 1970 and in 1971, as well as with Barse Miller, Millard Sheets, and Milford Zornes. She paints in watercolor, oil and acrylic, and her work reflects the New Mexico light.

She has "a womanly, sensitive awareness of the life and beauty around her," according to Mary Carroll Nelson, "and her own need to withdraw in order to express her own reactions to the world. She enjoys the partial subject—a bit of one tower rather than the whole church. Her work includes landscapes and close-ups in nature. She seeks a unity of nature's forms with man-made ones." She has exhibited at the American Watercolor Society since 1976 and at the National League of American Pen Women since 1977, is published by Starline Collector's Gallery, and along with her husband, Don , is represented by Arthur Sussman and Last Straw Galleries.

Bradley, Bernard H. Watercolorist of the Red Rock country, born in Chicago, in 1915 and living in Sedona, Arizona, since 1970. "I find that the actual process of painting becomes less important as the struggle to capture an 'essence' intensifies," he says. "Fundamentals are always vital but are secondary. To interpret the 'feeling' inherent in the subject is the real challenge."

After studying at the Art Institute of Chicago on a scholarship, Bradley attended the University of Texas and in 1941 received a Master's degree in architecture from the University of Illinois. A full partner in the Chicago architectural firm of Holabird and Root after ten years, he handled assignments on four continents while painting as a hobby. In the early 1960s, Bradley and his wife visited Prescott, Arizona, on a business trip and "came down Oak Creek Canyon. We'd never heard of the place, but before we left we owned a lot on Sky Mountain." Attracted by the climate that eased his spinal arthritis, Bradley designed his own home on the mountain in 1970.

He says about Sedona that "wherever you look, there is something to paint, and it is never twice the same. Light and shade are constantly changing." About the "Red Rocks," he has discovered that "they are not just red. They are also all shades of umber and ochre, with accenting tones ranging from off-white to deep purples. In many of my paintings of them, I don't use red at all." He is an unusual watercolorist in that he makes so many preliminary sketches, studies, and color notes that he completes only two or three paintings a month. His gallery is Husberg Fine Arts Gallery.

Phyllis Garoutte Brackett, GRANDMOTHER'S BOUQUET, watercolor, 18 x 24

Bernard Bradley, GHOST TOWN, watercolor, 22 x 14

Don Brackett, JEMEZ COUNTRY, watercolor, 15 x 22

David P. Bradley

Daniel

Bradley, David P. "Contemporary commentary" Indian painter, sculptor, and printmaker, born in Eureka, California, in 1954 and living in Santa Fe, New Mexico, since 1977. "I deal with the dualities of Indian existence today," he explains. "One is that truthful situation of him/her in the modern house, complete with light socket and a plug-in. The other side of the duality is the scene out the window. I have a modern Indian, who maybe collects art, and I have a prehistoric landscape, the pure land outside."

Of Norwegian and Ojibway descent, Bradley moved to Minnesota to live with a foster family when he was six. "I had a very unusual childhood and maybe very rough," he recalls. "I ran away and have been on my own since the tenth grade." Following a year at the College of St. Thomas in Minnesota, he managed a model farm for the Peace Corps in the Dominican Republic and then was a practical veterinarian in Guatamala. He came to Santa Fe in 1977 to attend the Institute of American Indian Arts.

"When I first went to the Institute," he says, "sculpture came easily to me, but to control my painting was a great battle. I couldn't arrive at a style," but he graduated in 1979 as valedictorian. "I do like to have fun with my art," he adds, "and I like to find humor. In some paintings I try to put humor in, but there are also some very grave, serious symbols there, too. I'll put symbols in my paintings that might suggest the state of the world today. Even though it's a scene from the Old West, all of sudden it will relate to what's going on today." In 1981, he received *Santa Fean* magazine's Artist of the Year award. He is represented by Elaine Horwitch and Judith Stern Galleries.

Brennan, Daniel, signs "Daniel." Colorist oil painter of Mexican fantasy, born in Hutchinson, Kansas, about 1941 and living in San Miguel de Allende, Mexico, since 1964. In the evolution of his paintings, he says that "reality is always the starting point. I must begin with something I see and the romantic aspect develops from that. I don't paint a purely fantasy world. It is always based on reality."

After service in the U.S. Army, Brennan studied journalism under the G.I. Bill at Kansas State University. He changed his major to art, transferred to Memphis Academy of Art, and then went to New York City to work with Will Barnett at the Art Students League. He returned to Kansas City, loaded boxcars to support his painting, and moved to the artists' colony at San Miguel on the strength of a sale of fifteen paintings to a patron. He has remained in San Miguel because "the magic caught me. I responded right away to Mexico, although for the first six months I painted like I had in Kansas City. The influence of Mexico took over gradually. I tried to see Mexico through the eyes of the children, for seen that way it becomes a magical place.

"I enjoy painting," Brennan says, "like some people enjoy sex." To enhance his naive colors, he sketches the preliminary lines in blue, like Gauguin: "I use blue because I feel that colors put on top of blue become more brilliant." His approach is "to see what can be done with colors. I paint the painting the first time and the viewer repaints it with his eyes." In 1979, Brennan's work was chosen for the *Encyclopedia of Contemporary Mexican Painters* and in September 1981 he was featured in *Southwest Art*.

David Bradley, CALL OF THE WILD, acrylic/canvas, 30 x 24

Daniel Brennan, MASQUERADE, oil, 21 x 40

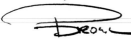

Brigham, Barbara. Sculptor of humorous Western dioramas, born in Newark, New Jersey, in 1929 and living in Austin, Texas. One of her collectors has said that "she has talent for a Yankee. I have studied her scenes and have shaken my head at the authenticity and the realistic detail such as the light glowing on a cigarette or the embers of a campfire. The characters come to life, yet they impart a bit of humor."

The daughter of a commercial artist and a pianist, she majored in art at Skidmore College and attended the Art Students League in New York City on a scholarship, studying painting under the famous Frank Vincent DuMond. She then moved to Mexico City and illustrated books before changing to modeling in 1974. Each of her scenes is original because she "refuses to use molds or go into any other form of mass production," and the detailing varies. The most popular subject is the old time Western saloon. Other works include campire scenes, doctors' and lawyers' offices, poker players, and individual characters.

"The bodies are constructed with wire wrapped with pipe cleaners to give form," she says, "then stronger wire goes up through the figure and down into the base for solidity. The heads, hands, boots, hats, etc., are modeled, baked and painted. Hair and beards are pieces or rope which I dye. The figures are then dressed from scraps to make them appear worn out. Whiskey and wine bottles, beer mugs, and hurricane lamps are made from thrown away syringes, needle tops, and tubing which I rescue from the hospital trash box." She is represented by Husberg Fine Arts Gallery.

Brinkman, Tracy Beeler. Traditional sculptor of bronze figures, born in Los Angeles, California, in 1958 and living in Mountain Home, Texas, since 1981. "Growing up in my particular family environment was my art training," she remarks. "My parents included me in all traveling and social situations, which all revolved around art, and while traveling, I always entertained myself with drawing. For Christmas, I wanted project materials instead of dolls. My interests changed many times, but they were always art oriented.

"I always *hated* school and made less than perfect grades. I was bored to tears in high school. For some unknown reason, I went to college at Northern Arizona University where I 'studied' general courses. After three semesters, I quit and went back to Sedona. Anything I know, I learned from my father and from art books, and I traveled through Europe for two summers with a student program, one of the best educational experiences for me.

"Right after my first show last October with Dad and Jim and Nancy Boren, I was married, but yes! yes! yes! I am still going to work. The Beeler name honestly does pressure me. I feel that if I am going to be a sculptor, I had better be a darn good one because I am Joe Beeler's daughter and have had many advantages other beginning artists have not had. My father never did pressure me to become an artist when my talent became apparent, but both parents always encouraged and supported any reasonable interest I pursued, naturally including sculpture. Discipline is important to me in my art life, as is being around other artists. I have to be with nature, too. It restores and inspires me." She has exhibited at El Prado Gallery of Art.

Broer, Roger L. Modern painter, mostly of animals and particularly of the hawk, born in Omaha, Nebraska, in 1945 and living in Kent, Washington. "I used to try to paint Indians with the same emotional magic as Fritz Scholder. First I realized it was a copy—like Fritz Scholder and not an original by Roger Broer. A friend told me that 'you need not paint Indians to paint Indian.' I now paint things, things that are precious to me. In doing that, I paint Roger Broer who is producing his own magic and essence of his own Indianness. I mostly fear copying myself."

Of Oglala Lakota descent, Broer received his BA in fine art from Eastern Montana College in 1974 and studied toward his MA at Central Washington University the following year. He then remained in the Northwest. He says that "I've always wanted to be an artist, and I guess I still do. The only difference from when I was a child is that I now have technical ability. My painting is the same, and it looks to me that my children are a lot like I was. When I work, I play. Art belies the whole Puritan work ethic.

"When I paint, I do that just for me. I do not consider anything. I guess that the reason I have achieved recognition is because intelligent people understand my work. If I find I have to rationalize my paintings verbally at any point, then I must look again at my work because evidently I must not be succeeding at making art. I perceive my major strength to be a 'no holds barred' approach to painting. How a painting is accomplished is of little value when in retrospect one observes the sense of spiritualism in the finished product." A member of the American Indian and Cowboy Artists, Broer has exhibited with the AICA since 1979.

Barbara Brigham, THE FIGHT (diorama)

Tracy Beeler Brinkman, AS FREE AS THE WIND, bronze, h 22

Roger Broer, FROM THE FLOOR LOOKING UP, mixed media, 14 x 18

CLARK BRONSON

Bronson, Clark Everice. Wildlife artist in realistic bronze sculpture and painting, born in Kamas, Utah, in 1939 and living in Bozeman, Montana. "In early 1969 I made a drawing of a mule deer jumping over a log. I knew that if I could draw that mule deer, I could sculpt it. Suddenly there was a whole new world of art open to me, a world I'd never considered before but one I knew I could be completely creative in. And in sculpture, just as in my wildlife painting, I had no one to teach me but myself."

The son of a Utah game warden, Bronson was experienced with animals before he was ten. When he graduated from high school, he won an art illustration "Draw Me" contest, took correspondence courses, and then studied at the University of Utah, but "I wasn't learning anything about wildlife art." He was an apprentice to Arnold Friberg for three years, until he was asked by Utah Fish and Game to do illustrations. By the time he was 30, his watercolors had been published in major magazines and he had illustrated four books, but "one day I just started a sculpture and I haven't lifted a brush since."

It took Bronson a year and a half to model his first four bronzes, and he still does only three or four pieces a year because "the research and details won't let me work any faster than that. I work on one piece at a time. Once I start, I continue straight through and I never entertain thoughts about any other work." He has been featured in *Southwest Art*, June 1975 and January 1980, and in *Art West*, spring 1978, is listed in *Who's Who in American Art*, is a member of the Society of Animal Artists, the National Sculpture Society, and the National Academy of Western Art, and exhibits at Trailside Galleries.

Clark Bronson, EAGLE'S CONQUEST, bronze, h 34, l 23½

Jonathan Bronson

Ginger Brown

HARLEY BROWN

Bronson, Jonathan. Traditional sculptor of wildlife bronzes, born in Chihuahua, Mexico, in 1952 and living in Pleasant Grove, Utah. "I see something," he explains, "that gives me an excitement or a thrill, or I see a particular thing that sticks in my mind as being exceptionally beautiful or has an exceptionally strong meaning or significance, or sometimes has a value in terms of something that's significant naturally or mentally, or something that has a value in a way. And these things come together over many years."

Raised in Utah, he is a cousin of Clark Bronson. By the age of six, he had begun drawing wildlife and by ten he had sold his first wildlife sculpture. He took care of orphaned owls and ravens, and of injured wild animals. Interested in engineering, physics, and astronomy, he also studied pre-medicine at the University of Utah for two years covering anatomy and hematology. In addition, he spent seven years at Wasatch Bronze Foundry, assisting in more than 30 monumental bronzes.

After ten years of sketching and field study cataloging in the Uinta and Rocky Mountain ranges, he has made four Alaskan trips, with special studies on wolves. In finding his ideas, he says that "there's just a perfect moment when everything comes together in a way that will never be that way again. There's just a certain split second that seems perfect." According to his representative, for several years his bronzes were sold before they could be produced. Recent editions were sold before they were sculpted, and the newest is being ordered before he has time to do the field studies. Bronson is represented by Nola Sullivan.

Brown, Ginger. Oil painter of nostalgic Texas scenes, born in Tarzan, Martin County, Texas, in 1936 and living in Midland, Texas, since 1949. "We have a ranch," she observes, "where I get a lot of my ideas. I know from first-hand experience what it's like to work on a windmill and help round up cows. I'm not very good at it, but I like to know how it feels so I can give more expression to my paintings.

"I have carried a pencil and paper around ever since I was able to walk. As a young girl, my daddy was a bus driver in Houston and I would ride with him in the summer and sketch my dad and the people on the bus. I went to elementary school there, won a scholarship to the Houston Museum of Fine Arts in 1948, and attended the museum school until my family moved back to Midland in 1949. I also studied privately from 1960 to 1964, and after I had started painting full time in 1975, I took another sketching class in Midland in 1980.

"I snap a lot of photographs at the ranch to use in my paintings and take pictures of my husband on horseback. He is my best source. He's been a cowboy all his life, so it makes him authentic. I hardly ever enter shows because I am very busy just painting and selling my prints and originals. I feel that I would be fortunate to master oil painting in my lifetime." Her four limited edition and one open edition prints are carried by galleries in Texas and New Mexico.

Brown, Harley. Traditional painter of pastel and oil portraits of Indians, born in Edmonton, Alberta, Canada, in 1939 and living in Calgary, Alberta, since 1966. "A person's day is filled with confronting one face after another. Each face is so different, not only in features but in angles of expression or the way light hits on it. Each face has secrets to uncover, and I interpret a reflection of the person's life and mind. This is why I am so interested in the Indian face. Its lines, furrows, texture, and color are as much a part of nature as the Superstition Mountains."

While growing up in Moose Jaw, Saskatchewan, Brown earned a teaching degree in music while still in high school. He then went to Alberta College of Art in Calgary where he played honkey-tonk piano and did dollar portraits in taverns, sometimes settling for a round of beer. "I had a lot of hangovers in those days," he recalls, and he auctioned all of his paintings to finance studies at the Camberwell School of Art in London. He sold pastel portraits of Indians in England and when he returned to Calgary, he began intensive research on the reservations.

To paint a portrait, Brown sketches and photographs the Indian and an assistant takes the history. In his Calgary basement, he wears Bermuda shorts and a Mickey Mouse T-shirt while he paints to the soundtracks of old movies. "I've tried art other than portraits," he says, "but I keep coming back to them." He was featured in *Art West*, summer 1977, and is a member of both the National Academy of Western Art and the Northwest Rendezvous Group. He is represented by Trailside and Shriver Galleries, exhibited in the Peking, China show and his pastel at the Settlers West 1981 silent auction carried a minimum bid of $6,800.

Ginger Brown, WORKING HORSES, oil, 8 x 10

Harley Brown, ESTELLA, lithograph, 13½ x 18, Edition 50

Jonathan Bronson, SPRING WINDS, bronze, h 4 ft, l 4 ft

Brown, Reynold. Impressionist oil painter of the Western scene, born in Los Angeles in 1917 and living in La Verne, California. Brown "sketches to keep up. He does pencil drawings while waiting for dinner. He experiments with different mediums." "Anything and everything," he states, "for it's like a musician practicing scales."

In the first grade, his teacher told the principal that "I've got him so he can write with his right hand, but I can't do anything while he's drawing. He always wants to draw with his left hand." When Brown was sixteen, he assisted in drawing a syndicated comic strip on flying and then worked as an illustrator for North American Aviation until 1946. He spent the next four years as a free-lance illustrator in New York City. In 1950, he returned to Los Angeles where he was a free-lance artist for major motion pictures and also taught head and figure painting and illustration at the Art Center College of Design, training many of the younger contemporary Western artists.

Since 1970, after 40 years as an illustrator, he has been doing easel paintings, traveling thousands of miles in his van to sketch the landscapes and talk to the old-timers who provide stories to be painted. His subjects are generally historical. "The difficult thing about doing Western art," he points out, "is that there is always someone who knows something about anything you do." He believes that accuracy is "important up to a point, but after much research, he is not sure that there is only one right answer all the time." Sometimes the experts do not know about the exceptions. Brown was featured in *Artists of the Rockies*, Fall 1975, and is represented by Trailside.

Brubaker, Lee. Traditional oil painter and illustrator, especially of the American Indian, born in Hollywood, California, in 1933 and living in Kirkwood, Missouri, since 1962. "The most personal painting I've done," he observes, "and would like to have kept was titled 'No Meat Today.' The situation dealt with an Indian hunter returning to his family empty handed. The summer of 1980 saw little paydays for me. Upon coming in the back door, often I was met with, 'Did you get paid today?' I've often wished I could tell this story to the owner of the painting."

Encouraged by his mother who was an artist, Brubaker studied illustration and fine art at the Art Center College of Design in Los Angeles for four years, worked as an illustrator for Douglas Aircraft Corporation until 1962, and then came to Missouri as a commercial illustrator. His pictures have appeared in *Time, Newsweek, Sports Illustrated,* and *Fortune,* for major advertisers. He was teaching art at Washington University in 1977 when he became friendly with a class model who was a full-blooded Sioux. The result was that Brubaker spent half his time illustrating and the other half painting the American West.

He says that "the one painting that stands out most in my mind dealt with Indians attacking a stagecoach. The couple who purchased the painting were psychiatrists and the husband grew up with Western movies in Greece. Their conversation dealt with feelings about violence. Why? I'm not a violent person but I do enjoy exciting action paintings. I try to steer clear of the romantic impressions of the movies, but you do have to put in a little romance." Brubaker is represented by Husberg Fine Arts Gallery which listed a painting at $3,800 in 1980.

Reynold Brown, TERRITORIAL JUDGE, oil, 24 x 36

Lee Brubaker, NO MEAT TODAY, oil, 16 x 20

Bruce

Duane Bryers

Budge

Bruce, John A. Realist painter of the California West in oil, born in Los Angeles in 1931 and living in Diamond Bar, California. "I was raised in the West just after the Great Depression," he says. "Memories of people then are material for my paintings. They were rugged, poor, and proud of their ability to face whatever came. Granddad Bruce typified the cowboy of the time. He was a circus strong man turned rancher. It was great adventure to stay with him in his log cabin near Rifle, Colorado. Even in the summer, the nights were chilly enough to make you run both ways to the privy.

"Grandma Haig lived in Sparks, Nevada. She owned an antique and second-hand store. My first recollections of Indians were from trips with her visiting reservation settlements, trading goods and blankets. There was a sadness in their eyes that I never understood until I read American history. I joined the Army, served in Korea, and was discharged in 1952. After studying art at the Art Center School and Chouinard Art Institute, I transferred to the state college system, earning a degree in psychology and art.

"I have been employed as artist-designer-illustrator and have held art director positions as well as doing free-lance design and illustration. This background as commercial artist and illustrator enables me to feel comfortable with most art media including egg tempera, watercolor, acrylic, and gouache; but almost all my serious work is done in oil. I have a rough time restricting myself to one subject because I enjoy painting a landscape as much as a character study." One of his original lithographs was purchased by the Smithsonian Institute in 1975, ten years after his first one-man show. He is represented by El Prado Gallery of Art.

Bryers, Duane. Traditional oil painter of the old and contemporary West, born in Lakefield Township in Upper Michigan, in 1911 and living near Sonoita, Arizona, since 1979. "You can't put into words," he observes, "what makes an artist. You do it, but you really don't know how you do it. Something happens between the brain and the fingertips and the tip of the brush so it comes out the way you feel."

As a young man, he was a champion pole vaulter and an acrobat, but by the time he entered junior college in Minnesota, he knew he would be an artist. Newspapers featured his 1931 sketching trip via freight cars, his winter ice sculpture in 1935, his national soap sculpture award in 1936, and his 1939 commission for a 100-foot mural that paid for his move to New York City where he studied at the Art Students League. While in the Air Force from 1943 to 1946, he created a nationally syndicated comic strip.

He continued in commercial art in Minnesota, Chicago, and New York City until 1958 when his calendar of "Hilda" was published and he moved to Tucson. A Western mural was commissioned in 1968, and he sold his first major Western paintings in 1970. After moving to Mexico to paint full time, he returned to Arizona in 1975. Bryers has exhibited at major invitational shows since 1978, including a solo exhibition at the National Cowboy Hall of Fame in 1980. *Rocky Mountain Magazine* featured him in December 1981, as one of eight leading contemporary Western painters. Written up in *Southwest Art*, March 1976, and *Art West*, January 1982, he is published by Jackie Fine Arts and a minimum bid of $16,500 was set on his painting for the 1981 silent auction at Settlers West Galleries.

Budge, Linda M. Realist oil painter and sculptor of the big game of the Rocky Mountains, born in Salt Lake City, Utah, in 1940 and living in Laramie, Wyoming, since 1972. When she moved to Wyoming, she painted Western ranch and rodeo scenes, but says that "I didn't have much to say about cowboy life." When she discovered wildlife as her subject, however, it was "a natural thing for me to paint animals. I don't know what's more important to me, the animals or the art. They just go together.

"When one grows up in the West, one tends to take animals for granted. I thought I really understood Western wildlife, but the more time I spend studying these animals, the more interesting they become. I have a very special feeling for animals and they for me." As a child, she tamed a trout in a stream, and now she can on location paint the background for a moose, expect the moose to enter the scene, and actually have it walk on in. "I feel good about the work I'm doing," she observes.

Self-taught, she began with "one of those little wooden boxes with paints and some canvases" to while away evenings, but her first painting sold for $15. She then "did lots of cat portraits—they sold well." Seeking a more rural environment, her husband and she chose Wyoming, and she started an art gallery in Laramie. In 1979, she sold the gallery to be free to paint full time in her studio. Each sculpture is finished at home in the evenings. She is a member of the Society of Animal Artists, attends the invitational shows sponsored by wildlife organizations, and was featured in *Art West*, January 1982. "I haven't had a whole lot of inventory left to send to galleries, but one would be Gallery West & Frame Plant," she adds.

Duane Bryers, SADDLEWORN, oil, 16 x 20

John Bruce, TETON TIM, oil/canvas, 18 x 24

Linda Budge, TIMBERWOLVES, oil, 18 x 26

Bunn, Kenneth Rodney. Sculptor of North American and African wildlife in bronze, born in Denver, Colorado, in 1938 and living there in 1982. "In my work now," he observes, "I am trying to create masses, a thing that evolves out of a lump of clay or wax with a minimum amount of protrusions or unessential air spaces or openings."

After studying at the University of Maryland, Bunn was an apprentice at the National History Museum of the Smithsonian Institution in Washington, D.C., because "in the beginning, I was interested in the scientific aspect of presenting animals—dioramas and that sort of thing." Now he says that "people or animals become secondary to creating something in bronze that has life. It is the struggle of seeing something beautiful and transforming it into bronze. It is capturing the feeling of the subject by using metal as a means of expression."

He has taken frequent trips to African game parks. "I have always been partial to cats, and the majority of the African pieces will be devoted to the cat family. In sculpture, you are continuously after beautiful lines and motion. Cats lend themselves to that. Their hunting attitude has the powerful expression of a predator. It is not so much the form of the animal but the form of what the animal is creating." Bunn is listed in *Who's Who in American Art* and was featured in *Southwest Art*, November 1974, and *Artists of the Rockies*, fall 1978. He exhibited in the Peking, China, show, is an Associate of the National Academy of Design, and is a member of the National Sculpture Society, Society of Animal Artists, and National Academy of Western Art. He has exhibited at Sandra Wilson Gallery.

Burk, Charles. Contemporary watercolorist of realistic Southwestern subjects, born in Albuquerque, New Mexico, in 1947 and living there again since 1971. "Although I paint in a very objective style, I am attracted to subjects I can portray as much more important than they are generally seen to be. My most successful works are often those of subjects that would be thought of as unattractive. Giving an unattractive object importance hopefully causes the viewer to wonder about other reasons for the effort."

"I attended high school in San Francisco and entered the University of New Mexico in 1965 to study architecture. I had to interrupt college for active service in the Naval Reserve in 1969, and started painting there. I returned to the University in 1971 as a fine arts student and began painting professionally while still in school. I graduated in 1973 and was fortunate to receive a commission which perpetuated my career for what would otherwise have been two precarious years." At the same time, he traveled around New Mexico looking for subject matter and had his first one-person exhibition.

"Most of my paintings are not of 'pretty' or 'arty' settings," he adds. "I am attracted by the discards, back lots, and unseen places. Figures of people are seldom in my paintings. I guess that's part of my feeling about not belonging. I paint Southwestern subjects because, as a native, I am part of them and they are part of me, but I am turned off by cliches in art that presume to represent my heritage." Burk was written up in *Southwest Art*, June 1979. He exhibits with the American Watercolor Society and is represented by Seth's Canyon Road Art Gallery.

Kenneth Bunn, WOLF CHEWING BONE, bronze

Charles Burk, WOOD AND WIRE, watercolor, 22 x 30

 WILL BURLINGAME

ML BURNS AWS

⊖ SID BURNS

Burlingame, Will. Realistic oil-glaze painter of the Old West, born in Glendale, California, in 1942 and living in Huntington Beach, California. "The single most important thing that made me want to do paintings of the West was a book granddad had at his house, Charles Russell's *Trails Plowed Under.* In it, along with the wonderful stories, was a picture titled 'Riders of the Open Range.' To me, that painting captured a real feeling of the West. The book was given to me when granddad died in 1966 and the painting still inspires me.

"When I was thirteen, my grandad gave me a horse and taught me the ropes. He was a cowboy who worked on a ranch near Pomona. I worked summers along with him and became caught up in the cowboy life. After high school, I attended a city college for two years, then enrolled in the Art Center School in Los Angeles and graduated with honors in 1966. I took a job as a designer and illustrator and stayed with that firm for fifteen years, painting Western pictures at night and on weekends that were exhibited beginning in 1974. In 1981, I quit my job to concentrate full time on my painting.

"I begin a picture by doing thumbnail sketches to find an abstract tonal pattern that suits me, and from there I'll develop that plan a little larger. Then I photograph models and horses, begin a full-size drawing on tissue paper, and trace it on gesso-coated masonite. The actual painting is a series of oil glazes, one over the other, each isolated by a layer of varnish. Most paintings require perhaps fifteen layers of transparent oil color to get depth and clarity. It takes about five weeks to complete a picture." Burlingame is represented by Husberg which listed an oil for $4,500 in 1981.

Burns, Mike. Realist watercolorist of old homesteads, schools, and churches in the Pacific Northwest, born in Seattle, Washington, in 1943 and living in Bothell, Washington. "What fascinates me about the old buildings is the starkness and simplicity of their settings," he explains. "With all the conveniences we have, it is difficult to imagine living 40 miles from the nearest town or rail head, trying to turn sagebrush into crops."

While in high school and college, he won eleven awards and a scholarship in the National Automobile Design Competition. He studied industrial design for a year at the University of Washington and then received his BA in art from Seattle Pacific University in 1965. After three years as a commercial illustrator, he became a self-employed artist in 1969, painting "the architectural relics of eastern Washington and Oregon. They're found amidst wheat fields and sagebrush, and the settings are, in one word, dramatic.

"The distinctive aspect of my paintings is their simplicity both in composition and the subjects. I use only what is necessary to tell the story or set the mood. Adding objects that are not there I find distracting, sometimes out of context, and it tends to make the painting look 'nostalgic.' Even though there is a historical aspect to my paintings, it is not nostalgia. I focus on the present, on what something has become. Many artists get lost between the historical truth and the present. They end up caught in a fairy tale, a land of make believe." A member of the American and National Watercolor Societies, he has been in more than 115 exhibitions, was in *American Artist*, May 1974, and *40 Watercolorists and How They Work*, and is represented by Foster White Gallery and Gallery West.

Burns, Sid. Self-taught sculptor in bronze of realistic frontier action themes, born in Tulsa, Oklahoma, in 1916 and died in Phoenix, Arizona, in 1979. "I always had a feel for sculpture," he said. "I was afraid to tackle it, though, because it has to look good from all sides."

Raised on family spreads in the Panhandle country and in Kansas, Burns was self-taught in works on paper, drawings and watercolors. A fourth-generation Western boot and saddle maker, he opened his first leather repair shop at twenty in Santa Paula, California. He made a variety of Western gear in addition to saddlery, and kept horses on his ranch in the upper Ojai. During World War II, he was an Army Air Force pilot flying "the Hump," and for the next fifteen years he operated a shoe repair shop on Forest Avenue in Laguna Beach.

At the age of 50, he overcame his fear of three dimensions and modeled his first statuette. The estimated cost of casting the bronze was $2,000 but Burns was confident enough to go ahead. Two years later, he met Leslie B. DeMille, the Western artist and gallery owner, and DeMille recalls that "one look was all he needed to recognize the special quality of Burns' work." He agreed to represent Burns and is still the representative of the estate. To sculpt without distraction, Burns moved to Prescott, Arizona. In his twelve-year career, he completed 24 bronzes, all released in small editions. The artist's copies of the bronzes are in the National Cowboy Hall of Fame where he had won a bronze medal in the Solon Borglum All Sculpture Show. His works are also in the Gilcrease Institute and the Favell Museum, and he was listed in *Who's Who in American Art.*

Will Burlingame, ENEMIES OF THE CROW, oil, 24 x 36

Sid Burns, SPOOKED, bronze, h 29

Mike Burns, VILLAGE GREEN MARKET, watercolor, 16 x 26

Calle, Paul. Realistic oil painter and pencil drawer of America's Western past, born in New York City in 1928 and living in Stamford, Connecticut. "I think that if I had to state a goal, a hope pertaining to my work," Calle says, "my aim would be to help keep alive that huge reservoir of our past, to draw strength and sustenance from it, to build upon it in ways that are new and different, but not reject it."

After graduating from Pratt Institute in Brooklyn in 1947, Calle worked in commercial art and is a member of the Society of Illustrators. In 1962, he was chosen by the National Gallery of Art as an official artist for the National Aeronautics and Space Administration, and in 1969 Calle's "First Man on the Moon" postage stamp had a run of 150 billion. He pointed out the connection between space exploration and the Western experience when he traveled the West for the National Park Service in 1967, and he commented on the "romance and beauty" that he saw and the "enormity of the country."

In 1973, he turned his talent to painting the West, particularly Indians. He still paints in the converted hayloft of a big red barn in Connecticut, but he is surrounded there by Western gear, garb, and guns that come from the regular sketching and photographing trips he takes. For each painting, Calle makes an exact-size pencil drawing in minute detail, so finished that one drawing won an award and has been released as a print. His work is in major collections like the Gilcrease Institute, Phoenix Art Museum, and National Cowboy Hall of Fame, he has been written up in *Art West*, March 1980, and he is a member of the Northwest Rendezvous Group. He is represented by McCulley Fine Arts Gallery and his publisher is Mill Pond Press.

Paul Calle, JUST OVER THE RIDGE, oil, 28 x 48

ANGELO CARAVAGLIA

Caravaglia, Angelo. Modernist sculptor in wood, bronze, stone, and cement figures, born in Erie, Pennsylvania, in 1925 and living in Salt Lake City since 1956. "I find vitality in working a new way," he comments, "in altering my style to accommodate a mood or expression. 'Style' is a great responsibility that has a lifetime commitment—one I cannot carry. To be held custodian of it would mark the end of my freedom. That freedom I value more than the art world's insistence that a particular style be maintained.

"I remember, as a child, the pleasure of carving a piece of wood, the delight in drawing and painting. The wood, knife, paper, and paint were very important to me. They were treated with reverence. I feel the same way today—enjoying the first strokes into the wood—the impact of lines on paper. Throughout my schooling, assistance in painting was always available, but to find real help in sculpture was difficult. After finishing school, I joined the Army. When applying to Cranbrook Academy in 1946, I was accepted on the basis of my sketchbooks. Sculpture was still something to be met alone.

"Now, the process of execution of a work of art is the important thing to me—more important than the final product. It's the pleasure in developing an idea, manipulating the materials, conveying the idea through plastic elements. As the work progresses, I begin to lose interest, my mind already caught by a new idea. As each piece is finished, I must move it out of the studio as soon as possible. I cannot live with them long; they are my ghosts." The winner of Fulbright, Tiffany, and five research grants, he is Professor of Art at the University of Utah, and represented by Ankrum and El Prado Galleries.

Carlson, George. Sculptor of figures in bronze, and painter, especially of Tarahumara Indians, born in Elmhurst, Illinois, in 1940 and living in Franktown, Colorado. "I started sculpting," he discloses, "because I thought it'd help my drawing. I grew convinced that if I knew what the other side of a man's head looked like, I could draw him better. From the first touch, sculpting has proved to be the most exhilarating experience of my life."

He was drawing seriously at seven and studied at the American Academy of Art, the Chicago Art Institute, and the University of Arizona, although he never stayed long enough to be influenced in style. After trying commercial art and finding that "slickness was choking off my creative ability," he moved to Taos and lived with painter Buffalo Kaplinski. For two years, he refrained from painting to flush out his commercial experience. He listened to the Indians and "was determined that my art would show the Indian's harmony with nature, not his savagery."

"I keep working towards the simplest style, the least number of statements needed in a work. I do whatever is necessary to get down the essence of a subject. Abstract shapes are foremost in my mind when I'm designing, but when the basics are neglected, freedom of expression is lost. An artist should at least understand muscle masses and think of these masses as designs." Carlson is a member of National Academy of Western Art, won its Prix de West in 1975, was featured in *Southwest Art*, October 1976, and *Artists of the Rockies*, summer 1980, and exhibited in the Peking, China, show. His exhibition of 20 Tarahumara bronzes and 20 paintings was at Kennedy Galleries in 1980. He is represented by Stremmel and Bishop Galleries.

Carlson, Ken. Realist painter of wildlife in Wyoming and the Canadian Rockies in oil, born in Morton, Minnesota, about 1940 and living in Missoula, Montana, since 1979. "You want to avoid a picture frame," he emphasizes, "that calls attention to itself. You need something which both contains the painting and also gives the eye the illusion of extending the field of vision. I've sometimes struggled with various moldings and proportions and surfaces for three days to achieve the right effect."

When he was confined to bed for a year with rheumatic fever, drawing was his distraction, but his parents "had never seen an oil painting and they didn't have the means to further my study." The winner of a "Draw Me" contest, he received a scholarship to the Art Instruction School and still remembers the excitement of running to the post office to get his lessons. At seventeen, he commuted to Minneapolis to study with the dean of the School, and when he graduated from high school he attended the Minneapolis School of Art for a year before going into commercial art.

For two years, he illustrated *Birds of Western North America*, moved to San Francisco, and then in 1970 began concentrating on large oil paintings of wild animals. "I don't want a chronological listing of my accomplishments and biographical facts," he says. "I would much rather that people think of me as painting from nature, all the time, constantly stimulated and inspired by my surroundings and by the theories of other animal artists. I want to avoid the static and lifeless and come closer and closer to the essence of the subject." Written up in *Southwest Art*, November 1980, he is published by Mill Pond Press and exhibits at Husberg Fine Arts Gallery and Trailside Galleries.

Angelo Caravaglia, ROUND TABLE, wood, h 4 ft

Ken Carlson, MASKED BANDIT—RACCOON, oil, 24 x 15

George Carlson, PERCHERON, bronze, h 16

Earl Carpenter

© Carson '82

Gary Carter Jr.

Carpenter, Earl. Panoramic land-scapist of the Grand Canyon, born in Long Beach, California, in 1931 and living in Munds Park, Arizona. After he moved to Phoenix in 1960, Carpenter concentrated on paintings of the Hopi and Navajo. "But when I came too close to the poverty, the superstitions, and the conflicts under which those people live," he says, "I couldn't paint them anymore. I can't paint a subject unless I love it," and he has come to love best the mood and sweep of the unpeopled terrain.

"A hitch in the U.S. Air Force in the mid-50s gave me time to think," and a course in weather was an introduction to clouds. "When I got out, I enrolled at the Art Center School of Design in Los Angeles." Four years there were followed by a year at the Chouinard Art Institute. He then worked in commercial art and taught in Phoenix, but soon began painting full time. His first direction was abstract. Recognition came when he switched to realistic land-scapes and now his oils are in collections in 38 states.

On location, Carpenter sketches in watercolor or oil to organize the subject and eliminate superfluous details. He uses a camera for cloud effects because "some patterns change so rapidly" over the Mogollon Rim where he lives. His oils are "noted for their transparency," showing a "wash-like application of the paint." Earlier oils were painted without white, "but I am gradually re-introducing it for the atmospheric effect." An admirer of the Impressionists who also "painted with the heart," he frequently does a series of paintings on one subject so that "the full development of the idea can be realized." Profiled in *Southwest Art,* January 1981, he is represented by The May Gallery.

Carson, James. "Figurative painter, more romantic than historical, of cavalry, Indians, outlaws, cowboys," born in Little Rock, Arkansas, in 1942 and living in Baldwin, New York. "My strongest childhood memories," he recalls, "are of cotton, hot flat land, and farm animals in Twist, Arkansas. My father was college educated, my mother one-eighth Cherokee. Raised in Memphis, I read much on the West and was an avid Western movie goer. One of the strongest influences on my pictures is those Western movies.

"At thirteen, I spent four weeks at Philmont Boy Scout Ranch in New Mexico and fell in love with horses and the grandiose landscape of the West. After college, I went to graduate school at New York University, but two summers in Europe convinced me that I was destined to be a painter. I graduated with a Ph.D. in chemistry and was teaching at Princeton University while I commuted to New York five nights a week for three years to attend classes at the Art Students League. I resigned my teaching position to become an illustrator of paperback novels, and within two years was illustrating nothing but Western stories. I had finally found what I wanted to do most.

"I research my pictures thoroughly and love painting the romance of the Old West, although I feel that liberties should be taken to enhance the portrayal of the subject. I have devoted full time to Western painting and illustration since 1978. In 1980, I took a trip out West, visited the Arizona galleries, photographed much of the landscape, attended the annual CAA show in Phoenix, and signed with the May Gallery." In 1981, his oil painting was listed by May Gallery at $3,500.

Carter, Gary. Realist oil painter and sculptor of historical Northwestern scenes, born in Hutchinson, Kansas, in 1939 and living in West Yellowstone, Montana. "My family started migrating during the Cherokee Strip land rush and settled in with the Kiowa. My folks started their migrating not too long after I made my debut. Seems like I've been rambling ever since. I have spent many of the happiest hours of my life packing with my father in search of another Kansan. The dreams and memories of their West have filled my mind with paintings.

"Started packing when I was five years old. I loved school because if I did well, I had three months on the east slopes of the Sierras. That was before the Sierra Club had to protect the environment." After unloading grocery trucks and serving in the Army, Carter went to the Art Center College in Los Angeles where his realism and Western subject matter were accepted. He then had one year as an illustrator before a one-person show of his Western paintings sold out in Tucson, Arizona. He moved to Tucson and turned to art full time when he was 33.

The historical subjects that he paints come from his reading and the southwestern Montana valley where he now lives. He composes the paintings on the basis that "if this had happened, it should have been this way." He works every weekday, "from the time he gets up until he gets tired," and likes to paint outdoors where the results are "loose and fresh." In 1978, Carter won Best of Show at the Montana Historical Society, and the following year he was a founding member of the Northwest Rendezvous Group. He sells his paintings himself, welcoming collectors to his studio, and has had a backlog of orders. His prints are published by The Wooden Bird.

James Carson, PRECIOUS CARGO, oil, 30 x 36

Gary Carter, oil, 14 x 30

Earl Carpenter, ANGELS GATE, oil, 24 x 48

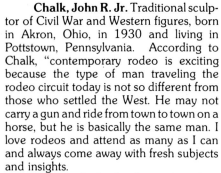

John Chalk

Gloria Champine 82

Bill Chappell

Chalk, John R. Jr. Traditional sculptor of Civil War and Western figures, born in Akron, Ohio, in 1930 and living in Pottstown, Pennsylvania. According to Chalk, "contemporary rodeo is exciting because the type of man traveling the rodeo circuit today is not so different from those who settled the West. He may not carry a gun and ride from town to town on a horse, but he is basically the same man. I love rodeos and attend as many as I can and always come away with fresh subjects and insights.

"From as far back as I can remember, a pencil and scratch pad were my faithful companions. I literally taught myself to draw. Movie matinees would prove to be an excellent resource for my fingers to draw the cowboys and heroes from memory. It just seemed to be something that came easy for me." Chalk graduated from high school and enlisted in the Marines in 1948 as a combat artist. After his discharge, he was employed as illustrator, art director, and account executive until 1980 when he began full-time sculpture work.

"My first commission," he says, "was for a life-size rodeo cowboy bronze. I am a great 'people watcher' and can sit in public places for hours studying faces, body postures, gestures, interesting folds and wrinkles of garments, etc. Then, as I begin to sculpt, I find myself structuring the nose of one person, the lips of another, an expression from a third, until the piece defines what I innately had in mind from the beginning. In constructing a full figure, I often use a full-length mirror to work out a pose. I then sketch that pose from memory. My background as an illustrator is a help to me in posing a sculpture that tells a story." Chalk exhibits his work in his studio.

Champine, Gloria. Traditional painter of Western wildlife, prairie schooners, and old homesteads in acrylic, born in White Sulpher Springs, Montana, in 1939 and living in Greybull, Wyoming, since 1970. "Feeling," she emphasizes, "is the most important element in a painting. In addition to mood, the artist needs a feeling for color and form. I like to paint to the accompaniment of music to reinforce the mood I want for my pictures—Chopin for romance, Debussy for his feeling for nature."

After painting her first picture as a child, she was encouraged to study art at Montana State University, and privately in San Francisco, New York City, and Baton Rouge where her husband's work took them. Widowed, she returned briefly to Montana. But, "I was so desperate for a glimpse of the sun," she recalls, "that I packed the trailer, piled the children into the car, and headed south." On the outskirts of the little town of Greybull, she saw a log homestead, "just had to paint it," and decided to make her home there because the people were friendly and art-minded.

Starting with classes in her home, she progressed to owning an art supply shop and to teaching courses at Northwest Community College and its extension classes. She had to quit teaching, however, when painting took all her time. "I am using animals more and more to express human emotions," she points out. "You get down to basics with animals, yet each one is unique, just as individual people are unique. I often have as many as six paintings in the works at the same time. If I'm having a problem with one, I can move on to another." Written up in *Art West*, July 1980, she is represented by her own Rustic Reflections Gallery.

Chappell, Bill. Traditional oil painter and sculptor in bronze of the cowboys and Indians of the Old West, born in Van Zandt County, Texas, in 1919 and living in South Fork, Colorado, since 1972. "One reason I stayed in grade school as long as I did," he mentions, "was to trade with the people at school. I was older at eight in some ways than a lot of people are at 21. When I quit school, I went to work steady, cowboyin' in Texas, New Mexico, and Colorado.

"I'd never seen a piece of leather carved—I started without any instructions at all. I'd never seen a swivel knife. I just studied the saddles on the ranch and as I got older, I ventured out to make a saddle. I made the tree out of the wooden blades of a windmill, and covered the tree with the hide from a steer that got killed by lightning." After two years in the Navy in World War II, he operated a saddle and boot shop in Seymour, Texas, and carved a life-size figure of Will Rogers.

In 1953, he moved to Colorado and began oil painting and sculpting. "I've done just about everything you could do with a horse," he emphasizes. "And then again, I have done everything you could from the standpoint of tack. This really gives you a good knowledge whenever you try to put it down on canvas or model a bronze. Most of my paintings are real complicated, requiring a lot of drawing. I ordinarily do one painting a week, or if a painting gets so wet I just can't go on with the detail, then I'll start another. As far as bronzes go, I make two models every year. I have never quit the cowboy thing. I enjoy it." A member of the Texas Cowboy Artists, he was written up in *The Western Horseman*, September 1971, in *Cowboy in Art*, and *Bronzes of the American West*.

Gloria Champine, COURTSHIP, acrylic, 24 x 36

Bill Chappell, DESTINY, bronze, h 20, w 16¼

John Chalk, WITH FATE AGAINST THEM THE DEATH OF CUSTER, bronze, h 24, Edition 15

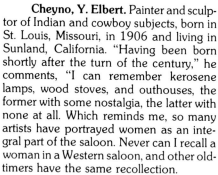

Cheyno, Y. Elbert. Painter and sculptor of Indian and cowboy subjects, born in St. Louis, Missouri, in 1906 and living in Sunland, California. "Having been born shortly after the turn of the century," he comments, "I can remember kerosene lamps, wood stoves, and outhouses, the former with some nostalgia, the latter with none at all. Which reminds me, so many artists have portrayed women as an integral part of the saloon. Never can I recall a woman in a Western saloon, and other old-timers have the same recollection.

"Well, kerosene gave way to gas and gas to electricity and as this was happening, Orville Wright patted me on the head and my destiny was revealed. Though the urge to draw and paint was always there, the adventure of the wild blue yonder held me tightly in its grasp for some six decades. I learned to fly in World War I airplanes, doing yeoman's work in exchange." From 1936 to 1971, Cheyno was employed in the aircraft industry, from American Airlines supervisor to operations research associate with Lockheed.

"From 1972 onward, I have been working as a full-time professional painter and sculptor. I was the founder of the American Indian & Cowboy Artists society in 1974, to bridge the misunderstanding between the peoples and to assist talented American Indian artists in the art world. In 1976, I proposed to San Dimas an annual Western art show, now in its sixth year. I also proposed that San Dimas consider a Western art museum, currently initially approved. I am a minority conglomerate, English, Japanese, and American Indian. In these times, I can stand on either side of the ethnic issues, scream that my rights are being abused or bewilderedly ask what all the fuss is about." He is represented by Files and Many Horses Galleries.

Chilton, Fred. Self-taught landscape painter and photographer of the Mesilla Valley, born in Las Cruces, New Mexico, in 1944 and living again in Las Cruces since 1979. "In 1978," Chilton says, "I was painting huge 20 by 60 foot billboards for National Advertising Co. The ads usually depicted 'happy people' enjoying cigarettes, beer, cars, etc. Painting these gigantic pictorials was the most fun I had had in a long time. In February 1979, I began painting in earnest."

Like most artists who profess to be self-taught, Chilton had some training and also worked in a field related to art. He attended the Center for Creative Studies in Detroit from 1962 to 1964 but quit because he was "discouraged with the avant-garde trend." Following examples of 18th-century American painters, he became a sign painter in Michigan. After 17 years, he turned to fine arts. But, with the midwest economy worsening, Chilton decided to head back to Las Cruces. "New Mexico seems like an endless supply of timeless material," he declares. "The Mesilla Valley, its farms, towns, and people, is the best source for my subjects."

When he started painting, Chilton found that he had already absorbed and retained a feeling for what a good painting should look like. In addition, he became an exhibitor as a photographer, providing an understanding of "the changes in color and quality of light as the day passes." He exhibited at the Solmagundi Club in New York City in 1982 and is represented by the Gallery Americana.

Fred Chilton, NOVEMBER, MESILLA VALLEY, oil, 24 x 36

Elbert Cheyno, VAQUERITOS, oil/linen, 22 x 28

E. Chiriacka   *Keith Christie*   *Robert Christie*

Chiriacka, Ernest. Impressionist painter of dramatic Western moods, born in New York City in 1920 and living in Great Neck, New York. "While doing illustrations for such publications as the *Saturday Evening Post, Esquire,* and *Cosmopolitan,* I developed a deep interest in the Indian and other figures from the history of the American West. My work in this field led me to make many sketching trips to the country west of the Mississippi, and eventually to devote my entire time to portraying the West in many facets and moods.

"I received my earliest art training at the Art Students League in New York. Because I showed promise in my work, I was urged to continue my training and therefore enrolled in the National Academy of Design Art School and the Grand Central School of Art in New York City. I began my career, as did many important Western artists, as an illustrator for national magazines. My interest in the West ultimately took me there. While in the West, sketching and gathering material for future work, I was commissioned to paint portraits of leading film stars and do posters and other works for the movie studios.

"My paintings are not just another rendition of Western life. While the incidents and characters portrayed are correct to the smallest detail, my endeavor is for more than that. To rise above the cold photographic and infuse the picture with a sense of the living moment required a more impressionistic treatment. This I achieved." In 1976, Chiriacka also began modeling bronze statuettes. He adds that "I continue to paint. Like a breath of life, it's always there, and there I am." He is represented by Kennedy and Country Art Galleries.

Christie, Keith. Traditional sculptor of bronze statuettes and painter in oil and tempera, born about 1940 and living in Browns Valley, California. "With a painting," he points out, "first I think of the theme, like a cutting horse. A painting, though, is only two dimensional, and I think two dimensional—I'm looking at it only from one direction. But for a bronze, I have to think differently. I don't have to worry about a pose, the anatomy of it or anything else. I'm thinking only in terms of the emotion—the feeling—of it. That's the thing that predominates.

"When I was just a tiny kid, practically my first word was 'horse,' and I was constantly pestering my mother to draw horses for me. Pretty soon, she told me to draw my own horses, and I've been doing it ever since. Whittling was just something I could do, too. Even a bar of soap wasn't safe in the house. It wasn't until later, when I saw Remington bronzes, that I was really interested in bronzes. I attended art school for one year, and that was a disaster. The instructor made some comment like 'You're supposed to outgrow cowboys and Indians when you're ten years old.'

"I became chairman of the arts and crafts department at high school and I turned into a real bear to live with, so I figured I would just build a little backyard foundry and turn out some bronze sculptures. Pretty soon I was making more money in art than I was at teaching. It seems a little unbelievable. The only way I can describe it is like a guy that works all week just to play golf on the weekend, then he finds out he can beat Arnold Palmer." He won the Phippen Memorial Show in 1979, and Pacific Coast Quarter Horse Association has a five-year program for buying his bronzes. Current galleries include Wadle and Moran.

Christie, Robert. Representational oil painter of sporting people, horses, and dogs, born in Brooklyn, New York, in 1928 and living in Atlanta, Georgia, since 1961. "I was always interested in animals and the outdoors," he recalls. "The milkman had a horse, and the junkwagon was horse drawn. I loved the horses, and I went to the zoo a lot. My basement was full of tropical fish and over the years I had many cats—but never a dog."

He went to Ohio Wesleyan University to work toward a degree in fine art but transferred to Pratt Institute in Brooklyn where he graduated in 1952. While employed as a commercial artist in New York City, he continued with portrait painting at Pratt and at the Art Students League. When he moved to Atlanta, it was to give full time to painting. He started out doing commercial art, found portraits to paint, included horses in the portraits, and then had his time consumed with equestrian portraits. His first portrait of field dogs resulted in a demand for prints.

In a painting of cattle judging at a fair, he "saw each of those men and the cattle separately, and the barn in still another place. The trick is to catch the feel of the moment. It's something that photography cannot do. Many artists sell themselves short in not trying to capture the spirit of a model. That is what gives a painting a third dimension, that keeps it from being a flat picture on canvas." One of his ideas is a double portrait with a close-up of the sitter on one side and the sitter in a field with horse or dog in the background. Written up in *Southwest Art,* November 1981, his prints are published through his own Backtrail Gallery and he is represented by Sigoloff Galleries and Nelda Lee Inc.

Robert Christie, POINT AND HONOR, oil, 24 x 30

Keith Christie, COWBOY CONFERENCE, oil, 24 x 36

Ernest Chiriacka, THE NEW LAND OWNERS (1979), oil/canvas, 32½ x 46

ROBERT CLARK

Cia, Manuel Lopez. Realist/Impressionist/Abstract oil painter of figures, born in Las Cruces, New Mexico, in 1937 and living in Albuquerque. When the time came to select a career, Cia had to choose among boxing, electronics, and art, "but boxers always got beat up, so I said, 'Forget that!' And when I saw those electronics books, I said, 'Forget that, too!' "

After serving in the Air Force, he studied at the American Academy of Art in Chicago from 1958 to 1961, then at the San Francisco Art Institute and the Los Angeles Trade Technical School for scenic and pictorial art. He was employed as a billboard painter and in 1972 went to work for Lockheed as a technical illustrator. Back in New Mexico, he developed his painting style, combining "realism with Impressionism through soft edges, impasto, and bright colors, and with abstraction in design patterns and unconcern with pure subject matter from corner to corner.

"When a viewer sees abstract qualities," he explains, "our conversation can lead us to Chinese Sung painting of the negative and positive space in its most simplified form, and to Zen using sense against nonsense. In color, I use the principle of divisionism where different colors are side by side and have an optical blend at a distance, and the Persian Rug technique where dominant colors are carried throughout the work." He adds that he is "not a religious person in an orthodox sense. I guess I picked up on my old man. He was pure Indio and didn't believe in temples. I don't know if he prayed or not, but he certainly had a great respect for animals and his fellow man. I am the same way." Written up in *Artists of the Rockies*, fall 1981, he is published by Dita Adam and Starline Collector's Gallery, and represented by his own Cia Bellas Artes and Woodrow Wilson Fine Arts.

Clark, Dane. Impressionistic painter of landscapes and figures in acrylic, born in Plainview, Texas, in 1934 and living in Kapaa, Kauai, Hawaii. "My paintings," he states, "are impressions of places and moments of time. In my landscapes, I use color and patterns to project the essence of a place, creating a mood that the viewer can identify with. For me, painting is a free and natural act devoid of theory. I don't like to talk about my art. I just like to paint. I shall always find painting a joy!"

Educated in a one-room Texas schoolhouse where his mother was the teacher, Clark had private art lessons while he was in high school. At Southern Methodist University, he studied art and played football, then graduated from McMurray College in Abilene after briefly taking architecture at Texas Tech. He also attended the Colorado Institute of Art for two years and later was the director of the Institute for a decade. He visited New Mexico frequently and cooperated in opening a short-lived Santa Fe gallery. In 1971, he decided to paint full time and went to Europe for six months.

When he returned to Denver, watercolor was his first medium, but he soon switched to acrylic. Representational painting gave way to abstract renderings, and then as he became influenced by the power of color settled into Impressionism. His early interest in architecture led to paintings of Indian and Spanish buildings, while his landscapes were sometimes real and sometimes a composite. His figures were generally subordinated to the entirety of a village scene. Clark was written up in *Southwest Art*, October 1973 and *Artists of the Rockies*, summer 1976. He was in the 1981 Peking, China, show and exhibits at Seth's Canyon Road Art Gallery.

Clark, Robert. Realist painter of the American scene in egg tempera, born in Minneapolis, Minnesota, in 1920 and living in Cambria, California. "You have to be strong enough," he emphasizes, "not to put in everything you see. I think the biggest problem the novice has is the inability to eliminate the non-essentials. You may have to use a certain amount of stagecraft, too. You have to know how to dramatize what you see. Every picture has a dominant idea to express. Dominance and subordination are part and parcel of the presentation."

Summers on his grandparents' farm developed his love for the homely objects of country life. After training at the Minneapolis School of Art and the Walker Art Center School, he had his first exhibition in 1947, following service in World War II. He moved to California in 1948, and four years later joined the staff of the Long Beach Museum of Art. Later, he created backgrounds for dioramas for the Los Angeles County Museum of History, Science, and Art and in 1965 completed a mural for Forest Lawn Memorial Park in Glendale.

He considers egg tempera to be "a very limiting medium. The mixture dries very rapidly and cannot be used outdoors, but it imparts a sense of realism and depth. My interest is in painting the particular, not the general. The objects we see have personalities, and I hope to reveal some of their inherent qualities. I think broad views are softer and less compelling than close views. The close-up has a magnetic quality. I'm interested in achieving an incisive, intimate look and I tend to make no concession to prettifying." Listed in *Who's Who in American Art* and written up in *Southwest Art*, January 1979, Clark is published by Mill Pond Press and represented by El Prado Gallery of Art.

Dane Clark, SANTA FE WINTER, acrylic, 18 x 18

Manuel Cia, LEE OF CHAMA, oil, 30 x 24

Robert Clark, INDIAN SUMMER (1979), egg tempera, 20 x 13

Clay, Gloria. Traditional sculptor portraying the ranch life she leads, born near Gillette, Wyoming, in 1930 and living in Laramie since 1959. "The day I was born," she claims, "the doctor didn't arrive before I did because he was at a horse race, and horses have been a part of my life ever since. We rode horses to school and all the games we played were on horseback. In the winter we pulled our sleds with horses and went swimming with them in the summer. Instead of 'cops and robbers,' our games were 'soldiers and Indians.'

"My grandfather was an artist, a great admirer of Charles Russell. When I was twelve, I got my first oil paints and my everyday life became the subjects that I used, going out on horseback to find new calves and watch the community brandings." After graduating from high school as Gillette's rodeo queen, she learned leather tooling in a saddle shop, married, moved to a ranch in Laramie, and began doing commissioned portraits of horses and bulls. In 1977, she attended her first art class, a ten-week session on sculpture.

"From then on, it was a case of learning by doing," she declares. "I may not be as prolific as some artists because I still spend part of my time outside living this life I try to portray; it's the best way to acquire the inspiration and authenticity that I want and to point up a rope dallied the wrong way, a crooked-legged horse, or a knot that's not tied right. So aside from the days when somebody says 'can you help?' when I go back to my jobs of hired hand, horse wrangler, dude wrangler, hay mower, tally keeper, vaccinator, gate watcher, etc., I'd like to spend the rest of my life as a sculptor, with a little painting thrown in now and then." Her work is in Troy's and Western Images Galleries.

Cleary, Shirley. Realist painter of Montana landscapes and found objects from outside the conventional historical viewpoint, born in St. Louis, Missouri, in 1942 and living in Helena, Montana, since 1978. "People in Denver said to me," she points out, "we like your figurative work, but why not do cowboys and Indians if you hope to sell. But that isn't my tradition. I'm not Western in a hokey sense. Instead, I deal with things I'm personally involved with like fishing and hunting. I also use abandoned machines as images."

She earned her BFA from Washington University in St. Louis, in 1964, studied at the University of Valencia in Spain in 1965, and at the Tyler School of Art in Philadelphia in 1966 and in Rome in 1967, receiving her MFA in 1968. After teaching art in Missouri and District of Columbia schools, she moved in 1971 to Montana, where she has taught workshops and in colleges. In 1981, she was artist in residence in Denmark where "the Danes could relate to my work because they have used many of the same machines that we do."

"The machines I paint are just old machines I come across. My main interest is how they contrast with their environment and I usually title the paintings by number rather than the name of the machinery. I was working on a grant at Montana State University and a student asked me why I was drawing a manure spreader. This reinforced my decision not to call the machines by their names. Also, many people want to know if I fish myself. The answer is yes. We originally moved to Montana, to be close to the blue-ribbon fishing streams here." She has been written up in *American Artist, Art West,* and *Montana Outdoors,* all in 1981, and is represented by Sportsman's Edge and Sportsman's Gallery.

Clendennen, Sandra. Traditional Western and wildlife painter in oil, born in Burnet, Texas, in 1939 and living in Tucson, Arizona. "Although many people think painting consists of sitting in front of a blank canvas with a brush and a stroke of genius, I have found research to be an integral part. Digging through reference books, magazines, setting up models, and treks into the surrounding countryside also constitute a good deal of the painting time. In addition, by teaching myself to use a camera, I have been able to freeze special settings for future use.

"I began to study painting and drawing at ten. After an early marriage, I attended Baylor University and then continued to study on my own. In Marble Falls, Texas, I opened an art school for children, conducted area workshops, and sold to private collectors. In 1975, I moved to Tucson where I attended the University of Arizona and began conducting workshops in Green Valley. In 1977, I became the manager of Settlers West Galleries, working for six months of the year, and devoting the remainder of my time to painting.

"I consider painting a lifetime commitment, with a growth in spurts preceded by a great deal of hard work and endless self-criticism. My work has been shown in the Grand Central Art Galleries in New York City, the Gallery at Shoal Creek, and Settlers West Galleries.

Shirley Cleary, TYING ON A FLY, gouache, 15 x 19

Sandra Clendennan, PACKING IN, oil, 18 x 24

Gloria Clay, BETWEEN HOOF AND HORNS, bronze, 20 x 14

John Clymer, LONG COLD WINTER, oil, 24 x 48

Clymer, John. Painter of Pacific Northwest game animals and history, born in Ellensburg, Washington, in 1907 and living in Teton Village, Wyoming. "When I was a kid," Clymer recalled, "I always wanted to live in the mountains. I wanted to get into forestry but my folks wouldn't listen to that at all. One day I got to thinking that if I could paint pictures, I could live wherever I wished. I was young and didn't know any better."

At thirteen, Clymer enrolled in a correspondence course in art and four years later he sold two drawings to Colt Firearms. After graduation from high school, he "moved to Canada. I did illustrations for leading Canadian magazines and traveled extensively over Canada, Alaska, and the Yukon." While in Canada, he studied with Fred Varley and J.W. Beaty and exhibited his work. He spent 1930 at the Old Howard Pyle School in Wilmington, Delaware, where he was influenced by N.C. Wyeth, then returned to Canada where he was elected an Associate of the Royal Canadian Academy of Art. In 1936, he moved to Westport, Connecticut, and studied with Harvey Dunn in New York City. He was in the Marine Corps with Tom Lovell during World War II and afterwards returned to commercial illustration that included 90 *Saturday Evening Post* covers.

In 1964, Clymer began painting full time. His two keys from the Pyle School were Personality, "an artist putting himself into the picture," and Mental Approach, "the way you feel about the people you are painting." Clymer is the subject of a book by Walt Reed, is a member of the Cowboy Artists of America and the National Academy of Western Art, and has been featured in *Persimmon Hill, Artists of the Rockies,* and *Southwest Art.*

M. Cobbett

COCHRANE

Cobbett, Marian. Painter of Indian portraits and dances in pastels and oils, born in Orlando, Florida, in 1929 and living in Albuquerque, New Mexico. "The play of light on the face, and on the figure, is what I want to paint," she states. "The figure in motion, in dance, inspires me to catch the color and emotion portrayed. Having always been a 'people watcher,' it is natural that I try to capture the essence of the subjects in portraits. I am striving for impressionism in my technique, both with brush and pencil."

She has spent most of her life in Albuquerque and received a degree in psychology from the University of New Mexico in 1951, studying mathematics, engineering, and drawing as well as taking private courses in painting and creative design. She became a full-time painter in 1968 and taught pastels at the Albuquerque Institute of Art in 1975. Her private teachers have been colorists, and she says that "I love color and find it difficult to sign and frame a black and white drawing. I always reach for the brilliant pastel sticks before I can stop."

She calls herself "a frustrated musician and dancer," and her forte is doing vividly costumed Indian dancers as single figures. "The color and pageantry of the dances at the Rio Grande Pueblo fascinate and delight me. I have studied them for years. I try to share the beauty and excitement with those who view my work." A newer specialty is flamenco paintings done in Santa Fe. But she will not sell a painting to a customer who must "first show it to my decorator." Marian Cobbett has been featured in *New Mexico Magazine*, September 1980, and is represented by The Pinon Tree Gallery.

Cochrane, Charles L. Traditional oil painter of scenes of the Old West, born in Bigelow, Missouri, in 1923 and living in Garden Grove, California, since 1958. "A woman at a Western show in Arizona came up to my painting," he recalls, "and told me she could hear in it the crunch of ice under a horse's hooves, and I thought, my gosh, so do I! Before I am through, I want to do a painting that would be so beautiful, it will make hard men think and women cry."

Raised in St. Joseph, Missouri, he drew on butcher paper as a child, cutting off the bloody corners. His father left the family early; he had "seven bad uncles living just outside the law," and his grandfather made whiskey, so Cochrane weaned calves when he was ten and as a teenager boxed for $5 a night. During World War II, he served in the First Marine Paratroop Division, then attended the Moran School of Commercial Art for a year and the Kansas City Art Institute for six months. After moving to California, he worked for ten years as an insurance claims supervisor.

He painted at night and quit his job after his wife sold his paintings at shopping malls. She says "it was amazing. I was bringing them in wet and people were arguing, waving money in my face." When he was invited to a major 1979 show, he asked, "How would you feel? Imagine if you were an actor and invited to be in a movie with Elizabeth Taylor." When painting, he listens to records like "The Ballad of Wrangler Joe," often taking a break to accompany the musicians on his violin. He never works from photographs, relying instead on books to tell him how things really were. Featured in *Southwest Art*, May 1978, he is represented by Files' Gallery of Fine Art and Newsom's Gallery.

Marian Cobbett, PABLITA OF SANTA CLARA, oil/linen, 10 x 8

Charles Cochrane, NOBODY WINS, oil, 36 x 48

B Coffin

Pola Winsky

Coffin, Barry. "Contemporary Native American" sculptor of satirical Indian figures in clay and bronze, born in Lawrence, Kansas, in 1946 and living in Santa Fe, New Mexico, since 1974. Known as a "Native American artist" rather than as just an "artist," he says that "whether I like it or not, that's how I'm referred to, how I'll always be referred to—but I'm proud to be an Indian. I try to show Indian feelings, reactions to how we were treated, and especially how young Indians feel."

Son of the athletic director of Haskell Indian School, Coffin "took art in high school, but they didn't teach you that art could be a career. I went to white public schools. The government wants it that way. They want Indians to be white but Indians won't be." Of Potawatomi-Creek ancestry, he "went to college a semester and dropped out, worked at all kinds of jobs" in factories and as a welder, served in Vietnam, and in 1974 was working as a laborer when he "looked at things on display" at an art fair "and thought, why couldn't I do that?"

Accepted at the Institute of American Indian Art in Santa Fe when he was 27, he sculpted and worked at Shidoni Gallery and Foundry where his pieces sold. His style is "a preoccupation with Indian political awareness and modern images, coupled with a reverence for ideas and images of traditional Indian culture." He adds that "when I start building a piece in clay, I have no idea what it will be. I just start and it comes to me," but his figures are not always traditional. An Indian hanging is titled "The Only Good Indian." Other titles are "Snake Dance Guy" and "Indian Guy." Sculptures that blew up in a kiln accident became the "Wounded Knee" series. Coffin is represented by The Squash Blossom and by Shidoni Gallery.

Coggeshall, Pola Winsky. Traditional sculptor of ranch animals in bronze, born in San Angelo, Texas, in 1945 and living in Dallas since 1958. "I love horses," she declares. "I was born thinking horses. I bought my first horse when I was thirteen. Sold a lot of Coke bottles and did a lot of babysitting to support a $40 green-broke mustang, and I've had one or more horses ever since, even though I've always lived in the city. For that reason, it's not difficult for me to sculpt horses. Sometimes I use photos and sketches but most often I work from live animals.

"I don't remember ever really starting in art. It's just something I've always done, sort of like growing. We lived on Long Island in New York from 1946 until 1958 when we moved back to Texas. Around 1961, I began posing as an artist's model. I started college in Denton while still living and working in Dallas, but when a Dallas artist offered me the opportunity to work in his foundry as an apprentice, I gave up school and quit posing to spend more time sculpting (which wasn't a difficult decision). I had complete access to supplies, studio, and knowledge.

"I married in 1967 and sculpted, rode horses, and studied anatomy. In 1974, two prospective buyers convinced me to make multiple castings and they became involved in selling for me. I often work on several pieces at the same time. Sometimes I'll be ready to cast after just a week. Other times I'll spend over a year. God gave me a gift and the desire. When I'm using it, I find great peace and happiness. I've always got a deep prayer of gratitude in my heart. The people at Shidoni Gallery and Foundry have been very helpful and I have exhibited through them."

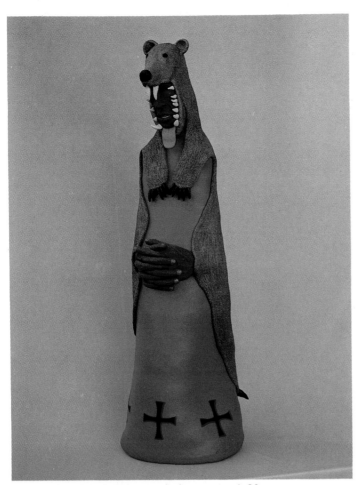

Barry Coffin, BEAR GUY, acrylic/stoneware, h 30

Pola Coggeshall, LIGHTNING, bronze, h 8, l 8

113

Coheleach, Guy Joseph. Realist painter of wildlife, including domestic birds and foreign mammals, in watercolor and oil, born in New York City, about 1933 and living in Plainview, Long Island, New York. "The hunter's trophy," he points out, "is the result of his quest. The photographer's photographs are the result of his quest. My trophy is my painting, and that painting is the result of a long stalk which is my quest. I am a predator. We are all predators to a degree.

"I started drawing in grammar school. I think all children are interested in animals and birds as they grow older. I guess I never grew up." Descended from Swiss immigrants, Coheleach (pronounced Ko-lee-ack) as a boy earned pocket money by keeping poisonous snakes in the basement and selling the venom he extracted. After serving in the Army in Asia, racing cars, and climbing mountains, he settled down to the commercial art for which he had been trained at Cooper Union in New York City.

While he illustrated sundries and drew dog portraits on black velvet, he maintained his interest in wildlife. His break came when bird painter Don Eckelberry turned a commission over to him in the mid-1960s. "My income dropped overnight to a third of what it had been," Coheleach recalls, "and I was scared, but at least I could look at the guy who had to shave every morning." By 1974, there were 40 prints published and by 1977, his personal donations of works to the National Wildlife Federation, National Audubon Society, and other such groups had raised over $3,500,000. He "intends to do more museum-quality painting and less commercial painting, and let professionals run" his Regency House Art.

Guy Coheleach, ROCKY MOUNTAIN CHASE, oil, 20

MICHAEL COLEMAN

Coleman, Michael. Traditional oil painter in 19th-century style of historical and contemporary Plains Indians, trappers, and landscapes, born in Provo, Utah, in 1946 and still living there. "He never waits until the inspiration hits, but works until it comes and then works some more. He works every day except Sundays from 8:30 a.m. until 6:30–8:30 p.m. Then he usually helps his framer or does research at the library."

He grew up fishing and hunting, always wanting to be an artist. After completing high school, he majored in art at Brigham Young University. They considered him an unusual student there because he was a representational painter. He quit the university when his instructor convinced him that nothing more was left to learn there, and went on to the San Francisco Art Institute. His influences have been 19th-century American masters, Henry Farny, Thomas Moran, and George Inness.

To stimulate ideas, he spends summers traveling. He paints on masonite primed with gesso tinted pink. Key areas like the horizon line are marked, and then he starts painting from the top down. The basic design is completed the first day, and "the tedious part begins." Details and highlights are added last. He stands the painting inside a frame and also looks at the painting in a mirror as final checks. Initially an oil painter, Coleman now works primarily in gouache, finishing 20 to 30 paintings a year. He exhibited at the National Academy of Western Art in 1975, at the Santa Gertrudis auction in 1976, had a one-person show at Kennedy Galleries in 1977, and was given a retrospective at the Buffalo Bill Historical Center in 1978. Written up in *Southwest Art*, February 1977, he is listed in *Who's Who in American Art* and is represented by Zantman Art, Kennedy, and Texas Art Galleries.

Michael Coleman, BUFFALO MEDICINE (1981), gouache/board, 27½ x 18

M.L. Coleman

Coleman, Michael L. Traditional oil painter of unpeopled Western landscapes, born in Livingston, Montana near Yellowstone Park in 1941 and living in Bremerton, Washington since 1982. "The ideal landscape," he believes, "is one that strikes a balance between reality and emotion, between observation and pictorial treatment, thereby capturing and expressing an eternalized moment in time. A painting should communicate an inner state, a yearning, a fantasy, a feeling independent of the subject of the painting, yet aroused by the reality of it."

Raised in Yellowstone Park where his father was a ranger, he was painting the landscape while in grade school. On the college level, however, the accent was on non-objective art so he earned a degree in accountancy. After two years in the Army, he spent eight years with a public accounting firm, painting and studying art in his spare time. In 1973, he moved to Montana, consulting on accounting and painting evenings, but he returned to Denver in 1975.

The next year, he moved back to Montana to be a professional painter, signing himself "M.L." to minimize confusion with Utah's Michael Coleman. He believes that his youth in Yellowstone taught him "to see nature with the same interest and intensity that a portrait painter would study a face." He sees no problem in switching from the science of accountancy to the emotion of painting, saying that "in my art I am primarily concerned with selecting and reorganizing nature according to my feelings. 'Creating' is over used and abused. Most artists don't really create very much." Written up in *Art West*, September 1980, M.L. Coleman is published by Salt Creek Graphics and is represented by Ponderosa and Flathead Lake Galleries.

James Collender

Collender, Jim. Traditional painter of the Hole in the Wall country of Wyoming and sculptor of rodeo subjects, born in Los Angeles in 1935 and living in Longmont, Colorado since 1966. "Some artists," he remarks, "line twenty canvases up against the wall and whip them out. But not me. The closest I come is moving to another piece while I'm waiting for an oil to dry. However, since I've begun work in sculpture, I find I can make the switch from three-dimensional to two more easily than changing from watercolor to, say, pastel.

"When I was two, I was trying to copy Mickey Mouse and I've just been into art ever since. In high school, my math teacher handed me a piece of paper at the beginning of each class and let me doodle." At eighteen, he enlisted in the infantry and found himself on the front lines in Korea. He then attended Chouinard Art School in Los Angeles but was turned off by "the beatniks who were flooding into the art field" so for the next twelve years he was a commercial artist in the aerospace industry.

At Martin Marietta in Denver, he "sat right next to Jim Boren and Roy Kerswill at work." His Western paintings were done at night, and by the mid-1960s magazines began using them for covers. By 1970, he was exhibiting, and in 1974, he was accepted by Denver and Santa Fe galleries that generated enough demand to let him paint full time. "I do believe in motivation," he points out, "and the strongest motivation is the need to pay bills. The Hole in the Wall country deserves to have its story told through art. I would do anything to stay there, except maybe rob a bank." Written up in *Southwest Art*, March 1979, Collender is represented by Two Grey Hills and Images Gallery.

Carroll Collier

Collier, Carroll Lloyd. Impressionist oil painter of Western landscapes, born in Dallas, Texas, in 1923 and living in Forney, Texas, since 1972. "Objects or potential subjects," he points out, "arrange themselves in different ways as a person moves through the landscape. The light from the sun as it moves casts shadows which are constantly moving, forming different patterns. At any given moment, we may see in these configurations a charm or magic."

After high school, he was apprenticed to his cousin, a Dallas artist, and then served in the Army during World War II, later illustrating for the Graphic Reproduction Department in New Orleans from 1943 to 1946. This was his art school, working with fifteen other artists and exchanging ideas. After his discharge, he returned to Dallas to work as a commercial artist and then a free-lance illustrator. In 1972, he quit illustration to become "an easel painter of landscapes."

Composition is his forte, and he "uses color prints in composing paintings. Working with oil paint, I paint in or paint out anything I want in the photograph to compliment the subject. Sometimes two photos are combined, cut out and pasted together on a piece of cardboard. Often, photography is used to capture the shape and detail of objects. The color and value of everything in the picture is taken from quick sketches made on location at the time I shot the photos. Although I sell paintings to make a living, I don't paint 'to make money.' This is a constant problem facing most young artists because there are always more paintings than there are buyers." Written up in *Southwest Art*, December 1979, Collier is represented by Baker Gallery of Fine Art and Gallery at Shoal Creek.

James Collender, ROUGH STRING, bronze, h 16½

Michael L. Coleman, EVENING GLOW, oil, 24 x 18

Carroll Collier, STILL NIGHT, oil, 13 x 30

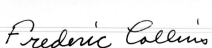

Collins, Frederic. Traditional sculptor of horses in bronze, born in Akron, Ohio, in 1910 and living in Santa Fe, New Mexico. "My multi-patinas," he explains, "are not painted, nor are they coated in polychrome temperas. The coloring of my pieces is accomplished by using combinations of classic patinas achieved with heated bronze and chemicals which bond the color permanently. This makes a sculpture more dramatic and more beautiful, yet the artist has been faithful to his medium.

"As a small boy, I pored over books on Russell and Remington and I determined some day to have a ranch and live in the West. When I was in my early teens, I would cut saplings and carve heads from the branches. These I sold to Abercrombie and Fitch for several years. I attended the University of Michigan Engineering School and my family moved near Cranbrook Institute where I met international sculptor Carl Milles who gave me valuable pointers. I did commissions of dogs and horses, and studies of horse breeds.

"My love of horses and the West finally took me to the Texas Hill Country where I purchased a ranch and did a commission of a half-size bronze horse. Soon after moving, my wife and I formed a manufacturing company of handbags decorated with ornaments which I sculpted. A few years ago, we sold the company and moved to Santa Fe for the art atmosphere. At present I am doing a series of horse heads of different breeds and types. After this, I will return to pieces of a more complex nature. As always, horses will be a part of the work. I find it thrilling to take a piece of wax and build it into an art form that tells a story. I have my sculpture in the Shidoni Gallery and in the Son Silver Gallery."

Comp, Norm. Impressionist painter and lithographer of Western scenes, figures, and wildlife, born in Fullerton, Pennsylvania, in 1932 and living in Issaquah, Washington. "I am a bit dubious," he points out, "about the immense popularity of Western art. As in any trendy atmosphere, a great many may enter for quick gain. I'm hoping that the collecting public will not be influenced by the subject matter and buy poorly executed art."

While growing up in Pennsylvania, Comp farmed and tended cattle. He went to the Philadelphia Museum School of Art part time until he entered the Navy in 1952 and was assigned as a draftsman/illustrator. After his discharge in 1956, he painted signs and returned to art schools part time until he moved to Allentown, Pennsylvania, as a commercial artist in 1957. From 1960 to 1975, he worked in commercial art in Chicago and in 1975 moved to Seattle, Washington, as art director for *Plants Alive* magazine. In 1978, at 46, he became a full-time painter.

"My family wanted to know just what I did," he says. "I couldn't show them. When they see one of my paintings now, they understand. They can *see* it. My main media were acrylics and watercolor, but I'm being drawn back to oils. I first try to achieve a unique and interesting view of my subject, through composition and color and mood. I leave the storytelling up to the mind and imagination of the viewer. If Western art does not endure, I really won't mind because I'm doing what I enjoy most. Maybe someday they won't have to label everything. It will just be called art." Written up in *Art West*, November 1981, Comp has exhibited in major Western art shows in the Northwest and has advertised his own studio.

Conaway, James. Modern oil painter of the Arizona landscape, born in Granite City, Illinois, in 1942 and living in Minneapolis, Minnesota. Comparing the Midwest to the Southwest, he says "the biggest difference is the light. In the desert you can sense the heat through the light. And all the colors are warm—there's nothing cool even about the greens. Midwestern landscapes are cool greens and blues and they're completely man-made, roads and fields. All the forms of the desert are natural."

A teacher of painting and drawing on midwestern campuses for 20 years, he is presently Associate Professor of Art at Hamline University and also "just loves to paint. I like the smell. I like the washes dripping down my arms. I like everything about it." When he was teaching in Iowa six years ago, he held classes on location and was intrigued by the landscapes. On-site work is essential to him because "I don't think you really *see* it unless you're drawing it."

In the summer of 1979, he made his first trip to Arizona and "fell in love with the desert." He had his initial Minneapolis showing of his Southwestern landscapes in 1980. Previously, he had a three year period when he didn't sell anything, continuing to try only because "I love to paint," but the Arizona subjects sold "very well." He works on canvases up to seven feet, covering with washes in ten minutes, although he takes as long as two months to refine the painting, scraping and redoing many times. He may do a series of 12 to 15 paintings at a time, working in his studio from field sketches and "smearing paints and washes all over." Written up in *Artists of the Rockies* fall 1980, he is represented by C.G. Rein Galleries.

Frederic Collins, SADDLED HORSE, bronze, h 13, l 14

James Conaway, VERDE VALLEY MONOTYPE, oil, 24 x 35½

Norm Comp, LONE GRAZER, acrylic, 20 x 30

Eileen Conn

Roger Cooke

Conn, Eileen. Woodcarver and painter of bird groupings, born in Uniontown, Pennsylvania, in 1948 and living in Lake Montezuma, Arizona, since 1974. "Birds are very special to me. I could watch them all day," she says. "When I carve one, it is as though I were becoming part of the bird and the bird a part of me. I feel as though I am about to create a living creature."

She attended art classes at Carnegie-Mellon University, studied at Carnegie Museum, and earned her BFA from Ohio University in 1969. After she married Ted Jay, they moved to Sedona where she painted and ran a gallery. She attended a demonstration by an English bird carver and was later asked to paint a bird carved in Sedona. That awakened her enthusiasm for carving and she made steady progress. Husberg, who became her dealer, declares, "she comes close to producing the illusion of living birds in their natural settings."

She starts out with leaves and blossoms cut from copper foil that is soldered to wire stems that are soldered to branches for the setting. The bird is carved with hand tools in basswood, with the head as the most important focus because "that's where the personality lives." Burning irons make the feather details. Then the birds are sanded and fitted with wire legs. Hips are added and the birds are fastened in place for sealing and painting. A small bird takes a week and a large grouping six weeks. A flying bird takes twice as long. Her most popular subjects are cardinals, chickadees, and quail, but she refuses to do roadrunners because she dislikes them. She was profiled in *Southwest Art*, April 1981.

Cooke, Roger. Oil painter of Plateau Indians and historic scenes of the Northwest, born in Portland, Oregon, in 1941 and living in Sandy, Oregon. "The reason," according to Cooke, that "Indians have had a negative attitude toward white folks is that they have been exploited ever since Columbus hit the beach. I try to show them from a positive viewpoint, and I give the person who poses a reproduction of the painting. They really appreciate it.

"The first step toward my painting was the 'Draw Me' school. It started me in the right direction. After military service, I attended Portland State University and graduated from the Art Center College of Design where I majored in illustration. I began work as an illustrator in Indianapolis but after two years, I moved back to Oregon as a free-lance illustrator. My goal was to become a full-time painter, and in 1974 when Alan Husberg convinced me he could sell everything I painted, I told my illustration clients to get somebody else.

"My choice of subjects dates back to stories my grandfather told of Indians and pioneers. The most difficult aspect of painting Indians is their heads. Indian skull features are completely different from those of Caucasians, furthermore the skulls differ from one region to another. For example, the Coastal Indian faces were broad and flat. If there is one mistake that occurs among artists who paint American Indians, it is that they paint a Caucasian face and widen the cheekbones, and then add a feather in the hair. The result still looks like a white man." Cooke was written up in *Southwest Art*, February 1976. He is published by Greenwich Workshop and represented by Husberg Fine Arts Gallery which listed a small 10 by 20 inch oil at $2,200 in 1981.

Eileen Conn, GOLDEN WINGED WARBLERS, woodcarving, lifesize

Roger Cooke, WINTER RAID, oil on masonite, 24 x 36

James Peter Cost

Shelley Anne Cost

R. Wm Couch

Cost, James Peter. Traditional painter of California landscapes and coastal scenes in gouache and transparent watercolor, born in Philadelphia, Pennsylvania, in 1923 and living in Carmel-by-the-Sea, California, since 1946. "The subject matter is the most important part of painting," he emphasizes, "and there should be no competition from the medium. I think you have real self-expression when none of the methods or principles interferes with the artist's statement.

"My interest in the American landscape goes back to Sunday afternoon rides through the countryside with my mother and father. I loved the Burma Shave signs and Chew Mail Pouch painted on the barns. I learned to spell by these symbols of Americana. In high school, I painted pictures of barns and the countryside and loved doing it, but when I went to college I gave up my love of Americana for the wild ideas being taught by my professors. I was an abstractionist in S. McDonald Wright's class at UCLA between 1946 and 1950. After teaching abstract art to hundreds of students, however, I found little challenge in my work.

"I decided to try traditional art. To my amazement, I lacked the basic skills of drawing through I had a Master's degree in fine art." By 1964, he "had reached the point where I wanted to paint full time." At the end of two months, he "had to raise prices to slow down sales, but even that didn't seem to matter." He painted 150 pictures that first year, 35 the second, and 20 the third as he made "each picture become more of a challenge. I love to paint, and what I love to paint, people care about." Shelly Anne Cost is his daughter. Written up in *Southwest Art* April 1976, he is represented by James Peter Cost Gallery.

Cost, Shelley Anne. Realist painter of northern California landscapes in various media, born in Santa Monica, California, in 1953 and living in Carmel, California, since 1964. "I find it very valuable," she observes, "to be working in a gallery situation and meeting and conversing with the collectors. I don't introduce myself unless it becomes critical, so that I can get as much 'feedback' as possible. It is inspiring to an artist to hear favorable comments and also a good thing to hear the criticism that really evaluates my work objectively.

"From the age of seven, I was making and selling necklaces to galleries. At twelve, I began painting in oil and sold my first painting. By the next year, I had sold 20 paintings, and when I entered high school, I just thought of myself as an artist. I received a BA from the University of California at Los Angeles in 1974 and from that time I have supported myself as a professional artist. I decided not to take a Master's degree because I was able to work very closely with my father for three years after graduating.

"I feel that a great artist can take any subject and make it a masterpiece. Many subjects could look like nothing when seen in real life but it is the artist's job to make that painting come alive on canvas. All of the paintings I create are from actual subjects. Though the composition may change, I do use actual barns, buildings, and homes that I have seen. It is the detail that is fun for me. In fact, it is often hard to complete a painting since it could really go on forever. I paint barns that are very old but I never paint them run down. I always try to preserve the dignity of the structure. Due to the strong demand and low production, I have not been exhibiting in any gallery but our family gallery since 1980." She was written up in *Southwest Art*, August 1981.

Couch, R. William. Representational oil painter of wildlife, landscape, and historical subjects, born in a mining town near Iron River, Michigan, in 1929 and living in Taos, New Mexico, since 1977. "Americans," he states, "are coming of age and have finally realized the richness not only of their historical heritage but their environmental treasures as well. This awareness came to some maturity in the 1960s, and I felt that I could contribute to this through my art because of the present-day pressures on the Western environment and natural wildlife habitat."

Raised in the northern Ozark town of Jefferson City, Bill Couch earned a degree in economics from St. Mary's College in Minnesota in 1952 and served in the U.S. Army of Occupation in Germany as a Counterintelligence Corps agent until 1954. He then took a course from the Famous Artists School and free-lanced in illustration for seven years. "In the 1950s and 1960s," he says, "it was difficult to make it on your own as a free-lance illustrator and almost impossible as a fine artist," so family pressures forced him into management positions.

In 1969, Couch started a fine arts studio he combined with illustration, and in 1977 he moved to Taos to pursue art full time. His interests are divided between the Western high country and the Southwestern desert, so he calls Taos "the best of these two worlds." He also models ducks and geese in wood. "I am best known for my wildlife art," he adds, "through gallery associations and illustrations in such publications as *Ducks Unlimited* and *Audubon* magazines, as well as *New Mexico Wildlife*." Prints are distributed by two publishers, and he is represented by Taos Art and Myles Galleries.

Shelley Anne Cost, AN AFTERNOON IN THE VALLEY
gouache, 10 x 15

R. William Couch, TETON ELK, oil, 24 x 36

James Peter Cost, CARMEL BAY, oil, 30 x 48

125

Cowley, Lois. Realist-Impressionist painter and sculptor of portraits and figures, born in Sutton, Nebraska, in 1936 and living near Denver, Colorado, since 1963. "Eyes are truly the windows of the soul," she believes, "and they must be captured exactly. While the eyes are reflections of that special inner essence, everyone's eyes reflect that spirit in a different way. In children, the eyes are like flowers unfolding, but in adults, eyes tend to mirror character, wisdom, and the particular knowledge they have gained."

She began her art career at fourteen with Saturday afternoon classes, "but it's hard to pinpoint just where the magnetism comes from that draws one into art. No matter what the outside influences of art may be, the final decision comes from within." From 1955 to 1959, she majored in fine art at the University of Nebraska and, by the time she was twenty, she was painting commissioned portraits. "I like to conduct extensive interviews with the subject," she emphasizes. "I try to find the best quality in each person—the true essence of their spirit. Then I consider the best elements of composition for them and the best colors to bring out these traits.

"In a commission, the inner essence of the subject may dictate that the portrait be more detailed in order to bring out specific traits, but a real excitement for me is to be able to loosen up in the features and background of the works I do just to please myself. Most of these paintings concentrate on Indians. Here the Impressionistic technique allows me to suggest endless spiritual implications." Written up in *Southwest Art*, September 1978, and *Artists of the Rockies*, winter 1975, she has been represented by Gallery A.

Cox, Tim. Realist oil painter of contemporary cowboy life in southeastern Arizona, born in Safford, Arizona, in 1957 and living in Clifton, Arizona. "I can never remember a time," he states, "when I wasn't drawing and painting. My mother tells me when I was less than three years old I drew a bird, and even included its ears. My first grade teacher still has some of the drawings I did in her class. When I was in high school, I was painting and selling oils, and after graduation I've painted for a livelihood."

He worked daytime as a service station attendant, cut and sold mesquite wood, and ran a trap line while painting at night. When Grant Speed, who was president of the Cowboy Artists of America, agreed to look at his paintings, Cox drove 200 miles to meet Speed and was persuaded to study with William Whitaker at Brigham Young University. It was the first time that Cox had sketched live models other than horses and cows, as he attended class for six hours a day, five days a week, for three months, while also painting at night to earn money to stay in school.

"I'm getting better at not letting every little thing distract me," he says, "but when I see a rider in the distance or hear a cow bawl, it's hard to concentrate on my work. When I need to research a subject, I do it right here where we live, surrounded by working cow ranches. I ride and help neighboring ranchers during the roundups, using my own horses." Speed introduced Cox to Texas Art Gallery which has represented him since 1977 and has published seven limited edition prints through Texas Art Press. He has been written up in *The Western Horseman*, September 1981, and at *Preview '82* three of his paintings were auctioned for a total of $36,000.

Crandall, Jerry. Realistic oil painter of early Western life, born in La Junta, Colorado, in 1935 and living in Riverside, California. "In order to get the true feeling of these Western people," Crandall says, "I believe that I must re-create the time as closely as possible in my own life. I know what it's like to be in a pistol charge on horseback and to fire blackpowder firearms. I've danced with the Indians and have even been in a gunfight in a Western movie. In this way I have a first-hand knowledge of a subject before putting it on canvas.

"As a boy, I played at the site of Bent's Fort, and vividly imagined the mountain men, wagon trains, and Indian encampments that had been there over 100 years ago. By age fifteen, I had made a complete Indian dancing costume, learned dances, and had read scores of books on Indian lore. My father, a creative artist in his own right, encouraged my interest in art." After high school, Crandall served in the Army from 1955 to 1957, attended Woodbury College until 1960, and worked as a commercial artist.

In 1972, Crandall began as a professional Western painter and calls research "really exciting for me. I ferret out pockets of history and I truly enjoy breaking new ground by painting an incident described in an old trapper's journal. I think of different paintings a hundred times a day, and can find dozens of ideas for new pieces in just one old diary." Crandall has been written up in *Southwest Art*, October 1974 and October 1980, is listed in *Who's Who in American Art*, participates in invitational exhibitions, has been historical advisor for movies and television, is published by Guildhall, and is his own representative for paintings.

Lois Cowley, NAVAJO SUNSHINE, oil, 16 x 20

Tim Cox, PARTNERS, oil, 30 x 40

Jerry Crandall, COUREURS DES BOIS, oil, 30 x 40

Crook, Don. Realist painter in acrylics and pastels of people in scenes of the Old Pacific Northwest, born in La Crosse, Wisconsin, in 1934 and living in Yakima, Washington. "I have had success with paintings that include children as the main subjects. People seem to relate to a child in a predicament, whether it be humorous or threatening. A collector may buy a child-related painting even though not a particularly Western oriented person. This gives me a little wider scope and allows my buying market to be diversified."

A long-time resident of central Washington near the Yakima Indian Reservation, Crook spent more than twenty years as an illustrator and art director. He designed animated films for television, an experience he carries over into painting. He first formulates a story line through research, then starts with charcoal sketches before collecting the exact gear and clothing in order to pose friends as models for photographing the scene. He remarks that "with older models this presents no problem, but try to convey this story to a three year old. I may go through two or three trial shooting sessions with different children before I come up with one.

"I paint six hours a day, every weekday," he adds, "with Saturdays and Sundays broken into two five-hour shifts. I try to do twenty major pieces a year. For the first time, I have added pastels to my repertoire. There has been a large demand for my work, and acrylics take more time. Pastels take one half the time of an acrylic and to my amazement brings two-thirds the price of an acrylic." A member of the Western Artists of America where he has won Best in Show, Crook is represented by Favell Museum and Trailside Galleries. In 1982, his painting was sold for $20,000 at the C.M. Russell Show.

Crook, Elaine Manning. Traditional oil painter of today's Indian people, born in Chicago, Illinois, in 1942 and living in Mesa, Arizona, since 1962. "I began experimenting with my present approach to painting," she observes, "when I bought a painting of about 1840 vintage that needed restoration. When I delved into the process, I realized I would have to learn the old technique to restore the painting. I also realized that most artists were not using the old methods. This is what launched me on my current style, a lengthy process incorporating multi-layered application of opaque and transparent paint.

"I became an artist because I really had no choice. There was never anything else so compelling as to dissuade me from this goal. As a child, I was always drawing people. I attended Saturday classes at the Art Institute of Chicago from 7th grade through high school and sold my first painting when I was in the 8th grade. It was an exhilarating feeling. In 1960, I won a scholarship to the Art Institute and moved to Phoenix in 1962. There I attended Arizona State University until I took a position as a television art director.

"I started doing research into the Indian culture for programs. Then I traveled to the reservations in Arizona and New Mexico. After assimilating my impressions, I began an absorbing painting journey from which I have yet to return. I don't limit myself to any one Indian culture because I find them all fascinating. Also, it is a learning experience and a good opportunity to create intercultural friendships." In 1978, she attended the American Academy of Art in Chicago to take a class in the old painting style she presently uses. She shows exclusively at El Prado Gallery of Art.

Crooks, Ron. Traditional oil painter of the nostalgia of the Old West, born in Glendale, California, in 1925 and living in French Gulch, California, since 1972. "I think the peak in art was the French Impressionists," he observes. "It is a looseness in style in the paintings that borders on abstract. I hope my style goes that way. My feeling is that if an artist lived to be 200, he would become an abstract painter, boiling down all he wants to interpret into its abstract essence. Basically, all painting is abstract. A good painting is a good abstraction."

Raised in Glendale, he enrolled in Otis Art Institute in March 1944 and "completed only three weeks at Otis before being drafted into the Army. Two and a half years later I returned home and enrolled again in Otis. After one year, I moved to the School of Allied Arts in Glendale. In 1950, I left school to go to work in the art department of an aircraft company. In 1968, after fifteen years in advertising art, I took the big step to fine art, painting all subjects but soon discovering you need an identity in one; I picked Western subjects because they let the artist use landscape, people, storytelling, etc.

"It was a rough go to begin with. It was a year and a half before I could see up," but "to me, somebody who works for somebody else is a paid slave. My philosophy is that not every day is a good day. Some days, you don't want to paint. If it's a bad day, though, it ends at midnight. Things will get better and they always do." He paints about 200 oils of Western scenes a year, and travels to about a dozen art shows. Written up in *Southwest Art*, November 1975, and a member of the American Artists of the Rockies, he is represented by the Flatlander and Trailside Galleries.

Ron Crooks, A LONE RIDER, oil, 18 x 24

E. Manning Crook, A FEATHER IN HER CAP, oil, 24 x 36

Don Crook, SUNSET CANYON TRAIL, acrylic, 30 x 40

Penni Anne Cross

Cross, Penni Anne. Painter of Crow Indian portraits in oil and hard pastel, born in Spokane, Washington, in 1939 and living in Crow Agency, Montana. "I have given my thoughts, paints, brushes, canvas, and time to God for His expression. I have asked Him to make my paintings a spiritual ticket into someone's life that they may be a better person and come closer to God, finding a peace inside that I have come to know. I love what I'm doing, both in my Christian work and my painting."

A convert to Christianity and married to a minister, she is a self-taught painter. In 1972, she gave a bible class on a Nevada Indian reservation that became the center of her thoughts and furnished the subjects for her paintings. Much time is spent by her in getting to know the sitters, and photographs are used as a reminder. "When I do a portrait of someone," she says, "I want the viewer to know what I know. I want that viewer to feel and see the same thing I feel and see in that person."

She began specializing in Crow Indian subjects, and in 1978 was adopted into the Crow Nation. Her name was "Travels the Good Road." After moving to the southern Montana reservation, she states that "it is essential to record what is going on in the Tribe at the present time. The goodness that I see in these people must be preserved. I want to do that through my paintings. My desire is to document the proud history of the Crow Tribe—its traditional ways and new influences." In "Preview '81" at the Texas Art Gallery, her 32 by 24 inch pastel brought $6,000. She was in the 1981 Peking exhibition and was written up in *Southwest Art*, April 1977. Her prints are published by The Wooden Bird.

Penni Anne Cross, SPEAK TO ME, hard pastel, 30 x 23

CROUSE

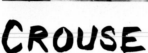

Crouse, Danny. Realist painter of Western scenes in oil on masonite, specializing in figures from the "Muzzleloaders Association," born in Hutchinson, Kansas, in 1938 and living in Toledo, Ohio, since 1972. "When I was eight years old," he recalls, "my cousin's girl friend would draw by copying the pictures from my coloring books. I continually pestered her to tell me how she could draw so well. Her answer was always the same, 'keep copying it over and over until you get it right.' By the time I got them right, I became known as 'the artist.'

"During my junior year in high school, I won a scholarship to a summer session for artists at the University of Kansas. This led to a BFA from U of K in 1961. My major was illustration. During the next years, I did very little painting for galleries as I was trying desperately to make a living as a commercial artist." Crouse worked in Hutchinson, Wichita, Kansas City, and finally in Toledo where his job for nine years was painting architectural art. He did the "entourage" for the buildings, that is, the cars, trees, scale figures, animals, etc., in full color casein.

In the past few years, Crouse has been a free-lance illustrator, working for New York City accounts, doing mass market paperback books. In addition, he has been teaching and is studying toward his MA through an Independent Study Degree Program. During the summer of 1980, when he was 42 and had been painting for 25 years, he heard about "the opportunities in painting in the Southwest. During December of 1980, I visited Arizona and accidentally stopped by Husberg Fine Arts Gallery in Sedona. I showed them some of my paintings and they took two. This was the beginning of my association" with marketing Western art.

Crowe, Thompson Phillip. Realist wildlife painter of ducks, big game, and upland birds in watercolor-casein, born in McMinnville, Tennessee, in 1947 and living in Nashville, Tennessee. "I don't kill anything in my paintings," he states. "Not even a rabbit in the talons of a hawk. I'm a conservationist at heart. I hunt game with a gun, but I don't take a stand on the issue and try to sell other people on hunting. Killing is part of hunting, but it is totally anticlimactic to the experience overall."

He grew up walking the outdoors with his father who was in the Air Force, attended high school in Puerto Rico, and entered the Ringling School of Art in Sarasota, Florida, where he "found out everybody else could draw better. By the time I finished school, though, I realized I had something to offer." He served in the Army and was chosen as European Artist of the Year, then returned to Nashville as a commercial artist.

When Gray Stone Press needed a wildlife artist, Crowe said "sure I can paint wildlife. Everybody can." He adds, however, "I found out shortly that everybody can't. Your research has to be right. Your anatomy has to be right. I had to do some serious studying. I try to paint what the average hunter, like me, sees when he goes afield. A hunter will remember the day he shot his first buck, or killed his first duck, so this is what I strive to put into my paintings, the visions people have in their minds of good times afield." A trademark is showing leg bands on his duck paintings, to encourage the waterfowl banding program. "It's just my own thing," he says, "my personal statement in support of conservation of wildlife."

Danny Crouse, AFTERNOON SHADE, oil on masonite, 18 x 24

Phillip Crowe, WINTER ELK, watercolor-casein, 21½ x 26½

Donald V. Crowley

Crowley, Donald V. Realist oil painter of the Southwestern "people and events as I find them today," born in Redlands, California, in 1926 and living in Tucson, Arizona, since 1974. "The captivating subtleties revealed in a painting cannot be conveyed through conversation or the written word. That's why I believe that every painting should stand on its own," Crowley emphasizes, "and the less said about it the better. Art is like sex. It's something that you do, not something that you talk about."

When he was ten, his family moved to Santa Ana, California. After high school, he served in the Merchant Marine and the Navy until 1948, and believes that the G.I. Bill that financed his education at the Art Center College in Los Angeles "was the greatest single thing the government ever did." Crowley graduated with honors in 1953 and then worked as an illustrator in New York City. He says that he "cannot recall having a single free weekend during the entire 21 years that I worked in that business."

In 1973, a friend asked Crowley to exhibit paintings in Tucson. One look at Arizona was enough to lead him to leave the "unbearably pretentious, tinsel" East. He began concentrating his "efforts on character studies of the Paiute and Apache Indians because they had been largely overlooked. My hours spent on the reservation are a revelation, watching those beautiful people." In gratitude, he presented the San Carlos Apaches with the proceeds from 40 artist's proofs of his 1981 Greenwich Workshop lithograph. He has been featured in *Southwest Art,* December 1974 and December 1977, and at the 1981 silent auction at Settlers West Galleries, his painting was listed at $28,000.

Donald Crowley, ROBERTA'S DAUGHTER, oil, 30 x 20

B. H. Cummings
'82

F. DADAY

Dagosta

Cummings, Ben H. Self-taught painter of California landscapes who has been exhibiting since 1945, born in Healdsburg, California, in 1909 and living in Santa Rosa, California, since 1963. "I experience a sense of well-being when I create something that is uniquely mine," he says. "A landscape becomes mine when I have chosen those elements from it that best express the sense of place and then organize those elements to lead the viewer into that place. I prefer landscapes that give a sense of cheerfulness."

After attending a one-room grade school, Cummings took art courses in high school and in Santa Rosa Junior College before transferring to the University of California at Berkeley to study chemistry as a more likely job opportunity during the Depression. He worked as a chemist in California, Texas, and New York before retiring at 55 to paint watercolor landscapes and to become curator of the Codding Museum of Natural History in Santa Rosa. He is currently finishing dioramas for wildlife exhibits.

Cummings believes that his training in science has made his paintings "tight." He declares that "the delineation of forms is painstaking. It is the artist's prerogative to use a medium as a tool to communicate his response to an environment. My way is explicit and direct." His method is to select a mood that expresses the essence of a particular landscape, so that "scenes in the Sierra Nevada mountains are in a high key, coastal scenes emphasize the interplay of fog and sunlight, and coastal hills speak of the golden light." Cummings is represented by Husberg Fine Arts Gallery.

Daday, Ferenc. "Colorist" painter of the landscape and people of the West in oil and watercolor, born in Kerkabarabas, Hungary, in 1914 and living in Burbank, California, since 1956. "In a mechanical world," he observes, "there are two possible routes that the contemporary painter can choose. He can express the anguish and crises, or, he can seek out that which is more fundamental to man's needs and render it sensorially. If he hopes the observer will pause for a peaceful moment and lose his anxieties, the artist must elect to follow the second footpath.

"After extended studies in Italy in 1936, I graduated from the Royal Academy of Art in Budapest in 1938. I then selected a new and fascinating field of activity by calling into life a firm that provided most of the set designs for the Hungarian film industry from 1938 to 1944. I also participated in exhibitions in the National Gallery in Budapest. In 1947, I was invited to organize an exhibit in Stockholm and also held a show of my watercolors painted there.

"In 1948, I received another invitation, this time from the Argentinians. In laborious years, I created one mural after the other to adorn the Assembly Halls. In 1951, there was a show of my watercolors and oils in Buenos Aires. In 1955, I left for the United States, and after a short stay in Atlanta, Georgia, I settled down in Los Angeles." Living in the West, he has painted cowboy scenes and other Western episodes that combine the two worlds, the old through his training in Europe's art academies, and the new featuring the themes and the history of America. His style is dramatic, emphasizing the clouds and the lighting. Written up in *Southwest Art*, March 1980, he has shown at The Hanging Tree Gallery and Copenhagen Galleri.

Dagosta, Andy. Traditional oil painter of the Old West, born in Omaha, Nebraska, in 1923 and living in Glendale, California, since 1946. "When I was a small boy, my passion was cowboy movies. In those days, almost all the boys who didn't want to be another Lindy wanted to be cowboys, so with my friends I spent Saturday afternoons at the movies watching Bob Steel, Hoot Gibson, Buck Jones, Randolph Scott, Gene Autry, and other Western heroes. I also spent Saturday mornings at the local art museum, studying the works of Albert Bierstadt, Thomas Moran, Charles Russell, and Frederic Remington, and sketching the Greek statues in the dark recesses."

After four years at Omaha Tech, Dagosta served in the 12th Air Force in Italy during World War II and then settled in California where he attended the Hollywood Art Center. In 1948, he opened a commercial art studio in Pasadena and twenty years later began to paint in oil as a hobby in order to put on canvas the knowledge of Western history that came from his research. His friendship with the artist Lloyd Mitchell provided advice, and he studied with Reynold Brown.

He went to the desert to photograph and draw. As he says, "I became familiar not only with the clothing, guns, saddles, stirrups, cookware, and buildings of frontier days, but I learned every detail of the work of those days, such as the loading of pack animals, so that everything I paint is exactly what it was in that place at that time for the function portrayed." By 1970, he won first place at the Death Valley Open show, and he was a founding member of the American Indian and Cowboy Artist Society. Written up in *Desert*, October 1975, he has exhibited at the California Fine Arts and the Paul Metcalf Galleries.

Ferenc Daday, ANOTHER DAY, oil, 24 x 30

Ben H. Cummings, SMITH RIVER BLUFFS MONTANA
acrylic watercolor, 18½ x 28½

Andrew Dagosta, GONNA RAIN LIKE HELL, oil, 24 x 36

D'AMBROSI

Jim Daly

D'Ambrosi, Jasper. Traditional sculptor of figures of the Old West in bronze statuettes and heroic monuments, born in Wilmington, California, in 1926 and living in Tempe, Arizona, since 1977. "There definitely is a genetic influence in the progression of man," he believes. "As we progress, we do so from our own genetic structure. In my case, that's northern Italy—a proven heritage in the Old World. If you let fly with your instincts, you will echo your heritage. That's what I'm doing here—working out from my genetic structure."

Son of an immigrant father and a mother descended from pioneers, he sculpted the mud in his yard while still in grammar school. After service in the Air Corps in World War II, he played football for the University of Southern California. "That scholarship paid the bills," he recalls. "Players were each given twelve game tickets and I sold the ones for the Notre Dame game in 1948 for 250 bucks." He graduated cum laude in 1951 and was employed by Douglas Aircraft as a technical illustrator, quitting in 1962 to form his own printing company in Los Angeles.

In 1970, he turned to art full time, and in 1972 he began to concentrate on bronzes of Western Americana. An edition of sixteen of his "Muddy Creek Crossin' " was priced at $15,000 and sold out. He now has 28 bronzes on the market and has completed four commissioned monuments in California, New Mexico, and Kansas. "I like clay," he explains, "because it's clean. You can build and destroy and work it until you've got the living curve that's exactly what you want. The response of this inanimate material to my touch can become really sexual. I work out my emotions on it." Featured in Broder's *Bronzes of the American West*, he is represented by Way West Gallery.

Daly, Jim. Realist painter of Western narratives, born in Holdenville, Oklahoma, in 1940 and living in Eugene, Oregon. As a youth, he says he "hopped trains and traveled with the hobos, staying in the Salvation Army missions in the bigger cities along with the down and outers. It was exciting, and I liked it. Some of my paintings reflect the memories of those old guys. I often recall stories they would tell, and use them for situations in my work. It's fun when you're sixteen years old, but tragic when you're older."

Of Osage and Cherokee descent, Daly served three years in the U.S. Army and then studied at the Art Center College of Design in Los Angeles. Influenced by Norman Rockwell's work, he became an illustrator and was staff art director of *Westerner Magazine* for three years. "All I want to do is paint," he states. "I love this country and its history. As a result, I'm happiest when painting Americana. I believe the artists in this country are the best in the world. I have to work very hard because the competition is so great."

Daly often stages his events with live models. Children in rural America are favorite subjects, as is the effect of the passing of the West. Sometimes he uses himself as a character, and adds that "I'm always looking for new faces. If I see an interesting one, I'll walk up to the person and ask if I can take his picture for use in a later oil." Photography plays an important role as guides for expressions and backgrounds. Daly uses an agent because "business matters confuse me, so I let them do the worrying, and I do the painting." He has been featured in *Southwest Art*, October 1975, has exhibited with the Northwest Rendezvous Group and is represented by Lesli Art.

Jasper D'Ambrosi, BLOSSOM TIME,
bronze, lifesize, edition 30

Jim Daly, AT LONG LAST, acrylic, 40 x 30

DARVAS

R. Daughters.

Dawson

Darvas, Endre Peter. "Expressive" painter of Western landscapes in acrylic, born in Kisvarda, Hungary, in 1946 and living in South Lake Tahoe, California, since 1971. "I seldom paint 'a picture' of something," he explains. "The subject matter is secondary. My primary interest is a mood—a single expressive visual statement. A painting is a thought, an idea executed in paint, expressing a visual language. I learn from nature by looking. I can find a thousand paintings in a clump of dry grass."

After escaping from Hungary during the 1956 revolution, the Darvas family landed in El Paso, Texas. He had his first one-man show at sixteen, but enrolled in the University of Texas on a math and physics scholarship. As art became the strongest influence, he moved to Taos, New Mexico, where he found "a compulsive creative atmosphere. I am never at a loss as to what to paint once I set to it. There are a rush of ideas, then one of hundreds emerges and brings with it the energy to tackle the toughest task, that of getting started. I am painting something that I know rather than something that I see."

His palette contains 40 colors. "Working with a limited palette is like walking with a limp. True, in theory you only need the basics. The theories are mostly about color and light, however, while we painters are stuck with pigment in goo, so it rests essentially on preference. I just happen to prefer every color on the market!" At 36, he has more than 3,000 paintings in American collections and he has received more than 40 one-man shows. He has now established his winter home in San Carlos, Sonora, Mexico. Written up in *Southwest Art*, May 1978, he has exhibited at The May Gallery.

Daughters, Robert. Impressionist oil painter of Southwestern landscapes and of Indians, born in Trenton, Missouri, in 1929 and living in Taos, New Mexico, since 1972. "It looked like the Cowboy Artists was a great organization and so I decided to join them. I went to see one of the heads at CA, and he explained the whole thing. You didn't just walk in and say here I am. When it comes to the CA, you are asked to join. I somehow got the feeling I wasn't on their 'Things To Do Today' list.

"I was raised in St. Joseph, Missouri, and was entering drawing contests before I was ten. I can honestly say I was never interested in anything else. After high school, I went into the service. When I came out I worked as a curator at the St. Joseph Museum of Natural History while attending the Kansas City Art Institute." After graduating in 1953, Daughters became a partner in an advertising art studio, winning more than 250 awards in twenty years.

It was about 1967 when he saw the CA show and said, "I can do this." He adds that "on my return, I did six canvases that were very, very Western. The paintings were accepted by a very good gallery, and I thought I had it made. I look back now and I realize that I made a terrible mistake in the subject matter. It just wasn't me. When I got into landscapes and Indian portraits, I felt better about myself. That must have come through because the happier I became, the more I sold." He regards van Gogh as a strong influence. Daughters was in the 1981 Peking, China, exhibition, was featured in *Southwest Art*, August 1980, and as one of the Taos Six in October 1974, and is represented by Trailside and Linda McAdoo Galleries.

Dawson, Doug. Representational painter of portraits and landscapes, born in Hinsdale, Illinois, in 1944 and living in Wheat Ridge, Colorado. "I've always been concerned with one thing," he points out, "and that concern is *saying something*. I don't care if a piece is as tight as a photographic image or so loose you have to stand back to see it. I'm concerned with statement. My work ranges from loose to tight since I work out of disorder. I push until I've gotten what I want or until I have to throw it away.

"Painting is something I gave into. While I've been consistently interested in art throughout my life, I've nevertheless rejected it for long periods of time. In school, it didn't seem to me that the artist made any valuable contribution to the world. I was eighteen and an idealist. But in the end I kept coming back to art. When I was a graduate student in biology at Drake University, I gave in because I found I was painting instead of being in the laboratory. I gave in to the compulsion to paint because I kept doing it no matter what."

In 1970, Dawson was teaching art and biology in the Denver public schools and painting in his spare time. He was accepted by his first gallery in 1971, received an award from the American Watercolor Society in 1974, and by 1975 was able to quit teaching. The family had been saving for five years and had nine months of "living money" ahead plus a basement stocked with food and 200 rolls of toilet paper. He has since been elected a member of the American Watercolor Society and of the Pastel Society of America, has been written up in *Artists of the Rockies*, winter 1979 and *Southwest Art*, January 1981, and is represented by Valhalla and Anne Magee Galleries.

Doug Dawson, RAVENNA, pastel, 15 x 13

Robert Daughters, CANYON SENTINEL, oil, 30 x 40

Peter Darvas, ASPEN GROVE, acrylic, 24 x 34

HLDEATON

Norman Neal Deaton

Deaton, Herman L. Realist sculptor of figures and animals in bronze, born in Newton, Iowa, in 1928 and living there ever since. "I had the good fortune," Deaton observes, "to be raised on the farm where a son can learn by watching and helping. It's also a good place to learn about animals, both domestic and wild. These animals contribute greatly to my awareness of life because I was around it all from conception, birth, life, and death. This is one reason that most of my sculpture contains animals.

"I was the typical farm boy, going to a country school, and listening to Jack Armstrong on the radio after rural electrification went through in the mid-1930s. After graduating from high school in 1946, I blundered into my future as a farm hand and eventually to twelve years of heavy construction on highways. Through these years I was dabbling in art work, and in 1964 I joined a museum exhibit firm owned by my brother. We worked for major clients like the Smithsonian Institution and it was here that I learned modeling, molding, and casting—from mastodons to wildflowers.

"In 1974 I decided to see if it was possible to survive on my own and I set up my studio. My professional sculpture consists of bronzes for galleries and miniature cold-cast bronzes of handpainted animals. I also accept commissions and have done a bas relief mural that measures seven and a half by 18 feet. Another is five by 37 feet and is shaped in a curve. The high cost of travel has about killed showings for me though I do belong to the Society of Animal Artists and have shown at their annual meetings. My bronzes are in various galleries to the west of here, including Husberg and Gallery of the Southwest."

Deaton, Norman Neal. Sculptor and painter of natural science subjects, born in Des Moines, Iowa, about 1930 and living in Newton, Iowa, since 1959. Talking about his Deaton Museum Studio, he says that "there are no textbooks on this subject, no reference materials. This is the kind of business in which you never stop learning. Fifty or 60 percent of it is experimental. We're always inventing new materials for molding and constructing."

Raised in Newton with his brother Herman, he practiced stuffing dead animals as a child, took art classes in high school, and studied a few art courses while in the Navy. Turned down as an apprentice at the Smithsonian, he obtained a temporary job at the Philadelphia Academy of Natural Sciences until there was an opening because of the Smithsonian's modernization program in the mid-50s. In 1959, he established his own studio in Iowa to cater to museums around the world. His speciality was "sculpture taxidermy" where the animal's body is sculpted and the skin is fitted to the model, thus eliminating "stuffing."

In his studio, Deaton applies "a naturalist's insight" to "recreate a world of wildlife and nature through painting, sculpture, and model making." In 1974, he was chosen to prepare lifesize specimens of buffalo, steer, horse, and grizzly bear for the Museum of Westward Expansion in St. Louis. Another statue, this one of a prehistoric mastodon, took 9,000 pounds of clay. In 1976, Deaton decided to change from anatomical modeling for museums to sculpture of the complete animal, going from artistic science to fine art, and from painting ecological backgrounds to the easel painting of wildlife. His gallery is El Prado Gallery of Art.

Norman Neal Deaton, AMERICAN BISON, hand-painted polyresin, 7 x 10

Herman L. Deaton, THE BULLFIGHTER, bronze, 5 x 9½

Thomas A. DeDecker

De Grazia

Chuck DeHaan

DeDecker, Thomas. Traditional painter in oil, gouache and watercolor of the Western Indian lifestyle before 1880, born in Appleton, Wisconsin, in 1951 and living in Redmond, Washington, since 1975. "The Native American Indian had the most fascinating natural culture, until the white man infiltrated it. The peace and harmony, especially of the nomadic Plains tribes, is envied by all. Thus I paint the peace and harmony they enjoyed and which I also want to experience. I feel I can recreate in my paintings what they felt 150 years ago.

"Previous to college, I did very little with art. My interests were toward archaeology and anthropology. As a result of a student art show at Brigham Young University, I was advised to pursue my talents full strength, and after two years I found myself involved in drawing. After college, I traveled throughout the West, trying to find a niche. During those years, I was influenced by deceased artists such as Corot, Bierstadt, and Tavernier. I settled in Washington, and became obsessed with the Plains tribes. I have been a student of their culture and of art ever since.

"My paintings are a constant challenge. Before I can sit down and start on a basic sketch on my board, I will struggle in my mind with the design, balance, and composition of that scene. An artist must pour his heart out on each painting. The mental labor involved in doing a painting is often so tedious that I feel weak by the end of a day. It takes full attention and total awareness of what I am doing in each painting, but almost always I find the hours passing away as if only minutes had gone by." DeDecker is represented by El Prado Gallery of Art and Copenhagen Galleri.

De Grazia, Ettore (Ted). Impressionist painter, sculptor, and printmaker of religious and Mexican figures, born in Morenci, Arizona, in 1909 and living in Tucson, Arizona. "When people ask why I paint the pictures I paint," he points out, "I do not answer because the paintings are my life. They are my experience. They are what I have felt and what I have known. How can I explain this in a few words? The onlooker must explain for himself. If he cannot, the painting is not for him.

"From childhood I have been interested in color. Often I went on long hikes with my father. We always came home with rocks which I crushed with a hammer for color. Sometimes we found clay which I molded and baked in the kitchen oven." At eleven, he went with his family to Italy where they lived for four years. After returning to Morenci, De Grazia was 23 when he finished high school. He gave up painting for a while and entered business, but "painting was beginning to bother me again." He took his work to the world-famous Mexican painters Diego Rivera and Jose Clemente Orozco in 1942 and received a one-person show in Mexico City.

De Grazia was 35 when he received his BS in music from the University of Arizona, and 36 when he received a degree in art. "I was a disappointment to my school," he recalls. "I had to go my way alone. I could not paint to please the public with pretty pictures in ice cream colors." In 1960, he was commissioned to do the UNICEF greeting card. He "has worked in all media," including plates, serigraphs, lithographs, and etchings, and claims to be "the world's most reproduced artist." Listed in *Who's Who in American Art*, he is represented by De Grazia Gallery in the Sun and by Buck Saunders Trading Post and Gallery.

DeHaan, Chuck. Traditional oil painter and sculptor of the 20th-century cowboy, born west of Fort Worth, Texas, in 1933 and living near Graford, Texas, since 1970. "Before you can paint a house," he declares, "you've got to build it. To draw it you've got to know it. The only way I'm able to paint horses is that I've known them and worked with them all my life. It'd be awfully hard for me to draw an airplane."

Self-taught, his drawing began early. "My interest in art started as soon as I discovered that pencils left tracks. From then on, I tracked up everything that would lay still." One of his first jobs was breaking colts at a dollar a day, and "there was times when it felt like I had to reach up to touch the bottom." His rodeo career started when he rode his first bull at thirteen. He preferred bronc riding because "I never saw a cowboy ride into a cowcamp on a bull and just couldn't put my heart into it." Eventually he turned to training cutting horses on his Cow Track Ranch.

Until the last few years, his paintings were used mainly for reproduction on the covers of Western magazines and catalogs. He ran his own advertising agency for twelve years, but now he has cut his commercial work to one account that is "like family." He adds that "when I paint cowboys and horses and tack, I know what I'm painting. I've always communicated with horses, and in portrayin' them I like to keep on close speakin' terms so I can paint what they're sayin'. Some Western artists don't know the fine points of cowboyin'. They have horses doin' things horses don't do." Published by Guildhall, Inc., he is represented by Trammell's Flying T Gallery and Copenhagen Galleri.

Chuck DeHaan
RIDIN' OL' PAINT 'N' LEADING OL' DAN
oil, 30 x 24

Ted DeGrazia, ALONE, oil, 20 x 40

Thomas DeDecker, THE PEACE OF THE CHEYENNE PEOPLE, oil, 15 x 24

Juan Dell   *de mayo*

Dell, Juan. Sculptor of bronze figures including "Fighting Indians of the West," born in West Texas and living in Santa Fe, New Mexico. "I like to develop an idea in my mind before I go to sleep or as I am awakening," she says. "At this time I can see the sculpture clearly in my mind, and I can quickly change it from one position to another. Some sculptors use preliminary sketches to develop a piece, but I have found a mental picture best."

Juan Dell is the nom de bronze of Glenna Juandell Mitchell. "My mother liked the sound of Juandell," she explains. "There were no problems until I separated it into two names. There are lots of Juans about—all men. I was born on the Llano Estacado, the Staked Plains. Their mysteries and history fascinated me." Her first lessons were in painting at South Plains College; she also took private instruction. She began sculpting in Taos in 1968, intrigued by the foundry there, and she has been allowed to work in foundries in the three places that she has lived since. The experience has given her a rare technical knowledge and she makes her own rubber molds.

She is totally absorbed when she is modeling, and "one of my worst fears is that I will accidentally drink the chemicals rather than the coffee." She often uses live models, and frequently they are women. "I admire pioneer women," she declares. "They were the stabilizing force in the West." Her bronzes are now in eight public collections. She is the only female member of the Texas Association of Professional Artists, and she won the Association's gold medal in 1977. The subject of the book *The First Lady of Western Bronze*, she is represented by Gallery Americana.

De Mayo, Louis. Stylized painter of contemporary Indian figures in acrylic, born in Philadelphia, Pennsylvania, in 1926 and living in Phoenix, Arizona, since 1973. When a gallery owner suggested that De Mayo tell people he is Indian to facilitate sales, De Mayo asked whether "if I wanted to paint a horse, would I have to say I was part horse?" His friend Carl Gorman who is Navajo told him, "Louis, if people ask what tribe you're from, tell them you're Awop-paho."

A first generation Italian-American, De Mayo was raised in the neighborhood that produced Mario Lanza and Frankie Avalon. "If you spit," he claims, "you would hit a singer." After serving in the Marines during World War II, he studied at the Pennsylvania Academy of Fine Arts under the G.I. Bill, then was employed in a series of commercial art jobs. He relocated to Phoenix as Art Director for *Arizona Highways*, a job he soon quit to establish himself as a full-time artist.

"I really have only one regret about leaving Philadelphia, and that is that I didn't leave it sooner. I choose Indians to paint because of their dramatic quality and their manner of dress," he states. "I had a strong emotional attraction to the Yaqui and their black garb. Maybe it's because I grew up seeing women in black. My people are all dark skinned. I don't want to make too much of a racial issue in my work, but it certainly could stem from such roots. I look at life as if it were a big slow-moving steamroller. It gives you a helluva lot of time to get out of the way if you fall down, but if you just want to lie there, it is going to roll right over you." Written up in and featured on the cover of *Southwest Art*, December 1980, De Mayo is exclusively represented by Morris Fine Arts Gallery.

Juan Dell, THE SACRED ROBE, bronze, h 36, Edition 25

Louis DeMayo, TRAIL BOSS (1982), acrylic/canvas, 60 x 48

De Mille, Leslie Benjamin. Painter of portraits, especially of Indians, in oil and pastel, born in Hamilton, Ontario, Canada, in 1927 and living in Santa Ana Heights, California. "To be a portrait artist," he declares, "takes a lot of study, a bit of psychology, patience, and the courage to look a sitter straight in the eye and smile when he or she says, 'It's lovely—but isn't there something wrong with the mouth?' "

At eight, he won first prize in an art competition. At thirteen, he attended Hamilton Technical Institute and then went on to the Art Students League in New York City. In 1947, he returned to Hamilton as a commercial artist, married, and had five children before moving to California. "I worked first at Knott's Berry Farm doing portrait sketches. From there I went to the Disneyland Hotel. Each year, I did over 400 portraits." Becoming serious as an artist, he took lessons from Leon Franks who taught DeMille "how to see" and "how to lose edges effectively," and he went on to paint Presidents Nixon and Reagan, among other celebrities.

One unusual style of pastel composition DeMille calls "the past and the present. The idea was to create a ghost image" of a large portrait in a monotone (the past) and contrast it with a smaller image of the same person in the lower left hand corner, this time in bright colors and contemporary styles (the present). DeMille has also written an instruction book and has his own thirteen-week television show for public broadcasting. He is listed in *Who's Who in American Art*, in *Western Painting Today*, has his own gallery, and was featured in *Southwest Art* in September 1981.

Desatnick, Mike. Realist/Impressionist painter of Southwestern Indians, born in Hammond, Indiana, in 1943 and living in Durango, Colorado. "I have been attracted to the American Indian," he declares. "I find their beauty, character, and simplicity of life which harmonizes with nature to be very special in these sophisticated times. My own heritage is filled with hard times, and I relate that to the Indian's experience."

During high school, Desatnick was offered a scholarship to the American Academy of Art in Chicago but family obligations required that he work in a steel mill. Being drafted for combat in Vietnam made him "decide that if I ever got out of there in one piece, I wanted to do something better with my life." After he was discharged, he entered the Academy and in two years won 22 awards. Before graduation, he was hired as a commercial artist and after another two years was offered a position as instructor at the Academy where he taught for six years.

"I don't get into preliminary sketches," he states. "As valid as they can be, they bore me. I get very excited about a subject that I'm going to paint. I'll study my material then I'll do the painting over and over in my head, maybe a thousand times. When the painting is resolved in my head, I go directly to the easel, make a basic sketch on the canvas, then paint. Each painting is so personal that if something comes up that takes me away, I'll never go back to finish it." Desatnick was featured in *Southwest Art* August 1978 and his painting was selected to become the poster for the first Western art exhibit to go to China. He is represented by Shriver, Trailside, and Texas Art Galleries.

Deuel, Austin. Traditional painter and sculptor of the modern and Old West, born in Pittsburgh, Pennsylvania, in 1939, and living in Scottsdale, Arizona. According to Deuel, "I know how to fight and how to survive, and especially how to work hard. I am not afraid in front of that blank canvas. You can't think too much about art. You have to do it. When you start off, it is a challenge. There are problems to be solved."

A city boy, he taught art in junior colleges for seven years, ran an art gallery, served in Vietnam as a Marine Corps combat artist, wrote a column called "Artifacts" for a San Diego newspaper, traveled abroad; collected Old Masters and contemporary art, has sculpted and painted murals, has been published in lithographs, greeting cards, calendars and plates, and has been winning awards in all categories since 1963. Concerning his murals, he says that "it is an artist's lifetime dream to be able to paint large important pieces that will be seen by so many people for so many years."

Concerning technique, he recalls that in 1966 he went to a teacher "to learn to paint. Since then I have talked to many fine artists, but he was the simplest and most correct. He told me he could tell me everything I had to know about art in two and a half hours. This sort of shocked me since most of the art institutions were set up for years of study. He said, 'These principles will never change.' When he finished the lecture, he said, 'Now it's just spending the rest of your life doing it.' He was right. His principles have not changed for me, and I have challenged them many times and lost." A member of the American Indian and Cowboy Artists, Deuel has been written up in *Southwest Art* three times and is represented by Signature Galleries and Kessler's Art Gallery.

Leslie B. De Mille, SPRINGWATER IN RED
oil, 24 x 36

Mike Desatnick, CORN DANCE TRADITION, oil, 40 x 30

Austin Deuel, UNUSUAL WEATHER, watercolor, 20 x 40

Jim Deutsch

Steve Devenyns

Deutsch, Jim. Traditional sculptor of Western cowboy, rodeo cowboy, and wildlife subjects in bronze statuettes, born in San Antonio, Texas, in 1926 and still living there. "My first attempt at art was in 1974," he recalls, "when I was 48 years old and president of a home building company. I had been looking for art to decorate our new home when I got an unexplained urge to sculpt something—anything. I sort of played around with the clay at first but as I worked on, it was almost as though I was reliving an instant in 1952 at the National Intercollegiate Rodeo Finals.

"I have never had any formal training in art, graduating from Texas A&M in 1953 with a BS in general agriculture. I founded my corporation and worked very hard in making it a success. When "In a Spin," my first bronze, passed the test in gallery sales, my wife and I voted to tackle the world of art. I like my three subjects equally well. And I have done enough to know my way around.

"Since I don't use any preliminary sketches or armature, I simply start forming the clay to resemble the mental image I have. The clay is a synthetic that can be baked in an oven. Once this clay is cooked, it becomes semi-hard and I can cut away from it or add raw clay that when re-baked becomes a bonded part. On complicated pieces, I often do the work in sections so that the foundry can separate the sculpture during the molding process. This can be done easily by placing saran wrap between the sections during the baking. The rest is simply a matter of transforming the meaningless mass of clay into that image in my mind. " Written up in *Southwest Art*, June 1979, Deutsch (pronounced "Dych") is represented by Escondido and Corpus Christi Art Galleries.

Devenyns, Steve. Realist painter of the contemporary West in oil, pencil, and colored pencil, born in St. Louis, Missouri, in 1953 and living in Cody, Wyoming. "To keep my ideas fresh," he comments, "I spend a lot of time helping friends on neighboring ranches. There I try to find the simple things in nature, a tired cowboy resting alongside his sweaty horse or many other things that people overlook, the innocence of a newborn Hereford calf or a colt exploring his world for the first time.

"At the age of fourteen in Colorado, I began to work as an apprentice saddlemaker. This interest has stayed with me. During junior high, I began rodeoing in Little Britches, in junior rodeo I competed in the three riding events, and throughout high school and college I limited competition to bareback and saddle horses. I have been on a horse in just about every angle imaginable, and while studying pre-vet medicine at Colorado State University I gained knowledge of animal anatomy. In 1974, an auto accident brought my rodeo days to an abrupt end.

"While recovering, I found a great deal of time to sit and draw. I realized there might be a future for me in art, and the well-known woodcarver John Kittleson supported me. I began traveling to art shows, met Ray Swanson, and began oil painting in Swanson's studio. In 1976, 1978, and 1980, I was a gold medal winner in drawing at the Phippen Memorial Show, and again in 1981 at the Texas Cowboy Artist show. For relaxation, I play fiddle, guitar, and saxaphone. There is many a night at the art shows when I 'fiddle around' with the artists who also bring their musical instruments. My paintings and drawings can be seen at Copenhagen Galleri."

Jim Deutsch, MOUNTAIN MAJESTY, bronze, h 14½

Steve Devenyns, SPRING'S NEWCOMER, oil, 15 x 17

GEORGE DICK

Thomas H. Dickson

DIECKHONER

Dick, George. Wildlife and Western painter and sculptor, born in Manitowoc, Wisconsin, in 1916 and died in 1978 in Albuquerque, New Mexico, where he had lived since 1947. Dick described his work as "simply putting down something to which I was long exposed—something I know and like. The somewhat Impressionistic approach is very much the way I regard nature. Most often I eliminate or subdue the background. To me, this adds to the feeling of the unknown, the vastness and the 'foreverness' of nature."

After graduation from Wentworth Military Academy, Dick received a degree in forestry from the University of Michigan in 1939 and joined the U.S. Wildlife Service, traveling about the West with a falcon named Margaret. During World War II, he served in the Tank Corps in Europe, then was hospitalized for many months and recuperated in a lean-to in Jackson Hole, Wyoming, eating the fish he caught and the sourdough biscuits he baked. His desire to paint wildlife brought him to Albuquerque where he earned his MFA from the University of New Mexico in 1950, studying with Randall Davey and Kenneth Adams. He also spent two years painting in Mexico.

"There's always something mysterious in nature," Dick believed. "When I have succeeded in presenting the subject and conveying these qualities, there is a definite sense of satisfaction." His concern was with the Southwest, quarterhorses, cow ponies, race horses, game, and wild fowl. His work was published in *Arizona Highways*, the *Saturday Evening Post*, and *New Mexico Stockman* magazines, on Christmas cards, in Ainsworth's *Cowboys in Art*, and in Hassrick's *Western Painting Today*. He exhibited nationally and is represented by Woodrow Wilson Fine Arts.

Dickson, Thomas H. Traditional wildlife sculptor in bronze and stainless steel, born in Denver, Colorado, in 1949 and living in Aurora, Colorado. "My efforts to progress sculpture beyond its known limitations are to be found in the medium, the metal I use," he notes. "I was the first representational sculptor to cast in stainless steel, a medium and process completely of the 20th century. I have progressed from this to bi-metal castings and mixed-media sculpture in bronze and stainless steel.

"My childhood was a blend of city life in winters and summers at the family home in the Colorado Rockies. After graduation from high school in Salina, Kansas, I attended the University of Denver for one year and then in 1968 enlisted in the Navy where I was an underwater demolition expert, served a tour in Vietnam, and in 1972 was a member of the Navy parachute team. In 1973, I went to a California welding trade school, attended Southwestern College, and began my sculpting career. After working in an art foundry and two gold mines and operating a gallery, I have sculpted full time since 1977.

"I am primarily a wildlife sculptor and am very concerned with mankind's blatant abuse of wildlife and its habitat. This makes no sense to me at all. To let a species of life become extinct is to tear a page from our only textbook and throw it into the fire. This is done for the sake of fuel and energy, in the name of progress. My purpose is not to compete with nature but to preserve it. I hope to help guide the viewer of my work to a higher plane of awareness of the physical and intellectual benefits of the existence of the animals I portray." Written up in *Southwest Art*, fall 1977, Dickson has exhibited at Mattson and Trailside Galleries.

Dieckhoner, Gene. Realist painter of wildlife in oil, watercolor, and pen and ink, born in Cleveland, Ohio, in 1940 and living in Ventura, California. "When I'm out," he remarks, "I'm inspired by the scenes I see. Quite often I come across tracks in the sand or snow and I imagine what circumstances caused them. I like to portray everyday events in the life of the animals. It's almost like following the animal around during its daily voyages and recording who or what it meets and the things it does."

After starting art studies in grade school, he concentrated on watercolor at the Cleveland Institute of Art and majored in watercolor and commercial art at Ohio University. While in the Air Force for three years he continued art studies at night, then in 1965 moved to Los Angeles for a job in an advertising agency. In 1971, the loss of a major account put him out of work and he began offering drawings at sidewalk art shows. "I discovered," he reports, "that pen and inks are little appreciated, so I started on paintings and people said, 'Hey, you ought to be in galleries.'

"I never was especially interested in the animal world, and spent a good portion of my life unaware of its beauty, humor, and charm. When I began painting wildlife, it was quite a learning process, but I did not want to look back on my life and have any regrets, so I took the plunge. Through my work, I can now get people to become aware of all that is happening around them. None of these subjects is exotic or unusual if you just open your eyes and see." A donor of art to conservation groups, he has won a National Park Service contract for art and has done a wildlife plate series. He is represented by Driscol Gallery and by Husberg Fine Arts Gallery, which priced his painting at $3,200 in 1980.

George Dick, POST OFFICE, oil, 20 x 30

Thomas Dickson, TRILOGY, bronze & stainless steel, h 38, l 28, Edition 12

Gene Dieckhoner, ALMOST LUNCH, oil, 15 x 30

SHANE DIMMICK

DINES

Dimmick, (Sandra Eleanor) Shane. Realist pen and ink artist of wildlife, born in Rawlins, Wyoming, in 1953 and living in Evergreen, Colorado, since 1978. "I feel that every hair, feather, and scale is necessary to my work," she emphasizes. "I love detail. I love to portray the animal as close to its physical nature as possible. Granted, I don't get carried away with drawing their fleas or ticks! But with detail, my work becomes not only 'stand back' but also 'come forward, come close and take a look' work.

"Because of my sisters' allergies, I was not allowed to have fur-bearing pets when I was young, and that may be where my love of animals came from. In 1976, I received a BS in biology from Fort Lewis College, with minors in art and chemistry. My wildlife art grew in college not from art classes but rather from my biology with animal anatomy and behavior. After graduating, I got a job in commercial art, then in 1978 became a free-lance commercial artist and started my own business, 'Animal,' to sell my wildlife prints.

"I portray wildlife because I envy their grace, their simple way of life. They don't create wars or pollute. Lately, I feel sorry for them. They are treated unfairly, abused, and all by one species, man. Although some people feel it trite to have a 'cause' these days, I do not. If through my work I can stop one person from buying a fur coat, then I have succeeded. We should share the earth with wildlife. It is their earth too. They are truly the 'voiceless.' Like human animals, non-human animals feel the pain, encroachment, and other fears that we do. I see it in the animals' eyes." A member of the Society of Animal Artists, she is represented by the Carson Gallery of Western American Art.

Dines, Bruce Eaton. Representational watercolorist of ducks, geese, and upland game birds, born in Denver, Colorado, in 1927 and still living there. "What motivates me most in painting," he says, "is my desire to share an experience in my love for the out-of-doors. Working only in watercolor, I try to paint game birds so that looking is to have been there yourself, watching the changing sky colors of dawn and dusk and hearing the calls of waterfowl and the sounds of nature."

A third generation native of Colorado, Dines served as an artist in the Air Force during World War II. After graduating from Denver University with a BFA in commercial art and design in 1948, he went to work for the First National Bank of Denver, the largest bank in the Rocky Mountain region, and retired in 1979 as Executive Vice President and a member of the Board of Directors. An avid hunter and fisherman, he had painted as a pastime since 1955, specializing in the birds of the marshy bottomlands of waterfowl flyways. After his retirement, he was able to paint full time.

As a dedicated conservationist, he was a founder of Trout Unlimited and has served as a Trustee of the National Park Foundation Board in Washington, D.C. and of the Denver Museum of Natural History. His "thorough knowledge of the habits of ducks and geese enables him to execute his waterfowl paintings with detail, subtlety, and feeling for line and color." His one-person shows have been in New York City in 1976, San Francisco in 1977, and Denver and Santa Fe in 1980. A watercolor brought $1,900 in Texas Art Gallery's *Preview '81*. Prints are published by Texas Art Prints and he is represented by Carson and Trailside Galleries.

Bruce Dines, NEARLY SNOWBOUND, watercolor, 21 x 28

Shane Dimmick, WOLF IN WINTER (timber/gray wolf, canis lupus), pen & ink and ink wash, 22 x 24

F. DiVITA

Eugene Dobos.

Jane Sprague Dobrott

DiVita, Frank. Traditional bronze sculptor of Northwestern wildlife, mostly birds, born in Genoa, Italy, in 1949 and living in Kalispell, Montana. "The influence for my work," he points out, "comes from the blending of two worlds. The old world which was my birthplace gives me a love for tradition, craftsmanship, and philosophy. The new world gives me a love of a more primitive and raw beauty of mountains, natural surroundings, and wildlife. I consider the Western art movement a renaissance movement similar to the movement in Italy in the 15th and 16th centuries."

The DiVita family moved to Missoula, Montana, in 1960. After earning his BFA in art and zoology from the University of Montana, DiVita worked as a graphic artist and then as a medical illustrator for the University. A career in medical illustration would have meant leaving Montana, so he took a job as wildlife illustrator for the U.S. Forest Service before becoming a full time sculptor and painter. "Most of my recognition," he states, "has come in the bronze field which is closer to what my mind conceives.

"I work mostly with birds. I chose birds because they have fascinated me since my youth. I remain with them because life is too short to devote to a multitude of ideas and do them all justice. I used to sketch my subjects first, but I found it hard to conceive a three dimensional piece on paper without drawing all angles. By the time I had done that, I felt I had lost some spontaneity, so now I mostly work directly with the clay," creating the model while watching the bird. DiVita participated in the Peking Exhibition of Western Art in China in 1981 and is represented in seven states including the Driscol Gallery.

Dobos, Eugene. Modern spray and stencil painter of floral shapes, and sculptor, born in Dnepropetrovsk, Russia, in 1933 and living in Taos, New Mexico, since 1963. "When you paint for money," he emphasizes, "you look in the mirror in the morning and it says, 'There's a hypocrite.' That's not a good feeling—I don't care how much money you make. When I get up in the morning, my mirror says, 'There's a good man.' That's worth everything. Financial security is not true art. Security and art are like oil and vinegar."

When Dobos was nine, the Germans brought his family to Hanover as forced labor. There he learned English and undertook private art training. After emigrating to Chicago in 1951, he studied at the American Academy of Art from nine until four, then worked as an engraver until eight thirty in the evening. In the summer of 1955, he painted in Taos for a month, and in 1957 he won a scholarship to the Art Students League in New York City. When he returned to Chicago, he said that "I used to take my work to galleries and they'd throw me out. Then an electronics engineer asked me if I'd store his welding gear. When he slammed the door I lit the torch, made a piece of sculpture, took it to the gallery, and they accepted it right away."

In 1980, he was ready for change. "I've been painting flowers, and I went to Arizona this spring to paint cactus. I also love to paint poppies, roses and iris. I'm doing a lot of thinking now, and I'm getting into another stage. I don't know what it will be, but honesty of pursuit is what counts. If artists cannot pursue their visions, who can?" Featured in *Margaret Jamison Presents, Southwest Art*, summer 1976 and May 1979, and *the Santa Fean*, June 1980, he shows at the Heydt-Bair and CJS Galleries.

Dobrott, Jane Sprague. Realist painter in transparent watercolor of life on the Gray Ranch, born in Tucson, Arizona in 1948 and living south of Animas, New Mexico, since 1978. "We are very isolated," she observes, "and I kept sitting around waiting for something to happen and finally decided I was going to have to make it happen. I started painting. The cowboys were an obvious choice, since I live with them every day. I do have to be careful to keep out of their way. They take their roles very seriously and consider it wholly their domain."

She earned her BFA from the University of Arizona in 1971, but her "technique has been mostly trial and error, teaching myself as I go. I attended the university when emphasis was on 'expressing' yourself and not on teaching fundamentals. All it taught me was frustration. Once you know the basics, you can 'express' yourself. They had the cart before the horse. I started painting professionally three years ago, just after we moved to the Gray Ranch, where they are still doing some things just as they did 50 years ago. What an opportunity for authenticity!

"Most of my subject matter is gathered during the 'works' in the Spring and the Fall, that is, branding and shipping times. The cowboys go out on what they call 'the wagon' for approximately a month to work the cattle, taking their bedrolls and remudas from camp to camp. It is my pleasure to give the viewer a peek at just what it's like to be a 'Diamond A' cowboy, and in doing so, accurately record events on the ranch," which spreads over 321,000 acres. She is represented by Troy's Cowboy Art Gallery.

Frank DiVita, WILD TURKEY, bronze, h 11

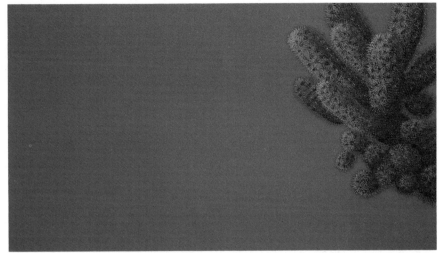

Eugene Dobos, CACTUS, oil, 48 x 89

Jane Dobrott, SSSSS, watercolor, 12½ x 16½

MEL DOBSON

Gene Dodge

Dobson, Mel. Wildlife painter in watercolor on scratchboard and in oil, born in Holden, Utah, in 1934 and living in Jackson Hole, Wyoming. "I liked to draw," he says, "and I took every art class I could find in high school, but I didn't imagine I could count on art as a career. If I could later have held a job as a wildlife biologist, I'd have been completely happy, but you have to do what you want to do.

"The best times of my youth were the times spent on horseback in the mountains," Dobson states as he recalls growing up on his father's ranch. An amateur painter, Dobson's father recognized his son's talent and found him outside art classes. For a while, Dobson worked for Kennicott Copper as an oiler, then he moved to Olympia, Washington to become a draftsman in the engineering department of the State game department. He took some commercial art courses that let him sketch for departmental promotions, and he also spent weekends photographing game in the forests so he could sketch what he'd seen, but he was not satisfied with the quality of his drawing.

After 18 years as a draftsman, he was introduced to scratchboard, heavy claycoated white paper covered with a thin layer of black ink that is scribed by the artist to make a line drawing. The sketches came to life, were accepted for publication, and were readily sold. Dobson promptly quit his job to devote full time to art, found an agent in Seattle, developed an additional technique of combining scratchboard with gouache, and in addition began to paint in oil. He was written up in *Art West*, spring 1978, became a member of the Society of Animal Artists, and is represented by Trailside Galleries which priced a small gouache at $1,600.

Dodge, Gene. Realist wildlife painter in oil, born in Riverside, California, in 1942 and living in Prescott, Arizona, since 1977. "Most of the time," he says, "I'll see something in nature that I like, and then I'll try to visualize a given animal in that setting. So in a sense, I work from the setting to the animal. The basis of a painting for me amounts to finding something in nature that turns me on and then rearranging it to find a composition that complements the various elements involved."

Raised on a small ranch in Ramona and in Riverside, his early life was centered around animals but he had no formal art training. As a child, he "didn't give art a second thought." He studied engineering in college in Riverside, then worked for the California Division of Highways for seven years and with a private contractor. In the mid-1970s, road construction became an unstable industry and Dodge decided that the time had come to test the artistic abilities he had thus far expressed only in pencil sketches for his children.

His two brothers-in-law were the Indian artist Ray Swanson and the wildlife artist Gary Swanson who both lived in Prescott, Arizona. "I always envied Gary's freedom to spend so much time so close to animals and nature," he explains, "and the more I went with him on trips into the field, researching animals and habitat, the more I realized how important his art was. I could see that combining my love of nature and my artistic desires would be a way of doing something really special with my life." He began an apprenticeship under Gary Swanson and in six months won first place in oil at the outside Phippen Memorial Show. Written up in *Southwest Art*, December 1980, he is represented by Overland Trail and Lido Galleries.

Gene Dodge, ON THE ALERT, oil, 24 x 30

Mel Dobson, TEEC NOS POS CATAMOUNT, scratchboard/watercolor, 20 x 30

Bev Doolittle

Doxey-

Dudley

Doolittle, Bev. Painter of wildlife and Indian scenes, born in southern California in 1947 and living in Joshua Tree, California. "Because my work is limited in volume," she points out, "I now approach every major painting as a print. I don't have the luxury of picking three or four or so of the paintings I do in a year and saying, 'These will make good prints.' Now I develop an idea for a painting with the thought that it will be a print first.

"I knew from the time I was in kindergarten that I wanted to be an artist. The rest was just sort of marking time until I could be one. As soon as I finished high school, I went right into the Art Center College of Design in Los Angeles. The school was oriented toward commercial art, and my goal was to succeed in the agency world. My husband and I worked together for five years, but what we were doing began to be awfully repetitious. We took off for a year, traveling and painting. We wanted to see if we could make a living as painters. At our first show, we sold 14 paintings for a total of $700.

"I'm a terribly slow painter. Right now I do three, four, or five—at the most—major paintings a year. This is because of the nature of my painting style. The picture evolves from a concept into thumbnail sketches, to a pencil study, to a color study and finally into the finished painting. Time sheets help me keep track of the time I spend on each painting. That's important to me. It helps establish a base price for a painting and it keeps emotions out of the pricing arena." Written up in *Prints*, January 1982, she is represented exclusively by the Carson Gallery of Western American Art which suggested the Greenwich Workshop for publishing prints.

Doxey, Don. Super-realist painter of Western still lifes, born in Ogden, Utah, in 1928 and living in Salt Lake City. "I guess I work in a sort of ivory tower," he declares. "With still-life painting, you work directly from the models, moving your subjects in any way that you want in order to develop the composition. I don't enjoy working outdoors. I don't like bugs, and I don't like the shifting sun. I don't want things in my paint looking back at me. I prefer the air-conditioned comfort of my studio."

With parents who were school teachers, Doxey was "raised on tales told by my grandparents and great-grandparents who were among the earliest Mormon pioneers." After earning his MFA from the University of Utah in 1955, he went to New York City for further study at the American Art School. As staff artist for a television network, "the pay was fine as long as you worked," but he did not work steadily so he came back to Utah to teach at Westminster College.

Doxey buys or borrows his props from antique shops. He starts painting at seven and continues until he gets tired. Then he does something physical to refresh himself. As for his paintings, "the objects to be used are arranged and lighted. They are drawn directly onto a prepared canvas. Color is then added, and for me the fun begins when I start painting the details—tarnish on metal, a stain on a lace handkerchief—that's what it's all about. I try to create a sense of immediacy. I want people to feel that the inhabitants of the room were there only a moment ago." His influence there was Harnett. Doxey was featured in *Southwest Art*, February 1981 and is represented by Husberg Fine Arts Gallery.

Dudley, Jack. Palette-knife oil painter of the landscape and wildlife "of the dry terrain of the West," born in Sonora, California, in 1918 and living in Laguna Beach, California. "Since I am preoccupied with the effects I can get utilizing hot sunlight and deep shadow," he observes, "I must paint the Southwest for it is there that these qualities abound. I don't paint 'pretty' pictures. I look for drama. To me, the dark shadows of a cliff or under an ancient arch can be as dramatic as anything could be."

After attending the Art Center College of Design in Los Angeles for five years on a scholarship, Dudley worked as a commercial artist. He has painted around the world, especially in Spain and Portugal, the Caribbean, South America, and the Orient, but he says that "in recent years, my paintings have been of the Southwest, such places as the Canyon de Chelly, Monument Valley, the Grand Canyon, and the four corners area. Pueblo and Navajo Indians and some of the wildlife (big horn sheep, pumas, deer) have also been subjects."

Described as "a master of the 'broken color' knife technique recognized by brilliant bits of pure color," Dudley declares that his "use of the knife in painting is to show a surface texture more compatible with the subject matter than I would capture with a brush. Whether it is the roughness of walls or boulders, all seem to be suited to the use of the knife, and the color-filled shadows as opposed to the brilliance of sunlight are laid down with clarity." Dudley has had 31 one-person shows and is represented by the Leslie B. DeMille Gallery.

Don Doxey, THE LONELY GAME, oil, 26 x 28

Bev Doolittle, PINTOS, watercolor, 21 x 21

Jack Dudley, THE CANYON, oil, 30 x 40

Duillo, John. Realist painter and etcher of scenes of the Old West, still-lifes, and military history, born in New York City in 1928 and living in Hicksville, Long Island. Duillo says he selected the Old West and Americana as his subjects because "they contain all of the ingredients that excite and inspire me in art—color, adventure, wide scope, and philosophical depth. The Western genre is a blend of artistic introspection and outward perception, created by the need to reconstruct a vanished era."

Educated at the High School of Music & Art and in a liberal arts program at the New School for Social Research in New York City, he served in the Navy as an aerial photographer in World War II and was discharged in 1948. He then studied art with Adja Yunkers and photography with Berenice Abbot before working in illustration, photography, art direction, and set design. Later, he painted hundreds of magazine illustrations and book covers for most of the major publishing houses in New York City, doing the pictures for stories by Zane Grey, Louis L'Amour, and Max Brand.

He says that "I try to bring intellect to bear in my paintings. Simplicity is not a virtue, either for the mature artist or for the mature viewer. Simplicity is for the simple-minded." When he is painting, he believes "that the artist must have his subject in front of him. No amount of reference to sketches, memories, or photographs can give you the same information to make judgments on, and it is judgment in changing, eliminating, and accenting that is crucial." Duillo is a member of the Society of American Historical Artists and is represented by The Grizzly Tree Gallery.

Duncan, Robert. Traditional oil painter of "people, sometimes mountain men, sometimes farmers and ranchers, but most often Indians," born in Salt Lake City, Utah, in 1952 and living in Midway, Utah, since 1976. "What inspires me, and is usually the underlying theme," he points out, "is people coping and making the best of their environment. I'm fascinated with the ability of the human spirit to overcome obstacles and the West is full of examples of this.

"I began drawing animals when I was five and did my first oil painting when I was eleven. I spent most of my summers on family ranches in the upper Green River area of Wyoming. It was these summers that had the greatest effect on my painting. I continued painting all through my school years in Salt Lake City and sold my first big painting for $55 to my junior high school. After high school, I attended the University of Utah for two years before deciding that I would learn more just painting full time.

"My neighbor Edward Fraughton was of great help. I later was lucky enough to meet John Clymer who has given me advice, and in 1977 I spent a month studying with Robert Lougheed. My friend Valoy Eaton has also been a tremendous help, but I think the greatest challenge for any young artist is to make 'the song' his own, to try to say something that comes from within, instead of just doing new versions of another man's idea. I get most of my ideas from just observing people because I don't think people have changed that much from the past in the basic ways they react to situations. I've never joined any art organizations or entered shows. It hasn't interested me." Duncan's gallery is Trailside Galleries which priced his painting at $7,200 for 1981–1982.

Robert Duncan, THE IRON POT (1982), oil, 20 x 28

John Duillo, THE ARTILLERYMAN, oil/canvas, 25 x 31

Troy Dunham   *Dunlop AZ*   *Cal Dunn AWS*

Dunham, Troy. Realist painter of "American Lifestyles, the people, places, and events that make our lives unique from life elsewhere" in oil, pencil, and colored pencil, born in San Luis Obispo, California, in 1955 and living in Corte Madera, California. "I make the best of each trip out of my studio," he says, "visiting museums, digging in archives, recording subject matter, meeting local artists, and taking in whatever good whitewater rivers or backpacking are in the area. The very best part of my work is meeting the people that I portray.

"While I have been drawing and painting since I was three, serious study began in high school and I turned down athletic scholarships to follow up my interest in art at College of Marin. In 1977, I earned my BA in art from San Francisco State University, but it was extensive private study that developed my discipline. I am largely self-taught. My artwork comes first, though I also pursue dramatics, music, film, and writing. Recreation and adventure are a necessary part of my artwork. I like to keep an aggressive attitude toward life. This keeps a certain vitality and vigor in the way I approach my work.

"When I am home, I spend twelve to fourteen hours each day in my studio, putting hundreds of hours of labor into each finished piece to produce realism. I have spent up to thirteen months on a single painting. Much of my work is so meticulously done that the viewer cannot tell what the medium is. My subjects include social and political commentary as well as insight into the subtle beauties and melodramas that we live out. In the last few years, I have had mostly studio sales, so relatively little of my work has made it to public viewing."

Dunlop, Paul. Realist painter of neon signs in watercolor, born in Jos, Nigeria, Africa, in 1953 and living in Phoenix, Arizona, since 1964. "In 1976," he recalls, "I was in San Francisco near a sign with about 2,000 bulbs in it. I was preparing for two shows, and I did a painting of the sign to show where my abstracts were coming from. I started to do more and more signs because I enjoyed doing them so much, and because I realized that neon itself is an abstract form, with its simplified lines and rows upon rows of tubes.

"My father was a Baptist missionary who had been in Africa for eight years when he met my mother who also was a missionary. We returned to the United States in 1955. School was boring so I left at fifteen to work for a carpet company. In 1970, I entered the service, wound up at Fort Huachuca in Army Intelligence, and as the result of an accident lost a leg. In 1973 I entered Phoenix College. Three years later, I received a degree in painting from San Francisco Art Institute and also took a degree in photography.

"The thing that opened my eyes to art was meeting real artists. I thought, 'Well, if you really want to, you can make a living at painting,' so I made it a point to paint 40 hours a week. I wasn't selling much, but luckily I had a coin collection and a race car. When I needed a hundred bucks I'd sell this, that, and I survived. Philosophically, I'm not a photo-realist. I rearrange lines. Toward the end of a painting, I make changes in color relationships to compensate color optically. Then the values come out right." Written up in *Arizona Arts*, summer 1981, and *Southwest Art*, January 1981, he is represented by the Suzanne Brown Gallery.

Dunn, Cal. Watercolorist of the New Mexico landscape, born in Georgetown, Ohio, in 1915 and living in Santa Fe, New Mexico, since 1980. "I love the West," he declares, "but for me there's a lot more here to paint than just cowboys and Indians ... ranches and pueblos ... horse and buffalo droppings. To me the West is an unbelievable bigness—vast configurations that stir the imagination. It's happy colors and forms that excite the eye ... it's subtle grays and grotesque shapes that stagger your reason ... it's a chosen land."

Dunn began his art career while a student in Central Academy of Commercial Art in Cincinnati from 1932 to 1934. He was an illustrator in Ohio, Michigan, and Iowa until 1943 when he became a freelance cartoonist for national magazines including *The New Yorker*. During World War II, he was an animation art director for the Air Force and the Navy, and in 1947 started Cal Dunn Studios in Chicago to produce industrial films and commercials for television. He won 60 national awards including an Emmy in 1958. Dunn was also painting, and as early as 1939 his work was exhibited at the New York World's Fair and reproduced in *American Painting Today*. He was elected to the American Watercolor Society in 1954 and was one of 100 American watercolorists selected to exhibit in England in 1963.

"When I'm painting," he adds, "I feel good all over, but it's not always easy. Sometimes I goof and I'm disgusted. Roll all these feelings together and it's one hell of a wonderful trip." Dunn has had more than 30 one-person shows and has received more than 30 awards. Listed in *Who's Who in American Art*, he is represented by Robiard and Fowler's.

Cal Dunn, RIO DE LAS VECAS, watercolor, 22 x 28

Troy Dunham, CHARLES AND MARIE, colored pencil, 23 x 15

Paul Dunlop, LAS VEGAS CLUB, watercolor, 21 x 29

FRANZ DUTZLER 1982   Ed Dwight

Dutzler, Franz. Sculptor of game fish in painted wood, born in Sierning, upper Austria, in 1940 and living in Sisters, Oregon, since 1975. "When I was five years old," he recalls, "an American soldier came by our house to exchange several trout for some potatoes. This first sight of fish started me on the pursuit of the trout. The next fifteen years I spent my free time watching, pursuing, and catching them. I finished school in Austria, excelling in art, but the future didn't look promising as only the rich can fish.

"At twenty I emigrated to Australia, became an apprentice cook, and spent my free time fishing. I then heard about the fantastic fishing in New Zealand and emigrated there, working as a buffet chef. After I came to the United States, I worked as night chef in Yakima and caught my first steelhead in the river. I started developing the idea that I wanted to preserve fish so I learned taxidermy. In San Francisco as night chef, I really learned how to fly cast, but I wasn't happy with my taxidermy.

"I looked on the map to see where I would like to fish the most and settled on Eugene, where I was again night chef. I finally caught my first steelhead on a fly. After five years, I moved to Sisters, where I continued as a chef. The idea that I might carve trout out of wood started to develop. One day I saw a carved bird that was really beautifully done and I decided to try carving. To ski is my second love, but then I broke my leg. That is when I started to carve in earnest and I came up with a pretty good fish. I now work with kiln-dried alder and carve the fins and tail out of eastern maple. Then I paint the details and mount the sculptures on pieces of driftwood." Dutzler is represented by the Carson Gallery of Western American Art and the Eddie Bauer Store.

Dwight, Ed. Representational bronze sculptor of statues and statuettes on Blacks in the Old West, born in Kansas City, Kansas, about 1933 and living in Denver, Colorado. "That's what I want," he stresses, "to show the total experience of Blacks in the West. I'm looking into the relations between Indians and Blacks, and I'm continuing to expand Black military experience. Then there were the Black cowboys who were the best rodeo riders. And a lot of Blacks made a living doing what they'd learned back East—farming.

"I guess I always really wanted to be an artist. I did my first oil painting when I was eight, but my father told me to forget art, and I almost did." After attending junior college, he joined the Air Force in 1953, earned a BS in aeronautical engineering at Arizona State University in 1957, became an Air Force experimental test pilot in 1962, and was the first Black astronaut trainee. In 1966, he resigned his commission and was employed by IBM in Boulder, Colorado. Assigned to decorate a building, he began sculpting modernist forms.

He had his first one-person show in Denver in 1967 and was doing graduate work at the University of Denver in 1975 when he was commissioned to model the bust of a Black politician. He taught himself how to do heads, and then was selected to do a series of eight bronzes of Blacks in the West. He made 28 that were exhibited as the "Black Frontier Spirit in the American West." Since then, he has modeled hundreds of additional bronzes, including the series "The Evolution of Jazz." He has been written up in *Southwest Art*, November 1977, and *Artists of the Rockies*, winter 1982, and is represented by Von Graybill and Leslie B. DeMille Galleries.

Ed Dwight, CORPORAL CLINTON GREAVES, bronze, h 26½, Edition 20

Franz Dutzler, MOUTHFUL, wood, h 17, l 26

Dyck, Paul. Painter of American Indians in 14th-century Florentine technique in egg tempera and oil glazes, born in Chicago, in 1917 and living in Rimrock, Arizona, since 1938. "Using this Florentine method," he stresses, "is assurance that the painting will last. Too many contemporary artists crank out paintings that look good today, but because they haven't learned the chemistry or the nature of the materials they are using, their paintings will begin to crack before long. Some of them look as though they were painted on alligator hide."

Descended from the Flemish Old Master Anthony van Dyck, he was raised in Calgary, western Canada, and then in Europe where he was apprenticed at eight to his uncle, a painter with studios in Florence, Paris, Prague, and Rome. At twelve, he was sent out on his own, and by the time he was fifteen he was back in Europe, exhibiting his collection of Indian artifacts. In Dresden, he met One Elk, a Sioux who was with the Hagenbeck Circus. Dyck was adopted by One Elk when he went to live with the Sioux in South Dakota in 1934 and was named Rainbow Hand.

In World War II, Dyck served as a Navy artist and then returned to his Arizona ranch where he painted the series "Indians of the Overland Trail" and wrote *Brule, the Sioux People of the Rosebud* to preserve the real image of the Indian "unspoiled either physically or ethnologically by the white man's contact. When they reigned, the land was not despoiled." Dyck's watercolors are painted in Sumiye ink and technique, using Japanese brushes with "bristles that come from the armpits of Mongolian ponies." He is listed in *Who's Who in American Art*, was featured in *Art West*, summer 1977, and is represented by Rosequist Galleries.

Eades, Luis. Modernist painter and collagist, born in Madrid, Spain, in 1923 and living in Boulder, Colorado, since 1961. "The paintings objectify several aspects which have interested me," he says, "some formal and abstract, some iconographical. The tendency has been to move away from self-oriented expressionism toward an art which makes use of images culled from the rich repositories of our culture and environment."

Eades was educated in England at Bath School of Art, Slade School, and Birkbeck College of the University of London. He also studied at the Instituto Politecnico Nacional in Mexico City and received his degree from the University of Kentucky in 1952. From 1954 to 1961, he taught at the University of Colorado in Boulder. Eades has had more than 23 one-person shows and his paintings are in numerous public collections including the Whitney Museum in New York City, the Museum of Fine Art in Houston, and the Dallas Museum of Fine Art.

"In my paintings," he explains, "I think in terms of contrasting elements. I bring together two different ways of dealing with three-dimensional space on a flat surface. Objects are painted factually, within the traditions of realistic painting. An intellectual allusion to volume is made by 'nets' of solid geometrical figures which intrude into the paintings. The juxtaposition of these diverse images intrigues me, but I intend no literary, social, or political meanings: no stories are told, no messages hidden." Eades' galleries are Carlin and Carson & Levin.

East, Barbara. Traditional painter of the Old West in watercolor and tempera miniatures, born in Boulder, Colorado, in 1950 and living in Collbran, Colorado. "I have been a long time admirer of the CA," she confesses. "I always wanted to be a CA. It was my belief they were real cowboys who could also paint. I don't think I could paint as well, but I could cowboy with any of them. After fantasizing for five or six years about being the first lady CA, I wouldn't want them ever to allow me in because women's lib said they'd have to, but I wish my paintings could hang in a room with theirs.

"Throughout my school years, I drew horses in all of my class notebooks. In college, I ran into a much less humorous opposition to my art. If it had been up to my teachers, I would have been another art teacher, but they pushed too hard. I remember being very down after quitting school. Then someone told me of Ace Powell. I learned more from him in two weeks in the winter of 1971 than during two years at the University of Montana.

"I started painting on cigarette papers at Ace's suggestion in 1971. A doctor bought the first 25 for $1 each. That was my first art sale." At the 1979 C.M. Russell auction, one of her 1⅝ by 2⅞ inch watercolors sold for $1,100, and a watercolor on a 1 inch square postage stamp sold for $500. During the seven fair months, she is responsible for 1,500 head of cattle on 90 square miles of high Colorado range, alone except for her horses, mules, and dogs. After the cattle are rounded up in the fall, she moves back to her studio to paint. She has exhibited with the Northwest Rendezvous Group and was written up in *Art West*, summer 1979.

Barbara East, SLIPPIN' AWAY, gouache, 12 x 12

Paul Dyck, SUNRISE MAN (1974), oil, 48 x 36

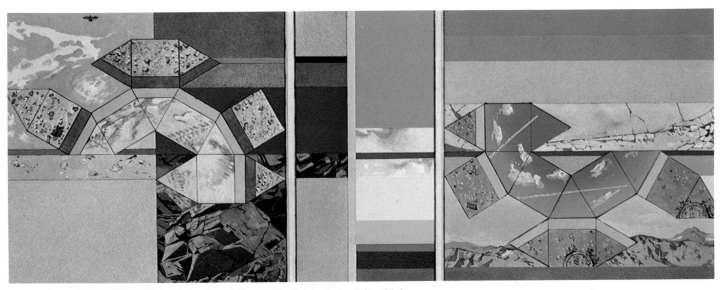

Luis Eades, MESA TRIPTYCH (projected model), acrylic, finished size 8 ft x 20 ft

VALOY EATON

Eaton, VaLoy. Traditional oil and watercolor painter of rural Utah, born in Vernal, Utah, in 1938 and living in Heber City, Utah, since 1971. For VaLoy Eaton, painting is "making honest statements about simple subjects. I consider myself to be more of an appreciator than a creator. I would like my paintings to say, 'Look what Eaton saw and how he felt,' instead of 'Look what Eaton can do'."

Country music was part of Eaton's childhood as his auto mechanic father and his mother played in a band. Eaton majored in painting and drawing at Brigham Young University from 1956 to 1960, on a basketball scholarship, and for the next ten years taught art and coached sports in the Salt Lake Valley. In 1971, he completed his Master of Arts and moved to Wasatch County as a professional painter, quitting teaching when the money he earned from painting equalled his salary. "I didn't feel there was much risk," he recalls, "for there was a demand for my paintings."

Eaton doesn't do preliminary sketches, fearing that he might lose the mental image. He sometimes paints on an oversized panel, starting the composition in the center so he can cut the Masonite to fit the finished picture. His palette is boards nailed against the wall at 45 degrees, with pigments piled along the length. He uses "spontaneous brushstrokes that melt into each other in such a way that they don't attract attention as mere paint." He calls a picture "a series of corrected mistakes," but by 1975 his painting was accepted for the NAWA annual. He is represented by Fowler's Gallery and by Settlers West Galleries where his painting was listed at $6,800 for the 1981 silent auction.

VaLoy Eaton, WARMDAY—INDIAN CANYON, oil, 30 x 48

Katalin Ehling

Bob Elgas
1982 ©

Ray G. Ellis A.W.S.

Ehling, Katalin. Dyer of art batiks of "Pueblo women doing everyday tasks" and printmaker, born in Kassa, Hungary, in 1941 and living in Cave Creek, Arizona, since 1969. "When I started," she points out, "batik was considered just a craft. When I first entered the Arizona State Fair in 1973, they didn't know where to put my work. They finally decided to put it up with the crafts, but my batiks ended up winning the prizes anyway. I haven't had to fight that bias too much. Being in good galleries gives my batiks credibility as fine art.

"My family left Hungary in 1944. We moved to the States in 1950." After high school, she studied at the American Academy of Art in Chicago for two years, then went to Paris in 1963 to learn fashion illustration. When she returned, she was employed by an advertising agency until she moved to Phoenix. After taking refresher courses in art, she saw her first batik in San Francisco in 1973 and began with a kit.

The process commences with drawing the pictures in charcoal on a single piece of cotton, then applying hot wax to the sections of the fabric that are not to be dyed in an immersion. There can be eighteen separate baths, taking up to two weeks for completion. Each batik is different from every other batik. In 1975, her dealer suggested Indian themes and she "decided to try it, but within certain limits, staying as universal as possible with subjects I knew about, families, mothers, children." By 1980, her prices exceeded $1,000 for large batiks and she was also making lithographs and serigraphs. Written up in *Artists of the Rockies*, winter 1977, and *Four Winds*, winter 1981, she has eleven galleries including Breckenridge and NI-WO-DI-HI.

Elgas, Bob. Realistic oil painter of the wild waterfowl of Montana, born in Wibeaux, Montana, in 1920 and living in Big Timber, Montana, since 1940. "Not many other artists have the opportunity to paint Emperor geese or Sandhill cranes," he emphasizes, "from a flock that eats from their hands every morning, and as a result, I should be able to—and do—paint them correctly. Another advantage is having had the opportunity to observe waterfowl, and other birds, all over the North American continent.

"In 1940, we purchased a cattle ranch. Spent 35 years raising Hereford cattle until the interstate highway system bisected the property. A tract of land approximately 60 acres was retained. This is our home, and the acreage has been developed into a wildlife habitat area. Included within our flock are representatives of nearly all the world's wild geese, various kinds of swans, cranes, and other assorted wildlife forms. There has been some scientific involvement as well, including many arctic expeditions. I may be the only artist in this book who has an Eskimo name.

"I did not become involved with art until I was past 40, and this began when I received a paint-by-number set. I do very much regret not having begun at an early age. An additional restraint has been a hereditary color blindness. I have learned to function within the capability I possess. My palette is very limited and I utilize earth tones that I do see reasonably well. Most people seem unaware that the problem exists. I do participate in various shows and have won numerous Best of Show awards. Prints are being distributed by Salt Creek Graphics and Texas Art Press, and my paintings are displayed by Texas Art Gallery and Trailside Galleries."

Ellis, Raymond G. Representational watercolorist of Southern seascapes and the West, born in Philadelphia, Pennsylvania, in 1921 and living in Hilton Head, South Carolina, since 1974. "I've been painting watercolors for longer than I'd like to remember," he points out. "It's been over forty years, I guess. Still, if I don't paint five paintings a week, I feel like I'm getting lazy. Other artists take weeks to produce one painting. I can't work that slowly."

He always knew that he wanted to paint. His parents had met in art school, and his father was a newspaperman who went into the advertising business. Ellis studied at the Philadelphia Museum School of Art from 1939 to 1941, then spent a year in a newspaper art department before serving in World War II as a contributing artist to the Coast Guard magazines. His first one-man show was at the Pennsylvania Academy of Fine Arts in 1947, but in 1954 he founded Ellis Advertising with offices in New Jersey and New York.

Ellis continued painting, and in 1968 he established a studio in Chatham, New Jersey. The following year, he was elected to the American Watercolor Society, and subsequently has received numerous awards and honors. In 1971, his coastal watercolors were published in a book, and in 1972 he was included in *Master Watercolorists at Work*. He established a second studio in Steamboat Springs, Colorado, that became a base for Western travels that culminated in a one-man show in 1974 at the C.M. Russell Museum. When a painting is 90 percent finished, he uses a trial mat to judge his composition, and even outdoors he uses a folding mat. He is published by Oxmoor House and represented by Carson Gallery of Western American Art and Trailside Galleries.

Bob Elgas, NUNICK (Eskimo for sandhill crane), oil, 30 x 20

Raymond G. Ellis, DOWNHILL PATTERNS, watercolor, 25 x 17

Katalin Ehling, AUTUMN HARVEST, batik, 36 x 30

Entz, Loren. Representational painter of contemporary Wyoming cowboys, cattle, and horses in oil and pencil, born in Newton, Kansas, in 1949 and living in Cody, Wyoming, since 1980. "The reason I became an artist," he observes, "is an inner driving force. When I was a boy, I spent long hours drawing pictures instead of playing outside. In my youth, while plowing fields I painted pictures in my mind. While riding as a cowboy, I was thinking about art. While driving down the highway, I'm thinking about art.

"I went to Frederic Remington High School, built out in the country near Brainerd, Kansas. It made an impression that a famous artist owned a ranch near where I grew up. In the courtyard was a reproduction of a Remington bronze, and in the classrooms there were reproductions of Remington paintings. I went to Hesston College in Kansas for one semester. Abstract art was in vogue. I have always been a realist so I was discouraged and left school. In 1975 I moved to Missouri to help Dad farm and realized I didn't want to be a farmer.

"In 1976, I went to Longview Community College in Missouri, majoring in commercial art, but I was turned down by commercial studios so I moved to Miles City, Montana, and pursued being a cowboy. Ranch hands work long hours, but I still made pictures and began to sell a little. In 1980, I moved to Cody and began working an eight hour job, carpentering, so I could spend more time making pictures. My first professional showing was in February 1981, and in May I received an award at the Phippen Memorial Show. I quit my job in December and now do artwork full time. The neat part is I'm making a living at something I love to do. My two galleries are Salt Creek Graphics and Sagebrush.

Eubanks, Tony. Representational oil painter of the old and the contemporary West, born in Dallas, Texas, in 1939 and living in Grapevine, Texas, since school days. "My ultimate objective," he emphasizes, "is to be able to make a living doing exactly the paintings I would like to leave behind. I sometimes find myself painting subjects that someone else wants me to paint, and this can be a very great handicap to an artist. My best work comes when I'm doing exactly the thing that I feel like I wanted to do or say.

"The earliest remembrance I have of wanting to be an artist was probably at the age of three. From the start, it was obvious that my greatest ability was in artwork. My parents encouraged me, although they didn't understand that there was any future to be gained from it. I took lessons from a lady in Corpus Christi until I was about eleven, and after we moved to Grapevine, I enrolled in the Famous Artists course, although the number of cowboys to be painted was very limited.

"After high school, I enrolled in Arlington State to major in agriculture and transferred to North Texas State University, getting a BA in advertising art. Abstract expressionism had reached its zenith and I learned very little artistically. After college, I worked as a technical illustrator and then attended the Art Center College of Design in Los Angeles. For financial reasons, I returned to Dallas and commercial art. I had always painted as a sideline and had done well in gallery sales, but I could not do true justice to either one so after fifteen years I finally decided to begin painting full time." His prints are published by Texas Art Press and American Western Collection, and he is represented by Reminisce and Texas Art Galleries.

Ewart, David D. Representational oil painter of "true-to-life characters and scenery of the area," born in Seattle, Washington, in 1939 and living in Salem, Oregon. "How many times have you heard the phrase, 'Oh, I can't draw a straight line!'" he asks. "The plain truth is that, since we aren't machines, no one can. An interesting crooked line is much more to be desired than one ruled along a straight edge, for it transcribes something of the person behind it, the pulse of life.

"I have spent my formative years in the Northwest, graduating from high school in Edmonds, Washington. I then spent a year at the Burnely School of Art in Seattle and two years in the Edison School of Art." During those three years, he worked to earn tuition and board and still managed to do about 5,000 portraits. "Sometimes I turned out 20 portraits a day. I began touring Washington, painting oil portraits for only $8, but there did not seem to be enough discipline in my life so I joined the Air Force.

"After a four year stint, I went to Los Angeles to attend the Art Center School of Design. This gave me the confidence to pursue a ten-year career in commercial art." On weekends, he would drive around, searching for subjects, and eventually he became known as the artist of the hippies. In 1974, he was encouraged to switch to Western art. "It's funny," he remarks, "that I'd always been intrigued by the history of the West but never thought of combining it with my art. I began buying books, talking with anyone who had expertise. The more I learned, the deeper my compulsion to paint the West grew." Written up in *Southwest Art*, November 1979, Ewart is published by Soaring Wings and represented by the Ace Powell Art Galleries.

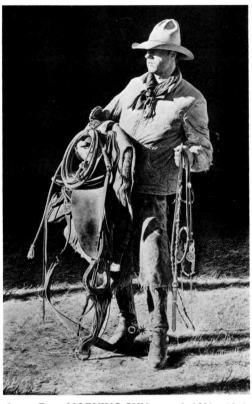

Loren Entz, MORNING SUN, pencil, 19¾ x 13¼

David Ewart, THE PATH FINDER (Canadian mountain man), oil/canvas, 18 x 24

Tony Eubanks, LAND OF THE UTE, oil, 30 x 40

Fairlamb, Burr. "Nostalgic" painter of historic and contemporary Western subjects in watercolor and acrylic, born in Norfolk, Virginia, in 1935 and living in Ft. Worth, Texas, since 1943. "I am addicted," he explains, "to giving my subjects nostalgic treatment, regardless of what they are. Certain tribes of American Indians had qualities that I find attractive in their everyday lives at the turn of the century, rather than today."

Raised in Texas, Fairlamb "amassed a record number of National Scholastic Art Awards," then he attended the University of Colorado and graduated from Texas Christian University. He also studied privately, because, as he says, "when I was in college, fine arts departments were stressing abstract painting, and realism was virtually ignored, for it was equated with commercial illustration and was thus not 'in.' I was caught up in the trend but changed when I discovered I could make visual statements about things which interest me if I painted in a representational manner." Words he uses are "craftsmanship, quality, comfort, graciousness, warmth, memories, heritage, and culture.

"I spend a lot of time," he observes, "in developing a situation in which I place myself in order to see if it is plausible, and if it fits within the restrictions imposed by size, by medium, and by my painting techniques. But all of my paintings, even the most realistic ones, can be broken down into abstract elements, so I rough out with thumbnail sketches and value studies until I am satisfied that the abstract elements hold together." Fairlamb is represented by Rainone and by Grand Central Galleries of New York City, and was featured in *Southwest Art*, August 1979.

Falk, Joni. Realist oil painter of still-life and landscape miniatures, born in Chicago, in 1933 and living in Phoenix, Arizona. "I have this wonderful feeling when I paint the pottery," she points out. "There are technical challenges and I try to imagine the potter, what he was thinking and how it was when he made the pot. Searching for new subject matter, I meet people with fabulous collections, but I'm very protective of my work and don't feel that I'm duplicating what a photograph can do.

"I'd never done anything in art," before giving craft classes in her hobby shop. "I'd sit there, madly reading directions they send with the craft supplies. I'd find out how to do something, and then the ladies would come in and I'd go back and teach the class. My students pushed me further and faster than I ever would have gotten on my own." Then, "I started at all the mall shows, and I sold out immediately. I began to paint pottery because I saw marvelous photographs in *Arizona Highways*.

"I wonder why my work appealed to me so much in the first place. Maybe there is something mystical about it. Maybe because it is created out of clay and I feel a need to express toward it a physiological response. I am in awe of the people who do pottery. I am putting my own sensitivity into how I present my paintings, and I do try to enhance people's appreciation of the pottery. I guess that maybe we (the potter and I) are sharing this mutual thing, but I worry that in some way I'm infringing on the potter's privacy, and his creativity. Sometimes I do feel that by painting someone else's work, I am removing myself from the creative process." Featured in *Art West*, September 1981, she has seven limited edition prints and is represented by May and CR Galleries.

Burr Fairlamb, THE DARE, acrylic/board, 16 x 20

Joni Falk, THE ENDURING SPIRIT, oil, 6 x 12

John Falter

G. Farm

A. Hooker Fay
NWR

Falter, John Philip. Narrative painter of early days in the West, born in Plattsmouth, Nebraska in 1910 and living in Philadelphia. "Most of the figures in my paintings emerge from my imagination," he points out. "Sometimes at three o'clock in the morning I can visualize a figure who ought to be in the picture. The next day that person goes in. Occasionally I put in a lot of people, and if it appears a little too crowded, I take some out. People go in and out of pictures just like people move in and move out of towns."

Raised in Falls City, Nebraska and in Acheson, Kansas where his father ran a clothing store, Falter entered the Kansas City Art Institute at eighteen and was awarded a scholarship to the Art Students League in New York City when he was twenty. He had already sold illustrations to the pulp magazines and he promptly caught on with the slicks. A chance visit to his studio initiated a connection with *The Saturday Evening Post* for which he subsequently painted 185 covers. During World War II he handled special art assignments including 180 posters for the Navy. In 1976, he was elected to the Society of Illustrators' Hall of Fame along with Winslow Homer and Harvey Dunn.

A dedicated jazz pianist who relaxes with jam sessions, Falter starts his paintings in the background, saying that "I want to create on canvas a stage set." His hope for his Western paintings is "to end up with a pictorial story of the pioneers and their great overland migration." He is listed in *Who's Who in American Art*, was written up in *Southwest Art*, October 1977, and *Artists of the Rockies*, winter 1977, and is a member of the National Academy of Western Art. He is represented by Husberg Fine Arts Gallery and Trailside and published by Mill Pond Press.

Farm, Gerald. "Story type" oil painter of Western nostalgia, born in Grand Island, Nebraska in 1935 and living in Farmington, New Mexico. "I am a painter of the moods of people," he explains, "and the story that is in them. I thoroughly enjoy painting people. It's always great fun to try and capture the many emotions people are capable of. A great deal of my models are from the local area, although I may change them slightly to show more expression—or to add a mustache so the character adds more to the painting."

After graduating from high school, he spent four years in the Navy. Part of the time was as an illustrator in Washington, D.C. where he completed the Famous Artist Course in commercial art in 1958. He earned his BS in art education from Nebraska State College in 1961, taught in high school for a year and was an industrial art director for seven years before starting his career in fine arts when his wife "got a job teaching school to make it possible." In 1976, he traveled through Europe studying the Old Masters.

Influenced by Norman Rockwell among others, Farm's painting has its story to tell and is designed as a conversation piece. The key is the models who "are selected with great care. Their faces, and especially their eyes, must reflect the kinds of emotion that should be put on canvas." At the San Juan College silent auction in 1981, a price "in excess of $10,000" was paid for a Farm painting. He is listed in *Who's Who in American Art* and was featured in *Southwest Art*, June 1974 and February 1979. He is represented by Texas Art Gallery and his print publishers are Mill Pond Press and Texas Art Press.

Fay, Arlene Hooker. Impressionist painter of Plains Indian portraits, primarily in pastel, born in Great Falls, Montana in 1937 and living there in 1982. "What is an artist," she asks. "Am I one or am I still practicing to be one. My creative process is to get the right color on the right number and to stay inside the lines—sometimes. Sometimes not. I do not consider myself particularly creative. I merely try to present the subject in an appealing manner."

She began drawing as a child. "We were isolated on a farm," she recalls, "and I imagine I was inspired by the drawings the older kids brought home from school." Confined to a wheelchair by a polio attack at fourteen, she painted a commissioned portrait at fifteen and had a painting reproduced at eighteen, but she used art as therapy while working at an office job. After moving to Browning with her husband, she "was decorating in 'early Indian' and decided to do a few Indian portraits to hang at home." The portraits were sought by dealers, sold, and she was a professional artist.

"It's because I love people that I paint them," she points out. "I've been told over and over again that I must paint other things. Why? I say I'd better keep painting people until I get them right." To compensate for her lack of training in art, she tries "to go to shows and look at the paintings and talk to other artists. They all seem to know more than me." She adds that her family comes before art because it "is the only organization to which I belong." A founding member of the Northwest Rendezvous Group, she won Best in Show for Mixed Media in 1978, was featured in *Art West*, spring 1979, and is represented by Finley Point Gallery.

John Falter, THE GUSHER, oil, 34 x 26

Arlene Hooker Fay, MARGIE WITH HER STAR QUILT
pastel, 25 x 20

Gerald Farm, GUIDANCE TEMPERED WITH WISDOM, oil, 30 x 40

179

Fellows

CA

Fellows, Fred. Realist painter and sculptor of the contemporary West, born in Ponca City, Oklahoma in 1934 and living in Bigfork, Montana. Because he regularly practices roping steers and has broken his arm and fingers, "people ask if I am not concerned about my hands, being an artist. I tell them an artist doesn't really paint with his hands but with his head. I could paint with a stub for a hand if there were some way to attach the brush to it, though I'd just as soon not lose a hand."

Ponca City was the home of Wild West shows and Indian reservations, and while Fellows went to high school in Los Angeles, he still competed in rodeos. He was a saddlemaker for two years, then learned commercial art on the job in industry and became an art director. In the evenings, he joined with other artists for seven years to do life drawing. The paintings were abstracts and coffee houses gave him shows, but he turned to realism when he asked himself "how anyone can understand something that is totally private to the artist." He had continued with his roping and he decided he preferred Western art because it is "about a period and a part of our country that has a deep fascination for me."

Fellows completes eight to ten major oils, seven or eight smaller ones, and one major sculpture a year. "On the basis of commissions," he says, "it would take me three years to finish what people have ordered." He has been a member of the Cowboy Artists of America since 1968, is listed in *Who's Who in American Art*, was featured in *Artists of the Rockies* and in *Prints*, publishes through Salt Creek Graphics, and is represented by The Peacock Galleries Limited and Flathead Lake Galleries.

Fred Fellows, SACRED TIMES, oil, 30 x 15

JOE FERRARA

m Fillerup

Ferrara, Joe. Traditional painter of the Old West and of wildlife in oil and tempera, and sculptor, born in New Haven, Connecticut in 1931 and living in Hamden, Connecticut. When asked how a painter from the East can do Western scenes, he replies that "I can be in the West today and the North Woods tomorrow. You get yourself involved in the subject matter of a scene and travel mainly through your imagination. When you do a painting, you live the event yourself."

Growing up on a farm, he drew constantly and his parents could never keep enough paper in the house. In the fifth grade, he won a radio art contest sponsored by Jack Dempsey, sending in a drawing of an octopus wearing boxing gloves. After earning his BFA at Pratt Institute in Brooklyn, he served in the Navy before employment in New York City art studios and then agencies in New Haven and Hartford. In 1962, he began his own studio in Hamden, offering complete art services because "commercial art is not just drawing pictures. You have to know type, printing, photography, and what can be put into print that is economical."

Ferrara is best known for his Winchester calendars that he started doing in 1967. At first, 25,000 were printed. These have become collectors' items as the distribution has grown to 400,000, in five languages. He also designs engravings and medallions for the guns as well as the gun box. In 1980, he designed the commemorative gun sleeve for John Wayne's gun. Another thrill "even after all my years in this business," is "when my son calls and says he saw my antique cars and songbirds on sugar packets in a restaurant." Ferrera is now concentrating on Western paintings and sculpture, and is represented by Biltmore Galleries.

Fields, Chester. Realist painter of wildlife and Western themes in acrylic and tempera, born in Dalles, Oregon in 1945 and living in Spokane, Washington. "Fifty percent of art is business," he believes. "If you are the best artist but not a businessman, you won't survive. Fortunately, there are shows and publications and opportunities for artists to gain exposure so there is no reason to starve." He himself has used the similarity of his name to the cigarette. Nicknamed "Smoky" in school, he signs as "Chester" rather than the "Chet" he is now called.

He began drawing insects at five and moved to British Columbia with his family when he was ten. Along with riding, hunting, and fishing, he continued drawing and took a mail order course when he was in high school. After graduating from Spokane Community College with a degree in commercial art, he was drafted into the Army and spent two years in Germany as draftsman and illustrator. When he saw the Old Masters in Europe, he "was tempted to throw my brushes away as I felt many of my goals had been accomplished 500 years previously."

After his discharge, he was employed as a commercial artist for four years before becoming a professional wildlife artist. He believes that there has been an increase in interest in wildlife art at the expense of Western art, "yet there is a demand for both and will be for a long time to come because the West is a part of our history and fascinating to most. That is my expression. I speak with a brush rather than with words. The latest and most exciting commission is the life of a Shaman, consisting of twelve large paintings for $100,000." Written up in *Art West*, summer 1978, he is represented by the Favell Museum.

Fillerup, Mel. Painter of Wyoming landscapes and figures, born in Lovell, Wyoming in 1924 and living in Cody, Wyoming since 1952. "When you have seven children, four of whom are in college, two serving on missions, one in high school, and you think of changing from a fine law practice to becoming a painter," Fillerup expounds, "it is not done without serious thought. I have become satisfied that in the long run I have much more to offer in the field of art than as a lawyer."

Brought up in Lovell, Fillerup went through the exercises in *Drawing Made Easy* a dozen times when he was a child, but he opted for the law at the University of Wyoming. After interruptions for military service in the Philippines during World War II and for a two-year mission to England for the Mormon Church, he graduated from law school in 1952 and began his law practice in Cody.

Fillerup states that "the legal profession has been good to me, but whenever there was available time I would be drawing or painting or studying the masters from books or in the galleries." He "would slip over to Jackson" for the Teton Artists School, attend the Art Students League in New York City, and get advice from seasoned professionals like Bob Lougheed. In 1975, he began painting full time and by 1981 had won the gold medal at the American Indian and Cowboy Artists show. His aim has become to have each painting "reach out and touch others" the way the subject painted touched him. He has been featured in *Southwest Art*, September 1980, and is represented by Trailside Galleries.

Mel Fillerup, EAGLE HEADDRESS, watercolor, 8 x 10

Chester Fields, SOLITARY HUNTER, mixed media, 30 x 40

Joe Ferrara, JOHN WAYNE COMMEMORATIVE GUN BOX COVER, oil, 2½ ft x 5 ft

Peter M. Fillerup (signature)

John Fincher (signature)

Nicholas S. Firfires (signature)

Fillerup, Peter M. Sculptor of historical Western figures in statuary and statuettes, born in Cody, Wyoming in 1953 and living in Wapiti, Wyoming. "I've always had a little romance with the wind," he muses. "Ever since I was a boy and my brothers and I could roam over the hills on our ranch, I've been in love with freedom and in love with the wind, because the wind, more than anything else, was free to go wherever it wanted." He has indicated the passing of the wind in some of his sculpture.

After studying art at Ricks College in Rexburg, Idaho in 1972, Fillerup went to Brigham Young University in Provo, Utah in 1973 where he won the Art Award Scholarship in 1976. He then became an apprentice to Dr. Avard Fairbanks, a leading American sculptor, and accompanied Fairbanks to Italy where they learned the art of enlarging models into heroic sizes, working with marble, and foundry technique. He also worked in plaster casting in Salt Lake City where his sculpture was accepted for a cultural center, in addition to sculpture at the Buffalo Bill Historical Center, Buffalo Bill's Memorial Museum, and Old West Trail Town.

Fillerup adds that in sculpture, "you're dealing with the imagination and you want to keep it that way. You don't want everything spelled out. Line as well as detail must be executed so as not to overwhelm the spirit." Concerning the texture of the finished work, he says that "people like to see where your hand has been. They like to feel that they have touched something living that has somehow touched them. That way they sense the presence of the artist." Fillerup is represented by Altermann Art and Carson's Galleries.

Fincher, John. Contemporary oil painter of New Mexican still lifes, born in Hamilton, Texas in 1941 and living in Santa Fe, New Mexico since 1976. "My subject matter probably would classify me as a regional artist," he agrees, "but I would identify Western Regionalism as the realm of those cowboy and Indian painters who cater to a type of nostalgia, painting what they know little about because the time has gone. If my work is regional, it is of a considerably more contemporary point of view."

Growing up near Lubbock, Texas, "it was hell to play out there" in his grandmother's yard "because I could get well-and-truly scarred if I fell down" in the prickly pear cactus, "but they had an enormous impact on me visually. Still do. What a curious, strange plant." After getting his BA at Texas Tech in 1964 and his MFA at Oklahoma University in 1966, he taught art at Wichita State University. In nine years, he was chairman of the department, an administrative job assigned "because I could spell and write a literate memo." Although he was economically in "an attractive trap," he quit to paint.

As a teenager, he had taken private lessons that featured still life, a style he returned to in Santa Fe where he moved because his money would last longer than in New York or Houston. For a subject, he chose cactus with its "built-in gestural quality. I like that thorny image. I do enjoy the tension of people wanting to touch the work, but this thorny, spiky element keeps them from doing it. They're torn, and they don't just walk by the piece. I cannot see myself doing paintings that work on the viewer like warm bathtubs. I prefer my images to say 'Wake up! Move'!" His prints are published by Sette Publishing Co. and he is represented by the Elaine Horwitch and Moody Galleries.

Firfires, Nicholas Samuel. "Realistic Impressionist" painter of Western action scenes, born in Santa Barbara, California in 1917 and living in Montecito, near Santa Barbara since 1971. "Painting is a lot like breaking a horse," he claims. "First you have to know how to do it. Then you have to have the courage to say, this is what I am going to do. And then, you must do it."

While attending school, Firfires spent his free time training horses on nearby ranches. He majored in art in high school and went to the Art Center School of Design in Los Angeles in 1937 and 1938, as well as Otis Art Institute in 1939 and 1940. He served in Europe in World War II, in combat and as an artist. From 1946 to 1958, he was a commercial artist in Santa Barbara, painting portraits and hundreds of Western illustrations. Since then, he has devoted himself to fine art. His first show was in 1960, portraying the ranch life he was living. Reviews of his exhibitions emphasize authenticity, enthusiasm, and skill.

"I paint from the ground up," he says. "That is, I paint standing, walking back and forth to see how my work looks from a viewing distance. I work directly on the canvas over a light charcoal sketch of the subject. For years I have sketched and painted on the spot from life. I utilize photographs for some reference, but I never 'copy' them. I find it sad that so many artists today could do nothing without a camera." Firfires is listed in *Who's Who in American Art, Western Painting Today,* and the *Biographical Encyclopedia of Western Artists,* and was featured in *Southwest Art,* June 1980. He is represented by Trailside Galleries.

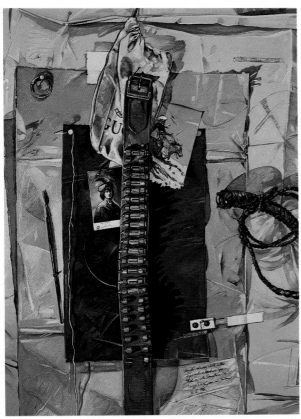

John Fincher, WESTERN MEN (1982), oil/canvas, 48 x 36

Peter Fillerup, LIVER EATIN', bronze, h 18½, Edition 51

Nicholas Firfires, THE CHUCKWAGON PILOT, oil, 24 x 36

Randy Follis

Flahavin, Marian. Painter of people and horses in candid natural situations in oil and pastel, rather than in traditionally posed portraits, born in Coltom, Washington in 1937 and living in Spokane, Washington. "Women artists," she says, "experience the same problems of acceptance professionally as women in general. They have to be twice as good and work twice as hard to be taken as seriously as the average man artist, and make half the money. Most women artists would tell you that the greatest help to them would be a 'wife.' Yet, the West was and is peopled with women and children as surely as cowboys and horses, and they certainly were responsible for carrying the West on.

"My life has always been rural and Western. Although I grew up on a wheat farm without a horse, and cowboys were not highly regarded by local farmers, I have been secretly smitten with them since I was six. I have been drawing people since childhood. Earned my BA in art in 1959, from Holy Name College, Spokane. However, since abstract art did not excite me, I did graphic design for fifteen years at the college.

"On quitting my job in order to raise a small son and quarter horses, I began to paint children and horses and discovered realistic art. Started to paint in 1974, seriously in 1976, and have been growing as fast as I can since. Showed in eight juried and nine invitational shows in three years. My first one-artist show in 1977 brought twenty commissions. I have a two-year backlog on my commissions which are half my work, and I have been invited to Rivershore to do a series of plates." A member of the Women Artists of the American West, her work is available in MONAC Gallery and Saddleback Western Art Galleries.

Follis, Randall L. Realist painter of the West in watercolor and oil, born in Corsicana, Texas in 1939 and living in Bloomfield, New Mexico. "Public reaction to an artist's work," he declares, "is an important factor to him. Criticism from the right source is welcome and usually helpful. The same criticism from a source that is unfamiliar to you can be a blow that sometimes puts a dent in your ego. Any compliment is nice to hear, but the one that makes it all worthwhile is the youngster who looks up at my work with wide eyes and states a simple 'WOW.'

"My father was a farm laborer so we moved around quite a lot. Most of my young years were spent on farms and ranches in West Texas. I graduated from high school in Dimmitt in 1958. No college. While living in Hobbs, New Mexico in 1966, I received a painting set and five art lessons as a gift. Though I surprised myself with the results, I painted only when I had nothing else to do. When I moved to Farmington in 1973, my interest in art increased. I began to read available art material and to paint regularly.

"About this time, I took a workshop and met the painter Curt Walters who has been a guiding light. Began to seek galleries to handle my work, but I think I have closed more galleries than most artists have been in. I was able to start painting full time in 1980, but I changed from oils to watercolor because we had small children for whose protection we had to put everything away each night. I always thought I was a reasonably good painter, until I decided that I really wanted to make it my life." At a 1981 San Juan College silent auction, his painting sold for more than $5,000 to "a Follis addict." His galleries are Aldridge Fine Arts and The Art Barn which also publishes a print.

Randy Follis, BEST OF THE BUNCH, oil, 30 x 40

Marian Flahavin, ALBERT NIPON, oil, 30 x 24

Dale Ford   *Pat Ford*

Ford, Dale. Woodcarver and painter, especially of 19th-century Western vehicles, born near Visalia, California in 1934 and living in Incline Village, Nevada, near Lake Tahoe since 1980. "My parents were merchants by trade but ranchers at heart," he says, "so I grew up in two worlds. I have been drawing, painting and carving as long as I can recall and was encouraged by my parents throughout. By age twelve, I was into all aspects of arts and crafts, but art in those days was a starvation occupation, not to be taken seriously, and I was expected to enter business.

"My formal education was business administration, but after a short time in the business world, I knew I was in the wrong place. I decided to move to the Monterey Bay area and open a commercial art shop that would incorporate everything I knew into a single business. I called it Dale Ford Originals and that it stayed for many years. Being original was the key to my success and I soon had more business than I knew what to do with.

"My work went through an evolution for several years, narrowing itself to the finer arts. Twelve years ago I went strictly Western and nine years ago I did my first miniature horse-drawn vehicles. I was commissioned to create the largest collection of miniature horse-drawn vehicles ever, and 86 of those are on display in Wisconsin at Sentry Insurance. I must admit that wood sculpture is my favorite medium. I sell about 75 percent of my work, nearly all to collectors." Ford has been written up in *Western Horseman*, *Art West*, and *Southwest Art* and is represented by Period Gallery West, Hall Galleries and McCulley Gallery.

Ford, Pat. Realist painter of Texas wildlife in acrylic, born in Tulsa, Oklahoma in 1933 and living in Humble, Texas. "I give one painting per year and its print rights to the Waco chapter of Ducks Unlimited," she explains. "The first year alone we raised $300,000, so this year should put us well over $1,000,000. The program will continue for ten years, with the original paintings held in Waco to be auctioned as a group at the end of ten years. The animals support me by letting me paint their portraits and I support them for the privilege.

"I studied art at Tulsa University on a scholarship. I did not pursue art while my children were growing up but when my youngest son started school, I entered a few things in local shows and a banker talked me into selling several pieces. I opened an art store that turned into a gallery, painting everything from people to places. The wildlife work was what clicked. It is the part that I am familiar with because I can hunt and fish with the best of them. Soon my work was outselling the other artists' work in the gallery so we closed the gallery. I needed time to paint and did not have the time to be a storekeeper.

"I no longer hunt with a gun but I do go along with a camera. I work from these photographs as well as mounts, but I don't try to make my paintings photographic because I feel cameras miss a lot. I try to paint the wildlife portraits as you would see them with your eyes, not through the lens of the camera. I strive to make them seem real, unafraid, and unaware that we are watching them." Written up in *Southwest Art*, March 1979, she is published by Somerset House and represented by La Galleria and Corpus Christi Art Gallery.

Dale Ford, STAGECOACH, hardwood & steel, h 21

Pat Ford, BOBWHITE QUAIL, watercolor, 16 x 20

Christopher Forrest

Howard Forsberg

FORSTER

Forrest, Christopher. Printmaker and painter in acrylics of wild birds, born in Trenton, New Jersey in 1946 and living in Willingboro, New Jersey. "The first step in etching is preparing the plate and applying the ground. It sounded easy, so I talked my wife into allowing me to use the kitchen stove for 15 minutes. Well, four hours later I was still at it. The kitchen was filled with smoke and smelled of chemicals. Eventually, it worked almost like the books said it would, and I began to really enjoy etching.

"I began painting at the age of seven, and at eleven I was painting in oils and exhibiting. I had grown up with the outdoors as a large part of life and thus chose to study engineering at a rural university and a career in the Army that would allow me to spend time outdoors. I was commissioned upon graduation from college in 1968 and when I received my Master's in 1974 decided to combine the outdoors with painting in my spare time and concentrated on wildlife. In 1976, I began experimenting with original graphics.

"Upon leaving the Army in 1979, I was a full-time etcher and lithographer. Developing a painting starts with time and experience in wilderness environments, then researching the bird using books and photos, obtaining a skin or mount from the museum, drawing extensively, and sometimes making clay models. I start the painting with the background, either realistic or impressionistic. Next I introduce the bird. I tend to think of myself more as a printmaker than a painter, however, having produced 70 original graphic editions carried by 350 galleries. My distributor is Hangups." Written up in *Southwest Art*, November 1981, Forrest is a member of the Society of Animal Artists.

Forsberg, Howard. Painter of historical Western subjects, born in Milwaukee, Wisconsin in 1918 and living in Rio Rancho, New Mexico since 1977. "Originally, when I got into this Western theme," Forsberg explains, "I was interested in the contemporary end of it—the practicing cowboy, the rural setting, and so forth. As I got deeper into it, I became more sensitized to the historic end, the strife of the Indians and their role in our country.

"My mother and grandfather were artists and encouraged my early attempts. I studied at the Layton School of Art before moving to Chicago in 1939 where I lived at the YMCA while apprenticed to a large art studio. At night I attended the Frederic Mizen art school. By 1946, I had assignments from major clients in New York City. We decided to spend the year 1949 in Tucson and in 1950 I continued my career in the New York area. The West was drawing us back, however, and in 1952 we settled in Pasadena, California where I owned a large art studio. In 1966 I was offered the job of painting instructor at the Famous Artists School and we moved to Connecticut.

"In 1976, I became interested in Western art and decided to become a serious easel painter. My book *Figure Painting for Beginners* was published in 1979. I feel that an artist is a truly creative person, and the group that should be considered artists is much smaller than the group that is given the name artist. People attach a sort of mysticism to 'art.' Everyone wants to be an 'artist,' but then comes the old classic, 'I can't draw a straight line.' Well, damn few people can draw a straight line. That's why you use a ruler." Forsberg is a member of the Society of Illustrators in New York City and is represented by The May Gallery.

Forster, Paul Peter. Representational painter of "quiet moods and remote scenes" of New Mexico in various media and techniques, born in Buffalo, New York in 1925 and living in Columbus, New Mexico. "My earliest recollections were caught up in the world of art," he says. "I remember being carried up through the green grass of the lake shore to the Albright Art Gallery and through the gallery, room by room. At eight, I was making three street car transfers for each of my solo visits.

"At eight, I also began studies in art at the Buffalo Museum of Science on Saturday mornings, and continued them for four years. At seventeen, there was the Army Air Corps, and two and a half years later the discharge. There was a stint of work in personnel studies, then a degree in art from Brigham Young University in 1952 and self-employment as an easel and mural painter. In 1961, I was called by the Church of Jesus Christ of the Latter-Day Saints to set up an art program in the Tongan Islands. I later taught at Brigham Young University from 1964 to 1969, and returned to the ranks of the self-employed in art.

"I shy away from philosophical statements about my paintings, but if one would corner me for a statement—then: 'My intent in producing a work of art is to view an idea, circumstance, an aspect of nature or man in his environment, and use all of the talent and skill I have to portray this in some unique and artful way. No artist is totally without reliance upon history or reference—but as one man resembles another yet remains unique as an individual—so does my work remain mine'." Written up in *Southwest Art*, February 1979, Forster is represented by the Biltmore Galleries and Tivoli Gallery.

Howard Forsberg, EAST TO WEST, oil, 24 x 36

Paul Forster, MASS AT MESCALARO, oil, 36 x 24

Chris Forrest, GOLDEN EAGLE, lithograph, 18 x 24

191

Lincoln Fox

C. FRAGUA

Forsyth, (Mary) Bryan. Traditional sculptor and painter of Southwestern figures and themes, born in Tucson, Arizona Territory in 1910 and living in Pecos, New Mexico. "When I became involved in commercial art," she recalls, "the agent counseled me to drop my first name (Mary) because 'people don't expect a woman to paint Indians and the out-of-doors' (Ha!), so my signature became 'Bryan Forsyth,' a happy blend of the Irish and the Scottish.

"I was lucky enough to be born in beautiful Arizona Territory where my growing years were based, with cooling off on the California coast and in the Rocky Mountains during the summers. My father opened my eyes to the natural world. As soon as I could walk, there were picnics and fishing expeditions into the Catalina Mountains and lessons about the activities of insects, birds, and wild animals. He played a game by drawing the outline of a bird or animal to see how quickly I could identify it.

"It wasn't long before these elements found expression with paint, pen, and clay. I won *St. Nicholas* magazine medals for drawing in 1921 and 1923, and was an honor student at the Maryland Institute of Art in 1929–30. I studied Western art with Frank Tenney Johnson at the Grand Central School of Art in New York City in 1931–32 and was invited to be his apprentice in California. From 1937 to 1968, my studio was in New York where I did portrait commissions and commercial art including newspaper, magazine, and book illustrations. In 1969, I moved to New Mexico. I was commissioned in 1978 to model a bronze of author Mari Sandoz for the Nebraska Hall of Fame, and in 1981 my bronze 'Victorio' was accepted by the New Mexico Museum of Fine Art. I am represented by Shidoni Gallery and Foundry and Sanders Galleries."

Fox, Lincoln. Traditional sculptor of bronze statuettes and statues, particularly of Indians, born in Morrilton, Arkansas. in 1942 and living in Alto, New Mexico since 1971. "I am first and foremost involved with the spirit of man," he declares, "and in this light, I have not found a more pleasing symbolic individual than the American Indian. His personal confrontation and co-operation with the creative forces captures my interest and excites my imagination.

"I hated school. I got poor grades until I went to college." In art, "I used to copy models. I figured if the instructors thought it was good, they must know." Meanwhile, he earned his BFA from the University of Texas, MA from the University of Dallas, and MFA from the University of Kansas. "I was supposed to be 'professional' but I said to myself, 'I know this work stinks.' Still I looked at history and saw that other artists had it—their work was alive."

He decided to study the works of famous sculptors he admired to find out what made their work alive. "It was like starting over again. It was devastating for me." Then he found that it was distortion that was the key to making the work come alive. "I started seeing it for the first time. The figures were wrong anatomically, but they had life. I realized that all of life that is communication is distortion. Exaggeration and distortion make the art exciting. After that discovery, I had twice as much fun. I let things happen." He has been exhibiting since 1968, including a one-artist show at the Smithsonian Institution in 1975. He was written up in *Southwest Art*, May 1980, and is represented by his own gallery and by Shidoni Gallery and Foundry.

Fragua, Cliff. Modern sculptor of Indian forms in stone, born in Albuquerque, New Mexico in 1955 and living in Jemez Pueblo, New Mexico since 1973. "There is one place where I wish to stay permanently," he emphasizes, "and that is here on the land where I am from, the center of the earth. Here is where I will find a meaning. Here is where I will continue to learn about stone and its way of life, its existence. I will pass it on to whoever has the strength and determination to see into the stone and to hear the stone speak.

"Upon graduation from high school, I hadn't the slightest idea of what I wanted to do. I got on the road and hitched a ride to Santa Fe and was accepted at the Institute of American Indian Arts. I started formal training in 1973. I studied painting and then in 1974 applied at the San Francisco Art Institute, but the atmosphere was so different. I knew that once I returned to New Mexico, I was home.

"Upon returning to IAIA, I took classes in ceramics and sculpture. Three dimensional forms had taken my interest. The excitement had built to where I would think 3-D—3-*Dimentality* as I called it. At the school I found the additive process and the subtractive process. This really blew my mind. Soon I viewed painting as a form of sculpture—2-D images on 3-D forms. I put aside the canvas and brushes and picked up the mallet and chisel. I could feel a presence in the stone and I was able to communicate with it. The force or spirit in the stone had made contact with my mind and body, and soon we came to understand each other. We would talk first, then compromise, then agree." Written up in *Southwest Art*, August 1980, he is represented by Galeria Del Sol and Wadle Galleries.

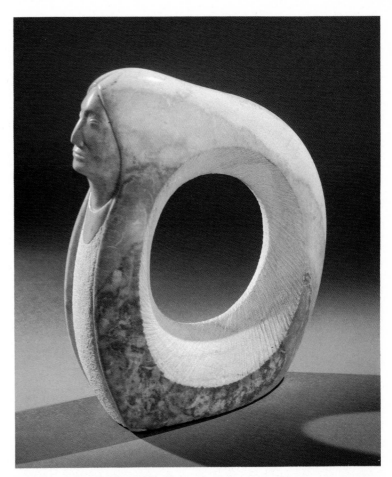

Lincoln Fox, SONG FOR THE DEER,
bronze, h 38, l 25½, d 15¾

Cliff Fragua, REMEMBERING, Colorado alabaster, h 13

Bryan Forsyth, VICTORIO, bronze, h 15, l 18

193

Edward Fraughton, WELLS FARGO, bronze, h 18, l 48

Edward J. Fraughton

Fraughton, Edward James. Sculptor of figures and animals in American classical style, born in Park City, Utah in 1939 and living in South Jordan, Utah. "First," he states, "art is technical. It represents a reverence for the use of earth's most basic substances. Second, man and art both succeed and survive on emotional expression. The spiritual aspect of the work is every bit as important as pure craftsmanship. One without the other is out of balance. Perfection is the best of both—perfect harmony."

Born to a poor family in a dying mine camp, Fraughton was the "town artist." He recalls that "a most intriguing realization of my youth was the discovery of myself. This stack of protoplasmic matter called 'me' appeared to consist of entirely two parts, some unexplainable portion I call 'soul' and the most obvious part, 'body.' Somehow, two little lenses called eyes seem to connect the body with the soul, as do the other senses." Fraughton earned a BFA from the University of Utah, with special studies from the sculptors Dr. Avard T. and Justin Fairbanks.

"In 1969, at the age of 30, I was finally off to Europe to seek my fortune." His first monumental sculpture was being cast in Italy, and he wanted to see the works of the masters at firsthand. He discovered that "classical forms of art link themselves together across time." Fraughton has been winning gold medals since 1973, has had seven public monuments commissioned, is in twelve public collections, is listed in *Who's Who in American Art* and *Bronzes of the American West*, has been featured in *Artists of the Rockies* and *Persimmon Hill*, is a member of the National Sculpture Society and the Society of Animal Artists, and is represented by Kennedy and Husberg Fine Arts Galleries.

John D FREE

Bill FREEMAN

Free, John D. "Naturalistic" sculptor and painter of Western animals and men in a traditional manner in bronze, oil, pastel, and pencil, born in Pawhuska, Oklahoma in 1929 and still living there. After growing up on his grandfather's ranch near McAlester, he claims to "have been opening and closing gates for cows and horses since I was tall enough to lift a wire hoop from a post. My grandfather was my boyhood idol, and he still is."

As long as Free can remember, he has been sketching and modeling cowboys and horses, but the idea that he could make a living as an artist did not occur to him. In college to study pre-veterinary medicine and animal husbandry, he took a few art courses but was turned off by the emphasis on abstraction. After cowboying and rodeoing, he tried his hand as a rancher but "almost went down the drain after three years. A successful rancher has to be a smart man." Because he "couldn't support a good roping horse and a good trailer and go to all the rodeos," he decided that it would be better to paint and sculpt cowboys than to be one.

When Free had taught himself all he could, he spent four years studying privately in Taos, New Mexico. He says that he has passed many hours sitting on a bucket, sketching or modeling from life as well as taking photographs. A quarter Osage with a little Cherokee blood, he calls himself an unallotted Osage—which means no money from the government. He was given a one-man show at the National Cowboy Hall of Fame in 1971 and was a member of the Cowboy Artists of America from 1972 to 1975; he is a member of the National Academy of Western Art and won the silver NAWA medal in 1979. Written up in *Persimmon Hill, Oklahoma Today,* and *The Oklahoma Cowman,* he has opened his own foundry.

Freeman, Bill. Painter and sculptor of Western wildlife, horses, and landscapes, born in Greensboro, North Carolina in 1927 and living in Scottsdale, Arizona in winter and Jackson, Wyoming in summer. Freeman's father was apprenticed to his artist uncle at thirteen and became a portrait painter and teacher by saying he was one. His father died when Freeman was three, and his mother, who had been the father's pupil, completed the unfinished portraits and set up her own studio in El Paso. She taught Freeman.

Raised on a flower farm in Ysleta, Texas, Freeman handled the livestock. After graduating from high school in 1945, he worked for the Forest Service near Silver City, New Mexico and began painting. He farmed again until 1951 when he made a painting trip with his mother. For the next ten years, Freeman was an itinerant cowboy in Arizona, New Mexico, California, Wyoming, and Massachusetts wrangling horses in summer and working cattle in winter on ranches and dude ranches. He tried college but dropped out. In Tucson, a gallery suggested that he join the Arizona Game Department to get the experience needed for wildlife painting. When he had been there for two years, assisting research biologists and illustrating publications, he decided to paint full time and has since done "over 3,000 paintings and a flock of sculptures."

Despite his practical knowledge of how to "shoe horses, pack, and ride," and how to dissect big game for study as the foundation for his art, Freeman admits that "it's so complicated, it's impossible to learn it all. You keep building on the knowledge each time, but there are still secrets that elude you." He is represented by Trailside Galleries.

Bill Freeman, UNTITLED, oil, 18 x 24

John D. Free, THE DAYBREAKERS, bronze, h 16, l 21

R. FREEMAN

Freeman, Richard A. Painter of the foothills, ranches, and cowboy life of Alberta and British Columbia, Canada, born in Leicester, England in 1932 and living in Peachland, British Columbia since 1974. "Nostalgia plays a part in much of my work," he emphasizes, "bringing a subtle reminder of dwindling frontiers. I combine soft tonal qualities with movement, draftsmanship, composition, and colour to project the viewer into my paintings. My works show knowledge of anatomy, in both human and animal form, but I try to keep it unpretentious.

"I have loved drawing and painting all my life. The eldest of four children, I attended school in Leicester, winning scholarships to Lutterworth and Leicester College of Art for my senior year. At the age of eighteen, I joined the R.A.F. Most of the two years were served in Northern Ireland where my off-duty hours were spent sketching and painting the moors, lakes, and rocky coast. Following my service, I joined an international advertising agency, constantly painting to improve my style, as well as taking university extension courses in the evening.

"Canada has always intrigued me with its open spaces. In 1955, I emigrated, living first in Ottawa where I worked with Crawley Films. Still the West beckoned. In 1957, I moved to Calgary as art director of a national advertising agency, eventually purchasing a small holding to raise horses and becoming a Canadian citizen. I spend many hours in the saddle and truly admire and respect the working cowboy of Western Canada and the United States. I have never regretted the discipline of my commercial training." Freeman's work is in twenty corporate and public collections. He markets his prints and paintings as Freeman Galleries.

Freeman, Robert. Modern painter and etcher of American Indian subjects, born on the Rincon Indian Reservation in 1939 and living in San Marcos, California. "To me," Freeman observes, "art is a thinking process. It is the ideas in your mind, not the ability to draw or paint. It is images. Also, I like to create shapes and play with colors nonobjectively.

"I was educated at Escondido High School, Mira Costa, and Palomar College where I graduated in 1971. I have no formal art training, which to me is an advantage. When I began to paint in 1961, I naturally painted what I knew: contemporary Indians, playing baseball, washing clothes, and working. I was influenced by the work of Jackson Pollock and Rufino Tamayo. People and their interactions with each other is still my subject matter.

"I live and paint where I was born in north San Diego County. I have tried to isolate myself from the art groups, because I do not want to be influenced by current art trends. Now, I am involved in etching. I learned the process about six years ago. Since then, I have been able to create and produce 60 different plates." One year after Freeman began painting, he sold his first work, and two years later, in 1964, he won first prize at the Scottsdale National Indian Art Exhibition. In 1966, he exhibited at the Gallery of the American Indian in Washington, D.C., and in 1968, he was a guest artist at the Cowboy Artists of America. He also won gold medals at the American Indian and Cowboy Artist show and in Italy. Two books have been published, *For Indians Only* and *War Whoops and All That Jazz*. His most recent one-person shows have been at Van Grabills Gallery and at Pacific Western Traders.

Robert Freeman, THE POTTER, etching, 14 x 18

Richard A. Freeman, COOL WATER, oil, 24 x 36

Arnold Friberg

Friberg, Arnold. Painter of Western people and horses, born in Winnetka, Illinois in 1913 and living in Holiday, Utah since 1949. According to Friberg, "I fill up my pictures with man and animal, and with just enough landscape to identify the setting. My natural way is to put figures all the way to the edges, to fill the canvas. The challenge is to put a lot into a painting without letting it get junky."

Raised in Phoenix, Friberg started cartooning at eight and was enrolled in an art instruction correspondence course at ten. He worked as a sign painter's apprentice, "making a man's living" while in high school, and then borrowed $500 in 1931 to study at the Chicago Academy of Fine Arts and later in New York City with Harvey Dunn. He was an illustrator in Chicago in 1937 when the Northwest Paper Company commissioned a series on the Royal Canadian Mounted Police that lasted for 35 years. The job required painting horses, and Friberg recalls that "I learned them fast.

"To me, the picturing of horses is next to worship. I am awed by how a hock joint is put together. I marvel, not only at the anatomy of animals, but also at the anatomy of trees, the whole thing, the design and engineering of it." He served in the Army in World War II, remained in San Francisco as an illustrator, and in 1949 was hired by the University of Utah to found a commercial art department. In serving his Mormon Church, he became known as "The Painter of Scripture," and was chief artist for the movie "The Ten Commandments." He has been featured in *Artists of the Rockies*, spring 1977, and *Southwest Art*, December 1981, and is represented by Husberg Fine Arts Gallery.

Arnold Friberg, WINNERS AND LOSERS, oil, 40 x

Fritzler, Gerald L. Watercolorist of Impressionist-realist landscapes of the Rockies and scenes near his studio, born in Chicago in 1953 and living in Mesa, Colorado since 1979. "Watercolor painting seems to forever move and excite me. There is no other medium that captures my interest more. It is a medium of many varieties and handling, and the freshness of spontaneity is overwhelming. I enjoy painting the landscape most of all because it's always new and exhilarating."

Fritzler studied on scholarship at the American Academy of Art from 1973 to 1976 and worked as a commercial illustrator in Chicago and Milwaukee, Wisconsin before moving to Colorado where he paints full time. He had been exhibiting watercolors nationally since he was a student, including one in the traveling exhibition of the American Watercolor Society, and was encouraged by winning an award at the 1979 AWS show and by the invitation to exhibit at the National Academy of Western Art. By 1981, he was exhibiting in four major shows. One was the first exhibition of American Western art in Peking, China.

"The quotes I think about often," he states, "are: 'accept challenges that seem unreasonable, because if you don't strive toward the challenge before you and give it your best effort, you might never know if you could overcome it. Press on, for nothing in the world can take the place of persistence and determination.' For those reasons, I love to paint watercolors because they are very challenging and I like to control them in various stages and degrees; and yet, to also let the medium work for you is the way I like to paint." He is represented by Shriver Gallery.

Frizzell, Charles. Realist painter of Colorado scenes and Indian figures in egg tempera and acrylic, born in Murray, in the mountains of Kentucky in 1944 and living in Victor, Colorado since 1979. "I have always painted," he drawls. "Even in high school, when a drawing or a sketch was needed, the solution was: 'get Charlie to do it.' When I finished college, I almost blew my art career and got a job."

He grew up in Kentucky and after graduating from Murray State University traveled throughout the states of Washington and Oregon and down the California coast. He moved to Oklahoma City and to support his family painted quick portraits in a shopping center. He heard about the beauty of the Colorado mountains, managed to scrape together enough money to visit Cripple Creek, and responded to the terrain by making a small down payment on a parcel of land, but was unable to afford to move there until 1967. During the first winter, he lived in a trailer with frozen waterpipes that required a visit to Colorado Springs to take a bath.

Frizzell spends days hiking through the mountains to find scenes to sketch. Then he puts the sketches aside until one generates a feeling of excitement as it triggers the memory, because without strong internal emotions he feels that the right mood to paint won't be there and the work will not be his best. From the sketch, he strips away the background and focuses on the subject, declaring that he uses his brushes like a writer uses words to evoke responses. Frizzell is a member of the National Society of Painters in Casein and Acrylics, was written up in *Artists of the Rockies*, for summer 1975, and is represented by Garden of the Gods Art Gallery.

Froman, Ann. Traditional sculptor of series of bronze figures, "Women of the West," "Women of the Bible," "Nude York," and "Dancing Bronzes," born in New York City in 1942 and living in Stanfordville, New York since 1979. "Women of the West,' was inspired by my exhibition in Phoenix in 1979," she explains. "I did not see there too many sculptures of Western women so I did my research and proceeded to create a collection of Indian women doing their chores and artistry, dance hall dancers flirting with the men, female bandits such as Belle Starr, plus a school teacher and square dancers."

Raised in New York City, she studied at the National Academy School of Fine Art and the Art Students League as well as the Fountainbleau School of Fine Art in France. "I was thrown out of my sculpture class," she observes, "because the teacher said that he couldn't teach me anything." Her first design job was in fashion, specializing in shoes. In 1968, she switched to sculpture, and when she visited Israel and Italy, she was influenced by seeing the Arab women and the churches. After that, her work began to "look very biblical" and she did the religious series in which Eve is nude and pregnant but "she has no belly button because she was created and not born."

In 1979, she and her husband decided that too much time was lost in commuting from home to studio to foundry so they moved to Stanfordville where her husband opened a foundry to cast her bronzes. They also travel together to her shows and have logged more than 40,000 miles a year in a specially equipped station wagon. She has won six national awards, is in ten permanent collections, and has exhibited from coast to coast including at the Gemini and Shorr Goodwin Galleries.

Charles Frizzell, ALBERT, acrylic, 30 x 24

Ann Froman, WORDS OF WISDOM, bronze, h 11

Gerald L. Fritzler, HOUSE AT ELK RANCH, watercolor, 18 x 26

Loren G. Fry

Stanley W. Galli

Joe Garcia

Fry, Loren G. Painter in acrylic of today's ranch life on the High Plains, born in Chicago in 1924 and living in Benton Harbor, Michigan. "Through my paintings," Fry says, "I would like to transport the millions, who can't experience ranch life, into the back-country where the cowhand and his horse do their job. At first, I couldn't believe how they negotiated rocky, waist-high sage country at a fast jog with only a rare stumble. My own horses have never put in a full day covering 40 miles of the rough country."

Fry claims that "the money-making hours of his life were spent in an agency while the money spending hours were with horses." He attended the Chicago Academy of Fine Art. After World War II, he helped form an advertising agency and worked as an art director in Chicago for 22 years. A horse owner himself, he painted a series of covers for *The Quarter Horse Journal* in the mid-1960s. He began taking Western vacation trips in the early 1970s and was accepted as "house artist" at the Fear Ranch in the Green River Valley near Big Piney, Wyoming. In 1975, Fry also began riding with the hands on the Cueno Verde Ranch in south central Colorado. That was the year he started painting full time.

In his desire to bring the ranch hands before the widest public, Fry declares that "you can only turn out so many paintings a year, and I feel that prints will make my work available to many more people. Many people have asked about them." Sage Brush is his publisher and May is his gallery. Fry has been featured in *The Western Horseman*, June 1977, and in *Southwest Art*, May 1978, and his paintings have been reproduced on the Dan Post Boot Co. calendars.

Galli, Stanley Walter. Painter of wildlife and of the Spanish Colonial period in the West, in oil and acrylic, born in San Francisco in 1912 and living in Kentfield, California. "Not being a genius," he says, "I have to slog. There are flashes sometimes of inspiration, but if I don't go through the drudgery, I don't discover anything." He adds that "I don't want agents. I don't want a gallery. I don't know if I can do it, but I'm fixing to try. And boy, I'm a fighter."

The only son of immigrant Italians, he was expected to become a lawyer, but when he won a scholarship to art school in the seventh grade, he was launched on "the adventure that is painting." Before he finished high school, the family moved to Reno where he was a baker's apprentice. After he returned to San Francisco, he drove a laundry truck until he had funds enough for the California School of Fine Arts, where he studied on a scholarship. In two years, his funds ran out and he began working for a local art agency. He served as an artist in World War II, then went back to the agency.

Despite local successes, he visited New York City to obtain free-lance commissions from the national magazines. He also designed 23 postage stamps and in 1969 went to Rome to study and establish a second home. In 1977, he decided to devote himself to fine art, "to paint what symbolizes the gracefulness or the boisterousness that existed. I cannot look at our California landscape without seeing those old Colonials and Indians running around." Listed in *Who's Who in American Art*, Galli is a member of the Society of Animal Artists and was elected to the Society of Illustrators Hall of Fame. His exhibitions are in museums and societies.

Garcia, Joe. Realist watercolorist of California landscapes, historic buildings, people, and animals, born in Escondido, California in 1944 and living in San Marcos, California. "I enjoy painting many different subjects," he says. "When I began painting birds about seven years ago, I had no idea that it would lead to the interest that has caused me to specialize in that area by necessity. I have also had the privilege of working with fine conservation organizations such as Ducks Unlimited and Safari Club International.

"Becoming an artist was not a goal in my early life, but after exploring different fields in my first two years at San Marcos Community College, I committed myself to commercial art and entered the Art Center College of Design in Los Angeles, receiving my BFA in 1970. After graduating, I did free-lance commercial art and became increasingly aware that I was impelled toward fine art, especially watercolor. I pursued watercolor as an avocation, and now perceive it as my primary goal in art.

"Although I have been trained in oils and acrylics, I prefer watercolor for its versatility and spontaneity. These factors and the textures of the paper and paint appeal to the part of me that reaches for the unaffected freshness of nature. My technique involves the use of wet into wet washes for background, contrasting the softness of this effect with the detail of the bird or animal. At times, I enjoy working in pen and ink or in pencil, which gives me increased awareness of form and line. In addition, the exactness of the ink or pencil allows me to explore detail and value, which in turn affects my watercolors." A member of the Society of Animal Artists, Garcia is represented by Troy's Gallery.

Stanley Galli, ONLY SPANISH SPOKEN, acrylic wash, 38 x 52

Joe Garcia, CANADA GOOSE, watercolor, 12 x 18

Loren Fry, THE BOUNDARY TREE, acrylic, 20 x 30

Garcia, Robert Arthur. Sculptor of figures in different media, mostly stone, born in Casa Blanca, French Morocco where his father was stationed in 1952 and living in Los Cerrillos, New Mexico. "Some of the stones come from different mountains here in New Mexico," he states. "Myself and a few other sculptors take four-wheel drives and all the tools we need. We camp there, dig the stones out all day and roll them down the mountains. We load the trucks to the maximum and the next day we divide the stones."

Of White Mountain Apache and Mexican American descent, Garcia graduated from high school in Tucson, Arizona, in 1971, studied film making and was an assistant camera man in Los Angeles, then he received his degree in sculpture from the Institute of American Indian Arts in Santa Fe. After working as an apprentice to Allan Houser in 1977, he became an independent sculptor. "Up there on the mountain," he says, "sometimes I'll get an idea looking at a particular stone, and then it's understood that that will be my stone. We don't compete with each other. Life is too short.

"Ideas come in different ways. It seems the stone has a soul of its own and it's up to me to bring that life out in the open. The basic shape of the stone sometimes holds the idea for me. I think design is most important. The negative space of the stone is as important as the positive. With that in mind, a simple design can be real powerful. Other ideas come from keeping your mind open. This keeps your eyes peeled and your soul clean. A lot of my ideas come from personal experiences and even dreams. I enjoy sculpting whatever I'm feeling at the time. It's a good release." Garcia is represented by Parke and Seth's Canyon Road Art Galleries.

Garriott, Gene. Realist painter of the rural West, born in San Francisco, California in 1930 and living in Albuquerque, New Mexico since 1961. "I have kicked around the West a great deal," he declares, "and, having acquired a traveling habit at an early age, I still do. As a result, I have never 'zeroed in' on any particular region or subject matter. Some of my recent works have covered such diverse subjects as a sidewalk sale in Denver and a gold mining operation in Alaska."

Because his father was a telegrapher with the Western Pacific Railroad, assigned to railway stations throughout the West, Garriott recalls that "we lived in box cars, tiny shacks beside the tracks, and in rented houses in small towns" in Utah, Nevada, and California. "Everywhere in the West" was his home. He earned a BA from the University of Nevada, spent two years in the Armed Forces, and later studied at the Art Center School of Design in Los Angeles before becoming a commercial illustrator. He especially enjoyed working for corporate clients, saying that "what makes this work so interesting is getting to go on location where research for each painting can be done firsthand." He has also done portraits for the corporate executives.

"Although I'm a Western artist," Garriott states, "I have never been a cowboy." Instead, "I paint the towns and landscapes as they are today, not as they once were." An example, his painting of an 1880s building in La Vegas, New Mexico, is in its contemporary setting. In oil, tempera, and acrylic, his paintings are in collections in New Mexico and Colorado. Garriott has been featured in *Art Voices*, September 1981 and is represented by Brandywine Gallery.

Gennusa, Ragan. Realist painter of wildlife and Western scenes in watercolor and oil, born in Rosebud, Texas in 1944 and living in Dripping Springs, Texas since 1981. At the University of Texas, he was the only art major on the football team and "was looked at very strangely by team members," he recalls. "Fortunately, I've always had a sense of humor and been confident enough about myself that I didn't care what they thought." After graduation, he began his art career painting football action scenes.

Raised in Port Arthur, he "spent a great deal of time on a farm, hunting and fishing. It was during this time that I became fascinated with the outdoors and its creatures. It was also on the farm with its row crop and cattle that I gained an appreciation for the hard work involved and was able to witness the olden ways and chores. I became interested in art at an early age and pursued art through high school." He went to the University of Texas on a football scholarship, playing split end and leading the team in receptions.

"I graduated from the university in 1968 with a BFA and went to work for the Texas Parks and Wildlife Department, illustrating animals. While painting wildlife for a living, I had a chance to visit many ranches. As I began to see the heritage of these ranches, I also started doing Western paintings. In 1972, I signed an exclusive contract with a gallery which gave me the opportunity to paint full time. After five years, I decided not to remain exclusive. Galleries over the Southwest handle my work from time to time. I also have special showings and I sell my own work, doing lots of special commissions. I work predominantly in watercolor, combining transparent and dry brush technique to arrive at the detail I want."

Gene Garriott, CANTINA, alkyd, 24 x 30

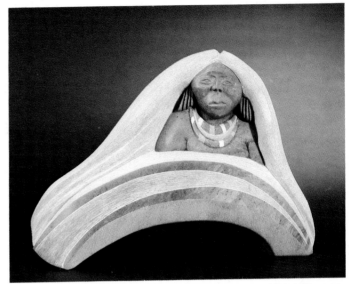

Bob Garcia, STAR CHILD, New Mexico alabaster, h 15½, l 21

Ragan Gennusa, ONE OF A KIND, watercolor, 24 x 36

William George

Lynn Gertenbach

Gessner '82

George, William. Representational oil painter of the historical West, born in Torrance, California in 1926 and living in Los Angeles. "My Western heritage," he explains, "comes from my father's family. They grew up in Brownsville, Texas; Morenci and Globe, Arizona; and Silver City, New Mexico. We all lived in Nacozari, Mexico, in the 30s. Life was primitive and rugged, but we kids loved it!

"I attended Chouinard and Jepson art schools on scholarships and with assistant teaching. My teachers included Pruett Carter and Norman Rockwell. Nicolai Fechin taught at Jepson's, but I was so young and in such awe of the man that I didn't feel I could qualify for his class—obviously that was foolish! I worked three years in Los Angeles as a beginning illustrator and then moved to New York at Rockwell's urging and painted many illustrations. After nine years, I returned to Los Angeles where I continued free lancing an immense variety of paintings.

"In 1970, following a period of growing dissatisfaction with commercial art, I began my love affair with easel painting by studying with three teachers. Though I admire historical accuracy, a painting without style, draftsmanship, color, texture, and design is nothing. Of immense difficulty for me is just discovering the 'authentic' William George. I love the Western subject, of course, but also enjoy painting nudes, European subjects, period pieces, and landscapes. I guess I have essentially been a loner all my life. I never joined any art organization or entered my work in art shows, though perhaps I will in the future. I am currently represented by The May Gallery, Biltmore Galleries, and the Jones Gallery.

Gertenbach, Lynn L. "American Impressionist painter of people and places in the hills and gardens of Los Angeles," born in Racine, Wisconsin in 1940 and living in Van Nuys, California since 1966. "When I was a small child, riding the bus to school," she recalls, "I found that my right index finger had a mind of its own. It began to trace the faces and features of people that I saw onto my schoolbook or the palm of my hand. It was impossible for me not to doodle or draw."

She received a National Scholastic scholarship when she graduated from high school in 1958, and in 1960 she earned a commercial art degree from Colorado Institute of Art. While working as a fashion illustrator, she attended Layton School of Art in the evening, then moved to California where she was a free-lance illustrator and did pastel portraits. In 1962, she traveled around the world, with eight months in India. In 1964, she painted in Mexico, and in 1965, went back to India.

"When I returned to Los Angeles," she says, "I produced work based on my travels and also began to move closer to my own environment. Since American Indians have always fascinated me, I looked to the rich heritage of Arizona and New Mexico. I traveled by car to see Old Oraibi. I felt both empathy and respect for Indians and could see how this land reflected the life-carved story lines in their faces. In recent times, after exploring myself further, experiencing new ways of thinking and experimenting with my art, I now feel less rigid about my attitudes. I don't need to prove anything. I simply enjoy being a painter, a woman, and always looking at life through a child's eyes." She has won more than 30 gold medals and is represented by Signature and Dassin Galleries.

Gessner, Debbie. Sculptor of Indians and horses in bronze, born in Portland, Oregon in 1954 and living in Philadelphia, Pennsylvania since 1978. "Art," she says. "I do it because I have to, monetarily and spiritually and every shade of grey in between. It is my living and my life. Sometimes it is good and sometimes it is bad. At times when the inspiration is not there and there is no money in the bank, it is very painful to create. Other times the ideas and creative juices flow in such abundance that I won't sleep for days.

"In 1963, our family moved to Arizona. I envisioned wild Indians and glorious wild horses, but Scottsdale looked like any other city. When I graduated from grade school, I finally got an Appaloosa and the cowboys taught me horse skills. As a teenager, I became fascinated by the cultures of the different Indian tribes. In 1973, I decided to go into art as a career, made three silver miniature sculptures for a show, got good responses, built up a starting inventory, and pounded the pavement till I found my first gallery.

"In 1977, I was invited to the George Phippen Show and took second place for outside sculpture. O'Brien's Art Emporium put on two shows for me. Things were really rolling, but I needed time to re-sort my thinking and moved to the East Coast. With a fresh perspective in 1980, I took up sculpting again and am 'back in the saddle' once more. The concepts that come are not always best adapted to a material form, but therein lies the real challenge of sculpture. How does one sculpt a dream or a longing or a vision. It is my frustration and my joy. I have a one-woman exhibition in Bern, Switzerland, and show my work with Trailside Galleries."

Lynn Gertenbach, BUFFALO CHILD, oil, 40 x 40

Debbie Gessner, TRICKY FOOTING, bronze, h 26, Edition 12

William George, JOE WALKER: EXPLORER, oil, 28 x 40

209

Lorenzo E Ghiglieri

Ghiglieri, Lorenzo E. Sculptor and painter, born in Los Angeles in 1931 and living near Portland, Oregon since 1956. A representational sculptor of dramatic Eskimo and Indian figures and wildlife, he "sees himself as a storyteller," modelling "in a style he relates to baroque realism," in "a language all can understand."

One grandfather was a sculptor, as was his Italian father. The other grandfather was a musician, as was his French mother. Lorenzo, as he calls himself, grew up on the edge of the barrio, playing bongo drums and classical guitar as a hobby. At 17, he won a scholarship from the Los Angeles Art Directors Club. During the Korean War, he served as a naval artist, painted a ship's portrait for official presentation to Great Britain in 1953, and then became a commercial artist in Chicago and New York City.

In 1956, he moved near Portland where his firsthand experiences became the basis for his art. He rode over the back country, lived with the Eskimos, and studied the Nez Perce. He did not turn to sculpture until 1974. By November 1979, he was featured in *Southwest Art*. Sculpting ideas come from sketches, and when he thinks everything through, "his hands are merely completing" the images. Compatibly with his six foot six inch and 265 pound stature, his commissions have included life-size bronzes of an eagle and of a striding Abraham Lincoln as well as a 4 by 12 foot bronze, "The Genesis of Love." The people of Oregon presented Ronald Reagan with a Ghiglieri statuette. "I must hurry," Ghiglieri declares. "I have a thousand years of work to do."

Lorenzo Ghiglieri, CHIEF JOSEPH, bronze, h 22, l 23

GINTER

GIORDANO

Bill Glass

Ginter, Mary Ann. Painter of acrylic abstracts of the Plains and the Southwest, born in Pawhuska, Oklahoma in 1926 and living in Annandale, Virginia. "My paintings are intended," she says, "to convey the beauty I perceive in all of nature. They are strong (many times people are surprised that they weren't done by a *man*) semi-abstract landscapes that often include hard-edge geometric forms as part of the overall design." She stresses that "any attempted explanation of her paintings merely detracts from their own individual statements. The statement that matters is the visible one contained in the paintings themselves."

After growing up in Columbus, Kansas she was a member of the honorary art fraternity at Kansas State Teachers College in Pittsburg, Kansas. She also lived in California before moving to Virginia where she has studied privately for eleven years. The constant theme in her work, she believes, is optimism, because "the great outside world is in fact a very good place indeed." Her goal is to give "each canvas a vitality of its own," to make "each one communicate that nature is good, colorful, exciting, and continually changing.

"My work," she says, "expresses a lifelong love for the myriad colors and shapes of the Plains and the Southwest." To simulate a "three-dimensional perspective," she uses "geometry, patterns of light, and texture to interrelate and communicate feelings of earth, sea, sky, and space in an orderly, disciplined, and architectural quality." Her paintings have been exhibited widely in federal and other public buildings in the Washington area. She is represented by Joan Cawley Gallery.

Giordano, Joseph. Realist watercolorist of wildlife and of "Situations in Nature" of domestic animals, born in New York City in 1935 and still living there. After graduating with art honors from The School of Industrial Arts at fifteen, he was employed at a publishing company "where his talent was discovered." His next job was at a greeting card company where he remained for 21 years. The promotions that he conceived and produced won "national recognition in the paper goods industry."

As a free-lance commercial artist, Giordano has illustrated books, packages, record album covers, and covers for the *Reader's Digest*. In addition, he is the president of a firm that licenses character designs that he creates, to publishers and manufacturers for application in product lines. One example is plush toys.

As a fine artist, Giordano paints in two formats. The first is a group of academic nature studies in almost photographic detail of wildlife subjects, particularly birds of prey, that are sold as Western Americana. The second is the whimsical "Situations in Nature" series of domestic animals that is also being published as limited edition prints. He spends his vacation time traveling to the national preserves in the United States and abroad. Many of the subjects that are used in his paintings are the result of hours spent photographing them in their natural habitats so he can "recompose various situations into the ultimate composition" back in the studio. For his watercolors, Giordano is represented by Trailside Galleries which has listed one at $4,000 in its 1982 catalog.

Glass, Bill. Cherokee sculptor of "strong Indian women" in clay and bronze, born in Tahlequah, Oklahoma in 1950 and living in Locust Grove, northeastern Oklahoma. "I don't want to get to where I'm stuck" in one direction, he stresses, "or where I have to do it a certain way. I want to use my research into my heritage, but I also want to be able to stylize it from time to time. I want to preserve something, but I also want to create something so that in the future another artist might say, 'that's what that Cherokee was doing'."

Raised on southwestern reservations where his father worked for the bureau of Indian Affairs, he did not think of art until he returned to his own tribal land. A business major at Central State College, he took an art class and discovered sculpture. "Getting into art stimulated me," he recalls. "I began to get into my tribe, to find out more about the Cherokee." He joined the Tahlequah Archaeological Society researching ancient symbolism to make his work historically accurate, studied at the Institute of American Indian Art in Santa Fe, and served as director of the Cherokee Arts and Crafts program for two years.

The choice of clay as his medium began at the Institute. "I like clay," he emphasizes. "Sometimes I will have a set plan for a whole piece, but the clay will give it a new twist or movement. It is as if the spirit of the clay is at work." The "strong woman" theme traces back to his great-grandmother who was on the Trail of Tears, "a subject that is so moving that artists will remember it forever." Written up in *Artists of the Rockies*, fall 1979, he has shown at Sloan-McKinney Galleries.

Bill Glass, MEDITATION
bronze, h 14½, l 11, w 12

Mary Ann Ginter, MOONSHINE,
acrylic/linen, 48 x 36

Joseph Giordano, RED SHOULDERED HAWK AND MEADOW VOLE, mixed media, 24 x 30

N. Glazier

glidden

Michael Gnatek Jr.

Glazier, Nancy. Wildlife painter of the Yellowstone, Tetons, and Black Hills, born in Salt Lake City, Utah in 1947 and living in Linden, Utah. "My paintings have become a direct link between the wild creatures and we civilized creatures," she said, "the canvas being the window. I can feel the spirit of each animal come alive at some point while I'm painting. It is almost like a hidden spark I must fan into a flame. It is the joy of creation."

Immersed in art and animals from an early age, Glazier took lessons from an old German artist in Cody, Wyoming, when she was fifteen. "He had white hair and a strong cigar," she recalls, "and he used to watch me paint, giving abrupt corrections. Once he caught me using black paint—then he really did get upset! I dreamed some day to paint like him. I hope he'll forgive me that I now use black." At eighteen, she decided to become an artist. "I just knew I had to paint. It was like a responsibility, not a choice. I was scared, yes, but I love adventure." She talks about years "of struggle and poverty, but it was worth it. The opposition fed my dreams."

Glazier moved back to Utah and began studying North American wildlife. She "set out alone to find the secret place of a moose cow and her calf, to spot the antelope buck who had spotted me long before, to gain time and trust with a royal elk, so close I can feel the moisture of his breath, to study eye to eye with a surly old bull bison." She is a member of Women Artists of the American West. Her prints are published by Wild Wings Gallery, and she is represented by Trailside and Laughing Horse Galleries.

Glidden, Kathy. Painter of New Mexican animals and people, particularly the Spanish Americans, born in Des Moines, Iowa in 1943 and living in Algodones, New Mexico since 1977. "I'm trying to become freer," she stresses. "I seldom sit down and decide to paint a particular thing. I like to just play around with colors and lines, pushing and pulling them, and when I see a familiar shape or color, I work on that. Do you see the mesas up in the right hand corner? Maybe I'll fool around a little up there."

Her mother was an artist who encouraged her talent. She studied at the Art Center throughout high school and became an art education major at the University of Kansas, also concentrating on drawing both the human figure and animals. After graduation, she moved to Albuquerque, New Mexico where she taught art to junior high school students. In 1973, she exhibited drawings at the State Fair. They were a hit. She was offered gallery representation and found that drawings had become her major outlet.

When she quit teaching after ten years, she said that she "never really thought that I could make a living from painting. In fact, I can't believe it when I wake up in the morning and don't have to leave here to go to work." She paints mainly from photographs, old magazines, and memories. The same faces can appear again and again. The faces are clear but the background floats off with "lost and found edges. I'd like that to be my trademark, if I have to be labeled at all." She now prefers working in acrylic. Written up in *Southwest Art* and *American Artist* in 1975, *Artists of the Rockies* in 1980, and *Art Voices/South* in 1981, she shows in her own studio as well as in Linda McAdoo and De Colores Art Galleries.

Gnatek, Michael, Jr. Painter of the American Indian, particularly in pencil and colored pencil, born in Hadley, Massachusetts in 1934 and living in Washington, D.C. since 1960. A commercial artist, he states that "the time I spend in my studio is not work. It is what I really enjoy. It's frustrating to be doing anything else. I'm a perfectionist, my own worst critic. I destroy one or two pieces for every one I finish, and there are five or six a year that I destroy after completion. I would much rather be satisfied than have a piece leave my hands that I'm unhappy with."

Raised on his father's farm near the Connecticut River, he demonstrated ability early and received several years of private instruction. After studying at Yale University's School of Design, he spent three years in the Marine Corps as an art instructor in Washington, D.C., where he has remained. He operates his own commercial art studio and each night averages six hours of fine art in his basement studio. He illustrated the "Jimmy, the eight-year-old heroin addict" article that won and lost the 1981 Nobel Prize.

He has changed from painting in loose, splashy oils in his fine arts to working in lead pencil and colored pencil to compose meticulously detailed drawings. He calls the process "tedious" and says that, as in watercolor painting, there is no room for error or overworking. As a subject, "the Indian has been my focal point for as long as I've been drawing." Research is through correspondence, especially with the Shushoni Mission, "but sometimes I go overboard on costuming." Gnatek is featured in the American Western Collection for 1982, with drawings priced at $2,600. He is represented by Morris Fine Arts Gallery.

Nancy Glazier, MATRIARCH, oil, 30 x 40

Kathy Gliddin, DONKEYS AT LAS GOLANDRINAS
(1980), acrylic, 32 x 24

Michael Gnatek, SITTING BULL, colored pencil, 24 x 29

Rod Goebel (signature)

Goebel, Rod. Painter of the Southwestern landscape "in powerful colors, lights, and shadows," born in Austin, Texas in 1946 and living in El Prado, New Mexico. "I grew up in the mountains of Mexico and Colorado," he recalls. "I had an empathy with what I saw in nature as a child. It was a feeling that what I saw I could do. Some people ask how they can learn to paint. That was never a question I asked myself. I just painted because I wanted to—I had to."

When he was eighteen and had a brush with death, he began to paint seriously. Formal instruction started at the University of New Mexico, followed by the Colorado Institute of Art and private training in portraiture. "There is no end to learning about art," he observes, "especially color. I'm fascinated by color. I'm not an intellectual painter, but rather a physical or emotional one. Many of my paintings are based on intellectual concepts of color or design, but as soon as I begin to work, the intellectual process ends.

"There are many variables that affect how I will approach a particular subject. Sometimes a subject will suggest how it is to be painted. I don't take a literal interpretation of nature, but rather I rearrange it in a more perfect, idealized whole. My paintings are purely personal things. I feel a kind of physical tension in responding to beauty. I want people to feel what I feel, to feel by seeing, to see in their muscles." Goebel was featured in *Southwest Art*, August 1980. He is one of the Taos Six, believing that "Taos has always had a special quality about it." A member of the National Academy of Western Art, he exhibited in the Peking, China, show and is represented by Trailside Galleries.

Rod Goebel, SEPTEMBER STILL LIFE, oil, 36 x 30

Ted Goerschner *Walt Gonske*
NAWA

Goerschner, Ted. Impressionist oil painter of Southwestern canyon landscapes, born on the East Coast about 1935 and living in Prescott, Arizona. "Canyons," he observes, "are totally different. Their shapes, size, colors, character, and moods are constantly changing. They are the beauty marks of the earth. The monoliths are dramatic, and the bottom where the water collects and invites life and regeneration tells the story. It is almost theology here. Canyons and their colors have a kind of nobility."

At six, his family spent a year in Arizona that determined his career. He was also motivated by his grandfather, "a Renaissance man" as a cabinetmaker and artist, "by the time I completed high school there was no other answer but art. It was the only life I really wanted, even in times when I would walk away from my palette and work as a finish carpenter to pay the bills." After two years in the infantry in the Korean War, he studied at the Newark School of Fine and Industrial Art, the University of Tampa, the Art Students League, and Temple University.

By 1971, he was established as an Impressionist oil painter. He left Florida for Arizona because "the demographics of art today are much the same as the social demographics. I fit in here, and the subject matter is unending. It's all earthtones, all from primary colors. Terra rosa dominates, but my palette is going down from twenty to eleven or twelve." He has not yet painted the Grand Canyon, asking "how do you do the face of the earth on a piece of canvas? You can only do a splinter of the Canyon." Written up in *Southwest Art*, July 1981, and featured in *Twenty Oil Painters and How They Work*, he is represented by El Prado Gallery of Art.

Gonske, Walt. Painter, born in Newark, New Jersey in 1942 and living in Taos, New Mexico since 1972. In his oils, his aim is to preserve the past by making a visual record of the old structures and scenes of the Southwest before they are destroyed. "Time hasn't yet changed in the West as it has in the East," he says. "The super reality is still here, and so is a new breed who appreciates it."

After graduating from the Newark School of Fine Arts, Gonske studied with Frank Reilly, a famous illustrator, and later at the Art Students League in New York City. He then became a free-lance illustrator in New York, fulfilling commissions for top publications like *Esquire, Life, Playboy,* and *The New Yorker.* "An illustrator's background is great training," he declares, "but it's a dead end if you don't move on. An artist grows and changes simply because he is creative. If he doesn't, he might as well put his materials in cold storage."

In New Mexico, "all my drawings and painting are done in my studio, working from 35mm slides taken with a Nikon FTN camera. This gives me great depth of field. When I find what interests me on a scouting trip, I fire off the camera a hundred times. I'll pick out several shots for paintings and more often than not, I'll use them pretty much as they were taken, changing composition, values, or color when necessary. I also might work from two slides, using the background from one and the center of interest from another." Gonske is a member of the National Academy of Western Art and his work is in the Gilcrease Institute. Profiled in *Southwest Art*, February 1975, he shows in Pelham and Trailside Galleries.

Walt Gonske, BLACKFEET CEREMONIAL DANCERS, oil/canvas, 44 x 32

Ted Goerschner, CANYON SPECTRUM, oil, 30 x 36

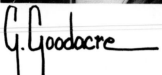

G. Goodacre

Veryl Goodnight

Goodacre, Glenna. Realist sculptor and painter of the figure, born in Lubbock, Texas in 1939 and living in Boulder, Colorado. "I grew up around cowboys in west Texas," she observes, "and I just don't find them all that fascinating. And I do not do horses. I'm not into animals at all. I'm into people. Indians have grown to be dominant themes in my work, and I do a lot of women because too few artists have really told their story well. I want to be thought of as a 'portrayer of people.'

"Fortunately, my parents recognized that I had talent so they arranged for me to receive private lessons. Beyond that, I majored in art all through school." She graduated from Colorado College and later studied at the Art Students League in New York City. Told by an instructor that she could never sculpt, she did not begin until 1971, but she doesn't believe that her sculpture "would be as successful if I hadn't painted. After you work with three dimensionals, then go back to paintings, you discover how much one complements the other.

"I want my work to do more than just stare out at people. Western art demands that you do more than just present a head study. I try to tell a different story about the people in my art. I always try to show happy Indians, especially when I work with children. Faces fascintate me, and I present the colorful, happy people that appeal to me." She is listed in *Who's Who in American Art* and was featured in *Southwest Art*, December 1976 and *Artists of the Rockies*, winter 1976. An exhibitor in the Peking, China, show, she has done heroic statues, is a member of the National Sculpture Society and the National Academy of Western Art, and is represented by Driscol Gallery and O'Brien's Art Emporium.

Goodnight, Veryl. Traditional sculptor and painter of wildlife, born in Denver, Colorado in 1947 and living in Englewood, a suburb of Denver. "It has become very unpopular," she says, "to admit that photography is used as an aid in art. And I can't understand why. When I'm studying an animal that is active, it would be a waste of time to make sketches. And of course I'd have no time at all to study the behavior. But if I use the camera, sometimes I record it all."

She opened her first studio at twenty and is largely self-taught, except for "the many friends and peers that I've drawn and painted with over the years. Even though I don't have an impressive list of schools to spiel off, my background in art is strong." The great-grandniece of Charlie Goodnight who charted a cattle trail from Texas to Montana, her ambition is "to ride the whole trail on horseback and do a series of paintings and bronzes of animals that inhabit the route."

The first step in her verification of authenticity in sculpting is field observation. The second is selecting photographs from her files to locate a group of likenesses that allow her to study each part of the anatomy separately. After the model is done, the third step is comparison of the sculpture with the live animal. Then, she has the piece critiqued by experts in wildlife and in sculpture. If the model passes, she still puts it away for long enough to let her look at it objectively again. She is a member of the Society of Animal Artists, has been featured in *Southwest Art*, July 1977 and *Art West*, December 1980, was in the Peking, China, show, exhibits with the Northwest Rendezvous Group, and is represented by Driscol Gallery.

Glenna Goodacre, NOT ALONE, bronze, h 16

Veryl Goodnight, HUNTER ALONG THE RIMROCK, bronze, h 19, l 21½

RC Gorman

Gorman, Rudolph Charles. "The Picasso of Indian artists," painting Navajo women in many media, born on the Navajo Reservation, Canyon de Chelly, Arizona in 1932 and living in Las Colonias, New Mexico near Taos since 1968. "I wish people would quit pushing my being Indian," he says. "The only time I was interviewed as if I were a normal person was by the Jewish Press in Tucson. It was the first time I felt international and almost white."

With sandpainters, silversmiths, weavers, chanters, and holy men in his ancestry, he lived a traditional Navajo life as a child, learning the Navajo ways and language. "When I was nine, in a strict Catholic boarding school," he writes, he developed the sandwich recipe: "While nuns are looking the other way, mash up some prunes with a fork, spread the mixture between two pieces of bread, and stick it in your shirt to eat later during chapel." After serving in the Navy and attending Northern Arizona University, he received a grant from the Navajo tribe to study in Mexico and reports that "the first time I went and saw Orozco's work, I was stunned. It was so close to my own people. Rivera went to Europe to discover himself. I went to Mexico and discovered Rivera and myself. Had I not gone to Mexico, I would have probably ended up depicting demented Indians or blue deer leaping over purple butterflies."

Gorman is "well known for his hospitality, friendliness, gregariousness, and pleasure in eating and fine wines." There are four books on him, *The Lithographs, The Posters, The Drawings,* and *Nudes and Foods.* He is represented by his own Navajo Galleries in Taos and Albuquerque and has been written up in *Southwest Art,* May 1974 and June 1978.

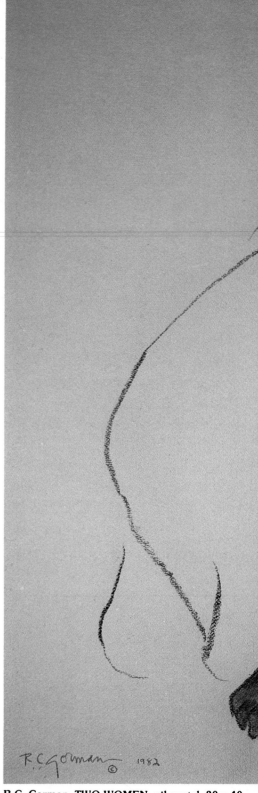

R.C. Gorman, TWO WOMEN, oil pastel, 30 x 40

Walter Graham (signature)

Joe Grandee (signature)

Don Gray (signature)

Graham, Walter. Realist painter in oil and watercolor and sculptor in bronze, born in Toledo, Illinois in 1903 and living in Wenatchee, Washington since 1950. "Even though the composition and design of a painting are based on the abstract," he points out, "the final result should have realism that needs no explanation." A commercial artist whose work as a cowboy on a Wyoming ranch gave him the background for Western and outdoors paintings, realism was to him a natural style.

Raised in Chicago, Graham attended the Chicago Academy of Fine Arts Institute and had private instruction. He became an illustrator for Street and Smith Publishers, painting cover art for *Western Story, Western Life, Appaloosa News,* and other magazines until 1939 when he helped form a commercial art studio in Chicago. During the summers, he went to Wyoming and Montana to paint and sketch. In 1950, he decided to become a full-time painter of animals and historical Western subjects. He sold his interest in the studio and moved to the West Coast.

In Washington, commissions for paintings, murals, and statuary were frequent, including sculpture for an industrial building and for bank buildings in Idaho and Washington, "Historical California" ranch paintings for the California Beef Commission, paintings for the Montana Cattle Association, paintings and murals of wildlife for the Alaska Ferry System, murals for the Rocky Reach Dam in Washington, paintings for the ocean liner "Polar Star," and a fountain sculpture for a Spokane bank. A member of the Society of Animal Artists, Graham is listed in *Who's Who in American Art,* has been featured in *Western Painting Today,* and is represented by Lesli Art.

Grandee, Joe Ruiz. Realist oil painter and sculptor of the Old West from the mountain man era to the 1890s, born in Dallas, Texas in 1929 and living in Arlington, Texas. "The American character," he believes, "was shaped by the Westward movement. It took a certain breed of highly individual people to accomplish what they did. Out there, they developed qualities that exemplify the American character. They were the ones who made this country. I am trying to portray these qualities in my paintings."

A hernia operation at six weeks restrained Grandee's physical activity in the rooming house his parents owned and as a child led to quiet play with toy soldiers and sketching. When at nineteen he saw Western landscape paintings by Thomas Moran, he "knew I had to do this too." He had been taking a correspondence course in illustration but now he bought oil paints and enrolled in the Aunspaugh School of Art in Dallas. After two years operating a small ranch, he devoted himself to painting and by 1956 was a full-time professional.

In the beginning, he went to antique and art shows and played the flamboyant buckskin-clad rustic. Since then, he has been the first "official state artist" of Texas, first to sell a contemporary Western painting for more than $10,000, and first Western artist to have a comprehensive exhibition at the Capitol in Washington. He was commissioned to paint Ronald Reagan for "Death Valley Days," the wedding portrait for Lyndon Johnson's daughter, and a Texas Ranger for Richard Nixon. Listed in *Who's Who in American Art,* he has been featured in *Southwest Art* and *People Weekly.* His biography is *The West Still Lives.* He is published by American Masters Foundation and represented by Corpus Christi Art and One Main Galleries.

Gray, Don. Super-realist painter of "stark and lonely" Oregon born in La Grande, northeast Oregon in 1948 and living in nearby Union since 1971. "I'm a Western person," he declares. "I was born and raised here and have attitudes that I think are uniquely Western. I paint things that are inherently Western because they're out here where I live. I like the contrasts you get in eastern Oregon, and I'm not just talking about visual contrasts, but psychological contrasts.

"I always felt, even in my early years, that I wanted to do something that had to do with art, but it never really entered my mind that you could just paint for a living. I got a degree in education instead, thinking that I'll teach art and that way be able to make a living, but teaching was not for me. To start painting full time, we moved back to eastern Oregon in 1971 and lived on a ranch. I showed that first year's work at a gallery in Portland. It was a complete sellout.

"Earlier in my painting, I was interested in the work of Andrew Wyeth and even visited him in Pennsylvania. I don't feel that way anymore. There must come a time when you realize you are you. Lately, I've been trying a direct approach, starting with a broad bristle brush, brushing the shapes and designs directly on the panel. I come in later and refine it, as I work the painting up. My composition is intuitive, rather than self-conscious. I like to create a painting that has some kind of unusual quality to it." Gray has had seven one-person shows, has had feature articles in *Art West* and *Southwest Art,* and is represented by Fowler's and by Schmuland and Hastings. He finds it irksome to have to "tape my smile on" to deal with galleries and customers.

Walter Graham, INDIAN VILLAGE, oil, 20 x 24

Don Gray, THE JIGGER BOSS (1981), alkyd/masonite, 26½ x 24

Joe Grandee, WOLVES OF THE DESERT DEMAND TRESPASSERS RANSOM, oil, 38 x 52

Greer, A.D. Traditional oil painter of Western landscapes and still lifes, born in Pondcreek, Oklahoma in 1904 and living in Austin, Texas since 1965. "I was expelled from public school for drawing in class," he recalls. "Some of the drawings were risque, and there was talk of sending me to the reform school. The probate judge, however, was a woman. She said I belonged in an art school, not in a reform school.

"I was about seventeen before I started painting with watercolors, and then I switched to oils when I was twenty. The first oil painting I did sold for $50. Even if I couldn't *sell* something, I'd draw a picture for something to eat. I took whatever I could get a hold of for money that was honest. In 1941, I was doing stage curtains, fine art for galleries, hustling pool. A man came to me and said he wanted to publish two of my paintings. I said, 'If I were your son, would you advise me to do this?' He said, 'Sure,' and so I did it.

"One of the paintings reproduced eventually sold more than a million copies. From then on, I didn't have to worry about selling. As soon as I'd get one done, I'd take it to a dealer and they'd *buy* it. If I see a thing—say the North end of the Grand Canyon—I look at it until I *memorize* it, and then I fly back to Austin and paint it. I also have files of pictures, but I don't paint *from* those pictures. If I would want to paint some grapes, I have a lot of pictures of grapes, and the night before I started I might take those pictures out and look at them, but then I'd put them away, go to bed, and get up the next morning and start painting." His larger landscapes have been sold for $100,000 by American Fine Arts Gallery, his exclusive representative since 1975.

A.D. Greer, A GOLDEN MOMENT, oil, 36 x 48

R.V. Greeves

Greeves, Richard V. Traditional sculptor of bronze Indians, born in St. Louis, Missouri in 1925 and living in Fort Washakie, Wyoming on the Wind River Indian Reservation since 1951. "I talked to a young commercial artist who had a painting of an old saddle, a .22 rifle, and a bunch of .44-40 caliber bullets. He'd photographed the 'still life,' projected it on the canvas and painted it, and then sold it for one hell of a price because it was Western art. Thank God you can't render sculpture photographically."

The son of an Italian tile layer, Greeves left home at 15. "I guess you might say that the Indian is my real love," he observes. "I've made them my life's work, and I was doing it long before it became popular. A lot of artists think you can know the Indian by coming out here on weekends, but you can't. You've got to love and hate with them. There's a magic for me here. I just feel it, the same feelings I had when I first came here as a kid. Right now, I'm working on a whole series of bronzes to try and capture this mysterious beyond of the Indian.

"You've got to get the inside right before you can get the outside right, and you've got to get the outside right before you can even begin to create a feeling or mood. If your work shows pain, you should be able to tear a clay finger off and throw it on the table, and by God, you should be able to look at that finger and see pain." Greeves exhibited in the Peking, China, show and is a member of the National Academy of Western Art where he received the gold medal in 1976 and 1979, the silver in 1978, and the Prix de West in 1977. He was featured in *Southwest Art*, summer 1975, and has his own gallery.

Richard V. Greeves, KIOWA, bronze, h 6

Russell Ulysses Greer

★ Martin Grelle

Grieves

Greer, Russell Ulysses. Carver of cottonwood figurines of Indians, born in Minnesota in 1922 and living in Bend, Oregon since 1968. Greer found painting to be "very competitive among lots of fine artists" and so concentrated on "the less crowded market for woodcarvings." He says that he likes "to see a perfection of details, but more important is the overall composition and expression."

At the age of seven, Greer moved with his family to Kalispell, in northwestern Montana. Toys and game pieces were carved from firewood with a pocket knife. After graduation from high school, he worked with his father as a timber faller and on remote ranches near the Flathead and Blackfoot reservations. Through the years, he continued carving as a hobby and in 1963 completed a home art course from the Famous Artists School. He also collected reference materials on Indians, including Curtis photographs.

In 1968, Greer moved to Oregon, "too young to retire but too old to work." Seven years later, his family dentist asked to display the figures in his office and the interest that developed led Greer to decide to carve full time. He uses cottonwood and has found "the best carving bark" in British Columbia. Lightning-struck cottonwoods are at a premium because they have the thickest bark. Features are shaped with chisels, gouges, and a small electric drill. Details of fur, feathers, beads, and hair ornaments are scribed, leaving uncut portions of the gray bark slab to serve as rough framing. Greer says that oil and varnish on the carving produce "the best natural skin tone for Indians' faces." His gallery is Husberg Fine Arts Gallery.

Grelle, Martin Glen. Realist painter and sketcher of contemporary cowboys of the Texas foothills in all media, particularly acrylic and pencil, born in Clifton, Texas in 1954 and living there since. After he won the gold medal for drawing and the Best in Show award at the American Indian and Cowboy Artists show in 1979, one of his sponsors said that "this is the first time, to my knowledge, that a drawing has won Best in Show, not just at San Dimas but in any Western art show. Usually it is a monumental oil painting."

Born on a small farm outside Clifton, Grelle's family moved when his father became the Clifton consignee for an oil company. Grelle first showed interest in art in elementary school, but sports soon took priority and he was president of his class and a member of the National Honor Society while winning painting awards. After graduation from high school in 1973, he worked for his father as a truck driver until he began taking painting more seriously. When he sought criticism from the artist James Boren, he was encouraged to keep painting.

He had his first one-artist show in 1974, attended McLennon Community College for a semester in 1975, and in 1976 had his second one-artist show. Fourteen of seventeen paintings were sold on opening night. The following year he won the bronze medal for drawing at the AICA show, and has sold out each year since then. By 1980, he was in a range of invitational shows and auctions and his paintings were on the covers of *Gulf Coast Cattleman*. His subjects are from central Texas, the hills, creeks, old houses, and neighbors, and his life is divided among art, community, church, and family. He was named to *Outstanding Young Men of America*, and is represented by Texas Art Gallery.

Grieves, Bob. Traditional sculptor of bronze statuettes of mountain men in the early West, born in Henry County, Ohio in 1922 and living in Detroit, Michigan. "Wax," he emphasizes, "doesn't have the same character as metal. With wax, you create the form, but once you cast it in bronze, it takes on life. When you put the patina on, you begin to feel things you didn't feel before. It's an emotion you're bringing out."

Leaving home when he fifteen "so my dad would have one less kid to feed," he worked on a cattle ranch in western Nebraska for his room and board. "I loved that country, and it's as though all the things that happened then were only yesterday." During World War II, he was a gunner in the Air Force, then worked in the Union Stockyards in Chicago and took night courses at the Art Institute. Since then, "when a horse moves, it's as though I can see inside him, just what his bones and muscles are doing, and when I study a man's anatomy, I relate it to the bones of a horse."

Grieves established a sign business that prospered and painted in his spare time "but I was never quite satisfied." In 1970, he tried carving, "but now I found myself fascinated by it. First I'd do a sketch with clay, and before I knew it I was doing just ceramic sculpture. An artist friend told me I'd never get anywhere unless I learned to handle bronze, so I started visiting foundries to find out about the casting process. A sculptor who turns his work over to a foundry has missed one of the most important parts of the creative process." Written up in *Southwest Art*, December 1980, Grieves is represented by El Prado Gallery of Art.

Bob Grieves, WITHOUT A BLAZE, bronze, h 31½, l 28

Russell Greer, SCOUTING PARTY, woodcarving, h 38, l 5½, d 6

Martin Grelle, MISERY LOVES COMPANY, acrylic, 18 x 24

R. Grinnell *Gwy*

Grinnell, Roy. Oil painter of the historic American West, born in Santa Barbara, California in 1934 and living in Santa Fe, New Mexico since 1978. "Western art is never repetitious," he points out. "I might come across a bit of Indian lore or something about the Old West I didn't know and be led off in different directions. I'll never get to a point where I won't discover new material. I'll never be able to paint all of it."

Following graduation from high school in Santa Barbara, he enlisted in the Navy for four years, then entered the Art Center School of Design in Los Angeles for one semester. He exhausted the G.I. Bill benefits by changing his major, and was able to get back into art only by winning a scholarship. After art school, "New York was the best possible training ground," he says. "There is no way I could have replaced the education I received from the seasoned illustrators I met there. I had to have so many styles and techniques." He stayed twelve years, and "came to a point where I had to break away because there were stories I wanted to tell."

In 1975, he returned to California where he continued to free lance but combined commercial art with more and more painting. When he moved to Santa Fe, he was painting full time. "There is also an element of pressure in fine art," he explains. "It's not the monetary thing, it's the opportunity to tell a story and have it last. A finished painting will be handed down within a family, or possibly go to a museum. That's what it's all about." He is now participating in major invitational shows, has become a member of the Society of American Historical Artists, and is represented by Wadle Galleries.

Gwyn, Woody. Realist painter of the northern New Mexico landscape in oil and acrylic, born in San Antonio, Texas in 1944 and living in Galisteo, New Mexico since 1976. "I've found that if I tell the truth, no more and no less," he explains, "people respond to it. I am a painter working in the Realist Tradition. If my work is to be tagged Post-Modernist landscape, then fine, but that is for others to decide—my work is my response to reality—realism.

"I was raised in Midland in west Texas. I went to the Pennsylvania Academy of Fine Arts in 1964 and returned to Texas and began my career as a painter. My main impulse has always been around landscape and I've always loved the work of the great landscape painters." When he reached what he calls a "death rattle" in the Texas paintings of hills, sky, and highways, he decided "that New Mexico was the place for me and moved first to Los Cerrillos in 1975." The following year, he was accepted as one of "12 Contemporary Artists in New Mexico" and exhibited at the university.

"The artist's greatest tool is concentration," he points out. "It's like meditation, and when the subject starts clicking, it's sort of like a tone sounding in your head, a silent tone. You just stand out of the way and let the truth come through. All art that matters responds in that way to reality. The important thing is not so much to have an idea or concept about your subject, but to respond to it directly and spontaneously. Art has nothing to do with ideas, theories, or interpretation. I don't impose expectations anymore. Intellect has no place in art." Featured in traveling exhibitions and public collections, he is represented by Heydt/Bair and Davis & McClain Galleries.

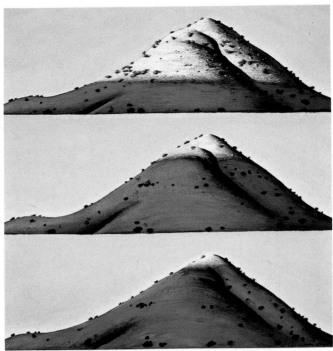

Woody Gwyn, DAWN ASCENSION, acrylic, 30 x 32

Roy Grinnell, AFTER THE HUNT, oil, 14 x 18

Hadley, Michael. Traditional painter of the Western landscape from the northern Rocky Mountains to the red rock country of Arizona, born in Ogden, Utah in 1948 and living in Centerville, Utah. "I have wanted a career in art for as long as I can remember," he says. "At an early age, I began experimenting with watercolors and oils, and at twelve was staying after school to watch one of my teachers paint. During my senior year in high school, I set up a studio and began to paint landscapes in oil.

"A painting by Farrell Collett in the principal's office of my school intrigued me, and fall semester at Weber State found me in a painting class studying under Professor Collett, who guided me in the fundamentals of design, color, and authenticity in painting the West, and was the primary influence in shaping my career. During my junior year in college, I accepted a call from the Church of Jesus Christ of Latter-Day Saints to serve a full-time two year mission in the Eastern states. What seemed difficult became a dream come true as I spent a year near the Metropolitan Museum of Art. When I returned, I enrolled at Brigham Young University, finishing in 1975 with a BA.

"When I found a summer job in Jackson, Wyoming, close to Yellowstone and Grand Teton National Parks, hard work began to pay off and my paintings began selling quickly. After several trips to Sedona and the Grand Canyon area beginning in 1981, the landscape became so irresistible to paint that a whole new avenue opened itself to me. The Grand Canyon is by far the most challenging subject that I have ever painted. The problems with perspective, color, and design make this Arizona landscape the premier among all landscapes." Hadley is represented by El Prado Gallery of Art.

Hagel, Frank D. Realist-Impressionist painter and sculptor of the historical Northwest, the trappers, mountain men, Indians, and wildlife, born in Kalispell, Montana and living there since 1972. "I like to keep a piece of sculpture going at the same time as I'm working on my paintings," Hagel states. "To me, being able to change media helps me produce better results in both. If I work too long with either one, I get bored."

After trying ranching, rodeoing, logging, and construction, Hagel was in the U.S. Navy from 1952 through 1955 and then graduated from the Art Center College of Design in Los Angeles in 1959. He moved to Detroit as an illustrator and by 1968 "had a job that required me to be there only during the 'car season,' January to August. Then I could spend the fall out here in Montana—I could paint and do some big game guiding. By 1972 I knew I couldn't put it off anymore, so we moved."

When the big game hunting season opens, Hagel is out of the studio and on the trail. "I do a lot of action sketches and also shoot a lot of pictures with telephoto lenses," he says. When the season ends in October, he packs out the animals and the gear and heads back to Kalispell. The first job is to sort out subjects for painting and sculpting, and then he works through June on an eight to five schedule. "I learned some rules as a commercial artist that help me keep at work even during my 'down' periods." He has designed and sculpted medals and painted murals. At the Kalispell Auction in 1980, a painting brought $3,000. He was featured in *Southwest Art*, October 1977, and is represented by Ponderosa Gallery and Settlers West Galleries.

Haines, Evelyn F. Watercolorist of Western subjects, particularly animal portraits, born in Pawnee, Colorado in 1920 and living in Scottsdale, Arizona. "Being a woman has interfered with my career," she says, "but not as much now as it did. A gallery in Tucson once told me that they couldn't sell women's work, even if the woman painted like a man. I wasn't sure what that meant, but I was sure it was his problem and not mine.

"Raised in a house my great-grandfather built on land he had homesteaded, I can't remember when I did not paint. My mother always encouraged me. There were many days spent sketching the horses on our farm. I became a professional in 1965. Painting can be a career; all that is needed is a clean sheet of watercolor paper and the courage to make the first mark. I do not paint on location. The air and the sun dry the paper; the bugs have a holiday. I work in the comfort of my studio. The radio is tuned to a music station. I adjust the lights and get a cup of coffee. By this time it is 9 a.m. If all goes well, I work until 4 p.m.

"Finishing a painting includes daydreaming and searching for authentic material. Animal portraits are slow but landscapes move along at a faster pace. If the painting goes sour, I work on address lists, wrap paintings and check inventories, cut mats, and photograph. There is more to the profession of an artist than the actual painting of the picture. Most men artists have their wives doing all of the 'other' jobs." Her private collectors include President and Mrs. Reagan. Honored as a distinguished alumna in art from Colorado Women's College, her gallery is Trailside.

Evelyn F. Haines, STARS AT NIGHT, watercolor/canvas, 16 x 30

Michael Hadley, EVENING WALKS SOFTLY, oil, 18 x 24

Frank Hagel, THE HIGH ROLLERS, oil, 20 x 34,

Joe Halko *B Haller*

Halko, Joe. North American wildlife artist in acrylic and oil and sculptor in bronze, born near Great Falls, Montana in 1940 and still living there. "I enjoy leaving my cozy home to camp out in the wilderness," Halko states, "even under miserable conditions. It's an exhilarating feeling and I appreciate it that the animals are out there too, experiencing it day in and day out."

After growing up on the family farm, he spent two years in the Army and studied art briefly in New York City. Back in Great Falls, he was hired as a taxidermist in a sporting goods store, earned a degree in biology at the College of Great Falls, and then returned to taxidermy until 1976 when he became a full-time artist. "Taxidermy is an art," he points out, "but in sculpture you can work with surface texture. Animals are furry or feathery whereas sculpture is rigid. Trying to give the illusion of softness, life, and movement is fascinating. I try to create the appearance of lots of feathers or hair without overdoing detail.

"Imagine an animal in motion," he adds. "There are only a few gestures that really look graceful. If you need more feeling of strength or emotion, you may have to do something anatomically incorrect to enhance whatever you are trying to convey, without your viewers knowing you have done it." A hunter, he contributes a bronze to Ducks Unlimited every year and has received $2,000 for a "Quick Draw" sculpture made in 30 minutes. He is listed in *Who's Who in American Art*, is a member of the Northwest Rendezvous Group and the Society of Animal Artists, was featured in *Art West*, March 1980, and exhibits at Fowler's and Settlers West Galleries where his painting was listed at $2,800 in the 1981 silent auction.

Haller, Bettie. Representational oil painter of ranch and pioneer life, born in Austin, Texas in 1946 and living in Amarillo, Texas. "An artist doesn't need to paint 'The Last Supper'," she says, "for the art to point toward God. Cowboys and cowgirls are people, and God moves in their lives today just as he moved in the lives of those written in the Bible. If I can convey His love to the viewers of my work, then I shall feel that my art has served a mighty purpose.

"As far back as I can remember, I watched my father, the Texas Hill Country artist Palmer Chrisman, paint. He could pour into me concentrated knowledge about art that would've taken me years to discover by trial and error. In 1969, I graduated from Texas Tech with a Bachelor of Advertising Arts degree. My first job was doing illustrations for a paper. Next I worked as an illustrator for a research organization, but I wasn't satisfied with my art career because I wanted to create work so I began doing Westerns in oils.

"People usually ask me why am I, a woman, doing Western art. My decision was greatly influenced by Texas Tech. We were encouraged to draw what we could see, and I saw a Western environment. I use cowboys and pioneer families to express feelings of nostalgia and sentimentality to the viewer. People also ask why I sign my name 'B. Haller.' The answer is that if they know I'm a female from the first moment they see the work, they might not give me a fighting chance! After they've established that they like it and find out I'm a woman artist, it doesn't seem to affect their opinion so much. I was invited to be in the OS Ranch, Nebraskaland Days, and Western Heritage in Colorado shows. Galleries representing me are Setting Sun and The Country Framer."

Joe Halko, INTO THE BASIN, bronze, h 7, l 14

Bettie Haller, THE GIFT, oil, 24 x 30

Hallmark, George. Realistic painter of the contemporary Texas cowboy in oil, mixed media (colored pencil, pastel, tempera, and acrylic) and sculpture, born in Cleburne, Texas in 1949, and living in Kopperl, Texas, in northern Bosque County. "My favorite subject matter," he observes, "is old cowboys. I enjoy meeting and talking to them. I feel I learn so much from them. They don't hesitate to tell you when something's wrong.

"I graduated from high school in 1967. My school had no art education and I didn't know art schools existed until much later. I attended Tarrant County Junior College, majoring in art, and took courses at Texas Christian University. Most colleges today teach that being a realist is 'old hat.' I could never believe that, and eventually dropped out and began educating myself. After working five years as a commercial artist for an architectural firm, I free-lanced for four years. During the summer of 1979, I studied with William Whitaker at Brigham Young University.

"I paint what I grew up loving. The cowboys of today are just as important as those 100 years ago, and also important are the women and children behind these men. Second, I paint what I know best. If I had grown up in New England, I'd paint seascapes. Today's artists can make a pretty good living, and the general public doesn't treat us as low-life. This is sort of a change from the past. Texas Art Press has reproduced one painting in a limited edition print. I have had several successful one-person shows including one for Texas Art Gallery where I have shown for five years and have been in four of their *Preview* shows. I also show with Trailside Galleries." In *Preview '81* his painting sold for $4,800.

Hampton, John Wade. Painter and sculptor of the Old West, born in New York City in 1918 and living in Scottsdale, Arizona. "I loved old Tom Mix movies," he remembers. "All boys are interested in cowboys, but most of 'em outgrow it after they get practical-minded. I never have got practical-minded ... yet. I like to paint the romance of the West, not somebody getting a saddlesore or a hernia."

After practicing roping with his mother's clothesline in Brooklyn, Hampton won first prize in a rodeo sketching contest in 1935. He began illustrating Western pulp magazines while he was in high school and served in Intelligence in World War II. On the proceeds of assisting Fred Harman in drawing the comic strip "Red Ryder," Hampton bought a small ranch near Silver City, New Mexico, and "became a one-cow cowboy" in order to act out the life so he could draw it. The experience he gained was part of the credo of the Cowboy Artists of America he helped form. He says that "it had to be a part of the recipe that to depict range life correctly, the artist had to know how to do some cowpunchin'. It's as simple as that. And this half-breed cross between an artist and a cowboy produces a cowboy-artist." After "we set the stage," he observes, "young kids, today, are making a killing in Western art."

In 1977, Hampton tried his first bronze and promptly won the gold medal at the CAA show. He now "likes doing bronzes" because he can "keep one for himself" and "the money is better than in paintings." Hampton was featured in *Southwest Art*, May 1974 and *Art West*, November 1980. He is listed in *Who's Who in American Art* and has exhibited internationally.

Hampton, Roy. Realist painter of Western portraits, horses in action, and landscapes, born in Los Angeles in 1923 and living in Woodland Hills, California. He comments that he "likes all types of art, but I always preferred Western movies and more or less preferred Western art because of it. American Indian art and Western art are original to our country. All other types of art are foreign ideas that have been transported to America. Western art is home-grown. It is our own.

"I rode my horse to school," George Leroy Hampton remembers, "and was always drawing." During World War II he was in the Submarine Service at Pearl Harbor and from 1946 to 1947 worked for Walt Disney Studios as an animator. "We had three life drawing classes during the week plus three in the evenings," he says. "Then I went to college for awhile." He built furniture, tried law school, sold, taught judo, became vice president of a mortgage company, and so "let 25 years go by and did not do any art until a car wreck changed my life and helped lead me back to art. I have been a full time artist since 1972."

Hampton now travels the West in a motor home. He declares that artists do live longer: "They're always looking forward to the next thing." After saying he is not sure about awards, he admits to having won the gold medal at the 1981 American Indian and Cowboy Artists show and to being in *Who's Who in American Art*. The three things he'll "never forget" include winning a gold medal in competition with CAA and NAWA artists, painting John Wayne, and spending a day with a medicine man. Hampton was featured in *Southwest Art*, August 1981, limits his galleries to those where he can have personal contact, and is represented by The White Gallery.

Roy Hampton, THE YOUNG BRIDE, oil, 20 x 24

John Wade Hampton, TURNING THE LEADERS, bronze, h 20, l 30

George Hallmark, SOMETIMES IT'S HELL GETTIN' STARTED, oil, 24 x 36

Una Hanbury

James M. Haney

Hanbury, Una. Impressionist sculptor of portraits and horses in bronze and stone, born in Kent, England in 1909 and living in Santa Fe, New Mexico since 1970. "My profession is often misunderstood," she explains. "The real role of a sculptor is essentially mental—the ability to envision a three dimensional work of art. Who actually executes the design has little to do with the concept. At least 50 percent of the work is thinking up the idea. Much study is involved in asking questions like what is the meaning of this thing.

"I grew up in the south of England and spent my childhood galloping on my pony. That style of living no longer exists. I had sculpting lessons by the time I was seven. I was told that that was what I was to be and I didn't question it. Much later, I studied painting for three years" in France. She also graduated from the Royal Academy of Fine Art in London and studied with sculptor Jacob Epstein. She left England for Washington, D.C., in 1944 to work at the British Embassy.

"I was a full-time sculptor in Washington when I could afford to be, but I had some difficult times." Her financial condition eased when she went into home construction and she was able to go back to sculpting, particularly portrait heads. She says that "because portraits expose a person's innermost being, one has to be very careful and gentle." She recognizes that she is "on the crest of a wave, so it is the best time of my life." She has been written up in Broder's *Bronzes of the American West, Artists of the Rockies*, summer 1979, and *Southwest Art*, August 1980, is listed in *Who's Who in American Art*, and is represented by Munson and Carson Galleries.

Haney, James M. Still-life painter specializing in Southwestern Indian artifacts, born in Matador, Texas in 1949 and living in Amarillo, Texas. "I have a container fetish," he says. "Even as a child, I loved to play with cardboard boxes. I love baskets and pots. Old broken things fascinate me. They tell a story. I like to combine different cultures and different ages. I see containers as mankind's oldest friends."

Haney calls himself a "Texas farm boy from Seminole." When he decided to go to West Texas State University to major in art, his father asked him "why would anybody want to do that?" He graduated in 1971 and taught art in school and drove the school bus until he was able to paint full time. John Sloan was an early influence, and E.I. Couse's paintings pointed him toward New Mexico.

His lighting is low key and the colors are natural, with brown and blue representing the "earth and the sky." He works in acrylic on masonite, rarely using real objects as models but rather combining sketches and photographs of artifacts that he selects from his research files. "Still-life painting must also have a touch of liveliness," he declares, so he adds butterflies, birds, and flowers to contrast their transitory lives with the timeless artifacts. The renderings can be meticulous. In the beadwork on the yoke of an Indian dress, he has found as many as 14,000 beads, each requiring four to five steps to paint. He has exhibited at the Museum of the Southwest and was featured in the August 1981 issue of *Southwest Art*. His gallery is his own, for paintings and prints.

Una Hanbury, DYMORIET, bronze, h 13, a young arabian stallion
bred by Richard Pritzlaff of Sapello, New Mexico

James M. Haney, TRILLIUM AND CHECKERSPOTS, acrylic, 30 x 40

Bob Haozous

Harbaugh

Hantman, Carl. Traditional oil painter of the Old West, born in New Bedford, Massachusetts in 1935 and living in New York City. "You hear about self-taught artists. If there is anything I'm not, it is self-taught. I think an artist should get as much professional training as he can. When you paint, you should not have to worry about *how* to paint. I think it takes as long to prepare to be painter as to be a doctor."

Raised in Florida, he graduated from high school in 1951 and attended the University of Miami before deciding that to get the training he wanted, he would have to go to New York City. For eight years, he studied at the Art Students League. Meanwhile, he worked as a commercial artist, winning awards for his paintings including one for his first cover for a Western paperback. Over the years, he did more than two hundred covers, particularly Westerns, for every major paperback publisher. As his paintings became more popular, he received inquiries from Western galleries and in 1974 started with a Texas gallery that he said "handles it all and I concentrate on painting." Deadlines were gone, and "I don't have to paint until 3 A.M. to get something finished."

For ideas, he has a collection of 5,000 stills from old Western movies, as well as clothing, gear, and artifacts. He starts with postcard-sized oil sketches, then develops more detailed renderings until he sets the final composition. Models are posed for photography on the roof of his city apartment, and finally the preliminaries are combined into the design for the actual painting. He was written up in *Southwest Art*, fall 1976, and is represented by Husberg Fine Arts Gallery which listed his painting at $4,500 in fall 1980.

Haozous, Bob. Modernist sculptor in various materials "of cowboys and Indians in whatever way I want," born in Los Angeles in 1943 and living in Santa Fe, New Mexico. "Many of the older artists, my father included," he points out, "seem to feel contentment in doing art however restricted or impersonal their art may be from my point of view. The fact that each artist had to acknowledge personal restrictions to achieve goals is very comforting. Therefore, my goal would probably be to portray my own reality as honestly as possible."

Son of the important Apache sculptor Allan Houser, Haozous (pronounced "Houses") attended Utah State University in 1961–62 and received his BFA from the California College of Arts and Crafts in 1970, the date of his first invitational show. Awards began in 1972, and his work is in seven public collections. "Many Indian artists," he stresses, "wish to be free of the stigma of cultural art and to compete with other artists as international artists. I have claimed to be an Indian artist because I believe the Native American people still have direct ties to their own life experience or reality. Therefore, the art produced by these people should and must have direct cultural ties.

"The concept of an international, universal man is ludicrous. The Native American has had, in the past, a direct reference between himself and nature, neither being the dominant. Even though flashy and commercial art forms with less personal cultural references are more and more common, the basis of Indian art has always been an honest interpretation of the individual's reality." For himself, he says that "the earth mother form is a very profound symbol." He is represented by Heydt/Bair Gallery.

Harbaugh, Ken. Impressionist painter of the Arizona landscape in oil and gouache, born in Osaka, Japan in 1953 and living in Phoenix, Arizona since 1971. "A lot of people look at me," he observes, "and see the athlete, and they sell me short as just another macho jock. I hope they're wrong. Sensitive is a big, overused word, but I am sensitive to nature—and I'm sensitive to the feelings inside me. I must get down what I see, the movement, the color, the essence and strength of the composition."

The son of a soldier, he says that when he "took art in junior high, I almost flunked. Sports were more exciting. I was going to play football on a scholarship to Glendale Community College, but I realized I had to make a choice. I couldn't give art the time it needed if I gave sports the time they needed, so that was it for organized sports. It was college art classes that did it. That's when I began to study art seriously.

"I love the Impressionists. The color. The brush work. These reach out and grab me. What I do is a natural progression of what they've taught me. I like to think I've taken their work and made it *move*. I keep wanting to get more movement into my paintings. Sometimes I think, if I ever get *everything* I want, the paint will just keep on going right off the canvas and I will be left with great big white nothings. I work directly from nature because there is really no color in a slide, from a technical standpoint. To people who know film, it's pretty obvious just by looking at a painting by an artist who uses slide reference, what type of film he used to shoot the slides." Written up in *Southwest Art*, January 1981, he is represented by Austin Gallery and The Glory Hole.

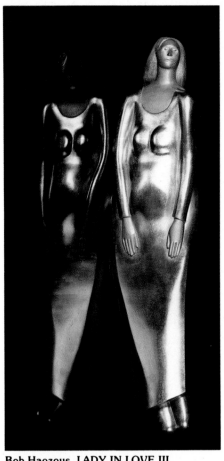

Bob Haozous, LADY IN LOVE III
cast stainless steel, h 5, Edition 6

Ken Harbaugh, FLOWER FARM, CLOSING TIME, gouache/panel, 30 x 36

Carl Hantman, LAND OF THE APACHE, oil, 24 x 30

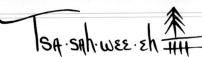

Tsa·sah·wee·eh 🌲

Pamela C Harr

R. M. Harris

Hardin, Helen. Painter in acrylic and printmaker of symbolic Pueblo Indian figures, born in Albuquerque, New Mexico in 1943 and living there in 1982. "My feeling about being Indian, a woman and me," she points out, "and expressing myself as all three, can be found in examples of my work. In one, I didn't go into anything about race or gender. I started with a big circle and I filled it and that's the way I started and the way it ended. I didn't invent any Indian mythological stories. I don't usually start anything with any wonderous idea."

Daughter of Pablita Velarde, traditional painter of Santa Clara Pueblo, and a white father, she was raised in the Pueblo for her first six years while her father was in the Army. She began winning art contests at six and was selling pictures at the Gallup Inter-Tribal Ceremonial at ten. After Albuquerque high school art courses, she attended the University of New Mexico and the Special School for Indian Arts at the University of Arizona. She signed with her Indian name Tsa-sah-wee-eh, Little Standing Spruce, followed by H.H. below a small tree.

"In recent years," she notes, "there's been a lot written about the Indian artist and his or her spiritual identity, whatever the devil that is. I think many of the artists who lay claim to this are really mouthing the words to sell their works. It's what the white man wants to hear. I just stay at home and work. I don't want to be the richest artist, or the most famous. I just want to be the best. I am fortunate to be in a position that I do not consign paintings to any gallery. I prefer working on a wholesale level or not at all. Written up in *Southwest Art* twice and in *Artists of the Rockies*, her work can be seen at Enchanted Mesa.

Harr, Pamela. Traditional sculptor of people in a Western setting, with emphasis on their character and emotions, particularly pioneer women, born in Palo Alto, California in 1944 and living in Bozeman, Montana since 1977. "In sculpture," she emphasizes, "there truly is a place for tragedy, as well as for happiness and action, in capturing the Western motif. I feel it represents the essence of the losses of so many courageous pioneering women—something that only an artist can preserve.

"When I was younger I didn't think I'd ever be an artist. Drawing was very difficult." She decided to become a physical therapist and received her BS from Oregon State University in 1966. Married to a career Army officer, she was employed as an illustrator for the Department of Agriculture and then worked with handicapped children for three years, using sculpture as therapy. In 1971, her husband was killed in Vietnam. She accepted a job on a cattle ranch in Oregon and in 1973 she took a bronze-casting course, moved to Washington, and adopted sculpting as her career.

Told that pioneering women as subjects would not sell, she concluded "that women could be portrayed in ways that could be just as salable if the artist would only use imagination. After all, that's why we're called artists." At a C.M. Russell Art Show, she met the Montana sculptor Harvey Rattey and moved to Bozeman when they married. According to her, "art occupies my entire life, and the business of selling art is just as important as creating it." Her works may be purchased from Bridger Foundry and Gallery "by direct sales, lease, or time payment." A member of the Women Artists of the American West, she was written up in *Southwest Art*, February 1979.

Harris, Roy M. Bronze sculptor of cowboys and "range critters," born in Ogden, Utah in 1928 and living in San Luis Obispo, California since 1954. "I've gone to the well, so to speak, three times in my lifetime," Harris reflects. "When I was younger, horses and cowboys were the most important things in my life. Then I wanted to teach and do research about animals, and now I'm totally captivated by sculpting them."

After growing up in northern Idaho, Harris put himself through Weber State College by roughing out a string of colts each summer. When the Korean war broke out, he was a horse trooper with a reconnaissance squadron in the Bavarian Alps. Two years later, he enrolled at Utah State University for his BS and then worked as cow boss on a ranch in eastern Arizona. He received his Master's in 1954, the year he joined the faculty in California Polytechnic State University's animal science department. In 1970, he earned a doctorate in animal genetics.

While teaching at Cal Poly, carrying on cattle and horse research, and working with the cattle industry in Baja California, Mexico, Harris started experimenting with modeling in 1974. "It's something that's been building up over the years," he explained. "It just finally emerged." He now completes three or four Western bronzes a year, in editions of ten to twenty at prices up to $3,000 per casting. He says that "if I could best describe myself, I would say 'I'm just an ol' cowboy that went wrong.' I'm still not sure why I quit cowboying full time and went to school, except that I reckon I have a curious and creative mind. In any event, at the present time I'm enjoying the best of both worlds." Dr. Harris is represented by Copenhagen Galleri.

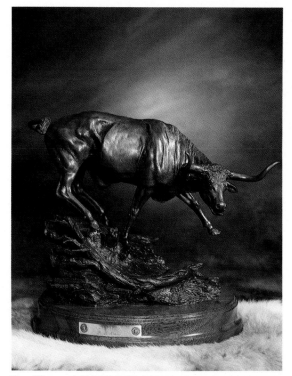

Roy Harris, A DASH FOR FREEDOM, bronze, h 9, l 11   Pamela Harr, FROM BELLE TO BANDIT, bronze, h 11, Edition 24

Helen Hardin, VISION OF THE ETERNAL HUNT, acrylic, 20 x 26

G. Harvey, THE OIL PATCH, oil, 40 x 60

Harvey (Jones), Gerald. Oil painter and sculptor of the way the West is now and the way it was, born in San Antonio, Texas in 1933 and living in Cedar Park, Texas. "I am not a cowboy artist," Harvey observes. "I am simply an artist. The reason I paint the Southwest is because I live here. These people and this land are the subjects I know and love best. All of my academic training was in fine art, not commercial art. French and American Impressionists were my greatest influences."

An authentic Westerner, Harvey's grandfather was on some of the last of the historic cattle drives. Harvey graduated cum laude from North Texas State University in 1956 and had a short period of private art study. He feels that his "greatest teachers were observation, painting, self-discipline, and hard work in an attempt to exercise a God-given talent." Believing that "an artist is only as strong as his last painting," he collected raw material in London, Paris, and New York as well as across the Southwest in 1981.

In 1977, Gerald and Texas Art Gallery had decided that he should paint for a year to produce enough work for a catalog, and then auction the whole collection in one evening. The first show sold out for more than $100,000. Gerald believes that the process helps him "live with and work on each painting to avoid duplication and bring each piece up to the finest quality he is able to achieve at this period in his artistic life," and so the procedure was continued. In 1980, his one-person show sold out for more than $1,000,000. Harvey was featured in *Southwest Art*, summer 1976, *Artists of the Rockies*, spring 1979, Ainsworth's *The Cowboy in Art,* and Hassrick's *Western Painting Today.*

marion haws *Elie Hazak* *Donald M Hedin*

Haws, Marion. Representational landscape painter and sculptor of the old American West, born in Vernal, Utah in 1947 and living in Newton in Cache Valley, Utah. "Generally," he emphasizes, "almost everything I paint is something I've been impressed with. I don't put anything on the market that I don't feel good about. Sometimes I'm strongly attracted to a painting and hate to see it go. Sometimes a painting I like is sold and I wonder where it ends up because often I don't know the people who buy my paintings."

He studied art with William Whitaker at Brigham Young University from 1969 to 1974 and was influenced by VaLoy Eaton, although he states that a lot of his painting is self-taught. He began painting full time in 1976 but he avoids what used to be thought of as the typical Western subjects in favor of the things around him that other people hurry by. His goal is to do the rural landscape so richly that "one almost experiences the fresh scent of grass and feels the warm sunshine on his back." He loves farm life and the old barns and wagons.

Being a professional artist is a "hard ballgame," he acknowledges, because there is a lot of competition and it is a slow process breaking in. "I don't paint for the galleries, though," he points out. "I paint for myself. If you paint what you like and the people like it, you've got something going." His wife and he sit down the first of each month and have a planning meeting on how the days will be spent. He tries to paint every day, to meet the goal of 50 paintings a year, but time is lost in taking pictures to the framer and getting them ready for shows. He is represented by the Four Seasons Gallery and by Husberg Fine Arts Gallery which offered a painting of his for $1,200 in fall 1981.

Hazak, Elie. Traditional sculptor of the Old West in bronze statuettes, born in Ismir, Turkey in 1945 and living in Thousand Oaks, California since 1969. "When I was a child," he recalls, "I used to dream of being on a horse running in the open spaces. For me, Western art is representative of not merely the cowboy or Indian figure but rather the beauty and freedom of getting on a horse and riding forever. Western art to me suggests freedom, the freedom we're losing every day."

Raised in Jerusalem, his parents' religious beliefs precluded modeling human images so he was sent to a Catholic school to learn languages. At thirteen, he met a celebrated art teacher Ayala Gordon, who Hazak says "is always in the back of my mind when I work." He also studied privately with a Russian painter and attended art school in Jerusalem. "When I reflect on all my schooling," he states, "I cannot remember the specifics of what I learned. We were taught basic anatomy and design for four years." He adds that after the Six Day War in 1967, "I could not handle the earth around me." For two years, he was a professional actor in Europe and finally in California.

He enrolled in art classes, then was employed in a foundry "to learn the casting business from the ground up. Now, I do most of the process in my workshop, except for the actual casting in bronze. Since I was not raised here, it has taken quite a lot of time and effort to research every aspect of the life of a cowboy. Up until now, I have done very little advertising and have gone to few shows, so people often want to know to whom I sell my bronzes. Most of my clients are private individuals who collect all or most of my pieces." Hazak was written up in *Southwest Art*, June 1980.

Hedin, Donald M. "Ultra-realist" painter in acrylic of still-lifes of the 19th-century West, born in New England in 1920 and living in Somers, New York. "Every artist," he points out, "has something he wants to say. The idea of trying to tell a story with the use of still-life props has, from art school days, intrigued me. Although I do not always try to suggest the human presence, as though he or she had just stepped away, I often employ this plan in doing a painting—a smoking cigar, for example.

"From the time I was a skinny little kid, there was never a time that I wanted to be anything but an artist. I was fortunate enough to have the opportunity to work under a competent local artist before reaching art school age. Another bit of luck was being accepted by Pratt Institute in 1938. The war years gave me another boost. I found North Africa, England, and Italy magnificent places to paint. The last year of the war found me in the state of Washington, and my enthusiasm for the great American West has never subsided. Only my career as illustrator and art editor for *Reader's Digest* kept me from the West.

"The hope is that one can record 19th-century props in an unusual and attractive manner, while recording the life-styles accurately. I chose a 19th-century style of painting to produce a compatible package. About half of my paintings fall into the category of trompe l'œil. A modest-sized painting will take over 100 hours, and one about twenty by thirty inches well over 200. The challenge is making objects so three-dimensional that with proper lighting, the objects invite the viewer to lift them." Written up in *Southwest Art*, August 1977, he is represented by El Prado Gallery of Art.

Elie Hazak, CHEYENNE HUNTER, bronze, h 23

Donald Hedin, ASA JACKSON'S WINNING HAND, acrylic/masonite, 21½ x 28

Marion Haws, AROUND THE BARN (1979), oil, 15 x 30

Heflin, Tom Pat. Realist and abstract painter of the Southwest and of Illinois in acrylic on crushed paper, born in Monticello, Arkansas in 1934 and living in Rockford, Illinois since 1948. "My work routine consists of four days a week spent at my studio which is an isolated farm. There are no telephones or passing cars to intrude. The day begins at 11 A.M. and ends around 3 A.M.. Taking time out to jog two miles each evening, I spend the other fourteen hours working on my paintings.

"I've always known what I wanted to be," he says. His first drawing at five showed his grandfather reading a newspaper. Encouraged by teachers, he attended Northeast Louisiana State University as an art major and also studied at the Chicago Art Institute. When he took a job in Rockford, it was as billboard painter, and after sixteen years he was vice president of the company. He had begun teaching art in 1968, and in 1970 he quit the sign company "to paint what I like." In 1979, he opened his own gallery.

"In most cases," he points out, "I simply paint my environment. If I'm in the Southwest, I paint Indians, cowboys, and Western landscapes. In the Midwest, I paint the landscape around my farm studio." His paintings are inscribed with the date he conceived the idea and a comment on the day, for example, "Tuesday, April 7, 1981, sunny, windy, warm, jonquils." He adds that "I have always had an appreciation for realistic *and* abstract art and find it quite easy and natural to move from one to the other when I paint. It has been my contention that both are valid as long as the work is good. The majority of my paintings are realistic." Listed in *Who's Who in American Art*, he is represented by Overland Trail Galleries and Flusche Fine Art Gallery.

Heinz, Ralph A. Painter of historical as well as contemporary Western scenes, born in Willoughby, Ohio in 1943 and living in Rollins, Montana since 1976. "The present popularity of Western art," he believes, "is a resurgence of the public's interest in realism, in things they can identify with. It is a reaction against 'modern' art which became so far removed from reality and from concrete images. Western art portrays the 'rugged individual,' and it gives comfort to individuals trapped in cities to know the West still exists to escape to.

"The grandfather I was named after died young on a cattle ranch in New Mexico. After traveling extensively with my parents, I left home at seventeen and worked as a horse wrangler on a ranch in Colorado. For the next couple of years, I competed in professional rodeos as a bull rider until I majored in English at Northern Arizona University. When I graduated, I enlisted as a paratrooper and went to Vietnam. I had worked for six summers for the U.S. Forest Service as a fire lookout, painting and drawing without distractions, and moved to Montana to be close to places of history.

"I am self-taught as an artist. My major interest is the Indian wars of the 1870s. My closest friends have not been other artists, rather they've been historians, and it is to them that I have been able to turn to for research. It is this group of viewers who are art critics not often heard from. They look at historical artwork with regard to their own specialized knowledge of firearms, clothing, saddles, military accouterments, etc., and it is for this reason I paint in time-consuming detail. I am a member of The Company of Military Historians." Heinz is represented by The Hole in the Wall Gallery.

Helbig, Erwin E. Traditional painter of the contemporary Western scene, born in Butte, Montana in 1919 and living in Kalispell, Montana since 1969. According to Bud Helbig, "as a little boy I had two persistent aspirations: to be a working cowboy and an artist. The first I achieved at an early age, as I grew up on a small cow and horse spread in Western Montana. The second goal, that of becoming an artist, took a longer and more circuitous route.

"While sketching everything around me, my imagination was further fired by tales of first-hand acquaintances of the colorful Will James. There were no art schools in Montana in those days so I enrolled in a Federal Art School correspondence course, which only whetted my appetite for knowledge of art. I worked for two years on a bridge-building crew for the Milwaukee Railroad to earn money for more schooling. Reluctantly leaving Bitter Root Valley, I headed east to art schools in St. Paul and Minneapolis. After a three and a half year interruption by World War II, fate led me to Chicago and the American Academy of Art. After three years studying under Bill Mosby, I worked for many years in the commercial field in the Chicago area as illustrator and art director.

"I kept my contacts with the West through frequent trips to Montana, Texas, and Colorado. Finally the call of the West became too strong to resist, and I moved back to Montana. A member of the Cowboy Artists of America since 1972, I concentrate most of my attention on the fast-changing contemporary West—the world of the rodeo and the cowboy. I work in all mediums except acrylic." Helbig was featured in *Art West*, July 1981, and is represented by Art of the West Gallery.

Tom Heflin, MEDICINE CROW, acrylic/gesso panel, 30 x 22

Bud Helbig, COW BELLES, watercolor, 19 x 29

Ralph A. Heinz, NORTH OF THE YELLOWSTONE, oil, 30 x 48

HENDRICKS

Hendricks, Kay M. "Trompe l'œil" painter of historical objects of the American West, born in northeast Colorado in 1923 and living in San Diego, California since 1959. "My 'Western' paintings," he observes, "are a departure from those that deal with the snow and dust, and the people and critters. Certainly, action and hardship typified the building of our West, but when darkness eased around the pioneers each day, most had the comfort of some kind of shelter. Within their wagons, bunkhouses, camps, or soddies, they rested, eating, drinking, repairing gear, making music, or telling stories, to be ready for tomorrow. My still-life paintings show some of the *things* those excellent people used."

His mother and aunt were both amateur artists and encouraged him to draw. He was painting at nine and spending summers on his uncle's ranch, helping with farming to be allowed to help with the cattle. At fifteen, he was a trail guide, discoving that work could be for wages, and in World War II at eighteen, he was in the cavalry in Europe. After the war, he was a saddlemaker and managed a shop until 1955 when he enrolled in mechanical engineering at the University of Arizona. From 1959 to 1968, he worked as technical editor for a publication, painting as a hobby until the demand for pictures exceeded the time available.

Hendricks feels "the same sense of attachment to those thoroughly used treasures that the original users must have felt. Few items were thrown away in the 'old days.' Instead, they were repaired and kept in service. Setting up my models and developing my scenario is like writing a short story of a tranquil interlude in what was the most colorful period in our history." He is represented by Trailside Galleries.

Hensley, Jackson M. Traditional painter of the New Mexico landscape and still lifes, born in Portales, New Mexico in 1940 and living in Taos, New Mexico since 1966. "My work is based on a classical approach," he explains. "Many studies are made prior to any major effort. I work solely from life—outdoors or in the studio. I paint outdoors in water-based paints on 100% rag paper. Paintings can take up to several years—drawings only moments. The framing is done in New York City."

After schooling in Portales and starting college with a major in architecture, Hensley was encouraged by Peter Hurd to study at the National Academy of Design in New York City where he won a scholarship. He then painted landscapes in New Orleans and in New England, and exhibited in New York City and at the Corcoran Gallery of Art in Washington, D.C. Ten years after his return to New Mexico, his painting "Christmas Promise" was purchased by the Museum of New Mexico and reproduced in the 1976 calendar published by *New Mexico Magazine* for the bicentennial year. He was the youngest artist chosen.

Hensley has exhibited in over 200 shows and his work is in over 200 collections, but he says that since 1964 he has stopped showing in national or otherwise open shows. "I work solely with private galleries—the freedom is worth the notoriety lost." He declares that his "work is mainly in watercolor, inks, conte drawing, and oil (once in a while pastel—some sculpture)." Andrew Dasburg called his style "authoritative realism" and his landscapes "distinctive." He is represented by Carr Gallery and his own Gallery of the Southwest.

Jackson Hensley, EARLY LIGHT, ARROYO HONDO, oil, 40 x 60

Kay M. Hendricks, BILLY'S PIPE, oil/panel, 12 x 16

Herring, Lee. "Traditional realist" oil painter of historical and contemporary Western scenes, born near Point in rural Raines County, Texas in 1940 and living in Dallas, Texas. "Without excuses," he says, "I am convinced that traditional realism requires the best effort from those artists possessing the greater abilities. It is a combination of draftsmanship, composition, design, perspective, and mastery of color, with the skill to make the subject dominant and understandable, producing a work of beauty and delight.

"During World War II, my father and mother were both in defense work and we moved from the Texas Gulf to Portland, Oregon. Near the end of the war, we began farming in Texas. With a scholarship to play football, I obtained both my BS and MS degrees in advertising art and art education. During the years from 1963 to 1974, I worked as a technical illustrator, illustrator, and cartoonist. I taught public school in Texas and Australia and in a technical college. I formed an advertising agency, went into sales and back to school.

"Although I was successful in what I did, all along I had wanted to paint. Finally in 1975, I quit everything else and painted full time. Art, to me, is traditional realism. If the piece is historical, I feel it is necessary to do a great amount of research, to find the extremes and plot a plausible course between them. Once I made a week long wagon train ride across empty back country. I made the trip in order to get some idea of what it must have been like. From dawn to dusk I was photographing everything of interest and riding horseback ahead of the wagons to wait with my camera. I am presently represented by the Overland Trail and Manitou Galleries."

Herrmann, Edward E. Oil and water-color painter of Colorado mountain landscapes, born in Fort Wayne, Indiana in 1914 and living in Estes Park, Colorado. "My general feeling about autobiographical information," he says, "is that it is unimportant, irrelevant, and overemphasized. The paintings should speak for themselves. One either relates to them or not. Since I have not as yet cut off an ear, a novel about me could be pretty boring."

Educated as a mechanical engineer for three years at Purdue, Indiana and Penn State Universities, he worked in industry from 1935 to 1958, including management of Interior Design and Color for Raymond Loewy Associates and Studebaker-Packard Corporation. He also painted as a hobby, taking workshops in 1946 and 1947, although he considers himself to be self-taught, and exhibiting in major shows since then. In 1958, he established his own design consulting firm in South Bend and also taught at the Art Center for sixteen years. He opened his fine art studio and gallery in 1969, and six years later moved to Colorado.

Herrmann prefers to paint watercolors directly on location where the light, seasons, and nature's moods "contribute to interpretations not possible in the studio. It's the idea of landscape that I like, to choose from the rich assortment of shapes, textures, colors, values, and movements that nature furnishes. I can be as analytical or emotional in my interpretations as my creativity will allow." Using these watercolors for inspiration during the winter, he paints in oil and acrylic in the studio where his style becomes "strong, vivid, and more Impressionistic." He is published and represented by his own Herrmann Gallery.

Herron, Ronald M. Sculptor in bronze of "the older way of life" in Montana born in Havre, Montana in 1943 and living in Helena, Montana. "I am a man astride two centuries," he claims, "the one in which I grew up and the one in which my ancestors forged a civilization out of the raw frontier. In my early years, I always had a menagerie at home. My teen summers were spent as a working hand on a ranch, my winters with a legendary mountain man in the wilds of Glacier Park. I spent countless times in the company of old Indians who spun out tales of their youth—an era long disappeared."

Raised in Kalispell where he kept dogs, fish, pigeons, weasels, and hawks, he was a cowboy from thirteen to eighteen when he "joined the U.S.A.F. to train security dogs." On his return to Montana he was "an avid falconer and a certified corrective horseshoer." It was while he was a state brand inspector that he "was encouraged to become a professional artist." Since then, "the demand for my bronzes keeps my painting to a minimum. My knowledge of wildlife, working ranches, and respect for the Indians is my expertise."

Herron models miniatures and statuettes as well as larger sculptures, but calls his "edition of one" bronze unique. He "has created over 300 of these 'one of a kinds' in thirteen years," in addition to his limited editions that extend to ten castings. He appears at numerous one-day shows and estimates that over 200,000 saw his work in 1980 alone. Moreover, his "Medicine Bundle" at the entrance to the gallery at the Mt. Rushmore Monument was viewed by over 3,000,000 in 1981. His gallery is Montana Gallery & Book Shoppe.

Edward E. Herrman, HALLETTS PEAK, AUTUMN, watercolor, 15 x 22

Lee Herring, HER FATHER'S LAND, oil, 30 x 40

Ronald M. Herron, MEDICINE BUNDLE, gouache, 15 x 30

Hick, Terrance. Impressionist oil painter of central Wyoming landscapes and rural scenes, born in Marshall, Minnesota, in 1950, and living in Casper, Wyoming since 1967. When he was 17, he "looked at Conrad Schwiering's work and said 'now that's the way I want to paint.' Six years later when I had a show, I overheard someone say 'he paints just like Schwiering.' I sat and thought there's only one Elvis Presley and there's only one me, so I took everything I'd done and threw it away and started all over again.

"I remember when we were living in Sioux Falls, South Dakota and I was in the eighth grade. Instead of doing test papers, I'd just sit and draw, and my teacher said 'you've got something.' She encouraged me." His parents bought him oil paints when he was in the tenth grade. He entered Casper College in 1969, switched to the Art Center College in Los Angeles for a year, then returned to Casper where he earned an arts degree in 1973.

After eight years of painting signs and painting pictures in his spare time, he began painting full time in 1979, having overcome misgivings about his talent by earning a black belt in karate. His favorite painters are Nicolai Fechin and John Singer Sargent: "If it's a good honest painting, I'll like it. I don't like showmanship. No Andy Warhol. That's a song and dance routine. It's not for me. When I go back to the studio, I'll think about the subject for awhile. I go over slides many times until I find the combination I want. The painting is almost like collage. When something doesn't work, I'll throw it out and replace it with something else." Written up in *Southwest Art*, September 1980, Hicks is represented by El Prado Gallery of Art.

Hill, William Lee. Impressionist oil painter and sculptor of "the West and its citizens, animal and human," born in Star Valley, Wyoming in 1922 and living in Mendon, Utah. "I was playing the piano one day," he recalls, "and it struck me how the different chords of music affect the people who hear them. It made me wonder if colors would not have the same effect. I did a lot of experimenting and learned to use small amounts of pure color which the eye blends. Of course, the French did this too, but they used mostly pastels. I am a Western painter and the West is strong and masculine and I use strong colors to get the effects I want."

Born "on a hard-luck farm, we were so poor that the Depression came and went and we didn't know the difference. I learned about it later from my school books. I was kind of alien among my own people. The folks called me a 'dreamer.' Now, when I paint a picture, I always try to reach into the humanities involved. I know those people—some of them were my family. I graduated from Brigham Young University in 1949 with an emphasis on English literature and education. I taught school while developing myself as an artist.

"I paint in an expressionist style that provides me opportunities to paint abstract qualities such as emotions, experiences of the senses, temperatures, personality, and natural, spiritual qualities. I regard myself as an American painter, in contrast to 'cowboy artist.' I'm an artist, not a cowboy." Written up in *Southwest Art*, December 1979, Bill Hill's prints are distributed by Western Profiles Publishing Co. and he is represented by Zantmann Art and Myer's Galleries. He is working now in two areas, one he calls Western humanities, and the second, Western action scenes.

Terrence Hick, GARDEN TALK, oil, 30 x 40

Bill L. Hill, SETTLING A WAGER, oil, 20 x 30

Tom Hill

Jack Hines

William Hoffman

Hill, Tom. Representational water-colorist of Mexican and cowboy figures, born in Texas and living in Tucson, Arizona. "A lot of people feel that watercolor is a 'lightweight' medium," he observes, "one that's okay for sketches and studies, but not for major works and one that is not permanent. This misconception is probably the result of having been given, as a child, watercolors to 'play with.' As it is so dynamically done today, however, watercolor painting is acknowledged to be one of the most difficult mediums and one of the most exciting. Properly taken care of, it is one of the most permanent.

"I was always sure I'd be an artist. When I was six, I would lie on the floor and draw on the backs of discarded envelopes. Even now, I remember the pleasure when I put pencil to paper and felt the tactile quality of the graphite rubbing onto the paper." Raised in California, he was an artist in the Navy, attended the Art Center College of Design in Los Angeles, was an artist for Universal Studios in Hollywood, and then became a staff artist for the *Chicago Sunday Tribune* and attended the Art Institute of Chicago. He left Chicago to become an illustrator in New York City.

"I always felt temporarily transplanted in the East," he says, and he moved to Arizona. "As I acquired more experience in drawing and painting, I began to realize that I desired more than just realism in my paintings. I also searched for more than reportorial art for myself. I wanted to be able to make statements in my paintings that would be understood by the viewer, and I wanted my work to have a 'feeling' about it, a soul, if you will." Hill is a member of the American Watercolor Society and an Associate of the National Academy of Design, was featured in *Southwest Art*, April 1977, and has written two books on how to paint in watercolor. He is represented by Settlers West Galleries which set a minimum bid of $2,750 for his oil painting in its 1981 silent auction.

Hines, Jack. Traditional painter of mountain men and Indians in watercolor, acrylic, and pencil, born in eastern Nebraska in 1923 and living in Big Timber, Montana. "While the hardy and courageous mountain men qualify as this artist's subject matter," Hines states, "their lives were, essentially, a distortion of the human condition. Looking at the Indian and his life, we find a complete existence. A rich, nature-based philosophy comes forth from centuries of life in our West, before the first white foot was placed tenuously upon its soil.

"I was born into an atmosphere of lingering memories of the great westward trek. My first steps in art were directed to an Omaha art agency. My needs in visual communication and I, found our way to the Los Angeles Art Center School with supplemental classes at the Chouinart Art Institute. My mecca was New York, and my arrival there was the opening of a 26-year odyssey. There were steady incursions into fine arts, with acceptances in major exhibitions. During those last years in the East, I was engaged in a series of pack trips into the Northwest's mountains. When an opportunity surfaced to take over management of a guest and cattle operation, I moved quickly to accept.

"And so, today finds me in the upper Yellowstone Valley, doing what I love most. Here is my subject to paint for a lifetime." In 1975, Jessica Zemsky and Hines were married in the studio in Big Timber. They are both members of the Northwest Rendezvous Group. Hines was written up in *Southwest Art*, March 1979, and *Art West*, May 1980, and is published by Salt Creek Graphics. His watercolor in Trailside Galleries was listed at $3,500 in 1982.

Hoffman, William. Representational painter of Western people and country, born on a ranch in Great Falls, Montana in 1924 and living in Big Bear Lake, California. "I've always been artistically inclined," he explains, "but my mother taught me that artists starve and art is a waste of time. I'd come home after a day's work on the fields of our ranch carrying a notebook filled with sketches and get scolded. This kind of discouragement gave me zero knowledge of what was going on in the world.

"Charlie Russell's studio was four blocks from our home. Whenever he passed our house, Mom would say, 'There goes that no-good drunk again.' At ten, I would sneak into the Mint Bar, looking at Charlie's paintings before I was kicked out, never thinking I would be an artist. When I first started painting, I was District Manager of a large office. About six months later, I showed a painting to a large wholesaler who told me they'd buy everything I did. I hung on for five years, until I was making more in my spare time than I was after eighteen years with the company. That's when I quit. In 1974, I visited my brother's cattle ranch and when I got home, I was a 'Western artist!'

"Westerns normally take me ten to twelve days to complete. This is an awful long time to spend on one subject. Therefore, I always get the hardest or most detailed portions out of the way first. Usually these are the animals and the people in the painting. Next would come any buildings. I breathe a sigh of relief when these are done because the landscape part of the painting goes relatively fast. About 75 percent of my paintings are snow scenes." Written up in *Southwest Art*, March 1979, he has "50 paintings in print" and is represented by Newsom's Gallery.

Tom Hill, STREET IN TAXCO, watercolor, 28½ x 20½

William Hoffman, WINTER CAMP, oil, 30 x 40

Jack Hines, THE FORBIDDEN VASTNESS, watercolor & crayon & pencil, 20 x 30

Joseph Holbrook

Harold Holden

Hopkinson

Holbrook, Joseph. Traditional oil and acrylic painter of the historical West, born in Toledo, Ohio in 1946 and living in Los Angeles since 1974. "Nature," he remarks, "gives us the concepts of design, color, line, form, and the basics for expression of what is inside and outside the realm of the material world. The artist focuses his creative abilities, pulls nuances of influence from unknown corners of his mind, feeds in information—and creates."

A resident of California since 1962, Holbrook received a degree in business management at California State Polytechnic College but after a few years became dissatisfied with the business world. While co-owner of a watercolor gallery in Laguna Beach in 1974, he began painting and exhibiting, self-taught except for a brief attendance at the Art Center School of Design in Los Angeles. In 1977, he began exhibiting at art shows in California and Nevada, and in 1980 won an award from the Western Artists of America.

"Unless your purpose is scientific in nature," he says, "you wouldn't explain a flower cell in order to express its beauty. Instead, you choose words that you feel will give the least complex but most meaningful expression of its beauty. You give special attention to those words that translate what you personally feel about its beauty. In expressing the same flower through painting, I would choose the elements of art that I feel will give the least complex but most meaningful painting of its beauty. As the purposes of painting change, so do the results." He is represented by Lesli Art.

Holden, Harold. Painter and sculptor of contemporary cowboys in traditional settings, born in Enid, Oklahoma in 1941 and living in Kremlin, north of Enid. "I paint contemporary now," he says, "but when all the cowboys go to motorcycles, then I'll be painting the 'old' West." His cowboys are described as "the cowboys of the 1880s in modern clothing, a little older perhaps, but still working in the old ways. They are better mounted and the cattle have shorter horns, but little else has changed."

Raised in Enid, Holden attended Oklahoma State University and graduated from the Texas Academy of Art in Houston in 1962. He worked in commercial art and as art director for *Horseman* magazine. Three years after he began painting in 1970, he moved back to Enid to paint full time. Some of the people in his work are real, but they are few now. "I used to use a lot of models," he declares, "but the more you do it, the more you can do without it. You don't need a model with sculpture. In fact, some artists sculpt a piece first and use that to do their painting from."

He claims that he will never get rich on sculpture: "I price a bronze three times the casting price. If you sell it in the gallery, they take a third, the foundry gets a third, and you get a third. It may look like you are making a killing but you aren't." Husberg prices most of his paintings, and Holden thinks "some of the prices are a little high." In 1981, he won first place for painting and sculpture at the Texas Cowboy Artist show at The Galleries. Few people in Enid see his work because he sells in Sedona, Arizona, Tulsa, Oklahoma, and Houston, Fort Worth, and San Angelo, Texas.

Hopkinson, Harold I. Painter of Indians and cowboys in northern Wyoming, born in Salt Lake City, Utah in 1918 and living in Byron, Wyoming. "Some of my methods of working are unorthodox," he says. "If I plan the foreground to be a sagebrush color, I'll paint the intended area in a thin wash of red. If the sky is to be blue, I'll use a wash of orange. I use these opposite colors and allow bits to purposely shine through, giving a certain vibration to the painting which could be called impressionistic.

"I feel I have lived a very fascinating life," he adds, "with so many stories in the background. Every painting I do has something of those distant memories." He was raised on the family ranch near Fort Bridger. Although some relatives were Sunday painters, his only encouragement came from the "Draw Me" magazine ads. His father's judgment was "if you want to starve to death, just keep on painting," and Hopkinson did not enter his art career until he was 28. He earned his M.A. from the University of Wyoming in 1952 and went on to study at Brigham Young University and at the Art Center School in Los Angeles.

"I usually start by making little scribbly sketches," he declares. "I scribble around until I happen on what to me appears to be a rather dramatic moment. During these scribbles, I create the specific design. I look for one spectacular impact." He avoids a preliminary color sketch because that would take the "zest" out of painting the oil. Hopkinson is in Ainsworth's *The Cowboy in Art*, Hassrick's *Western Painting Today*, and *Who's Who in American Art*. He was featured in *Southwest Art*, September 1976. His gallery is Voris.

Harold Hopkinson, CHIEF JOSEPH, oil, 24 x 36

Joseph Holbrook, AMERICAN MAN, acrylic/panel, 28 x 22

Harold Holden, WORKIN' FOURSOME, oil, 30 x 40

261

Allan Houser, DINEH, bronze, 39 x 35 x 60, edition 6

Houser

Houser, Allan. Modernist sculptor of American Indian figures in bronze and stone statues and statuettes, born in Apache, Oklahoma in 1915 and living in Santa Fe, New Mexico since 1962. "By the time I went back to finish school, I was nineteen and overage for the school near home," he recalls. "All the kids seemed young. Instead, I went to the old Indian School in Santa Fe, the one founded by Dorothy Dunn. It was the only art school an Indian could afford to go to in those days, because it was free."

Grandson of the Apache chief who was Geronimo's interpreter, Houser had to "drop out of high school to help with the farm." In Santa Fe from 1936 to 1938, he was the only Indian working in sculpture. He also painted murals in Washington, D.C., exhibited in the 1939 New York World's Fair, and had a one-person show at the Museum of New Mexico. During World War II, he lived in California and worked as a factory hand and ditch digger, but in 1948 he won a sculpture competition at the Haskell Institute in Kansas and modeled his first eight-foot stone monument.

In 1949, Houser received a Guggenheim fellowship. He began teaching in Indian schools in 1951, was awarded the Palmes d'Academique by France in 1956 for contributions to Indian art, and retired from teaching in 1975, "a long time for somebody who had wanted to free lance. You never think of getting old. Sometimes I lie awake all night, thinking of the new project for the next morning. I want it to tingle my back when I look at it." Houser's sculpture is in six museums, he was written up in *Artists of the Rockies*, April 1979, and *Southwest Art,* June 1981, and he is represented by The Gallery Wall.

Houston, (Patrick) Cody. Traditional sculptor of figures and wildlife, including ranch scenes, in bronze, born in Mooresville, North Carolina in 1941 and living in Augusta, Montana since 1976. "Don't peg me wrong," he emphasizes, "cowboys and ranch life have definitely influenced my work, but other interests like hunting, fishing, and skiing are additional sources of inspiration. Authors Mark Twain and Robert Service and artists Norman Rockwell, Winslow Homer, and John Singer Sargent have also had a bearing."

He whittled his first sculpture in wood at eight and joined the Army in 1961 after two years at Brevaard College. Moving to Montana in 1965, he spent summers as "foreman of a forest service trail crew in the Bob Marshall Wilderness, a wonderful opportunity to study wildlife in primitive country." In 1969, he graduated from Montana State University with a degree in biological sciences and then went to work for the Montana Livestock Commission as stock inspector and undercover detective.

Assigned to Kalispell, he "hung around the Ace Powell Art Foundry so much that they finally offered me a job. It was there that I learned the entire foundry process and spent my last year as foreman. In 1976, I left the foundry to begin working as a full time sculptor." By 1979, he was receiving certificates of award, and the following year he was Best of Show in Sculpture at the Russell Show and High Bid Award at the Western Experience Sale. "I obviously lean towards the realists in literature and art," he adds. "I don't like photo-realism at all. What I do like are bold, positive statements in art and implied, not graphic detail." He is represented by Sierra and Biltmore Galleries.

Howell, Frank. Painter of Indian portraits in "mysterious detail and spiritual quality" in many media, born in Sioux City, Iowa in 1937 and living in Englewood, Colorado. "I'll stretch a canvas," he says, "then just stare at it for maybe three hours. During this time, I must have complete silence about me. Once I start to paint, the radio can blare, people can talk, but in its initial stage, silence must be absolute. As I sit before the canvas, sometimes images emerge so clearly in my imagination that I can see them on the canvas. Once that happens, I can start to work. I know exactly what I'm going to do."

Educated at the University of Northern Iowa with a BA in art and graduate work in creative writing, he taught art in high school and college for eleven years. His choice of the Indian theme was influenced by his residence in Taos, New Mexico, where he found that "the Indian is a vehicle to express my feelings. I find myself in harmony with Indian philosophy. It used to be that I'd paint completely realistic people or landscapes. My work still has an element of realism—that interest in detail—but now it is more surreal.

"I painted the face of an old Indian once and, almost immediately, I sensed something special about it. Every time I started to paint on a different part of the work, I began experiencing strange feelings like someone was being critical of me. Finally, I realized that the haunting eyes in the painting were making me sick. I had to cover the eyes of the subject before I could complete my painting." Listed in *Who's Who in American Art* and written up in *Artists of the Rockies, Southwest Art,* and *Art Voices/South,* he has shown at K. Phillips and Putney Galleries.

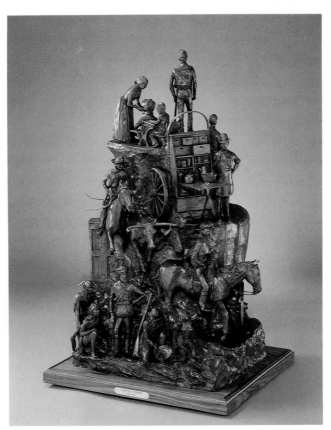

Cody Houston, FRONTIER SPIRITS, bronze, h 36, l 20, d 18

Frank Howell, ARIZONA RIVER, acrylic, 24 x 24

S.Hubbell

Huber

Hubbell, Stephen J. Painter and sculptor of ranching and packing as they are today in Trinity County, California born in Pasadena in 1933 and living in Weaverville, California since 1971. "If you're an artist and you live where it's beautiful," Hubbell claims, "it influences your artwork. If I want to paint a big sky scene, it helps to remember what the sky looks like. I try to use as much of the local scenery as I can, and most of the models are local ranchers and packers that I photograph."

Raised in southern California, Hubbell points out that his "parents died when I was in high school, so after I graduated I had to go out and get a job. I couldn't afford to go to art school or something." He had one year of training in technical illustration and went right to work for Lockheed Aircraft in 1952. For almost 20 years, he worked as a commercial artist for companies and as a free lancer. An urban type, the closest he had been to cowboys was "watching a lot of cowboy movies," but in 1964 he illustrated *Appaloosa Breed Characteristics* and thereafter he became increasingly interested in horses and ranches.

Moving to Weaverville, he says, was "a gamble that paid off. I have a studio separate from my home and go to work six days a week and treat it as a regular job with regular hours. I average around 35 new pieces of art a year. That includes large and small paintings and some sculpture. My working habits are to take one piece at a time from start to finish." Hubbell is a member of the American Indian and Cowboy Artists and won the gold medal for watercolor in 1980. His studio is open to the public as a gallery.

Huber, Dan. Traditional sculptor of the historic and contemporary Western scene in bronze statuettes, born in Yankton, South Dakota in 1941 and living in Milwaukie, Oregon. When asked what Western art is, he replies that "hanging a label on art as to a geographic area is absurd. I don't believe that I've ever heard the terms Southern art, Eastern art, or Northern art. To the general public, the label itself confines both the artist and his subject matter. In fact, the subject matter is as varied as the interests of the artist."

Named for the Yankton Sioux, Huber's birthplace on the Missouri River was the Dakota Territorial capital and a jumping off place for Western migration. His family had been settled there for three generations. Through his school years he earned extra money breaking horses for farmers. After serving with the Army in Germany for three years, he returned to Yankton and competed in bareback and bull-riding events in Midwestern rodeos. He also began sketching the cowboys and the animals of the arena.

A professional sculptor since 1973, he starts with working sketches to resolve the design. Subjects range from contemporary ranch scenes to whimsical action to serious anatomical studies. He states that "I think I'm my own harshest critic. The most rewarding part is watching and listening to the responses different people have to my work. Sometimes people see something in my bronzes that I had never seen. Then I, in turn, enjoy them even more." Huber participates in invitational shows and won Best of Show for sculpture at the 1974 C.M. Russell Auction. Written up in *Art West*, fall 1978, he is represented by Husberg Fine Arts Gallery and Trail's End Gallery.

Stephen Hubbell, **A MAN CALLED MIKE, watercolor, 24 x 18**

Dan Huber, EPHRIAM AND BUFFALO ROBE, bronze, h 20, l 17

Clark Hulings, LA GRANJA, oil, 17⅜ x 26

Hulings, Clark. Representational oil painter of Mexican and New Mexican scenes, born in 1922 and living in Santa Fe, New Mexico. When asked "how" he paints, he has replied that "there is no reason to expect an artist like me to be articulate about what he is doing. He just does it—a good deal of it subliminally."

Raised in Spain where his widowed father remarried in 1926, Hulings returned to elementary school in New Jersey. Visits to the Metropolitan Museum sparked an interest in painting and Hulings began private lessons at fourteen. Following high school, he attended the Art Students League, then was influenced to study physics at Haverford College. A tubercular lung disqualified him from working on the atomic Manhattan Project, but he remained in Santa Fe where he had a one-man show in 1945. After decades of painting that included portraits in Louisiana, further study at the Art Students League, commercial illustration in New York City, three trips to Europe, exhibiting in New York City, and a painting of the Grand Canyon for the Interior Department, another painting of the Grand Canyon won Hulings the Prix de West of the National Academy of Western Art in 1973 and he moved back to Santa Fe.

Concerning illumination of his paintings, he explains that "I have learned to create light effects by observing nature, by remembering what my teachers told me, and by studying other people's paintings. My method of working is pretty much trial and error—I put something on the canvas and correct it until I cannot improve it." At the 1981 Western Heritage Sale, his oil "Kaleidoscope" sold for $310,000. He was featured in *Artists of the Rockies, Persimmon Hill,* and *Southwest Art,* is a member of NAWA, and has shown at Fowler's Gallery.

Susan T. Huntington   *WilsonHurley*   D. HYDE 𝝖𝝖

Huntington, Susan Terpning. Representational painter of Plains Indians and horses, born in Elgin, Illinois in 1953 and living in Albuquerque, New Mexico since 1978. "My subject matter," she points out, "is realistic Western art, mainly of American Indians and horses in appropriate natural settings. I also occasionally paint mountain men, wildlife, and landscapes. Each painting is the result of accumulated historical and ethnographic research combined with many trips taken throughout the West to photograph scenery."

Raised in Connecticut, she has been active in art since childhood, learning from her father Howard Terpning and beginning formal training in high school. Studying art and anthropology with a special interest in American Indian ethnology, she attended Beloit College and the University of Maryland and received her BA from Drew University in New Jersey. She helped illustrate the American Indian artifact collection at Beloit College and has studied the collections of other major museums.

Art and ethnology led her into Western art and she began painting professionally in 1976. "The painting medium I started with was acrylics," she adds, "but I have since changed to alkyds and oils. I also work in charcoal and pen and ink. The move from Maryland to New Mexico has greatly changed my perspective on the West and I think this is reflected in my paintings. Two of my paintings were included in the first exhibition of Western Art to be shown in Peking, China, in 1981, and I am currently represented by Troy's Gallery. My prints are distributed by National Print Galleries. My hobbies are birdwatching, bird painting, and photography."

Hurley, Wilson. Representational painter in oil, especially known for broad landscapes of the Western United States, born in Tulsa, Oklahoma in 1924 and living in Albuquerque, New Mexico since 1952.

His early childhood was spent in Leesburg, Virginia, after the family left Tulsa in 1928. In 1936, they were spending summers in New Mexico, and he was enrolled in Los Alamos School where he graduated in 1942. He entered the U.S. Military Academy in that year, graduated in 1945, was commissioned a second lieutenant, and flew in an air-sea rescue unit in the Philippines until 1949. At that time he resigned his commission in the Air Force and entered George Washington Law School where he earned a degree in 1951. He practiced law in New Mexico, primarily in Albuquerque, for thirteen years.

His commitment to painting began at an early age. He was exposed to many fine painters in New Mexico during his childhood, and while practicing law and flying in the New Mexico National Guard, he continued as a Sunday painter. He has devoted himself full time to painting since 1964. Hurley's interest in broad vistas, mountains, canyons, and clouds is probably the result of his flying experience, although he enjoys painting still lifes and a variety of other subjects. He has been featured in *American Artist, Persimmon Hill, Artists of the Rockies, Art West,* and *Southwest Art.* He exhibits in regional group shows and had one-man shows at the National Cowboy Hall of Fame in 1977 and at the Utah Museum of Fine Art in 1980. He is represented by The Taggart Trust.

Hyde, Doug. Modern Nez Perce and Assiniboine sculptor of Indian figures and animals in stone, born in Hemiston, Oregon in 1946 and living in Santa Fe, New Mexico since 1971. "My sculpture," he points out, "is drawn from the mythology and stories of my ancestors, handed down to me by my grandparents during my childhood near Lapwai, Idaho. I like to work directly on a piece without using preplanned ideas. Thus, the shape, color, and striation of the various stones that I use all combine to suggest ideas. The resulting spontaneity is, I feel, an essential characteristic of my work."

After attending school in Idaho, he came to the Institute of American Indian Art in Santa Fe in 1963 and studied under the sculptor Allan Houser. On graduating in 1966, he attended the Art Institute of Los Angeles for a year, then enlisted in the Army. Wounded in Vietnam, he was discharged in 1969 and returned to the Nez Perce Reservation where he trained as a tombstone cutter. In 1971, he became a graduate student and teacher at the Indian Institute, and established his own studio in 1974. One gallery says it sold "hundreds" of his pieces in five years.

"When I begin a sculpture," he explains, "I start with raw chunks of stone that must be specially prepared. This process which may take from eight to ten hours involves cleaning to discover and remove flaws, washing to determine coloration, and finally grinding with power tools into an approximate shape. At this point, I begin the sculpture. An idea emerges and the qualities which I have discovered in the stone help to determine the completed work." Written up in *Artists of the Rockies,* spring 1975, and *Southwest Art,* July 1978, Hyde is represented by Artistic Gallery and Fenn Galleries Ltd.

Doug Hyde, THE GAUGUIN GIRL, alabaster, h 22

Susan Huntington, WINTER RAID, oil, 24 x 20

Wilson Hurley, ONATE'S ROUTE, oil/canvas, 40 x 48

Jackson

Jackson, Harry. Sculptor of cowboy figures in bronze that may be painted, born in Chicago in 1924 and living in both Lost Cabin, Wyoming and Camariorre, Italy. "It's just plain jack-ass-ery to say that painting my bronzes makes them look like wood. Hell, nobody complains that painting over canvas detracts from the intrinsic quality of the canvas, but critics still believe I'm defiling bronze when I paint over it."

Brought up near the stables and stockyards, Jackson recalls that "all I was good at was drawing, riding, and running away." At fourteen, he hopped a train for Wyoming and became a cowboy. Encouraged by a local artist, he was soon proficient enough to serve as the youngest official combat artist for the Marines in World War II. After the war, he studied painting with the Abstract Expressionists in New York City. A trip to Italy in 1954 returned him to realistic themes, and in 1956 he was commissioned to paint two heroic scenes of the American West. Among his studies for the paintings were figures in wax. When the patron saw the waxes, he ordered them cast in bronze, and Jackson became a full-time sculptor. His 1960 New York City show helped pay for the studio in Wyoming and the foundry in Italy.

Jackson's bronzes are now in public collections around the world and have been featured in *Life* and *Time*, as well as *Southwest Art*. His commissions include heroic statues of historical subjects and portraits that are not always Western, but he lives on a 40,000 acre ranch where he breeds horses and raises cattle. He is a member of the National Academy of Western Art and the National Sculpture Society, is represented by Wyoming Foundry Studios, and exhibits at Trailside Galleries.

Harry Jackson, SACAGAWEA, polychrome bronze, h 10 ft

John Jarvis (signature)

M. Johansen

Jacob, Ned. Painter of the Westerner today, particularly Indians, born in Elizabethton, Tennessee in 1938 and living in Denver since 1966. "My goal in drawing," he states, "is to describe the subject accurately and expressively with a minimum of means. I work quickly. I have a strong tendency to put things down simply. I just can't seem to work slow." A dealer described his technique as "Ned draws the way other people talk." A painter asserted that Jacob's work "makes a strong first impression. He hits you as hard as he can."

After growing up in New Jersey, Jacob hitchhiked to Montana with $50 and a high school diploma. He had worked as a guide and as a trading post clerk when he met the painter Ace Powell who taught him art fundamentals. Without funds, Jacob lived with the Blackfeet until he hitched to Taos in 1961 because he was impressed with Nicolai Fechin's colors. Bettina Steinke taught him drawing, A.D. Greer advised on colors, Robert Lougheed took him on field trips, and a circle of other young painters offered support. By 1966, Jacob's skills had matured.

His practice in painting is to make a small color sketch for each work because "If it's a small painting and you find a problem, it's a small problem." In Denver, friends gather in Jacob's loft where he says, "I'm the mouthpiece." He has gone to Spain, Russia, Morocco, and the South Seas to study and sketch and has been featured in *American Artist* and twice in *Persimmon Hill* and *Southwest Art*. Elected to membership in both the Cowboy Artists of America and the National Academy of Western Art, he quit both because he doesn't believe in competition with his peers. He is represented by Fowler's Gallery.

Jarvis, John. Traditional painter in gouache and watercolor of "landscapes peopled with Indians," born in American Fork, Utah in 1946 and living in Pleasant Grove, Utah. "My art is very personal," he observes. "I find it difficult to do commissioned work with creative restrictions. I never wait until inspiration hits, but work until it comes and then work some more. I spend most of my time painting, partly to make a living but mainly out of pure love for the profession. I would like people to experience my emotions through viewing my art.

"When I was eight, my parents gave me a John Clymer scrapbook. I still have this book along with many other drawings and oil paintings I did while in grade school. I had a one-man show my senior year in high school and received an art scholarship to Snow College, a small southern Utah junior college. Not clear on what I could do with art, I decided to major in fishery biology and minor in art. I graduated from Utah State University in 1971 with a BS, and because art was becoming more important to me, enrolled in Brigham Young University for a Master of Fine Arts.

"My painting was influenced by Andrew Wyeth's technique. With continued development, many hours of painting, and exposure to other artists, my own art began to emerge. My love of nature and outdoor activities has had a great influence. Translating these experiences to my painting with the use of the Indian seemed a perfect solution. Their respect and reverence for nature coincided with my own feelings." Jarvis is represented by Husberg Fine Arts Gallery which listed a watercolor at $7,000 in 1981.

Johansen, Melvin. Traditional sculptor of wildlife in bronze statuettes, born in Oakland, California in 1915 and living in Merlin, Oregon since 1981. "I started as an apprentice taxidermist for the Snow Museum of Natural History in Oakland where I developed skills in diorama preparation by constructing foregrounds and painting backgrounds under the guidance of specialists. I also gained an excellent foundation in animal anatomy.

"With time out for work on delicate optical and aircraft instruments at the Alameda Naval Base during World War II, I continued my museum work. I went into the field in remote areas throughout the Western states, Mexico, and Canada, collecting data and material and sketching and photographing wildlife. My photographs appeared on sporting calendars and natural history and outdoor magazines, and a solo exhibition of 'Birds in Flight' was shown in California and Nevada museums. Motion pictures were used in Disney and other Hollywood nature films."

An interest in art and archaeology has taken him to ancient sites throughout Mexico and the Mediterranean. He also pursued his own development in his spare time, sculpting and painting. In 1972, he retired early as a Senior Curator of Natural Sciences to devote full time to creating bronzes. Once a keen hunter who decorated his own guns, he has long since traded his guns for a camera and he donates bronzes to conservation groups for fund raising. He "strives to achieve a simple impression of the spirit of the animal rather than the literal interpretation he'd been accustomed to in the museum." His bronzes are being shown in The Sportsman's Edge and The May Galleries.

Melvin Johansen, HASTY EXIT, bronze, h 20, w 17

Ned Jacob, DREAM SHIRT (1981), pastel, 30 x 16

John Jarvis, ON THE TRAIL, gouache, 19 x 14½

hw—johnson R   *JAMES RALPH JOHNSON*   *lois johnson*

Johnson, Harvey W. Traditional painter of historical Western scenes, born in New York City in 1921 and living in Santa Fe, New Mexico since 1975. "My father was a sculptor," he says, "my mother a landscape painter. I studied art for three and a half years at the Art Students League (as had my father and mother). Despite all this family interest in art, no one ever pushed it on me."

Raised in the East, Johnson also studied in WPA adult art classes, and went to the League after serving in the Corps of Engineers in World War II. To get started as an illustrator, he worked in an art studio for six months with no pay, then painted Westerns for men's pulp magazines. When the pulps declined, he spent nineteen years as an instructor at the Famous Artists School in Westport, Connecticut, where the well-known illustrator Harold Von Schmidt told Johnson about the market for Western paintings. Johnson was named a charter member of the Cowboy Artists of America and was in its first show in 1966. His oil paintings won silver medals at the 1978 and 1979 shows.

Johnson believes that "artists need the stimulation that comes from associating with other artists. Since my particular subject is in the Western vein, Santa Fe is the culmination of years of dreaming. Western art has had to pass more tests than most people realize, but I feel that we have established Western art as fine art." Johnson is listed in *Who's Who in American Art* and in virtually all Western art texts. He has been featured in *Artists of the Rockies* and twice in *Southwest Art*. Prints are issued by Salt Creek Graphics and Greenwich Workshop. His yearly output of paintings is committed in advance to five shows and to a waiting list that he is trying to reduce.

Johnson, James Ralph. Painter of realistic landscapes and historical Western scenes, born in Fort Payne, Alabama in 1922 and living in Santa Fe, New Mexico since 1964. Twenty-two years in the Marines have predisposed him toward the military, especially the horse cavalry that has become a primary subject for his oils.

A native Southerner proud of Confederate cavalryman, Bedford Forrest, Johnson was introduced to the West by visits to his ranching uncles in four Western states and Canada. He has painted all his life, studying art for four years and graduating from Howard College in 1943. Sketches made during his military service include infantrymen in World War II battles. After leaving the service, he became a writer and illustrator of Western and wildlife books. His wife B.F. Beebe and he wrote 44 books, most of them illustrated by Johnson, on the Civil War and on wildlife habitats from Alaska to Africa. Three of their books were made into movies, three were book club selections, and several were reprinted in Europe.

Johnson has worked full time as an artist since 1970. He paints fresh and sunny scenes of the Southwest because his philosophy is that "if you cannot live with a painting and enjoy it daily, there's no point in having it around." His oils and acrylics are shown in galleries from New York City to California, including the Grand Central in Dallas, Trailside, and Merrill's in Taos. A member of the Western Writers Association and of the American Indian and Cowboy Artists, Johnson is represented in 600 collections and is listed in *Who's Who in American Art*, *Western Painting Today*, and in *Contemporary Authors*.

Johnson, Lois. Representational oil painter of figures and portraits, particularly of Indian children, born in Shafter, California in 1942 and living in Flagstaff, Arizona since 1965. "Early in my career," she observes, "I was certain that talent alone brought success. It has been my experience since then that just surviving as an artist takes an inordinate amount of perseverance and brainpower. To go beyond mere survival to any success at all requires Herculean effort."

Raised in the San Joaquin Valley, she took art courses at Fresno City College in 1959, at North Texas State University in 1962, privately in 1964, and at Northern Arizona State University from 1970 to 1975. "I never felt the need to seek a degree," she says, "because it had little relevance to what I wanted to do." When she moved to Arizona, she began painting portraits of the Navajo and Hopi Indians. "I often choose to paint children," she points out. "I respond to their innocence. In a world which taxes our overburdened psyches, my desire is to bring attention back to the clarity and force of simplicity.

"I have great respect for the people that I have painted on the reservation. When I paint studies from life, I attempt to recreate on canvas their humor and their dignity. These quick studies are painted more from emotion than from thought. As they are transferred to larger, more complex paintings, a great effort is made to sustain that original emotional response. My goal is to interpret the subject, to give the painting a life of its own rather than let it just be a copy of life." She is represented by Wickenburg and Lido Galleries.

Lois Johnson, **A PRIVATE PERFORMANCE**, oil, **36 x 28**

Harvey Johnson, **THE TRADER'S SOLDIER**, oil, **24 x 42**

James Ralph Johnson, **SCOUTING PARTY**, oil, **18 x 36**

Padre Johnson

R. BRADFORD JOHNSON'S

Johnson, Ray "Padre." Representational oil painter of portraits and contemporary ranch scenes, born in Minneapolis in 1934 and living in Cody, Wyoming since 1979. "I have been able to project an effective mood," he points out, "because I have tasted and smelled and listened and observed as an actual working member of the few remnants of what still is a vital historic figure in the contemporary 1980s. In many respects, he is the same cowpuncher, and as alive today as his rugged predecessor of 100 years ago."

After being recognized for achieving unusual portrait likenesses when he was ten, Johnson was a college athlete while working at blue-collar jobs and serving as an emergency room technician in a hospital. Changing his vocation, he entered religious training, was ordained a minister in the Lutheran Church in America, and completed doctoral studies.

Following a campus/community ministry at Dartmouth and Middlesex Colleges in New England, he was a Navy Chaplain from 1966 to 1969, including a paramedical chaplaincy to a Special Forces unit in Vietnam's Mekong Delta. Wounded twice, he was the third-most-decorated chaplain in Navy history. He then left the active ministry, holding a variety of executive jobs, working with urban and reservation Indians, and traveling on all continents. Presently on a leave of absence from the church, he has been a ranch hand in Montana and Wyoming since 1979. This has provided the experience for his Western, outdoor, and portrait art. At first, his paintings served only as "trading stock," but now he is published by Voyageur Art and is represented by the Center Art Galleries and Many Horses Gallery.

Johnson, R. Bradford. Realist painter of acrylic miniatures of rural American scenes on watercolor board, born in Monterey Park, California in 1942 and living in Atascadero, California. He admits to being influenced by Wyeth but explains that "we differ greatly. Wyeth paints versions of his own ethereal world and I paint the real world that used to be. It's really rural Americana—a sort of tragedy of time— frozen on canvas.

"I was encouraged by my parents to pursue my artistic whims, but it wasn't until high school that encouragement was coupled with technical assistance." The first paintings he made were "murals" he daubed on the walls of his home when he was two. He stayed in Orange County, attending Whittier College where "the curriculum was somewhat limited and I exhausted all of the paintings and art history classes in three years." When he graduated in 1964, he opened his own commercial art studio but gave it up because of his "desire for unlimited creativity." He opened three art galleries that prospered before moving to Morro Bay in 1972 and becoming a policeman.

Since 1966, he has entered his paintings in competitive shows where he has received more than 75 awards. He began covering the central California area in his vintage Pontiac, recording county landmarks in afternoon shadows. Most of his painting is done in his studio that is stacked with things from the past including old-time radios through which country-Western music is played while he paints, and says that he applies "plenty of artistic license to move trees and buildings to enhance a painting." His book *Farewell to Fond Memories* and his prints are published by Pine Mountain Publications, and he is represented by Zantman Art Galleries.

Ray P. Johnson, SUNDOWN AT THE DIAMOND BAR, oil, 30 x 24

R. Bradford Johnson, TRANSITION, acrylic/watercolor board, 12 x 24

Stan Johnson

WM. E. JOHNSON

Donal C. Jolley

Johnson, Stanley Quentin. Sculptor of Indian legends in bronze, born in Murray, Utah in 1939 and living in Mapleton, Utah since 1977. Stan Johnson's philosophy centers around his Mormon religion and its influence. He says that "you cannot separate art and religion. They both have a spiritual message to give. When the content is as sacred as one's religion, it deserves an art form of equal worth and should contain our highest spiritual aspirations."

After graduating from high school in Salt Lake City in 1957, Johnson spent two years at the University of Utah before undertaking a three-year mission to Denmark for the LDS Church. When he returned, he enlisted in the National Guard and became the company artist. This influenced him to go back to the University of Utah for art courses, but the only compatible instructor was Avard Fairbanks so Johnson studied sculpture. He also took commercial illustration and was able to obtain commissions while in school. When he felt that the courses had no more to offer, he quit to enter commercial art. A motorcycle accident following ten years of illustration led him to the conclusion that he should proceed with what he really wanted to do, sculpting, and he took a teaching post for financial support.

By 1978, he was able to sculpt full time. In 1981, he sold 200 limited edition bronzes from twelve of his originals that were cast in his own foundry. On one model, his "Eagle Boy," the edition was 37 and the pre-publication price was $6,000. Within 40 days of issuance, Johnson had raised the price to $16,000 in order to slow the sales, and the 34th casting was to be priced at $18,000. He is represented by his own gallery.

Johnson, William E. (Bill). Representational oil painter of the Old West and sculptor of bronze statuettes, born in Charleston, Illinois in 1925 and living in Trinidad, Colorado since 1965. "Charles Russell," he says, "told Harold von Schmidt, when he was young and working for Maynard Dixon—'paint your *own* pictures, kid, your world is different than mine, paint your own pictures.' Harvey Dunn put it another way, 'paint epic pictures, not incidents or fragments, paint the epic.' Von Schmidt learned this from Harvey early.

"My background as a boy was on farms and ranches, raising cattle and in the feedlot and agriculture business near Gunnison, Colorado. In the summer of 1947, I studied under Harvey Dunn at Western State College and from 1947 to 1949 under A.R. Mitchell at Trinidad State Junior College. I studied under Frank J. Reilly at the Art Students League in New York City in 1949 and 1950, and graduated from the Art Center School of Design in Los Angeles in 1954. From 1954 to 1965, I worked in New York City as a commercial artist.

"I moved back to Colorado in 1965 as head of the art department at Trinidad State Junior College. Trinidad is an old town on the Santa Fe Trail, quite diversified and paintable. My pictures are made from spots, places, and locations, but a picture is an assemblage. I see so many copied photographs today, just that, copied photos—too bad. There is a mind's eye and it isn't being used as it used to be. I don't think you can paint without *looking* at things. Nature is always changing and rewarding for the person who *looks*, and *who* looks more than someone who is trying to paint? At present, I only show my sculpture in El Prado Gallery of Art, but I sell most of my work on my own."

Jolley, Donal C. "Sometimes traditional sometimes abstract" watercolorist of "Western landscapes, buildings, steam locomotives, horses and people," born in Zion National Park, Utah in 1933 and living in Rimforest, California since 1970. "My art comes out of my past," he observes. "I've thought about why I do big flat panels and large monolithic forms. When I was growing up, that's all there was to look at. I don't paint pictures of Zion very often, but those kinds of divisions, shapes and forms are present in much of my work.

"My dad was chief ranger. I came a bit prematurely and as far as I know, I'm the only person ever born in the park." His high school taught basic drawing and watercolor and "by the time I finished high school, I liked drawing and disliked everything else." While studying at Brigham Young University, he was drafted into the Army and won an Army Commendation for illustrations. After graduating from the University, he worked as an illustrator, painting in his spare time, but "the day I got my ten-year tie pin, I left.

"I'm not considered a 'cowboy' artist, although many of my best works are cowboy or Indian themes, but I think all my work is 'Western' in nature. Many of my best pieces are not quite traditional and not quite abstract. If I can't get an idea moving right away, I soak my watercolor tray to keep the paint moist, and if the blankness continues too long, I may inspect the woodpile to see if there's something I should do to get ready for the winter. Then the inspiration to paint is suddenly there!" Listed in *Who's Who in American Art* and written up in *Southwest Art*, March 1980, he is represented by In The Spirit Gallery and Ragland's Woodland Gallery.

William Johnson, OLD TIME RANCHER, bronze, h 15

Stan Johnson, MINITARI WAR DANCE, bronze, h 36

Donal C. Jolley, AMERICAN NATIVE, watercolor, 22 x 30

Covelle

Thomas William Jones

Jack Jordan

Jones, Covelle. Sculptor of Western figures in bronze, born in Bremond, Texas in 1940 and living in Waco, Texas. "Self-discipline is important for anyone who works at home," he asserts, and "one of the things that really gets to me is that people don't believe that a person at home can possibly be working. It is easy to sluff off and procrastinate. I don't have time for that, but other people say 'Oh, it's okay to call Covelle. He doesn't work. He's an artist.' "

With a BS in art education from Tarleton State University and a Master's from North Texas State University, Jones taught in Hobbs, New Mexico. He says that he "started out with an intense desire to express myself as a painter, but that medium didn't accomplish for me what a three-dimensional one did. I then turned to clay, and I knew that sculpture was what I wanted to do." When he gave a sculpture demonstration to his class, he "couldn't put it down. I worked there in my classroom until after dark, and I haven't stopped since."

After almost twenty years perfecting his technique, Jones observes that "when they talk about Willie Nelson being an overnight success, it's like an artist. No one thinks of all the one-night stands Willie had to play. For an artist, no one thinks of the years of sweat that have gone into his work before he makes that questionable overnight success status. I find that as I get deeper into my work, I have to do more and more study. People expect me to get better." He has exhibited at the Western Heritage Show and in the Texas Ranger Hall of Fame, has had three commissioned editions, was featured in *Southwest Art*, April 1978, is represented by Corpus Christi Art Gallery and Cross Galleries, and signs his work—"Covelle."

Jones, Thomas William. Representational watercolorist of "whatever catches my eye," born in Lakewood, Ohio in 1942 and living in Bellevue, Washington since 1967. "People are grabbing for something to sink their teeth into," he believes, "something to hang on their wall that's close to them, some meaningful object or place. People have had too much of the hard-edge style. They're looking for something to enrich their lives, something like representational realism.

"Raised on the shores of Lake Erie, much of my early impressions about art were given to me by my father. While I was attending the Cleveland Institute of Art, an interest in aviation led me to paint historical aircraft scenes. This along with my landscape painting helped pay for my education. After graduating in 1964 and moving to the Pacific Northwest, I concentrated on gallery representation, juried national exhibitions, and commissions. This was a turning point. The first of sixteen solo gallery exhibitions took place in 1970.

"A good representational painting has an image which has been pulled out of a lot of abstract underpainting. Lots of paintings never make it past the abstract underpainting stage. Even at that early stage, it's possible for a painting to start to get stagnant and lose its flow. When you look at a good piece of work, you can't tell where the artist started. Things go together—there's control, mastery, a refinement of technique that allows some areas to be just suggestive and others detailed. When I start a new painting, I have it practically painted before I start." Written up in *American Artist*, September 1979, and *Artists of the Rockies*, winter 1980, he is represented by Carson's Western American Art Gallery and Foster/White.

Jordan, Jack. Traditional oil painter of the Old West, born in St. Louis, Missouri in 1928 and living in El Cajon, California since 1972. "There is a romance to the horse," he declares, "but basically a horse is not very bright. Where a horse will run right into a barbed wire fence, a mule will back off. A horse isn't a pet. His size alone makes him dangerous for the uninitiated. They are marvelous to paint, but perhaps too glamorized in Western history. Handsome, but dumb."

Raised on a farm near Des Moines, Iowa, Jordan checked traps and trout lines on the way to school. At twelve, he took art lessons for a year as part of a WPA project, and in high school studied commercial art. After graduation in 1946, he joined the Marines, and then spent three years touring night clubs and carnivals as a professional magician. When he returned to Iowa, he became a newspaper artist and next moved on to a paper in San Diego where he also studied at Coronado School of Art. He later attended Otis Art Institute in Los Angeles and paid his way by selling Western paintings.

In 1971, he studied in Mexico and decided to become a full time painter with the Old West as his subject because, as he says, "I like the excitement, the romance, and the spirit that goes along with the era. I feel drawn to paint the beginnings, even before the cowboy, when the Indian and the trapper and the scout were the only intruders in that vast country. I love paint to be juicy," he adds, "and the best painting I've ever done is always the one I'm working on now." Jordan was featured in *Art West*, spring 1979, and *Southwest Art*, June 1979. He exhibits at invitational shows and is represented by Burk Gal'ry and Artists Union Gallery.

Thomas W. Jones, MURRAY'S FRIEND (1979)
watercolor/paper, 20 x 22

Covelle Jones, MAN WITHOUT FEAR
bronze, h 19½, l 17, Edition 20

Jack Jordan, THURSDAY'S CHILD, oil, 24 x 36

Jungbluth, Mimi. Painter of pastel portraits of "the Native American as he is today," born in Kansas City, Missouri in 1934 and living in Ruidoso, New Mexico. "I was born," she emphasizes, "into a family where the parents encouraged creative expression from each child. Mother and Daddy made as much drawing material available to us as they could. The emphasis was on the joy of just drawing. Both of my parents contributed to our appreciation of "ethnic-ness" and to the opportunity to love old people. No doubt these ethnic encounters had an effect on why I portray the Native American.

"During my junior year of college, I received a call from my junior high school teacher asking me if I would like to do a portrait of a little boy. I did the portrait from life, but I've never done another work of a small child from life again. One thing led to another, and by the time I moved to Austin in 1968, I was very much 'in demand' as a portraitist. When I found myself living in an area where I knew no one, I went to a gallery and the woman there suggested I become more acquainted with the people of the Southwest. To me, that meant *Indians*.

"I began painting from published photographs, but each time I went to a show I would see another artist's rendering of the same photo. In 1975, we were told about the Indian Market held in Santa Fe each year. We headed out and have been blessed with some beautiful friendships. Since moving to Ruidoso, we have been more personally involved with the wonderful Mescalero Indians." She is a member of the Pastel Society of America, and was featured on the cover of *Southwest Art*, March 1981.

Justus, Wayne. Realist painter of the contemporary American cowboy in opaque watercolor and oil, born in Escondido, California in 1952 and living in Pagosa Springs, Colorado since 1979. "I help ranches work their cattle in the spring and fall in trade for the opportunity to gather authentic subject matter on the American cowboy. One truth I am trying to portray in my art is that cowboying still exists much as it did 100 years ago. They still work from a wagon and do the work on horseback.

"For years I lived on a horse ranch and later became an exercise boy on a thoroughbred ranch. Most of my grade school days were spent drawing pictures. I studied with an artist from Spain who gave me lessons in drawing in charcoal in 1966 when I was in seventh grade. Since then I have studied under Austin Deuel from 1967 to 1968 and several later sessions. I studied under Donald "Putt" Putman in 1976 when my wife and I modeled for him in exchange for his knowledge. 'Miles on the brush' is most of my art education.

"My early ranch life was still in my blood so I combined cowboying and art. We left California in 1979 to spend ten months on two big cattle ranches in New Mexico before moving to our property on the western slope of the Rocky Mountains of southern Colorado where we paint and raise quarter horses.

"I get the idea, draw sketches, and then use photographs as a tool, not a device. Photos help me to get detail that I wouldn't be able to get otherwise from memory. The authenticity of my paintings is very important to me and getting it first hand is to know that that's the way it actually is." Justus is a member of the American Indian and Cowboy Artists.

Mimi Jungbluth, RAELYNN, pastel, 14¾ x 9¾

Wayne Justus, YOU'RE NEXT, oil, 24 x 36

Kaplinski, Buffalo. Painter of Western landscapes in acrylics, born in Chicago in 1943 and living in Elizabeth, Colorado since 1967. "What I like to do," he declares, "is paint outside, get the emotional experience you can't get in the studio, then go into the studio and translate the abstract elements, develop them in a way that the work becomes stronger, maybe take the color and expand on it. I enlarge the experience in the studio and give it a more intense personal interpretation."

Kaplinski studied at the American Academy of Art and the Art Institute of Chicago from 1961 to 1963. In 1966, he was in Taos, New Mexico, where he said that "a lot of values move closer to each other" in painting. The next year he moved to the high country and remarked that "it's a new form of reality for me. And the pure design forms, the repetition of shapes and lines, they turn me on."

Fellow painter Ned Jacobs says that "Buffalo has no preconceived notions. He lets the landscape dictate to him. He has no conventions at all, either in subject matter or approach. Buffalo knows that doing one thing is like staying a child all your life. And he is constantly changing. If you don't like what Buffalo's doing now, wait, because the next day he'll be doing something different." Kaplinski adds that "if nobody else likes what I'm doing now, that's their problem. Every artist wants to be known as a good artist, not just for doing one thing." He has been in twenty one-person shows and 75 national shows like those of the American Watercolor Society and the National Academy of Design. He was featured in *American Arts, Southwest Art*, and *Artists of the Rockies*, is listed in *Who's Who in American Art*, and is represented by Trailside Galleries.

Keese, Travis. Oil painter of central Texas wildlife and Big Bend subjects, particularly wild turkeys, pronghorns, and eagles, born in Lyons, Burleson County, Texas in 1932 and living in Kerrville, Texas. "When I go into the field, I carry binoculars, camera, canvases, a complete oil kit, pencils, sketchbook, a pad to sit on, and food and water. When I find a suitable location, I sit and paint for three to four hours, returning each day until I have the landscape pretty well complete. The bird or animal is usually placed in the studio with finishing touches added to the background.

"I graduated from Blinn Junior College with an associate of arts degree in 1951 and from the University of Houston with a BFA in 1954. I then served in the Army from 1954 to 1957, and was trained as a photolithographer. I was a free-lance artist until 1959, was employed in photo-engraving, and was staff artist at the Houston Museum of Natural Science from 1964 to 1970, producing diorama backgrounds, illustrations of wildlife, posters, and murals.

"I had been entering competitive painting exhibitions regularly. In the mid-1960s, I began to study Western habitats, cacti, etc., and my interest turned westward. I became a member of the Texas Association of Professional Artists in 1977. My method of working varies. Sometimes I start with a sketch and carry the painting through to completion. Sometimes the painting begins as a fragment and I will develop a composition without doing a sketch. Most of my paintings are composites. Because of the drying time required by the oil technique, I often have ten paintings underway at once." He is represented by Keese-Southwest Gallery and his prints are published by Arts Limited Inc.

Buffalo Kaplinski, KAYENTA PRAYER—PSALM 63, acrylic/canvas, 60 x 60

Travis Keese, BURRO MESA BUCK, oil, 24 x 30

T.D. KELSEY

Kelsey, T.D. Traditional sculptor of Western cattle, saddle bronc roping, and team roping in bronze statuettes and statues, born in Shelley, Idaho in 1940 and living in Kiowa, Colorado since 1972. "I used to read Will James," he states, "and something he wrote has stayed with me: 'There's nothing as good for the inside of a man as the outside of a horse.' And I guess horses have always made me feel that way."

Raised near Bozeman, Montana, he rodeoed while in high school and continued as a spare-time saddle bronc rider for twenty years. His father flew as a crop duster and Kelsey bought his first plane when he was sixteen, raising the money by selling his hunting rifles. He continued flight training while he was studying pre-med at Montana State University and at twenty was hired by United Air Lines. Based in Denver, he bought a ranch 60 miles southeast and in 1969 acquired his first Texas Longhorns, the start of a herd that has included Grand Champions.

In 1970, he was modeling terra cotta as a hobby when George Phippen's widow suggested casting the piece in bronze. His early castings were accepted by Saks Gallery, and in 1977 Kelsey decided that "more than anything else he wanted to sculpt." In 1979, he resigned from United Air Lines to concentrate on art while continuing to fly his own plane as a hobby and to travel. He has received a commission from the Professional Rodeo Cowboys Association for three bronzes for their Hall of Fame in Colorado Springs, and another for a life size bronze for the new museum of the Longhorn Breeders Association of America in Fort Worth, Texas. Written up in *Artists of the Rockies*, fall 1981, he is represented by Saks Gallery and Peppertree Fine Art, Inc.

Kerswill, Roy. Watercolor and oil painter of historical material in traditional style, born in Bigbury, Devon, England in 1925 and living in Jackson Hole, Wyoming since 1960. "I have entered hundreds of shows over the years and have collected numerous awards and the only thing I have to show for it is a huge collection of ribbons hanging in a bunch on my studio wall. Basically, I just plain enjoy painting and make a good living at it."

Because his father was in the Royal Navy, Kerswill grew up in English seacoast towns before winning a scholarship to the Bristol College of Art. During World War II, he served with the British forces in New Zealand and then came to this country in 1947. He traveled extensively, working as a surveyor on the Alcan Highway and taking a 7,000 mile trip in an 18-foot cedar canoe from the west coast of Canada to New Orleans, paying his way by painting portraits. In 1951, he began illustrating for the Martin Company in Denver, drawing imaginary space vehicles while building a clientele for art.

"The game of the artist is sharing," he declares. As he travels the West, he often comes across a spot that says to him, "something interesting could have happened here" to the mountain men, the settlers, the scouts, or the Indians. As to technique, "I have a complete mental picture before I begin to paint. Then I just paint what I see and how I feel. I don't have any secrets. I paint with the same need as I eat. I'm addicted to painting, to this inner urge to create and communicate." Kerswill was featured in *Southwest Art*, summer 1976. He publishes his own prints and is represented by The May Gallery.

Kettlewell, Neil M. Realist sculptor of wildlife in bronze, born in Evanston, Illinois in 1938 and living in Missoula, Montana since 1969. "I spent years in dissection classes taking animals apart," he asserts. "Now I've decided to put them together. I term myself a realist, a wildlife sculptor in the world of Western art. I don't really like the description much, but there is some truth there. Unless an animal is recognizable to the viewer, the communication is lost."

After earning a doctorate in physiological psychology from the University of Michigan in 1968, Kettlewell is now an Associate Professor of Psychology at the University of Montana. Sculpting is a second career, begun in 1977 when he decided he wanted a bronze of a big horn sheep to display. He had neither training nor experience but he bought a chunk of wax and modeled the sheep. By 1979, he had modeled fourteen statuettes that sold in galleries and he was featured in *Art West*, November 1979.

Kettlewell has no studio. After his regular day at the university, he retreats to his den with his wax and he models while watching television. He uses no armature and makes no sketch. "Wildlife sculpture appealed to me," he explains, "because of the variety of forms, textures, and movement. My task is doing what the piece demands, listening to it, rather than forcing wax into shapes previously decided upon." He relies on his taste for Chinese sculpture, his knowledge of anatomy from medical studies, and his experience as a hunter. His scientific training aids modeling, too, because "art is essentially another form of communication." His gallery is Husberg Fine Arts.

Neil Kettlewell, ILLUSIONS, bronze, h 7, l 6, d 6

T.D. Kelsey, ESCAPE ARTISTS, bronze, h 13, l 8

Roy Kerswill, EDGE OF THE VILLAGE, oil, 40 x 68

289

Janet W. Kimberling

B'ee D'xŏ

Kimberling, Janet Wensley. Romantic realist painter of New Mexico adobes and landscapes, born in New Rochelle, New York in 1925 and living in Santa Fe, New Mexico since 1975. "I do not follow any 'ism' or school," she declares. "I believe a painting should have something to say, and the emotion expressed by the artist should be readily felt by the viewer. Bizarre technique for its own sake doesn't interest me.

"Talent shows up early, and my mother saved the drawings I did at six. I won poster contests, and when I was ten wrote home from camp that 'I have to go now, and finish the painting I started yesterday.' My father was an amateur artist and I was taken to exhibits and demonstrations. I worked my way through college. The summer before my senior year I had a job in an art studio. I was the only girl among seven men who said they would hire me only if I said nothing when they told off-color jokes. 'That's all right with me,' I replied, 'but I'm not cleaning the sink, either'."

She took time off to work as a draftsman in New York City during World War II. After graduating magna cum laude in 1948, she was a package designer for a year, had a show of watercolors in Boston, and in 1955 began making free-lance architectural renderings in Milwaukee. She started painting full time in 1967, doing large oil landscapes. Now, she is "enchanted with New Mexico and may often be seen by the roadside, painting its quaint adobes." She makes color studies, never photographs, and develops her larger works in the studio. Current subjects are Spanish Colonial history and the Rocky Mountains. She is represented by Gallery Americana and D'Oros.

King, James. Full-blood Navajo painter of portraits, landscapes, still lifes, and nudes in oil and acrylics, born in Shiprock, New Mexico in 1951 and living there in 1982. A poem of his, titled "Money," sums up his determination and artistic ambition. "They say in a few years, I'll be able to/Buy seven cars without having to borrow,/Have one house in Phoenix and/One in the mountain of the reservation./They say I will probably travel in my/Own Lear Jet,/In a successful man's suit;/This talking may be loud or true,/It don't matter to me none,/ Whether rich or poor I will continue/To paint till I'm seventy-nine,/After that I'll just draw.

"In the second grade I did a small painting and kids started calling me an artist. I hated that word and vowed I'd never paint again, but in high school I did small paintings and sold them for five dollars. After graduation in 1971, a friend who was pushing the brush showed me how to paint and I received a grant for art training in Salt Lake City. I graduated from there and moved back to Shiprock but I could not get a job so I became a babysitter and then got a job as a soil technician at Navajo Agricultural Product Industry.

"I was still painting and well-known artists said 'you have a future' and they would have awarded me best of show. With this in the back of my mind, I ran across Joe Tanner, quit my job, and started as a self-employed artist in 1978. In 1980, I walked away with three best of shows and now it's a 'Labor of Love: It's when you bound your head in/Bandages to keep your hair from disturbing you/And don't notice your sister is watching/Till she says something and scares you to death./Labor of love is continuous till the phone/Rings or a knock on the door.' " King is represented by Tanner Indian Arts.

Janet W. Kimberling, THE BLUE DOOR, oil, 24 x 36

James King, MEMORIES OF A SAILOR, oil, 40 x 53

Tom Knapp

R.L. Knaub

John Knowlton

Knapp, Tom. Bronze sculptor recording the modern Western scene, born in Gillette, Wyoming in 1925 and living in Ruidoso Downs, New Mexico since 1971. "There's a Western art fad in progress," Knapp declares, "and things that happened 100 years ago are currently being reexamined for use as subject matter. I feel that this is largely wasted effort. After all, such artists are trying to breathe life into something they didn't actually experience."

During his adolescence, a Plains Indian tribe camped near his family's ranch every summer. There were no museums, but Army service during the Korean War exposed him to sculpture and painting shows. After the war, he attended the California College of Arts and Crafts in Oakland and the Art Center School of Design in Los Angeles when he was nearly 30. His first job was as an animation artist for Mountain Bell Telephone Company in Albuquerque, New Mexico. He decided that he would quit Mountain Bell "whenever commissions from sculpture equalled my regular salary." After quitting, he "suddenly realized that self-employment had cut my total income in half." He has been a full-time sculptor since 1969.

Knapp casts his own bronzes in the backyard of his studio, as part of a neighborhood "Pour In" that has been described in *New Mexico Magazine*. His series of contemporary American Indian ceremonial dancers was featured in *Art West*, which quotes Knapp as claiming that "vitality, movement, is the most important thing in sculpture, not the detail." His work is in five public collections, he is listed in *Who's Who in American Art*, and is represented by Fowler's Gallery.

Knaub, Raymond L. Representational painter of the Plains and the Southwest, born in Gering, Nebraska in 1940 and living in Lakewood, Colorado since 1968. "I look for a sense of place," he says. "When I stopped at one of those empty old farmhouses in western Nebraska and stepped inside, the sense of exhaustion and collapse in the place invaded me! There I was, alone with all these sensations, and when I heard the noises upstairs that I knew were only mice, the fact is, I was scared as hell and could not go up those stairs."

His German-Russian grandparents emigrated from the Ukraine to Nebraska where Knaub grew up. He says that "to consider myself self-taught would be ludicrous, when I have attended three universities:" Baylor from 1958 to 1960, Nebraska where he earned his BFA in 1963, and Colorado. He is an admirer of Andrew Wyeth who "has to be recognized as one of the major 20th-century artists."

Knaub has taught art in county schools since 1968. He paints in the afternoons and evenings, working on three or four pictures at a time. "I have a persistent need to put something down on canvas," he declares. "If I do not, I get very irritable. Painting is a necessity, like eating or sleeping." He believes that "the passage of time has a physical presence" that remains, and he is "moved by the thought of all of the life that once went on" at a given location. Knaub has had five one-person shows, has work in Colorado and Texas collections, and exhibits nationally. He was featured in *Southwest Art*, September 1978, and is in *Who's Who in American Art*. The Baker Gallery of Fine Arts and De Colores Art Gallery represents him.

Knowlton, John. Oil painter of Western and marine scenes, born in Los Angeles in 1923 and living in Morro Bay, California. "My style," he explains, "is a loose 'painterly-realism' rather than photo-realism. I pay attention to the realism of the life and legend of the American cowboy and the Western scene. My viewpoint is strong on storytelling quality for I paint and live my subject based on my own 27 years' experience as cowboy, cattle buyer, and cattle feeder.

"I started painting at ten. The big influence on me was Frank Tenney Johnson. Viewing his exhibit at the Biltmore Salon in 1931 started me thinking cowboy." Knowlton grew up sailing around Alamitos Bay and was a naval officer on Pacific duty in World War II. After receiving his BS in animal husbandry from the University of California at Davis, he entered the cattle business where he was in the Northwest, Deep South, and all the Western states and saw "the very last of the disappearing Old West, with cattle trains, chuck wagons, line camps, and trail drives, living the lifestyle of the modern cowboy.

"Although I studied with Frederick Taubes and others, and at Questa College in San Luis Obispo, I am basically a self-taught artist. My technique is oil on canvas, but I use bold colors with glazing imprimatura or impasto. Regarding both my seascape and Western works, a critic wrote that I 'deserve the title of sailor on horseback as much as Jack London did'." Knowlton has won awards from 1937 to 1981 and is represented by the Double Check Western Gallery.

Tom Knapp
SPRINGTIME IN THE ROCKIES
bronze, h 30

John Knowlton, NIGHT VISITOR, oil, 18 x 24

Raymond Knaub, SALT CREEK, WYOMING, ABOUT 1927, oil/canvas, 24 x 38

KONIS PSA

Howard Koslow

Kolliker, Bill. Contemporary watercolorist of the landscape of the Mexican border, born in Bern, Switzerland of an American mother in 1905 and living in El Paso, Texas since 1953. "Painting is like driving a car," he explains. "Once you've learned the skills, you don't think about the mechanical operation of moving the car. You're too busy thinking about where you're going. In the past ten years, my hand has become freer and I'm not as concerned with details. I don't think about color. I feel it."

He emigrated to New York City at fifteen when his father died. Landing a job as office boy in the art department of the Hearst newspaper from 4 P.M. until midnight, he took art classes at the National Academy of Design from 9 A.M. until 3:30 P.M. In 1930, he was employed at the *American Weekly*, rising from illustrator to art editor in twenty years. When he moved to El Paso, his "house was the city limit. I knew this was a special, strange land." While working in advertising, he also designed a mural, 7-foot eagles and plaques, and had solo exhibitions in El Paso and Juarez, Mexico.

In 1965, he decided to devote himself to painting, saying that "I simply changed jobs and went into business for myself. I never wanted to be anything but an artist, so I feel like I've never worked a day in my life." Each morning, he awakens with an idea of what he will paint that day. "I formulate the composition while still lying down," he points out. "If I don't plan ahead, I flounder all morning." While working, he listens to Mozart or ragtime so "the brush dances across the paper, creating its own melody." Listed in *Who's Who in American Art*, he is represented by Gallery Westside.

Konis, Ben. Pastellist of the Southwest Indians, born in Perth Amboy, New Jersey and living in Amarillo, Texas since 1969. "Fifty years from now," he says, "people can look at my work and see the 1980s. Maybe the Indians are wearing a blanket from J.C. Penney's store instead of a handwoven one, but it's authentic."

Of Lithuanian descent, Konis spent two years in the Army during World War II. His untrained sketches led him into the Caton-Rose Institute of Fine Art in New York City. After graduation, he was a fashion illustrator and a partner in an ad agency for 15 years while he continued his art education. Interest in the Southwest was fostered by vacation trips, and when he bought two Amarillo houses, it was the first time he had not lived in an apartment. "When I first saw Taos and the dancers in their regalia," he declares, "it floored me. New York had no color for me like that." Within a year he had a one-man show and he was teaching.

While painting oils, he thinks of the letters C C D, meaning contrast, color, and detail, and in his pastels he will "still strive for that unique blending property that only the oils have." Color is his forte, and he "takes license with what I see to enhance its artistic qualities, especially the color. I invent color schemes." In some paintings he will incorporate a "secret," a portrait hidden in the landscape background. He begins painting after his children are off to school and continues until they return, a discipline that followed triple by-pass heart surgery in 1975. He has written on pastel technique in *American Art* and has been featured in *American Artist*, *Southwest Art*, and *Accent West*. His paintings are shown in Wickenburg and Rainone galleries.

Koslow, Howard. Realist painter of Western mountains in acrylic, born in Brooklyn, New York in 1924 and living in East Norwich, Long Island. "To record the American landscape in realist paintings," he emphasizes, "the mountains, the rivers, the beaches, the national parks, the canyons, and the back roads, before they disappear under the force of the bulldozer, that is a *goal*. There is so much to see and chronicle that I am certainly not about to exhaust my subject matter, only the time and perhaps the energy to paint it.

"I was awarded an Art League scholarship to Pratt Institute, graduating in 1944 and going directly to an apprenticeship with Jean Carlu, the French poster artist, at his New York City studio. After about a year, I worked in commercial illustration studios and in 1948 took time off to revitalize my paintings by studying at Cranbrook Academy. When I returned to New York, I continued with free-lance illustration, incorporating the painting techniques, and still do but I have actively pursued gallery painting during this entire period.

"I have traveled extensively for the Air Force Historical Art Program, and for the Postal Service—designed stamps for 1971, 1972, 1980, and 1983. A painting trip to Yosemite Falls sponsored by the National Park Service in 1976 opened a whole new vista for me. The American West has always been a magical place for me. I recall the John Ford movie epics with their extraordinary landscapes, the marvelous Remington prints, and the many illustrated books on the West. I have been a member of the Society of Illustrators since 1958 and am represented by Grizzly Tree Gallery."

Bill Kolliker, YUCCAS, watercolor, 30 x 22

Ben Konis, HANGING LOOSE, pastel, 22 x 18

Howard Koslow, NORTH FROM KAYENTA, acrylic, 19 x 36

Krahn
P.S.A.

JAMES KRAMER

Krahn, Pat. Representational painter in oil and pastel of "subjects from the nature she knows," born in Bartlesville, Oklahoma in 1930 and living in Lubbock, Texas since 1958. "My work is representational," she explains, "because I want to share what I have seen and the emotions I have felt. Painting is the way I have found to do that. I want to make others aware, those that look but do not see.

"I was first influenced to pursue art by my 5th grade teacher and then by the art teacher at Amarillo High School. I selected Texas Women's University because of its art school. I love to draw and especially enjoy working with the pencil. I found the public preferred my paintings that incorporated color so now I satisfy my love of drawings by doing a completed value study in charcoal under my oil paintings. This drawing is so complete that once the 'underdrawing' for an oil painting was exhibited and it won a jurored show.

"I work every day, either setting up for a still life painting, figuring out a composition, or working on a painting in progress. The only way I know to perfect my craft is by working at it. Sometimes they don't come off as I had pictured them but even when they are 'throw-aways,' I believe I've learned something because there's always some area that was just what I was looking for in color relationships or paint application. I know I'll never learn all there is to know about painting, and through it all I'm enjoying the experience." She has had twenty one-person shows, is in eleven permanent collections including the Diamond M Museum, is a member of the Pastel Society of America, and is represented by Sagebrush Galleries.

Kramer, James. Traditional watercolorist, especially of architectural subjects, born in Columbus, Ohio in 1927 and living in Santa Fe, New Mexico since 1976. "A fresh, clean sheet of paper is delightful," Kramer confesses, "but intimidating. I hate pure white paper. Machine-made paper is stark white. Handmade paper has warmth. I like old paper and I buy it wherever and whenever I can. I also like brushes."

After two years at the Cleveland Institute of Art where the instructors taught Kramer "to draw, to paint, to know what good materials were, and the composition and character of paint and paper," he transferred to Western Reserve University and then Ohio State University because "the responsibilities of family life turned him to the field of architecture. He practiced architecture in Ohio and in California until 1970 when he could again turn full attention to his painting." He calls Santa Fe "a community of representational painters. I felt at home from the beginning.

"All of my larger watercolors," he explains, "are painted in the studio from sketches made in the field. I use color slides for further reference. In the studio, I begin with thumbnail sketches, then make an accurate line drawing for projection onto a preliminary study. Once ready, I project my study onto a full sheet of watercolor paper, wash the paper, and begin painting. I do what I want to do. The medium can produce things you don't expect, but I want control." Kramer is listed in *Who's Who in American Art*, has been featured in *American Artist*, August 1973, and *Southwest Art*, January 1982, is a member of the National Academy of Western Art, and is represented by Shriver Gallery.

Pat Krahn, INNOCENCE, pastel, 19 x 25

James Kramer, MERCADO GATO NEGRO (1982), watercolor, 14 x 21

Kuczynski, David. Impressionist-realist oil painter and printmaker of "seascapes, landscapes, American Indian subjects, and family portraits, anything that touches me," born in Plains, Pennsylvania in 1947 and living in Lomita, California since 1974. "I hate labels," he emphasizes, "but if I had to qualify myself, I'm somewhere between Impressionism and realism. My work is realistic insofar as people can identify with the subject, but it's loose because of my style. It's a form of communication, a form of self-expression, not a profound social statement."

Interested in art since his childhood memories in Pennsylvania where he was raised, he enrolled in the American Academy of Art in Chicago in 1965. In his fourth year, he won the Mosby Fine Arts Scholarship and then went into the Air Force where he was assigned to meteorology. A tour of duty at Malmstron Air Force Base in Great Falls, Montana, introduced him to the Western landscape and "created a desire to know more about the proud people who had fought to save their land."

After military service and free-lance commercial art jobs, he moved to southern California in 1974 to make "his sole occupation that of art." Several more years of study and selling paintings at local art shows followed, until he mastered the technique of "saying 'something' to someone" while "fulfilling myself and my spirit." Although he favors the American Indian and horses, he states that his "themes are unrelated. It is important for artists not to limit their subject matter because their skills and imagination will also become limited. Ultimately, a good (or bad) painting boils down to an indescribable feeling in the mind and heart of the viewer." He is represented by El Prado Gallery of Art.

Kuhn, Bob. Realist-Impressionist painter of animals in acrylic on masonite, born in Buffalo, New York in 1920 and living in Roxbury, Connecticut. "If you are only painting the outside of the animal, you may come up with an attractive result, but it doesn't say anything about that animal. If you love the animal, you want to know about it. Then you want to tell everybody else what you found out—and your means of telling it is paintings.

"Studied: Pratt Institute, Brooklyn, N.Y." is the opening of Kuhn's autobiographical listings. "Work published: Many paintings for books, magazines, calendars, starting in 1941, pause for time in maritime service, then steadily until 1970. Books and prints: *The Animal Art of Bob Kuhn.* Several limited edition prints. Prizes: 2nd and 1st prizes, oil, National Academy of Western Art. 1st prize, Wildlife Art Show. Expeditions: Numerous trips to Africa, Alaska, Canada. Membership: Society of Animal Artists."

In *Profiles in American Art* in 1982, Kuhn as "The Man Who Paints Animals" says, "I don't know why I paint animals. All I know is when I was a very little boy, there was something about animals that grabbed hold of me. To me, the fun of painting animals is to be the stage manager, the arranger, the fellow who selects out the stuff that doesn't abet the subject and the mood, and to bring in the things that would enhance the mood. Having the temerity or courage, having figured things out, to bend them or change them when the painting calls for it, is the final test of whether you're functioning as a naturalist or a painter." At the 1981 Settlers West silent auction, Kuhn's painting elicited a minimum bid of $16,500.

Kuka, King. Abstract/Impressionist painter of Indian figures in watercolor, born in Browning, Montana on the Blackfoot Reservation in 1946 and living in East Glacier, Montana. "I enjoy my work, now," he states. "I was for a long time caught up in the Indians of Charlie Russell. That's what I thought art was. So that's how I painted. And when I could paint realism, I found out I hated painting and I didn't like the results."

His grandfather had been a poor Indian rancher who painted oil portraits of Blackfoot to help make ends meet. At twelve, Kuka discovered the paints in a trunk and tried them. As an Indian in a white high school though, "you were really looked down on." A newspaperwoman led him to the Institute of American Indian Art in Santa Fe, New Mexico, and "it just changed my whole life. I felt like I was someone and my life was important. I saw people making it. That was the key." He sold his first painting, graduated in 1965, served in the Army until 1967, earned his BFA from the University of Montana in 1973, and then taught high school art.

In 1978, he studied in the graduate school at Montana State University and then began painting full time. "I went to work experimenting," he recalls, "unlearning realism and trying to find myself. Now I like what I'm doing. In my sculpture and my painting, I have a great fear in the beginning and a slight fear all the way to the end. But I feel without that fear, I might become overconfident, proud, and end up with an inferior piece." He has won honors in all media and in most national Indian art exhibitions since 1969, and his work is in museum collections. Prints are published by Wolf Chief Graphics and he is represented by Anne Magee and Magic Mountain Galleries.

David Kuczynski, PLAINS INDIAN, oil, 20 x 16

King Kuka, CONTINENTAL DIVIDE (1981), watercolor, 30 x 22

Bob Kuhn, WOLVES TESTING A HERD, acrylic, 24 x 48

Kunstler, Mort. Realist painter of commissioned subjects, including Westerns in oil, born in Brooklyn, New York in 1931 and living near Oyster Bay, Long Island. "Most illustrators," he points out, "like what they do. Michelangelo was an illustrator. His client was the Church. His 'page' size was rather large—the ceiling of the Sistine Chapel. The Pope was his art director and told him what to paint, but Michelangelo hated painting the ceiling because he wanted to sculpt.

"I was encouraged to draw by my parents, and I think I can truthfully say I drew as well at twelve as I do today. Of course, they were done without the facility I have now. I was graduated from high school at fifteen and found myself at Brooklyn College where I became the first four-sport letterman. I was the first person ever to go to Pratt Institute because of athletic ability, and then went to work for an illustration studio. I quit after a while and started to free lance, and have been at it ever since.

"When Jimmy Bama moved to the West, he put me in touch with a gallery out there. I sent it some of my paperback illustrations, and the people told me the works sold as fast as they hung them. It surprised me, but it was nice." One man bought 39. "I tried to dissuade him, but he wanted them." In 1979, *Mort Kunstler's 50 Epic Paintings of America* was published with text by Henry Steele Commager. Kunstler is also an official artist for NASA, and "wants to be the first artist in space. Can you imagine what it would be like? Rembrandt was 'there' in his time, Russell in his, and I want to be 'there' in my time." He was written up in *Southwest Art*, June 1978, and in *Prints*, January 1981, and is represented by Hammer and Trailside Galleries.

La Fontaine, Glen. Cree sculptor in molded paper, clay, and ceramic tile of the designs and philosophical Indian concepts of the Plains horse culture, born in Seattle, Washington in 1950 and living in Portland, Oregon. "I make a clay tablet and from that I create a mold of polyester resin" to form the paper, he explains. "The design element of the cast paper transcends the material, and old feelings are translated into 20th-century media. That's the beauty of the modern Indian art movement."

Raised in Bellecourt, North Dakota, as a member of the Little Shell Band of the Pembina Crees on the Turtle Mountain Reservation, he was "always drawing and making little sculptures—not Indians but dinosaurs." At eighteen, he enrolled in the Institute of American Indian Arts in Santa Fe, New Mexico, where the sculptor Allan Houser "influenced me. Whether I was conscious of it or not, I was his student." The following year he received a scholarship to The Center of the Eye Film School, then went to the Rhode Island School of Design, spent 1971 with the silversmith Charles Loloma, and in 1972 toured Mexico on a grant.

Mexico, he says, "was a cathartic experience. I realized I wanted to do northern Indians," so he started work on the Colville Indian Reservation in eastern Washington, "an intense period." In 1975, he was part of a six-man invitational at the Heard Museum, and the following year had his first one-man show at the Amon Carter Museum. In 1978, he created an 8 by 10 foot tile mural of the Plains culture for the Daybreak Star Arts Center in Fort Lawton, Washington. Four of his sculptures are touring Europe. Written up in *Southwest Art*, February 1982, he is represented by Westwood Galleries.

LaFord, (Carol) Grende. Painter in scratchboard and oil and sculptor of wildlife and horses, born in Grangeville, Idaho in 1955 and living in Clarkston, Washington. "I am proud of being self-taught," she declares. "None of the media in which I work is favored over the others, so what I enjoy most is being versatile. I love to create the things I know, and having raised and trained Appaloosa horses, I believe I am a natural in portraying all breeds of horses, from the horses of the historical mountain men to the rodeo cowboy's horse and those of the women of the West."

Her love of animals has inspired her to draw them since early childhood and she began painting in oil at ten. A 1974 graduate of Lewiston High School, she has ridden sidesaddle in the area of the Snake and Clearwater Rivers most of her life. She has worked in scratchboard since 1976 and says that "of course there are secrets involved so I give a brief answer to questioners. The board I use is made in Europe. It is clay coated and I ink it by spraying on a light coating, mainly for base colors. Then using a very sharp knife, I scratch out each line, down to the clay. The color is stained into each scratch, using ink, watercolor, or acrylic. Unusual as it is, colored scratchboard has become my best-selling medium.

"Sometimes I think up a title for an idea. At other times I have an idea with no title until it is completed. Most ideas are from life experiences or are historical subjects which I research on the spot for sketching, feelings, and meditation." A member of the Women Artists of the American West, she has works on display at the Favell Museum and Hells Gate Park. Most sales are from her own Grende LaFord Western Art Studio.

Mort Kunstler, HAIDA INDIAN POTLATCH, oil/canvas, 28 x 40

Glen LaFontaine, TALKING EYES, ceramic sculpture, h 23

Grende LaFord, AUTUMN SNOW (1982), colored scratchboard, 12 x 24

Charles LaMonk (signature)   *Armond Lara* (signature)

La Monk, Charles. Traditional painter in oil and mixed media, portraying pure-blood American Indians of today and Tarahumara Indians of Central Mexico, and, pictographs and petroglyphs of ancient American Indians, born in Kemmerer, Wyoming in 1910 and living in Palmdale, California. "I try to capture on canvas," he points out, "the haunting emotion of the Indian people whose every ounce of strength is consumed in daily survival. The somber features and the costumes reveal a determination to live on as they have for generations."

A graduate of the art department at Los Angeles Trade Tech, La Monk also studied privately with Will Foster and at Chouinard Art Institute. His work has been displayed in the White House by Presidential invitation and has been exhibited widely in museums and universities, including the Los Angeles Museum of Natural History, Southwest Indian Museum, Heard Museum, University of New Mexico, and Denver Museum of Natural History. A member of the American Indian and Cowboy Artists, he won the gold medal in 1977 and the silver in 1978.

His paintings also show the caves and canyons of the Southwest to contribute to American archaeology and history by recording prehistoric Indian art, the pictographs and the petroglyphs. La Monk does art demonstrations for groups by painting a portrait of a specific living Indian from memory while lecturing the group on the family and lifestyle of the named subject. The conclusion of the narrative is the completion of the portrait. La Monk's gallery is The Artist's Gallery.

Lara, Armond. Modern collagist, painter and sculptor "of the natural world," born in Denver, Colorado in 1939 and living in Santa Fe, New Mexico since 1981. "I am a great believer in simplicity," he explains. "I love East Asian art, and have come to see a similarity between it and American Indian art. One talks about the essence of something and the other talks about the spirit of something. To me, it's the same thing. Art says who you are and where you come from. I am very much a part of the Southwest. How could it be otherwise? It is where I came from. It is what I know. It is who I am."

Raised in Walsenberg, Colorado, he listened to the stories and learned the beliefs of the Navajo from his grandmother. He studied architecture at the Colorado Institute of Art for three years before transferring to Glendale College to get his BA in art in 1962. He later became Arts Advisor to Bellevue, Washington, in 1975 became art director in Redmond, and in 1977 was chosen Artist in the City of Seattle. Because "I don't relate to blackberries, I don't know how to swim, and I don't like fish," he considered the Pacific Northwest an alien environment and moved to Santa Fe where "the roots of my past come alive in the beauty of the land.

"I am painting," he adds, "and doing some lithography, but my favorite medium so far is working with handmade paper. Last year I was able to plant a field of corn and sunflowers, and those leaves are ideal for making paper. What I do with the paper depends on what kind of result I'm after. All of my best work has a simple theme which comes to me spontaneously. Some of my pieces are folded and creased so they take on a sculptural form." Lara is represented by Heydt/Bair and W.A. Taylor Galleries.

La Monk, BLACKFOOT CHILD, oil, 16 x 12

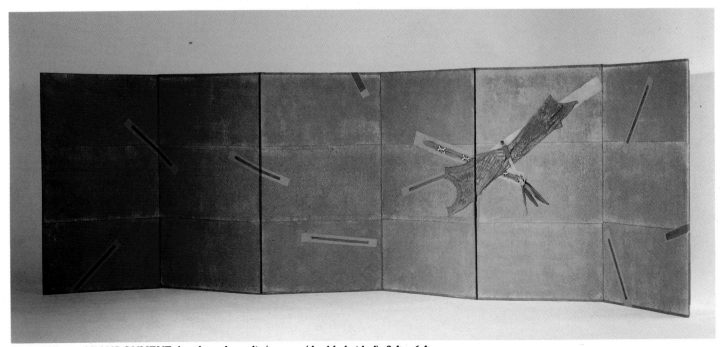

Armond Lara, ABANDONMENT, beads and acrylic/canvas (doubled sided), 3 ft x 6 ft

HANK LAWSHE' NWR

BOB LEE ss

Lawrence W. Lee

Lawshe, Hank. Traditional painter of the historical "Fur Trade Era," born in Los Angeles in 1935 and living in Kalispell, Montana since 1975. When his commercial art employer was moving East, he says, "I had come to that point in life where I had to make up my mind whether I was going to go on living for work, or start working at living." His career as a painter has proved the correctness of his choice, professionally and personally. "I tell you," he observes, "this art business can be tough. You have to stretch out the pay and sometimes you have to eat beans, but I wouldn't trade it for any other business in the world."

After growing up on the family farm in central Illinois, he worked as mechanic and soldier, with five years as a champion racing car driver, and began his career in art as a sign painter. In 1966, he accepted a job as commercial artist with a new advertising agency in Fort Collins, Colorado, and was promoted to Vice President in 1971, in management rather than art. He continued to paint in oil as a hobby, selling the paintings through Bob Wolf's Montana sporting goods store. When his employer asked him to move, he quit and became caretaker of a remote Montana ranch.

Teaching himself to switch to fine art was difficult. "There seemed to be no use trying to produce a major painting before you could do one good, single subject," he found; but within two years his "clean and simple" pictures "with a lot of feeling" were successful. In 1977, he won the Best of Show at the C.M. Russell exhibition, and in 1979 he was elected a member of the Northwest Rendezvous Group. Featured in *Artists of the Rockies*, spring 1978 and *Art West*, March 1981, he is represented by American Western Collection and Art Enterprises.

Lee, Bob. Traditional oil painter of New Mexico ranch scenes, born in Alamagordo, New Mexico in 1933 and living in Belen, New Mexico since 1964. "Through some friends who knew of my interest in art," he recalls, "I had a chance to meet Gordon Snidow who was painting Western subjects and had a good educational background. I invited him to the ranch to learn about cowboying and in turn, I learned numerous things about painting. I also borrowed his Famous Artist Course books.

"From the time I was a little kid, I had tried to draw and paint. At Alamagordo High School, I got my first public recognition, but it was for football. I chose the University of New Mexico, was the leading ball carrier, and took a drawing course from Randall Davey who encouraged me. Since I thought I would be a rancher, I didn't take him up on it. I graduated in 1956 and spent a couple of years in the Marine Corps. After my release, my brother and I took over management of the family ranch. In 1964, I was elected a State Senator, another family tradition, and then I registered in a painting course that was of little help.

"In my study of the Famous Artist Course books, I discovered many areas of painting that I knew nothing about. Through Gordon Snidow I met Bill Moyers who taught me a lot and in 1968 the Cowboy Artists of America held their first trail ride at the ranch. I was invited into the 1968 Saddleback Gallery show, in 1969 into Taos Art Gallery, in 1972 the OS Ranch Show, the next year the Stamford Art Foundation Show, and in 1973 the Texas Art Gallery Preview Show. By continuously studying, I hope to continue improving." Lee was written up in Ainsworth's *The Cowboy in Art* and in *Southwest Art*, July 1979.

Lee, Lawrence W. "Representational and illusionistic" painter of character studies of Indians, born in Fort Smith, Arkansas in 1947 and living in Tucson, Arizona. "I remember one of my professors telling the class," he states, "that you don't become an artist until you have worn a hole in the floor from standing in front of your easel and painting. When I took my easel from its former location and looked down, I saw that I had worn a hole in the linoleum right where I stand to paint. In the professor's book, I was an artist."

His parents were educators and "to hear them tell it, I was a child prodigy, but I don't think I was. I am color-blind. When my college advisor found out, it did keep me from painting during college. All I did was draw, which was okay because drawing is never a wasted discipline. However, I soon learned that a BA would not assure me a job," so he went back for his master's degree in art education. "It was a year before I could get a job, so I could start painting."

During a trip to Flagstaff, Arizona, "I stopped at a gallery and began showing there. I have always been a mystery to myself, a stranger. As each work reveals itself to me, I often feel that part of me has changed —or has even been stolen by this stranger. I wonder what will happen when I do finally recognize myself there on the canvas. Will I then be looking out at the world from another stranger's eyes, merely a dream looking out upon another's reality? Sometimes I wonder, and as I wonder, I paint." A recurring motif is a dragonfly in a bubble, the sphere of wisdom and the insect of creativity. Lee's work is in twenty public collections. Written up in *Southwest Art*, December 1980, he is represented by Amerson and Joy Tash Galleries.

Hank Lawshe, RUSTY, oil, 18 x 14

Lawrence Lee, WINTER MAGIC, acrylic, 48 x 36

Bob Lee, THE WRANGLERS, oil, 24 x 20

Roland Lee

Bill -Leftwich-

Lemon ©

Lee, Roland L. Watercolorist of pioneer Utah and landscapes of the Southwest, born in Alhambra, southern California in 1949 and living in St. George, Utah. "The moods of Southern Utah are intriguing," he states. "Crumbling adobe houses and sagging wooden barns whisper sadness and loneliness, while brilliant red cliffs and purple mesas shout exuberance as they catch fire at sunset. My special hope is that I will interpret the stories correctly, so that others may enjoy the spirit of the country I love."

Raised in California, Lee received his BA from Brigham Young University in 1971 and worked as illustrator and graphic designer at an advertising agency and as art instructor at Dixie College. This commercial and educational experience lasted for ten years which, Lee says, gave him plenty of time to develop discipline and his own style. When he moved to Utah in 1979 to paint full time, it was to a town that had been settled by his own pioneer ancestors. He began winning first place awards in 1980 and is now participating in national invitationals.

He keeps a family cabin near Zion National Park and says "it's really thrilling to watch the cliffs light up and explode with color in the late afternoon sun." He also paints his heritage "to preserve the old pioneer buildings in my artwork before they're all gone." After being "spotlighted" in an art investment newsletter in 1981, the value of Lee's work doubled. At one show, a collector purchased a painting before it was hung. At another, twelve of fourteen watercolors were sold the first day. His work is featured in the book *Mormon Arts* and he is represented by Mammen Gallery II.

Leftwich, Bill. Realist painter and sculptor of Indian, cowboy, Mexican, and military subjects, born in Duncan, Oklahoma in 1923 and living in Fort Davis, Texas. "Every picture or bronze I create," he stresses, "I consider and plan and think over for a good while because I want it to have significance. I want it to be interesting and significant in ten or twenty years from now. I try to avoid trends or fads, and create a work from my experience that has never been depicted before."

Of Chickasaw descent, Leftwich studied at the Dallas Institute of Fine Art under Olin Travis in 1933 and the following year at San Antonio Academy of Art under Hugo Pohl. In World War II, he was in General Patton's Armored Cavalry in the ETO, won a Silver Star, studied sculpting in England in 1945, and served in the horse cavalry at Texas A&M. Since then he "has made many tracks from Mexico to Montana—speaks Spanish, some Apache and Navajo, and is at home in rural Mexico as well as on the reservations." He adds that "my years on the border and in Mexico give me an edge when it comes to doing Mexican subjects."

Leftwich has "cowboyed in Texas and Old Mexico and worked at many jobs from Big Bend Park Ranger to Utah smelter." His first magazine article was published in 1951 and he later wrote and illustrated seven books as well as painting many magazine covers and ten murals. "I plan to concentrate on the Mexican vaquero, rurale, and revolutionario in the years ahead," he says. He is a member of the Texas Cowboy Artists Association, The Company of Military Historians, and Western Writers of America, and is represented by Big Bend Art and La Casa Galleries.

Lemon, David. Traditional sculptor of figures of the Old West in bronze statuettes, born in San Diego in 1945 and living in Sandy, Utah. "I was a Navy brat until my eleventh birthday," he recalls. "As a child I lived in Hawaii, California, Guam, Rhode Island, Iowa, Tennessee, and Utah. When I was in kindergarten, I drew stick figures, then eventually started to draw box figures. The turning point was in the twelfth grade when I came across a copy of *The Agony and the Ecstacy*. I entered the yearly art show with my sculptures, won two university scholarships, and sold three pieces for $150. Boy was I on cloud nine!

"Neither of the universities could give scholarships because my grades in other classes weren't high enough so in 1965 I joined the Navy for a four-year hitch. When I got out, I worked in a printing plant for the next eleven years. I took a class in illustrating, but the instructor asked me, would I be interested in trying my hand at abstract art, and I quit the next day. For the last three years at the printing plant, I had so little work to do that I started to bring in my clay.

"During the summer of 1977, I sought out the advice of Edward J. Fraughton and he'd literally tear up my work if it wasn't just right. One day I found a copy of *Southwest Art* and the thought struck me, if those sculptors can make it, then maybe I'll have a chance to do the same. I made up a brochure at work and sent out copies to galleries listed in the magazine. Two days later, I received my first reply, from Texas Trails Gallery, and I decided to give it a try. *Southwest Art* did an article on me in August 1981, and this helped. I have found out you need to be a showman to a certain extent."

David Lemon, EAGLE THAT FLIES, h 16½, w 12

Bill Leftwich, I'D LIKE TO BE IN TEXAS, oil, 24 x 18

Roland Lee, RED RUSTING ROOF, watercolor, 19 x 30

Wayne Lewis (signature)

Lightfoot (signature)

Lewis, Wayne. Traditional sculptor of the old American West, born in Washington, D.C. in 1947 and living in Oak Harbor, Washington since 1979. "At ten," he recalls, "I attended the Corcoran Gallery's School of Art. Children were expected to be serious students, and I sculpted my first horse. At eleven, we moved to rural Maryland and every weekend I could be found competing in a horse show. At sixteen, I was a stable boy at the racetrack, sketching the horses and the characters.

"In high school and college, my major was art. My first two jobs were lacking in creativity so I quit and enrolled again in the Corcoran which was not the learning experience of the first time around. It was 'do your own thing' art and I moved on to find out what else the world had to offer. After a year at the F.B.I., another back in college working evenings, and two as an illustrator, I decided to quit to spend time painting. Early in 1973, I came across some of Harry Jackson's bronzes. This was a dramatic turning point in my life, a theme that I took to naturally, and I was on my way.

"Due to the cost involved, I began working for a publishing company, illustrating. With lunch hours and evenings spent sculpting figures from the Old West, the days passed quickly. A visit to Washington led to the move there, and the slack job market led me to take the hobby that I loved and turn it into a full-time adventure. With the financial backing of a local Western art collector, I have been able to cast pieces in bronze. None of the excitement has been lost. Lunch hours and evenings are still spent sculpting, but so is the rest of the day. I am a very happy sculptor indeed. My galleries include Old Town Art and Gainsborough Galleries."

Lightfoot, Jon Forest. Painter "of a moment in the life of Southwestern Indians," born in Kansas City, Missouri in 1939 and living in Tucson, Arizona since 1971. "I can only paint what moves me," he stresses, "and I have tried to paint what I see with the empathy I feel from within. For me, the Indian is a heroic figure; and to show that strength is the challenge I have set for myself. Even though they have been victimized, what is important is that they are surviving and that they will succeed."

Son of a Cherokee father and a Swedish mother, Lightfoot's earliest memories are of a farm in Minnesota and then attending grade school on the Cherokee reservation in Oklahoma. His primary interest was the theater, so he tried a drama scholarship to all-female Bennington College, moved to New York City, and combined acting with commercial art. He was apprenticed to the modernist painter Lowell Nesbitt for three years, traveled to Italy, and began to paint figures. In 1971, he returned to Tucson where he had gone to high school, practicing Mexican decorative art for two years.

In 1974, he started painting full time and the following year found his personal style of posing somber, realistically painted Indian faces against a backdrop of abstract blanket designs. He says that "to develop one's own statement is what art is all about," and he points out changes in his "canvas size, going into the 4 foot by 5 foot range. And I think, too, my new work is looser, more painterly, and I feel more comfortable with color." He was featured in *Artists of the Rockies*, spring 1978, and *Southwest Art*, August 1978, was included in the Peking, China, exhibition, and is represented by Trailside and In the Spirit Galleries.

Wayne Lewis, SPRING RUN, bronze, w 31

Jon F. Lightfoot, LAS TORTOLITAS, acrylic, 24 x 36

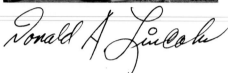

Lincoln, Donald A. Sculptor of "wild animals in their natural habitat" in bronze, wood, and stone, born in Grinnell, Iowa in 1920 and living in Rollins, Montana since 1975. "The question I am most frequently asked is 'how long did it take you to do that,'" he observes. "I am unable to answer the query because I don't punch a time clock and I have several projects going at one time. I'm always chasing perfection but never catching it.

"Moved to Missoula, Montana, at an early age and graduated from Missoula County High School. Attended business college before entering the service. Spent 49 months as a pilot in the Army. After discharge, I worked in construction, logging, and owned and operated a general merchandise store in Hot Springs, Montana. Self-taught as an artist, I moved to Sacramento, California, in 1955 where I spent twenty years in graphic arts. After retiring in 1975, I returned to northwest Montana to devote full time to woodcarving and sculpture.

"I am fond of bronze but find wood and stone sculpture more of a challenge. One mistake and you start over. Also, it is one of a kind. My greatest satisfaction is having others enjoy my creations as much as I enjoy doing them. I built my studio and gallery on the west shore of beautiful Flathead Lake, at the base of the Mission Range of the Rockies. Most of my work is sold there. The Sagebrush Gallery in Kansas and Rosemary's Galleries represent me." His "The Honey Bucket" wood sculpture was Best of Show in three dimensions and Popular Choice at the 1981 Kalispell Art Show and Auction. He also carves life-size figures of Indian women and wood doors and does pen and ink drawings of wildlife.

Lingren, Rod. Sculptor of miniature and medium-size Western bronzes, born in Santa Barbara, California in 1931 and living in Alpine, California since 1977. "To me," he observes, "Western art is about our roots. It was a personal struggle, what the person did with his hands or ideas. No writing, just the doing. As Western art becomes more popular and the public becomes more knowledgeable I'd expect it to become broader. The super-realist schools will be supplemented by looser, semi-abstract schools."

Raised in La Mesa, Lingren "drew my way through school, instead of spelling, arithmetic, and English. My time was spent drawin'—while the other kids were playing." He took a college-level class in printmaking when he was thirteen. At sixteen, he accompanied his father on a European tour for a year and at eighteen was in the Near East and India. He attended Grossmont College and worked as a leather designer and a master printer, studied music and played the guitar professionally, then learned casting and finishing as a dental technician before participating in sculpture seminars.

He says that he "didn't choose miniatures, they chose me. One of my models of wild horses seems pretty big after sculpting teeth. When I'm pouring bronzes, I often think of Cellini and of the Greek founders. I bet given the chance we'd know each other pretty quickly. They'd do the same things I do: Know the color of the metal, color of the crucible, check everything ten times, and when pouring hope to hell things go well. I make my own patinas. I can vary the color infinitely to my taste." Lingren is represented by Husberg Fine Arts Gallery.

Lipetzky, Pat D. Realist painter of American wildlife in oil, watercolor, ink, and on china, born in Minnesota and living in Whitefish, Montana. "Antelope," she explains, "are animals of the open plains, steppes, and foothills. Their defense is their alertness and speed which is approximately 50 mph. The pronghorn buck will reach a weight of 110 to 160 pounds and has a maximum lifespan of twelve years.

"I have lived in Minnesota, New Mexico, Wyoming, and Montana, so I have studied the big game animals in their natural habitats, via 4-wheel drive vehicles and on horseback. I studied art at the University of Minnesota in Minneapolis, the Minneapolis School of Art, the Walker Art Center in St. Paul, and Art Instruction Inc., and continued my art training at the University of New Mexico in Albuquerque and in an arts seminar with Frederic Taubes in Amarillo.

"The latest award I received was from Art Instruction in December 1981, the first place in professional animal painting, with an article in the *Illustrator* for April 1982. I also entered the Safari Club International at Las Vegas, the C.M. Russell auction, and the MONAC show at Spokane. I am a member of the Women Artists of the American West and enter all of their shows, receiving awards in the 1979 and 1980 national competition." She also won the Best of Show award for an Indian warrior painting in the National Federation of China Painters show in Albuquerque in 1974. She is published by Salt Creek Graphics and is represented by her own Lipetzky Studio.

Pat Lipetzky, AMERICAN PRONGHORN, oil, 24 x 18   Rod Lingren, TOE DANCER, h 6¼

Don Lincoln, HONEY BUCKET, walnut carving, h 10, w 12

Oed Long

Bernique Longley © 1982

Long, Ted. Oil painter and sculptor of historical Plains Indians and Western scenes, born near North Platte, Nebraska in 1933 and still living there in 1982. When on the subject of the perils of field trips, Long describes one into British Columbia in 1978: "The hunting was not good and fog had started to move in. The pilot said we'd better get out. We didn't make it over the mountain ridge. Fortunately, he wasn't hurt at all. I was lucky that I wasn't killed. I sustained a broken vertebra and have been recovering slowly ever since."

Raised on the ranch that his great-grandfather homesteaded before the turn of the century, Long has been drawing and painting pictures of Indians and ranch life since he was six. The Oregon and Mormon Trails were within sight and the Sioux, Cheyenne, and Pawnee Indians had followed the buffalo there. At thirteen, he began rodeoing. He served in the Army during the Korean war and then returned home to paint. Although he was untrained, he was able to get commercial work. His first job was cartoons of rodeo performances.

For his studio, he moved to a century-old log cabin that had been a museum to the homestead along the North Platte River. Outside in pens are bison and elk he "keeps on hand because they are excellent models for my paintings and bronzes." Long usually researches the Ogallala Sioux at Pine Ridge, but one honor he appreciated was the commission to model the sculpture of Standing Bear for the Nebraska Hall of Fame. He produces about three major sculptures per year and about 50 paintings. An exhibitor in invitational shows like Cheyenne Frontier Days, he is represented by Copenhagen Galleri and Overland Trails Galleries.

Longley, Bernique. Stylized oil painter of Mexican market scenes, of Indians, and of florals, born in Moline, Illinois in 1923 and living in Santa Fe, New Mexico since 1947. "I always wanted to be an artist, even when I was a little girl in Chicago. I see something, respond to it, and hope other people will, too. One thing just seems to stimulate another. My work may not be what is currently fashionable, but then that's not what I'm trying to do. I just feel my way and create."

After attending scholarship classes until she was seventeen, she studied at the Art Institute of Chicago and received her degree in 1943. Two years later, she was awarded a fellowship and spent a year in Mexico. She says that "it was such a wonderful time. Rivera was still painting. Tamayo was just coming up, and it was wonderful to be able to watch them work. But most of all, there was the color of Mexico. I had lived in Chicago all my life, everything gray and dull." By 1946, she was exhibiting in the Annual Chicago Show and the following year she had a one-person show at the Museum of New Mexico. Color was her forte.

In 1948, she won an honorable mention in sculpture, too. She said in 1975 that she had "studied sculpture in art school and did quite a bit of it. Now I'm going back to it, and that means going back to school." Another addition to her repertoire had taken place in 1971 when she began painting multi-figured scenes rather than single figures. More recently, she started a series on American Indian women. She is listed in *Who's Who in American Art*, was featured in *Southwest Art*, May 1975, and is represented by Santa Fe East and Summer Gallery.

Bernique Longley, BUFFALO DANCER (1981), oil/panel, 40 x 26

Ted Long, BRIDGERS BEAVER MEN, oil, 24 x 48

Lisa Danielle Lorimer   *Thomas W. Lorimer.*

Lorimer, Lisa Danielle. Realist painter of still lifes of Old Western subjects in watercolor, born in La Jolla, California in 1948 and living in Sedona, Arizona since 1981. "Still life," she observes, "is my unique way of describing how life was, and what motivated these people, how they thought, what was beautiful to them. When I can, I like to capture that mysteriousness of dark people huddled near smoky fires, for whom every day was a struggle for survival, yet driven to take hide, bone, and sinew and turn their few possessions into art.

"My parents were both frustrated artists during my younger years. My father taught me how to draw horses and my mother negotiated the sale of my first painting. I won several art awards during my school years and was awarded a scholarship to California State University at Long Beach. 'Pop Art' and Abstract Expressionism were in, and after three years I was only a little better educated, so I went to work for an advertising studio. It was a terrific education, but my parents by then had turned welded sculpture into a business, traveling to art fairs. They encouraged me to frame my paintings and join them.

"When my husband pursued his dream of exhibiting in an all-Western show in 1974, he encouraged me to find my niche and I became fascinated with 'portraits' of Indian artifacts displayed against a loose but definitive background. I love to play on the intricacies of the design, or the strength or subtlety of the colors chosen. So fascinating a study is this—really a study of us all—that I think it may be worth a lifetime of wondering about in paint." A member of Western Artists of America and of Women Artists of the American West, she is represented by Husberg Fine Arts Gallery.

Lorimer, Thomas W. Traditional oil painter of Indians and cowboys on the northern Plains, born in East Chicago, Indiana in 1941 and living in Sedona, Arizona since 1981. "The American West has set a stage for the artist," he observes, "in which there is virtually unlimited source material for storytelling. Here the elements abound that spark an artist's imagination, allowing him to become familiar with the material culture, and to color it with respect for the people and places."

While growing up in Indiana, his father's stories of adolescence on a North Dakota farm and later cowboy years in Montana fed his curiosity about the West of an earlier time. He made up his mind to be either an artist or an archaeologist, and then opted for art as less lonely. The claim money from a motorcycle accident paid for study at Chicago's American Academy of Art. After graduation, he found studio jobs, but it was clear that more specialized instruction was required to compete with the top illustrators so he enrolled in the Art Center College of Design in Los Angeles.

Before graduation in 1970, he was selling drawings and watercolors at outdoor exhibits in sufficient quantity to support himself. In 1974, he went to the Death Valley Days show with six panels of artwork and sold every piece. That show was his turning point. Since then, he collects early cowboy and Indian gear and travels the West at his own speed, not to snap photos from a car window but to walk the terrain. He doesn't paint every day or keep a schedule, but when he's into a "painting set," he paints without "coming up for air" and he'll not be interrupted. His favorite show is the Charles Russell Auction and he is represented by Husberg Fine Arts Gallery which listed an oil at $3,200 in fall 1980.

Thomas W. Lorimer, WE GIVE THEE THANKS, OH GOD, oil, 29 x 25

Lisa Danielle Lorimer, A CELEBRATION OF BEAUTY, watercolor, 21 x 36

Lougheed, Robert Elmer. Painter of animals in the outdoors, born in Gray County, Ontario in 1910 and living in Santa Fe, New Mexico since 1970. "I always use nature as my model," Lougheed says. "If I should paint a horse from memory, it would be a Bob Lougheed horse and not a real horse. All the horses, in fact all the animals in my paintings, are real. To the young, unspoiled artist, I would say ... learn to draw and paint from life. Don't get trapped by photography."

As a child on a Canadian farm, Lougheed sketched animals from nature and at nineteen was employed to do illustrations for a catalog. He went to the Ontario College of Arts and the Ecole des Beaux Arts in Montreal and worked as a commercial artist on the Toronto *Star* for six years. To perfect his skills, he studied with Frank Vincent DuMond and Dean Cornwell at the Art Students League in New York City, supporting himself by continuing in commercial art. One product was Mobil's "Flying Red Horse." To get closer to his peers, he moved to a barn in Westport, Connecticut, a town where 60 artists lived.

When they were starting out, fellow painter John Clymer told Lougheed to "forget doing those horses. Do pretty girls. That's what's selling." Lougheed declares that he "never did learn to paint girls. I kept on doing horses and cornered the market for ads that called for animals. Now, John is doing horses." Lougheed usually begins an animal picture by painting the landscape on the spot and the animals from life, on location or at a zoo or game farm. He is a member of the Cowboy Artists of America, has won its "most popular" artist award, and is published by Mill Pond Press.

Love, Harrell L. Painter and stylized wood and stone sculptor of Indian and wildlife figures, born in Wynne, Arkansas in 1940 and living in Santa Fe, New Mexico since 1978. "No deposit, no return," Love asserts. "Whatever is put into a piece by the artist will usually return to the observer. In contrast with some contemporary sculptors, I feel that my work should be readily understandable by everyone. My most successful pieces project a flow and motion that capture the attention, the same as an appealing song."

After receiving a BS in art from the University of Arkansas at Pine Bluff in 1961, and being listed in *Who's Who Among Students in American Colleges and Universities*, Love worked as an art instructor at Wiley College in Marshall, Texas, from 1962 to 1964 and took summer classes at Wayne State University in Detroit. He attended the University of New Mexico in 1964 and 1965 and then worked as an art instructor at the University of Arkansas at Pine Bluff from 1966 to 1968. He took additional courses at Memphis Academy of Art in 1968 and the University of Oklahoma in 1977 while being employed as a counselor and sales representative in Oklahoma. He has also worked as a commercial artist.

Love's credo is: "he who works with his hands is a laborer, with his hands and head is an artisan, and with his hands, head, and heart is an artist." A religious man, he states that "when I watch birds, as well as when I artistically create them, I'm reminded of the total trust they show in the Father's care." He is represented by his own Touch of Love Gallery.

Love, Ralph. Traditional oil painter of the Western landscape, born in Los Angeles in 1907 and living in Temecula, California since 1958. "I could be called a traditionalist," he emphasizes, "but not a literalist. When I do landscape, I try to capture the feel of the place rather than just what it looks like. A painting, after all, is not a legal description of property."

One of nine children, he had an independent spirit at an early age. As a boy, he painted posters, riding his bicycle to pick up and deliver orders. "I liked the smell of turpentine even then, but the smell of beans was better so I painted posters." His education included two years studying with the artist Sam Hyde Harris, two years of life study in night classes, and two years of Bible College. During the Depression, he painted signs and posters, did lettering, "or anything that would bring in income. Paintings were traded for dental work, a new washing machine, and medical attention." At the same time, he was an ordained minister.

In 1940, Love began teaching art while a pastor in Yucaipa, California. His paintings won prizes commencing in 1945, and in 1947 he started traveling the Western states as an evangelist while continuing to paint. In 1958, he built a home and art gallery in Temecula where he also taught, lectured, and illustrated. By 1968 when he stopped competing, he had won 28 awards. As he said, "I preached and painted for years and most of the money came from painting." Written up in *Artists of the Rockies*, fall 1977, Love is a member of the Society of Western Artists. His prints are distributed by Connoisseur's Gallery and he is represented by Son Silver West and Munson Gallery.

Ralph Love, SKETCH AT BODIE, oil, 12 x 16

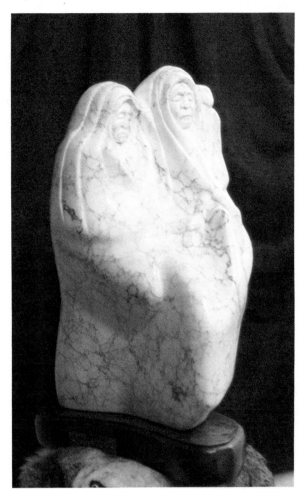

Harrell L. Love, COMFORT, alabaster, h 10, w 14, d 23

Robert Lougheed, NAVAJO TAPESTRY, mixed media, 20 x 40

A.I.C.A.

Lovell, Tom. Traditional painter of Western history, born in New York City in 1909 and living in Santa Fe, New Mexico since 1977. "I like people," Lovell says. "If I can communicate some of this feeling in each painting, common ground may be established with the casual spectator. I believe the artist has a certain obligation to interest and inform without being encyclopedic about detail.

"I enjoy recreating the past," he adds. "As a boy, books of adventure in far off times and places were real. At seventeen, I shipped as a deckhand on the *Leviathan* and various other jobs followed. Enrollment in the College of Fine Arts at Syracuse University was the next step. At this time the newsstands were filled with 'pulp' magazines and I produced a cover in oils and eight or ten dry brush illustrations a month during my senior year. The message on the covers had to outscream a hundred others. After graduation I continued to free lance for the pulps for six years before tackling the 'slicks.' In 1944 I enlisted in the Marine Corps and was assigned to an easel. Illustration continued to flourish after the war."

In 1969, a commission for fourteen large paintings of southwestern history caused Lovell to shift his focus to the American West. Since then, almost all of his work has been Western history. In 1974, he won the National Academy of Western Art's Prix de West, was elected to the Society of Illustrators Hall of Fame, and won the Franklin Mint gold medal for prints. Lovell has been featured in *Artists of the Rockies*, summer 1980 and in *Persimmon Hill*. He is a member of the Cowboy Artists of America and NAWA, has exhibited at Altermann Art Gallery, and is published by Greenwich.

Lubo, F. Bruce, Sr. Realist painter of Indian portraits and scenes, born in the Pueblo of Laguna in 1911 when New Mexico was still a territory and living in Palm Springs, California. "I'm always on the lookout for great Indian faces, wrinkled and aged," he explains, "but the older people don't always like being sketched. Fortunately, I'm blessed with a photographic memory and I can recreate them on canvas with no difficulty."

He started sketching at an early age. "Wherever I went," he recalls, "I always had a pencil or crayon with me. I don't remember when I began to draw. Drawing seemed to be an extension of my right arm." Raised in California by his uncle, he took his uncle's name and was educated in Riverside schools, from elementary through college, where he majored in engineering and art. In 1940, he was employed as a design engineer of aircraft. "When thirty years were finished," he says, "I decided that was long enough to paint only when I could grab the time. I'd take an early retirement and devote my life to painting."

Encouraged by his first exhibit at Pala Mission where he sold out, he opened an Indian Shop in Palm Springs. "Working twelve hours a day on art," he pointed out, "doesn't give me much time for anything else. I paint in oils during the day in the shop window, and at night at home in watercolor. My paintings are in over 200 collections around the country and for some reason, I can't think why, my biggest out-of-town buyers are doctors." A member of the Roadrunner clan, he signs his paintings with a roadrunner. He has won many awards, is a member of the American Indian and Cowboy Artists, and has exhibited at Kachina Gallery and Tanner's Indian Arts.

Bruce Lubo, CRACKER JACK, watercolor, 28 x 22

Tom Lovell, THE DECEIVER, oil, 20 x 36

Lundeen, George W. Realist sculptor of people in bronze and terra-cotta statuettes, born in Holdrege, Nebraska in 1948 and living in Loveland, Colorado. "Rough preliminary sketches help to crystalize my ideas for my work," he points out. "I can't imagine a good sculptor who can't draw. I believe one should have the experience of rendering figures with accuracy as well as drawing with absolute freedom—preferably alternating between the two. Drawing sharpens the perception. You begin to see more, and more importantly, to coordinate the eye, the hand, and the mind."

The grandson of a calligrapher, Lundeen studied art and cast his first bronze at Hastings College. Believing that "the study of art should mean the study of life," he went on to his MFA in sculpture from the University of Illinois and to a Fulbright-Hays grant to learn from the Masters in Italy. After one year of teaching in Nebraska, he became a full-time sculptor and moved close to his foundry in Colorado.

"Like drawing and painting," he stresses, "sculpture can be realistic or abstract. As a matter of fact, when I begin my work, it is in an abstract state—then I model it out into realism. I'm always aware in my work of 'mass' and 'space.' My use of vignettes gives me some interesting negative effects, but it would take me a lifetime to complete all the ideas I have for the human figure." Artist in residence at Texas A&M, Lundeen has exhibited with the National Sculpture Society and the National Academy of Design, has been featured in *Artists of the Rockies*, spring 1981, and is represented by Driscol Gallery and O'Brien's Art Emporium.

Lutrell, Richard. Realist painter of Indian portraits in pastel, born in Galesburg, Illinois in 1926 and living in Sedona, Arizona since 1975. "While I am mostly known for my Indian portraits," he emphasizes, "I paint many other subjects such as scenes, flowers, birds, and old buildings. To me, anything put down on canvas is the 'face' of something, be it the face of a questioning child or an abandoned barn in a Kansas field.

"In the small farming community of Alpha, Illinois, where I grew up, no one ever dreamed of becoming an artist. After all, you were going to have to make a living, weren't you? So, because I always liked to draw, I became a closet painter. My father didn't actively discourage me, but he worried. I had no thought then of pursuing art as a career." In 1948, he worked as a trail guide at the Grand Canyon, then attended the University of California at Santa Barbara for two years and in 1962 enrolled in Brooks Institute of Photography where he also taught until 1965.

Because of his love of Indian country, he moved to Flagstaff, Arizona, where he was incapacitated by the 1970 recurrence of a chronic back injury. For a year and a half, he was unable to work at an outside job but "could and did paint between bouts. I'd never had any formal training, and now I could experiment. Once my health was restored, I could go full steam ahead. Although I have had more training in photography, now that painting is my profession I no longer take 'good' photographs per se. Instead, I photograph components that may become part of the composition in a painting." Lutrell was written up in *Southwest Art*, June 1981, is a member of the American Indian and Cowboy Artists, and has won its gold medal.

Lyon, Harold Lloyd. Representational oil painter of the Western ranch scene as it is today, born in Windsor, Ontario, Canada in 1930 and living in Westbank, British Columbia. According to Lyon, "if you set up your painting so that it's just like a little road and you take out all those things that aren't necessary, then the painting is easily understood and the mind enjoys this. It enjoys looking into it. You're entertaining the mind when you do a painting."

After having filled his schoolbooks with sketches, Lyon left sawing pulpwood in northern Ontario to study at the Ontario College of Art in Toronto and also the Meinzinger School of Art in Detroit. In 1956, he was employed as art director and he taught art fundamentals for Canadian television. He was an art director in Calgary, then spent five years in the United States as a free-lance illustrator. He had been painting since art school, and in 1965 he returned to the Okanagan Valley in Canada where he has been painting ever since.

In the beginning, he painted florals as "something I could have in my studio." Next he worked on old buildings and fishing boats and portraits before coming to feel that "there's a combination of those things that makes for good paintings." He believes that "some of the best paintings in the world are being produced today, and the better paintings are yet to come. So that is why I'm working hard to—maybe, maybe—be one of those painters." Not a "10 o'clock to 2 o'clock in the afternoon painter," he works seven days a week. Listed in *Who's Who in American Art* and written up in *Artists of the Rockies* for winter 1981, he shows at Shriver and Martin G Galleries in the United States and The Collectors and The Harrison Galleries in Canada.

Richard Lutrell, MEDICINE MAN (1982), pastel, 28 x 22

George Lundeen, FLATLANDER, bronze, h 36

Harold Lloyd Lyon, NIGHT RIDERS, oil, 24 x 36

Mabry, Jane. Oil painter and pastellist of Southwestern subjects including New Mexican Pueblo and Navajo Indians, born in Roswell, New Mexico about 1911 and living in Albuquerque. "While painting eight hours a day doing landscapes for the National Park Service in Washington, D.C.," she states, "I went to the Corcoran School three nights a week and on the weekends I studied with Catherine Critcher, the only woman member of the Taos Founders group. She gave me extra help because I loved Taos and the Indians so much, and it was a wonderful experience to study with her.

"Growing up in a small town in New Mexico had offered little chance to study drawing or painting," she points out, "but I persuaded my parents to buy me a few essentials and at the age of six I started by copying the Santa Fe Railway calendars which reproduced the Taos Masters in living colors." Daughter of a writer from a pioneer family, she earned her BFA from the University of New Mexico and then studied for four years with Gerald Cassidy, the Indian painter from Santa Fe, before going to Washington. She also attended the Art Students League in New York City.

After returning to New Mexico, she concentrated on portraiture, especially a series on the Indians to record native costumes and environments. In school, she had had "a year of drawing casts in charcoal" that she calls invaluable and "something that contemporary schools are sadly neglecting." Listed in *Who's Who in American Art* and a member of the Pastel Society of America, she is represented by and is a part owner of Galeria Del Sol.

Macdonald, Grant. Acrylic painter of the Texas landscape and wildlife in "interpretive realism," born in Leesburg, Virginia in 1944 and living in Kerrville, Texas since 1971. "Some people regard artists," he points out, "as nothing more than a reflection of contemporary society, for better or worse. They seem to think that when society catches a cold, the function of the artist is to sneeze, frame his handkerchief, and call it art."

Raised in Baird, Texas, he began to draw at six and took private instruction while in grade school. After completing his secondary education in Virginia, he received his BFA from the University of Mississippi in 1966, served as an officer in the Air Force until 1970, and settled in Kerrville to paint. The "primary interest was portraiture, but my move to the Texas Hill Country resulted in a new awareness of landscape and wildlife which is abundant here. Also, my long-time interest in the human form has found new expression in my portrayals of contemporary ranch life.

"I believe the viewer brings his own experience and imagination to a painting, but an artist should not depend on his viewer. An artist should also be a craftsman. He must have mastered technical skills. An untrained child wildly banging on a piano is expressing himself, but we would hardly call him a musician. The same standard should apply to artists. People who paint as a hobby think 'wouldn't it be great to do this for a living,' but I do ten times as much painting as I would for my own enjoyment." Written up in *Southwest Art*, October 1979, he is published by Concho Gallery, Inc., and represented by Altermann Art and Concho Galleries.

Machetanz, Frederick. Representational oil painter of Alaska as it was in the mid-thirties, born in Kenton, Ohio in 1908 and living in Palmer near Anchorage, Alaska since 1948. "You see polar bears on the ice pack," he explains, "and for a split second you have seen them exactly right. That impression must imprint itself upon your mind so that you have a criterion against which your future paintings of polar bears may be compared. This holds good for all wildlife."

After receiving his BA from Ohio State University in 1930, Machetanz studied at the Chicago Art Institute and the American Academy. When he earned his MA in 1935, his uncle offered him the present of a visit to Umlakleet, Alaska. As he stepped off the plane, a chief's daughter mistook him for her dead son and gave him access to village activities. Machetanz remained for two years, filling a portfolio he brought to New York City where he wrote books on Eskimo life. After serving in the Aleutians in World War II, he returned to New York City for further study at the Art Students League and then moved permanently to Alaska.

From 1948 to 1961, Machetanz and his wife made a winter lecture tour to pay for painting in Alaska during the spring and summer. His glazing technique on blue and white underpainting was adapted from Maxfield Parrish. In 1962, Machetanz had his first exhibition and the proceeds allowed him to paint full time. He has done 50 lithographs, and Mill Pond Press is his publisher. In 1981, *American Artist* chose him as artist of the year. Listed in *Who's Who in American Art* and featured in *Southwest Art*, November 1981, he is a member of the Northwest Rendezvous Group and his gallery is Artique Ltd.

**Fred Machetanz, FACE TO FACE,
oil/masonite, 52 x 32**

Jane Mabry, KIOWA GIRL, oil, 20 x 16

Grant Macdonald, HIDIN' OUT, acrylic, 30 x 40

Mails, Thomas E. Realist oil painter of historical and contemporary American Indians, born in Groveland California in 1922 and living in Lake Elsinore, California. "I have a profound regard for the Indian religion," he emphasizes. "Everything about the native American centers in religion, and all they undertake begins with and is thereafter influenced by this single base or source. My deep interest lies in conveying, in words and pictures, their ceremonies, and the ceremonial costumes."

After serving in World War II, Mails entered the College of Arts and Crafts in Oakland, California. His teachers found him a job as instructor in architectural design at Heald College in San Francisco, and in 1947 he moved to Seattle where he worked in architecture until 1955 when he entered the Lutheran Theological Seminary in St. Paul, Minnesota. He was ordained in 1958 and became a pastor. Because the record was incomplete, he began to document the Indians in 1962.

"I paint and write about the Indians of yesterday," he states, "because of their unique and accomplished life way, because of their outstanding philosophical, creative, and religious attainments, and because of their suffering, endurance and character—as a suppressed people. I paint and write about the Indians of today not because they and their life way are (as once believed) vanishing, but because they are *not* vanishing. There is a ceremonial renaissance taking place." His paintings are first used in his books which are studied by almost every Western artist. Featured in *Southwest Art*, summer 1976, he has written eighteen religious and five Indian books and is represented by Biltmore Galleries and The Galleria.

Makk, Americo. Impressionist painter of three continents including the historical American West, born in Hungary in 1927 and living in Honolulu since 1967. Asked what his research on the West entailed, Makk replied that "first comes books. Then museums. Then we visited Indian reservations, and then the bars and saloons in some of the old-time towns. I also used imagination from the cowboy movies. They can give you the action of the past that you can't now find in the ghost towns, but you very much have to go and feel and live in the area you want to paint."

Makk began his painting at the Hungarian National Academy in Budapest. He won a scholarship that allowed him to study Italian Masters, and in Rome he won the Vatican Portrait Award. Makk and his wife Eva Holusa were both appointed Professors at the Academy de Bellas Artes in Sao Paulo, where they became official artists of the Brazilian government. In 1962, they emigrated to New York City to find political stability and have since exhibited at international shows. Makk's portrait of President Carter was presented to the White House by the Governor of Hawaii.

Now specializing in Western themes, Makk was sent by the Los Angeles Museum to sketch California ranches. In Texas, the headline for their visit was, "Hungarians Find Happiness in Desert?" Makk said that the men were friendly: "First I had to learn Texan. Finally we got together and had a nice time." The paintings of the three Makks, Americo, Eva, and their son A.B., tour mainland museums and galleries on a regular basis. They are listed in international reference books and were featured in *Southwest Art*, November 1977.

T.E. Mails, THE HOPI SIO HEMIS KATCINA, oil, 48 x 24

A. Makk, STARTLED, oil, 30 x 40

A.B. Makk

Eva Makk

DMALONEY

Makk, Americo Bartholomew. Scenic painter of the natural world, born in Sao Paulo, Brazil in 1951 and living in Honolulu since 1967. Son of Americo and Eva Makk, A.B. says that reality is in flux: "The flash of sunlight on a leaf, in a certain season, at a certain time of day, from a certain angle, will never again be exactly the same, and yet these events will be repeated, with variation, through all the ages in which leaves grow."

In Brazil, A.B. exhibited at five and was called "the little Picasso." He completed high school in New York and graduated Phi Beta Kappa with a degree in psychology from the University of Hawaii. Makk says that he was never "forced to take up a brush," but his parents were primary influences: "My dad is from the Italian and Hungarian schools. What he paints is realism, with very heavy contrasts. My mother studied at the French schools, so her paintings are more Impressionistic. They have light colors and a loose finish. My style is a combination of the two."

A.B. adds that in the West, "we have been on digs where we looked for arrowheads and different artifacts. Once my parents were walking in the desert. There was a car trailing behind them, but they wanted to walk. They wanted to know what it was like to have to walk across the land, to think of people crossing barren areas in a covered wagon." Makk began to exhibit with his parents in 1975, agreeing with them that "realistic copying is inadequate, like trying to create life without soul. We need that extra spark, that conviction that life is beautiful and exciting." As the Makk without an accent, A.B. tours the country showing the family paintings.

Makk, Eva Holusa. Impressionist painter of Indian and pioneer women and children, born in Ethiopia in 1933 and living in Honolulu since 1967. "For every ten thousand men who have tried to become artists," she declares, "one woman may have tried. This is changing now, and I wish to help it change, to show by my own work that a woman can be a master." As women, "we try to express the human spirit, often impulsive, unpredictable, always truthful, not simply the truth of realism but vibrant, vital, whole."

Her father a diplomat and her mother a Hungarian baroness, Eva Makk began painting at four, studied modern and Impressionist techniques in Paris, and graduated summa cum laude from the Rome Academy of Fine Arts. She met Americo Makk in Rome and married him in Brazil where they were official artists of the government, painting murals including the largest single-theme fresco. On one expedition, they were thirteen months in the Amazon jungle. The Makks moved to New York in 1962, painting church murals and exhibiting internationally and settled in Hawaii in 1967.

Both Makks have been attracted to the American West. In Texas, "they touched the tumbleweeds ('that gives it soul when you paint it'), went without water as many of the pioneers were forced to do, and even spent several nights in the desert." They both agreed that the desert is beautiful, but Eva said that "it can also be a frightening place." She adds what she calls the feminine touch to her work. Her paintings depict the women and children and "the tiny creatures like the lemon butterfly which frequents the desert in fall." The Makks are listed in *Who's Who in America.*

Maloney, Dave. Realist/Impressionist painter of contemporary Montana in watercolor and acrylic, born in Akron, Ohio in 1942 and living in Great Falls, Montana. "Weather permitting," he points out, "I prefer to paint outside. I feel that it is necessary for one to paint in the environment directly, so that one can capture the light, the wind, the quietness, and even the feeling of solitude of an abandoned homestead which at one time was a home with people, their livestock, and their occupation of the Old West."

Raised and educated in Akron, Maloney came to Billings, Montana, on a football scholarship to Eastern Montana College. After earning his degree as an art instructor, he taught in the Great Falls schools and has served such professional organizations as the Montana and the National Art Education Associations and the Montana Institute of the Arts. He also continued his own education as an artist, experimenting with all the materials of the art media in painting and in printmaking, until he reached the realization that he would rather paint than be a teacher of painting. He has since entered more than fifty invitational and competitive national exhibitions, specializing in watercolor.

Maloney feels that it is not necessary for a Montana painter to dwell on the past because "the essence of life today deserves delineation and appreciation too." He "spends his time exploring and recording the fields and mountains of Montana and all that has been built or is living within this environment." Much of his achievement he credits to painting out-of-doors, with contemporary people hunting and fishing. Maloney was written up in *Art West,* winter 1977 and exhibits paintings at the C.M. Russell Museum and Gallery 85.

A.B. Makk, ROCKIES, oil, 24 x 30

Eva Makk, TIGUAS, oil, 24 x 30

Dave Maloney, HONKERS INTO PARKER LAKE, acrylic, 30 x 40

Manuel, Dave. Traditional oil painter and sculptor in bronze of historical Western figures and wildlife, born in Walla Walla, Washington in 1940 and living in Joseph, Oregon since 1977. "The highlight of my career to date," he points out, "was the unveiling of the 8-foot John Wayne bronze owned by the Frontier Museum. The event took place at the museum's grand opening, April 1982. The statue was unveiled by Tonie La Cave and Melinda Munoz, children of John Wayne. Michael Wayne presented me with a commemorative John Wayne rifle. The daughters pulled the veil off the statue and then I received a hug and kiss from each of them. I still haven't quite settled back down to earth yet.

"At the age of nine, I won my first award, presented by Grumbacher and *Parent Magazine*, judged and signed by Norman Rockwell. My art education is self-taught. Between 1974 and 1976, I painted a series of 36 paintings on the Marcus Whitman story, used in a government film for the Whitman Mission Museum in Walla Walla. Each year since 1978, I have received best of show bronze awards in Washington, Oregon, and Nevada.

"In 1980, I was commissioned by the Frontier Museum, Temecula, California, to do 250, 30-inch and three 8-foot statues of John Wayne. The statue has been endorsed by the Wayne family. The edition of 250 is sold out at $4,850 each. As for the three 8-foot statues, one is on permanent display at the Frontier Museum, the second the Wayne family owns, and the third is owned by the U.S. Repeating Arms Co. In 1981, I had a museum-art gallery built to house my Indian artifact collection and artwork. The museum is open during the summer months. I am a member of the Western Artists of America."

Manzo, Anthony J. Realist oil painter in a "technique based on craft and traditions handed down from the past," born in Saddle Brook, New Jersey in 1928 and living in Taos, New Mexico. "Nothing has been said," he believes, "that hasn't been said before, so each of us must find our own way to tell an old story. When I finish a painting, what do I want to see? First, I know what I don't want to see, unrelated objects. They confuse the story. A work of art tells the full story, and I am a teller of tales. It just so happens my medium is the canvas."

He studied at the National Academy of Design School of Fine Art before completing a course in illustration at the New York Phoenix School of Design. According to Manzo, his teacher in fine art "would say, 'Anthony, do not waste your time trying to find yourself. If you have anything, you can't stop it from coming out.' Through professionals, you will have at your disposal years of experience to guide you around the potholes, past the dead ends, thus shortening your journey to the main throughway.

"Just as an artist has an obligation to use the best materials with the proper technique, so must he try to create a work that can be measured. A society's culture is measured by its art, which is nurtured by the intellect of its patrons. An artist's work is the reflection of his mind. Great art will survive in spite of critics and the lack of patrons. In art we strive for simplicity, for the most beautiful things are simple, and simplicity and knowledge go hand in hand." Listed in *Who's Who in American Art* and written up in *Southwest Art*, October 1978, Manzo is represented by The Collectors Gallery of Fine Arts and Grand Gallery.

Marcy, Douglas C. Realist painter of the contemporary West in pencil and colored pencil, born on the family farm and ranch in western Nebraska in 1949 and living there now, in Hay Springs, Nebraska. "As fast as the modern world moves," Marcy points out, "it is conceivable that today's West with its vast open ranges, huge feed lots, colorful ranches, and pickup trucks will become just another chapter in America's history. Just as past artists tried to capture a part of their times, so does the contemporary Western artist.

"I didn't draw much as a youngster. I was too busy ridin' horses and puttin' up hay. So although I was always interested in art and fooled around some, I never had any formal training until my college years at the University of Nebraska. I started out in mechanical engineering school. When they sent me to drawing classes to strengthen my draftsmanship, I never returned to engineering. Following graduation in 1972, I spent some time in Florida making hand-thrown pottery, until gas shortages shut down my kilns in 1977.

"After a variety of jobs, I wound up on a large Florida ranch where they raised everything from hogs to buffalo. While there, I began drawing ranch scenes. Sales developed along with my skills, and soon I was making more money drawing than I was on the ranch as a division manager. About that time, I decided that if I was going to 'draw the West' I'd better get there, so I moved back to the family ranch. There, I began again living the life I portrayed. I have the best of both worlds. I live what I paint, and I paint what I love." Written up in *Southwest Art*, August 1980, Marcy is represented by Altermann Art Gallery.

Doug Marcy, PIPE POWDER, color pencil, 20 x 16

Dave Manuel
CHIEF JOSEPH, OLLOKUT, CHIEF LOOKING GLASS
bronze, h 28, w 24½, d 39

Anthony J. Manzo, TO THE GOD OF THE HUNT, oil, 36 x 48

Sajos Karlos (signature)

GB. MARKS (signature)

JOHN MARSH (signature)

Markos, Lajos. Impressionist oil painter of the Old West and portraitist, born in 1917 in Transylvania, Hungary and living in Houston, Texas. "I love the old times" in the West, he emphasizes. "The people were tough and strong. They lived hard lives, and all that would show in their faces. There was violence and killing because these people had strong beliefs. It makes them colorful characters for study. That's why I am anxious to paint them."

He studied under private tutors at home and then at seventeen at the National Royal Academy in Budapest. After his father died when he was nineteen, he obtained a scholarship to the Academy and worked in a sign painter's shop for his board. "When you want to study, you'll go hungry," he stresses. "Nothing will stop you." Following World War II, he was an internationally known portrait painter in Italy and then came to the United States in 1950 where he was commissioned to do art training films. For nine years, he operated an art school in New York City and painted portraits of celebrities.

Markos moved to Houston in 1967, saying that "the history of Texas is so colorful. They are such great and important subjects. Take the stagecoach, for example. I studied it the same way I studied anatomy of man and horse, from the inside out." His big palette contains 41 colors, twice as many as most artists use, because "to work with many colors makes the work go faster. If you have only a few out, you must stop for more or spend too much time with the mixing. I don't like to stop and fumble for another color." Written up in *Southwest Art*, April 1975, and *Artists of the Rockies*, summer 1977, Markos exhibits at Texas Art Gallery.

Marks, George. Traditional painter and sculptor of the West today, born in Conrad, Iowa in 1923 and living in Albuquerque, New Mexico since 1965. According to Marks, "a Western artist such as myself can contribute a pictorial record of life in our Western United States," but not enough has been said about the importance of "collectors, art patrons who follow our progress, attend our exhibits, and purchase our work, for they provide the means by which we can continue to produce the paintings and sculpture about the life and heritage we all love.

"There was no specific event that led me to an art career because I had liked to draw animals ever since I was a kid. My pioneering grandfather brought his cattle from Montana and branded them, so we got a little of the 'Wild West' in the Midwest in those early days. My grandfather's influence, my mother's encouragement, and getting acquainted with the art of Charles Russell had more to do with me getting into Western art than anything." During World War II, he enlisted in the Marines. After three years, he entered the University of Iowa and earned his BFA in 1950, then remained an additional year for graduate study. Summer months were spent in the West.

Marks had been a commercial artist for fifteen years when he moved to New Mexico, applied for membership in the new Cowboy Artists of America in 1966, was accepted, exhibited in the first show, and eventually won two silver medals. He has been written up in three books, Ainsworth's *The Cowboy in Art*, Broder's *Bronzes of the American West*, and Hassrick's *Western Painting Today*, exhibited in the 1981 Peking, China, show, and is represented by Galeria del Sol.

Marsh, John. Realist painter of Western and genre subjects in transparent watercolor, born in Glen Falls, New York in 1936 and living in West Point, California since 1972. "I paint people I know well," he points out, "especially older people because I see in them an entire lifetime reflected in their faces, hands, and bodies. The fine detail in my work serves to create the reality, heightening the emotional impact of the subject. Thus, there is a lifetime record of experiences expressed in the painting, in addition to the illusion of three-dimensional space."

Raised in Wallingford, Connecticut, he elected to enter a technical high school to be able to study design, drawing, and painting. In 1955, he attended the University of Bridgeport on a scholarship, then transferred to the Art Center School of Design in Los Angeles where he earned a degree in professional art in 1959. After two years in design for General Motors in Warren, Michigan, he joined in establishing an industrial design firm in San Francisco and in 1972 moved to the foothills of the Sierra Nevadas in northern California to paint full time.

"I begin by looking for an interesting design to be the vehicle for the particular moment I wish to depict. In order to arrive at an original, strong design, I make numerous studies. Pattern and texture are very important to the harmony. I develop a detailed line drawing from my design of the final image and then I make my final color roughs. After this process, I begin the final painting by applying layer upon layer of transparent washes to build up the many different textural and spatial elements of the painting." Written up in *Southwest Art*, October 1977, he is represented by El Prado Gallery of Art.

George B. Marks, THE FORTUNE HUNTERS
bronze, h 18, w 12

Lajas Markos, OLD JAKE, oil, 24 x 36

John Marsh, HIGH ON THE FROZEN CARSON, watercolor, 19 x 29

Martin, Jean. Realistic painter of the New Mexico landscape in various media, primarily oil and watercolor, and print-maker, born in Dorchester, Massachusetts in 1924 and living in Albuquerque, New Mexico. "I begin an oil painting," she states, "with freely applied color, using fingers, fist, and palette knife to block in all major shapes. Slowly, with copal medium added to the paint to keep the surface workable longer, I develop the painting, refine it, and gradually use smaller brushes. The final strokes are done in a nearly miniature technique. I use a jeweler's magnifying glass fixed to my drafting table to relieve the eyestrain, adding glazes and varnish after the paint is completely dry."

She majored in both marketing and art, studying art at Lasell Junior College and Massachusetts School of Art. After working as a draftswoman in Boston, she served in the Navy from 1943 to 1945, then moved West. Additional studies were at the University of New Mexico and in workshops. "It takes a lifetime to become an artist," she points out. "There are no shortcuts.

"Several times a year, I feel the need to go out into nature, to recharge my batteries. On these working vacations, I will make sketches and take photographs. I also capture new memories of images that may not find their way into paintings until months later. I am exclusively a studio painter and do no final work on location." She has done a painting demonstration for television and has created prints for Saga. When she turns to graphics, she stops painting in oils. Written up in *Artists of the Rockies*, summer 1975, she is represented by Galeria Sigala and the Aldridge Gallery. Both have given her solo shows.

Martinez, Juan H. Traditional sculptor of Western art bronzes, born on a ranch near Albuquerque, New Mexico in 1927 and living in Pico Rivera, California. "The first day I attended the one-room school in the mountains east of Albuquerque, the teacher handed me a piece of paper and pencil," he recalls. "I didn't know what to do so I looked out the window and drew that scene and I was kicked out of school. Later we moved into town and I began to carve figures. In those days, there wasn't anything else to do at night. I would take my things and along with the Pueblo Indians we would sell to the passengers as they got off the train on Saturdays.

"After returning from the Army, I moved to Los Angeles and enrolled at the Art Center, but this type of fine art was not in the books. In 1958, I went to see a man who was a representative for an importing company, and as I walked into his house, my whole future changed. This man had been collecting Western art and this was the first time I saw Western bronzes of Indians, cowboys, and wildlife. I realized right then what I wanted to do.

"I went on to do my own research and found that the only art foundry that had ever existed in the Western states had gone out of business at the start of the war so I decided to build my own. I did my own casting until 1962. It was then that I discovered that a couple of other guys were doing Western bronzes, George Phippen and George Carlson. We were the only ones in those early days. I am a member of the American Indian and Cowboy Artists and now show at Overland Trail and Son Silver West. It has been fun doing art bronzes, and it is a lot of hard work."

Martinez, Miguel. Painter in oil pastels and acrylics and printmaker of northern New Mexico figures and landscapes, born in Taos, New Mexico in 1952 and still living there. "My main subject matter is Spanish women," he points out, "because in the life of the Spanish people, the women are very strong and sensitive. They are the ones who hold the family together. They raise and protect this family all through their life. A child can survive without its father but cannot without its mother.

"I grew up and have been working professionally in Taos for twelve years. My parents are both from Taos and also grew up here. My studies included the Taos School of Fine Arts and private studies with Ray Vinella and Vladin Stiha. I feel I have total control over my paintings and my life. I can express what I feel not in words but by what I put down in my paintings. It is a homage to the Spanish women. I also paint the landscape of northern New Mexico.

"I paint mostly thirty inches by forty inches but I also do drawings which are smaller. I use either models or photos depending on what gesture I am looking for. Then after the drawing is sketched in, I discard everything and paint what I feel I want the mood or expression to be. My work is closely related to my personal life." As one of the Spanish artists who has succeeded in penetrating the contemporary marketplace in New Mexico, Martinez has participated in Hispanic art organizations dissatisfied with being locked into traditional art and "museumry." The goal, he believes, is the Hispanic artist who will not only pull from the past but who will also carry the culture forward. He is represented by Navajo Gallery and Gallery G Fine Arts.

Miguel Martinez, SPANISH WOMAN, oil pastels, 40 x 30

Juan Martinez, WIND RIVER TRAPPERS, bronze, h 22, w 20

Jean Martin, ISLETA PUEBLO, watercolor, 18 x 24

Pat Mathiesen ✳

Mathiesen, Pat. Realist sculptor of
Crow Indian and horse bronzes in polychrome, born in Hollywood, California
and living in West Yellowstone, Montana
since 1978. "I consider polychromed
bronzes three dimensional paintings," she
notes, "but I polychrome selectively, primarily the Indian garb that just cries out to
be colorful. Ceremonial figures in particular
seem to lose something when their brilliant
dress is a solid patina."

While she was studying art in San
Francisco, she "drew everything in detail
and the instructor would come along and
mark my work as too photographic. I
cannot function in the abstract or impressionist style. I see things in the tiniest detail
and it is fun to be accurate." She married in
Phoenix and moved to Alaska where they
ran an outfitting and guide service, specializing in wildlife photography. Wiped out by
the 1964 earthquake, they returned to
Arizona where she modeled a few Alaskan
wildlife figures in wax because she missed
the Far North.

To preserve the models, she took the
waxes to a Prescott foundry to have them
cast in bronze. The pieces were seen by collectors at the foundry, purchased, and by
1966 O'Brien's Art Emporium in Scottsdale
began to show her work. She started to
travel the northern Arizona Indian reservations and produced a series of Apache,
Hopi, Mandan, and Navajo bronze figures.
When she was divorced in 1976, she
destroyed many of the Southwestern molds
and in 1978 moved to a log house in the
Montana wilderness where she has modeled
Crow and equine bronzes, saying that "my
artwork and my self-confidence have both
grown." She was featured in *Southwest Art*,
March 1981, and is represented by The
May and In the Spirit Galleries.

Pat Mathiesen, BLACK BUFFALO WOMAN (left) & SPIRIT OF CRAZY HORSE (right), polychromed bronze, h 24, Edition 25

Jay H. Matternes   MAUGHAN

Matternes, Jay H. Representational painter of the natural sciences, animals, and the West in oil and acrylic, born in Corregidor, the Philippines in 1933 and living in Fairfax, Virginia. "Painting is a way of life," he says, "and even when I am doing other things, such as trotting my dogs, taking a long drive, or being read to by my wife, I am often absorbed in some vexing problem in painting. So, in effect, I am working on a picture even when not standing before my easel."

Son of an Army surgeon, Matternes' "first exposure to the depiction of prehistory was when I was a sophomore in high school. I would literally go every weekend to the Academy of Natural Sciences or to the Philadelphia zoo. I made reams of drawings." He attended Carnegie Mellon University on a scholarship and received his BFA in 1955, then was employed as staff artist at the Cleveland Museum of Natural Sciences. Drafted in 1958, he served as exhibition artist in the Army until 1960, when he turned to free lancing.

Since then, he has illustrated major books on the natural sciences for the National Geographic Society and for Time-Life, has participated in exhibitions on animal art, has his work on permanent exhibition in fifteen museums, and has joined expeditions to every state and to six foreign countries. Thus, when he is asked whether he actually saw his subject matter, he can reply that "in some cases, where my subjects are extant wild mammals or birds, I can answer quite truthfully 'yes,' although not necessarily in the way I have chosen to depict them, for a painting is usually an idealization" A member of the Society of Animal Artists and listed in *Who's Who in American Art*, Matternes is represented by the Carson Gallery of Western American Art.

Maughan, William. Painter of the early exploration of Western America, born in Long Beach, California in 1946 and living in Vista, California. "I began my career as an illustrator," Maughan observes, "as did the artists who influenced me as a child—Howard Pyle, N.C. Wyeth, and Frederic Remington. After seven years of illustrating, I felt I had the experience and ability to do what I desired most, to be a painter of pictures to be enjoyed for the sake of the painting itself and not just to advertise a product."

Great-great-great-grandfather Maughan was the first to settle in Utah's Cache Valley in 1856. Family stories concerned the Indians in their daily experience with the white man. Maughan went to Ireland on a mission for his church from 1965 to 1967, after one semester at Brigham Young University, and then was drafted into the Army. He served in Vietnam, and in 1970 entered the Art Center College of Design in Los Angeles. When he graduated with distinction in 1973, he was selected as an apprentice to leading New York City illustrators and remained there for another three years as a commercial illustrator.

In 1977, he returned to Southern California as a commercial artist, but "advertising and illustration didn't seem enough," so in 1980 he began concentrating on historical Western art. In his painting, he puts the values of the complete composition down in brown and white, then adds opaque and transparent glazes. His goal is "a mood created by story and color," with interest achieved by contrasting texture, complexity, light, warmth, and edges. "Overlapping elements create the illusion of depth and composition." His gallery is Husberg Fine Arts.

William Maughan, MOUNTAIN MAIL, oil, 24 x 36

J.H. Matternes, PISHKUN: BUFFALO JUMP, oil/linen, 3 ft x 6 ft

McCain, Buckshot (Buck) Frederick. Oil painter of the West "as mythology—a story of people—not history," born in San Diego in 1943 and living in Tucson. "I drew constantly in those early days on the ranch," he recalls, "recording the Indian and cowboy life around me, but I knew little of painting, and had no thought of becoming an artist. In fact, until I went away to college, I had never seen an oil painting."

Son of Buster and Boots McCain, he was raised on the 186,000 acre ranch that had been settled by his family in 1836 in what is still McCain Valley on the Mexican border. The victim of dyslexia, a learning disability that his mother's discipline overcame, he wanted to be a doctor and won a pre-med scholarship to the University of San Diego. When his father died, McCain helped manage the ranch and quit college after three years. Injured in a fall from a horse, he taught himself painting while recuperating. A year later, a San Diego gallery began representing him.

For a year, he painted in Europe, doing Western subjects with a Swiss background that he sent back to California to sell, and studying Old Master techniques. When he returned, he rented a mining ghost town in New Mexico where he spent nine months of the year in solitude. He also invested in two New Mexican ranches and raised cattle before moving to Santa Fe in 1975 and then to Tucson. "I do not paint the violent or the ugly," he emphasizes. "Fine art is beauty, and beauty is harmony, balance, and coordination. I choose to 'walk in beauty,' as the Navajo says." Written up in *Southwest Art*, when he won a 1974 Franklin Mint Gold Medal, he has exhibited at the Biltmore Galleries and Joe Wade Fine Arts.

McCann, Gerald Patrick. Traditional painter of Western scenes, born in Brooklyn, New York in 1916 and living in Madison, Connecticut. "Living and working in the New York area," he says, "has given me the opportunity to study the Old Masters, as well as the Impressionist school. I believe painting is like music—rather than paint in brushstrokes you paint in passages, then into seas of tone from which the thin line of the melody emerges. People often ask me how I keep coming up with fresh ideas. I tell them I drink a lot.

"I attended Pratt Engineering School, and then switched to the Art School where I studied painting and anatomy with a teacher who gave me the key to his studio, enabling me to study his extensive collection of slides showing dissections of the human body. I later studied illustration, and was privileged to hear von Schmidt and Harvey Dunn speak. Both were strong influences on my work, and I believe that Dunn was one of America's most creative artists.

"I began doing illustrations for Street & Smith, specializing in black and white dry-brush Westerns, and from this learned to create the strong light and dark patterns to which all good painting can be reduced. Over the years, I did covers and illustrations for a variety of men's magazines, always with a Western motif or outdoor background. I also taught landscape and composition at the Famous Artists School. My most recent trip to Arizona and New Mexico gave me much new material. The ethereal quality of distant mountains has rarely been captured in Western art because the realism that characterizes much of today's Western art cannot capture this Impressionistic landscape. I have exhibited at Kennedy and The May Galleries."

Buck McCain, STORM OVER SANTA FE (1979), oil, 36 x 48

Gerald McCann, THE SCOUTING PARTY, oil/canvas, 24 x 36

McCann, Leonard. Traditional sculptor of historical Western cavalry and Indian figures in bronze statuettes, and painter, born in Burley, Idaho in 1939 and living in Aurora near Denver, Colorado since 1952. "The West is what I knew first," he observes, "from the places I've been and the things I've seen." His family moved across Idaho to Montana, Oregon, and Nebraska before settling in Colorado. His first saddle-horse was given to him at five on a ranch in Oregon, and Plains Indians and their artifacts were plentiful near his home in Dakota City, Nebraska.

In high school in Denver, McCann belonged to the rodeo club, then left school in 1957 to join the Air Force. Discharged in 1958, he saw Western art in Taos, operated the family service station, and tried a succession of jobs. When he married in 1961, he finished high school by correspondence, found the abstract philosophy at Colorado Institute of Art to be objectionable, and finally graduated from Rocky Mountain School of Art in 1969 with a degree in commercial art. After six months as Assistant Director of the school, he was employed for two years by sculptor Ken Bunn and learned modeling and foundry practice. In 1972, he became Assistant Curator of Sculpture at the Denver Museum of Natural History, and three years later left to model Western themes full time.

He feels that design "is the number one thing that goes in with the armature" which may be "baling wire, coat hangers, anything at hand." He models as many as ten figures a year, including dancers and nudes, but the Western and the military subjects are the ones that get cast. Featured in *Art West*, May 1981, McCann is a member of the Northwest Rendezvous Group and is represented by Artists' Union Gallery and Gallery Select.

McCarthy, D. Michael. Traditional oil painter of mountain landscapes, born in Los Angeles in 1951 and living in Sedona, Arizona since 1976. "The landscapes I paint are derived from energetic pursuits in my daily life. That people associate them with paintings of the past, I take as a source of pride. Before I ever climbed a mountain, I loved mountains through the art of the Masters. The Hudson River School is the school I feel closest to. It's as though Moran and Bierstadt were my friends."

In grammar school, Mike McCarthy waited impatiently for the weekly art period, but he followed his father's career by taking accounting in college. The few art classes, however, "touched something in me" and he earned his BFA at Fontbonne College in St. Louis, Missouri, in 1973. After eighteen months "re-teaching" himself to paint, he began his "visual odyssey" of summers in the wilderness and winters painting. Outdoor sketching is in watercolor, in early morning or late afternoon, and he finds it "imperative to climb and hike to those viewpoints" that he needs.

In his studio, though, he paints after dark, using a "true light" tube and incandescent floods because that is the way paintings are seen. "The vibration of the world is different at night," he explains, "and you have more space for thinking." His palette is a glass-topped table on wheels. He takes the phone off the hook and goes to bed about seven in the morning. Figures are rare in his landscapes, but he believes that the sky is critical because it contains the "illumination for the entirety." He was featured in *Artists of the Rockies*, fall 1978, and *Southwest Art*, December 1980, and is represented by Husberg Fine Arts Gallery.

Len McCann, PLENTY COUPS, bronze, h 15, w 17, d 6½

D. Michael McCarthy, THE REPLENISHED EARTH, oil, 14 x 30

McCarthy, Frank C. Realist painter of the Old West, born in New York City in 1924 and living in Sedona, Arizona. "Some Western artists document, some do scenery, animals, and portraits of Indians. I paint to achieve a visual impact—trying to redesign the beauty of the West. I put into this setting the characters that roamed it as well as the vehicles that crossed it. My paintings are based on truth and their settings in reality, but the events are not specific."

McCarthy's fascination with the West started before he was five, when he saw Buffalo Bill. While going to high school in Scarsdale, New York, he studied at the Art Students League in New York City during the summers. Then came an illustration course at Pratt Institute in Brooklyn, followed by a studio apprenticeship. In 1948, McCarthy began as a free-lance commercial artist, painting hundreds of paperback covers and movie and business ads. Within two years he was doing Westerns. In 1969, he placed his first easel paintings in a New York City gallery, and by 1971 he had no more time for commercial work.

He paints in casein oil, starting with abstract scribbles to find patterns of light and shade. As he progresses with the paintings, changes are made on the canvas in the search for beauty and form, emphasizing objects like rocks and dirt as well as the play of light and color in action. At his first one-person show at Husberg Fine Arts Gallery in 1973, 23 paintings were sold in 20 minutes. His paintings now go to a waiting list and his limited edition prints by Greenwich Workshop are sold out. McCarthy is a member of the Cowboy Artists of America and the Northwest Rendezvous Group, and is listed in *Who's Who in American Art*.

Frank McCarthy, THE TOLL OF A SHARPS RIFLE, oil, 24 x 36

McCauley, Don. Painter of "nature's forms" in oil and "Indian-like abstractions" in watercolor, born in Louisville, Kentucky in 1938 and living in Ridgecrest, California since 1978. "If I chose one word to summarize art," he says, "it would be *perhaps!* A second choice would perhaps be *sincerity!* And perhaps a third *wit!* Questions worth asking ourselves as artists net us more truth, entertainment, knowledge, wisdom, and friendship when they can be answered with a simple, 'Perhaps—with sincerity and wit!'

"I began my professional life as a scientist—Ph.D. in Physics from the University of California in 1970. From 1970 until January 1978, I worked as a civilian scientist for the Navy. My research dealt with holography—the science of making optical gadgets using lasers and special films. But since 1960, I'd been a 'Sunday painter,' one among the masses of perpetual 'amateurs.' In January of 1978, I quit my job as a physicist and began drawing and painting full time—for a living! I had made the shift from the sciences to humanities.

"I became an artist by simply saying, 'I'm an artist. I'm a *doer!*' Artists are *doers* and always have been. There's some artist in each of us, to the extent we're doers. You ask, 'What about talent? You have to be born with the talent for art, right?' Wrong! It's easier showing the art-making process to someone with artistic talent because he knows that talent isn't the answer." In the year he began painting professionally, McCauley won a Best of Show award and by 1981 he was in Texas Art Gallery's *Preview*. Written up in *Southwest Art*, November 1978, he is also represented by Peppertree Fine Art, Inc.

McCaw, Dan. Impressionist oil painter of "scenes of the American West and Mexico, figure studies, landscapes, portraits, and romantic nostalgia," born in Butte, Montana in 1942 and living in Hermosa Beach, California. "Too many artists," he insists, "paint what the galleries want. So, they lose their individuality. There are plenty of paintings around that were done with the wrist, not the heart." Instead, "artists should be sensitive to their world. They have to be honest with themselves. In a painting, aesthetics should be the first concern."

Growing up in Butte, McCaw "began to sketch many of the characters who populated the mining community." At twenty, he received a scholarship to the San Francisco Academy of Art and later continued his studies at the Art Center College of Design in Los Angeles. After several years as a commercial artist, he decided "to give up commercial art for fine art." He believes that "the term 'life enhancement,' coined by art historian Bernard Berenson best describes his own approach in interrelationships with life."

He emphasizes that "it takes years of experimentation, dedication, and searching to develop a personal idiom. The painter must show people more than what they already know. He must show them with so much understanding and sympathy that they will recognize what the artist portrays as though they had seen and experienced it themselves." His own oils are designed to "reveal a world of color, emotion, and special moments. Instead of rejecting earlier movements of the century," his approach is to "turn reality into visual poetry by creating a world of personal involvement." McCaw teaches at the Art Center College of Design and is represented by Shriver Gallery and Settlers West Galleries.

McCoy, A.J. Representational wildlife painter in oil and watercolor, born in Painesville, Ohio in 1936 and living in Ennis, Montana. According to her, "I don't know of another field that has more people telling you how great your work is than art. When they should be telling you that it stinks, they tell you how gorgeous it is. If you tend to be so proud of yourself that you believe all of this, you will never advance very far. Be your own worst critic, but be honest, too. If it is good, say so. If it stinks, say it, but be able to tell the difference.

"I grew up in stark poverty, determined to rise above this type of life. In high school, I worked for the faculty for a small salary. To become a nurse, I worked during the summers and on campus but did not have the entrance fee for the third year. Much to my surprise, I got a job in a publishing house in the Washington, D.C., area. Here I remained for eight and a half years. Most of the male artists had formal training and they taught me all they knew. Then I went back to school and received my R.N.

"We moved to Heart Butte, Montana, on the Blackfoot Reservation where I nursed in the daytime and painted at night. After much thought and prayer, I decided to hang up the bedpans and paint full time. While so close to Glacier Park, I became very much interested in the wildlife, and so was launched my career. People keep telling me that Indians and mountain man scenes are big, but I am not about to start painting something that I am not interested in just for a few bucks. I was a guest artist at the Northwest Rendezvous, was elected into the Society of Animal Artists, and am a charter member of the Western Artists of America." Jeannie McCoy is represented by Troy's Gallery.

A.J. McCoy, LESSON IN STEEL, oil, 18 x 24

Dan McCaw, THREE FRIENDS, oil, 30 x 40

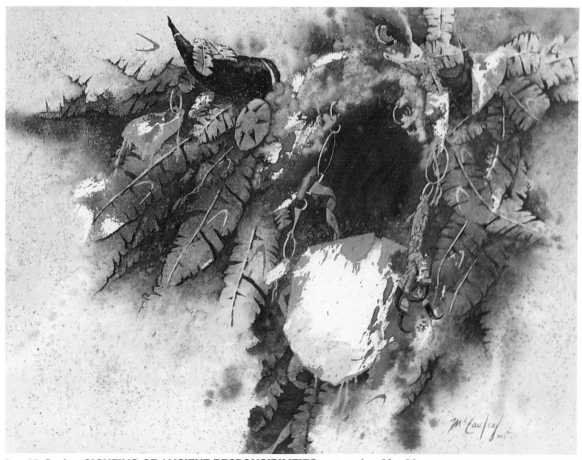

Don McCauley, SIGHTING OF ANCIENT RESPONSIBILITIES, watercolor, 22 x 30

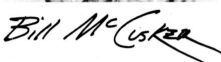

Bill McCusker

Tom McGary

DAVID McGoffin

Marlene McGoffin

McCusker, Bill. Representational watercolorist of "soft core" Westerns of Washington scenes, born in Dickinson, North Dakota in 1929 and living in Yakima, Washington. "If my paintings have a story to tell," he explains, "it's a quiet story. Most of my paintings that people buy are ones that relate a particular experience or memory to them. I just paint what I know and see. It's also part of the West—not just the cowboy and cattle, but the part that is also disappearing—the small farm, the homestead.

"I have been drawing since I was in grade school—it was something I just 'did.' I never did seriously consider being an artist, let alone make a living at it. It was taught to me that you had to learn something to get a 'job,' and I drifted into the lure of show biz. I spent one season on the road as a magician and studied drama at the University of Washington, but my stint in the Army changed that. After the Army, I went into the 'brand new' TV business and it was while at a station in El Paso that I got re-bitten by the need to create in paint.

"About twelve years ago, I let myself be talked into showing my work. To my amazement, some even sold. My God! I really don't paint the 'Western scene,' although horses and cattle and riders sometimes appear. I'm primarily a landscape artist who paints the West. They're mostly nostalgic things. Some are moody—abandoned places and things. My entry that won Best of Show was just a campfire in a dark snow scene that could have been anytime, anywhere. I was 'artist in residence' at the Museum of Native American Culture in 1979 and 1981, as well as a founding member of American Artists of the Rockies. My galleries include Trailside and Ponderosa."

McGary, David. Traditional sculptor of bronze statuettes of Plains Indians, born in Cody, Wyoming in 1958 and living in Alto, New Mexico. "I couldn't be a painter," he points out, "and paint on a slick surface. I'd have to use a palette knife to give depth to the strokes. Textures and patinas are important in sculpture. The texture creates contrast between the parts of the piece, and the patina highlights the tones. They give a piece the added depth that I need to really show its feelings."

He says that a jewelry class in school and sketches in the museum led to study with Harry Jackson in Italy. "I spent my seventeenth birthday there at the base of the Alps," he observes. "I wanted to work on the details of a piece, but Harry persuaded me to pay more attention to the anatomy of the structure, and it's really paid off." When he returned, he established his studio and foundry near Ruidoso, New Mexico, stating that "having all your work done in-house goes a long way to insuring the quality.

"The historical details are very important to me. I put in three incorrect historical details and challenge my collectors to pick them out. If they can, I give them the piece. I used to put just one flaw in, but one collector came real close so I started putting in three. That one time got me scared." In the four years up to 1981, he produced fourteen major bronzes and raised his editions from 15 to 22, but he is "not going to start increasing those editions just to make money. I've seen where other people have done that and the quality drops. It gets to the point where I don't dare show anyone a new piece until after I've had a show. Otherwise, I wouldn't have any pieces to show in the galleries." He is represented by Dewey-Kofron and Wagner Galleries.

McGoffin, Marlene and David. Dyers of batiks of Southwestern Indian women, born in Euclid, Ohio and Tucson, Arizona respectively, both in 1947, and living in Phoenix, Arizona. "We don't think in terms of composition, design, and color," they point out, "because neither one of us has been artistically trained. We're technically proper because we've taught ourselves to be proper. You can teach mechanics, however, but if a person doesn't know what looks and feels right, then he's not going to make a good artist.

"We began as a team," David explains, "about six years ago. Prior to that, Marlene was the only one doing batiks. I had a job and was doing macrame and weaving on the side. One day I decided that if I was going to be an artist, I had to support myself as an artist, so I quit my job. I didn't begin to do batiks until I became allergic to wool and had to stop weaving. Marlene always puts action in her drawings; mine just sit there. I like to show backs and I like my ladies to be sexy. When I first wanted to do a woman whose back was turned, everybody told me it was artistically incorrect, but I did it and I love those ladies. You can't give batiks the same rules you do paintings, because you can't work with shadows. You have to work with the drawing to get dimension.

"We start out," Marlene adds, "by each of us doing a number of drawings. When we are finished, we review and criticize them. The ones that survive are batiked. When we are finished batiking, we again review and criticize. The ones that survive this battle are framed. It's not a very relaxed period and we do it about eight times a year. There is a lot of tension until the batiks are completed." They are represented by their own The Gallery-McGoffin.

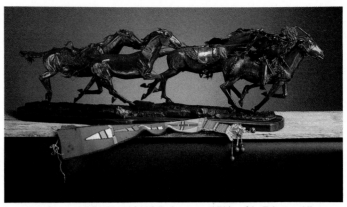

Dave McGary, STOLEN HONOR, bronze, 17½ x 61, Edition 15

Bill McCuster, NOVEMBER SOLITUDE, watercolor, 15 x 22

Marlene McGoffin, BONITA, batik, 42½ x 56

David McGoffin, EMPTY BASKET—FULL HEART, batik, 54 x 41

McGrew, Ralph Brownell. "Classico-Impressionist" oil painter of Southwestern figures, primarily Navajo and Hopi, born in Columbus, Ohio in 1916 and living in Quemado, New Mexico. "When our family lived on the Coachella desert in California, one of my favorite sketching spots was the lovely valley called La Quinta, about 20 miles from home. I made dozens of excursions there. After about ten years, we moved to La Quinta, and of course I never sketched there again."

After studying for four years on a scholarship at Otis Art Institute in Los Angeles, McGrew taught at Otis and studied privately while painting society portraits in his classical style. He then moved to Palm Springs where he lived for eighteen years. Sketching trips into the desert with the painter Jimmy Swinnerton led to a meeting with Shine Smith who introduced McGrew to the Navajos and Hopis. After that, McGrew had "a wealth of Indian faces stored in my sketch pads, in photographs, and most importantly, in my experience from trips. Every time I start to do a landscape, I think of an old Indian that I would rather do.

"I am an Impressionist in the classical sense. Reality comes from the suggested rather than from the detailed or the finished. My paintings are not exact copies of any of the scenes I see. I prefer the natural way of painting, and am fond of working different methods in the same canvas." In 1978, the McGrew Retrospective featured 116 works at the Laguna Beach Museum of Art. At the 1981 Western Heritage Sale in Houston, his painting brought $107,500. Written up in *Artists of the Rockies*, spring 1979, and *Southwest Art*, May 1980, he is represented by O'Brien's Art Emporium and Trailside Galleries.

R. Brownell McGrew, WAITING FOR A RIDE, oil, 42 x 66

Gregory I. Mc Huron ©

Carol McIlroy

McHuron, Gregory I. Realist oil and watercolor painter of the Tetons and of wildlife, born in Syracuse, New York in 1945 and living in Moose, Wyoming since 1973. "The majority of my works are executed on location," he points out, "as I am a firm believer in going to the source. If you want to paint mountains—go to the mountains, live with them, watch the interplay of light and environmental values affecting them. You must know what you paint, and it is this constant changing of factors that is so exciting. You can draw from everything that is going on around you."

Raised in Colorado, Wyoming, Alaska, and California, McHuron was schooled in forestry, fisheries, and wildlife as well as fine arts at Oregon State University. He has been painting in the Tetons since 1973. A member of the Society of Animal Artists, he has gone to Banff and Jasper Parks to find backgrounds for his wildlife paintings and he uses the Okanagan Game Farm in Penticton, British Columbia, for studies of the wildlife. He was invited to participate in the National Cowboy Hall of Fame's First North American Wild Animal Exhibition in 1979.

McHuron says that the reason he prefers painting on location is that "the drama that occurs all around you is difficult to recreate. Only the final pulling together of the painting is done in the studio where you can be critical without distraction. I try to make each new painting better than the ones before. It is this constant attempt to narrow the distance between what is envisioned and the end product that keeps an artist growing." He is represented by The May Gallery, which calls him "an artist on the move."

McIlroy, Carol. Traditional oil painter of impressions of New Mexico, born in Sandpoint, Idaho in 1924 and living in Albuquerque, New Mexico since 1955. "It may sound dumb," she explains, "but I will look at a painting upside down, sideways, or in a mirror. If it doesn't look right reading backwards, it won't work reading forwards. You have to keep adjusting till you have it. There is an instinctive point reached when you know you have conveyed the scene just the way it should be."

After growing up in a village in the Montana forest and in Washington State, she studied at the University of Colorado and the University of New Mexico. "I am motivated to paint a place or a scene," she stresses, "by the patterns of light that fall on the ground or on a building surface, or by an especially dramatic sky. The qualities of light in New Mexico are extraordinary, prompting color ranges from deep russet to shades of grey. For me, the trees are gorgeous, with or without leaves. I work on several paintings at the same time—when one is not developing, I put it face to the wall and start another."

She confesses that "the most wonderful thing about being an artist is that you can select a scene to paint and then combine elements, taking away or adding those things that convey the feeling you want to present. Painters are lucky, but they are unsure individuals for they recognize that they can never achieve ultimate perfection." She is listed in *Who's Who in American Art* and in *American Artists of Renown*, was featured in *New Mexico Magazine*, 1973, and in *Southwest Art*, April 1981. She is represented by Galeria Del Sol.

Carol McIlroy, AUTUMN, oil, 30 x 24

Gregory McHuron, THE LAST WARM RAYS, oil, 24 x 36

McLAUGHLIN

McMahan

John L. MENDOZA

McLaughlin, Nancy. Impressionist sculptor and painter of Blackfoot Indian women and tribal legends, born in western Montana in 1932 and living in Newport, Washington. She signs her work with just her surname because she does not think of herself as a "woman artist" and wants her work to be judged on its merits rather than on her sex. She has found that "a professional artist," regardless of gender, "needs to be prolific to make a living, as well as patient, strong as a horse, and very stubborn."

She was born six weeks prematurely, the result of an auto accident, and spent the first days in her grandmother's oven. When she was four, the family moved to a logging camp in northern Montana. During World War II, her stepfather worked on a ranch on the Blackfoot Indian Reservation. They lived in a sod-roofed log cabin and she "always got stuck milking the Jersey heifer—my hands were small and so were the faucets." At the elementary school there were fourteen children, and the other thirteen were Blackfoot. Her first art lessons were in Flathead County High School. After a two-year college course in education, she taught art for a year before going to Montana State University for fine art.

She first specialized in painting Blackfoot children, her "Indian Baby Syndrome" that founded the family joke that she had "produced more Indian babies than the reservation." She illustrated a book on the Blackfoot and painted a series on the Pacific Northwest Makah Indians, but she considers herself more adept at sculpting. She was featured in *Southwest Art*, February 1975, is a member of American Artists of the Rockies and Western Artists of America, and exhibits at Select Gallery.

McMahan, George E. Realist oil painter of wildlife and horses of the Pacific Northwest, born in Roundup, Montana in 1926 and living in Klamath Falls, Oregon. "I was raised in the country," he recalls. "My father's place in Klamath Falls included a swamp that was full of wild game and birds. It was so close that I could have shot honkers without getting out of bed, although the killing part didn't interest me."

At 21, an accident ended his career in the lumber yard. "After six months of being unable to do much," he explains, "I figured I'd better make some plans." He began studying medical illustration, "maybe because I was hurting real bad and thinking about this type of thing." He attended the Oregon Institute of Technology, the Art Center School, and the University of California in San Francisco, but after three years quit to become a field service technician for a computer company where "I got my day's work done in a half day. The other half was free to pursue art.

"I had an excellent education in art, but there were two things they never taught me—how to paint a picture and how to sell one! Those two prime things that every artist needs to know were not even discussed in school." For ten years, he used his half days to remedy his education, then began painting full time. "I don't think you can really paint until you quit thinking about the paint and start thinking about the picture. I've drawn for so many years, it's pure instinct, so when I'm painting, I'm painting my subject, not a painting. My paint is not paint, it's a voice." Written up in *Southwest Art*, April 1980, and the subject of the book *G.E. McMahan, the Man and His Art*, he is represented by the Favell Museum.

Mendoza, John L. Abstract-realist painter of southern Colorado in watercolor, born in Trinidad, Colorado in 1938 and living since then in Pueblo, Colorado. "You have to believe in yourself," Mendoza emphasizes. "Success in life is determined by how much confidence you have, brought about by some talent and a heck of a lot of hard work." He adds that he "has chosen watercolor to convey his feelings because it is a naturally spontaneous medium and he feels it complements his personality."

Born in a small mining town, he and his family moved to the St. Charles Mesa outside of Pueblo when he was an infant. He states that his "earliest memories are those he has now preserved in watercolors, with the vast horizons of the semi-arid prairie, the sunrise over the mesa, and the sunsets over the Wet Mountain Range." After earning his MA in fine art from the University of Northern Colorado, he taught art for two years before becoming the full-time professional he has remained for more than twenty years.

Influenced by de Kooning and Pollock, Mendoza began painting as an abstract expressionist, but he believes that the Oriental school left the prevailing influence on his work. He calls his style "a blending of realism based on his own Southwestern heritage "with the abstraction he learned. A member of the National Watercolor Society, he has had more than 30 one-person shows, has won more than 25 awards, has paintings in eleven permanent collections, and has been in the traveling shows of both the National and the American Watercolor Societies. His book *Southwestern Echoes* was published in 1979 and he is represented by De Colores Art Gallery.

Nancy McLaughlin, CONSORT TO THE WIND
bronze, 18 x 12

John Mendoza, AMONG THE ANCIENTS, watercolor, 22 x 30

George McMahan, HEADING TO TOWN, oil, 36 x 48

353

Merfeld, Gerald Lydon. Contemporary Impressionist painter and teacher who does some Western subjects, born in Des Moines, Iowa in 1936 and living in New Lenox, Illinois. "The big moguls in publishing and in museums," he declares, "find shock art to be newsworthy. This leads the public to conclude that any fool who works in a representational manner is a misguided unfortunate born 150 years too late. This insures the employment of a goodly number of culture snobs who keep the public off balance and humbled by their ignorance."

Able to dramatize his ideas, he says he "studied with William Mosby at the American Academy. I didn't even know the difference between commercial and fine art when I went there, but I soon decided I didn't want to spend my life doing ads for underwear." He graduated in 1957 and "Mosby was the one who told me Dean Cornwell (the New York illustrator) needed an apprentice. Cornwell taught me the value of precision and that 'when a line is right, leave it alone'."

Each summer, Merfeld paints on location in the West and makes sketches for completion in his studio. He explains that his style of "contemporary Impressionism is more than using little spots of broken color—it is catching an image and through it reflecting a mood, an emotion, or perhaps a memory." He adds that "I'm the kind of guy who functions best when he's scared. I have to convince myself every day that I can paint." Listed in *Who's Who in American Art* and featured in *American Artist*, December 1978, and in *Artists of the Rockies*, fall 1981, Merfeld has exhibited at the National Academy of Western Art and other national shows. He is represented by De Colores Art and Trailside Galleries.

Metz, Gerry. Realist painter and sculptor of the Old West in opaque watercolor, born in Chicago in 1943 and living in Scottsdale, Arizona since 1971. "Time," he points out, "is not how long it takes me to do a painting, get it framed, or drive to the studio each morning, but rather a place to be where paintings happen. This new way of looking at time has allowed me to inwardly 'get a handle' on the entire painting while not fully conscious of it. When I look at a blank white canvas or board, I already see the image—it's just a matter of getting the white out of the way."

Raised in Chicago, Metz attended Wright Junior College and the School of Professional Art, worked as a commercial artist from 1962 to 1965, and was director of the Village Art School until he moved West. "When I arrived here," he declares, "I tried to imagine what it must have been like a hundred years ago. Although I have no way of knowing what the personal dangers and struggles actually were, surely my life as an artist has been as lonely, and at times, almost as difficult as theirs must have been.

"True, hundreds of artists have painted the West, but thousands of artists have painted the tree and it doesn't stand to reason that one should no longer paint the tree. That's like saying all songs have been sung, so why sing any more.

"It's not the song, but the arrangement that counts." Metz is listed in *Who's Who in American Art*, participates in leading invitational exhibitions, was written up in *The Western Horseman*, June 1980, and *Southwest Art*, December 1980, and is published by The Stuart Collection, and is represented by The May and Casa Delores Galleries.

Michael, Gary. Traditional representational painter "of moods in people and places," born in Denver, Colorado in 1937 and living there in 1982. According to Michael, "only traffic-court judges listen to more lies than artists. From friends who ask for extra invitations to a show, to customers who don't abide by payment schedules, to galleries that promise to get back to you, to publishers who encourage a submission, there's just no end to the misrepresentations stuffed into the ears of the ambitious artist. And there's the rub, *ambition*."

As a boy, Michael spent hours drawing birds, but in adolescence his interest turned to tennis and he attended Denver University on an athletic scholarship. After getting an M.A. in English at Colorado University and a Ph.D. in Humanities at Syracuse University, New York in 1970, he returned to Denver to teach humanities at Metropolitan State College. On a leave of absence in San Francisco, "my wanderings turned me on about doing art again." He taught another year while auditing art classes, then quit in 1973 to paint. In 1975, he became an art instructor.

"Anything that excites me visually," he emphasizes, "is a potential painting. Finding motifs is easy. They're everywhere. Thinking of a way to treat them is what's difficult." For an artist, he says, "cream rises. Promotion is everything. These are opposite extremes for explaining success in the art market. The former is idealistic, the latter is cynical, but one thing is sure: Cream won't rise without promotion, though good promotion can push a lot of sour milk to the top." Written up in *Southwest Art* twice and in *Art West*, he is listed in *Who's Who in American Art*, is a member of the Pastel Society of America, and is represented by Rosenstock Arts.

Gerry Metz, PACKIN' OUT, opaque watercolor, 20 x 30

Gary Michael, TETON LILY POND, oil, 40 x 55

Gerald Merfeld, SISTERS (1981), oil, 20 x 24

Michaelsen

A. Mickelson

Michaelsen, Ken. Realist painter of "creatures of the wild," particularly birds, in gouache and oil, born in San Francisco in 1936 and living in Fort Bragg, California since 1970. "My birds and animals," he emphasizes, "cannot be done justice in any way except realism. Their beauty and charm deserve all the detail I can give them. I study them to discern their major characteristics, then play those qualities to the utmost. Such as the eye. In animals, all you have for the most part is the eye to show expression.

"My father is an artist. We always had some sort of art project going on, so I never had much question in my mind what I was going to be. I latched on first to a high school art teacher, found a lot of good experience in the Air Force where I moved my drawing board right next to the best pros, and then got with a newspaper and found another hero, my art director. I got most of my art education by working with and watching closely these other artists. I have painted almost every type of creature, but I chose birds to settle on because of their ability to leave the earth and become one with the sky. I can truly get into an eagle painting.

"When I first won the 1978–79 California Duck Stamp contest I went limp in the knees. Then, nine months later, even before the swelling in my head went down, I won the federal contest! When the call came from Washington, D.C. I couldn't talk. I just sort of gurgled. I jumped up and started dancing when the phone rang again and didn't stop ringing for two years. I believe we made somewhere around three hundred thousand dollars after taxes. How do I feel? Only like the luckiest guy who ever decided to pick up a paint brush!" He is published by Bloomfield Collections and represented by Swanson Art Galleries and Mayhew Wildlife Gallery.

Mickelson, Arlene Jo. Sculptor and intaglio printmaker of the art and mythology of the Indians of the Pacific Northwest Coast, born in Seattle, Washington in 1938 and living in Issaquah, Washington. "My art," she explains, "is about the Indians from the Columbia River north to Juneau. Not much is left of their culture because after the whites moved in, the Indians were all but wiped out with the smallpox and measles. The culture was matrilineal and today it is the women who are recording, writing, and teaching the heritage.

"It was on Bainbridge Island that I spent my first years. I loved to lie in the sand and dream about great dugout canoes on Puget Sound. When I was ten, my parents began to fill my time with art materials. During my last two years in high school, they enrolled me in pottery classes at the University of Washington night school. After I graduated, I was at the university for two years, then got married and went to work in an office. When I got my children into school, I reached into my past and found an interest in the Indian cultures of this area.

"I began to adapt the design principles to my pottery. The demand became bigger than the supply and I was tired of the repetition of making pots. I enrolled in a night class in bronze casting, a chance to portray the Northwest Coast Indians in a way that was even more explanatory than the pottery. At a show, I was encouraged to start doing flat art. It was hard to do drawing without something that was three-dimensional so I took classes in intaglio printing. Recently, I became a member of the American Artists of the Rockies. My galleries include Trails West Gallery of Fine Arts and Trails End Gallery."

Arlene Mickelson, MY SACRED SONG, etching, 18½ x 24

Ken Michaelsen, FEMALE MALLARDS, gouache, 30 x 40

Dan Mieduch

Herb Mignery

Don Miles

Mieduch, Dan. Representational oil painter of the historic and contemporary cowboy West, born in Detroit, Michigan in 1947 and living in Phoenix, Arizona since 1975. "Started drawing at age seven," he recalls. "Enrolled in Detroit Institute of Arts Drawing Program. Studied Rembrandt's paintings. Since I was only seven, and 4 feet 1 inch tall, and the paintings were hung much higher than me, I guess you could say I studied 'under' Rembrandt.

"Took night classes in painting in high school. Began watercolors at twelve, oils a year later. Sold wildlife paintings in Dad's bar for $40. Swept the floors for a lot more. Entered Michigan State University, left for the University of Michigan, which was closer to home and obtained a BS in industrial design in 1969. I was broke but my mom said, 'cheer up.' No sooner had I cheered up, when I was drafted. Spent eighteen months in the Army Medical Corps. Don't ask me why they made me a medic. I guess my name is spelled similarly. They sent me to a MASH unit in the Canal Zone. There I managed a three-month stint as command artist.

"After the service, I went to work for a major Detroit commercial illustration studio. Worked up to staff artist before they gave me my walking papers for having an overdeveloped sense of humor. Worked a few other studios in Detroit before they gave me my walking papers for having an overdeveloped sense of humor. Since it seemed that I was destined to work for myself, I considered what I most liked to do—to paint a simple way of life on the last bastion of the American 20th-century frontier and to perish or prevail on the ability to be quick on the 'draw.' The rest is history," as recounted in *Southwest Art*, October 1979. Mieduch is represented by El Prado Gallery of Art.

Mignery, Herb. Traditional painter in various media and sculptor in bronze of Western figures, born in Bartlett, Nebraska in 1937 and living in Hastings, Nebraska. "For serious subject matter," he observes, "I like the mountain man types because of the flowing garments and colorful appearance that characterizes them. Also, their faces contain a wealth of character. The same can be said of our 'older' cowboys of today.

"My early life centered around the ranch that my father and his brother own in the Nebraska sandhills. Roping was my pastime. Afoot or on horseback, it is the only thing that fascinates me as much as art. I've been drawing since I can remember. First it was pencil sketches of horses, cowboys, etc. After high school, it was cartooning for the college newspapers, a year on construction, then two years as an Army illustrator. After the Army, I worked at sign painting, bartending, and singing in a country Western band. In Hastings, I was employed as a commercial artist for a printing firm, and did free-lance work for the Thomas D. Murphy calendar company and advertising agencies.

"Eight years ago, I opened my studio and began to do bronze sculpture on a full-time basis. Although it goes quite slow at times, I've found it to be my most 'comfortable' media. I don't start out with any detailed sketches, but just 'jump in' and do my experimenting on the actual piece. If a part of it doesn't look right, I cut it away and start over. I feel too much 'paper preparation' takes the spontaneity from a sculpture. Since 1974, I have completed 21 bronzes, many of which deal with the subject matter of my early life." Mignery is represented by Folger Ranch Gallery and is published by Cornhusker Press.

Miles, Don. Painter of the natural scenery of the West as it is today, born in Lincoln, Nebraska in 1912 and living in Pasadena, California. "In painting," according to Miles, "the ability to draw is of primary importance. Composition comes next. Once an artist has a good drawing and a well-balanced composition, he has created a good design and from then on it is only a matter of following the plan to completion.

"My schooling took place in Long Beach where I went through my first year of college. I had enrolled in engineering courses but found I was really more interested in drawing. Because of this, I went to trade school in Los Angeles. In 1933, my first job was in architectural design and I continued there for six years." His interest in painting had begun when he was twenty. While supporting himself in mechanical engineering, he studied landscape painting under Henry Richter and for four years under Sam Hyde Harris who "loved the desert." Miles started painting professionally in 1964.

Miles declares that he "does not believe in beginning a painting by haphazardly splashing something on the canvas and then backing off to see what it suggests. Careful planning through drawing and composition is of utmost importance. Value and color are the two remaining items, and value is the more important. A painting can be off in color but if it is right in value, chances are it will be successful. I try to put the finish color on correctly the first time and leave it alone, without resorting to undercoats or glazes." Best known as a desert painter, Miles has won more than 90 awards and is represented by Leslie B. De Mille and Cody Galleries.

Don Miles, UNTITLED, oil/canvas, 24 x 30

Herb Mignery, OPPORTUNITY, bronze, h 16

Dan Mieduch, ONE ORNERY S.O.B., oil, 24 x 36

359

Miley

Frank D. Miller

Stan Miller

Miley, Douglas. Representational oil painter of Western landscapes, born in "an isolated farmhouse near Continental, Ohio" in 1941, and living in Prescott, Arizona since 1977. "By the age of four, I had established my preferences for activities, sketching the scenery with my colored pencils. Recognizing my talent, my parents gave me a beginner's set of oil paints for my eighth birthday. I had found my medium.

"During the next decade, I taught myself the fundamentals of painting and developed the techniques I felt essential to my style. By my early twenties, I was recognized for my realistic style, specializing in nostalgic landscapes. When I was drafted into the Army in 1963, I was classified as an illustrator and midway through my two-year stint was transferred to Fort Dix, New Jersey, where I was placed in charge of the sign shop. After my discharge, I returned to Ohio and worked as an illustrator for Campbell Soup Company for eleven years.

"In 1977, I moved to Prescott and went to work for an art conservation and restoration laboratory. The opportunity to closely examine the painting styles of Keith, Bierstadt, Moran, the Hudson River School, and many European artists has greatly contributed to my style and technique, especially in smaller paintings. Today, much painting is surface. We are not painting emotion, illusion, and atmospheric change as the 19th-century artists did. Everything today, including art, is just trends that last a second, and then change. There is no permanence in art now. I would have liked to have gone back to a more peaceful time and be able to think things through more thoroughly. My works are currently on display at Merrill's, Troy's, and Whitney's."

Miller, Frank D. Traditional painter of the old and the contemporary West, born in Burley, Idaho in 1939 and living in De Borgia, Montana since 1978. "I received my first art training from my father, a commercial artist," he recalls. "I can remember knowing that I was going to someday be an artist. I came from a large family and leaving school seemed like the thing to do. I moved to Ogden, Utah, and started working as a carpenter, studying the Art Instruction correspondence course at night.

"In those learning years, I found that I could be taught the basics, but the best art teacher was hours practicing. I believe that even though an artist might have degree after degree attached to his name, it still amounts to artists are mostly self-taught. In 1966, I took some paintings to Las Vegas that were well received, but not enough to go at it full time. In 1969, a gallery in Salt Lake City decided to handle my art and suggested that I 'soften up.' I looked closer at nature for those soft edges and they were there.

"I had the gold fever from 1968 to 1977, but instead of getting richer I was getting poorer. Shortly after, I had a dream, and in the dream I was told that if I would go to Montana it would go well in my art. In a few days, I had a job as a superintendent for a construction company in Great Falls and also worked doubly hard on my art career. From that time on, the dream has been fulfilled. In 1977, $600 was my top price for a sold painting. In 1980, I received Best of Show for a painting, and in 1981, 'The Winner Takes All' sold for $11,500. I am a member of Western Artists of America, and my galleries include J. Harken and Associates, and Miller Studio."

Miller, Stan. Realist painter of rural scenes and figures in watercolor and egg tempera, born on a farm near Freeman, South Dakota in 1949 and living in Spokane, Washington since 1966. "I find the two mediums adequate for expressing everything," he explains, "from an explosive sky to a pig's hair. Why I paint the subjects I do is hard to say. Certainly my early experiences play their part. The intense realism of Andrew Wyeth's work also casts its impression on me. I hope the Lord has His hand and influence on me and my work for I credit Him for His part by signing a small cross after my name.

"Perhaps it was on our farm that early impressions of the rural scenes began to fill my mind. Time went quickly, but the memories of this special farm and all that went with it remain strong. Then in 1956 we packed our things, auctioned off the farm, and moved to Sioux Falls. In 1966, we moved to Spokane where I went on to major in physical education and minor in art at Spokane Falls Community College.

"I practiced commercial art for two years working with a Christian Relief Organization in Pennsylvania from 1970 to 1972, then returned to Spokane for one more year of education in art. I really started to enjoy painting and I have been making my living as an artist and part-time watercolor instructor ever since. People want to brand me as a barn painter or a wagon painter but I am finding more interest in other areas. I've painted friends of mine and I also enjoy painting animals. I love to paint pigs. I'm keeping more of my paintings. I used to try to sell everything I did but now that's not important. At present, there is no particular gallery that represents me." Miller was written up in *Art West*, May 1981.

Frank D. Miller, HUPA HUNTING GROUNDS (1979), oil, 30 x 24

Stan Miller, THE CISTERN, egg tempera, 28 x 19

Douglas Miley, MONTANA ROCKIES, oil, 14 x 20

Vel Miller

T. Mimnaugh

Miller, Vel. Realist painter and sculptor of "Western themes through the eyes of a woman," born in Nekoosa, Wisconsin in 1936 and living near Atascadero, California. "It's refreshing to go back and forth between painting and sculpting," she observes. "I think you get stale if you stay in one medium all the time, and I have noticed in transferring from sculpture to painting or vice versa, those problems inherent in one are solved in the other. I enjoy both, even though the bronzes require a lot of time."

When she was six, her parents homesteaded a small working ranch in the Sacramento Valley of northern California. She was constantly drawing, and in high school also played guitar and sang while looking to a career in fashion design. After she married, she ran a ranch household and still made time to sketch and to take lessons. "I think that if you really want to do something bad enough," she emphasizes, "you can arrange it." Later, she studied at the Valley College and the Art Students League of Los Angeles. Beginning in 1963, she taught art, eventually at the Art Students League itself and at Long Beach State College, until after more than a decade the demand for her work made her quit teaching.

"I feel the need to depict the West through the eyes of a woman," she stresses. "There are many things that haven't been told. I paint and sculpt what I sincerely feel, and strive to put into each something that will capture the audience." She was accepted into major invitationals by 1971, with one-person shows by 1974. Written up in *Southwest Art*, November 1976, and *Artists of the Rockies*, summer 1981, she is listed in *Who's Who in American Art* and is represented by Overland Trail Galleries.

Mimnaugh, (Mary Theresa) Terry. Traditional sculptor of heroic figures and statuettes in bronze, and painter, born in Renton, Washington in 1954 and living there in 1982. "While I was growing up," she points out, "I could do anything I was capable of and was not restricted by gender. Now, I'm in a profession where my work stands on its own merit, as it should. It does the competing for me, without bringing gender into it. There is no excuse for a woman artist to claim discrimination. A name can be signed with the first initial and the work is back on even keel competition.

"After finally getting to take art in high school, I had a 'don't bother me' teacher. When I decided to go to college, the 'teacher' in my first class said, 'You should have had all your basics by now.' Things like building an armature I had to learn on my own. It's like learning to speak a language. First you have the talent, then you learn the words. After graduation in 1976, I apprenticed myself to a cowboy-artist-foundryman. I not only learned the foundry business but also broke horses.

"It was while working there that I applied for the commission to model Jeannette Rankin. I won the commission over 37 other artists from five states and Canada, and the heroic bronze was dedicated in 1980. Since then I hibernate six months a year. I need that time to put a dent in what I want to accomplish. I think that most artists have a constant drive to create but are plagued with the frustration of interruptions. The motivation, though, comes from within. Someone can tell you which way to go over a mountain, but the only way you're going to get there is by your own two feet." She is represented by Sherwood and Ponderosa Galleries.

Terry Mimnaugh, THREE BOYS WITH A MOUSE, bronze, h 11

Vel Miller, PRIDE OF OUR PEOPLE, oil, 30 x 20

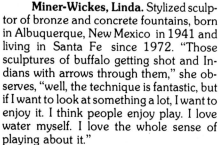

Miner-Wickes, Linda. Stylized sculptor of bronze and concrete fountains, born in Albuquerque, New Mexico in 1941 and living in Santa Fe since 1972. "Those sculptures of buffalo getting shot and Indians with arrows through them," she observes, "well, the technique is fantastic, but if I want to look at something a lot, I want to enjoy it. I think people enjoy play. I love water myself. I love the whole sense of playing about it."

Raised in Santa Fe, she was "good at mechanical drawing, physical education, shop, and geometry." A pupil of the painter Josef Bakos, she went on to the California College of Arts and Crafts where she was "a beatnik. At least that's what the kids on the block called me. I carried a tool box instead of a purse. You don't carry watercolors in a purse." After living in Europe and then Colorado, she returned to Santa Fe and worked at Shidoni Foundry where she was encouraged to sculpt. "I like the three-dimensional aspect. I like being able to walk all the way around it and see it as a whole."

When her family objected to the frog in their fountain, she sculpted a new head of two children under an umbrella and that was the start of her water sculpture. Her fountain in a Santa Fe park is of a young girl with a hose in a water fight with a young boy squirting a water pistol. Other subjects are "concrete animals that for some reason always turn out sort of comic," she explains. "Isn't that amazing? I'd like to do big pieces for cities. People could climb on them and enjoy them and play in the water. The element of water and the way it flows through our lives has been the inspiration. In the future, I will incorporate water, wind, fire, and sound and light." She is showing at the Von Grabill Gallery and at Shidoni.

Minor, Wendell. Representational painter of northern New Mexico in acrylic, and printmaker, born in Aurora, Illinois in 1944 and living in New York City since 1968. "My first awareness of my interest in art was in the fourth grade where I spent a lot of time drawing buffalos," he remembers. "My friend accused me of tracing the animals, but every one was drawn freehand. Unfortunately, my parents looked on my talent as a hobby, not to be pursued as a career.

"To get away from home, I chose a small art school, Ringling, in Sarasota, Florida. Ringling was a blessing because its curriculum was a lot of basic painting and drawing. People didn't get involved in gimmicks." After graduating in 1966, he was recruited by a greeting card manufacturer in Kansas City, and in 1967 moved back to Aurora. By 1970, he was a free-lance designer and illustrator in New York City where he has won over ninety awards including two Edgars and a National Book Award nomination for design.

Every summer since 1971, he has visited the Southwest, saying that "the real atmospheric light in the Southwest visually washes out the natural color. The seemingly overstated colors of Georgia O'Keeffe's paintings really are the true colors without the harsh sunlight. They seem unreal but the blues are that blue and the whites that white." On the site, he sketches and takes black and white photographs "that allow me a formal reference point. They even help isolate the object I wish to paint, but all colors come from my memory of that place." Featured in *Southwest Art*, *Prints*, and the *Society of Illustrators Annual*, he publishes his own prints and is represented by Hadler/Rodriguez and Silo Galleries.

Moline, Bob. Realist painter and sculptor of contemporary Indians and cowboys in acrylic watercolor, born in Amarillo, Texas in 1938 and living in Fort Worth since 1961. "Some painters do beautiful work," Moline observes, "but they paint Hollywood cowboys. And the Indians—they'll be going to war and have on every piece of clothing they own, whereas real Indians would strip down only to a breech cloth and spear. Most folks who don't know history think that's the way it was."

A Comanche, Moline grew up near Amarillo, Texas, where his father was a horse trader. Together, they broke green horses and sold them. Moline had read about a saddle shop near Fort Worth's stockyards and went there to learn that trade. "I had always liked to sketch," he recalls, "so I started designing my own patterns for hand tooling. In my spare time, I played with a few small paintings. I bought a 35 cent set of watercolors and began to experiment during my noon breaks. It took seven years to do a painting that was halfway decent."

During those years, he would sell paintings for $1.50. Then his boss put Moline's paintings on the saddle catalogs, and "between what I sold to the saddle shop customers and what I had put through a gallery in Amarillo, I was making more money in my spare time than in my full-time job." By 1973, he had more orders for paintings than he could fill so he abandoned the saddlemaking. In his second painting show, he won the watercolor prize and every year since then he has won a gold medal. He was a founder of the artists' group XIT, or Ten in Texas, that was publicized in the XIT book. He was also featured in *The Cattleman*, October 1981, and is represented by Signature Gallery and Trailside Galleries.

Linda Miner-Wickes, A CLOSE CALL, bronze, h 12¼, w 14½

Wendell Minor, DAY OF THE BUFFALO (1976)
acrylic, 21 x 13

Bob Moline, COURTSHIP, mixed media, 15 x 22

George Molnar

Molnar, George. Realist oil and watercolor painter of contemporary Western subjects, particularly Navajo portraits, born in Somerset County, Pennsylvania in 1953 and living in Prescott, Arizona. "I attend some pow-wows for the many colors," he observes, "but the greatest creative times for me are when I'm with a Navajo family and the kids take me to their favorite places near their home. Navajo children accept the past and are untroubled by the present. They love the land and the animals they raise. I try to capture this in my paintings.

"My family moved to Beaumont, California, when I was four. There I grew up. My parents enrolled me in a correspondence course with Art Instruction Schools, and I was encouraged by my future father-in-law, who introduced me to the work of Brownell McGrew and Ray Swanson. After a year in a small college where I studied under two outstanding art professors, I decided to go on my own. I knew I wanted to be in fine art so I worked for a grocery store and I painted in oils and watercolor anything with a history—old barns, small antiques, WW I airplanes, model T cars.

"All the while, McGrew and Swanson's work was in the back of my mind, so I took a trip to the Navajo Reservation. The urge to paint these people overwhelmed me. It was not only the people, it was the land, the sky, and a quest for deeper understanding of past traditions mingled with the present that drew me back again and again. I get just as excited when a storm hits as when I meet a really neat Navajo person." Molnar won the gold medal for oils at the 1979 Phippen Memorial Show and was featured in *Southwest Art*, October 1981. His prints are published by The Wooden Bird and he is represented by Overland Trail Galleries.

Elizabeth Montgomery

Montgomery, Elizabeth. Painter of small oils of scenes and creator of pencil drawings of Western objects, born in Walla Walla, Washington in 1935 and living in Cedar Crest, New Mexico since 1971. "I live with many of my subjects in my studio before I draw them," she points out. "In this way I see them not only as objects but I allow my imagination to dwell on what they were used for, by whom, and even what they themselves may have seen. I develop a rapport with them by such fantasizing."

Raised in Oregon, she is the daughter of a Methodist minister who was transferred frequently. An elementary school teacher first encouraged her interest in art. Although her father objected to a major in art at Lewis and Clark College in Portland, she persisted. After graduation, she worked as model and bank teller while painting in her spare time, but when she married, her husband also opposed her painting. Divorced, she began sketching in the Sandia Mountains near Albuquerque in 1971 and she soon embarked on a career that has brought her scores of awards.

She taught herself the technique she uses, finding her own material "in the most remote areas possible, in ghost towns, etc., that have been left to change in their own time span. My animal portraits are started only after I have met the animal and owner, seen the interaction between the two, and sensed the character of the animal. In my oils, I don't include people or traces of them because they are in most other places. The wilderness is disappearing too fast." The author of an article on pencil drawing in *Today's Art*, December 1976, and written up in *Art West*, November 1981, she is represented by Aldridge Fine Art Gallery and Galeria Sigala.

Wm. A. Moore wa

Moore, William A. Representational painter and sculptor of "the history of early man and the wilderness in which he lived," born in Glendale, California in 1936 and living in Reno, Nevada since 1968. "While working as an industrial designer in Reno in 1968, I began painting something for myself for the first time in my career. My childhood interests in paleontology, archaeology, and history were rekindled. This became an obsession. I worked by day in the commercial world and would paint until three or four in the morning, every night.

"I had won the first Senior National Scholarship Award in the General Motors Fisher Body Craftsman's Guild contest in 1956. This allowed me to enter the Art Center College of Design in Los Angeles where I studied until 1958. I then worked as a commercial and technical illustrator for missiles and aircraft until 1963 when I left to form my own company to offer graphic art services and industrial designs to customers mostly in the automotive industry. From 1968 to 1978, I was employed in Reno as director of advertising and as corporate art director. In 1978, I became a full-time painter.

"The move to Nevada, with its rugged beauty and rich visual texture, reawakened my basic interest in nature, prehistory, and early man. My first subjects were the Indians of North America, particularly those of the Sierra Nevadas. In 1975, I expanded my study of early man to include bronze sculpture. My intense interest in the past led me to the study of archaeology, wildlife, and the terrain where ancient man had lived. I began to collect and fashion early tools as they had done, and I visited many of their habitation sites. Galleries that handle my work include Riata Gallery and Artists Co-op Gallery."

George Molnar, TIME FOR A CHEW (1980), oil, 38 x 31

William Moore, HOLD UP AND LOOK, wax-base pencil, 24 x 19

Elizabeth Montgomery, EVENING PAUSE, oil/canvas, 15 x 30

Bettie J. Moran

maher morcos

Moran, Bettie, J. Traditional, non-objective, and abstract oil and acrylic painter and bronze sculptor, born in Wellington, Texas in 1925 and living in Albuquerque, New Mexico since 1968. "I am a most imperfect human being," she says, "and am fully aware of the audacity on my part to aspire to attain a great measure of order and perfection in all the work I do, and suffer great discontent with most of it. I create or re-create that which is most meaningful to me to the very best of my ability.

"No years were wasted searching for direction. My mother was a fine painter, and I knew as a very young child what my life's work would be. I was a painfully shy child but was 'volunteered' many times to pose for artists and students so they would not have to pay a model. Posing was not the easiest thing in the world for a youngster but it was wonderful to always be on the fringes—watching and listening. I have a deep respect for all dedicated artists.

"I have been steadily productive for over 45 years—good, bad, or indifferent! I have an insatiable appetite for new subjects or new approaches and media. Some can 'specialize' in doing one or two subjects for a lifetime. Perhaps the fear of losing enthusiasm or stagnation is the underlying reason for the way I work. The work I do is highly controlled and demanding. Some of the models for my bronze pieces required eleven months to execute. Certain acrylics took six months to complete. I work with tremendous joy, tears welling up. A certain loneliness persists though I'm seldom alone." Her oil painting was selected to appear on the 1982 New Mexico art calendar, and she has exhibited at the Museum of New Mexico since 1949. She is represented by Lundeen and Mountain Road Galleries.

Morcos, Maher Naguib. Traditional painter and sculptor of the romantic Old West, particularly Indians, born north of Cairo, Egypt in 1946 and living in San Diego, California. "In all the old movies I saw," he points out, "the Indians were always shown as the bad guys you couldn't trust. The more reading I did, the more I came to realize that they were a proud nation. Their struggle for survival and their eventual decline represent a unique composite of my vision of human experience.

"As a child in Cairo," he says, "Indians appeared to me as a symbol of America." At age fourteen, he won top awards in an Egyptian competition, and at fifteen, he was illustrating textbooks. "Sometimes," he recalls, "I'd open a book in class and there would be some of my illustrations. It was great." Despite his talent, he was encouraged to study architecture at Cairo University. He earned his second degree in art, concentrating on anatomy. While practicing architecture, he continued painting.

In 1972, he came to the United States to join his family near Chicago. He had planned to keep on with architecture, but when his Indian portrait was reproduced on the cover of a national magazine, the demand for his work led him into art as his career. Today, when viewers ask why a foreign-born artist concentrates on scenes of the Old West, he replies that it is "because of the challenge to me as an artist, to express creativity, talent, and imagination, which must be backed up with historical research." He has won best of show and gold medals for both sculpture and painting at invitational shows, and is a member of the American Indian and Cowboy Artists. Written up in *Southwest Art*, April 1978, he is represented by Eagle Art Gallery and Circle Galleries.

Maher Morcos, FINDING HIS WAY IN A BORDERTOWN, oil, 41 x 33½

Bettie J. Moran, EVENING IN TAOS, oil, 34 x 42

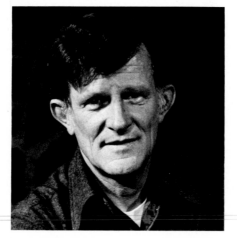

Jim Morgan.

Morgan

Regina

Morgan, Jim. Representational painter of wildlife in acrylic, born in Payson, Utah in 1947 and living in Mendon, Utah. "The amount of detail I put into a painting," he explains, "depends mainly on the distance and movement of the subject. For example, you cannot see every feather on a Canadian goose flying past at 40 mph. I like to present the subject to the viewer as if he were out in the field observing the animal first hand, where detail is not so obvious. I try to capture the feeling and essence of the wild animals.

"I was raised in a small town and have been interested in the outdoors since I was a small child tagging along with my father. With the encouragement of my parents, I have been drawing and painting wildlife since I can remember. There were no art classes at all in high school, so eight of us pooled our money and hired an instructor to teach a night class. Upon getting my BFA from Utah State University in 1970, I didn't think I could be content working in commercial art because I would have to relocate. I got a 40-hour-a-week job to make ends meet and painted at night and on weekends.

"Following that, I painted ten big-game paintings for the Utah Division of Wildlife Resources and some illustrations for the Bureau of Sport Fisheries and Wildlife concerning upland birds. I also did the cover paintings on *New Mexico Wildlife* and the Ducks Unlimited magazine. Since I decided to make the jump into painting full time, I have been doing commission work for private collectors. In my paintings, I emphasize the background and surroundings. Without these natural areas, there would be no wildlife for anyone to enjoy. Galleries showing my work include Hill's Art Center and Bernhart Fine Arts Gallery."

Morgan, Robert F. Realistic painter of a "Montana that is gone" and of wildlife, born in Helena, Montana in 1929 and still living there in 1982. "I am interested in my birthplace, my hometown," he asserts. "History has always been my great love, so it is only natural that combining the two provides me with great satisfaction. I portray a West that is gone, but with few exceptions it still lives here in Montana. The costuming changes and we civilize more and more, but basically we are similar to the past.

"I graduated from Helena High School in 1947, did not attend college, but began working in advertising and display. In 1952, I began working for the Montana Historical Society as exhibits designer until, because of economic considerations, I went to work full time for the Montana National Guard. I returned to the Montana Historical Society in 1960 as curator and for one year was acting director. I designed and constructed the Centennial Train which toured the United States.

"I resigned from the museum in 1970 to pursue a full-time career in art. My formal art education ended when I graduated from high school, but I have, over the years, taken beneficial courses of study. To research and interpret on canvas is to leave a legacy for others to enjoy and know what happened in the creation of this civilization. There is no greater place to do this than Montana." The fourth generation of his family in Montana, he has painted a major mural for the airline terminal and twelve major murals for a new hotel. He was featured in *Art West*, summer 1979, was a founder of the Northwest Rendezvous Group, and is represented by Montana Historical Society and by The Western Flyway.

Morris, Regina Stahl. Traditional sculptor of bronze statuettes of horses, born in Westport, Connecticut in 1945 and living in Bradyville, Tennessee. "I grew up in Sarasota, Florida," she remarks, "receiving my art education at home under the supervision of my father, Ben Stahl. This included access to the studio and its contents, as well as critiques and encouragement. Most importantly, I was able to watch and absorb as my favorite artist worked.

"During frequent trips to Canada, Mexico, Europe, and most of the United States, our family visited every important museum as well as towns where the masters worked. I also studied bronze sculpture at the Shortridge School of Equine Art for three years. My main interest has always been in horses, which have been the subjects of painting and sculpture through the ages. I feel the medium seems to have been created especially to depict animals. Regardless of whether he may be a hairy little range pony, an Irish hunter, or a heavyweight shire, his esthetic beauty and natural fluidity were created for us to enjoy, both astride and from ground level.

"Since I have never particularly liked to put backgrounds in my paintings of animals, sculpture allows me to devote my full attention to the animal itself. I usually make loose sketches of an idea, mainly so I won't forget what particular thing it was that I liked. This also carries me through while I build the armature. Once the original wax is completed, I make my own molds and finish the poured wax which is then sent to the foundry. I use my firsthand experiences as references for my work." Sales are through her own Godolphin Farms.

Jim Morgan, TIN CUP RIDGE, acrylic, 18 x 24

Regina Morris, GRIZZLY ATTACKING, bronze, h 9

Robert F. Morgan, HIGH ON THE HOG, oil, 16 x 32

Claudine Morrow

G. Morton

[signature]

Morrow, Claudine. Painter of the contemporary Indian in oil on canvas, born in Oberlin, Kansas in 1931 and living in Page, Arizona since 1956. "It is not my intention to romanticize the Indian or to mourn his change but to create studies of the contemporary Indian which capture individual personalities as well as tradition. I paint the Indian because in him I find a dignity that is often disguised in the more 'civilized' social order."

Daughter of a federal Bureau of Reclamation construction engineer, she was moved from one isolated dam project to another as a child, into seven Western states and Alaska. As her father told her, "The Bureau doesn't build dams at Hollywood and Vine." At seven, she had private art instruction in Fresno, California, and she had her first one-person show of prospectors, mountains, and Indians when she was fourteen. She also studied privately with Odon Hullenkramer in Santa Fe for two years.

In 1956, her father was assigned to the Glen Canyon Dam Project in northern Arizona. She developed her admiration for the Navajo while visiting her parents and in turn was given the Indian name of "The Woman Who Carries the Rainbow." Each summer, she returned to the locality that became Page, finding models at the Corporate Trading Post. She has since extended her studies to the Hopi, Pueblo, Arapaho, Shoshone, and Sioux, and has widened her subject matter to landscapes and still lifes. The first native-born woman in the permanent collection of the Whitney Museum of Western Art, her paintings have also been reproduced on Santa Fe Railroad calendars. She is represented by O'Brien's Art Emporium and Voris Gallery.

Morton, Gary. Realistic painter of the modern working cowboy in opaque watercolor, born in Tucumcari, New Mexico in 1951 and living in Tinnie, New Mexico. "An artist," he says, "must be emotionally linked to his subject. I know every one of the people I paint. I know the country and the horses. Cowboying isn't just a job. It's a way of life, and you live it 24 hours a day. These are real people doing what they do best, and doing it everyday, just as you see them in my paintings.

"I never took any art classes in school, but was always involved in art. After graduating in 1969, I went to work on the Bell Ranch, about sixty miles from Tucumcari. I was far from being a cowboy when I went there but I finally earned my boots. All this time I was still painting and drawing. I just really enjoy painting. I began to copy Will James, Russell, and George Phippen and then started on ideas of my own. I also began to sculpt. Bob Lougheed came out to paint quite often, and taught me the first lesson I ever had.

"So here it was 1977 and it came to me I could try art on my own. Still a little leery, I took a job taking care of a bunch of yearlings. When the season ended, we moved to the Hondo Valley. The first two years were anything but glamorous. I was no longer a working cowboy and couldn't call myself an artist either. Bob Moline helped me get in a few invitational shows and showed me something about art. I have never had a bad show. This past year I was in the OS Ranch Exhibit where I sold out in the first thirty minutes of the preview show. I signed with Guildhall to do prints, have won a couple of awards, and have been featured in several publications." Morton is represented by Signature Gallery and Artisan's Shop and Gallery.

Moses, Forrest. Contemporary painter of the northern New Mexico landscape in oil, born in Danville, Virginia in 1934 and living in Santa Fe, New Mexico since 1969. "I definitely feel," he observes, "that one's habits affect one's attitude. You are what you eat—well, you are what you live in. Santa Fe is an oasis. There are mountains where water rushes. Descending toward the West, the landscape quickly changes to bad lands of dry arroyos. These alternatives are always at hand. I felt I could get down to essentials in such a place."

At nine, Moses studied at local colleges. He graduated from Washington and Lee in 1956, served for three years as an Air Intelligence Officer in the Philippines, and then toured Europe in 1960. After taking interior design at Pratt Institute in New York City, he practiced in Dallas and Houston until 1965 when he decided to paint full time. While living in California, he had his first one-person show, taught for a term, and then was drawn to Santa Fe by its "continuity and rightness." He put "a lot of energy into a background that doesn't scream for attention. I'm attracted to an Oriental sense of sparseness.

"I like to think of my paintings as recreational rather than intellectual," he adds. "I can only intellectualize after the fact because art is intuitive with me while I am working. If I can't get it freshly and immediately, it loses something vital." Moses has had eighteen one-person shows and is represented in 48 public and corporate collections. He was featured in *Artists of Santa Fe, Southwest Art,* February 1973, and *American Artist,* April 1977, and is represented by Tibor de Nagy Gallery.

Gary Morton, QUIEN SABE WAGON, opaque watercolor, 24 x 30

Forrest Moses, GALISTEO RIVER BED, oil/canvas, 22 x 40

Claudine Morrow, HOZHONI, oil, 30 x 40

Sid mountain

Geoff Mowery

Mountain, Sid. Realist oil painter of wildlife, canyons, and mountain men, born in Jefferson, Ohio in 1918 and living in Pagosa Springs, Colorado. "I hunted, fished, canoed, tied trout flies, and tossed clay pigeons with my dad," he recalls. "Now, I'm a wildlife artist. Ninety percent of my paintings are wildlife. I paint what I love, and I love them all. That's what I learned from my father, love and respect for wildlife."

His mother was a professional painter of still lifes and he started painting at an early age. After attending the Cleveland Institute of Art and Cooper School of Art, he was "painting old barns and covered bridges then, but I painted wildlife too, always have, and always will." He has also been a teacher, leading canoe trips into the Canadian wilderness, pack trips into the Colorado Rockies, and mountaineering expeditions into the Sierra Nevadas.

"The only way to study wildlife," he points out, "is in their natural habitat. The weather, wind, and time of day have to be right. The grass has to be blowing in the right direction for a painting to look real. Animals know what's going on around them. As a painter, I must have the same awareness. A bighorn is always alert. Capturing his alertness is important to me. What is he looking at? What does he smell? That's what my paintings are all about. I'm a realist in the sense that my paintings have detailed accuracy." As a conservationist, he adds that "forty years ago, I saw rivers so full of ducks you could hardly see the water. You go back today and you're lucky to see any." Written up in *Southwest Art*, November 1980, he is published by Deer Creek Publishing and represented by Gallerie Marguerite and Parke Gallery.

Mowery, Geoff. Realist painter of wildlife in egg tempera, born in Cleveland, Ohio in 1945 and living in Bainbridge Township, Ohio. "My family went camping every summer when I was growing up," he recalls, "and I had seen every state except Alaska and Hawaii by the time I was nineteen. I always enjoyed spending time in the woods and watching animals prepare for winter, build their nests, and care for their young. I learned to recognize their prints along the creek, and to know who had a nest and where.

"I grew up in Orange Village near Cleveland and after graduation from high school I went to Los Angeles to study at Chouinard Art Institute. After several years, my instructors told me that I should paint on my own to develop an individual style. I started concentrating on surrealism, began blending animals into my surrealistic paintings in 1970, and by 1972 I was painting wildlife exclusively. The one thing that I do differently is that I paint my subjects close up. This enables me to achieve a lifelike quality. The texture of wood, rocks, and even foliage is a challenge to paint close up.

"Spring has always been my favorite time, not only for the wildlife and their young but for the woods itself. The colors of the leaves, flowers, and new growth are so unique that I feel I will never be able to capture them. I often bring in moss, bark, and even weeds to study as I paint them. I find this to be the best way to blend my colors and get the textures close to the real thing. I never pre-sketch a picture. I have an idea in mind. It grows and changes as I work along. When I'm painting, I lose all track of time and seldom even hear the phone if it rings." He is published by Triton Press and represented by El Prado Gallery of Art.

Sid Mountain, NASTY DAY, oil, 16 x 12

Geoff Mowery, ORCHARD SENTRY, egg tempera, 28 x 48

WM. MOYERS

CHARLES E MURPHY

Richard G. Myer

Moyers, William. Painter and sculptor of objective scenes of Western life, born in Atlanta, Georgia in 1916 and living in Albuquerque, New Mexico. "I paint what I do," Moyers observes, "because I find the working cowboy, past and present, such a harmonious outgrowth of his whole environment. He accepts the action, weather, loneliness, and responsibilities as a normal existence. Too, there is a lot of nostalgia in it for me—a chance to recapture something of which I can no longer be a part.

"When I was fourteen," he adds, "I had the fortune to come to the San Luis Valley of Colorado for a summer on a ranch. I did not return to Georgia for five years, and then just for two months." Before long, his competence as a cowboy helped pay his tuition at Adams State College where he graduated in 1939. He also studied at Otis Art Institute in Los Angeles before getting a job with Walt Disney Studios that showed him that "competent art could be produced on regular hours." He taught school in Colorado and then served in the Army in World War II. For the next fifteen years he worked as an illustrator in New York City.

"By about 1962, Western art mushroomed," he recalls, "and I started putting all my time into that, but I'm no missionary. The West is a real part of my life." He became a member of the Cowboy Artists of America in 1968 and won the gold medal for sculpture three times by 1975. At the CA show in 1981, his oil "Clearing the High Country" sold for $8,000 and his bronze "The Warming Cup" for $5,000. He is listed in *Who's Who in American Art*, was featured in *Southwest Art*, March 1980, exhibited in the Peking, China, show, and is represented by Taos Art Gallery and Trailside Galleries.

Murphy, Charles Edgar. Painter of game birds and birds of prey in watercolor and oil on canvas, born in East Liverpool, Ohio in 1909 and living in Sedona, Arizona since 1973. "I paint birds in a way that will appeal to sportsmen," he says, "and they know the subject very well indeed. The collectors stand ready to trip up the artist if he makes the slightest mistake."

Raised in Sebring, an industrial town where his father was in the pottery business, Murphy "majored in portraiture at the Cleveland Art Institute. Upon graduating in 1931, I was awarded a scholarship to Europe." He spent the next two years in Munich. When he returned, he found a job as pottery design director for Red Wing Potteries on the upper Mississippi where he was able to study "the birds and animals from a hunter's point of view. Duck hunting is such a beautiful activity. I believe that if it were not for the efforts of Ducks Unlimited and the hunters and others who support it, there would not be many wild ducks today.

"Soon, as recreation, I began to sketch, and more and more I found myself absorbing the details." Murphy's studio is filled with birds mounted to his specifications, on walls, shelves, bookcases, and in specimen drawers. "I get some from sportsmen," he declares, "but most come from game farms. There is such a variety of game birds that it is necessary to have them available for research." He has painted only wildlife since 1967, simplifying the compositions to make the birds dominant. His career has been featured in *Southwest Art*, and *The Illustrator*, and he is represented by Husberg Fine Arts Gallery.

Myer, Richard A. Bronze sculptor of Western, Indian, and historical statuettes, born in New York City in 1927 and living in Glendora, California since 1971. "How remarkable it is to me," he observes, "that I am able to make a living doing the thing I love to do more than anything else, and to know that my bronzes will be around long after I'm gone. That is all the motivation I need! And as I go through life, the more I work at it the more it seems I am just getting started."

While a boy scout, Myer built a 7-foot Eiffel Tower with 33,000 toothpicks. Summers were spent at his grandfather's farm in Pennsylvania and in 1940 the family "visited Indian reservations and historical ruins throughout the West." After graduation from high school, he was in the Army Special Services in Japan, painting murals, and then received his BA in art from Brigham Young University in 1952. Following his return to the East, he took a course at Sculpture Center to supplement study with William Zorach, the famous sculptor.

Myer painted, exhibited, and taught while working as an assistant art director in New Jersey, then in 1970 became head designer for Classic Bronze in California where he learned the casting process. He began sculpting Indian and bronze pieces and by 1975 was winning awards. "Still, it frustrates me," he complains, "that life is passing me by and there is so much more to create, so many ideas and so little time. I'm constantly striving to make a better piece than the last." Myer is a member of the American Indian and Cowboy Artists and was featured in *Southwest Art*, July 1976. His galleries include Trailside and O'Brien's Art Emporium.

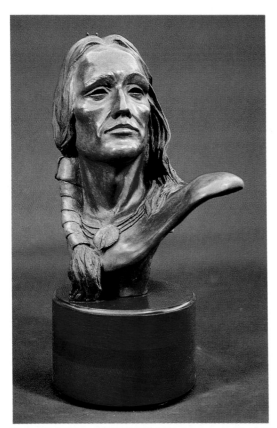

Charles E. Murphy, THE SILENT INTRUDER, watercolor, 18 x 26

Richard A. Myer, GREAT EAGLE, bronze, h 19, Edition 24

William Moyers, COLORADO HAYING TEAMS, oil, 24 x 36

Myrah, Newman. Realist-Impressionist painter of the Northwest, born in Holdfast, Saskatchewan in 1921 and living in Portland, Oregon since 1949. Myrah says that "my interest in the horse and what the animal meant to the West determines the subject matter of many of my paintings. Painting is my profession, my hobby, and a way of life."

When Myrah was five, his family moved to Deer Lodge, Montana. "I was raised in a little town," he recalls, "and I was the only kid that could draw, so I was encouraged." He earned pocket money on a sheep ranch because "there wasn't much choice." After high school, he went to Portland with an uncle and worked in commercial art. He served in Japan in World War II and then enrolled in commercial courses in the Art Institute in Pittsburgh, becoming a free-lance artist back in Portland in 1949. Commissions for national accounts and periodicals tapered off in 1970 and he began doing Western paintings in his spare time. In 1980, he quit as an illustrator because "I'd better get going."

He admits that Charles Marion Russell's "style had an influence. That was art as far as Montana was concerned." Myrah completes an average of one painting a week: "If it's well planned, it should move right along. If you're waiting for things to happen, then it goes slow. I've been very fortunate, and I sell. I work hard at my painting, and now that I can devote all my time to it, I should be better. That's one of the things that keeps you painting—the hope that the next one is going to be really terrific." Myrah was a charter member of the Northwest Rendezvous Group and is represented by Husberg Fine Arts Gallery.

Myrup, John L. Photo-realist oil painter "of the world around him," born in Salt Lake City, Utah in 1945 and living in Lewiston, Utah. When he is accused of enlarging photographs, retouching them, and exhibiting them as paintings, he points out that he says "thank you. It's really a compliment. Sometimes they say it in a mean way, but mostly as a compliment. I don't know if other artists object to photographic realism in paintings. I don't know if they don't want to achieve it themselves, or if they can't.

"I come from a family of artists. I was the youngest in the family, and there was a lot of inspiration to become an artist. You know how people will tell you your stuff is good, so you keep on doing it." A biology major in college and self-taught as an artist, he did a lot of work on commission, "but then the economic pinch came and a lot of people who had made verbal commitments for a painting didn't come through, so I decided to paint for an exhibit.

"I throw things in my bus and get to an environmental area I like, and let the view flow. I take a camera and get the physical image, and try to hold the emotional effect in my mind. I use the camera like a sketch pad." He doesn't like to paint outdoors because "there's nothing worse than to have a wet fly walk across a canvas. And the intensity of light outdoors is such that it distorts the way you paint." Back in the studio, "I sort out my feelings, manipulating the environment to fit the feelings. I am happiest when I am painting in a happy environment. If it's cold and wet, I get a good book or whatever and just relax." His galleries include Tivoli Gallery of Art and Meyer Gallery.

Namingha, Dan. Modern painter in acrylic and sculptor inspired by his Hopi-Tewa heritage, born in Keams Canyon on the Hopi Reservation in Arizona in 1950 and living in San Juan Pueblo and on the Hopi Reservation. "It used to bother me when people labeled me an Indian artist," he states, "but now it doesn't. I know who I am. People always try to put you into little corners, but if you don't let them, they can't get away with it. An artist should not be limited. In fact, that is one of the reasons why you become an artist—to have the freedom to follow your ideas.

"I was reared on the Hopi Reservation and even when I was little, I observed things and drew them. It was just a matter of time until I learned how to bring out my art in the way I wanted to execute it." At sixteen, he received a summer scholarship to the University of Kansas, and then went to the Institute of American Indian Arts in Santa Fe and the Academy of Art in Chicago. "Like any young artist, I was impressed by the work of others—Picasso, Matisse, and Paul Klee—but I have my own way of looking at things.

"My big inspiration has always been based on my tribe. All my ideas evolve from that heritage. In the beginning, I had real doubts about being able to make a living at it. One day, I realized that there were people out there who were responding to what I was doing." He has had sixteen solo exhibitions, including a "Retrospective at 29," and is in fifteen public collections. His largest work is a 27-foot mural in the Phoenix Airport. Listed in *Who's Who in American Art*, he was written up in *Southwest Art*, April 1973 and June 1981. His representative is The Gallery Wall which also publishes his prints.

John Myrup, THE COMFORT OF VICTOR, oil, 16 x 20

Dan Namingha, KACHIN MANA, acrylic, 60 x 48

Newman Myrah, LINE SHACK, oil, 18 x 24

Michael A Naranjo (signature)

Bill Nebeker (signature)

Naranjo, Michael A. Traditional Tewa Indian sculptor of bronze statuettes and larger figures, born in Santa Clara Pueblo, New Mexico in 1944 and living in Espanola, New Mexico. "I feel fortunate to have the ability to create sculpture," he says. "When I was younger, when I could see, I would sculpt for pleasure, in a spare moment. Later, when I was blinded in Vietnam, I wondered if I had lost that gift. One day, lying in a hospital bed in Japan, I found out that I could still create sculpture with one hand. People ask me how I do it. I don't know."

After attending Highlands University in Las Vegas, New Mexico, from 1964 to 1967, he dropped out, was drafted, and when he returned from Vietnam a year later, he was sightless and his right hand was crippled. He studied sculpture in Taos in 1969 and 1970 and began exhibiting in 1971 and winning awards in 1973. "At first," he points out, "being able to work with only one hand, it was hard getting the pieces the way I wanted. It is an adjustment being blind, too, but in familiar situations it is not as difficult as one would think. My work is changing. The detail is finer. The anatomy is finer.

"I often feel my sculptures talk to me," he declares, "and 'Summer Hawk' is a prime example. When I started on him, he told me he needed to be larger, so I started again. At that point, the size was right, but 'Summer Hawk' was dissatisfied with the movement. Finally, we were both happy. When the original wax was first cast into bronze, I was able to see him. 'Summer Hawk' came alive. I liked what I saw at that moment and each time I see him again I like him a little bit more." Written up in *Southwest Art*, April 1977, Naranjo maintains a gallery at his home.

Nebeker, Bill. Traditional sculptor of the modern cowboy in bronze statuettes, born near Twin Falls, Idaho in 1942 and living in Prescott, Arizona since 1950. "If I wanted to pretend I was a cavalry trooper when I was a child," he recalls, "my mother would sew a yellow stripe on my pants and I would spend hours making my own gun, carved out of wood. I spent five hours getting ready to play for every hour I played but that is what I really liked about it, making my own toys."

After Nebeker developed an allergy, the family moved to Arizona. He studied geology for a year at the University of Arizona, then transferred to Northern Arizona University at Flagstaff "where the country is closer to town." He participated in college rodeos and was influenced to try sculpting on his own when he saw a George Phippen exhibition in Prescott. After Phippen's death in 1966, Nebeker worked at the Phippen Ranch foundry for four years. He was also allowed to study the books on sculpting in the library. "I learned a lot there," he states.

By 1978, Nebeker had won the gold medal for sculpture at the Phippen Art Show, and in the same year he was elected to the Cowboy Artists of America. His greatest personal satisfaction, however, came from his statuette of the late John Wayne as the actor appeared in the movie "The Searchers." Wayne saw the model, titled it, and signed it to indicate his approval. According to Nebeker, "I like to do working cowboys and their horses. I want somebody to look at my bronzes a hundred years from now and say 'That's the way it was'." Written up in *Southwest Art*, October 1981, he is represented by Trailside and De Mille Galleries.

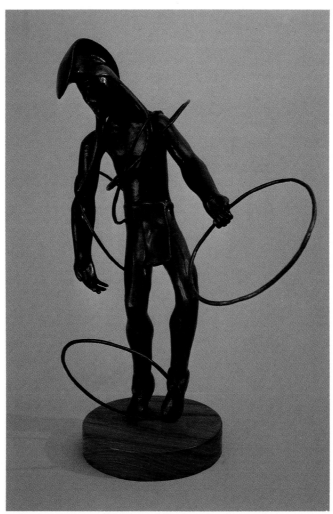

Michael Naranjo, SUMMER HAWK, bronze, h 23, Edition 10

Bill Nebeker, MIDDAY AT GRANITE SPRINGS, bronze, h 20, w 23

JAN ess

pat niblack

Gary Niblett GA

Ness, Jan. Oil painter of miniatures of Montana scenery and of old homesteads, born in Kenmare, North Dakota in 1944 and living in Bozeman, Montana since 1966. She points out that "on both sides of my family are ties to the historical homesteads of North Dakota. Part of the original homesteads are still in our family. I feel a strong commitment to preserving this heritage. I also have the same feelings for the natural beauty of the American West because that one moment that I capture will never again be exactly the same."

Her "growing years" were spent on the family farm. She moved to Montana in 1966 and began painting seriously in 1971. Because she "loves being a part of my kids' lives while I'm working" and enjoys both cooking and painting, she uses the kitchen as her studio. Rather than building a conventional new studio, the plan is to add on to the kitchen. Since 1979, she has been painting miniatures full time on one-eighth-inch-thick canvasboard. Although these paintings may be as small as two-and-a-half-inches square, she emphasizes that "the intricate detail carries at a distance" and that "the painting continues onto the sides of the canvasboard," another example of "the uniqueness of my work."

She documents the Montana homesteads because there is "a need for these places to be saved in some way." Also, she adds, "I feel it necessary to have control of every piece up to the framing. I know the mood and beauty which I have captured in each piece and feel it should be enhanced by the final step, the framing." Among the juried exhibitions she participates in is the Annual Miniature Art Society Show in Washington, D.C. She is represented by De Gallery and Cowhand Collections.

Niblack, Pat. Representational sculptor and painter of figures of children and Indians, born in Wichita Falls, Texas in 1924 and living in Santa Fe, New Mexico since 1969. In 1956 when she was only a painter, she recalls, "I loaned my studio to a portrait painter. He suggested that I sculpt his ear, then his nose, eyes, etc., and finally his head. When I finished, he looked, clicked his heels and bowed, saying 'you're a natural.' I had wanted to sculpt to understand volume and planes better, and there I stayed."

When she was five, she says, "I would sit on a stool between the doors of our large radio, listening to opera and drawing. After graduating from high school at sixteen, I audited art classes at Texas State College for Women that summer and enrolled that fall as a student. After the war, I settled in Tulsa, Oklahoma. where I went back to art full time in 1955. At Philbrook Art Center, I had private classes and in 1956 I won the award for representational painting." She switched to sculpture in 1956, moved to Fayetteville, Arkansas, in 1959 and then to Santa Fe "where I had spent many summers."

Her specialty is commissioned portrait sculpture that starts with "a three-hour photographic session. I work from those photographs. When the sculpture is near completion, the subject returns to Santa Fe for three days to sit for the final, exacting work. The cost of a bronze bust 'lifesize' is $6,000, 'heroic size' (1½ times life) $10,000." She operated the Pat Niblack Gallery from 1976 to 1978 but "my production work went down and I sold the gallery." She exhibits at Margaret Jamison Presents and is represented by Munsons and Gallery of the Southwest.

Niblett, Gary. Representational painter of the working cowboy in the high country, born in Carlsbad, New Mexico in 1943 and living in Santa Fe, New Mexico. Niblett was profiled in *New Mexico Business Journal* as an example of art for investment because he can't paint enough to meet the demand. "I'm two years behind," he declares. "I've got a waiting list a mile long. A lot of my paintings are being sold at much higher prices, but at my age, I must try to hold my prices down."

He says that "my ambition ever since I can remember was to be a painter out on my own." When he was in high school, his parents paid $380, "a tremendous sum" for them, for his correspondence course from Art Instruction. After a year at Eastern New Mexico University, his evident talent caused him to transfer to the Art Center School of Design in Los Angeles, but his "funds ran out real quick. The rest has been on my own." He was soon recruited by Hanna-Barbara animation studios as a background artist. After nine years, he had saved enough to move to Sedona, Arizona, to paint full time.

"I don't like anything modern," he says. "My goal is to paint loosely but accurately. I paint with a brush and it should look that way." A turning point was his election in 1976 as the youngest member of the Cowboy Artists of America. When he travels now, he claims that "you'd think we were movie stars," but Western artists don't get much attention in Santa Fe and "in a way it's nice." He has been profiled in *Artists of the Rockies*, spring 1978 and *Southwest Art*, May 1980, and is in *Who's Who in American Art*. His gallery is Biltmore.

Jan Ness, A GLIMMER OF WELCOMING WARMTH, oil, 2 x 2½

Pat Niblack, DESERT FRIENDS, bronze, h 12, w 10, d 10, Edition 12

Gary Niblett, THE TRAIL OF THE DEER, oil, 28 x 40

Nichols, Marjorie. Watercolorist of the Navajo and of Western birds, born in Laurium, Michigan in 1912 and living in Tubac, Arizona since 1960. "The creative urge in me seems to be the driving force. The watercolor technique I've developed," she explains, "is strictly my own, much of it Oriental in character. My favorite subjects are Navajos, birds and horses. Since there is a theory that the Indians migrated from the Orient by way of the Bering Straits, it gives my Indians some legitimacy."

Originally from the upper peninsula of Michigan, she came to Tubac in 1948 to attend an art school operated by Dale Nichols, the famous "red barn" painter whose work is in the Metropolitan Museum. In 1955, she went to Pass Christian, Mississippi, where Nichols was then running his art school and they married. She credits Nichols as her teacher but the marriage was brief and she moved to Palm Springs as a designer. Nichols had been among those transforming Tubac into an artist colony. When she settled in Tubac, the first art festival featured 25 artists. In 1980, the festival was dedicated to her and 200 paintings were shown.

"An artist needs peace and quiet. Especially this watercolor work requires concentration. I can't stand to paint with people looking over my shoulder, although I never worry about what I'm going to paint," she adds. "My head is all full of images. They just come out, but art is not really something you can sell. It must sell itself. People are in and out of galleries all day long and there is a person for each painting so you just have to hope the right person comes in for your painting." She has exhibited nationally and is represented by her own Windsong Gallery.

Nieto, John. Expressionist painter of the celebration of life through Indian figures in acrylic, born in Denver, Colorado in 1936 and living near Santa Fe, New Mexico. "I am in the habit of painting on my knees," he explains. "It comes naturally to me and it gives me a certain perspective, like looking up at a statue. Of course, it affects the scale, too. In this way, the face isn't overemphasized. I'm working toward a silhouette of a face without features but with the story told.

"I was raised around Roswell and Albuquerque. I am half Mescalero Apache and that is the side I relate to. When I was younger, I wanted to be different. I didn't want to study 'Indian art' so I left to go to Southern Methodist University and worked my way through in art-related jobs. Then I went to Europe for a year, which was a big influence. The German Expressionists knocked me out. I sketched in the Louvre. As Rothko said, art is a lonely trip that takes courage, but this appeals to my sensibilities as an Apache warrior on a vision quest.

"I'm not a reporter. I have no packaged message. I like to push paint around in ways that stimulate people. I use traditional values and ideals, but in a modern idiom. Light shows from the 60s and contemporary pop culture in general have had a big influence on me. I always paint to loud rock music for the energy. You can see that in my color." Nieto has exhibited in the American Indian Artists show in Paris, a one-man show at the Embassy in Barbados, and "Night of the First Americans" and "American Indian Contemporary Art" in Washington, D.C. Interviewed on The Voice of America and written up in *Southwest Art,* July 1980, he is represented by Houshang's and Galeria Capistrano.

Nordahl, David. Traditional painter of the Apache Indian of the 19th century, born in Albert Lea, Minnesota in 1941 and living in Santa Fe, New Mexico since 1979. He has been painting the Apache exclusively since 1979, he says, because the lack of public knowledge and the misconceptions about them fascinate him. He plans to make the Apache his life's work, depicting all the customs and everyday life of the different Apache tribes. There is, he believes, a mystery about them and their night movements.

"Everything I know about art is self-taught," he states. "The grade school I attended had nine kids enrolled. My art instructor in high school was the wrestling coach, but I studied every art book I could get my hands on. I sold my first painting when I was thirteen." By the time he was fifteen, he had his own studio and all the commissions he could handle. Through a customer, he got a job with a commercial art company, "and pretty soon I was drawing and working all phases of commercial art."

In 1968, Nordahl opened his own commercial art studio in Minneapolis and in five years was able to sell his interest. He spent four years on a Wisconsin farm, then went to Steamboat Springs where he was influenced by the mountains and by exposure to Western paintings he saw in the galleries. He "discovered that painting something was better than doing nothing, and I'd been doing a lot of nothing. My goal all my life had been to devote full time to painting. It just took me until 1978 to get it together." He moved to Santa Fe, began painting Apaches, and was featured in *Southwest Art,* March 1980. He is represented by Husberg where an oil painting is priced at $6,800.

Marjorie Nichols, THE MORNING RIDE (1980), watercolor, 24 x 30

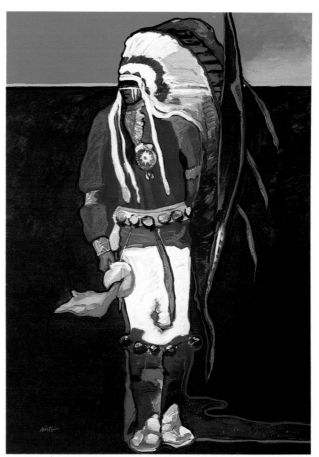

John Nieto, BUFFALO MEDICINE #2, acrylic, 60 x 48

David Nordahl, THE INTIMIDATORS, oil/panel, 24 x 40

Northup, George O. Traditional wildlife sculptor of bronze statuettes, born in Detroit Lakes, Minnesota in 1940 and living in Moose, Wyoming since 1967. In 1974, a friend interested him in the metal casting work he was doing in a small foundry. The friend offered a metal casting class, and Northup was captured by the possibilities in bronze. He began working with wax and clay to create a variety of animal shapes. That same year, his first major work emerged, was cast in Colorado, and the edition was sold out within eighteen months.

Raised in a large family where he was exposed to sculpting, painting, commercial art, and music, he spent most of his time outdoors in the northern woods country. Formal education ended after three years of taking liberal arts and business courses in colleges in northern Minnesota and in Bozeman, Montana. He worked in Chicago and in the Twin Cities, but in 1967 moved to Jackson Hole, Wyoming, to bring his family up in the mountains. In this resort area, he was plumber, welder, restaurant manager, and ski shop assistant manager.

For seven years, he was also the owner and outfitter of a company conducting raft trips on the Snake River in Grand Teton National Park and the whitewater section of the Targhee National Forest. He says that since becoming a sculptor, the question most frequently asked him is, " 'how long did it take you to do that?' The answer is that the idea may be part of your thoughts for months until it takes form, and then the actual process from wax to mold to metal may take only a month or two." Northup is a member of and exhibits with the Society of Animal Artists and is represented by Trailside Galleries.

Odell, Lad. Realistic painter of the historical and the present West, born in Los Angeles in 1947 and living in Manitou Springs, Colorado since 1980. "Western art," Odell declares, "is a delightful contribution to the lives of people all around the world. It reaches the imaginations of adventurous people everywhere. It truly is art from the heart of the average man. It is art to be lived with, to inspire."

By the time Odell was ten, he had traveled across Europe and the Middle East. In four more years, he had lived in fourteen different places, ending up again in California. Odell himself was interested in the history and anthropology of the American Indian. He graduated from Westmont College in Santa Barbara with a degree in psychology and human relations, having spent one college year in Holland where he was exposed to Rembrandt's works. After several years as an account supervisor, he discovered Western art and that shelved his plans for a master's in psychology. Because he had no funds for art school, he taught himself in pastel and watercolor, and what began as a hobby became full time.

He talks about Western art as a philosopher, saying that "Western art believes in external reality and man's responsibility to handle the real world. It is not introspective or self-indulgent. The criticisms about Western art are not artistic but philosophical. Western art reflects absolutes, a *real* world, a *real* bad, a *real* good, a *real* right, a *real* wrong. It is philosophically reassuring to a world which is beginning to realize it cannot survive if there is no down and no up." Odell is represented by Trailside and Texas Art Galleries. He was profiled in *Art West*, November 1980.

George Northup, BLUE WINGS, bronze, h 39

Lad Odell, DAY DREAMER, pastel/watercolor background, 30 x 40

Harry O'Hanlon

O'Leary

© JACK Osmer A.I.C.A.

O'Hanlon, Harry. Traditional sculptor of "Blackfoot camp life, hunting, scouting, and religious practices of the legendary past" in bronze statuettes, born in Edmonton, Alberta, Canada in 1915 and living in High River, Alberta. When 15,000 people gathered at the Bow River for the 100th anniversary of the treaty between Queen Victoria's government and the Blackfoot, Stoney, and Sarcee Nations on July 6, 1977, the gift from the Blackfeet to the English monarchy was "Trailing the Buffalo Hunters," a bronze that was the first in the Blackfoot series by the Alberta sculptor O'Hanlon.

O'Hanlon and his two brothers had decided to sail around the world forty years earlier, but they were wrecked in southern California. O'Hanlon made his way to Panama and worked for the Canal Company until World War II when he enlisted in the Armoured Corps. After the war, the brothers put together an expedition to locate buried Costa Rican gold. That failed, but in 1952 O'Hanlon struck oil near Cutbank, Montana, bought a ranch, and "took up cowboying." In 1956, he began painting Blackfoot portraits in oil on deerskin stretched "Indian style" over black birch frames that found their way into the Glenbow-Alberta Institute of Calgary.

In 1963 when he had painted 54 Indian portraits, he discovered the Moulton Pool oil field in Montana. He moved back to Canada, continued researching the Blackfeet, and found that he could recreate the traditional scenes better in sculpture than in paint. By 1979, he had completed fifteen models that he cast in editions of twelve priced at $3,900, and he was building his own foundry. The bronzes are in the collections of Canadian and English museums. O'Hanlon was written up in *Art West*, spring 1979, and is represented by Gainsborough Gallery.

O'Leary, Diane. Comanche painter of the legends of the Indian people in tempera and oil, born in Waco, Texas in 1935 and living in Scottsdale, Arizona. "One lone artist," she feels, "doesn't count for much, but taken as a body in any society or historical period, artists are the most faithful of historians. We rank with geological formations as evidence of what transpired on this planet during any given era since our arrival on the scene.

"I had the usual secondary schooling and then attended Texas Christian University, and Bacone College, Wichita University, Harvard, and Stanford University, finishing with graduate degrees in Southwestern archaeology and baroque literature (music). Nothing that I did before 1967 contributed directly to my becoming a painter, and I have not one single formal art credential to my name. Additionally, I had a family to support. There never seemed to be enough time to do special paintings for shows or competitions. Somebody's tuition was always due or the rent had to be paid first or the tires were smooth as glass, etc.

"So, there is no impressive list of shows and awards, but O'Leary paintings are in most of the major public and private collections of American Indian art in the world. I paint because it is the activity I most enjoy. There is no endeavor in my personal experience that even comes close to the production of a painting for sheer excitement. I consider creative endeavor of any sort the most important of all human undertakings. The product of that effort is surely a faithful index of the advancement of our species." She studied with Eric Gibbard and Georgia O'Keeffe and is represented by Enthios and Signature Galleries.

Osmer, Jack. Bronze sculptor of statuettes of Western saddles and Indian dancers, born in Prescott, Arizona in 1932 and still living there in 1982. "I was born and raised into the tradition of preserving the past by generations of ranch families and Indian friends. These good people are the real inspiration for my art. I want to tell about this land and the many peoples caring for it."

One-quarter Cherokee, Osmer was the son of a salesman who moved the family as much as twelve times a year. Home base was Prescott where the grandparents ran a hotel. Osmer's only formal art training was during his senior year in high school, and for fifteen years he fell in and out of jobs as equipment operator, automotive body man, surveyor, and engineer. In 1965 when there were only about six art foundries, Osmer began casting his own models in a garage. Other sculptors brought in work, and the foundry was enlarged into the House of Bronze for custom casting. A multi-toned patina was developed to add color effects.

In 1976, Osmer's collectors demanded that he become a full-time artist in order to enhance the value of his bronzes. He sold the foundry and returned to sculpting. His set of ten bronze saddles is in the Museum of Science and Industry in Washington, the Cowboy Hall of Fame, the Rodeo Hall of Fame, and President Reagan's Oval Office. His research notes for the saddles are in the Smithsonian Institution, and his newer Indian "Drum Dance" bronze has won awards. Osmer says that "sculpture should have a story to be told, no matter what direction you look at it." A member of the American Indian and Cowboy Artists, he has been written up in *Artists of the Rockies,* fall 1977, and his gallery is House of Bronze Fine Arts.

Harry O'Hanlon, ENEMY HUNTER
bronze, h 20, w 14, d 5, Edition 12

Sallie Ritter, HIGH MOUNTAIN SERIES #6 (1982) oil, 12 x 12

Jack Osmer, KIOWA CHANTER, bronze, h 13, Edition 20

ANNE ALLER
OVERSTREET '82 ©

Bill Owen A

Ottinger, Kenneth. Traditional sculptor of Western figures in bronze statuettes with colored patinas, born in Greenville, South Carolina in 1945 and living in Sedona, Arizona since 1979. "A sculptor is at the mercy of his foundry," Ottinger says, "but getting sculptor services is great. He makes the molds from the original, pours the waxes, cleans them, gates them, then takes them to a foundry. When he brings the bronzes back, he does the necessary finish work, and for most sculptors he applies the patina, but I do my own."

Raised in St. Louis and in Los Angeles where he received his BFA from the Art Center College of Design in 1968, he became a free-lance illustrator. He also taught at the Art Center College and spent 1975 as artist-in-residence at the University of South Dakota. "I began as a painter," he points out, "and, though I was always interested in sculpture, it was not until 1971 that I felt my work in that area had reached an adequate level. Now I'm comfortable with it and it's the only thing I want to do."

For ten years, he has been keeping a journal that "is much like a diary. I not only sketch in it, I talk to it, let off steam in it, and put down titles and ideas for pieces. I've got enough ideas now for years down the road." For him, a sketch is "a transition, not a finished drawing. Chiefly, I see the piece in my mind's eye, and I rough in the image in the clay or wax—I'm always in a big rush to get the concept visible—and later I refine the details." For patina, "I use a combination of different acids because each gives its own color subtly and unobtrusively." Written up in *Artists of the Rockies*, fall 1980, he is represented by the Hamburg Art Gallery and The Peacock Galleries Ltd.

Overstreet, Anne Aller. Painter of contemporary Montana ranch life, including miniatures, in watercolor and drawings, born in Livingston, Montana in 1949 and living in Big Timber, Sweet Grass County, Montana. "She is a real live cowgirl and her art shows it. Nearly all her pictures depict some aspect of modern American ranch activity and she has been successful in combining her abilities with subject matter close to her heart. Whether portraying cowboys in a blizzard or horses sunning themselves, her aim is to capture the West in a quiet way."

Raised on a working ranch south of Big Timber, she grew up doing the chores of a hand. Art has always been part of her life, beginning with childhood sketches of horses. After graduating from Montana State University in 1972 and studying privately, she has been a full-time professional artist, dedicated to "finding the grace in a situation without losing the reality." Her works show the influence of her own experiences.

She is one of the few Western artists who handle the minutiae of miniature paintings in watercolor and she won Best in Show at the 1978 National Miniature Exhibition. She does not use a magnifying glass. Eye strain could be a bother, "but I have checked with doctors and I follow their instructions, work on the painting no more than thirty minutes with a ten-minute break." At the other end of the scale, her pencil drawings are large and detailed. Her work is included in the 14th Annual Charles M. Russell Exhibition and Auction in Great Falls, and another watercolor will be released as a limited edition print. She exhibits at the Hole in the Wall Gallery and Gallery 85.

Owen, Bill. Realistic oil painter and sculptor of the modern working cowboy, born in Gila Bend, Arizona in 1942 and living in Flagstaff, Arizona. "Cowboys don't show their emotions," he observes. "They never show pain—even when bucked off real bad. They are tough and they live with pain and misery because they have to—they've learned to accept it. They think that anyone who complains is unpleasant to be around. I feel that I use the cowboy's body more than his face to show his expression.

"I've always drawn. I've never had any formal training. I feel that this is something you are born with, and that art training doesn't give anyone talent. Sure, I go to museums and study Russell and the Old Masters, and I have some favorite artists like Wyeth, Russell, and Remington." Raised in rural Arizona, it was "chores first, art second." He began painting in 1970 and decided to paint full time in 1971. "We almost starved," he points out, "but we finally made it." He joined the CAA in 1973 and won a silver medal in 1975.

"Ya know," he says, "people think that cowboys should all have that Southern draaawwl, but lots of 'em don't. They can come from all over. Cowboys have their own vocabulary." He prides himself on accuracy in art because "it's like telling a lie to paint what's not authentic. I'd have a guilty conscience. Integrity and morality are the two themes I'd say run through this kind of art. I'd lose my heart if I didn't paint cowboy art. It's that simple—and that complex." Written up in *Who's Who in American Art* and *Art West*, November 1979, he was in the 1981 Peking, China exhibition, is published by Salt Creek Graphics, and has a waiting list for his paintings.

Ken Ottinger, HORSESTICK DANCER, bronze, h 19

Anne Aller Overstreet, WORKING COWBOY, watercolor, 5 x 3

Bill Owen, THE WORKING COWBOY, oil, 24 x 50

Packer, Gita. Representational sculptor of animals in bronze statuettes, born in Jones County, Texas in 1922 and living in Fort Worth, Texas. "I don't consider myself a 'Western artist,' but an artist interested in the West as it used to be with its farmers and animals. I am a sculptor of animals in the realistic manner, which I am happy to say is art of the West. My heart is here, and so is my past.

"My parents and grandparents, ad infinitum, seem to have been farmers. I did not plan my life to involve sculpting. I was a journalism major at Hardin-Simmons University when World War II created an immediate demand for women in journalism and I became a reporter and photographer in Abilene, Galveston, and Fort Worth where I was amusements columnist. Toward the end of the 60s, I enrolled in a ceramic sculpture class. Clay was unkind to my hands and I bought a wad of wax and two nut picks. I made a blob of a baby, and by 1973 I was beginning my limited editions.

"I am frequently asked questions that have to do with my age and the fact that an ex-newspaper woman with no formal art education should 'expect to live long enough to get famous.' So many animals are waiting in my wax to be shaped into bronze that I am never at a loss for subjects. I feel almost as if my subjects decide on me. My hardest tasks have been the marketing of my art. The sheer creation of my pieces in wax is escape, sublime, but to sell—that is the work of my friends." She has participated in major invitational exhibitions, national and Western, was featured in *Southwest Art*, April 1979, is a member of Women Artists of the American West, and is represented by Hobe Sound and Cross Galleries.

Page, Raymond. "An innovative" oil painter of landscape and seascape "based on the Old Masters," born in Venice, California in 1945 and living in South Laguna, California. "My work never includes a human figure and seldom includes animals," he emphasizes. "I want my work to reflect the soul of the ocean or landscape. I want my colors pearly and pure and I want the contrast between the pearly and pure to show. The innovation comes in my use of light and color. I try to use subtle beams of light and often use black lighting.

"A third generation Californian of pioneer stock, I grew up in rural Riverside County and returned to the Los Angeles area to attend Art Center College. Found the commercial art courses very helpful, but not in harmony with my aspirations to be a fine artist. I studied the Masters privately. My work is a combination of approaches, innovations, and my own striving toward a unique conclusion that will contain the purity and depth of what the Masters obtained, but in the context of the 20th-century conception of beauty.

"I work from sketches. Beauty is my goal. In my mind's eye, I want every color to be jewel-like and the finished painting to contain all that is wonderful in fine art. I try to make my paintings larger than the frame that confines them by having my compositions extend out in large arcs and return to an invitation to look into thirty or so layers of thin translucent paint. In 1973, my first one-man show was launched on the 'Queen Mary.' This year, I will have my fifth annual one-man show at Haggenmaker Galleries. I have also been represented by Atlas Galleries." He is published by Edward Weston Graphics.

Raymond Page, CREPE MYRTLE TREES, oil, 20 x 24

Gita Packer, CHIN UP, bronze, h 10, w 4½

Parker, Ron S. Realist painter of Rocky Mountain wildlife in watercolor and gouache, born in Vancouver, British Columbia about 1943 and living in Wasa, British Columbia. "In Vancouver, where I spent most of my life," he explains, "raccoons are common night visitors in the suburbs. I've seen them in this setting on many occasions. This painting of two four-month-old raccoons with the salal in the background, the hollow stump, and the vine maple reminds me of my West Coast roots. Hollow trees play an important part in a raccoon's life, as this is where he is born and raised as well as where he spends his daytime sleeping hours. Curiosity has brought these two out into the daylight, interrupting their sleep."

Both of Parker's parents had artistic ability so it was not surprising that he displayed talent as a child. Because he was six feet tall when he was fourteen, however, his future seemed to be in basketball, although he elected to follow high school with four years of apprenticeship in commercial art. He studied architecture at the University of British Columbia but dropped out to return to commercial art, then went back to the University for a degree in education while becoming Canada's decathlon champion in 1966.

After serving in track and field administration, he worked as a carpenter until he caught the flu and began painting during his convalescence. His family approved of his choice of art as a vocation and supported him for two years of self-training. When his wildlife paintings started to sell, he moved to Wasa, in the Rocky Mountain trench on a waterfowl flyway where he hikes, photographs, and paints close to his subjects. His prints are published by Mill Pond Press.

Parkinson, Lee K. Representational oil painter of Western landscapes and figures, born in Ogden, Utah in 1913 and living in Layton, Utah. "My wife," he says, "is one of my dependable critics. We have a standing joke, though. If she tells me that she doesn't like a particular painting, I'm almost certain to sell it. It seems to be a barometer of success!

"I don't know where my talent came from. All I know is that since I've been old enough to hold a pencil, I've been messing around with some kind of drawing or painting. I remember the first day I went into the art room in junior high school. The smell of oil and paint permeated the air. It was at this time that I decided what I wanted to do. The first time I told my dad I wanted to go to art school, he was disappointed. By the end of the year, though I had saved enough to enroll in Otis Art Institute in Los Angeles.

"My first major job was with Universal Studios in the model-making department. In 1938, I returned to Utah. There were no jobs available but I was able to get work in commercial art. In 1942, I began working at the Ogden Arsenal and as the war ended I opened a G.I. Art School. At the end of this experience, I opened a jewelry display business and then by 1961 was running a picture-frame business in the daytime and painting pictures at night. I gradually found myself more and more involved with teaching. By 1972, I no longer had time to teach and devoted myself entirely to painting and research. My life has been fulfilling, and each new challenge has helped me grow. Everything I've done, I've tackled with gusto." Parkinson's galleries include Merrill's and Overland Trail, and he was written up in *Southwest Art*, January 1980.

Parson, Delwin O. Realistic painter of the Indians of the Tetons and the Yellowstone "in a simpler time," born in Ogden, Utah in 1948 and living in Rexburg, Idaho since 1980. "The beauty and history of the Teton-Yellowstone area intrigue me," Del Parson states. "The subjects of my paintings usually deal with the stories of those mountains when life was simpler and man lived in harmony with nature. I only wish I could have observed the Plains Indians firsthand at the height of the fur trade."

Raised in Springville, Utah, where his father Oliver Parson was a high school teacher and curator of the art museum, Parson recalls being impressed by Indian and buffalo statues in the museum. When Parson was six, his father became head of the Ricks College art department in Rexburg, eighty miles west of Jackson and south of West Yellowstone. Each summer, the family traveled in their station wagon into the mountains, with the father setting up his easel and painting everyday while the nine children were hiking, exploring, river-running, fishing, hunting, and dreaming of Indians and mountain men. Parson also worked summers for the U.S. Forest Service and rode in the rodeo.

In 1969, Parson began painting seriously while majoring in art at Brigham Young University. He started traveling again on his father's art trips and by the next summer was winning awards for his first paintings of the Tetons. He received his MA in 1975 and since then has been a portrait and gallery painter, represented by Trailside, James M. Haney, and Voris. From Rexburg where he returned in 1980, Parson travels to the terrain of the Indians he paints and employs his research to portray each tribe according to its lifestyle and costumes.

R.S. Parker, RACCOON PAIR, gouache, 18 x 14

Del Parson, WHITE MAN'S FIRE, oil, 24 x 30

Lee K. Parkinson, SATURDAY EVENING GET-TOGETHER, oil, 24 x 36

Leon Parson

Dave Paulley

Ken Payne

Parson, Leon. Representational painter of wildlife, particularly the Western mule deer, in oil and in graphite pencil, born in Provo, Utah in 1951 and living in Rexburg, Idaho since 1954. "I have felt the hair on the back of my neck stand on end," he confesses, "as I laid in the rain-soaked grass thirty yards away as the elk go through their mating challenges. Or, I love to see a mule deer materialize where only a few seconds before there was only sagebrush and pines.

"In my family, there are four professional artists. My dad was the art department chairman at Ricks College, and when I was fifteen, I saw a cover by Bob Kuhn on *Outdoor Life* that grabbed me. Even though I was a biology major in college, I took art courses. I served a mission of the L.D.S. Church, and at the conclusion changed to an artist. After two years, I went to the Art Center in Los Angeles with the idea that I was going to become an illustrator. Slowly I began realizing that every time I had a free assignment, it would be an animal. When I went through the things I had done as a child, they were all animals, and I saw that my life had gone in a circle. I was back where I should have been all along.

"In 1977, I graduated from the Art Center, and after about a year of freelancing, I said, 'do, die, or starve, I'm going back to Idaho' and I was hired to teach at Ricks College. After illustrating for the National Rifle Association for three years, I sent my portfolio to *Outdoor Life* and have been illustrating for them ever since. During 1982, I will produce ten of their twelve covers. I still find time to fill commissions from collectors, although sometimes they have to wait a long time." He is represented by Trailside Galleries.

Paulley, David Gordon. Traditional oil painter and sculptor of the West "as it was and is," born in Midwest, Wyoming in 1931 and living in Cheyenne, Wyoming. "Any person who can make a living doing what he really enjoys has to be one of the luckier ones," he believes. "I am one. Somewhere down the line, people will know that my brush was where my heart is."

Raised in the small town of Osage, Wyoming, in "the foothills of the Black Hills," Dave Paulley recalls that he was "surrounded with the lore of the Plains Indian and cow country history. My artistic inclination began early during my school years, so, having grown up in this environment, it seemed only natural for me to depict the countless stories and scenes that it offered." After service in the U.S. Navy from 1951 to 1955, his only formal art training was a correspondence course in drawing and a few short painting classes with the Denver artist Pawel Kontney.

A full-time artist since 1968, Paulley states that he "is dedicated to recording the West as it was and is, through my favorite medium, oil. I also work in watercolor, pen and ink, and bronze. Whenever possible, I travel to obtain fresh ideas and to research data for paintings. I recently toured the Southwest Pacific area, including Australia, for new material." A high percentage of his work is done on a commission basis. Listed in *Who's Who in American Art*, he has won the 4th Regional Eight-State Award for the best oil painting. His work is in public collections including the Buffalo Bill Historical Center and the Wyoming State Museum, and he is represented by Wild Goose Gallery.

Payne, Ken. Sculptor of cowboy figures in bronze statuettes, born on his grandfather's ranch in Lincoln County, New Mexico about 1937 and living in Nogal, New Mexico since 1973. "There are hundreds of bronzes of Indians. I shied away from those. I wanted to say something that hasn't been said. I like the humor of the cowboy life. There are ten million stories that have never been told. It's exciting to me.

"I was born and raised on ranches," he recalls, "working with horses. When you've been around it, you know it, but I never did like the work. I hated it. It was hard work and I never was prone to working cows." Instead, he became a flyer in 1955, lured by the thrill and excitement. He "was a smoke jumper in Montana," then in 1965 became a pilot for Texas International because he "couldn't afford not to go to the airline." Meanwhile, he was sketching as a hobby and in 1973 he quit flying to paint full time. By 1975, he had one-person exhibitions in four galleries.

He had "always wanted to do a sculpture" and in 1977 he began. His first bronze was the first bronze ever purchased by the New Mexico State Fair. Bill Moyers of the CAA "helped him learn composition." Payne says that "anyone can draw a horse. But look at his ears. They tell when he's fixin' to teach you how to fly. I'm not famous, but I make a living and I know what I'm doing." He casts his own bronzes: "When I started, I didn't know beans but a foundry let me come work sometimes and I learned it." He is represented by Leslie B. DeMille Gallery.

Leon Parson, HIGHER THAN EAGLES, oil, 30 x 24

Ken Payne, OUTNUMBERED, bronze, h 16, w 15½

Dave Paulley, NEW DAY FOR THE FUR SEEKERS, oil/canvas, 24 x 40

Jeannie PEAR

Raymond S. Pease

Pear, Jeannie. Impressionist-Expressionist oil painter of women and children, born in Las Vegas, New Mexico in 1922 and living in Denver, Colorado. "After our daughter was born," she recalls, "I free lanced book jackets, illustrations for books, and illustrations for magazine fashion-art advertisements. While I raised her, I could stay at home and be a housewife and work too. It was fun. When a piece of work was finished, I scrubbed floors with great joy, if you can believe that."

Both grandparents had homesteaded in New Mexico; her father was City Controller and led a jazz band, and her mother was an art potter. Raised in Denver, she had private lessons at twelve, worked in commercial art as an apprentice, and studied at Colorado Women's College. She married, went to Washington, D.C., worked in fashion-art and studied at the Corcoran Institute of Art at night. "I loved fashion-art," she observes. "It's demanding work, and I learned the discipline of drawing and the skills and pressures of the craft." She received four awards of merit for retail advertisements.

After she moved back to Denver and studied at the university and privately, she was the only woman invited by Johns-Manville to go to its Red Rocks ranch and paint for the "Heritage" collection. One oil portrait was of the ranch foreman "who was big and brawny, had a cowboy's spindly legs, and was as nervous as a pregnant pole vaulter. I had just blocked him in when he walked around and stared and said, 'Well, look how you got that wristwatch in.'" She has also painted angels and church banners. Listed in Hassrick's *Western Painting Today*, she was featured in *The Santa Fean*, July 1979, and is represented by The Frightened Owl.

Pease, Raymond S. Representational oil painter of the West, sports, and portraits, born in Burlington, Vermont on Lake Champlain in 1908 and living in Prescott, Arizona since 1978. "There is no substitute for good drawing," he emphasizes. "Today, many people count on color or paint handling to make up for a lack of intelligent draftsmanship, but it never works. It takes good drawing to make good pictures.

"As a young boy, my interest in the West was stimulated by the writing of James Willard Schultz who lived with the Blackfeet Indians. My firsthand encounter with the West was when I was twelve and my father took me to visit an apple ranch in Washington. In 1926, I drove to the West coast in an air-cooled Franklin, camping the entire distance. Roads were then unpaved west of Kansas City. I studied at the Grand Central School of Art, the National Academy of Design, and received my BFA from Yale where I had three teaching scholarships. In World War II, I was a captain in the Air Force overseas, attended the Ecole des Beaux Arts and the Academy Julien in Paris, and spent fourteen years as an instructor in the Famous Artists School.

"While living in Connecticut, I was an illustrator for the leading periodicals and publishers as well as painting murals, portraits, and easel paintings for galleries. I commence my work in fine art by making small charcoal sketches showing the broad pattern and something of the expressive quality desired. The advantage of sketches is that one can see the overall design at a glance and not get lost in detail. I select the one that appeals to me and develop a small color comprehensive. As I proceed with my painting, I constantly refer to the color sketch. Currently, my galleries include May and Nevada Arts."

Jeannie Pear, NAVAJO SCOUT, oil, 48 x 36

Raymond A. Pease, ALL IN THE DAY'S RUN, oil, 24 x 36

amado maurilio peña. 11/79

Pena, Amado Maurilio, Jr. Watercolorist and printmaker of Chicano folk art themes, born in Laredo, Texas in 1943 and living in Austin, Texas since 1973. "I went to apply for a phone in Santa Fe," Pena says, "and, for the first time, I came face to face with the occupation category. The woman at the phone company asked if I was employed and I said, 'no.' For some weird reason, I thought an artist is not really an employed person. It's not like a legitimate job."

Of Mexican and Indian descent, Pena received his BA from Texas A & I University in 1965 and taught high school art. After military service, he obtained his Master's in 1971 and moved to Cristal, Texas, the heart of Chicano political activism, where he was an art consultant. His exposure as an artist was through the political movement. When he became head of the Austin high school art department, he directed his art toward a broader significance. By 1978, he found that the art career was more demanding than teaching.

Now Pena can be "in Austin to print, then I can go to Santa Fe to paint. I have my studio and house there, too, and I can get away from all that's going on. How it will affect my work, I don't know, but I do know that emotionally and physically being in another environment makes a change in how I wake up in the morning." He says that his current work "synthesizes my strong love of the culture and landscape of the American Southwest." He is listed in *Who's Who in American Art*, was in the Peking, China, show, has been featured in many publications including *Southwest Art*, November 1979, and exhibits in 50 galleries internationally. He is represented by his own El Taller.

Amado Maurilio Pena, LA TAZA, mixed media, 30 x 20

Dennis R. Pendleton   *Les Perhacs*   **PERIllo** © 82

Pendleton, Dennis R. Impressionist painter of Colorado landscapes and of still-lifes in watercolor, born in Columbus, Ohio in 1943 and living in Denver, Colorado. "Being in touch with the galleries is really important for an artist," he points out, "yet the business side of any artist's life is completely neglected by art schools. I know it was at mine. They taught the fundamentals and discipline, but they omitted things like how to deal with galleries, taxes, and general finances. I had to learn those things on my own.

"I had an insatiable desire to draw from an early age, and the subject never mattered." At Ohio State, " I started in liberal arts, then switched over to fine arts and began to believe I could make a living as an artist." After school, he taught for three years "to pay off some loans," went to Chicago as an interior designer for two years, and then "left, hitchhiking, with about a hundred dollars in my pocket and one suitcase." He chose Steamboat Springs and stayed there six years, taking odd jobs with "a lot of time off. That's when I started working seriously as an artist."

Other artists "encouraged me in my work" and "suggested I move to Denver." There, he says, "we get a chance to talk about what we're doing in our art. That's really the most stimulating time." He thinks of himself as a "traditional, representative painter. I work outdoors, often in inclement weather. Now, whenever I'm outside, instead of just looking at the beauty of a scene, I look at the scene as a painting. Being there, and being aware, is perhaps the most important phase of my art." Pendleton was in the 1981 Peking, China show, was featured in *Southwest Art*, January 1982, and exhibits at Seth's Canyon Road Art Gallery.

Perhacs, Les. Stylized sculptor of wildlife of the Pacific Northwest in bronze, born in North Hollywood, California in 1940 and living near Puget Sound, Washington since 1968. "When I first began," he explains, "my pieces were mostly single forms. After I was married, I found myself doing more pairs. And later, after my son was born, I began doing groups of three. The changes in my life have made me more aware of how the dynamics of groupings function in nature.

"My dad had come from Budapest and was involved with the research and manufacture of electric cars. I never had any toys from the store. He always made me make them. I started welding when I was six. I never really went to high school but spent every afternoon in my dad's shop making things. When I was sixteen, I went to work in a tool and die shop, and then I was a technical illustrator, but I vowed I would never hold a dull job again. Fortunately, I was awarded a scholarship to Chouinard Art Institute. From there I went to Pratt and subsequently to Art Center and USC.

"My first job out of college was as model maker and designer for toy development. In the meantime, I longed to become more involved with nature again and to do more sculpture because art is my soul thing." By 1968, he had found wilderness acreage where he built a house, studio, shop, and foundry. "I live in the woods," he points out, "because it's possible to observe the forms I sculpt. The raven is a magical bird for me, and I have always had at least one. There is an intelligence and playfulness in these birds. I try to express these qualities through my art." Written up in *American Artist*, August 1979, and *Southwest Art,* March 1980, his galleries include Meinhard and Carson.

Perillo, Gregory. Realist painter, sculptor, and printmaker of American Indians, born in Greenwich Village, New York City in 1929 and living on Staten Island. "My father was a Neopolitan," Perillo recalls, "who wanted to be a painter, but he had no talent. He loved art and American history. Every Sunday while I was growing up, he took me to all the New York museums and galleries. At night, he told me wonderful stories about the West and the Indians.

"After school, kids who were welcome in my house couldn't ask me to theirs because their parents said I was, you know, an Italian, so all day I drew. That was one thing I could do better than anybody, and I kept telling myself, I'm gonna be big someday." At ten, he studied with other young artists, and in his early teens, he was a sidewalk portrait artist. At seventeen, he joined the Navy and was assigned as a cartoonist. The G.I. Bill paid for studies at Pratt Institute, the School of Visual Arts, and the Art Students League, and he met privately with W.R. Leigh. After that, he became a cartoonist for the U.S. State Department.

When he had hitchhiked to Montana in 1948, a Blackfoot couple had called him "the first curly-headed Indian they had seen." Fifteen years later, he went West as a painter. A member of what he calls "the Neopolitan tribe," he toured the Indian reservations, determined "to paint the Indians with the pride and dignity that once was theirs." Later, he started modeling bronzes, and in recent years there have been limited edition lithographs, plaques, plates, and figurines. Occasionally, he does a ranch subject, but for every cowboy, Perillo paints a dozen Indians. He exhibits at the Kachina Gallery.

Gregory Perillo, ARAPAHO BRAVE, oil, 38 x 50

Les Perhacs, THREE HUMMINGBIRDS
bronze & 24 carat gold on polished areas, h 8, w 6

Dennis Pendleton, AFTER THE STORM, watercolor, 17 x 23

403

PERKINSON

Roger Tory Peterson

Perkinson, Tom. Abstract-realist watercolorist of Western landscapes, born in rural Indiana in 1940 and living in Norman, Oklahoma since 1977. "I believe that the most exciting adventures are within ourselves," he says. "When one counsels the inner being with respect, humility, and faith, wondrous things happen. I am awed by what I see every time I begin a new painting. I can't wait for the journey.

"My work had its foundation in my formative years. As a child in Indiana, I would spend many hours alone, studying, watching and creating make-believe worlds in the forest and fields. Some of my strongest memories are of the vast blue skies, the undulating colors of wind-blown wheat fields, the ribbon-like wandering streams. These early dream/fantasy experiences were the beginnings of my imagery." He attended John Herron Art Institute, earned his BS from Oklahoma Baptist University in 1964, and received his MA in drawing from the University of New Mexico in 1968 where he was also an instructor in drawing. Since then, he has been a full-time painter.

"I regard drawing as a fundamental technical tool upon which my paintings have a solid foundation," he declares. "Drawing was also a discipline through which I developed not only my skill but my trust in my intuition and my deep communication with the inner self. I discovered that the inner world is limitless and important, and I have reached the profundity of the spirit. Through my paintings, I invite you to view the infinite world within." He was written up in *Southwest Art,* December 1978, and is represented by Gene Mako Galleries and by Husberg Fine Arts Gallery which listed his watercolor at $1,800 in 1980.

Peterson, Roger Tory. Realist painter of birds in mixed media, born in Jamestown, New York in 1908 and living in Old Lyme, Connecticut. "The ultimate observation," he emphasizes, "is that man is the endangered species. Each species is a mine-canary, and we are all down the mine shaft together. If we create the physical, political, chemical, and moral environment that other forms of life cannot survive, by what insane arrogance do we think we could survive?"

His interest in birds began while he was in high school, and he studied at the Art Students League and the National Academy of Design in New York City. He then moved to Massachusetts where he taught art science from 1931 to 1934 when he became art editor of *Audubon Magazine.* At that time, there was no handy identification system for birds, so his *A Field Guide to the Birds* published in 1934 was an instant success. The invention was to group birds by appearance rather than genetic lines. A completely revised edition published in 1980 contains 136 newly painted originals by Dr. Peterson and was a best seller.

"Birds are far more than cardinals and orioles to brighten the garden, ducks and quails to fill the sportsman's bag, or warblers and waders to be ticked off by the birdwatcher," he points out. "They are indicators of the environment—a sort of 'ecological litmus paper.' They reflect changes in the ecosystem rather quickly. They are an early warning system, sending out signals. It is inevitable that the intelligent person who watches birds (or animals or fish or butterflies) becomes an environmentalist." The world's most honored artist/naturalist, he was written up in *Southwest Art,* November 1980 and is published by Mill Pond Press.

Tom Perkinson, PEACEFUL VILLAGE, opaque watercolor & colored pencil, 30 x 40

Roger Tory Peterson, ROADRUNNER (1976), acrylic & watercolor, 26¼ x 35

Jacob
Pfeiffer

Rusty Phelps

Gordon Phillips

Pfeiffer, Jacob. Traditional oil painter of "the American Indian and the mountain man at a time that is long since past," born in Reszitza, Romania in 1936 and living in Aurora, Indiana. "I did not aspire to be a 'Western artist,'" he emphasizes, "but an artist portraying America's history as accurately as research and my talent would allow. My goal was to develop a painting style that would stand out from all others. I strive to create an atmosphere with technique rather than with illustrative design."

In World War II, his father was conscripted into the German Army for service on the Eastern front. The family was reunited in Austria, after the war, following imprisonment and flight on foot. A young priest in school introduced Pfeiffer to tales of the American frontier and he studied art in Linz, Austria, from 1948 to 1955. He emigrated to the United States in 1955 and also studied at Cincinnati Art Academy. "Never having pursued commercial art," he points out, "I have devoted my time to developing my career as a fine artist.

"Arranging my mental concepts is the struggle. When this process is completed, transferring my thoughts onto canvas is exciting but less challenging. My canvases are systematic and meticulous in their construction. I develop the scene I envision, stroke after methodical stroke, from beginning to end. I never begin a canvas which I don't finish. I portray routine occurrences as well as dramatic conflicts. My characters are often simple, humble individuals." He has never lived any farther west than Indiana. His print publisher is Art First and he is represented by Closson Gallery and by Husberg Fine Arts Gallery which listed his painting for $4,800 in 1981.

Phelps, Rusty. Sculptor of Western figures, born in Colorado Springs, Colorado in 1936 and living in Peyton, Colorado since about 1952. "As long as I can remember, I've liked to draw and carve figures from wood. I grew up on the prairie land of eastern Colorado. Nine of us lived in a house so small I could put the whole house inside the living room of the house I live in today. There was the ranch and farming work that always needed doing, school to go to, and also there were the stories of the old timers about bad times, the great drought, the last Indian raid, and driving longhorns on the trails.

"My inspiration as an artist came from these memories and many, many more. Everywhere I went, every ranch I worked on, every job I held, when people would see my drawings, paintings, or carvings, they would tell me how I should do something with my art, but no matter how much they said about how they liked what I did, they just couldn't imagine having to pay money for it. For spending some time in the Navy, I had the G.I. Bill available to me, and I thought maybe if I went to school, they might show me some short cuts.

"With the encouragement of my professor, I went to Taos to look at the art being done. Upon leaving, I knew that I could do as good. I borrowed $300 from my mother, returned to Taos, spent my money, and took home my first bronze. I have been doing this now for the past dozen years, was chosen for the all sculpture show at the Cowboy Hall of Fame in 1975, and have won too many awards and ribbons to mention. I belong to the Professional Artists of the Rockies, and the galleries I show in include The Garden of the Gods Gallery and the Kansas Gallery of Fine Arts."

Phillips, Gordon. Realist painter in oil and watercolor and sculptor of Western Americana, born in Boone, North Carolina in 1927 and living in Crofton, Maryland. He lives in the East, he says, because "I am overwhelmed by the West's power. Only when I am away from it can I fully appreciate its beauty, and only then can I paint it. If I actually *lived* there, I would probably paint seascapes." When he visits the West as he does every summer, he rarely sketches and never photographs, just "immerses" himself. "It's simply my way of working. I am interested in conveying an overall feeling, not making a carbon copy of something."

As a child, he resented his talent because teachers asked him to draw pictures on the blackboard during playtime. After high school, he served on a Navy destroyer during World War II, then studied at the Corcoran School of Art in Washington, where he later taught. He worked as illustrator and art director for eighteen years, mostly as a free lance. When he decided to switch to fine art, he took a nine-to-five job so he could have evenings and weekends free to paint. After three years, he painted full time.

His technique is to draw and paint directly on the canvas, without preliminary sketching, to "let the painting come naturally, by second nature-ness. At some point in the work, you have to forget the basics intentionally." He does only one painting at a time, from beginning to end, and lets "the painting itself tell me when it is completed." Some paintings, he says, fight back, while others "almost create themselves." Listed in *Who's Who in American Art*, he is represented by Kennedy Galleries.

Gordon Phillips, READY TO RUN, oil/canvas, 40½ x 28½

Jacob Pfeiffer, ALL THEIR WORLDLY POSSESSIONS,
oil, 18 x 24

Rusty Phelps, WHEN TRAILS CROSS, bronze, h 22, w 23, d 15

Tom Phillips △

Judith Pierce

Phillips, Tom. Painter of livestock and ranch scenes in watercolor and oil, born in Chickasha, Oklahoma in 1927 and living in San Francisco since 1975. "God is the only creator," he declares, "and any time I lose sight of this my work falls apart. I can't make it happen. I can only let it. My art teacher told me when I was eleven that I shouldn't think about 'selling' a picture because I wouldn't do as well and she was exactly right. Even today if I let myself think about the money I am making, I can't do the painting as well. This may be true of anyone in any field."

The great-grandson of an 1850s settler who had become a citizen of the Chickasha Nation, Phillips had five years of traditional art training by the time he graduated from high school. He served in the Merchant Marine and the Army in Korea, until 1952, worked as a commercial artist in Oklahoma City, New York City, and Colorado Springs, and painted for *Western Horseman* until 1962. After moving to Missouri, he became resident artist for the American Hereford Association, visiting breeders on their spreads to study and sketch their operations. He had been painting the contemporary Western cattle scene since 1955.

When Phillips went to San Francisco for further study, it was as a leading livestock illustrator, and he continued to tour the West as an easel painter. His specialty remains the recording of today's ranching where the gear and the clothing are modern, as are vaccination and shipping by truck, but the horse and the open pen branding can still be seen. Phillips is represented by John Pence and Shriver Galleries.

Pierce, Judith. Contemporary painter of "mystic and mythic" symbols in opaque water media, born in Indianapolis, Indiana in 1934 and living in Pueblo, Colorado since 1960. "I have been greatly influenced by the writings of Jung who gave me the courage to look into myself and my dreams," she explains. "I listen to the music of Liszt and Chopin, Beethoven, Brahms, DeFalla and many more while I paint so those themes seem to find their way into the paintings. Painting is my response to life and the joy of it.

"I graduated from DePauw University in 1956 with a BA and a major in art and taught art in Indianapolis public schools for three years. In 1960 I moved to Colorado, where I have had over twenty one-woman shows. I am best known for the technique of tempera and ink resist. My work is highly stylized and designed interpretation of my environment. I see all the elements of the prairies—rocks, bones, feathers, animals, fossils, etc.—as symbolic in both a personal and universal way.

"There have been several series on which I continue to work including 'The Women' which I began in Chicago as 'The Tea Ladies' and prostitutes, and have developed into Indian and prairie women. The later ones have really evolved into mystic and mythic women who inhabit the canyons and prairies and are at one there with the animals and birds. I believe these women to be some part of myself. My latest paintings 'The Cave and the Canyon Series' are a result of my fascination with and joy in the canyons of southeastern Colorado, where I spend much of my time hiking. Articles about me and my work have been in *Southwest Art,* April 1979, and my work can be seen currently at the Saxon Mountain Gallery and DeColores Art Gallery."

Judith Pierce, CAVE & CANYON #1, tempera & ink, 23½ x 32

Tom Phillips, MAKIN' FOR WATER, watercolor, 24 x 36

Pilatos, James. Representational painter of architectural and angling subjects in oil, watercolor, gouache, and pastel, born in Sioux Falls, South Dakota in 1932 and living in Carmel, California. "My work is based upon realism within a painterly approach," he declares. "Early training made me aware that content is the single most important ingredient and it takes precedence over all other forms in art. I make compositional studies and color notes in the field, doing all the finished work in the studio.

"At an early age I had a consuming desire to draw and paint, mostly draw. My interest was sparked by the great early-American illustrators. In my teens, my art education began at The Museum School in Portland, Oregon, and in 1951 I started four years at the Art Center School in Los Angeles. My career commenced in advertising, turning to full-time painting in 1964. I have made extensive travels throughout Europe, Mexico, and the American West.

"Most of my work is based on an idea, somewhat like telling a story within the painting as the illustrators did. I have no interest in painting 'scenes,' just to be painting, but attempt to select subjects that can offer a creative solution. I want to express a very personal experience, concocted with an imaginative vision. Whether it be an American trout stream or a back road in a foreign country, I always seek the challenge of creating art out of the everyday world. The satisfaction of knowing when all of the pieces fall into place is immense." In 1979, Pilatos won the silver medal at the National Academy of Western Art, and in 1981 he participated in the first American Western art exhibition in Peking, China with the Driscol Gallery.

Pitcher, John Charles. Representational painter of birds and flora of Alaska in opaque dry brush technique in watercolor and gouache, born in Kalamazoo, Michigan in 1949 and living in Anchorage, Alaska. "In illustrating," he points out, "you try more for an exact attitude and likeness of the bird in a position of repose. There's less room for action. In fine art, the bird should be identifiable and correct, but it doesn't have to show all the field markings. It is a work of art, not a field plate. In painting the bald eagle, I have brought these elements together in an effort to heighten the effect of magnificence and freedom that this embattled bird symbolizes so well."

Never in doubt about his career, Pitcher's interest from childhood was in nature, particularly birds. At nineteen, he hitchhiked the 3,500 miles to Alaska to observe the wildlife and the wilderness for the first time. Three years later, he moved to Alaska and since has traveled throughout the state sketching, photographing, and leading natural history tours. His bird illustrations have appeared in the *World book Encyclopedia, A Guide to the Birds of Alaska*, and in magazines.

"Fine art," he says, "goes beyond the senses and makes it possible to give, through my easel, a clear vision of the ideal. We spend too much time in the mist of the valley. We need to be raised occasionally to the clear blue sky." He feels that his "naturalistic works should be educational as well as aesthetically pleasing." A member of the Society of Animal Artists since 1975, he exhibits at Leigh Yawkey Woodson Museum's Annual International Bird Show. Written up in *Alaska Magazine*, he has shown at Artique Ltd Fine Art Gallery and is published by Mill Pond Press.

Pletka, Paul. Painter in acrylic of Plains Indians of the late 19th century, born in San Diego, California in 1946 and living in Tesuque, New Mexico. "The timeless struggle of a man with his humanity," he emphasizes, "was no different for the Indian than the ancient Greek or 20th-century man. My paintings show the spirit of man from the inside to the outside, and right now the outside happens to be the American Indian. The Indian as I know him is a mystical being. This is the total message of my work. I am not political."

Raised on the western slopes of Colorado, near the Utah border, he was drawing portraits when he was in the first grade. "I am lucky," he states. "They let me draw a lot and my interest in Indians was encouraged." He began winning national medals in high school, studied at Arizona and Colorado State Universities, and was artist-in-residence at Mesa College. Before he was 21, he was chosen to paint an 80-foot frieze in the Historical Museum in Grand Junction.

A non-Indian, he has remarked that if he "knew more about the theories of reincarnation, I might have greater insight into my obvious preoccupation with the Indian, his magic, and his sacred objects. Naturally, I would also like to know where my desire to create came from. There is not one single artist in my family." He adds that "Indians are not, nor have they ever been, savages. I continue to marvel at their oneness with nature. Those not destroyed morally, physically, and emotionally by the 'other' people are timeless beings not of this century but of all centuries. That is what my painting is all about." Written up in *Southwest Art*, summer 1973, Pletka is in 28 public collections and is represented by Gallery Ten and ACA Gallery.

John Pitcher, MORNING FLIGHT—BALD EAGLE
mixed media, 48 x 34

James Pilatos, PATCHING THE OLD HOUSE, oil, 30 x 40

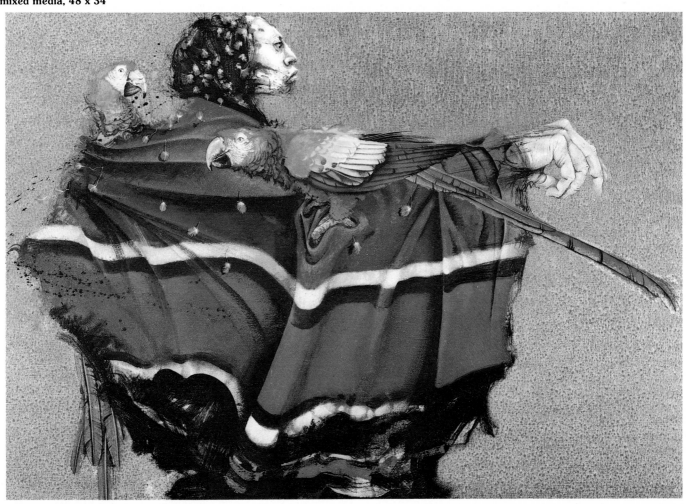

Paul Pletka, CACIQUE, acrylic, 40 x 58

Wolfgang H. Pogzeba

Frank Polk A

POLLAND

Pogzeba, Wolfgang. Abstract-realist painter, sculptor, printmaker, and photographer of the West, born in Munich, Germany in 1936 and living in Taos, New Mexico. "Many of my pictures," he states, "are developed through a negative world of vision, stressing the abstract quality of nature and its design. The viewer becomes caught up in an intellectual involvement as well as an emotional participation, rather than witnessing the mere literal, familiar image. I strive to evoke a harmony of the senses."

Son of an art restorer, Pogzeba attended cloister schools in Bavaria and sang in the Boy's Choir before the family settled in Denver in 1950. He spent two and a half years in engineering at Colorado School of Mines, then studied architecture and art at the University of Colorado. In 1958, he exhibited in Paris, while a student, and when he graduated in 1960 he was given a one-person show at the Historical Society Museum in Helena, Montana. The profit from the show was over $10,000. While in the Air Force stationed in Alabama, he had a one-person exhibition in Montgomery and also in New York.

After two years of graduate study and a short try at teaching, he began painting, sculpting, and photographing full time. He had already had seven one-person shows, with impressive public collectors. Over the years, he has experimented with different forms, saying that "I do one thing, refine it, then go on to something totally new. When you can get an idea, you can't afford to look back. The way to put it is versatility." His theme is still the West, and he notes that he "has become a more integral part of this land with each passing year." He is represented by Gallery G Fine Arts.

Polk, Frank Fredrick. Sculptor of bronze statuettes of cowboys "from 1918 to the present day," born in Louisville, Kentucky in 1908 and living in Mayer, Arizona. "I am a self-taught artist," he observes. "I was first known as 'The Cowboy Whittler,' later 'The Western Woodcarver,' and now as 'The Western Sculptor in Bronze.' I started sculpting in wax in the mid-60s. I am overly precise on authenticity and action, having experienced most of my themes, or at least seen them firsthand.

"Arizona has been my home since I was very young. I began cowboying for Arizona ranches at the age of fifteen, when there was no fencing and the cattle were wild." He had started his rodeo career at ten when he performed in Prescott with his trained burro, an act he continued for twenty years. He was a singing cowboy with his own show on the radio, worked as a stunt man in cowboy films, and was a dude wrangler. In 1946, he was voted best all-around cowboy.

Whittling had always been Polk's hobby. As he moved out of cowboying, he concentrated more on carving. Encouraged to develop his talent, he began whittling seriously, studied anatomy, and his work evolved into bronze casting that was successful with collectors because of its authenticity, whimsy, and his own personal appeal as a "dyed-in-the-wool cowboy" whose "image rubs off." "I was approved for membership by the Cowboy Artists of America in 1967," Polk says. "In 1968, I won the award presented by the Rodeo Cowboy's Association at the Cowboy Hall of Fame. I like to record in my sculpturing the way things were done in my cowboying and rodeo days." Polk is listed in *Who's Who in American Art*.

Polland, Don. Realistic sculptor of Western figures in miniature bronzes, born in Los Angeles in 1932 and living in Prescott, Arizona. "I have experienced no little prejudice on the subject of miniatures," he observes, "size being a very heavy topic of discussion. So often today, the distinction lies not in the quality of the work, the creative effort involved, but in whether the work is gallery size or museum size or whether it is fine art or a trinket. I feel that size has no place in the judgment of art."

When he was fifteen, he became a stable boy on a thoroughbred horse farm. A jockey for two years, he quit because he "had a terrible fondness for eating which jockeys weren't allowed to do much of." He had modeled in clay as a child, and through the years continued toward his goal of preserving the Old West and the Civil War in art while he served in the Navy, and then was electrician, farmer, commercial artist, tool designer, art director, and teacher in his own art school. He also studied modeling, mold making, and foundry practices on his own.

"Of all the arts," he feels, "the one that offers the third dimension is the one in which I can place myself in the middle of things. I can dream of experiences past or wished for." In 1966, he was influenced toward 4 to 6 inch high miniature bronzes, "intrigued by the enjoyment in being able to hold the thing in one hand. Today's collector is often one who has limited space, if not limited budget." His work is in the Whitney Gallery, C.M. Russell Gallery, Favell Museum, and Montana Historical Society, and was in the Peking, China show. He was featured in *Southwest Art*, October 1975, and is represented by Trailside Galleries.

Frank Polk, TWO OLD-TIMERS, bronze, h 17

Wolfgang Pogzeba, TWINING CANYON—ASPENS
oil/board, 20 x 16

Don Polland, WAR PARTY, polychromed bronze, h 6½, w 4, d 8¼

Polt, Allen. Watercolorist of Southwestern landscapes and portraits, born in Newark, New Jersey in 1941 and living in Santa Fe, New Mexico since 1973. "I don't always enjoy painting," he observes. "A temptation with everyone is to achieve a certain competence and then relax into a comfortable rut. We all do it. However, once you're aware of doing it, you can stop it, so I push the edge by not operating in a state of safety. I get into trouble on purpose and then get out of it. That's the fun of it, and usually the results are more exciting to look at."

After graduating from high school in Montclair, New Jersey he earned a degree in illustrating from the Newark School of Fine and Industrial Art, then worked in a Florida advertising agency for a year and served in the Army Reserve. Moving to New York City, he was employed drawing black and white portraits for the *Wall Street Journal* while also studying drawing and painting at the Art Students League. In 1967, he abandoned painting to become a model and to attend acting school, but did not find the satisfaction he was seeking and moved to Taos to reacquaint himself with painting.

"Many viewers," he points out, "are under the impression that watercolor is not a final medium, but instead only a training ground for oil. That is, of course, a misconception. I chose watercolor as my medium because it is unforgiving. I like that. Increasing the risk heightens awareness of a potential mistake and suddenly I'm in a pressure situation. I like that, too. It's a little like a chess game—you should plan at least six moves in advance before you pick up a brush." He is represented by Pelham Gallery and Many Horses Gallery.

Pond, Gordon Goodwin. Traditional oil painter of desert landscapes, Hopi and Navajo scenes, and ghost towns, born in Santa Ana, California in 1920 and living in Winslow, Arizona since 1976. "In 1961," he recalls, "the coroner's office sent me a woman's severed head to be sketched as an aid in identification. I was also asked to make a casting of the face. A young woman identified my side view drawing as that of her mother. The killer turned out to be her stepfather.

"In 1931, I was stricken with polio in the right arm, but exercise restored near-normal usage. I took art classes in high school and attended Saturday classes at Chouinard Art School in Los Angeles. Upon graduation, I enrolled in the C.C.C., building trails, then enlisted in the Marines in 1940. After my discharge in 1942, I worked as a scenic artist and attended Art Center School evenings. In 1943, I secured papers in the Merchant Marine and later built a boat and sailed to Mexico. I returned to studies that led to an MA in art education and in 1953 was employed as an art instructor at Compton College.

"I remained there for 22 years, publishing two books on art and papers on archaeology. Most of my paintings in the 50s were seascapes. In the 70s, I began to draw from experiences in ghost towns and desert locations. My work was selling very well and teaching conditions were dismal. I felt that art was my life, and that I should take the early retirement and get out of southern California. This proved to be the wisest decision I ever made. In Winslow, the paintings flow in great variety." Written up in *Southwest Art*, August 1979, Pond is represented by the Anasazi Gallery of Art and Saddleback Western Art Gallery.

Poppleton, Craig. Painter of Western figures in oil and in drawings, born in Logan, Utah in 1946 and living in Hyrum, Utah. "I feel that the way to produce an end result worthy of a collector's attention is in using a technique to create an effect, and not to be misled by gimmicks. The value of the work is equal to the honesty of its conception, uniqueness, and the height of the artist's emotions during its creation. This pragmatic approach to quality will ensure the utmost in craftsmanship."

Descended from Utah pioneers and from a great-grandmother who was captured by Indians, Poppleton spent his youth working on farms and ranches owned by his father and the neighbors. When he was 22, he enrolled in Utah State University's Illustration Department and in 1972 became a staff illustrator in Salt Lake City. Because of a family illness, he returned to his northern Utah birthplace and built his home on the spot where his great-grandmother was abducted. The land is now a working dairy farm that he runs in partnership with his father.

Poppleton believes that "this rustic environment has begun to nurture the old interest in portraying Indians of the past against the majestic landscape, as a product of his family's history, thus giving his paintings a personality and character that are distinctive." His illustrations that were published in magazines, he adds, "produced an acute awareness in him for demanding detail in draftsmanship and for creativity in subject matter." He is represented by Studio III Gallery and by Husberg Fine Arts Gallery that listed his 20 by 40 inch oil painting at $2,700 in 1981.

Allen Polt, NIGHT DANCER, watercolor, 34 x 22   Gordon G. Pond, RETURN TO THE KIVA, oil, 18 x 24

Craig Poppleton, UNEASY PAUSE, oil, 18 x 24

Poulsen, M.C. "Old Master" oil painter of contemporary Western scenes and figures, born in Akron, Ohio in 1953 and living in Cody, Wyoming since 1966. "I would paint anything that excites my imagination," he explains, "whether it be a nocturne, landscape, flowers, pack train, or people. It just so happens I was raised on a ranch and I paint what I know, the hunting camps and the people who inhabit them, but I have never thought of myself as a Western artist per se."

When he was attracted by a smell coming from an Akron building while he was a child, it proved to be oil paints, an odor he still loves. At ten, he saw paintings by C.M. Russell and was so impressed that for years he reversed his own initials to match. The family had been summering in the West and in 1966 they bought a dude ranch in Wyoming where Poulsen's father was outfitter and guide. Poulsen assisted his father in ranch work and also became a licensed guide and professional outfitter.

During a hitch in the Marines, Poulsen studied art privately in Hawaii for eighteen months. When he returned to the ranch, he was persuaded to enroll in Arizona State University, majoring in art, but he quit when he felt he would learn more on his own and from neighbors like Jim Bama. He prefers "doing people situations" rather than wildlife or landscapes because "people are my interest—people are the main part of the world." His technique is to build up color by placing one thin layer of paint over another for maximum transparency, up to thirty or more layers, and he averages twenty paintings a year. Written up in *Art West*, January 1981, his prints are by Sage Publishing and he is represented by Grizzly Tree Gallery.

Powell, Dave. Traditional sculptor and painter of figures of the Old West, born in Kalispell, Montana in 1954 and living in Santa Fe, New Mexico since 1977. "I don't always know whether an idea should be done in clay or paint, so I'll try it both ways to see which works better. I guess I'm riding a rail by trying to do both. I've heard you can't do both well and that one has to win out. Now I feel sculpture will win, though I love painting dearly."

The son of artists Ace Powell and Nancy McLaughlin Powell, who both painted and sculpted Indians and cowboys of the Old West, he was raised in Hungry Horse, and then the Olympic Peninsula, where he "missed the Blackfeet and moved to Kalispell, in 1968 to live with my father. I'll never forget that the Indians' clothes emitted the smell of sweet grass, and sometimes that fragrance comes back to me when I'm painting or sculpting an Indian figure.

"In the fall of 1973, I went to work for Bob Scriver, making molds and plaster patterns. Upon leaving in the spring, I found a job doing costuming and props for films. After that, I lived in Denver with artist Ned Jacob, doing life drawing classes, and then was hired for a season of 'Grizzly Adams,' doing costume and makeup. Following 'Adams,' I came to Santa Fe where I have done consultation for films and a special for NBC in between study with Bob Lougheed. I'm taking basic training, sort of like the Marines, so I can paint or sculpt in fast-moving light or in any weather. If I can get a true impression, if I can nail down the little details like marking the spot where I'm set up so I can come back to the same place the next day, I'll be a happy artist. My galleries include Wounded Knee and Wood River Gallery."

Dave Powell, MOUNTAIN CHIEF'S CHARGE, bronze, h 16

M.C. Poulsen, BILL STAMBAUGH WORKIN' FOR THE BRAND, oil, 19¾ x 23⅝

John F. Prazen

Don Prechtel

Roger Preuss

Prazen, John F. Sculptor of welded metal busts of American Indians, born in Price, Utah in 1939 and living in Salt Lake City. "Right from the time I was six years old," Prazen recalls, "I was by my dad's side, working with him, helping him in the forge. He would show me how the various metals were tempered, the different types of steels, and so on. This is why metalworking has become an extension to my way of thinking. With the skills taught me by my father, I share with the world my love for art.

"In the area where I was raised," Prazen adds, "the old Indians used to come in to pull the sugar beets. They were so different that as a little kid I used to follow them around." Today, Prazen is president of Pioneer Welding, the business started by his father in Salt Lake City in 1934, and he has improved on the old metalworking techniques to model more than fifty welded sculptures of Indians. These pieces are different, even to welders. *Welding Journal* has called "realism the keynote of the work of this son and grandson of blacksmiths" and has noted that "the artist uses a variety of metals and several welding processes—including a unique 'painting with metals'—to infuse his sculpture with life and individuality."

Prazen tack-welds steel pieces onto a curved steel sheet that is to be the face and then uses arc welding to form the features. The back of the head is hammered on a stump and welded to the face, and contours are refined with a grinder. The skin is a silicon bronze overlay, and the detailing involves a variety of metals and shapes. Color comes from variably controlled heat. Prazen was featured in *Southwest Art,* August 1979, and is represented by Voris Gallery.

Prechtel, Don. Traditional oil painter of "our American Heritage, past and present," born in Los Angeles in 1937 and living in Creswell, Oregon. "I'm more enthusiastic now than ever before about painting," he observes. "I'll paint anything. Things that I never thought I would paint, like flowers or fruit or landscapes. I never used to like landscapes but I like them more all the time. I used to think unless it had a cavalry charge running across a ditch, it wasn't worth looking at. Not anymore.

"I've been wanting to paint the Old West, ever since I can remember. Antique guns—things like that. Just the romantic swashbuckling era. I used to go to the movies to watch good triumph over evil." At fourteen, he sold his first painting to a friend for $5. After graduating from high school in 1955, he attended the University of Oregon, and worked as a car salesman and then as an optician while painting as a sideline. When he lost his job in 1968, he began selling paintings "and from that point on things just got better and better."

He operated an art gallery for five years and then started painting full time. "When I'm painting," he states, "I really don't think much about anybody and anything. I paint for myself. I don't like formulas about how to paint. Painting is an emotional thing, I don't think you should ever be finished with your work and say 'I'm really good.' All a guy has to do is look around and he can find ten guys that can do a better job." Prechtel was a founding member of the Northwest Rendezvous Group, was written up in *Art West,* December 1980, and is represented by Trailside Galleries.

Preuss, Roger Emil. Realistic oil painter of American wildlife, born in Waterville, Minnesota in 1922 and living in Minneapolis. "I regret to say that I couldn't study wildlife painting in art school," he points out. "They just did not offer that type of class. This is still largely true today. Formal art schools offer little or no training in this highly technical art, and most future painters of wildlife will have to be self-taught, as I was. Once they pick up the basic knowledge, they must go out into the field and apply it.

"As a youngster, I grew up very close to the outdoor scene. I used to do a lot of hunting and ran my own trapline. I didn't give art a thought, really, until after I got back from serving in the Navy in World War II. I wrote a few outdoors stories, but I thought the story might be better told in pictures so I enrolled in the Minneapolis College of Art and Design." He worked as a hunting and fishing guide while continuing to paint, and his break came when he got a chance to show his paintings in the Hollywood Fine Arts Center, in 1947.

In 1949, Preuss became the youngest artist to win the Federal Duck Stamp competition. Since 1953, his "Geese from Beyond the North Wind" painting has been reproduced 31,000,000 times. Fifty-five of his works have been published by five major publishers. Art donated to conservation causes has produced over $2,000,000, and in 1976 he was America's Bicentennial Wildlife Artist. "Wildlife," he says, "has been my inspiration to be an artist. If it weren't for wildlife, I wouldn't care to be an artist." Listed in *Who's Who in America* and featured in *Art West,* December 1980, he "seldom participates in invitational shows nowadays." He is represented by Wildlife of America and Cornell Norby.

Don Prechtel, TRACKIN' SNO', oil/canvas, 18 x 24

John Prazen, SUMMER HAWK (present day Comanche)
brass, copper, steel, and stainless steel, h 36

Roger Preuss, YELLOWSTONE CUTTHROAT, watercolor, 9¼ x 16¼

Price, Clark Kelley. Traditional oil painter of the cowboy—past and present, wildlife, and the early Western trappers and Indians, born in Idaho Falls, Idaho in 1945 and living in Thayne, Wyoming since 1981. "I love to play with light," he explains. "It seems to be the magic that brings my subjects to life. A dark foreground and lit background, or vice versa, or the way light and shadow patterns occur in various conditions in nature, thrill me, and challenge me to capture the essence of it.

"In my early years in Montana, wildlife was close to us. I remember seeing elk, deer, and moose from our log house. When I was five, my family moved back to Idaho Falls. After high school, I served a two-and-a-half year mission in the Fiji Islands, for The Church of Jesus Christ of Latterday Saints. On my return, I enrolled in Ricks College and later transferred to Brigham Young University, graduating with a BA in painting. I was out of school in 1971 but received my degree in 1973 when my loan was paid off.

"I tried to paint in my spare time while working at various jobs, but my heart was not happy. To my surprise, Trailside Galleries was interested in selling my work and I became a 'full time' artist in 1973. They sent advances on paintings unsold when I was desperate. The gallery calls me a mood painter, and I guess I am. Detail is relatively important to me, but is secondary to the 'mood.' Life and circumstances create so many moods that I am captivated by. I find my strongest subjects usually deal in simplicity. Not too many things to see, but sort of zeroing in on the subject, the background being fairly simple, almost an understatement." In its 1981/1982 catalog, Trailside priced his painting at $4,500.

Price, Gail. Abstract-realist painter in mixed media washes, born in Ohio in 1944 and living in Saratoga, California. "I have to have recognition," she says. "I'm willing to work hard for it. I have unreasonably high goals for me—but when I'm at Georgia O'Keeffe's age, or Louise Nevelson's, I want to be on the same kind of pinnacle."

Price earned a Fine Arts degree from Ohio University, with teaching credits. She became a fashion illustrator in Cleveland and a portrait painter in Lake George, New York, before moving to Colorado to teach high school art. Her students won national awards. She then studied ceramics at the University of Hawaii and returned to teaching art at Colorado Mountain College, in Glenwood Springs, where her students again received national recognition. To express her philosophy that "we all have the power within us to create," she conducted three workshops a day in Grand Junction, Colorado, and she wrote and narrated film strips on drawing.

She painted and exhibited barn, ranch, and split-rail fence subjects in Colorado, but after she moved to her secluded Carmel studio with its porch over a stream, her technique softened. "I'm not into total abstraction," she declares, "because I feel it cuts off too many people. I want to underpaint and let the shape and the form and the pattern predominate." Some of her paintings "are a result of the alpha state." Her hobby has been endurance horseback riding where she covers up to 100 miles a day in competition. She was featured in the September 1981 issue of *Southwest Art.*

Clark Price, RANGE TELEGRAPH, oil, 24 x 48

Gail Price, DAYBREAK, acrylic collage, 22 x 30

H Kelly Pruitt

Carl Pugliese

pummill

Pruitt, A. Kelly. Traditional oil painter of Western scenes, born in Waxahatchie, Texas in 1924 and living in Taos, New Mexico. "Planning," he declares, "just sets you up for a disappointment because nothing ever works out the way you plan it. I just trust that when I begin to paint, that something worthwhile, perhaps even with a message, will begin to develop." He never knows for sure what he is going to paint and just puts the brush on the canvas and starts to paint and the picture forms itself.

The son of an oil field pipeline walker who picked cotton in the Depression, Pruitt started working cattle along the Mexican border when he was twelve. He served with the cavalry in Asia during World War II, remaining in India to study art and philosophy under a Buddhist monk. When he returned, he worked as a cowboy in Arizona, painting on stones that he gave away as presents. The daughter of his employer showed the paintings to an agent who began selling them.

Although Pruitt never went beyond the third grade, he wrote an autobiography about two and a half years spent hiding in Mexico, because of a skirmish with the law and he has had poetry published. He doesn't call any one place home, just wherever he sets up his 30-foot teepee saying that "Indians had lived that way for a thousand years." When he sought counsel from a Sioux medicine man, he was given the name "Thunder Bow" that he signs to his more metaphysical paintings and also is the name of his gallery. He never uses photos in painting but proceeds from what he calls an emotional level of personal awareness. He never uses models, either, because as soon as they start to pose, "their spirit leaves them." Listed in *Who's Who in American Art,* he is featured in Ainsworth's *The Cowboy in Art* and Broder's *Bronzes of the American West.*

Pugliese, Carl J. Traditional sculptor of bronze statuettes of historical Western subjects and an illustrator, born in New York City in 1918 and living in Yonkers, New York. A founding member of the Society of American Historical Artists, he says that he "felt this group of artists and students of American military and historical happenings would complement each other in important areas of American history, uniforms, arms, and accouterments."

A native New Yorker, he displayed as a youth what has been his abiding interest in the American West and in United States military history. Four years in the Army deepened his devotion to the military, and after his discharge he enrolled in the School of Visual Arts in New York City. Among the books he has illustrated are *Confederate Edged Weapons, Classic Bowie Knives,* and *Literary Places: New England and New York.* He also republished *North American Bows, Arrows, and Knives* by O.T. Mason, with his own addendum, and has lectured on the Golden Age of American Illustration, 1880 to 1950.

Since 1970, Pugliese has devoted himself almost entirely to the sculpture of Indian and military figures. As a Fellow of the Company of Military Historians and a member of the Historical Arms Society of New York, he has done extensive research in museums and in his own library that has been assembled through his activities as an antiquarian bookman. His bronzes are in the permanent collection of the West Point Museum of the U.S. Military Academy, and have been exhibited in the Western Heritage Sale in Houston and in the National Sculpture Society. He won the general excellence award at the 1982 SAHA show and exhibits at Grand Central Art Galleries in New York City, and at the Grizzly Tree Gallery.

Pummill, Robert. Impressionist oil painter of the Old West, born in Loveland, Ohio in 1936 and living in Duncanville, Texas. "The artists I admire," he says, "are Sargent, Remington, N.C. Wyeth, many of the Flemish masters, and some of the French Impressionists. I feel many of the world's greatest artists are alive today, however, and many are painting Western subject matter. It would be difficult for me to pick a favorite.

"I took my first art course at eleven," he stresses, "and have been serious about it ever since. As with most artists, the interest has always been there." Raised in Ohio, he joined the Air Force at eighteen and served nine years, specializing in electronics. His art education was correspondence courses with Famous Artists School and Art Instruction. After employment in Mississippi and Florida, he went to night school at the Art Center School of Design in Los Angeles, while working as an industrial artist, then moved to Texas in 1968 as an illustrator for Vaught Aeronautics.

He had sold through galleries for most of the time since leaving the service in 1964, and in 1977 he became a full-time painter at 41. "From these experiences," he points out, "I acquired discipline and the ability to meet a specific goal, both timewise and subject-wise. In Western art, just as in commercial art, you have to know what you want to end up with before you begin. The most important aspect of doing a painting is the ability to analyze what is necessary to re-create a mood or feeling." Written up in *Southwest Art,* July 1981, his prints are published by Texas Art Press and he is represented only by Texas Art Gallery which has conducted an annual one-artist show and auction.

Robert Pummill, A MATTER OF RIGHT OF WAY, oil, 40 x 60

Carl Pugliese, STILL WARM, bronze, h 6½, w 8½

A.K. Pruitt, WHILE THE WARRIOR WAITS, oil, 20 x 30

Putman, Donald. Traditional painter of the old and the modern West in acrylic, born in Spokane, Washington in 1926 and living in Redondo Beach, California. "Why do I paint the West?" he asks. "Because it includes the whole scope—beautiful women, rugged men, landscapes, interiors and exteriors, and I have the freedom to relate an exciting idea in a way which I believe shows through to those viewing my works."

Raised in a fatherless home in California during the Depression, "Putt" studied art at Alhambra High School and at five feet three inches played football. After serving in the Navy for one and a half years during World War II, he completed high school in Idaho and won a football scholarship to Fresno State College before studying illustration at the Art Center College of Design in Los Angeles. In Florida, on a visit, he was hired to manage a railroad car for the Ringling Brothers Circus and then was an acrobat in a circus traveling in South America. When he settled in California, in 1961, he was employed as a scenic artist for MGM Studios.

After one year, he returned to the Art Center College as an instructor, saying that "every artist should at some point be a teacher, for the association with students and the need for a close observation disciplines the eye to see why a painting is good or bad." During his ten years as a teacher who influenced tens of the leading contemporary Western artists, his personal goal was to become a gallery painter, and when his own paintings took all his time, he quit teaching. Featured in *Artists of the Rockies,* summer 1976, his paintings brought $7,200 at Texas Art Gallery's *Preview '81* and he exhibited in the Western Rendezvous of Art in 1981.

Putnam, Jack D. Traditional sculptor and taxidermist of wildlife, born in Edgewater, Colorado in 1925 and living in Franktown, Colorado since 1978. He "took a Big Horn sheep on Pikes Peak" in 1970 and was so "struck by the beauty of the animal, I got busy and made a sculpture of it. It was something I had wanted to do for a long time, but I was busy making a living. You've got to take time and do it if you're ever going to, and I'm so glad I did."

In kindergarten, he modeled miniature clay animals, and he mounted a squirrel at eight. At fourteen, he discovered the Indian burial ground that was then professionally excavated as the Magic Mountain Site. After graduating from high school, he was drafted into the Navy and served in Hawaii, during World War II, assisting during surgery. Discouraged about studying medicine because "a doctor's life is not his own," he returned to Denver and was employed by a taxidermist. Trained as a zoological preparator, he went with the Denver Museum of Natural History in 1950, becoming curator and traveling widely to collect specimens.

Despite his lack of formal art training, he left the Museum in 1975 to create wildlife sculpture full time, working eight or nine hours daily "because I enjoy it." By 1981, he had completed thirty bronzes, including two that were life-size and one miniature of a running sheep three-quarters of an inch long and cast in gold. An avid conservationist, he donates art to conservation groups. His works are in eight museums and he won Best in Show for taxidermy at the 1981 Safari Club show. Written up in *Art West,* November 1981, he is represented by Cosmopolitan Fine Art and Stremmel Galleries.

Jack Putnam, WOLFPACK: DOWNWIND, bronze, h 12, w 21, Edition 15

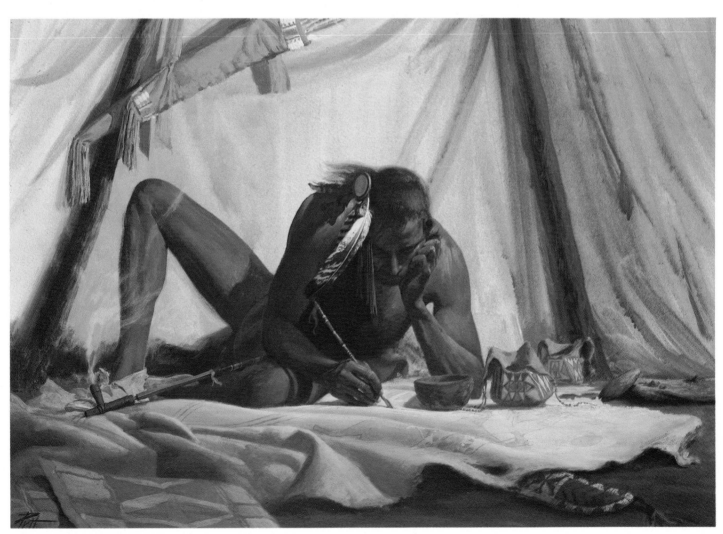

Donald Putman, THE ORIGINAL, acrylic, 30 x 40

Raffael, Joseph. Impressionist painter of California images in oil and watercolor, born in Brooklyn, New York in 1933 and living in San Geronimo, California since 1969. "My work is all autobiographical on an illusory level," Raffael says. "I seek to make an art that looks at you rather than have you look at it. I am a viewer, too. Painting is like having a wonderful conversation with someone or meeting someone—a continual discovery. Artists are servants of God in the sense that they have insights into the universal. They live in a mysterious place. Their will has nothing to do with it and that's why making art is, in some ways, very religious."

After receiving his certificate from Cooper Union Art School, Raffael accepted a summer fellowship at Yale-Norfolk School and then earned a BFA at the Yale School of Fine Arts. He won Fulbright and Tiffany awards and painted in New York until 1966 when a teaching visit to California influenced him to move because he preferred the wider artistic view there to the more intense New York focus. He began working on California paintings while still in the East, and sought teaching jobs at the University of California in Berkeley, and Sacramento State College. In 1971, after he had been living in Marin County, he began his series of impressions of huge animals.

By 1972, he was experiencing a change in his art. "I had lost the power of criticism," he observed. "I was amazed that the painting was coming out of the brush. I just loved it." Raffael is listed in *Who's Who in American Art,* has work in the Metropolitan Museum of Art, exhibited in the 1981 Peking, China show, was featured in *Southwest Art,* May 1980, and is represented by Nancy Hoffman Gallery.

Rakocy, William Joseph. Modern painter "of nature as a point of departure for interesting color, shape, and design" in all media, muralist, and museum curator, born in Youngstown, Ohio in 1924 and living in El Paso, Texas. Since becoming curator of the El Paso Museum, he has begun a series of representational watercolors of the old missions of the Southwest and has collected legends about them. One story he tells is of the 300 year old statue of San Miguel in Socorro Mission that was reputed to be full of gold. The statue needed repairs in 1938 but the residents protested moving it so the statue was loaded on a truck, taken to the bishop for blessing, returned to the mission, and repaired in its niche.

After studying at the Butler Institute of American Art from 1939 to 1941, Bill Rakocy served with the Sea-Bees in the South Pacific, in World War II, went to the American Academy of Art in Chicago, in 1944, and earned his MFA from the Kansas City Art Institute, in 1951. He received a grant to study in Italy in 1953, began as an instructor in painting and drawing in 1954, started exhibiting in 1955, and won an award in watercolor in 1956. He obtained a commission as a muralist in 1956 and continued with murals in Pittsburgh, Youngstown, and El Paso, through 1978.

In 1966, he had moved to Artesia, New Mexico to establish an art department. A ghost town buff, he bought an old building in Mogollon and was president of the association that developed the town into an art center. As curator in El Paso, Rakocy used his art to record the Casas Grande ruins for duplication in the museum as murals. He is listed in *Who's Who in American Art,* was written up in *Artists of the Rockies,* winter 1977, and has exhibited in Jinx Gallery.

Rane, Walter. Realist oil painter of Western figures, born in San Diego, California in 1949 and living in New York City since 1973. "What intrigues me most about painting," Rane explains, "is the recording of light and texture. I enjoy coming in close on something, seeing the patterns that occur and how they contrast with the atmosphere of the surrounding landscape. Pure landscape, though, seems empty without showing how some living thing relates to the trees, rocks, dirt, etc.

"The earliest work of mine which survives," Rane asserts, "was done at age five and is a crayon drawing of a cowboy. My kindergarten teacher sent it home with a note stating that my parents should encourage me. At ten I was given a 'paint-by-number' set but I disregarded the numbers and painted from my imagination. In 1969, I toured France with religious paintings I did for the Church of Jesus Christ of Latter Day Saints." Rane graduated with distinction from the Art Center School of Design in Los Angeles in 1973 and moved to Westport, Connecticut to study illustration. By 1974, he was working as a freelance commercial illustrator in New York City for book covers and magazines.

In 1981, Husberg Fine Arts Gallery began representing Rane in fine arts. "Although I have experimented with nearly every painting material," Rane adds, "I always 'come home' to oil paint. I make a lot of mistakes, and oil paint allows me to correct them. Oil also allows a variety of procedures, working with heavy impasto, thin washes and glazes, textures or smooth. Over the years I have arrived at a procedure that comes down to doing whatever seems right at the moment for the desired effect."

426

Bill Rakocy
PANCHO VILLA RETIRES TO THE RANCH C1920 (1979)
oil, 4 ft x 8 ft

Joseph Raffael, RISING (1982), watercolor, 53½ x 44

Walter Rane, LATE SUMMER, oil/canvas, 22 x 34

Rattey, Harvey L. Traditional sculptor of bronze statuettes of Indian and cowboy life, the rodeo, and wildlife, born near Chinook, Montana in 1939 and living in Bozeman, Montana since 1972. "We are all natural-born storytellers, but we choose different ways. Writing was not my forte. Working with my hands and eyes and imagination in clay or wax was, and as I shaped the things I knew, I experienced a creative joy which compensated for the hours spent. I could tell endless stories with my hands."

His youth was passed helping his parents on their ranch and listening to his grandparents tell about their life before the land was settled. For many years, he was foreman of a 44,000 acre cattle ranch "where a man could saddle his horse in the morning and ride checking cows, never seeing another person." Free time was spent as a calf roper in rodeos. In 1971, when he couldn't afford to buy a bronze of calf roping that he wanted, a friend gave him wax and suggested that he model his own. He did, others asked to buy copies, and he was embarked on an art career.

Part Assiniboine and part French, he "was able to bring back my ancestors' love for tribal customs, shape wild horses on the rimrocks, fashion a steer straining against a lariat, or relive my rodeo experiences. I do my work to please the lover of the West who appreciates what it's like to feel a bronc about to 'bust loose' underneath him, to break trail, to fix fence, to pitch your rope, and to have the friendship of the old-time Indians, to represent 'where the pavement ends and the West begins.'" Rattey is a member of the Western Artists of America. In 1977, he married sculptor Pamela Harr and together they run Bridger Foundry and Gallery.

Redlin, Terry. Realist oil painter of wildlife, born in Watertown, South Dakota in 1937 and living in Mound, Minnesota. "There are two major categories of wildlife artists," he points out. "One does landscapes and uses deer, ducks, and pheasants to make it complete. The other type concentrates on the subject, the species of bird or deer. I don't really like to do just the bird itself, but sometimes I'm forced to. I compete for duck stamps, so I have to change."

Growing up near the Central Flyway with the dream of becoming an artist, he entered the School of Associate Arts in St. Paul in 1955. He quit his first job as layout artist to go home to work in architectural rendering, but returned to commercial art in St. Paul, in 1967. "As a magazine art director," he says, "I evolved out of painting into management. By 1974, I was crowding forty. I looked around. There were no drawing boards, no brushes, and I thought, 'This isn't what I went to school for.' I hadn't picked up a brush in years, but I always wanted to be a wildlife artist."

In 1979, he decided to concentrate on wildlife art and devoted himself to field research. In 1981, he won the Minnesota Duck Stamp competition and was named Artist of the Year. In 1982, he won the Trout Stamp contest and placed second in the Federal Duck Stamp competition. He says that he likes to paint the fall and winter because "everything is too green and too thick in the summer. Sometimes I see something I've overlooked. I never throw away slides. I don't try to take too many thoughts ahead, though. By next year, my thoughts will have changed." Published by The Wooden Bird, his consecutive sold-out editions approach thirty, and his originals sell for as much as $50,000.

Redman, Mikael. Sculptor of miniature Indian figurines in precious metals, born in Flagstaff, Arizona in 1941 and living in Scottsdale, Arizona. "In contemporary times," he observes, "to my knowledge I am the only one to work with jeweled miniatures in precious metals as a major art form. I feel that I've opened the door. Sometimes, though, I have misgivings about my work. I'm a Ferdinand the Bull type. I love to smell the flowers. I love the gentle things in life."

Raised in Flagstaff, he took ballet lessons after school and before Little League practice that was followed by rodeo training and lessons in classical organ. "I don't do well unless I'm busy," he points out. "I feel that I am an artist today in spite of my education." He dropped out of Northern Arizona University and a music scholarship, sang and played on the stage, and then "in 1964 when I went back to school, I told my parents that I was going into art. I don't know why I said that," but in ten years he had an international business with 27 employees before he had to "re-establish his goals."

He believes that a smaller operation provides greater control, because "out of maybe ten castings, I'll get maybe one that is worth anything." He adds that "I wanted to capture the Kachinas, but I have no urge to chronicle the state. I'm not a Southwestern artist. In fact, my Arizona audience is small. I don't do shows. My work is so expensive that it is hard for me to assemble a collection." The pieces are also available in bronze at lower costs. Written up in *Southwest Art*, December 1973, and *Art West*, November 1979, he is represented by his own Mikael Redman Studio.

Mikael Redman, HEM'S KACHINA
18 carat gold with
24 carat gold overlays, h 3½

Harvey Rattey, MAIL WAGON, h 18, Edition 1

Terry Redlin, APRIL SNOW, oil, 24 x 36

Red Star, Kevin. Painter and print-maker, born in Lodge Grass, Montana, on the Crow Reservation in 1943 and living near Santa Fe, New Mexico. A modern Indian artist, he says that "basically, I'm a romanticist. I like that life of the old days. I try to capture the era" at the turn of the century "when the tribe started to change."

His father played Western music in the all-Crow band and his mother did intricate beadwork. They both "really liked Western art, especially Charles Russell. We had prints of his, but I never liked them much. In the early '60s I learned about Rothko, Rauschenberg, and other people like them. Picasso was one of my early heroes." Red Star attended the Institute of American Indian Art in Santa Fe, the San Francisco Art Institute, Montana State University, and Eastern Montana State, then in the early 1970s returned to teach art on the reservation. "In Montana, people're still stuck on the superboy Russell. I needed the stimulus of Santa Fe," and so he moved back to New Mexico.

At 6 feet 4 inches tall, Red Star is slender and graceful. He has exhibited in London, Paris, Munich, Tokyo, and Peking as well as in more than 50 group and 20 solo shows. He usually begins painting without a preconceived composition. Once he starts painting, the spirit takes over. Portraiture is bold and flat, in subjects taken from old Crow photographs, with vivid colors added. "Sometimes," he declares, "I portray things with underpainting—a man or a horse beneath the surface that appears like a ghost." He was featured in *Southwest Art*, February 1976 and April 1980, and is represented by Whitney Gallery.

Kevin Red Star, CROW INDIAN SPIRIT WARRIORS, acrylic & mixed media, 44 x 40

Maynard Reece

Howard Rees

Wm F. Reese NAWA

Reece, Maynard. Representational oil painter of wildlife, particularly game birds, born near Des Moines, Iowa in 1920 and living there in 1982. "I am fascinated by water and water action," he points out. "One reason I paint so many waterfowl is because they are always around water. This gives me a chance to tackle the problems of water in most of my paintings. I find my greatest challenge in depicting water, whether a ripple in a pothole or an ocean or whatever."

The son of a Quaker minister, Reece was exploring marshes and fields as a boy. "I didn't get much formal training," he declares, "but artists are seldom self-taught. You get training from someone, and I received mine from a whole series of very kind and helpful men." His first encouragement came from the director of the local museum where he sketched. After two years as a layout man for a publisher, he "went back to the museum and became staff artist and museum assistant, doing taxidermy and field work."

During World War II, Reece painted the Signal Corps in action in Europe and then returned to the museum. In 1948, he won the Federal Duck Stamp competition, the only artist to win this honor five times. He turned full time painter in 1950, and "it is possible that more people possess a print from a Reece painting than from the work of any other wildlife artist." According to Reece, "my goal still is to become a good artist. People say, 'You're already a good artist. You're just pulling my leg,' but the more you work in this field, the more you know how much farther you have to go." Written up in *Southwest Art,* November 1980, and *American Artist,* September 1978, his prints are published by Mill Pond Press and he has exhibited at Trailside Galleries.

Rees, Howard. Representational watercolorist of the old and the contemporary West, born in Wales, Utah in 1941 and living in Auburn, California. "I work mainly in transparent watercolor," he states, "a challenging medium I am totally dedicated to. I don't remember the last time I allowed myself the luxury of putting the white back into a painting with an opaque medium. There is something about the 'sparkle' of the white paper that can't be achieved any other way.

"Wales was a small coal mining town that is almost deserted now. I grew up in central Utah in the town of Pleasant Grove where I graduated from high school in 1959. From 1960 to 1964, I attended Art Center School in Los Angeles where I graduated with a BA. From 1964 to 1969, I worked as a concept designer for Ford Motor Company in Dearborn, Michigan, responsible for a great deal of design on the Mustang and Continental. One year was with Ford of England. From 1969 to 1974, I was a toy designer in California where I won the Toy of the Year award and was responsible for "Hot Wheel" cars.

"During this time, I started painting seriously, during lunch hours, etc. I started showing in a local gallery and sales were brisk. In 1974, the 'terrifying' decision was made to attempt painting full time, the best decision I ever made. I guess the question most frequently asked me is, 'how long did it take you to paint it?' My paintings go rather fast, after the 'nitty-gritty' preparation is done. I usually find that the quicker they are done, the fresher and cleaner they are. Anyone who is familiar with transparent watercolor, however, knows you can never stop 'thinking' while you are painting." He is represented by The May and Singletree Galleries.

Reese, William Foster. Figurative and objective painter, frequently of American Indian subjects and Indian artifacts, born in Pierre, South Dakota in 1938 and living in Bellevue, Washington. "All intellectualizing must be done," he points out, "before you start to paint—just as all decisions must be made without thinking throughout the whole painting process. The artist must call upon the sum of all his senses. When a musician is called upon for a concert, that is not the time to learn to play the piano."

Raised in Washington, Bill Reese was encouraged by his parents to become an artist. He studied at Washington State University and then at the Art Center School of Design in Los Angeles. To support his family, he was employed as a sign painter for a billboard company, an experience that helped him because he "formed the letters in space working with negative shapes, did the drawings, and laid on the colors." By the summer of 1971, he had saved enough to permit becoming a full time artist, but he avoids large, epic scenes.

"Much like the blooming of a flower, the painting should unfold gradually, each part in harmony with the other. If a rose were to bloom one petal at a time, it would be incongruous. A painting finished one area at a time would also be incongruous. The relationship of one part to another is essential." Reese has been featured in numerous publications including *American Artist, Artists of the Rockies,* and *Southwest Art.* He is listed in *Who's Who in American Art,* is a member of the Northwest Rendezvous Group, Pastel Society of America, and National Academy of Western Art, has exhibited in China, and is represented by Trailside and Shriver Galleries.

William F. Reese, CHIAPANECAS, pastel, 30 x 40

Howard Rees, RED ROCK CANYON, watercolor, 21 x 29

Maynard Reece, DARK SKY—SNOW GEESE, oil, 24 x 36

Ren, Chuck. Realist painter of sporting and Western figures in acrylic, born in Ajo, Arizona in 1941 and living in Vista, California since 1978. "I grew up in a small copper mining town," he explains, " and there wasn't all that much to do. It was always so hot that I'd spend most of my time indoors, drawing. When I was twelve, I sent in for the Famous Artist School test that you'ld always see offered in ads. They sent back my work with a grade of B plus, but told me I was too young to enroll. I was really crushed."

After taking his freshman year at Northern Arizona University, he earned a BFA from the University of Arizona, in 1964, but he "almost dropped out of college. They put you through elementary design and some other basic courses before you get to anything like figure drawing. It was pretty boring." He then became a technical illustrator. "Whenever I had the chance," he says, "I'd also do free-lance work for whatever it would pay. I started making a lot of contacts. The free-lance work increased to the point where I couldn't do both, so I quit my full time job in 1976 and went totally free lance."

A $75 ad in the Los Angeles Illustrator's Catalog produced calls from movie studios, record companies, and the National Football League. Compared to employment as an illustrator where he was "tired of the lifestyle that had company heads telling designers what to design," the NFL called him "perfect." By 1980, he had done over 200 illustrations for the NFL and a dozen covers for *Pro! Magazine*. Sixty percent of his work was football oriented. By 1982, however, the bulk of his output was fine art related to the American West, published by Gray Stone Press and exhibited by the Altermann Art Gallery.

Reno, Jim. Sculptor, born in Wheeling, West Virginia in 1929 and living in Simonton, Texas since 1952. He sticks to the contemporary West in modeling bronze monuments as well as statuettes, "to do only the things I have seen in my time," and has not joined the groups of cowboy artists who he feels are reworking old themes.

As a youth in New Castle, Indiana, Reno was always drawing horses, "not to be an artist but because I liked horses." He attended John Herron Art Institute in Indianapolis on a five year scholarship, then went to Texas to get a job as assistant to a sculptor. When he could not find a sculptor who was making a living, he took a job training cutting horses until his own sculpting paid the bills. By 1973, a bronze that was commissioned of the thoroughbred Secretariat was true enough so that "it just looks like it ought to eat oats." Reno has also modeled an equestrian statue for Texas A&M and both a 9-foot figural statue and "The Brand Inspector" for Fort Worth.

Reno lives on seven acres of wooded Brazos River bottomland. "I don't start very early in the morning," he says, "but I usually stay real late." He applies small light-green clay strips to his armatures, to build the figures out, not cut away. When the mold is completed, the foundry returns the clay for use on the next model. Some of Reno's clay is thirty years old and has been everything, horse, bull, and cowboy. He has exhibited statuettes at the National Academy of Design, the Pennsylvania Academy of Fine Art, and the White House, and is represented in the National Museum of Racing. Reno's gallery is Meredith Long & Company in Houston. He was featured in *Southwest Art*, September 1975.

Reyes, Jimmi. Representational pencil artist of Western subjects, particularly Indians, born in the land of the Maharlikas, the Philippines in 1957 and living in Los Angeles since 1972. "I grew up," he points out, "in a family of ten children who are all artists including my parents, a family of musicians, writers, actors, and painters who gave me as the eighth child an environment of sensitivity, creativity, and expression which became the basis of my learning and growth as an artist.

"I came to the United States at the age of fourteen and started going to art shows with my oldest brother Buddy. At sixteen, I was already showing in galleries and was voted in as the youngest member of the American Indian and Cowboy Artists. By 1974, I had won four first place awards, and in 1978 I won first place in the Second Annual AICA exhibition. My interest in Western art started with my respect for the Indians. I thought of them as people of great wisdom, living in harmony with the earth.

"Pencil, the medium I prefer, is the simplest, as simple words are better understood. Drawing focuses and aligns my consciousness and allows me a clearer perception and better understanding—therefore, seeing. This seeing is learning and growth, and itself is life which brings together the life of the subject and the understanding of the artist. As an artist, one draws with one's own life and one's own breath. Life in a drawing, something 'created by the created,' grows with the sensitivity of the beholder. I have eighteen drawings in limited edition lithographs distributed by Vintage Art and the galleries that represent me include Park Fifth Avenue Gallery and El Mundo Magico. The demand for my work is much greater than what I produce."

Jimmi Reyes, SOUL CALL, pencil, 14 x 12

Chuck Ren, DOUBLE TROUBLE, acrylic, 21½ x 32

Jim Reno, THE BRAND INSPECTOR, h 17½, w 26¼, d 12

Reyes, Norbert "Buddy." Traditional oil painter of Southwestern scenes, born in Subic, Zambales, Philippines in 1942 and living in Canoga Park, California. "When I first came to the United States, I was hungry a lot and I turned out scores of paintings so I could survive. Doing one after another like that gave me a chance to experiment with different styles. I eventually settled on my own method of communicating."

After playing cowboys and Indians on his grandfather's ranch in Mindanao, he copied Western characters from American comic books. Educated by the Jesuits, he earned a degree in architecture at the University of Santo Tomas, while entertaining as "The Elvis Presley of the Philippines" and as "Buddy" in a television serial. Self-taught as an artist, his paintings hang in the Manila Museum. He entered the United States on a tourist visa in 1967 and managed legal delays until he became a citizen in 1973.

"When tough times came," he says, "I just listed my options. Of course, when most of the list was crossed off, I got a little nervous." His breaks arrived when his portrait of Martin Luther King, Jr. won a prize and when his portrait of Apollo astronauts was part of the Bicentennial exhibit. He explains that "the Norman Rockwell charm was not just in the people he painted but in the little story he suggested as well. He influenced me to try for this effect. I look for a moment that has been overlooked or forgotten." The President of the American Indian and Cowboy Artists in 1981, he says that people "see my long black hair, the shape of my eyes, my cheekbones, and they ask what tribe I am from." Written up in *Southwest Art,* August 1981, he has shown at Files and Many Horses Galleries.

Reyes, Stephen. "Romantic realist" oil painter of sophisticated women, born in Waco, Texas in 1948 and living in Albuquerque, New Mexico. "My subject is woman," he points out. "My subject is light and shadow. My subject is beauty. I consider myself a realist and romantic painter. My main influences in art have been the paintings and teachings of Degas and Edward Hopper. I have also been influenced by advertising art and fashion art. I believe it is impossible for any person today not to be affected in some way by these two media.

"We have a family history of artists. My folks did not encourage me to go into art, but they didn't discourage me either. They just let it flow. When I became older, I learned that my grandfather who was of German descent was an artist. Those who knew my grandfather say I take after him in looks and attitude. I attended a Catholic high school and my art teacher was a nun. She made it clear that becoming an artist was not an easy road to take. How right she was! I have found nothing more challenging.

"I like white. It can be warm. It can be cool, virginal, pristine. It is versatile. It can be seductive and sophisticated. Even if I don't plan on using white in my painting, I still have a generous glob squeezed out on my palette which happens to be a glass-topped table. I am of the philosophy that artists are as much entertainers as anyone. They need an audience to get feedback, to find out if their work is making a statement and communicating. Sometimes the response hurts, but the majority of the time it is reinforcing. It gave me the courage to go into galleries with my paintings." Written up in *Southwest Art,* September 1981, Reyes is represented by the Joy Tash Gallery.

Reynolds, James E. "Broad realist" painter of contemporary cowboys at work, born in Taft, California in 1926 and living in Sedona, Arizona since 1967. "Critics don't bother me a bit," he declares. "I'm just doing my own thing, with no phony nonsense. I just like to paint cowboys. I'm a realist in every sense of the word, but in painting I lean toward impressionism. As far as my goals are concerned, I just want to be a good painter. And naturally, I want to leave something behind."

When Reynolds was a boy, summers were spent in a small town in the Sierra Nevadas, near Donner Pass. "The whole town was just so full of the mood of the Old West," he recalls. His interest in art was heightened by getting a calendar with a Frank Tenney Johnson painting that "just turned me on." After service in World War II, he studied at Kann Institute of Art in Los Angeles and the School of Allied Arts in Glendale, became a free-lance commercial artist, worked for Lockheed Aircraft as an illustrator, and then for fifteen years sketched and painted for the major movie studios in Hollywood. When he resigned his high paid job to paint full time, his supervisor was concerned, but Reynolds made more money his first year of painting than he had in Hollywood.

In 1974, Marlboro chose a Reynolds oil painting for billboards and magazines around the world. He is a member of the Cowboy Artists of America and has won the "public choice" medal twice. Franklin Mint has published his prints and he has been featured in *Southwest Art,* February 1977 and *Artists of the Rockies,* fall 1981. Yet, he sees his role only as "documenting a period of time that will be history later on." His publisher is Mill Pond Press.

Norbert "Buddy" Reyes, WARMTH OF FRIENDSHIP
oil/gesso panel, 30 x 36

Stephen Reyes, BLUE CHAMPAGNE, oil, 42 x 34

James Reynolds, SPRING CALVES, oil, 24 x 36

RICKER

Gary Riecke

Richter, Henry Charles. Representational sculptor and painter of the Old West and the West of today, born in Cleveland, Ohio in 1928 and living in Phoenix, Arizona since 1958. "Artists," he emphasizes, "are the last bastion of individuality. They depend on their own enterprising natures. They cannot force anyone to like or buy their work. They cannot be lazy. They must produce. They must have the courage necessary to put their souls out for everyone to view in their work, and to bear criticism without letting it put out their spark."

At four, he made drawings of animals, and at eight was offered a scholarship. His practice was to do a drawing everyday after school, before going out to play. After high school, he volunteered for the Army in 1946, then tried engineering courses before switching to the Philadelphia Museum College of Art in 1949. When he graduated in 1953, he was employed by ad agencies in Philadelphia and Cleveland, and started his own agency in Phoenix. "I know many articles have been written about the phony side of Western art," he declares, "how most of the paintings and sculptures are conjured by soft-butt saddle heroes from fancy art schools, but I can identify with the men of the West.

"Often what happens off the ends of my fingers in clay, or the extension of my brush or pencil, takes place without any conscious effort on my part. I work from what I call 'mind pictures,' working out the expressions and attitudes along with the design of the finished piece before my hands ever touch the clay." Written up in *Southwest Art,* March 1978, Richter is a member of the American Indian and Cowboy Artists and is represented by Son Silver West. His pewter sculpture and prints are through Jolyn Art Ltd.

Ricker, Irene. Realist watercolorist of Southwestern landscapes, born in Hot Springs, New Mexico in 1928 and living in Albuquerque since 1939. "Why do I paint?" she asks. "Well, I can become so totally immersed in a painting that my mind is free of the endless details of daily life. If the end result pleases me enough to add the frame, I realize this is something I have created in my own style. The fluidity and accidental character of transparent watercolor on paper cannot be duplicated or counterfeited. These are the good times that keep me fired up.

"My father was an artist turned jeweler so he became my first teacher," she recalls, "often using drawing games to keep me entertained." She won the statewide blue ribbon for grade school children and later won a scholarship in art at the University of New Mexico, where she graduated with a BFA in 1950. After working as a commercial artist, she studied with Robert E. Wood in 1969 and made the transition from oil to watercolor in 1970.

"When I work in watercolor," she explains, "I wet the entire sheet of paper and am committed to stay with it as long as I want to work wet into wet areas. I like to combine this with details in dry brush later. Other times I enjoy the change of working in gouache as this enables me to correct my mistakes or use opaque white if a highlight is needed. A positive approach in what I plan to do gives my work strength. I am not timid about using color, and working in the commercial field influenced my style to become quite realistic." She is listed in *Who's Who in American Art* and *American Artists of Renown* and is represented by Galeria Del Sol.

Riecke, Gary. Traditional wildlife sculptor in black walnut or Carrara marble, born in Spencer, Iowa in 1946 and living in Bigfork, Montana. "It is the challenge of working in a medium that allows no margin for error that intrigues me," he emphasizes. "After having worked in marble, I simply cannot find modeling clay very interesting. I want to be known as a sculptor in the traditional sense of the word. The bronzes which are cast from my clay studies are to me the same as prints are to a painter—an inexpensive reproduction of the original work.

"I grew up on a farm outside the small town of Ruthven, Iowa. My father and I spent our spare time in his basement workshop. We took our vacations at our summer home in Glacier National Park, and I first became interested in woodcarving watching neighbor Ace Powell work on a carving of a bear and two cubs. This interest stayed with me through the years, while I received a BS in mathematics and physics from Mankato State University, in 1968 and taught in Montana and Iowa.

"In 1977, we moved back to Kalispell, where I accepted a position at the Ace Powell Bronze Foundry. I soon left to pursue a professional art career. When I began, I had the idea that detail was all important, but I soon learned to portray character, personality, and emotion. I start on a very small, very crude model in clay. When I have it looking the way I want, I go to a full-sized clay model. Once the clay study is completed, it is used as a reference to produce the finished piece in wood or stone. Then, using the clay model, an edition of bronze castings is made. Because these are only reproductions I keep the price and the edition size low. My work is currently handled by Settlers West Galleries and El Prado Gallery of Art."

Hank Richter, DURN, bronze, h 7, w 19, d 14, Edition 30

Gary Riecke, GOING TO THE SUN, black walnut, h 16, w 9, d 9

Irene Ricker, VILLA NUEVA, watercolor, 14 x 23

Rigden, Cynthia. Sculptor of ranch animals in bronze statuettes, born in Prescott, Arizona in 1943 and living in Kirkland, Arizona since then. "When I went to Arizona State, I wasn't all that interested in sculpting. I got into it by accident. We enrolled alphabetically. Being Rigden, I was quite a ways down the line, and many of the courses were already closed. Drawing & Composition and Basic Design were filled, so I asked for Sculpting and loved it."

Her grandmother and mother were amateur painters. They "encouraged my interest in art. I never outgrew it." Horses were and are her favorite subject, as "the second most frequently depicted figures in the history of art." In 1966, she attended a summer seminar in Italy, and each year since she has traveled to horse fairs, shows, and contests. Her secret in modeling horses is to watch the "two pivot points, one above the rear legs, the other above the front legs. That is where all their motion is focused."

She lives on a cattle ranch in the high desert, the third generation to do so, and practices both art and management. When her father lost his sight, she shared the ranch responsibilities with him and is Vice President of the Yavapai Cattle Growers. She lives in a separate studio with hundreds of books on art history and on horses, along with miniature lead cavalry figures in battle array, and she models mules, burros, sheep, goats, pigs, and cattle as well as horses. When she wanted a longhorn steer as a model, she bought one, and ended with twelve. She has been written up in *Southwest Art*, December 1980, and *Arizona Highways*, June 1981, and is represented by Troy's Gallery.

Riley, Jack. Traditional sculptor of Western figures in bronze statuettes, born in Weatherford, Oklahoma in 1917 and living in Yukon, Oklahoma. "One day while my wife and I were at the Cowboy Hall of Fame, I was admiring the bronze sculpture of Remington and Russell and I said that I sure wished I owned one. 'Why don't you just make one,' she challenged. I tried it and entered one in an art show, and won! So I started doing some more.

"When picking up some of my old school books and flipping through the pages, I find that nearly every page has sketches of horses, Indians, and cowboys, so art must always have been my first love, although I didn't realize it for almost fifty years. I attended Southwestern State Teachers College and studied art for three years but in 1940 I faced the reality of finding a livelihood. I entered the Kansas City School of Horology, graduating in 1941 as a watchmaker and jeweler. Aboard the aircraft carrier Hornet until 1942 when it was sunk. I returned to the States until discharged in 1945.

"For the next 32 years, I was a watchmaker and jeweler in Oklahoma City, working evenings and weekends on painting, picking up honors in the process. I turned to sculpture in 1970. Despite my training, I consider myself self-taught because the college didn't even have a class in sculpture. Before long, I found I couldn't meet the demand. That's when I decided, in 1977 at the age of 57, to get out of the watchmaking business and into full-time sculpting. People wonder how I can do horses, cowboys, and Indians and not be a cowboy. My answer is you don't have to be a cowboy, anymore than you have to be a horse, to depict one accurately." He is represented by Sculptured Arts Gallery and El Prado Gallery of Art.

Riley, Kenneth. Realist oil painter of the historical West, born in Waverly, Missouri in 1919 and living in Tucson, Arizona since 1971. The intensity of the light "probably triggered the whole excitement about coming West," he commented, "especially the breaking light when you could see patterns. When you get into a big space with immense patterns moving across the countryside, it's unbelievable. Trying to get some of these effects is a lifetime right there."

Raised in Kansas, Riley went to the Kansas City Art Institute to study with Thomas Hart Benton in 1938 when his high school art teacher offered to pay for the first semester. In 1941, he moved on to the Art Students League and Frank Vincent DuMond in New York City, with evening classes at the Grand Central School of Art and Harvey Dunn. Soon Riley was selling illustrations to the pulps at $15 each but he enlisted in the Coast Guard for World War II and became a combat artist. In 1945, he returned to illustration, working for the *National Geographic*, the *Saturday Evening Post*, and other national publications. One painting was accepted by President Kennedy for the White House collection.

Painting Yellowstone and the Tetons for the National Park Service and teaching at Brigham Young University influenced Riley to move West. Also, he says that he "became excited about painting this country and tying in the historical aspects of it." Riley has been written up in *Artists of the Rockies, Art West*, and *Southwest Art*, was part of the Peking, China show, is a member of the National Academy of Western Art, and is represented by Fowler's Gallery and by Settlers West Galleries where his painting was listed at $18,000 in the 1981 silent auction.

Jack Riley, THE WINDBREAK, bronze, h 8, w 10, d 6

Cynthia Ridgen, QUADRIGA, bronze, h 9, w 17

Kenneth Riley, THE YUMA CONNECTION, oil, 24 x 44

441

Morris Rippel (signature)

Rippel, Morris. Realist painter of New Mexico buildings in watercolor and tempera, born in Albuquerque, New Mexico in 1930 and living there ever since. "I've always wanted to do very complex paintings," he says. "I'm doing paintings now of subjects I first sketched years ago. It's a matter of practice and confidence. Having talent is one thing, but learning to apply it correctly is another. I never did look at painting as just having fun. I was always serious about it."

At the age of ten, Rippel had five-dollar art lessons, "and that was half a week's grocery bill." He attended the University of New Mexico for two years, was called into the Korean War because he had joined the National Guard, and then returned to the university to study architecture. After graduating in 1957, he began doing watercolors as a hobby and in 1964 his paintings were accepted for sale in Santa Fe. When he had earned enough to support his family for one year as an artist, he began painting full time.

His influences have been Edward Hopper for showing the solidity of a building, Andrew Wyeth for abstract compositions with realistic focus, and books on drawing and egg tempera. In 1974, the National Academy of Western Art invited him to enter its watercolor show and he won fourth prize. He became a member of NAWA in 1975 and won gold medals for watercolor in 1976, 1977, and 1978. In 1979, his egg tempera on a gesso panel won NAWA's Prix de West. Rippel was featured in *Southwest Art*, August 1980, is listed in *Who's Who in American Art,* and is represented by Fowler's Gallery and Settlers West Galleries where his painting was listed at $19,000 in the 1981 silent auction.

Morris Rippel, SPANISH GOLD, egg tempera, 18 x 30

443

Robt. C. Rishell

B.J. Ritchie

R.H.R.

Rishell, Robert Clifford. Traditional oil painter who "captured the sunshine" in the Southwestern desert, born in Oakland, California in 1917 and died there in 1976. "I have always seen beauty around me in the simplest aspects of nature," he said, "and this is what I paint. There is so much that is sordid and ugly in the various fields of art today, but fine art has the duty of offering an inspiration to people. A painting should be more than a pleasant scene. It must touch the intellect of the viewer as well as his emotions."

Son of the former mayor of Oakland, he received three art scholarships and graduated with honors from the California College of Arts and Crafts in 1938. He served in the Navy in World War II, painting portraits and making three-dimensional invasion maps, then returned to college to earn his MFA and his teaching credentials. He also studied privately and taught from 1953 to 1974, saying that "I feel I continue to learn from the problems of my students. I try to encourage them to really *see*.

"Light and atmosphere," he emphasized, "play the greatest roles in my paintings. I paint 'into the sun' to achieve the contrasts that create the feeling of captured light on the canvas, and add a message if I can. I begin most of my paintings on location to catch the mood of the scene or area. The painting is finished in my studio where I may change the composition, by eliminating or extending. I feel a spiritual quality in the desert. They say one picture is worth a thousand words. If my paintings can intrigue or stimulate, then I will have contributed." Rishell won over fifty awards and was written up in most standard references and magazines.

Ritchie, Betty Jean. Representational oil painter of the West, born in San Antonio, Texas in 1934 and living in San Marcos, Texas. "I sign my paintings B.J. Ritchie," she points out. "I used to think that if I signed my full name, people wouldn't take me seriously. I was told by a lot of people to let the viewer think I was a male artist and my paintings would sell better, but I don't find that to be the rule. There are a lot of good women artists very serious about their work.

"Art has been the love of my life as far back as I can remember. I worked mostly with pencil and watercolor and at seventeen someone gave me a box of oil paints. I tried these out on an old canvas window shade tacked to my bedroom wall, the only canvas I had. I have had very little formal training but I have tried a lot of different techniques and learned mostly by trial and error and read every bit of material I could get my hands on. If I am working on a painting that I have already laid out and it seems to go in another direction, I don't have any qualms about abandoning my original idea and going with what is happening. I think that's real inspiration.

"I like to read biographies of old cowboys telling about an experience they had. Many times, I get a mental picture of the happening and I will make a quick sketch of my first impression. I get really excited when I see it in my mind's eye. I have learned to recognize the feeling I get and I know when it's going to be a special one and then I can't wait to get started. It seems to fall into place. I don't mean my brushes are magic and I don't have to work at it. I do, but it's just like you are there watching it materialize. I am represented by Morgan and Texas Trails Galleries."

Ritter, Sallie. Painter of the New Mexican landscape and buildings in oil and watercolor, born in Las Cruces, New Mexico in 1947 and still living there. "My daily schedule," she observes, "revolves around my studio. I do not begin to paint until I know exactly what I'm going to do. Sometimes, I may sit quietly until three in the afternoon. I *must* have a visual image. To actually put this image down accurately is a long, long way from *knowing* what I'm going to do.

"I have yet to recall a time when I did not believe that I would be a painter. It was an assumed fact. My formal training ran to the University of Rome in Italy, the Edinburgh College of Art in Scotland, and to a B.A. at the Colorado College in Colorado Springs. I know that I benefited from notes here and there, but I found that I learned more from looking at forms, movements, reflections, than I ever learned in art school. Once convinced that I could see beyond things in their practical functions, the hard work began.

"After I have sorted through stacks of photographs from my source files, I do a series of thumbnail sketches. I then go directly to my white primed masonite panel and free-hand in the drawing with pastel pencil, moving very quickly. Cheap hairspray fixes the first drawing, and I then move in with soft pastels to suggest color patterns. The shadow pattern is also suggested. Another bout of fixative and I begin with oil glazes that will be *underneath* later scumbled areas of opaque paint applied wet-in-wet. Nothing that has been applied will be obliterated completely." She has had eleven one-person shows and is represented by Woodrow Wilson Fine Arts.

Diane O'Leary, THE MEETING, oil, 50 x 40

Robert Rishell, EVENING RAP, oil, 40 x 30

B.J. Ritchie, MISSED BY A MILE, oil, 24 x 36

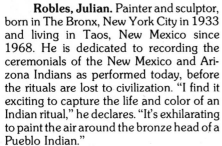

MARJORIE RODGERS

Robles, Julian. Painter and sculptor, born in The Bronx, New York City in 1933 and living in Taos, New Mexico since 1968. He is dedicated to recording the ceremonials of the New Mexico and Arizona Indians as performed today, before the rituals are lost to civilization. "I find it exciting to capture the life and color of an Indian ritual," he declares. "It's exhilarating to paint the air around the bronze head of a Pueblo Indian."

His mother who was an artist recognized his talent by the time he was six. He studied art in high school in Jersey City, New Jersey, and then at Pratt Institute in New York City before serving as a technical illustrator in the U.S. Air Force from 1953 to 1958. Posts in Cheyenne and Amarillo allowed painting trips to New Mexico. He remained in Amarillo to teach and to paint portraits until 1961 when he returned to New York City to work as a commercial artist. He also studied at the Arts Student League and the National Academy of Design until he moved to Taos where he was a founding member of the Taos Six.

At some Indian ceremonials, photography and sketching are not permitted so Robles memorizes the details and he sketches them in his studio where he has a collection of artifacts. To compose the details for a painting, he immerses himself into a recreation of the ritual as if he were a participant. His approach is the same as an actor's in making a role come alive. His canvases glow with light, from the midday sun to oil lamps underground, and his colors are the purple, red, and turquoise Indian costumes. He exhibits at Trailside Galleries and is represented in five collections.

Rodell, Don. Painter of wildlife, born in Alliance, Nebraska in 1932 and living in Sedona, Arizona since 1979. "Wildlife around the world is in big trouble today," he declares. "There are many animals that we know in our time that will never be seen by future generations. Painting them now may be the only way we can preserve them for posterity."

At 26, Rodell decided on art as a career and entered the Chicago Academy of Fine Art. He became an illustrator for magazines and books, discovering an aptitude for painting animals. As his concern about animals developed, he found that "wildlife has become my life. I never want to paint anything else." He moved to Wyoming "to be where the wildlife is," bringing his commercial accounts with him. Paintings he was asked to exhibit as fine art sold readily in a local gallery, but he kept the commercial accounts "until the painting sales matched these in income. Only then did I make the final switch."

Rodell says that the ancient cave paintings of early wildlife are the oldest form of art, but it is only "during the past fifteen years that contemporary wildlife art has come into its own," concurrently with "the increasing threat to many species. Wildlife artists have become dedicated conservationists and have raised millions of dollars for a variety of causes through the donation and sale of their works." Rodell donates to World Wildlife Fund, Ducks Unlimited, Nature Conservancy, and many others. His paintings have been shown in national and international exhibitions and are in public collections. He was featured in *Southwest Art*, August 1981 and is represented by The May Gallery.

Rodgers, Marjorie. Painter of Taos scenes and of California's High Sierras, born in Kansas City, Kansas in 1927 and living in Fresno, California since 1951. She says that "we tend to think that Russell and Remington captured it all a long time ago, but they didn't. There's the 'today' New Mexico to do and the 'today' cowboy and Indian." As a native Kansan, she is enthused that "like Dorothy in the 'Wizard of Oz'," she has come home again to exhibit in a Kansas gallery, "after traveling in the land of Oz, our Southwest."

Her family moved to Los Angeles during the Depression. She studied at the Best Art Foundation School and graduated from Frank Wiggins' School of Art in 1947, with additional fine art courses at California State University and Fresno City College. While she was employed as a commercial artist in Los Angeles, she married and then moved to Fresno where she became an art director. In 1972, she visited New Mexico to see her son who was working as a cowboy and she found what she calls "truly an enchantment in the Southwest. The Indians are independent and cherish their traditions, while the Westerners show a love of the outdoors in their ranch life."

In Taos, she also discovered Whitaker Galleries to represent her and to sell 250 of her paintings over the years. After a study trip to Europe during which paintings were sold in Germany, she returned more Americanized, in the sense that "we have a great country and a great history also." She has since established a studio in New Mexico's Sangre de Cristo Mountains to supplement her studio at the base of California's Sierra Nevadas. Her galleries are Whitaker and In the Spirit.

**Julian Robles, PUEBLO INDIAN DANCER
(1981), pastel, 26 x 19**

Marjorie Rodgers, DANCING AT AZTEC KIVA, oil/canvas, 22 x 28

Don Rodell, ON GUARD, acrylic, 36 x 60

A. Rodriguez ©

Gary Roller

⌃⌃ YAMBRACH
ROSE ©

Rodriguez, Alfredo. Impressionist painter of Navajo, mountain man, and Spanish-American figures, born in Tepic, Nayarit, Mexico in 1954 and living in Corona, California since 1979. "Thank God I am able to paint to live," he says, "and I hope I will continue living to paint. Painting has always been my life. Everything I see, I see from an artist's point of view. Every tree, every rock, everything under the sun, even the food I eat I analyze for the color combinations I would need to paint them.

"In the summer of 1967, my parents spent their savings to take me to the studio of Santiago Rosas, an elderly well-known Mexican artist, who taught me the basic art principles. All of this was in just six hours of lessons. That was all my parents could afford. My home town is surrounded by sierras, behind which lie the Indian reservations. At my first show, I felt a great surge of pride to see the ribbon hanging from my portrait of a Huichol Indian.

"It was not long before I made my first trip to the United States. One of my friends took me to a Navajo reservation. I also had the opportunity to meet some of the contemporary mountain men who still hold to their traditions of the past, and I had found a new subject. I myself am part Indian, but I am not a cowboy, and I do not care to limit myself to just one style. I am an artist who paints Westerns, not a Western artist. I think I paint intuitively—it is a natural state of being. I cannot remember why I did what I did in a particular painting. During my recent trip to Europe, I visited the house in which Rembrandt lived, and this was a tremendous inspiration to me." Rodriguez is published by South West, and represented by Overland Trail Galleries and Taylor's Gallery.

Roller, Gary. Traditional sculptor and painter of Southwestern portraits, particularly Indians and old-time cowboys, born in Amarillo, Texas in 1951 and living in Taos, New Mexico since 1980. A professional "Western swing" musician as well as an artist, he says that when he turns to music, "it has an immediate feedback. You've communicated. I got lonesome in the studio." When he returns to art, he says that "by comparison the music seems superficial. With the band, it is a group statement. Art is my personal statement."

At ten, he was a Kwahadi Indian Dancer and at seventeen he began his professional music career. After a year as an art major in Amarillo College, he left to study with Lincoln Fox near Santa Fe, but then broke away to help form the Pleasant Valley Boys. He quit the band the next year, studied portraiture, and painted portraits professionally. In 1975, he rejoined the band and also painted, remaining with the band until 1978 when he opened a studio in Amarillo to sculpt and paint full time. The next year, he went back to the band.

When he settled in Taos, art came first, and "by day he is Gary Roller, artist, with emphasis on bronze." Taos Arts, though, interviewed local musicians, and the first story was on Roller. "By night, he is a musician, the bass player in the Sagebrush Trio." He says that his "art work is a celebration of the other arts, like music," but that his "main problem has been one of finding the correct balance between music and art." In addition to his Indian and Western themes, he has modeled busts of The Beatles and of Walt Disney because they were inspiring to him. The bronzes are shown at Grycner Gallery and at Shidoni Gallery and Foundry.

Rose, Cheryl Yambrach. Realist painter of oil portraits of northern California loggers, born in Poughkeepsie, New York about 1951 and living in the Siskiyou Mountains of northern California. "When I was in England and Cornwall several years ago," she believes, "a strong feeling swept over me that I had been there before, living in Britain of the sixth century. As a result, I did a number of Celtic paintings. To carry the reincarnation feelings still further, I know that I have found my home and place to work now in the American West. For some reason, there is a correlation for me.'

Raised in California, she started painting in oil at twelve with help from her father who was a naturalist and her aunt who was a portrait painter. After high school, she studied at the Kachina School of Art and traveled abroad before settling in the remote Siskiyous where "the wind is always blowing through the junipers and the howls of my huskies are mingled with the coyotes. These are a special breed, and they are a part of a rapidly disappearing Americana."

Being the wife of a Bluegrass musician and gunsmith, "with a very full life of growing vegetables, feeding and caring for my daughter and all the animals, has helped me to become more deliberate in my work. I don't have time to sit and fuss over it all day. I spend a lot of time thinking out my next moves while I'm doing other chores. I could stop myself during any project during the day and I'll be thinking about art. I have to paint every day. As I finish one painting, I already have the basic idea of the next one worked out in my head." Written up in *Art West*, November 1980, she is represented by Meiners Gallery.

Cheryl Yambrach Rose, THE ARTIST'S FATHER, oil, 16 x 12

Gary Roller, EAGLE SPIRIT DANCER, bronze, h 16, Edition 25

Alfredo Rodriguez, MASTER OF HIS OWN DOMAIN (1982), oil, 22 x 34

449

E. Robert Ross

Paul A Rossi ℞

James R Oybal

Ross, E. Robert. Realist "Koda-chrome" painter of the Ontario wilderness, born in Hamilton, Ontario, Canada in 1950 and living in Victoria, British Columbia since 1982. "I have loved the outdoors for as long as I can remember," he points out, "and I care passionately about man's inhumanity to nature—his willful disturbance of the natural order by flooding the air and water with corroding, often lethal pollutants. I realized long ago that to care is not enough, and I recognized that my own means of 'doing something about it' is in my ability to paint."

Mostly self-taught, his inspiration came from his high school art teacher, Bob Bateman. He studied architecture in Toronto in 1972 but has had no other formal art training, "avoiding the influence of contemporary painters of nature and jealously guarding his individuality through solitary dedication." He is "concerned not to learn more about nature so as to make more commercially valuable paintings, but to learn more about painting so as to be able to say more perfectly and powerfully what he has to say."

He "records the as yet unspoiled areas to bring home not the negative aspect of the problem, but all that is magnificent about the natural wilderness. He aims to inspire, not incriminate." Despite "finely grained and textured detail," he emphasizes that "every mark on the canvas is made with a brush alone." He is "so dedicated to the preservation of the beauty of nature that he painstakingly and lovingly attempts to reproduce each leaf, rock, and crevice, each cloud and ripple, exactly as it is." His first one-man show was in 1977 at the Beckett Gallery which represents him. He is published by Mill Pond Press.

Rossi, Paul A. Painter and sculptor of the horsemen and horse culture of the historical West, born in Denver, Colorado in 1929 and living in Santa Fe, New Mexico. "A special interest in Western horsemen," he says, "their equipment, clothing, mannerisms, and methods of working, has resulted in the miniature bronze series, 'Great Saddles of the West,' a set of twelve."

His grandparents were pioneer ranchers near Leadville, Colorado, where he visited during vacations. From 1946 to 1950, he attended Denver University where he majored in advertising design, won letters in four sports, and during the summers worked on cattle ranches and followed the wheat harvest from Texas to Canada. After serving in the U.S. Air Force during the Korean War, he worked at the Colorado State Historical Society until 1956 when he opened a commercial art studio. From 1959 to 1961, he was an illustrator for Martin Aircraft Co., and then spent the next twelve years at the Gilcrease Institute in Tulsa, Oklahoma. "To show history through the eyes of the artists," he was co-author of *The Art of the Old West* in 1971 and resigned from the Gilcrease in 1972 to devote full time to art.

Rossi specializes in "frontier military history, the cattle industry, fur trade era, Plains Indians, and natural history of the West, working in all media, sculpting, painting, drawing, etc." His work has been featured in *Quarter Horse Journal*, *American Artist*, and *Persimmon Hill*. He has illustrated books, written articles, consulted, lectured, appraised, and acted as juror at exhibitions. He is represented by his own Canyonland Graphics.

Roybal, James. Sculptor of Old Western figures in bronze, born in Santa Fe, New Mexico in 1952 and still living there in 1982. "I grew up right in the center of Western art," he indicates, "but you can bring new life to anything. It's the way that you carry it off. A lot of sculptors get wrapped up in details. I think that since we're not God or nature we can't duplicate every muscle and hair and eye, so we should exaggerate the forms that people recognize, and the finished piece should be appealing from all angles.

"I grew up in Jaconita, a small village a few miles north of Santa Fe, where I was nicknamed "the Inventor" because I was forever building mechanical things from found objects. In the seventh grade I got my first taste of casting jewelry and bronze from a local sculptor, and had my first juried show in 1971. I attended Highlands University on a scholarship, finished my education at New Mexico State University after winning an art scholarship there, and studied under the artist Ernest Berke in 1975. I had gone to college thinking I would be an architect, but when I found out how many houses were being designed by contractors, I changed my mind.

"I have worked with a number of art foundries, casting my own work and other artists' bronzes for six years. On my sculpture, I do it all, from the concept to the making of the rubber mold, wax copy, ceramic shell mold, pouring the bronze, metal finishing, patinaing (color finish), to the walnut base." He feels that his experience designing silver jewelry when he was a teenager has helped him. He has exhibited and judged sculpture at the Santa Fe Festival of the Arts and his work is displayed at Signature Galleries.

Paul A. Rossi, ON THE WIND OF AN EAGLE'S CRY (1976)
oil/canvas, 30 x 24

James Roybal, EAGLEBONE WHISTLE, bronze, h17, w12, Edition 20

E. Robert Ross, RIVER RAPIDS, acrylic, 32 x 24

451

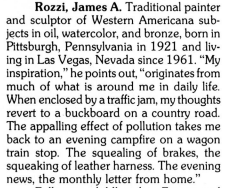

Rozzi, James A. Traditional painter and sculptor of Western Americana subjects in oil, watercolor, and bronze, born in Pittsburgh, Pennsylvania in 1921 and living in Las Vegas, Nevada since 1961. "My inspiration," he points out, "originates from much of what is around me in daily life. When enclosed by a traffic jam, my thoughts revert to a buckboard on a country road. The appalling effect of pollution takes me back to an evening campfire on a wagon train stop. The squealing of brakes, the squeaking of leather harness. The evening news, the monthly letter from home."

Following childhood in France and Italy and then New York City where he sketched the Old Masters in the Metropolitan Museum of Art, his teen years were spent in Utah. In World War II, he was a training aid artist and learned silkscreening. Despite his lack of an art education, he taught at San Bernadino Valley College in California from 1949 to 1960 and then after he moved to Nevada, at the Art League.

"I will not depict violence," he declares. "I paint for the family living room. I create the drama, romance, and industry of the West. The development of the West through transportation is of special interest to me. The idea of transversing these great open spaces intrigues me." For almost thirty years, he has also designed the custom roulette wheels, Big Six tables, and other gambling equipment for the casinos, and that has limited his art production so that "invariably I wind up showing already sold pieces. I have a collectors list that has prevented me from putting on a one-man show." Listed in *Who's Who in American Art*, Rozzi was written up in *Art West*, fall 1978 and is represented by Newsom's Gallery.

Ruehle, Jon. Traditional sculptor of North American wildlife in bronze, born in Oakland, California in 1949 and living in Sebastopol, California. "Not unlike the ritual magic of primitive hunters," he points out, "I need to establish a bond to the animal I'm attempting to capture. I begin to sense something of what it feels like to have that animal's unique shape and habits, to move like it does and to have the personality traits it needs to live the life it does.

"I attended the University of California at Berkeley on a scholarship as a pre-med student majoring in anthropology, but after four years I began migrating back to my early loves of art and nature. Moving to the Sierra Nevadas, I then backpacked down the Andean Coast of South America for six months, took printmaking classes at Cal and bronze casting classes at the De Young Museum in San Francisco. On the advice of an instructor, I went to work at a foundry and was soon casting a few of my own pieces.

"I like to focus the piece around some internal tension in the muscles and bones that culminates in the facial expression. Whether twisting to reach an obscure itch or straining to catch a faint ribbon of scent, the piece must work to convey the body language. Often this means avoiding violent or overly dramatic poses. I find that an animal about to spring conveys much more power and energy than one suspended in mid leap. I once had a collector tell me that my sculpture shows these animals as they might portray themselves, rather than how we choose to view them." He is a member of the Society of Animal Artists, has exhibited at the National Academy of Design, and currently shows at the Maxwell and Sporting Galleries.

Rule, Gallagher. Traditional sculptor of portraits in bronze, born in Oklahoma City in 1930 and living in Ponca City, Oklahoma. "There's always a moment of apprehension when the person sees himself. It's almost as if he's afraid some secret has been exposed he doesn't want shown. But you have to remember that you sculpt for the person who commissioned it rather than for the person himself."

Named after his father's wrestling coach, Rule went to school in Oklahoma City, Guthrie, and Newkirk before lying about his age to join the Marines at sixteen. While reaching the rank of major, he "discovered a talent for three-dimensional control. I'd had no prior sculpting experience although I'd taken some correspondence courses in commercial art." When he was in the hospital, he did "seventeen portraits as working exercises." After the war, he earned Bachelor of Philosophy and Bachelor of Science degrees and studied engineering, was employed in Switzerland and Spain for eight years, spoke five languages, and operated a large cattle spread near Newkirk.

At that point, he asked himself, "Who am I? A cattleman? An engineer with a hobby, or was I a portrait sculptor who had a hobby of engineering or cattle. If the latter, I should orient my life around the primary interest for happiness." He didn't sell a piece for two years, but then in 1971 and early 1972, he attained technical proficiency and confidence. In modeling portraits, he says, "likeness is no problem, and frankly, I believe there's an overemphasis on live sittings. I have to have some conviction about the person himself, and you can't acquire that in just a sitting. I like to have four to six months to complete a portrait, longer if necessary." Rule is represented by Troy's Gallery.

Gallagher Rule, JOHN WAYNE, bronze, h 17, Edition 50

Jon Ruehle, JUST LONG ENOUGH (1982), bronze, h 10, w 6, d 10

Jim Rozzi, THE HITCHHIKERS, oil, 24 x 36

Rumohr, Lois. Sculptor of bronze statuettes of figures, particularly the Western Apache of Whiteriver, Arizona, born in Bakersfield, California in 1922 and living in Arcadia, California. "When I tell my clients that I make most of my molds," she declares, "they usually look at me in puzzlement and then ask the question, 'How can such a small person lift such huge heavy molds?' My answer is always, 'With great difficulty!' What a person lacks in size is made up for in determination."

Of Spanish, Indian, Irish and Scotch descent, she began drawing as a child. After taking basic art courses in school and one year at the Art Center College of Design in Los Angeles, she studied for seven years with the sculptor Ralph Rathbone Preston. She also studied anatomy and learned mold making, casting, and patina application. "For twelve years," she points out, "I have been making trips to the Indian pueblos and reservations for photographing and sketching.

"One question that I await with trepidation is, 'How do you get it from the wax into the bronze? Is it dipped in bronze?' or I'll be asked if I carve directly in bronze! Considering the complexity of the process, I don't wonder that such questions are asked. For this reason, I will show a small sample mold or a hollow invested wax. I look forward to gallery receptions and meeting the people. This is because I am essentially a 'people' person, whereas my work is solitary in nature." A member of Women Artists of the American West, she has won awards since 1976 and participates in invitational shows. She exhibits at Thor's Royal Danish Restaurant and Gallery and at Sanders Galleries.

Ryan, Tom. Traditional oil painter and printmaker of contemporary Western ranch life, born in Springfield, Illinois in 1922 and living in Stamford, Texas since 1973. "An interest in Western history, the ability to draw and paint well, and an outdoor urge for nature's handiwork and the rugged life, led me on sketching trips in the 1950s to an area in West Texas that was the hunting grounds of the buffalo hunters. I have been painting and enjoying that area since then."

Although he had been drawing cowboys and Indians since grade school, Ryan had not chosen a career by the time he graduated from junior college. After he returned to Illinois following World War II service with the Coast Guard in the Pacific, just seeing N.C. Wyeth illustrations "ignited a feeling in me that burns today. With the magazine in hand, I made the decision to become a painter." While waiting for admission to the American Academy of Art in Chicago, he worked as an advertising artist, then studied at the Art Students League in New York City.

Between 1954 and 1962, Ryan painted nearly 300 book covers. The proceeds let him travel to the Southwest, and Ryan "found the contemporary cowboy and his work to my liking." As part of a 1963 commission, he went to the colt branding at the 6666 Ranch in Texas, and in 1967 he moved to Lubbock, close to the cow country. Ryan was an early member of the Cowboy Artists of America and won the Best in Oil award in 1968 with a painting that was reproduced as a Marlboro cigarette ad. He was written up in *Southwest Art*, September 1976, is published by Salt Creek Graphics, and is represented by Grand Central Art Galleries of New York City.

Lois Rumohr, SHY MAID OF SHIPOLOVI, bronze, h 16, w 15

Tom Ryan, SPLIT DECISION, oil, 24 x 30

 Sabo

Sherry Sander

T. Sander

Sabo, Betty. Realist oil painter of the disappearing way of New Mexican life, born in Kansas City, Missouri in 1928 and "grew up" in Albuquerque, New Mexico. "I know some artists isolate themselves," she says, "but I think a woman artist's studio should be in her home. The woman artist with a family has to get up, straighten the house, prepare the meals—and only then can she begin to paint. A man artist may get up, have breakfast, and go directly to his easel. A woman artist must have great discipline."

After majoring in art at the University of New Mexico, she studied with Carl von Hassler for five years. "I finish my paintings in my studio from detailed sketches, notes, and photographs made on location," she explains. "In any of the seasons, all I have to do is take an hour's drive in any direction and I can find a dozen subjects. I particularly enjoy recording the old adobes nestled in the snow. The warmth of the buildings and the underbrush against the cold colors of the snow are a perfect blend.

"Though a constant source of pleasure," she adds, "painting is a consuming, exhausting business, and after a period of steady working, there must be a time to refill the well. I close my studio door and forget all about painting. I never force it because I know there is nothing there. Then one day something will trigger an idea and in a minute I'm full of ideas for new paintings." She has been featured in *New Mexico Magazine*, September 1973, and in *Southwest Art*, December 1977, is listed in *Who's Who in American Art*, and has exhibited nationally including shows at the National Academy of Design and the National Arts Club. She is represented by Galeria Del Sol.

Sander, Sherry. Sculptor of bronze statuettes of animals, born in McCloud, California in 1941 and living in Kalispell, Montana. "Bronze in itself," she points out, "is a cold and heavy element. It is a contest to work with this physical material, portraying warmth and a feeling of movement or mobility. The fun is in pushing a subject as far as possible for dramatic effect, but still making that movement believable."

She has attended colleges in Oregon, California, and Montana. Married to the wildlife painter and sculptor Tom Sander, she moved to Wyoming with her family in 1963 and has lived in the Rocky Mountain area since then. She shares field trips with her husband, including a flight into northern Canada with a bush pilot who "knew a lake where the grizzly bear was invented." In addition to Canada, she has studied animals in the wilderness of Alaska, the Yukon, and the Northwest, and recently went to Africa.

"I mostly work with animals as a subject," she emphasizes. "I feel the artistic possibilities they offer are endless. The simple animated gesture studies are an absolute necessity, furthering the understanding of the animals' nature and anatomy. They are also the most exciting for me to portray" and to characterize them in bronze. In addition, she trains and shows thoroughbred horses as hunter-jumpers, and has modeled leaping horses as well as wildlife. A member of the Society of Animal Artists, she received an award of merit in 1979 and won the Best Three-Dimensional Award in Kalispell in 1980. She was invited to the Cowboy Hall of Fame Wildlife Show in 1979, had a one-person show at the C.M. Russell Museum and is represented by Trailside Galleries and the Sportsman's Edge.

Sander, Tom. Traditional wildlife painter in oil and watercolor, and sculptor, born in Bellingham, Washington in 1938 and living in Kalispell, Montana. After staying at a lake "where the grizzly bear was invented, we left with a better understanding. Not just what their anatomical layout was, but what they were, out in their own world. It's funny, but when you're working on a painting of an animal you've spent time with, things will come out in your work that you might not be aware of until you see it happening in the paint or clay.

"Raised in southern Oregon, I graduated from the University of Oregon and have worked in the outdoors all my life. Jobs as taxidermist and guide have been helpful because most of my painting and sculpting concentrates on animals and people of the outdoors. A major part of my year is still spent outdoors, and my travels have taken me from Alaska and the Yukon to the tip of South Africa. My work is in the C.M. Russell Museum, American Wildlife Foundation, and the Cincinnati Museum of Natural Science, and I am a member of the Society of Animal Artists.

"If I had one painting left to do, I would choose Canadian geese on a snowy day. Big-horn sheep—I've always had an affection for those, too. But if I had just one left, I'd do my sled dog team. I own some great animals and to do them justice would give me the most satisfaction. If sled dog drivers thought it said something about the sport or showed some insight not gained cheaply, I would feel it was successful." Featured in *Art West*, winter 1978, Sander is published by Salt Creek Graphics and is represented by Sportsman's Edge and by Settlers West Galleries where his oil painting had a minimum bid of $3,800 in the 1981 silent auction.

Sherry Sander, OTIS, bronze, h 14, w 12, d 9

Betty Sabo, LAS TRAMPAS, oil, 24 x 36

Tom Sander, WILD TURKEY, oil, 24 x 36

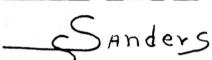

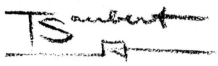

Jim
Savage

Sanders, Gerald L. Traditional sculptor of Old West figures and wildlife in bronze statuettes, born in Krum, Texas about 1924 and living in Pampa, Texas. "I get a lot of my ideas from my ranch and rodeo days," he explains. "I get lost in my work. I do my best creating after midnight when things quiet down. I just don't consider myself a real artist. I have a God-given talent, and I have decided to put it to work. To me, a true artist is one who came up the hard way by spending all of his life on his work.

"As a kid, I grew up around the stockyards on the north side of Fort Worth, Texas. I left home at an early age, living on a ranch around Denton, and riding for 'mount money' in a small rodeo. Art has always been a part of me. As a boy, I would make woodcarvings. I was working on a ranch when Uncle Sam called me to serve in World War II. After the war in 1946, I went to work as a lineman for Bell Telephone Company. As part-time work, I made custom gunstocks and went into taxidermy, searching for something.

"One day as I was making a knife handle out of stag, I decided I would do some carving in the horn. I ended up with fifteen carvings. In 1976, the Panhandle artist Kenneth Wyatt saw them and encouraged me to do bronze sculpture. I didn't even know where to start, but he said, 'If you can carve wood and horn, you can carve wax. At least, you can stick your mistakes back on.' So I got a block of wax and literally punched it out. In 1977, I sold my first piece, and have been doing pretty good ever since, for a country boy. I retired in 1981 so I could devote more time to my artwork. I consider myself one of the lucky ones." Sanders exhibits with the Texas Cowboy Artists Association.

Saubert, Tom. Realist painter and sculptor of contemporary and historical Northwestern people and wildlife, born in Missoula, Montana in 1950 and living in Kalispell, Montana since 1973. "I want to leave behind something that will say that Montana was here," Saubert emphasizes, "not necessarily that Tom Saubert was here. Everything I do is based on this relationship with the life around me. I would like to give back as much love as I am capable of. I feel blessed to be able to give it back through my art."

Raised in Billings where his father was a sportsman, Saubert attended Eastern Montana College for two years, then graduated from the Cleveland Institute of Art in 1973. "Any form of realism was considered mundane by my modernist influenced peers," he observes, but though he studied design and illustration, he turned down commercial art offers from New York to California in order to return to Montana. Self-styled "terrible" at promoting his own career, his first years were "a long, slow, tedious process" at getting exposure. He "didn't use a colored medium" until 1978, but by the end of 1981 he had a two-year backlog of commissions to fill.

When he paints, "music sets the mood" as he selects from country, jazz, and classical records. The models for his portraits are likely to be people he has met at ranches, at the auction yard, or in the grocery store where he appears with sketchbook and camera. He says his art is drawn from the "interaction" between the subject and him, and "love always comes into it." Saubert was featured in *Art West*, September 1981 and is represented by Ponderosa and Sanders Galleries.

Savage, Jim. Sculptor and painter of Western figures and Indian portraits in wood, born on a farm near Sioux Falls, South Dakota in 1932 and still living there. During 25 years as a carpenter and foreman of a construction crew, his hobby was collecting antique tools. When he acquired a hundred-year-old woodcarving set in 1967, he tried modeling some small pieces of wood including "a goofy little witch's face as a joke" on his wife. She displayed the carvings in her home until she ran out of space, then took them to a Sioux Falls gallery where they were accepted and sold. The first piece to go was the witch's face.

In the initial exhibition he entered, he won Best of Show, and at the National Woodcarvers Convention he won first place. In 1975, he was awarded the gold medal for sculpture at the Phippen Memorial Outdoor Show, after saying that "there were 33 bronze sculptures and mine was the only wood. I didn't think I had a chance." At that point, he decided to make carvings his full-time vocation.

To get color in his carvings, he rejected the idea of polychroming in favor of the "natural look" resulting from inlays of different kinds and colors of wood. He uses as many as sixteen varieties in a single sculpture that may be composed of 2,200 separate pieces of wood. He says that how to put wood together is almost as important as the carving because it's necessary to know about shrinkages. For this reason, he prefers hardwoods. When he became a professional carver, he had to begin serious research on the history and characters of the early West, and to acquire memorabilia to go along with antique tools that have long since been replaced by more effective tools. His "Grabbin' Leather" is in the collection of the Favell Museum, which represents him as does Kern Collectibles.

Tom Saubert, BY FIRELIGHT, watercolor, 20 x 22

G.L. Sanders, PRICE OF A FEATHER, bronze, h 15

Jim Savage, FANCY DANCER, black walnut with inlayed maple
butternut, honduras mahogany, ironwood, h 17

Savitt, Sam. Representational painter of horses and horse-related subjects in oil and other media, born in Wilkes-Barre, Pennsylvania, and living in North Salem, New York. "This racetrack," he claims, "could be anywhere. What was important was the threatening sky and the horses running hard as if to reach home before the storm broke. The chestnut is rapidly moving up on the outside. I know he will win this race. In three more strides, he will overtake the leader. The finish line is just ahead and he'll cross it five lengths in front."

After graduating from Pratt Institute in Brooklyn, he traveled and worked as a ranch hand throughout the West and then served four and a half years in the Army. He continued his studies at the Art Students League after the war and also studied drawing, painting, and sculpture privately. Horsemanship was learned from the equestrian teacher Gordon Wright. Savitt has been lecturing on horses in art since 1955 and has declared that "the horse is beauty, strength, rhythm, and action. To really know and understand him, to capture his magnificence with pencil or brush, will to me be forever challenging."

Official artist for the U.S. Equestrian Team since 1960, he has covered all horse breeds in every area of activity—polo, racing, steeplechasing, fox hunting, rodeoing, and horse show jumping. The *Sam Savitt Horse Charts* were published beginning in 1963, and he has written fourteen books and illustrated more than 100, in addition to his illustrations for national magazines. A member of the Society of Illustrators, he is listed in *Who's Who in American Art*, has exhibited with Arthur Ackermann & Son, and is published by Mill Pond Press.

Saylor, Steven. Photo-realist portrait painter in glazed miniature watercolors, born in Munich, Germany in 1948 and living in Dayton, Nevada. "My studio is near my home," he says, "in a renovated 1868 wooden boxcar. I heat the studio with wood which I cut on weekends. I paint with a northwest light, standing at my drawing table. The work lies flat. I put in a five day week, plus a day for riding and family, a day for chores."

Saylor's parents moved to Reno, Nevada, where he started school. The family also lived in Alaska when he was twelve and in Gettysburg, Pennsylvania, where he attended high school. He received a Master's degree in art from Kent State University in 1971 and was employed as an art director in Ohio and Nevada. After he began to paint full time, he discovered the technique of glazed watercolors that is similar to the glazed oils of the famous Maxfield Parrish at the turn of the century. "Glazed watercolor is a delicate building up of transparent colors with varnish between each color," he explains, "thus providing optical mixing of colors and transmitted light." Each painting may take weeks, the result of meticulous work and the application of 200 layers.

"Half of my work is commissioned," he declares. "For the rest I use the people and environment of my own area. I have projects eighteen months ahead and mull them over with doodles, drawings, and discussion. Each evening I take my current painting home and I study it. This way I can better attack the areas in the morning." Saylor is a member of the Society of Illustrators and is represented by Husberg Fine Arts Gallery.

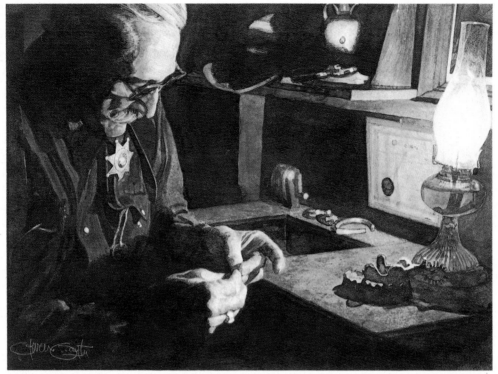

Steven Saylor, LAST OF THE CONSTABLES—ROCKY ADAMSON, glazed watercolor, 17 x 25

Sam Savitt, LAST RACE OF THE DAY, oil, 27 x 36

Schaare, Harry. Representational painter of the Civil War and the post Civil War era, born in Jamaica, Long Island in 1922 and living in Westbury, Long Island. "My objective," he points out, "is to capture the drama in the lives of those who shaped the Old West. My focus spotlights crucial situations in which split-second decisions, sound judgment, and decisive action were vital to the survival of early pioneers and settlers who braved the challenges of the harsh Western land."

In 1940, he attended the New York University School of Architecture and then transferred to Pratt Institute in Brooklyn, New York, to study illustration. After serving as a European Theater pilot in World War II, he returned to Pratt where he graduated in 1947. He was briefly employed in commercial art studios, then became a free lance commercial artist. By 1951, he was painting paperback covers including Westerns where the original art was not returned to him and he was "sure the originals were sold in Mexico or Europe" for more than the $350 he got.

In 1953, he broke the ranks of the *Saturday Evening Post* illustrators. He has also painted for *Reader's Digest*, has created posters and billboards for MGM, RKO, and other studios, has illustrated books for many of the New York City publishers, and has illustrated for advertising campaigns. A member of the Society of Illustrators since 1960, he has pursued a career in fine art, too. He says that "it's a kind of natural progression from a field in which next to impossible deadlines become daily routine" to explain the emphasis in his paintings on men "caught in the midst of trouble" during the late 1800s in the West. Schaare is represented by El Prado Gallery of Art.

Schelling, George Luther. "Semi-historical realist" oil painter of the American West, born in Worcester, Massachusetts in 1938 and living in Laceyville, Pennsylvania since 1967. "The Western paintings that I am working on," he observes, "I call semi-historical: the events happened but I do not want to put an actual date on them. An Apache raid on a wagon train must not be a specific one. Conflict in this case would be the essence of the picture. I seek *adventure* in my painting!

"Led a very normal childhood; only interest was in drawing and painting. In high school, took a correspondence course in commercial art from Art Instruction, the only training I have had in art. From 1956 to 1960, I worked for advertising agencies. From 1960-1980, full time free-lance illustrator and painter. Illustrator: 90% for magazines. Painter: mostly wildlife in natural habitat for galleries. I have had thirteen solo shows. I developed a reputation as a marine-wildlife artist because I did so many paintings and illustrations of the creatures of the oceans and rivers.

"Contemporary: Commercial art is over for me. I live in the wilderness. Art is still my only interest. The adventurous side of the West. The exciting and melodramatic. Although much of the past work you will see in my brochures and magazines is aquatic-oriented, the Western field is the field I desire to pursue. Doing the marine-wildlife was a wonderful and rewarding period in my life; however, it is time to crawl back on the land, dry out, and evolve into the American West." Written up in *The Conservationist* and *The Illustrator* and a member of the Society of Animal Artists and the Society of Illustrators, Schelling is represented by Husberg Fine Arts Gallery.

Schenck, Bill. Photo-realist oil painter of contemporary "Pop" Western figures, born in rural Ohio in 1947 and living in Mesa, Arizona since 1975. "While an art student, I worked for Andy Warhol. Everything he was doing had a tremendous impact on me. Not just his art, but the entire mystique that he built around himself fascinated me. I thought that changing my birthplace every year was going to lead to a profound mystique for myself. The only problem with this is that no one has taken notice yet."

He attended the Columbus College of Art and Design but left in 1967. Already using photographic references, he graduated from the Kansas City Art Institute in 1969. In New York City, in 1971, his first solo show of photo-realist cowboy subjects sold out, but the 1974 recession soured him on the East where he had to use movie stills for his cowboy images. After trying Wyoming, he moved to Arizona where he "was offered a show, so I came."

The Scottsdale gallery "hadn't sold a penny's worth of my work," but he survived by selling "very slowly, a very small inheritance of stock." In 1977, there was an opening for a solo show at Elaine Horwitch Galleries, and he "said, 'Elaine, give me that slot,' so she did, and we began to sell paintings." He claims to have invented a paint-by-numbers system where he "does the original drawing from the projected slide." He numbers each section of the drawing, mixes paints in pails and numbers the pails, and then assistants brush the paints on the drawings to match the numbers. "I retain absolute control of what appears in these canvases," he says. Written up in *Southwest Art*, August 1979, and *Arizona Arts*, autumn 1981, he is represented by Elaine Horwitch Galleries and Main Trail Galleries.

George L. Schelling, BOUNTY HUNTER, oil, 27 x 39

Bill Schenck, BLUE MIST CAFE, oil/canvas, 54 x 60

Harry Schaare, A.W.O.L., oil, 24 x 36

Schildt, Gary. Impressionist painter and sculptor of Western figures, particularly Indians and children, born in Helena, Montana in 1938 and living in Kalispell, Montana. "I kind of build up to a high to go to work," he observes, "and I have to do that with painting a lot more than I do in sculpture. Sculpture is just a real enjoyment physically, but painting is not physical enjoyment and just about anything can distract me. It's all mental, but once I get going I'm okay. Then, after I'm totally into it, hardly anything will be distracting."

Eleven - thirty - seconds Blackfoot, Schildt grew up on his family's ranch on the Reservation near Browning. As a youth, he evidenced a talent that was sharpened when he studied commercial art and photography at the City College of San Francisco. After he returned to Browning, he painted a "Reservation Series," moved to Great Falls where he did a "Western Series," then settled in the Flathead Valley. His approach to art is to look for "holes," the subjects that other artists avoid or find uninteresting.

He refuses to be labeled a "Western" or an "Indian" artist. "Unless it's a union that's kind of like the nose on your face, I feel strongly that an artist has a commitment to himself to remain independent in what he does. One of my problems is that I haven't settled down to one subject, but it's been my greatest asset, too. I haven't painted myself into a corner." He also objects to "the prevailing trend toward the slaughtering of living artists in the big business of art auctions." Schildt was written up in *Art West*, winter 1977, is a member of the Northwest Rendezvous Group, and is represented by Western Art Investment.

Schilling, Richard. Representational watercolorist of wildlife, particularly waterfowl in their natural habitat, born in Lincoln, Nebraska in 1933 and living in Loveland, Colorado since 1960. "The question asked me most frequently," he observes, "is 'why don't you give up dentistry and paint pictures?' I sometimes think this question might imply that if you are dead serious about a vocation, you should spend 100 percent of your efforts in its pursuit, although strangely enough, no one has ever asked 'why don't you just give up painting and spend your time practicing dentistry?' "

At thirteen, his first painting was accepted into a juried exhibition. He graduated from the University of Nebraska, with BS and DDS degrees, worked for the Public Health Service, and began painting in watercolor when he set up his private practice in 1960. In addition to evenings and weekends, he keeps Mondays free to paint but says that "in my mind, dentistry is one of the highest forms of art. The ability to prosthetically restore a mouth to natural beauty and functional harmony without suggesting to the observer that the result was accomplished by artificial means, is a true test of artistic accomplishment. I am using my God-given creative, and artistic ability in my practice of dentistry.

"I can only allocate part of each week to painting. And yet, I am 100 percent serious about my painting. For me, the actual process of painting a watercolor requires a very special moment. The creative spirit must be flowing to produce an exciting result. In recent years, my interests have also included the carving of wild birds in bass wood." Written up in *Southwest Art,* March 1980, Schilling is represented by American West Galleries.

Schimmel, William B., Jr. Representational oil painter of the Southwestern landscape, born in Tucson, Arizona in 1954 and living in Phoenix. "I am a representational landscape painter," he notes. "I paint the world around me as I see it. My subject matter consists mainly of the southwestern United States, particularly the deserts of Arizona. One of the saddest things for me to see is the tremendous amount of growth that is destroying what is left of our beautiful desert areas. This devastation has given new meaning and importance to the landscape painter.

"Having lived in Phoenix all my life, I've come to know the desert in an intimate way. I did not grow up drawing all the time. My Dad never pushed me. It wasn't until I was 19 that I decided I wanted to paint. I attended Arizona State University for two years and learned absolutely nothing except what I did on my own. I studied with my father from 1975 to 1977. His concise and practical teaching methods made it so much easier, and I began teaching with him.

"I learned to paint in watercolor and switched to oils later. I work mainly from photographs I take on location in the desert or perhaps the Grand Canyon. In the studio, I will work from three, seven, or a dozen photos, using them as reference only. I usually start with a light charcoal sketch, not detailed, to block in the major elements. Then I begin painting, sky first, distance second, foreground last, top to bottom, light to dark. I enjoy depicting the immense cloud formations, rugged mountains, intimate deserts, and lush forests. I believe in the necessity of art, and I believe in a world full of beauty." "Schim" is represented by Troy's Cowboy Art Gallery.

Gary Schildt, BLUE SATIN DRESS, oil
30 x 15

William B. Schimmel, ON THE BRINK OF A MIRACLE, oil, 20 x 30

Richard Schilling, POOL AT ACOMA, watercolor, 13 x 18

Schmidt, Dennis. Representational painter of a variety of Western subjects in acrylic, born in Victoria, Texas in 1950 and still living there. "If you're painting to please others," he emphasizes, "it's easy to burn out. If an artist is only motivated by the desire for financial success, it's the same thing. It becomes just another form of exploitation. Some artists, however, are in the fortunate position of being able to make a good living doing just exactly what they want to do, motivated by the things they truly love and enjoy."

A self-educated artist who enjoyed drawing as a child, he started out as an art welder. He began painting in 1972 as a means of self-expression and soon received attention for his portraits. When he "went full time in 1977," he discontinued portraits in favor of landscapes, wildlife, and Western "action scenes." The following year, he was given the first one-man show held at The Texas Ranger Hall of Fame, and in 1979 he won the Popular Painting Award at the Hall.

In 1979, he also started publishing his limited edition prints, saying that "my wife and I maintain complete control over subject matter, quantity, papers used, and overall quality. At least one of us is always present when the prints are actually run and for many proofings. Aside from quality, we also realize considerably higher profits, so this works best all around for us. The prints are distributed by Frost Fine Art Co. To me, Western art doesn't have to include a cowboy, a horse, an Indian, or cattle. It just has to project the spirit that emanates from this powerful, incredible part of the world. Most of the originals are sold by my wife and me and by The Texas Ranger Hall of Fame."

Schmidt, Jay. Realist oil painter of Western people, particularly Navajo Indians and cowboys, born in Wichita, Kansas in 1929 and living in Cottonwood, Arizona since 1979. "I am essentially an entertainer," he stresses. "The artist does not have to perform in public, but he does have to entertain an audience. He must 'hold' the audience every bit as much as does the singer or actor. Boredom is a crime too often perpetrated in the galleries of our land.

"My drawing started in kindergarten, oil painting began in the eighth grade, and in 1947 I won one of the two yearly scholarships offered by the California School of Fine Arts in San Francisco. My BA came from Bob Jones University and I spent seventeen years in the Baptist ministry, ending in ill health. I returned to painting in 1968, studying with Ralph Love. I also operated California art galleries until 1975 when I devoted myself full time to painting, influenced by my son Tim's interest in Western art. My two sons, two daughters, and son-in-law are all professional artists in the Western scene.

"I have swung to painting people exclusively. First, I have become enamored of the Navajo people. Second, I have come to admire and almost envy the rugged working cowboys of our time. My third reason is that people are the ultimate subject. I started in landscape and seascape, went on to animals, horses, cows, roundups, but now I'm zeroing in on the figures. I am after something very elusive, very difficult to define." Schmidt is a member of the Society of Western Artists, won second place in oils at the Phippen Memorial inside show in 1981, is reproduced by Scafa Tornabene, and is represented by Overland Trails and Lido Gallery.

Jay W. Schmidt, NAVAJO YEARS, oil, 20 x 30

Dennis Schmidt, COMING IN, opaque watercolor, 15½ x 22

Scholder, Fritz William, V. Painter of "the Indian real not red," born in Breckenridge, Minnesota, in 1937 and living in Scottsdale, Arizona. "The whole subject of the American Indian is loaded, of course," he says. "I hadn't realized it when I started the Indian series, but I touched on nerves and immediately became controversial. This was a surprise to me because the painting is not that far out."

His father, the administrator of an Indian school, was of California Mission Indian, German, and French descent. His mother's ancestors were English and Irish. That makes Scholder one quarter Indian, but he grew up in a white culture and has never thought of himself as Indian. In high school in Pierre, South Dakota, he studied with the Sioux, Oscar Howe, who was influenced by Cubism. After graduation from Sacramento City College, he "was literally starving. I really didn't know where the rent was coming from. So then there was a Rockefeller project that started in Tucson and I was contacted because I was part Indian. So that was how I discovered the Southwest." He received his Master's degree from Arizona State University and became an instructor at the Institute of American Indian Arts in Santa Fe in 1964.

He still had not yet painted an Indian by 1967, but he decided to try. "Most people," he declares, "think of the Indian as the Plains Indian with feather headdress and all that jazz. Well that was such a small part of the Indian. Most minorities want to be accepted in the mainstream. The Indian has never wanted it. If anything, he just wants to be left alone." Scholder became a full-time painter in 1969. He has been featured in most art periodicals and was given a retrospective in 1981. He is represented by ACA Galleries and Marilyn Butler Fine Art.

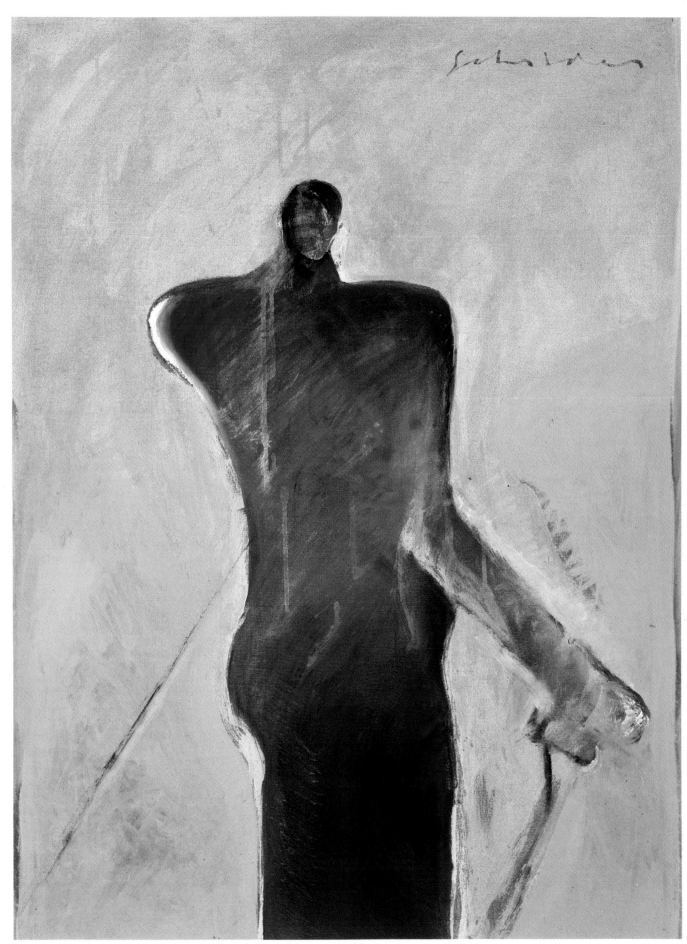

Fritz Scholder, AMERICAN PORTRAIT #25 (1981), oil/canvas, 40 x 30

Schwiering, Conrad. Mood painter of the Tetons, born in Boulder, Colorado in 1916 and living in Jackson, Wyoming since 1947. "Maybe I've painted the Tetons a thousand times, maybe two thousand. It's been a lifetime. You have to live with these mountains every day to know their moods. They're always changing, every hour, every day, every season, every year. No, I never grow tired of the mountains. I think of them as my good friends.

"When I was seven I started drawing horses," Schwiering remembers, but his father suggested studying business at the University of Wyoming. Summers were given to art classes in Denver, Laramie, and Taos. After he graduated, he decided to paint full time and attended the Art Students League in New York City. In 1941, he returned to Laramie, served in World War II, and then moved to Jackson to paint the mountains. "We sold two paintings that first year," Schwiering recalls, "one for $35 and another for $40. Beans were scarce. It took us thirteen years to acquire land and build our home and my studio."

Schwiering asserts that "many people have called me an Impressionist painter. If Impressionism is the study of sunlight, then I am an Impressionist. But rather than an Impressionist, I consider myself a mood painter. Painting is not an intellectual matter. Now, the technical knowledge has to be there, but art is a gut process, and there is no substitute for sweat." Schwiering was in the 1981 exhibition in China, has been featured in *Persimmon Hill* and in *Southwest Art,* is listed in *Who's Who in American Art,* was the subject of a television documentary, is a charter member of the National Academy of Western Art, and is in major public collections. He is represented by Trailside Galleries.

Schwindt, David. Western landscape painter in oil and acrylic, born in Aurora, Illinois in 1947 and living in Albuquerque, New Mexico since 1973. "We traveled a lot when I was growing up in western Colorado," he points out. "As soon as I was old enough to drive, I was helping my father haul horses to shows. We watched the land speed by at all times of day or night. I believe it was those experiences that contributed more than anything to my landscape painting today."

Son of a Methodist minister, Schwindt entered Colorado State University in 1965 as an engineering major "with art as an elective and found himself in the Commercial Art School instead." The following year, he studied fine art at the University of New Mexico, then transferred to Fort Lewis College where he graduated in 1971. He continued to study privately while holding a full time job as a sign painter. As an artist, "my total experience with color and light seemed to be tied with the landscape," he observes. "People were incidental. It was always the landscape that prevailed.

"There is no particular mystery in the way a landscape is painted when one understands the visual language for recording what one sees, yet one must feel something of what he sees as well. The Western attitude toward space was, and is, necessarily a large one. It takes a lot of space in the West to support only a few people. There are vast distances between towns, and there are many places in the West where I can see as the eagles see, looking down over great expanses of land. It is the point of view I have wanted to express." He has exhibited throughout the Southwest and is represented by Aldridge Fine Arts.

Scott, C.A. Representational sculptor concerned with 18th and 19th century Western American images, particularly the Western landscape, in bronze, born in San Diego, California in 1940 and living in Bellingham, Washington since 1970. "The intention of my work," he stresses, "is to record the Western landscape and to show the deep relationship which exists between the landscape and its peoples."

As a child, Scott made motor trips with his parents through the Southwest and "became attracted to the types of landscapes and their ranging colors." He earned his BA from San Diego State College in 1968, majoring in art and sculpture, and his MFA in sculpture from the University of California at Santa Barbara in 1970 where he also taught for a year. For seven years, he taught at Western Washington University, then traveled in Europe and worked on sculpture at an Italian foundry.

"Through my traveling in the West," he says, "I have documented through drawings and photographs various landmarks, trailmarkers, and other historical sites. Of main concern are those I find of particular sculptural quality that were and are spiritually and geographically significant to the migratory cultures of the area, some examples being Yei-bi-chi, Delicate Arch, Canyonlands area, Montezuma Castle, and Tombstone Rock. The scale in my sculpture is obtained by including accurate representations of people, architecture, animals, and objects related to the early American West. I am presently the only sculptor of Western art who is solely creating realistic Western landscapes in bronze." Scott has exhibited in Northwestern shows including American Art Gallery and Western Art Association.

C.A. Scott, DELICATE ARCH—SOUTHERN UTAH
polychromed bronze, h 10½, w 12, d 12, Edition 12

David Schwindt, AUTUMN ON THE RIO GRANDE, oil, 24 x 36

Conrad Schwiering, WHEN THE FLOWERS BLOOM, oil, 24 x 40

John Scott (signature)   *Peter Scott* (signature)

Scott, John. Painter of the people of the early West, born in Camden, New Jersey in 1907 and living in Ridgefield, Connecticut. Scott is the dean of the so-called "Remington Traditionalists," the painters of the Old West who maintain studios near Ridgefield where Frederic Remington died in 1909. Since 1978, Scott has worked almost exclusively in recreating the West as it was before the turn of the century.

At the age of sixteen, Scott went to art school in Philadelphia and became a commercial illustrator for publications that included Western pulp magazines. He has estimated that before World War II, his drawings and cover paintings for pulps like Dell and Street and Smith numbered into the thousands. During the war, he was a traveling artist-correspondent for *Yank,* covering events on the European battlefronts. These drawings are part of the Army Historical Archives in Washington, D.C. For the next 33 years, he painted hunting and fishing illustrations for *Sports Afield,* a series on the famous fishing areas of the United States for the Garcia tackle company, another series on early days in the Texas and Oklahoma oil fields for the Oil Museum in Midland, Texas, and 12 by 32 foot murals commissioned by the Mormon Church for Salt Lake City and Washington.

Scott is now concentrating on easel paintings of the West "in the time of the mountain men, starting around 1820." Although he still lives in the East, he was a founding member of the Northwest Rendezvous Group and is represented by Fowler's and Settlers West Galleries where his painting was listed at $10,000 in the 1981 silent auction. His prints are published by Mill Pond Press.

Scott, Peter. Representational oil painter of birds and of portraits, born in England in 1909 and living in Slimbridge, Gloucester, England. "It is a day of intermittent sunshine," he describes, "with a fresh northerly breeze and the sky full of cumulus clouds. At noon a flock of 24 geese came upwind to the marsh where some 50 ducks were sitting in the shallows and along the shore—mostly mallards with a few pintails. The geese ultimately landed among the rushes upwind of the ducks, but it was during the few moments before 'touchdown' that they looked especially beautiful against the sunlight."

The son of an Antarctic explorer, he roamed the countryside as a child, learning natural history as a scientist and a hunter. After earning his MA in zoology at Cambridge, he studied art at the Munich State Academy and at the Royal Academy Schools in London. "I was likely, I thought, to paint best those things which moved me most. That meant my wildfowl. They had never been painted in the way I saw them." His first exhibition sold well, and the Queen Mother bought a painting for her collection.

During World War II, he commanded small ships and was decorated both for bravery and for inventing a method of camouflaging warships. In 1946, he established The Wildfowl Trust where 200,000 people each year see tame waterfowl from all over the world, as well as wild native species. In his early work, he was preoccupied with detail, but he now paints on large canvases in oil. He works quickly, often beginning a second painting while the first is drying so as not to lose the freshness. A Knight Bachelor, explorer, and author, he has exhibited at Ackermanns Gallery in London and is published by Mill Pond Press.

Peter Scott, CANADA GEESE COMING INTO THE MARSH, oil, 20 x 24

John Scott, THE WATERFALL, oil, 15 x 30

Scott, Sandra Lynn. Representational printmaker and illustrator of wildlife, Western, and rural subjects, born in Dubuque, Iowa in 1943 and living in El Paso, Texas since 1979. "I love both wildlife and Western subjects," Sandy Scott says, "because I've had so much contact with each of them. I find my work is leaning more and more toward wildlife, but I will never lose touch with the Western theme. It's a great part of my life. I was brought up in that environment.

"In Tulsa, where I grew up, my dad was a rancher. My mother was a trick rider with the rodeo." Scott studied for a year at the Kansas City Art Institute, but "when I was offered a great job as an animation background artist, I couldn't refuse." She had her pilot's license at 21 and for three years was a stewardess for Eastern Airlines before becoming a portrait artist in California. On a visit to Hawaii, she tried etching and she "knew I had found my medium. I just knew I had.

"I presented my first portfolio of etchings to several galleries in the winter of 1976. Within the first few weeks it started selling" and each year since then she has brought out a portfolio of sixteen subjects in editions of 100. Her primary studio is in El Paso, but she flies her own plane to other studios in Canada and Ruidoso, New Mexico. "I live alone," she declares, "and my work is my life. These are my productive years." In 1981, she also began stone lithography. She was the first to display etchings at the National Cowboy Hall of Fame, exhibited in the Peking, China show, and was written up in Southwest Art, May 1979, and Prints, July 1981. She is represented by Driscol Gallery among many others.

Scriver, Robert Macfie. "The Cowboy's National Sculptor" who also models wildlife, men of American history, and Blackfeet, born in Browning, Montana in 1914 and still living there. "The thing that is unique about typical Western art," he observes, "is its story-telling quality. In other world, the story it tells is of more importance than design, composition, etc.

"The important stages of my life," he adds, "have involved music, teaching, taxidermy, and finally the warm feel of clay in my hands." After earning his Bachelor of Music degree in 1935, Scriver taught in Browning public schools until 1940 when he returned to college for his Master's. During World War II, he played cornet in the Air Force Band and then went back to teaching. He was also a member of orchestras including Ted Weem's. The taxidermy career began in 1951. In 1953, he built a shop for taxidermy and for the casting of miniature animal figurines he modeled, becoming the best known taxidermist in Montana, especially for big game.

By 1956, he was established in his new career as a sculptor, starting a series of wildlife bronzes. He cast sixteen models in 1962, had a one-person show, was a charter member of the Society of Animal Artists, and had arrived as a professional artist. He has since exhibited at the National Academy of Design and in China, has been featured in American Artist and Art West, has been commissioned to model major statues, has been included in famous Western collections, is listed in Who's Who in American Art, and is a member of the National Sculpture Society, the Cowboy Artists of America, and the National Academy of Western Art. He is represented by his own Scriver Studio.

Seabourn, Bert D. Cherokee Indian watercolorist, born in Iraan, Texas in 1931 and living in Oklahoma City, Oklahoma. "I am not glib and fast at talking," he says, "but I am a sentimental man. The Native American belief that all creation is related provides reason for my conception of using the beauty of the birds of the sky and the animals of the land to record the Indian Way of Life."

Raised in Texas, Arkansas, and Oklahoma, Seabourn was "labeled non-white" because he is one-quarter Cherokee. Before he was twenty, he was a Navy illustrator in the Korean War, despite his lack of training in art. When he was discharged in 1955, he was hired as a commercial artist while studying art at night, and after seven years, he had his degree from Oklahoma City University. In the early 1960s he began to investigate Indian history and culture. A few years later, he was able "to combine what I felt about the Indian culture with the abstract approach I'd been working in. It wasn't easy for a long time, but eventually a composite face began to emerge combined with the symbolism of animals and birds and the forces of nature."

Painting in a "dream-like" and visionary style in opaque and transparent watercolors, Seabourn states that "I don't want my work to tell a complete story, just enough to catch the eye of the viewer and challenge him or her to fill in the missing pieces, like a puzzle." Seabourn's paintings are in ten public collections including The White House and the Vatican. He is listed in Who's Who in American Art, was featured in Southwest Art, June 1981, and is represented by Signature Gallery and by his own Seabourn Studio for prints.

Bob Scriver, RETURN OF THE BLACKFEET RAIDERS
bronze, h 15, w 25

Sandy Scott, PINTAILS AND CATTAILS
etching, 10 x 18, Edition 100

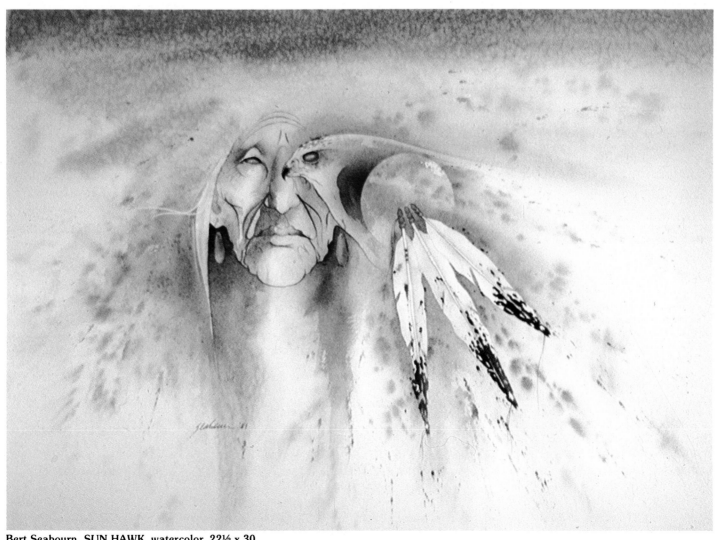

Bert Seabourn, SUN HAWK, watercolor, 22½ x 30

JL SEARLE

Sandi Seckman (signature)

Searle, J.L. (Jan). Sculptor of Indian people and oil pastellist, born in Ellensburg, Washington in 1938 and living near Walsenburg, Colorado. "I am familiar with Indian people," she emphasizes," and I want to show the American Indian as a sensitive person. So much Western art depicts the Indian as a 'savage' and this is simply not true. And, a lot of art shows the Indian as he is imagined by the artist, with no accuracy. It is 'imaginart' and it's bad art, even if it's done well."

During her youth, the family moved throughout the Northwest and she graduated from Alameda, California high school before attending Central Washington University to study art. She left college to become an illustrator and progressed to fashion illustrator, design artist, art director, and art agency owner. In late 1977, she came upon a box of clay and began "to mess around with it" until by nightfall she had "a fairly decent piece. I didn't know what I was doing, but working with that clay was very natural. I was hooked.

"Every piece I do is checked out by several knowledgeable Indian people before it goes to the foundry to be cast. I refer to photographs for close-up detail—but also for refreshing my memory on the movement and feeling of a certain dance. I also use a video tape recorder at pow wows, but you first have to be there and see the dance." The Colorado Commission of Indian Affairs has certified that "the bronzes of J.L. Searle are a totally accurate depiction of our heritage. I can guarantee that the bronzes are accurate in every way." She was also the featured American Indian artist at the Knoxville World's Fair. Written up in *Southwest Art,* July 1979, she is represented by Peacock Ltd and American West.

Seckman, Sandi. Watercolorist "of feeling and/or emotion," born in Denver, Colorado on Christmas Eve 1946 and living in Littleton, Colorado. "When my art was going well," she recalls, "I decided it was time to approach galleries. I made a list—first, what galleries I would like to be in—second, did they hang you on the floor or on the wall. Everything was to be first class or not at all—no compromising. That eliminated a lot of galleries.

"I have always loved art, something I was born with—always doodling and sketching in class, and inspired by an uncle who was one of the first Walt Disney artists back in 1936. I knew watercolor was my destiny. I combined contemporary and traditional which is hard to do and make it look right. I loved the response people would make about my paintings—everyone saw what they wanted to see. Once someone said, 'Even though you are not here—in your paintings you are. It's strange.'

"Most of my ideas come when I'm sleeping. I dream what I'm going to do from sketching to actual finished colors. The most exciting thing is I can paint what I saw in my dreams except for the washes. The washes can only be controlled to a certain extent and then they explode with color, imagination, and mysticism. Someone asked 'why you use only three colors in your paintings.' I feel only three colors create the mood for the setting—nighttime, after a rain, autumn, sunset, etc. Music is the most important factor when I paint. I love all kinds of music from classic to contemporary, whatever mood I'm in. I show in various galleries but the main two are Galeria del Sol and Art Resources."

J.L. Searle, THE LITTLE DANCER, bronze, h 28

Sandi Seckman, WINTER CALM, watercolor, 29 x 36

W, S, SELTZER

SEYBOLDT

Bill Shaddix

Seltzer, W.S. Traditional oil painter of historical Western subjects, especially Plains Indians, born in Great Falls, Montana in 1955 and living there again since 1976. Grandson of the famous Montana painter Olaf C. Seltzer, Steve Seltzer acknowledges that "naturally I was influenced to a great degree, particularly growing up in a home with my grandfather's pictures covering the walls. Many people don't realize that O.C. did many paintings of non-Western subjects, and I think these were of as much interest as the Westerns."

As a youth, Seltzer thought of art only as a hobby. He studied architecture at Montana State University, worked briefly in that field, then was in the real estate business for three years before deciding to paint full time. Although he had no training, he moved to Redondo Beach, California in 1974 and rented a studio in a building near Donald Putman, the California painter who taught at the Art Center College. "A student should be able to have a model that he can emulate," Seltzer says. "Finding someone who is willing to share his knowledge is a tall order," but he learned technique from Putman.

In 1976, Seltzer returned to Great Falls because his chosen subject matter was in Montana. His procedure in painting is to begin by sketching the basic shapes directly on the canvas with his brush. "Although preliminary drawings and color roughs can be helpful and often can prvent problems," he observes, "I feel that it can bog me down and destroy the spontaneity of a piece." He was written up in *Art West*, September 1980, is a member of the Northwest Rendezvous Group, and is represented by Husberg and Flathead Lake Galleries.

Seyboldt, Carl Eugene. Representational painter of the West and of wildlife in acrylic, born in Salt Lake City, Utah in 1945 and living in Eagle Point, Oregon since 1977. "My great-grandmother crossed the plains in a covered wagon," he says, "and I've always had an interest in historical transportation, especially covered wagons and stage coaches. Ever since I was small, horses and cowboys also interested me. Hopalong Cassidy was my favorite as I was growing up.

"My father was in the Air Force so we traveled quite a bit, to Germany, Illinois, Washington, Alaska, California, and Mississippi. After I graduated from Lompoc high school in 1963, I worked at Vandenburg Air Force Base and then served a full time mission to France for the Mormon Church. When I returned, I went to Grossmont Junior College where I graduated in 1969 with a degree in technical illustration that led to my assignment as an illustrator while I served in the Army. After I was discharged, I went to the Art Center College of Design in Los Angeles under the G.I. Bill and graduated BFA in 1975. Since then, I have worked as an illustrator and instructor at the Oregon College of Arts and Rouge Community College.

"I really didn't get interested in painting until I went to the Art Center and then a new world opened up. Animals have always interested me, and I now incorporate them in my paintings. A covey of quail can be seen spooking a pack train, or a Chinese ringneck pheasant scaring the Concord Stage. Action in a painting is important, along with lighting and mood. Like most illustrators, I leave the climax up to the viewer." Five prints have been commissioned and his galleries include Favell's Museum and Quintana's Trails End Gallery.

Shaddix, Bill. Traditional oil painter of the old and the current West, born in Colony, Caddo County, Oklahoma in 1931 and living in Sedona, Arizona since 1970. "I haven't entered many exhibitions involving awards," he recalls. "The first real recognition was in the third grade. I drew a picture of the teacher on the sidewalk. I used chalk as my medium and naturally I signed the teacher's name and my own. It was not a flattering picture, and I got swats as an award.

"My parents worked as farm laborers after they lost their own place during the early years of the Depression. They were very transient, never staying any place more than a few months. It was hard on us kids. From infancy, I was dragged on the foot of my mother's cotton sack. By the time we ended up in Rivera, California, I was majoring in fine arts in the high school. We worked with live models and were taken on sketching trips, the only formal training I have received.

"I served in the Army in Korea. After returning home, I was a mechanic's helper and then a deputy sheriff. One of the reserve deputies offered to finance all the material if I would paint him a picture. I agreed and was off and running. Prosecutors and attorneys began purchasing them and soon my painting career was interfering with my job. I gave my notice and hit the art circuit full time. The comments from observers are that they like the effect I get on lighting. I search the back country for new subjects. I use 35mm film and have a viewer beside my easel so it's like being on location without the bugs, and the sun doesn't keep moving. The galleries that represent me include Overland Trails and Saddleback Western Art Gallery."

478

Bill Shaddix, THE OUTLAW, oil, 20 x 30

Carl Seybolt, BAD NEWS, acrylic, 24 x 36

W.S. Seltzer, COLD DAY WARM TRAIL, oil, 30 x 54

Shoemaker, Vaughn. Impressionist oil painter of contemporary Mexican and foreign figures, born in Chicago, Illinois in 1902 and living in Carmel, California since 1952. "I paint mostly foreign subjects because America is made up of foreign born and because I am in a position financially where I can go to a foreign country to get my material. The average artist has a bunch of kids around the table who have to be fed and he cannot go out and spend five thousand dollars to travel to Europe to get a few painting subjects. That is the reason I have the field to my own."

In grammar school, he never learned to read well and dropped out of high school after a year to attend the Chicago Academy of Fine Arts. At nineteen, he was assistant cartoonist on the *Chicago Daily News*, and at 23, he was chief cartoonist. His work was syndicated to 101 newspapers, reaching 20,000,000 readers every day, and he won Pulitzer Prizes in both 1938 and 1947. After he moved to Carmel, he mailed the cartoons from there until 1972.

He had exhibited watercolors in Chicago in 1935 but his first solo show in oils was in 1973. According to Shoemaker, "a painting to a great extent, in my case anyway, is accidental. It is not exactly closing your eyes and swinging a brush but it is taking chances. If I don't take chances and free up, I will usually get something that looks tense. Sometimes I am free and get a swipe on the canvas and it produces a special effect. I can sit there for hours, not admiring it, but just enjoying an accident, knowing I can never do it again." He is listed in *Who's Who in America,* was written up in *Artists of the Rockies,* fall 1980, and exhibits at El Prado Gallery of Art.

Short, Richard. Painter of the West in a variety of subjects, born in Drumright, Oklahoma in 1935 and living in Lawrence, Kansas since one month after he was born. "Some Western artists do documentary paintings," he points out, "some do scenery, animals, or portraits of Indians, but I like to do it all. I feel there is no finer subject matter than the mountain men, traders, cavalry, cowboys and Indians. Add to this, wildlife, wagon trains, stagecoaches—well, there is just no end to possibilities. Indeed, it is a problem to decide which of the ten ideas I have backlogged to put on the panel next.

"I had pencil in hand well before kindergarten and spent my time drawing the cowboys and Indians of the Western movies I saw on Saturday afternoons. Educated in the Lawrence public school system, I am what is generally described as a self-taught artist. My only claim to art education was private instruction, and drawing was something I did for fun. I did not consider a career in art until midlife, when I was a construction supervisor and production manager. I quit the security of my salaried job five years ago.

"When developing a painting, I start with a drawing that could best be described as abstract and I proceed to a detailed drawing on a gesso-covered masonite panel that is large enough to be cut to final size when the composition is finished. At this stage, values and textures have been decided, leaving freedom to work out the color balance. I then paint with oils ala prima. When the painting has dried, I begin with glazes. This sounds fast, but it is slow, slow, slow." Prints are published by Master Art Renditions and he is represented by In the Spirit Gallery and Merrill's Gallery.

Richard Short, HUNTER AND MOUNTAIN LION, oil, 24 x 30

Vaughn Shoemaker, LULL IN THE MARKET, oil, 21 x 28

Shufelt, Robert. Delineator in pencil of Southwestern cowboy life, born in Champaign, Illinois in 1935 and living in Wickenburg, Arizona since 1976. "When you're an artist," he says, "you have plenty of time to think. I have a lot of statements to make about today's cowboy. One project I'm enthused about is portraying the ranch wife. I don't think many people know much about that way of life. They're incredible ladies and most of them can do just about everything."

"Shoofly" grew up in Chicago, spent two years in the Army, and went to the University of Illinois on a football scholarship. As a fine arts student, he drew Indian scenes despite his avant garde professors. He also played semi-pro football, raced sports cars, and worked as a free-lance illustrator in Chicago for twenty years. "I wanted to do easel painting, though," he declares, "so that became something I started building for. I knew I could draw and those twenty years as an illustrator were good training. Finally it was time to make the break and we just did it."

In his pencil drawings, "Shoofly" expresses his admiration for the working cowboy: "These guys are a breed unto themselves. They're fiercely independent and really don't make any money to speak of. They do it because they love it. You have to. They really go in style. It's their story I'm telling and they have given me the opportunity to live it with them. I've got to record that life. So much of the good ranch land is being eaten up by development. As a result it has to change." "Shoofly" has been featured in *Southwest Art*, October 1979, and in *Artists of the Rockies*, Winter 1981. He is represented by Trailside Galleries.

Silvertooth, (Carl) Dennis. Realist/Impressionist sculptor of Indian figures in bronze, born in Killeen, Texas in 1957 and living in Corpus Christi since 1980. "You begin to daydream while you are working on a piece, and it takes you on a nice little journey. The only thing that you are aware of is that your feet are connected to the floor. When you are really working, you wander off and at the same time you keep working on the piece and that is your only contact with what is real."

The son of a Cheyenne-Cherokee enlisted man and a German woman, he was raised partly in Germany and partly in Corpus Christi where he went to school. At sixteen, he took a job as a carpet layer to pay for sculpting tools and materials, studying privately and through a scholarship. In 1974, he met the sculptor Harry Jackson and was encouraged to try wax. In three months, he had three statuettes in bronze, the basis for his first exhibition. The next year, a bronze was auctioned for $4,750, and in January 1976 he was featured in *Southwest Art*.

Since then, his sculpture has been widely exhibited and has taken awards at every juried competition in which it was entered. "I'm not making anything to do with traditional Western art at all," Silvertooth emphasizes. "I'm not trying to preserve anything, except something of what you think the Indian was. People envy the Indian because the Indian knows who he is. He knows who his father was, and who *his* father was, and who *his* father was. They know exactly where they were, from very early, because they're still there." His sculpture is cast at Shidoni which represents him, along with Two Grey Hill Gallery and Many Horses Gallery.

Simms, Frank Young. Draws realistic charcoal portraits of Southwestern people and of animals, born in Albuquerque, New Mexico in 1951 and living in Ranchos de Taos, New Mexico since 1979. "My family has farmed and ranched in New Mexico and Colorado since the 1930s," Simms says. "This has had a major influence on my life and also my art because I am a working cowboy running a summer steer operation on my family's ranch near Chama, New Mexico. I derive much of my material from ranch life."

Raised in New Mexico, Simms went to high school in Colorado Springs, Colorado and to college at the University of New Mexico and Colorado State University. He attended the American Academy of Art in Chicago, from 1975 to 1979, earning degrees in fine arts and in graphic arts. "My medium tends to be charcoal," he declares, "and can be described as 'realistic,' not photographic. The 'honesty' of the medium is what appeals to me most as there is little room for miscalculation.

"I do not 'fictionalize' my drawings," Simms states. "I believe strongly in attempting to illustrate the underlying character of my subjects who are so unique to New Mexico. These subjects tend to be the 'real' people of northern New Mexico and southern Colorado, the Old Spanish, the Indians of the area, the cowboys I know and work with, and also the animals." His gallery is Shriver.

Frank Simms, LOOKING FOR STRAYS (1981), charcoal/rice paper, 21 x 33

Dennis Silvertooth, CALLS HIS GRANDFATHERS bronze, h 34

Robert Shufelt, GET TH' GATE, pencil, 18 x 26

Singer

Stan D. Sinnett

Singer, Ed. Modern oil painter and lithographer of the contemporary Navajo, born in Tuba City, Arizona on the Navajo Reservation in 1951 and living in Cameron, Arizona. "If you are an Indian showing drawings or paintings today," he points out, "your work is instantly measured against the yardstick of either Scholder or Gorman. It's irritating. It's true that I am affected by everything I see, and Gorman is very visible, but I started drawing in this style long before I had ever heard or seen Gorman's work.

"My father was a home builder. I drew this way as a boy on pieces of sheetrock and plywood. Half of my family was Christian and half was traditional Navajo." When he was in the sixth grade of a government boarding school, a teacher traded one of his watercolors for a new shirt for Singer who recalls that "I didn't even like the shirt. I sure would like to get that watercolor back." After studying at Southern Utah State College and Northern Arizona University where he was on the rodeo team, he taught high school for three years in Yuba City.

In 1977, he moved to Albuquerque to paint but found Flagstaff more compatible. His studio is 40 miles away, on the border of the Reservation. "I don't do portraits," he emphasizes. "I use the figure in the same way that you would use a flower arrangement. The main intent is on the line. I always have to keep in mind, for instance in doing a hand, that the fact that it is a hand is not as important as the fact that it is a line. My work doesn't ask for sentimental or romantic response. It is more like an abrupt confrontation." He has been winning awards since 1977, was written up in *Southwest Art*, June 1981, and is represented by El Taller Studios and Enthios Gallery.

Sinnett, Stan D. Realist painter of Plains Indians, born on the Blackfoot Indian Reservation at Browning, Montana in 1925 and living in Downey, California. "Realism," according to Sinnett, "is only a word that most of us use to describe images that represent the world as we think we see it. As an artist, the only realism is the canvas. This allows me to see the canvas as the real world, and to leave out or distort any shapes that I paint.

"Of Indian and French parents, I was reared by my grandparents on their ranch along Cut Bank Creek. The stories that were told were of great value later. I went to Cut Bank High School and later worked as a mechanic in California, studying art in night school after 1953. Injured on the job, I entered Chouinard Art Institute in 1959 and in 1964 went to Chicago to work as an illustrator. I returned to Chouinard to receive my BFA in 1970 while teaching illustration and art. In 1973, I received my Master's from the University of California at Fullerton and became interested in Western art.

"I am a traditionalist with a love for the impressionist color. I start by making thumbnail sketches until I have the idea fully developed. Then the final idea is drawn on the canvas and the painting is started. I paint my darks in first, then middle tones, and last the highlights along with the detail. I draw upon my background of stories of ranch life, the Indians, their horses, travois and wagons loaded with all their possessions and on the move, cowboys looking for strays, drifters riding the grub-line, and an assortment of hired hands." Sinnett is represented by Files Gallery.

Ed Singer, SUNDOWN, state 1 serigraph
34 x 24, Edition 40

Stan Sinnett, AT THE END OF HIS ROPE, oil, 30 x 40

L. Sisson

Barbara Joan Smith

Carl J. Smith

Sisson, Laurence P. Contemporary/classical painter of New Mexico and Arizona, in oil and watercolor, born in Boston, Massachusetts in 1928 and living in Santa Fe, New Mexico since 1979. "Thirty years of trying to express the beauty of the coast of Maine had reached a stalemate," he observes. "Now the Sea and I are friends, but I am in love with New Mexico. Having lived four seasons in Nambe, observing the dramatic changes in the sky and the woods and the mountains, I am at home with the landscape."

At seven, he was painting seriously. At 12, he was studying privately, and at 15 he had his second solo exhibition. When he graduated from high school, he was accepted by an important Boston gallery and won scholarships to the Worcester Museum School and to the Yale Summer School. Military service was with the Eighth Army in Japan where he could "absorb much of the Japanese culture and art." He then settled in Maine for 25 years while he had seventeen solo exhibitions including a retrospective at the Portland Museum and was in fifteen museum collections.

"I had a classical training," he points out, "but I am also part contemporary, and have an element of abstraction in my work. I am somewhat of a surrealist as well. I love to go beyond realism—to a degree. I don't want to be photographic, but I also don't wish to be so abstract that a subject loses its identity. I want to leave some mystery in a painting and something to the imagination of the beholder, but I want him to be able to identify. Maybe in this sense I am an impressionist. My work is many things to many people." Sisson is represented by O'Brien's Art Emporium and Frost Gully Gallery and was written up in *Southwest Art,* July 1981.

Smith, Barbara Joan. Still-life and figure painter of Western subjects in the style of the French Impressionists, born in Laurium, Michigan in 1933 and living in Pleasanton, California since 1971. "On my Finnish grandparents' farm in northern Michigan, one of my most vivid memories is drawing on brown paper bags by the kerosene lamp. Its flickering flame cast images against the walls that would inspire impressions. I won a first award in the children's division when I was five years old."

Her family moved to Tucson, Arizona in the 1940s. The Homecoming Queen in 1949, she studied dancing, singing, and piano and sang with a New York City orchestra for a week, while her twin brother became an actor in television and the movies. "Growing up with professional artists, my mother and stepfather Dale Nichols whose works hang in the Metropolitan Museum, exposed me to the fine arts," she adds, "as well as direction with my art." When she was living in Palm Springs in the 1950s and then in Honolulu, she drew Victorian women's figures and stilllifes in pastel.

Back in Tucson in 1958, she began painting in oils and had her first shows in Tubac and Phoenix, Arizona in 1960. She declares that "the great works of Renoir, Monet, and Lautrec inspired me over the years." Her subjects became the American Indians and the Mexicans. "I try," she says, "to capture on canvas the eternal 'spirit and soul' of a people rich in heritage. I continue to spend a month each fall in Tucson and Tubac where I paint daily. I find the serenity of the desert atmosphere solace for my soul." Her gallery is Windsong.

Smith, Carl J. Mood painter of the settlers on the Southern plains of the Texas Panhandle, born in Kress, Texas in 1928 and living in Canyon, Texas since 1966. Smith recreates atmospheric Victorian views of the pioneers. "I have lived what I paint," he says, "or else the subjects are so familiar to me, I might as well have lived them. Caring counts. I deliberately soften the harsh realities of the time with the overriding kindness people had for one another."

The grandson of a circuit riding Texas preacher, Smith graduated from West Texas State University in 1952, spent two years in the Army, and then taught art in Portales, New Mexico schools for twelve years. Smith paints rapidly, working a 40 hour week from nine to five. Sometimes he sits on the floor with his canvas propped against the wall, painting in time to majestic symphonies that provide "sweep," recording his and his family's recollections without the aid of a preliminary sketch or a photograph.

Smith prefers the homely message of love triumphant over the cruel environment. "I have an obsession about my childhood," he declares. "The memories of those times are hazy. My paintings have that dream-like quality about them." Collectors claim that Smith's paintings make them happy. "I've never found a person who does not like Smith's paintings," one insisted. Some canvases contain small indistinct figures so that "the viewer must make up his own story" to explain the simple parts being played in the caught moment. Smith has had 24 one-person shows, including an exhibition at the Gilcrease Institute in Tulsa. He is represented by Sagebrush Galleries.

B.J. Smith, TAOS MAIDEN, oil, 18 x 14

Laurence Sisson, ANASAZI RUINS, oil/board, 36 x 24

Carl J. Smith, A STRANGER'S FIRE, oil, 24 x 36

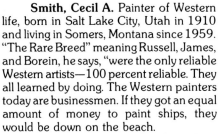

Smith, Cecil A. Painter of Western life, born in Salt Lake City, Utah in 1910 and living in Somers, Montana since 1959. "The Rare Breed" meaning Russell, James, and Borein, he says, "were the only reliable Western artists—100 percent reliable. They all learned by doing. The Western painters today are businessmen. If they got an equal amount of money to paint ships, they would be down on the beach.

"I grew up on my family's Idaho ranch that had been started by my grandfather in 1880 and I attended the University of Utah and Brigham Young University with summers spent as an open range cowboy in the free grass years. In 1937, my painting depicting Western America was included in the United States art exhibit at the Paris Exposition. In the late 1930's, I went to New York City to further my studies, and in the early 1940s I studied privately under the expressionists." Smith was in Naval Intelligence during World War II, making the Normandy Beach and Iwo Jima invasion maps.

After the war, Smith helped run the 89,000 acre ranch until 1959 when the family got out of the cattle business. He settled down to painting full time, from motion picture cartooning to 90-foot murals. He believes that "the moderns frown upon any art that is pictorial, but great art has always been descriptive of the life and times of the artist. I want every painting to tell a story." Smith is listed in *Who's Who in American Art* and in Hassrick's *Western Painting Today,* has been featured in *Western Horseman,* January 1977, and *Southwest Art,* February 1978, and is represented by Cottonwood Gallery.

Smith, Donald C. Realist oil painter and sculptor of Western scenes, born in New Orleans, Louisiana in 1929 and living in Metairie, Louisiana. "My approach to art," he says, "is the search for simplification, to make a painting that is the symbol of an event, not merely its journalistic recalling. I constantly ask myself the question, 'Is there anything in this painting that could be left out and not weaken the central theme?'

"My first exposure to the West was on a vacation trip we made to Colorado in 1946. I saw my first C.M. Russell print on a motel bedroom wall and I was hooked—not on motels but on Western art. From 1946 through 1956, we made yearly junkets West and I began collecting books and photographs. In 1957, I bought my first quarter horse and started riding in Western shows. I had graduated from Tulane University with a BA in 1950 and it was during this 'horseflesh' period that I was selling Western paintings to national magazines.

"In the mid-60s, the low paying Western paintings began to give way to a much more lucrative area of portrait painting and watercolor landscapes. When the family was grown enough to trade diapers for saddle blankets, we began to travel again. I became enamored of the bullfight and had a major one-person show of bronzes of bulls and matadors. In the mid-70s, I did some Indian studies and after 30 years, I had come full circle to painting Westerns again, although bronze is probably my favorite medium for self-gratification. Casting bronze is tantamount to a woman giving birth, I suppose—it is painfully slow, physically exhausting, and no matter how the piece turns out, you still love it. I currently exhibit in Troy's and Merrill Chase Galleries."

Don Smith, A CHANGE FROM BEEF 'N BEANS, oil, 18 x 34

Cecil Smith, BISCUITS ARE BETTER THAN GRASS, oil, 18 x 24

Jack Smith

Jaune Smith

Linda K. Smith

Smith, Jack. Sculptor of animals and figures in stone and bronze, born in Wichita, Kansas in 1947 and living in Santa Fe, New Mexico since 1974. "Whatever you can imagine," he believes, "you can find within the block of stone. If you're light enough with your touch, stone can be shaved thin enough to show light through. That's the great thing. There's an object within the volume of stone that will respond to you. I've shaved jet so thin that it would bend. And of course, once you've brought it out, it's there for all time."

For several years, Smith lived in the shadow of the Black Mesa on the San Ildefonso Pueblo in northern New Mexico. When he attended Wichita State University from 1966 to 1969, he studied anthropology and geology as well as commercial art. At Washburn University, he studied psychology and studio art from 1969 to 1971. "I started as a jeweler," he explains, "making beads for necklaces and small fetish styled pendants. Eventually the pendants grew till they were too big to wear. At that moment, I was a sculptor.

"I've carved a great many bear sculptures," he points out, "as it is the 'lion' of North America. America has stylized the bear in our history, so that while we're scared by the grizzly, we love the begging brown bears. Children have a 'Teddy' and television has bombarded us with bears that talk! In my bears, however stylized, I've tried to regain the majesty of these giants of the wild. The spirit of Audubon lives on in the Western artist who has a chance to show what the unspoiled West and its people and animals were like. I've chosen animals to represent my view of that part of nature." He has exhibited at McCormick Art and Shidoni Galleries.

Smith, Jaune Quick-To-See. French-Cree, Flathead, and Shoshone modernist painter of landscapes and Indian figures in various media, born on the Flathead Reservation, Montana in 1940 and living in Corrales, New Mexico. "I look at line, form, color, texture, etc. in contemporary art," she explains, "as well as viewing old Indian artifacts in the same way. With this, I make parallels from the old world to contemporary art and gain support for what I synthesize from both societies. It is finding my own vision.

"As far back as I can remember, I wanted to be an artist. Before I knew the word, I liked to draw. That's what I got attention for in school. I worked in fields when I was ten as a farm hand, and I used that money to send away for the Famous Artists course because I knew that's what I was going to be. I went to five different colleges, and it took a long time, working nights and days, mainly just surviving—so I've been a plugger and I've kept at it and it's all right, because the things have come together. I've got staying power now.

"Indian women are raised differently. Most of us have had to do farm labor the same as a man. We weren't raised to 'think pink.' The women in my family have always been strong, and I think I've done enough creditable things that it will help some of the stereotypes of what an urban Indian does, or what an Indian woman painter does. Maybe my ideas will affect some young person who needed to hear something that would encourage. Certainly my story is an encouraging one." Written up in *Southwest Art,* April 1981, and the subject of a 1981 documentary for PBS Television, she is published by Tamarind and represented by Marilyn Butler Gallery.

Smith, Linda K. Abstract/realist painter of natural forms such as plants, rocks, and ground in mixed media on paper, born in Los Angeles, California in 1933 and living in Moraga, California. "Visually," she explains, "I'm forever seduced by the play of light and shadow patterns on the complicated forms we see, dying cornfields or spikey cactus, tangled grasses, a stark isolated rock on barren ground. While the images might be homely ones on a traditional scale of beauty, I may become fascinated, returning many times and in other seasons to look again, photograph, and then paint them."

Raised in Los Angeles and San Angelo, Texas, she attended Stanford University as a creative writing major, the University of California at Los Angeles as an art history major, and then went to California College of Arts and Crafts as a drawing major where she received her BFA in 1975 and her MFA with distinction in 1978. Since 1978, she has taught chalk pastel drawing and composition at the college.

"Working from photographs has resulted in a certain strength that was missing in my earlier more traditional landscapes. I think that the camera in translating to two dimensions helps me distance myself from the too romantic reaction to the subject, so that I can see the essence more clearly. The original visual attraction for me is an abstract one, and the light patterns, often exaggerated or simplified, are significant elements in each piece. When this abstraction has in addition the qualities of recognizable form and surface and space, I believe that an extremely important emotional element is added." Written up in *Southwest Art,* April 1980, she is represented by Ivory/Kimpton and Davis Mc-Clain Galleries.

Linda K. Smith, SEDONA (1980), mixed media, 39 x 26

Jack Smith, WINNETKA AND THE FISH, marble, h 8½

Jaune Smith, RED LAKE SER. (1982), acrylic/canvas & collage, 56 x 84

491

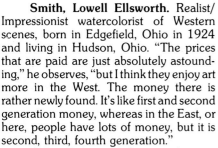

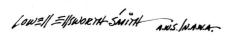

Smith, Lowell Ellsworth. Realist/Impressionist watercolorist of Western scenes, born in Edgefield, Ohio in 1924 and living in Hudson, Ohio. "The prices that are paid are just absolutely astounding," he observes, "but I think they enjoy art more in the West. The money there is rather newly found. It's like first and second generation money, whereas in the East, or here, people have lots of money, but it is second, third, fourth generation."

Although he was the son of an art director, music was his first love and in high school he formed a dance band. After serving for three and a half years in the Air Force during World War II, he opted for art despite having never painted, and received his BFA from Miami of Ohio in 1948. He was then employed as a commercial artist for 12 years and took the Famous Artists correspondence course, graduating in 1952. In 1960, he decided to devote full time to painting and teaching so he could "lay back and do the paintings as they come.

"I like to feel that the basis for all my painting is abstract. If you squint your eyes way down, you should see a light and dark abstract pattern. The basis is design and shapes, and shapes are an abstraction of nature. Take away the identifying surface features of a shape and all you have left is a colored shape. Take this even further and abstract the color out, and all that is left is a dark shape." The painter Ramon Kelley introduced Smith to the West and paints with him on location. A member of the American Watercolor Society and the National Academy of Western Art, Smith was featured in *American Artist,* and the book *40 Watercolorists.* He is represented by Seth Canyon Road and Shriver Galleries.

Smith, Tucker. Realist painter in oil and watercolor of scenes near his home, born in St. Paul, Minnesota in 1940 and living in Clancy, near Helena, Montana. "I am not personally interested," he points out, "in telling a story or illustrating history. I would rather convey a mood while portraying reality. I want to paint the actual rather than the ideal and I try to avoid sentimentality and nostalgia. I believe in subtlety.

"When I was 12, my family moved from our Minnesota farm to the mountains of Wyoming. While I always had an interest in art, I graduated from the University of Wyoming in 1963 with a degree in math and spent eight years as a computer programmer and systems analyst. If anyone had told me then that I would soon be doing this, I would have laughed. My art education was in abstract art, but I was basically always a realistic artist. After my schooling, I got back to realism.

"I choose subjects that are timeless, the things I see today—landscape, wildlife, rocks. I do outdoor sketches, but I am a studio painter. If I lived in the East, my paintings would be different. I live in the West, so my paintings reflect the West—but I hate to be categorized. People in the West like realistic art because they think of Westerners as realistic people. They are straightforward, honest, and unpretentious, so the art has to reflect these things. In the East, the audience goes with the critics, but I don't think Westerners give a darn about critics. They go with what they like." A founding member of the Northwest Rendezvous Group, Smith was featured in *Art West,* January 1980, and *Rocky Mountain Magazine,* December 1981, is published by Greenwich Workshop, and is represented by Carson Gallery.

Smyth, Ed. Realist watercolorist of contemporary cowboys, horses, and Indians, born in New York City in 1916 and living in Story, Wyoming since 1970. "I believe in honest art," he stresses. "If I haven't been there myself to know what I'm painting, then I won't even touch it. The West is what I know best, and I don't believe in fooling around with unfamiliar subjects. The things I paint are still in existence, but they're giving way to industry."

After going to school in New York and working summers on Eastern dude ranches, he moved to St. Louis to become head of advertising for horse-related programs at Purina-Ralston. He continued doing commercial art, photography, and copywriting for 24 years, until, as he says, "I'd followed a lot of cowboys down the road. I'd met Indians and learned about their ways. There was one time I went on a roundup with Casey Tibbs. I knew these were the people and the environment I wanted to make my life with. So, I packed my things and moved.

"If people are true Westerners," he adds, "they won't be drastically affected by outside influences. The true spirit of the West is the desire to be at least partially alone and self-sufficient. The challenge between the individual and his environment is all part of the West, and Western art is about real people, real animals, and real land." Smyth's camera has recorded it all, and he paints only from photographs he has taken. Paul Rossi who was director of the Gilcrease Institute has written that Smyth is high in the handful of Western artists who know the subject and have the ability to project it. Smyth's primary gallery is his own, The Line Camp.

Ed Smyth, THE RAMROD, watercolor, 15½ x 13¼

Tucker Smith, ROAN DRAFT HORSE, oil, 16 x 20

Lowell Ellsworth Smith, WEIGHING BANANAS, watercolor, 19 x 27

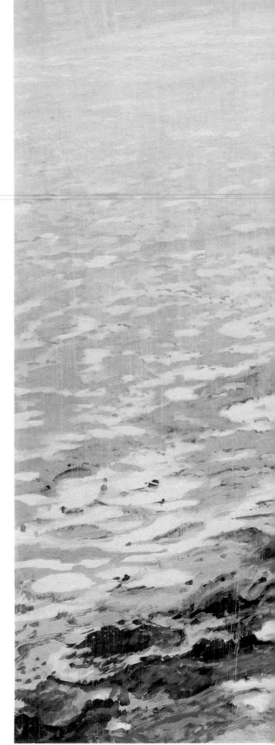

Snidow, Gordon E. Realist painter
of the contemporary cowboy in opaque
watercolor, born in Paris, Missouri, in 1936
and living in Ruidoso, New Mexico. "I like
to think I had something to do with the
popularity of Western art," Snidow says.
"Hell, I was doing it when it wasn't paying
anything. Now it's doing well and I wouldn't
leave it for the world. I feel very fortunate,
and my life couldn't be better.

"I remember my first art show in the
second grade in Tulsa. I also had instruction in junior high in Sherman, Texas. Dad
found a teacher to give me private lessons
in Enid, Oklahoma, and enrolled me in the
Famous Artists School. Then I discovered
the Gilcrease Museum when I was twelve
and I decided I wanted to be a cowboy
artist." After high school, he went to the Art
Center School in Los Angeles, graduating
in 1959 and selling his first Western painting for $125 in Tulsa. He sold two more
Western paintings in Taos, New Mexico but
to support his family became a commercial
artist in Albuquerque. In 1965, he joined
the new Cowboy Artists of America who
banded together for art shows, and in 1971
he became a full-time painter.

"Rembrandt has a place in my life,"
he adds, "not because I paint like he did,
but because he has influenced me philosophically. He painted the people of his
time. My approach to the cowboy is a
Rembrandt approach, because I am painting the people of our time." Snidow has
won seven gold and seven silver medals at
the CAA shows, plus the Popular Choice
Award twice and the Best of Show twice. In
1981, his painting sold for $70,000 at the
Western Heritage Sale in Houston. Those
are the only two shows at which he exhibits,
and he is two years behind on commissions
from collectors.

Gordon Snidow, HEADIN' FOR THE BARN, gouache, 24 x 36

Morten E. Solberg

Don Spaulding SAHA

Solberg, Morten E. Impressionist/ contemporary and realist/traditional painter in acrylic and watercolor, born in Cleveland, Ohio in 1935 and living in Carmel, California. "I start a painting in the contemporary style," he explains, "by concerning myself with the abstract quality and the feeling more than anything else. In this painting, I combine shape and color to create a feeling, a pleasing environment. I often don't know at this point what the painting will say. I will sometimes hang the unfinished painting until something that I've thought about comes through the shapes and color."

After graduating from high school in 1955, Solberg attended Cleveland Institute of Art at night while working for a design studio. That was his only formal training in art. Beginning in 1958, he joined the Marine Corps Reserves and for the next ten years was employed as a separation artist, sales representative, and art director for a greeting card manufacturer. In 1968, he moved to California to become art director for another greeting card company. After three years, he started his own design studio.

During all the time he worked at commercial art, he was also painting but "at first I was afraid to paint fine art because of lack of confidence in myself." By 1970, he was exhibiting, but completing only ten paintings a year, with little exposure. He began doing gallery painting full time in 1974, after displaying eight paintings at a 1973 watercolor exhibition where three of the eight won awards, and one was purchased for the National Gallery of Art. A member of the American and National Watercolor Societies and the Society of Animal Artists, he is listed in *Who's Who in America* and was written up in *Southwest Art,* May 1976. His prints are published by the Greenwich Workshop.

Spaulding, Don. Oil painter of the post-Civil War U.S. Cavalry, born in Brooklyn, New York in 1926 and living in Pound Ridge, New York. "My love affair with the U.S. Cavalry and the American West really blossomed in 1949 when I saw *She Wore a Yellow Ribbon.* I had already been affected by Frederic Remington's paintings, but it was the movie that turned me into a cavalry buff. I still watch *She Wore a Yellow Ribbon* when it shows on television. Now the inaccuracies in uniforms and equipment amuse me, but I still find the visual excitement.

"I grew up in the golden age of magazines, all filled with illustrations by the finest artists in the country. Those illustrators were my heroes, and from an early age I knew I wanted to be a picture maker." Spaulding spent four years at the Art Students League in New York City, and during lunch breaks took the subway to Bannerman's to shop for cavalry items like those in the movie. After private study with Norman Rockwell, he became a commercial artist and spent his free time collecting gear.

During a one-person exhibition at West Point, he was recognized as "distinguished by a careful attention to the accuracy of military articles," and it was stressed that the paintings shown were "reliable tools for military historians to enjoy and study." Spaulding says "it is time to lay to rest the inaccuracies and the Hollywood cliches. There is no great mystery about the way cavalrymen looked. Anyone interested can consult Army regulations." He is a member of the Society of American Historical Artists and of The Company of Military Historians, was featured in *Art West,* September 1981, and is represented by Grizzly Tree Gallery.

Morten Solberg, ONE WITH EARTH AND SKY, watercolor, 30 x 40

Don Spaulding, HOSTILE FIRE FROM THE RIGHT FLANK, oil/panel, 20 x 30

Speed, Ulysses Grant. Traditional sculptor of bronzes of the Old West, born in San Angelo, Texas in 1930 and living in Lindon, Utah. "There is a mystique about the West," he observes, "that has captured people in all walks of life throughout the world. In the United States, there are movies, television shows, rodeos, books, and magazines all depicting the West. In the midst of this worldwide enthusiasm for the West, there is a growing interest in Western art."

Raised during the Depression, Grant Speed never doubted that he would be a rancher. At twelve, he began to summer on a ranch that was "the neatest place on earth." After he graduated from high school at seventeen, he was a working cowboy. Itchy feet took him to fifteen ranches by the time he was twenty-two, despite two hitches in the Air Force, but he wasn't any closer to buying a ranch of his own.

He enrolled in animal husbandry at Brigham Young University, spent two and a half years on a mission for the Mormon Church, was a professional bronco rider in the rodeo until he injured a leg, and in 1962 qualified as a teacher. In two years, he knew he was in the wrong job. He had kept to himself his interest in art, but now he "decided very seriously that I was going to give art everything I had in me." After teaching school all day, he taught himself to sculpt, and by 1965 was selling bronzes at Trailside Galleries. The next year he was accepted into the Cowboy Artists of America and his career was established. He was featured in Ainsworth's *The Cowboy in Art* in 1968, then quit teaching. In 1970, the entire edition of his bronze was sold out at the CAA show, and in 1976 he won the CAA gold medal. His biography *From Broncs to Bronzes* was published in 1979.

Grant Speed, TWISTERS AND OUTLAWS, bronze, h 28

D. ALANSON SPENCER A.W.S.

Sprunger

Michael Stack

Spencer, Duncan Alanson. Representational painter of the landscape of the Four Corners country and of northeastern California, born in Los Angeles, California in 1911 and living in Mariposa. When asked if Western American art is all he paints, he replies that while he is by no means limited to this, the Four Corners country is his favorite because he "hasn't worn it out yet." He visits the area around the reservations about once a year.

Raised in the San Joaquin Valley where he attended a country school, he went to Hollywood High School and to Chouinard Art School, then served a two-year apprenticeship under the chief artist for the U.S. Navy. He was then employed for five years as a blueprinter for the Los Angeles Engineering Department before beginning a career in 1937 that would span 38 years and more than 400 movies. He started at MGM Studios, and painted scenic backgrounds for films like *White Christmas* and *The Wizard of Oz*. His final film was *The Fortune Cookie*. In 1962, he painted backgrounds at the New York World's Fair, in 1965 for the Los Angeles County Museum of Natural History, in 1972 for a 192-foot-long mural in Memphis, and a diorama of the Capitol for the Smithsonian Institution.

Slightly color blind, he used his training on the early black and white films to learn shading and color value. He also credits his membership in the Painters and Sculptors Club of Los Angeles in the early 1930s where he gave his first exhibitions and where the members would critique one another's works. A member of the American Water Color Society and of the Audubon Artists, he has been represented by O'Brien's Art Emporium for 26 years and also shows at Carson's Gallery of Western Art.

Sprunger, Elmer. Representational oil painter of Montana wildlife, born in Kalispell, Montana in 1919 and living in Bigfork, Montana. "The best settings for wildlife," he points out, "are during autumn and early winter, not always the most comfortable time to be outdoors. That's when the animals are the most beautiful—fully antlered and full coated. The best time of day, of course, is morning and evening (color is bleached out at midday). Animals and birds are more active at these times, too."

Raised in Bigfork at the foot of Flathead Lake near Glacier National Park, the Bob Marshall Wilderness, and the Moiese Bison Range, he worked in the woods as a young man. While he was in high school in Butte, he took private art lessons from Elizabeth Lochrie and subscribed to the Famous Artists correspondence course. During World War II, he was a commercial artist for the Army in Hawaii, then worked as a carpenter in heavy construction in the Puget Sound area. In 1950, he returned to Montana and was a sign painter and artist for an aluminum company for fifteen years.

In 1972, he became a full-time wildlife painter, convinced that "people interested in art, especially wildlife art, have a deeper feeling for the earth, its creatures, and their fellow man. Being a wildlife painter, I cannot help but be a strong environmentalist. I guess it goes with the game. I'm glad that as a lover of nature, I can express myself by painting what I see. It's a pleasant situation. Most people retire and take up painting to occupy their time. I'm never going to retire. I don't have to, because I enjoy what I'm doing." He sells paintings from his home studio and also at the Flathead Lake Gallery, and is published by Salt Creek.

Stack, Michael. Traditional oil painter of southern Arizona landscapes "reminiscent of the Old Masters," born in Monticello, New York in 1947 and living in Taos, New Mexico since 1981. "How I paint," he says, is "I get an idea for a painting and usually rough it in real fast on a stained canvas. After it dries, I will go in and start putting on paint, then I start glazing and scumbling and applying paint where needed and whatever it takes to make the painting look right. From that painting, I usually get an idea for another.

"I moved from New York to Southern California at three and lived there until 1971. I have been interested in drawing and painting as far back as I can remember and became interested in oil painting in junior high school. A self-taught artist, I have had no formal art education other than in public school classes. After high school, I did odd jobs and traveled extensively throughout the U.S. and Canada, always hoping to be able to make a living from painting. In 1971, I moved to Sonoita, a small town in southeastern Arizona.

"Five years ago, I decided to give art a try after saving enough money. Because where I lived in Sonoita was somewhat isolated, I didn't get out to associate with other artists. The first year was very tough, but each year things began improving. Since 1978, I have sold every piece of work entered into shows, but most has been purchased from my studio by private collectors. When I left my studio this past year, I had over thirty commissions to complete for collectors. I do not like to have my work sitting around because if I do, I am constantly going back to it and trying to perfect it. My galleries at present are Shriver Gallery and Johnson Gallery where I started out."

Elmer Sprunger
AUTUMN EVENING
oil, 20 x 7

Michael Stack, SHOWERS IN ARROYO SECO, oil/linen, 24 x 36

D. Alanson Spencer, OWL ROCK, watercolor, 20½ x 28½

Stahl (signature)

Oleg Stavrowsky (signature)

Ross Stefan (signature)

Stahl, Ben. Impressionist painter of the Old Western scene in oil, watercolor, and charcoal, born in Chicago in 1910 and living in San Miguel de Allende, Mexico since 1972. "In the East," Stahl says, "any mention that the artist was once an illustrator, even a good one, is deadly. Whereas in the West, artists brag about it, and are even hung in museums. But they are two different things. Illustration has a function. It tells a story. Pure art has no practical function. The only purpose is to move the viewer intellectually and emotionally.

"My first crude drawings were either of cowboys chasing Indians or of World War I scenes. When I was about thirteen, I started going to the Art Institute of Chicago on Saturday mornings. My first job was in a commercial art studio at $10 a week, and by the time I hit twenty, my work was being accepted in exhibitions. I was doing illustrations, but I was also, on my own, doing landscapes and nudes. Great painters painted pictures which told a story and remained great art. They put emphasis on the abstract structure and they minimized the story content. I began pushing in this direction.

"In the subsequent years, I illustrated a multitude of subjects for all of the slicks. I wrote a couple of books. Nine years ago we moved to central Mexico and my subject matter returned to my first love, cowboys and the Western scene, but this time I concentrated on indoor activities." In 1979, Stahl was elected to the Society of Illustrators Hall of Fame. He has received the Saltus Gold Medal of the National Academy of Design, is listed in *Who's Who in the World,* was featured in *Southwest Art,* July 1978, and *Artists of the Rockies,* winter 1982, and is represented by Settlers West Galleries and Fenn Galleries Ltd.

Stavrowsky, Oleg. Realist painter of the contemporary and the historic West, born in Harlem, New York in 1927 and living in Waco, Texas. "Most 'artist biographies,'" he says, "are pure drivel and claptrap, but I know the business demands it and for some reason clients are incurably curious about the personal lives of artists. For the life of me I don't know why but I know that's the way it is. My problem is that my 'career' in art has been boring to someone who is looking for juicy and exciting details.

"Very few people know me personally and I have heard that I don't really exist, that I am black (because I was born in Harlem), that I am from the 'old country' (because of my name), and that I don't speak English. Of course none of it is true. I got through two years of high school, was drafted into the Armed Forces in 1945, and got honorably discharged as a staff sergeant in 1949. I fooled around with ten thousand incidental jobs and finally when I was thirty decided I liked graphics.

"I got a pretty good job as a technical illustrator and I was really cooking. Then I got interested in fashion drawing and got into free-lance art. My only teacher was a book, but I had a solid reputation as a hot dog. I was in Oklahoma City, about ten years ago, decided to see what was in the Hall of Fame, and made up my mind I'd like to try that. I guess we all like cowboys and Indians. It was pretty good right from the start and I've been at it ever since. One big factor in my life is jazz. When I paint, I am listening to music. Sixty-four bars of good saxophone is like four square inches of good brush licks on a canvas. Western painting is my life, my joy, my income, my everything." Stavrowsky is represented by La Porta Art Gallery.

Stefan, Ross. Impressionist oil painter of the Southwest as it is today, born in Milwaukee, Wisconsin in 1934 and living in Tucson, Arizona since 1950. In declining to join an academy, Stefan wrote that "perhaps for a non-artist, it is difficult to understand that any art that is worthwhile must reflect the life of the artist, not the critic, committee, or jury. An artist competes with himself. If an artist is to be a rising star in life, all must grow from within the artist."

At thirteen, Stefan won a student art contest and later that year was taken to southern Arizona, to recuperate from pneumonia. In 1950, the family moved to Tucson where Stefan exhibited pastels. He switched to oil painting at eighteen, graduated from the University of Arizona in 1955, and established his first studio in Tubac, Arizona. He stayed with the Navajos during that year and his paintings of the land and the people became authoritative. In 1959, he signed an exclusive contract with the Rosequist Galleries in Tucson.

He says that he "makes no preliminary composition sketches or line drawings on the canvas but begins working with brush and color. Virtually all my painting is done in the studio, from ideas in my head. For detail, I sometimes refer to notes I made in the field, but those are seldom carefully rendered. I paint fast and don't hesitate to discard unsuccessful canvases or scrape out the offending members and paint in new forms until I am satisfied." Stefan is listed in *Who's Who in American Art* and in Hassrick's *Western Painting Today,* exhibited in the 1981 Peking, China show, and was featured in *Southwest Art,* March 1976, and *Artists of the Rockies,* fall 1979.

Oleg Stavrowsky, ROBBER'S MEET, oil, 40 x 72

Ben Stahl, HAVING THEIR PICTURE TOOK, oil, 48 x 58

Ross Stefan, MUTTON AND FRYBREAD, oil, 28 x 50

Steinke, Bettina. Representational painter of Southwestern and other portraits and figures, born in Biddeford, Maine in 1913 and living in Santa Fe, New Mexico. She describes a portrait as "the whole beautiful head, the way it turns, the way it sits on the neck, the great big shapes of the planes of the cheeks and the way they roll into the nose. The nose contains no lines. It's a lump of flesh. It's formed. There are no lines in a head. They're all big shapes."

Brought up in New York City where her father was a cartoonist and show-business personality, she began winning portrait prizes in high school and went to the Fawcett Art Institute in Newark, New Jersey, and to Cooper Union and Phoenix Art Institute in New York City. She believes that her "generation was the last to receive a purely classical education in art, including anatomy, drawing, perspective, still-life, history of art, murals, and experimental work in mediums." Her first big job was a series of 108 heads for the NBC Symphony Orchestra when she was 23.

For the next ten years, she painted portraits and illustrations in New York City. "In portraiture," she explains, "the subject is important. I compose on the full canvas, starting with the head and then adjusting all related parts. I believe the head is sacred. Everything must work to glorify it." She made her first Western visit in 1947 and moved to Taos in 1955. She was a charter member of the National Academy of Western Art in 1973, won the Prix de West in 1978, exhibited in the Peking, China show, is listed in *Who's Who in American Art*, was featured in *Artists of the Rockies* and *Southwest Art*, and has shown at Fowler's Gallery.

Steider, Doris. Painter in egg tempera and sculptor in bronze of the old Southwest, born in Decatur, Illinois in 1924 and living in Albuquerque, New Mexico. "The West we know is moving rapidly into the atomic age," she points out. "Lovely tin roofs, hand-hewn fenceposts, and the crumbling adobes with so many stories to tell are giving way to plastic, steel spikes, reflective glass, and cement block. We need yesterday's reminders to show us where we've traveled and painting them is for me a journey of love."

After earning a BS in applied design from Purdue and becoming a lab technician at Kirksville College of Osteopathy, she began painting professionally in 1959 and received her MA in Fine Art from the University of New Mexico in 1965. She has also done theater costume designs and interior decoration. "Painting for me is a necessity like breathing and sleeping, a spiritually energizing food that keeps awareness and sensitivity alive," she asserts. "The scenes I paint are often quiet or unobtrusive but for a moment in time everything is where it needs to be, its imperfections perfect, its spirit the only possible synthesis for that moment."

Her painting technique is to "keep files of slides for reference by subjects. I might use many slides for material and then paint a free interpretation, but I want to paint truths, real facts about posts or the direction of branches." Her small bronzes are of Indian figures. Since 1958, she has been in 180 major exhibitions and has won 74 awards, is listed in *Who's Who in America* and *Who's Who in American Art*, has been featured in *American Artist*, *Artists of the Rockies*, and *New Mexico Magazine*, and is represented by Baker Fine Art and Galeria Del Sol.

Stephenson, Louis L. Realist oil painter of mountain man portraits, born in Gillette, Wyoming in 1947 and living in Manitou Springs, Colorado. "I believe the most important aspects of a portrait," he emphasizes, "are the eyes, mouth, body language, hands, color scheme, and clothing, in pretty much that order. For example, when a person looks at you on the street, the first things we, as part of the animal kingdom, respond to are the eyes, mouth, and body language of that person.

"I grew up on ranches in Wyoming and Montana, joined the Air Force in 1967, and attained two degrees of black belt in Korean karate. My art career began in 1969 while I was in an Air Force hospital with a lot of time to spare and the man next to me suggested I draw a picture. I did a couple and, although they looked terrible, decided right then and there I wanted to become an artist. I have never regretted the decision. My art training began in 1971 in Santa Barbara, California. After graduating from college, I worked at the Santa Barbara Museum of Art until 1977 when I decided to go into art full time.

"I work both from life and from slides, and strive to evoke in my portraits not just a picture of someone, but more importantly, to show the soul, if you will, of that individual. By doing so, each portrait becomes alive. From a person's eyes, we gather information about how his spirit perceives and responds to the present and past experiences of the world in which he lives. The mouth, body language, and hands of that person are the continuous communicators of his soul. I am, among other things, a Christian hypnotherapist." Stephenson is represented by Carson and the Wild Goose Galleries.

Doris Steider, BLOWING IN THE WIND
egg tempera, 18 x 12

Louis L. Stephenson, CROWING A LITTLE, oil/canvas, 36 x 30

Bettina Steinke, HARVESTING DRINKING WATER (Cambridge Bay, N.W.T.), oil, 20 x 24

V. Stiha (signature)

Stiha, Vladin. Impressionist oil painter of Pueblo Indians and the New Mexico landscape and sculptor of Indian children, born in Belgrade, Yugoslavia in 1908 and living in Santa Fe, New Mexico since 1970. "Art is beauty, life is beauty," he says, "and both should be made up of the proper proportions of composition, design, action, and color. Above all, you must be yourself, you must be you whether dealing with other persons or choosing colors from your palette. One critic wrote of my work that he was reminded of Degas and Monet. I cried out 'No! I am Stiha. I paint like me.'"

The son of an artist, Stiha studied art in Yugoslavia, then learned the classic disciplines at the Academy of Fine Arts in Vienna and privately in Rome. After World War II, he moved to Argentina where he held more than twenty exhibitions. In 1958, he began ten years in Brazil, making his U.S. debut in 1968 in Beverly Hills, California. During an extended painting trip, he grew to love the Pueblo Indians of New Mexico and northern Arizona as subjects and settled in Santa Fe.

"I have learned to resolve every problem each day and I have reached a very agreeable age. I do not think I will change either my style or my motifs. It is the person who matters, each and every one of us, and we must all experiment with, and individually choose, our own composition, design, action, and color we are to make use of in life. They will speak for us as nothing else can." Stiha does commissioned portraits and also models naturalistic bronzes of Indian children in action. He has been written up in *Southwest Art*, summer 1973 and August 1979, and maintains his own gallery.

Vladin Stiha, CORN STILL LIFE, oil, 40 x 30

Stirnweis, Shannon. Representational oil painter of the historical West, born in Portland, Oregon in 1931 and living in Wilton, Connecticut. "I think," he points out, "that a successful historical Western painting could be seen by analogy as a three legged stool. Historical accuracy is one leg. The second leg is the drawing and painting skills that go into it. The third leg is the mood, the feeling, the ability of the artist to be moved and to translate that emotion to a flat piece of board and move others. The emotional content is my greatest concern and has the most to do with why I paint.

"I spent my first 26 years in Oregon except for art school in California and two years in the Army in Germany. My grandfather registered a Lazy "S" Stirnweis brand on his homestead in Eastern Oregon about 1903. I came to New York in 1957 as it was the center for illustration. I have since left that field, but I still find the associations built up over 20 years valuable to my work. There is much precedent for living here and painting the West. Schreyvogel did it, Frank Tenney Johnson lived here for much of his life, Remington's last home is five miles from mine, and Von Schmidt is ten miles away.

"I would like to say I have a consistent approach to painting but it keeps changing, perhaps evolving. An idea results in pencil scribbles. I costume models and photograph them. Charcoal studies and a pencil drawing follow. After a color sketch, the drawing is transferred to a toned board and the painting is slowly built up." A past president of the Society of Illustrators and written up in *Southwest Art*, October 1977, Stirnweis is published by American Masters Foundation and represented by May and Meinhard Galleries.

Stivers, Don. Realist painter of historical Western subjects in oils, born in Superior, Wisconsin in 1926 and living in Wilton, Connecticut since 1966. "I don't have to wait for a phase of the moon to paint," he emphasizes. "I'd rather be painting than anything else. I only take vacations to research and photograph. I seek absolute authenticity in a historical Western subject, but I interpret it through characterization. Landscapes are a foil for the people and horses I love to paint, and to involve the viewer in the action, I move in close to the subject."

Raised in rural Foxboro where his father ran the general store, Stivers was a draftsman and then enlisted in the Navy. He earned a BA from California College of Arts and Crafts in Oakland in 1950 and worked as a commercial artist in California until 1966 when he moved to Connecticut to free lance for books and magazines. In 1974 he began on easel paintings and in 1979 decided to paint full time.

Stivers may take 400 black and white photographs on a trip. He then examines the prints with a magnifying glass to find elements he can use. The elements are fitted together to make a composite where one horse may be reconstructed from three shots. When the values and shapes are established, Stivers starts painting. "I know exactly what the finished painting will look like before I begin," he says. He tapes the composite to the upper left corner and starts his brushwork in the upper right because he works from the top down. He exhibited in the Peking, China show, was featured in *Southwest Art*, October 1980, is published by Greenwich Workshop, and is represented by Troy's Gallery and McCulley.

Stonington, N(ancy) Taylor. Representational watercolorist of contemporary landscapes of Alaska, Idaho, and Washington, born in Suffern, New York in 1944 and living in Ketchum, Idaho since 1973. "I'd say that painting is not satisfying except indirectly," she observes. "The words I would use to describe painting, literally painting, are frustration, excitement, anger, tension, and disappointment. It's never peaceful or relaxed. A painting is ultimately satisfying maybe two weeks after it is done.

"I drew and painted my way through school but never gave a thought to being a professional painter. The only connection with art was in scientific illustration and cartography while I studied physical geography at Middlebury College and the University of Colorado. In 1970 I moved to Sitka, Alaska, began teaching geomorphology and meteorology at the community college, and started to paint again regularly. After my paintings sold in Sitka, I moved my home base to Ketchum to work on shows there."

She now has a full-time business manager, two framers, a shipper, three galleries, and a staff of 20 salespeople. She has had 41 one-person shows. Eighty-eight prints have been produced, with 23 sold out, and she has herself published and wholesaled 83 of them. Currently producing her first lithographs, she has also begun designing large metal sculpture. The author of articles in *American Artist*, April 1979, and *Southwest Art*, April 1979, she is frequently asked how she can possibly paint all those paintings with her left hand. "I assure them," she says, "that it would be a much more formidable task if I had to paint them with my right hand." Her work is also shown at Artique, Ltd. and Peterson Gallery.

Don Stivers, HURRY AND WAIT, oil, 24 x 43

N. Taylor Stonington, BAKER CREEK, watercolor, 22 x 18

Shannon Stirnweis, KIOWA WELCOME, oil, 24 x 36

Mark Storm (signature)

Tim Stortz (signature)

JOHN PAUL STRAIN (signature)

Storm, Mark. Realist oil painter and sculptor of the historic and contemporary West, born in Valdez, Alaska in 1911 and living in Houston, Texas since 1946. "In my opinion," he says, "Frederic Remington and Charlie Russell stand out from all the other Old West artists. They both did a faithful job of recording the spirit as well as the visual part of the life they portrayed. Alike as they are in these respects, Remington was more of the reporter while Russell was a joiner."

Son of a mining engineer, Storm went to grade school in Juneau, Alaska, Ashland, Oregon, Alameda, California and El Paso, Texas after one year in the mountains near Mazatlan, Mexico. Home became a small ranch in the Ruidoso Valley, New Mexico, and Storm went to high school in Austin. At the University of Texas, where he graduated in 1934, he had some art training, then worked at map drafting and commercial art until 1953 when he opened his own agency. It was said that "he would do an illustration with a horse in it for nothing, charging only for the background."

He had been painting Western art on the side since the 1940s, and in 1963 he started phasing out commercial art. A member of the Texas Cowboy Artists Association since 1973, he was featured in the book *XIT* and was Texas Cowboy Artist of the Year in 1980 and 1981. Listed in *Who's Who in American Art,* he has been in *Horseman Magazine* and *The Quarter Horse Journal,* and was commissioned to do the poster for the 1982 Houston Livestock Show. He believes that "today's West is very much like it always has been except that things are done quicker." His prints are published by Random Press and he is represented by Southwest Galleries.

Stortz, Timothy E. Impressionist oil painter of "people, their feelings, history, ideas, goals, and dreams," born in Independence, Iowa in 1952 and living in Denver, Colorado since 1972. "I'm not the type of artist to support the image of 'walking on water' or being some so-called 'star.' Not at all. My work is just that, work. I see myself as any construction worker, teacher, lawyer, etc. sees himself, putting in his time, his contribution to society. I enjoy what I do and the life I'm living."

Raised in small towns as the son of a traveling businessman, he had moved seven times by the age of fourteen. Studying art at the University of Northern Iowa in 1970 and at the University of Iowa in 1971 did not work out because the philosophy was "if it's new, it's art." He transferred to the Colorado Institute of Art "to paint and draw and create, and I saw graphic design as a way of making a living. If you look around, there are more artists out there with this type of background than anything else.

"I began to paint more and was doing a lot of Taos Indians and Colorado subjects when the opportunity came up to go to Mexico with Ramon Kelley, William Reese, and Lowell Smith. It was a big break and led to the 1981 four-man show on Oaxaca at the Frye Museum in Seattle. My work does not have any great new style or innovative approach to it. It is just my personal statement. The means are as important to me as the end, including the forms, orchestrating colors, and slowly developing the ambience. Every artist has his own language of visual self-expression and it is only through time that his expressions are revealed to others." Stortz was written up in *Southwest Art,* March 1981, and is represented by DeColores Art and Pelham Galleries.

Strain, John Paul. Painter in oil and gouache of life in the early American West, born in Nashville, Tennessee in 1955 and living in Benbrook, Texas. "The style of my work," he says, "has been called reminiscent of the romantic landscapes and portrayals of Indian life of Henry Farny and Thomas Moran. I try and attain a certain mood and atmosphere in each of my paintings. I feel many of the great artists of the past such as Moran and Farny have that quality.

"I began painting at an early age," he adds, "and decided to become a Western artist when I was in high school. I attended the University of Redlands in California and Brigham Young University in Utah as an art major. After college, I was employed as an illustrator for the Department of Energy for a year and then I launched out on a career as a full time Western artist. I have since participated in major art shows such as the Russell Auction and the Phippen Memorial, and my work has been featured on the cover of *The American Cowboy.*"

Strain's access to the Old West has been by traveling to sketch and photograph the backgrounds and by research. His 1981 series of Indian portraits was on the Tarahumara Indians, "a group that live in the Sierra Madre region of northwestern Mexico. They have changed very little despite 300 years of contact with Spanish soldiers, missionaries, and the Mexican people. I based these paintings on photographs." He also paints wildlife and landscapes, and has been represented by Trailside Galleries since 1977.

John Paul Strain, WHITE MAN RUNS HIM
gouache, 7¾ x 4¾

Tim Stortz, THREE MARKET WOMEN, pastel, 20 x 34

Mark Storm, MATAGORDA EXODUS, oil, 30 x 40

Jinx Stringham, A.A.R.A.

Paul Strisik

Stringham, Jinx. Representational oil painter of the Old West, wildlife, and landscapes, born in Whidby Island, Washington in 1926 and living in Jackson, Wyoming. "My influences," she stresses, "were Albert Bierstadt and Thomas Moran for their fidelity to the study of the play of light, John Clymer for his dedication, humility, and search for authenticity, and Ace Powell for his love of his fellow man and his willingness to help others.

"I was raised on an Idaho cattle ranch and recall my father spending endless hours teaching me the ways of the wilderness and wild animals." Educated at Boise Business University in Idaho, and Auerswald's in Seattle, Washington, she also studied art at the Seattle School of Fashion Illustration and privately. Since starting to paint full time, she has herself served as an instructor for ten years in Washington, as a juror, as a speaker, has operated her own gallery for six years, and has traveled throughout the West gathering reference data.

After moving her Jackson studio, she said that "much material remains elusive. I'm firmly convinced that every artist, male or female, needs a good wife." Her philosophy is that "an artist who paints a subject which he or she has not thoroughly studied, researched, or produced from personal knowledge fails self and viewer. Without the insight gained through such study or knowledge, it is impossible to capture the character of the subject. She has participated in the C.M. Russell Western Art Show since 1976, is a founding member of both the American Artists of the Rockies Association and the American Historical Artists Association, and is represented by Art Eclectic and The Art Galleries.

Strisik, Paul. Painter of landscapes, particularly the Rockies, in oil and watercolor, born in Brooklyn, New York in 1918 and living in Rockport, Massachusetts. About the Canadian Rockies, Strisik declares that "I was tremendously impressed. Each one is constituted differently, and there are such fine weather effects. I seem to have a rapport with these mountains, and painting them comes naturally to me."

While studying at the Art Students League in New York City with Frank Vincent DuMond, Strisik went on sketching trips that "were truly inspirational. He had a unique way of teaching. By orienting our thinking and putting us and the surroundings in perspective, he made us the type of painters who could tackle problems on our own. He never gave us the answers." Strisik paints on location, "first a small sketch in pencil, then I wash in the oil colors on a canvas in the fashion of a watercolor. I eliminate some features and introduce others. After about two hours, I stop and look at the painting back in the studio, keeping in mind that to the viewer, the painting becomes more real than the subject."

Strisik's credo is that "it is the artist's role to show people the poetry of their everyday surroundings." He has painted over North America and Europe, but he prefers the Rockies where "composition becomes a challenge." He has written *The Art of Painting Landscapes* and was featured in *Southwest Art*, March 1981, and *American Artist*, April 1971 and June 1979. He is an Associate of the National Academy of Design and a member of the National Academy of Western Art and the American Watercolor Society. He has won more than 125 awards and is represented by Settlers West Galleries, where his painting was listed at $8,500 at the 1981 silent auction.

Jinx Stringham, TRAVELERS, oil, 10 x 30

Paul Strisik, LAKE PATZQUARO, MEXICO, oil, 24 x 36

Virginia A. Stroud
GGG~S

[signature]

Robert Summers

Stroud, Virginia Alice. Acrylic painter of visual Indian oratory in pictographic style, born in Madera, California in 1951 and living in Austin, Texas. "Traditionally, Indian women didn't paint," she points out. "That was the men's area. I would love to be a Georgia O'Keeffe. With my paintings, I want one to see the Indian people as individuals and to relate to them as individuals, with all the personality, humor, and pride that makes us unique. I want to expose Indian-ness to people who never thought about it."

Orphaned at thirteen, she moved to Oklahoma, graduating from Muskogee Central High School in 1969 and then attending Bacone Junior College from 1969 to 1970 and the University of Oklahoma from 1971 to 1976. Traditional Cheyenne artist Dick West was her mentor at Bacone, but the academic influence at the University was frustrating. While still in college in 1970, she was the youngest Indian artist ever to win a Philbrook award. The following year, she was selected as Miss Indian America XVII for her beauty. In 1972, she won a museum award, and honors have continued. She was named Indian Artist of the Year in 1981.

"Through my art," she explains, "I am a visual orator. Art is a means by which the Indian culture will live on, perhaps the only means." For centuries, she adds, the Indians had no written language and used clear pictures to record events in the life of the tribe. The events may have been of great moment or a record of everyday activities, now or in the past, in order to preserve and nurture tribal experience. The style is simple, but it is "not naive." She is represented by El Taller.

Sumida, Gregory. Painter of the San Joaquin Delta in California and of Indians, born in Los Angeles in 1948 and living in Stockton near the Delta. "An artist is not a painter of subjects," Sumida says. "He is a recorder of feelings. Art is a private thing for me. It's an emotional and very serious part of my life. Emotion and feeling are as much a part of my paintings as is technique."

Of Japanese descent, Sumida was raised by a Spanish-speaking housekeeper. When he started school, he spoke only Spanish. His parents separated and his mother provided housing for itinerant farm workers who were his friends. High school art teachers told him to study the Old Masters, and Andrew Wyeth in correspondence advised him not to "study under any artist. You have a real quality for watercolor. Work it out your own way. Your pictures are rich and exciting to look at."

Sumida states that "I never want to stay the same and become stagnant" so he has moved from watercolor to oil to tempera to gouache. He spends days outdoors, sketching from life. He may take paints in a back pack or pedal the canal roads on a bicycle to avoid disturbing the Delta residents who become his subjects. Self-taught but sophisticated, he then studies the pencil and watercolor field sketches to compose the paintings that may take him weeks to complete. Now critically regarded as "one of the talented young artists," Sumida has had five one-person shows. His works are in a dozen private collections in the Hollywood colony and in such public holdings as Palm Springs Desert Museum and Oakland Museum. He was profiled in *Southwest Art*, August 1977, and is represented by Fowler's Gallery.

Summers, Robert. Representational oil painter and sculptor of the contemporary West, born in Glen Rose, Texas in 1940 and still living there. "I paint the people and things I know," he observes. "I find it hard to paint anything unless it relates to my own experience. Occasionally, I'll read some historical story and try to recreate that moment, but I have to be careful to make the costumes and weapons correct. Cattle ranching may be a vanishing way of life, but the basic principles are still much the same as they were a hundred years ago.

"I was brought up in a small country town, among normal people, and I intend to keep it that way." Son of a judge, he was encouraged when he began drawing as a boy. After he finished high school, he worked for a construction crew, took correspondence courses in art, and then was employed as a technical illustrator. "That was good training," he says. "We had to take blueprints and try to picture what the finished object would look like."

In 1964, a cousin paid Summers' living expenses for a year so he could paint full time. "Things got pretty tight," he recalls, "and if we hadn't lived in a small town, it would have been impossible." By 1966, he was exhibiting successfully. In 1969 he sold twelve paintings at a solo show in Odessa, and in 1973 his work was reproduced by Franklin Mint. He was the official Texas Bicentennial Artist in 1976, and in 1979, the five paintings he exhibited at the Western Heritage Show in Houston were sold, one for $29,600. In 1980 he was commissioned to model a heroic memorial of John Wayne. Written up in *Southwest Art*, July 1980, his prints are published by American Masters Foundation and he is represented by Altermann Art Gallery.

Virginia Stroud, AUTUMN HARMONY
acrylic, 48 x 36

Robert Summers, SLICKER TIME, oil, 24 x 36

Gregory Sumida, PLATTE RIVER CAMP, gouache, 10 x 15

Duke Sundt

AHSussman

HAL SUTHERLAND

Sundt, Duke. Traditional sculptor of ranch life in the present and the recent past, born in Fort Leavenworth, Kansas in 1948 and living in Sapello, New Mexico. "I put a lot of importance on titles for my bronzes," he points out, "and it is usually quite a chore but often I will have a title before I start a piece and actually design a work around the title. Occasionally friends will suggest a title and sometimes one of my brothers or my wife will think of one. Generally I stumble upon a title while creating the original."

From ages nine to thirteen, he lived in Copenhagen, Denmark where his father was in the military and where he "would make special excursions across the city to view certain bronze monuments." When he returned from abroad, he spent summers on a family ranch in New Mexico and went to school in Las Cruces where he enrolled in New Mexico State University as an engineering student in 1968. "My final decision to become an artist really never entered my mind until I was twenty when I transferred into the art program. In the summer of 1969, I landed a job at Nambe Mills north of Santa Fe, working in the foundry, and was fortunate enough to begin selling some bronzes through Nambe.

"I received my BFA degree in 1970 and was 'turned out' to make it on my own. I had worked the bareback bronc riding event while I was rodeoing off and on, and I then chose the next hardest way to make a living—being an artist. I was glad I had ranching experience to rely on to provide a steady income while I worked on my art, and I gradually was able to spend my time on my artwork and less time devoted to making ends meet by working as a ranch hand. I am represented by Texas Art, Jamison, and Shidoni Galleries."

Sussman, Arthur. Painter between realism and abstraction in biblical and Indian themes, born in Brooklyn, New York in 1927 and living Albuquerque, New Mexico since 1965. "In the early 1970s," he explains, "I began painting an Indian brave. This was after many years of painting the Old Testament. As I researched more into Indian lore, Blue Feather emerged. He is the aesthetic force that keeps coming up in my work. He rides Cloud Horse his stallion. Each painting in this series has a specific title implying an ongoing narrative."

After serving in the Navy, Sussman graduated with honors from Syracuse University in 1950, then attended the Brooklyn Museum School of Fine Art while working as a free-lance designer and illustrator. In 1960, he moved to Taxco, Mexico where he started painting biblical themes with a Mexican setting. He found the same inspiration in Spain and Israel. When he returned to the United States in 1964, he was given major one-person shows and the next year moved to New Mexico, because of the climate and sense of space. The West became the biblical background and also a new theme, Blue Feather.

According to Sussman, Blue Feather "is handsome (in his way) and barbarically instinctive. The works focus on quietly powerful action or impending action, but horse and rider are always part of a complex composition. I aim at emotional quality, using Old Master transparent glazing. It's gotten so that I think that someday there will emerge an actual story." Sussman is listed in *Who's Who in American Art* and is a member of the National Society of Mural Painters. He has been featured in *Southwest Art, American Artist,* and *El Palacio.* He is represented by his own gallery in Albuquerque.

Sutherland, Hal. Painter of the Northwest in brilliant acrylics, born in Somerville, Massachusetts in 1929 and living in Bothell, Washington since 1972. "During my early years," he recalls, "many milk wagons were still horse drawn, and I used to wait each afternoon for our local milkman to come by. I'll always remember the day he asked me if I'd like to sit on the horse's back. Wow! A great portion of my interest in the West was born right then and there, with that homely raw-boned nag."

After his parents separated, Sutherland lived with his grandparents. He quit technical training school because of the lack of art courses, and took odd jobs before enlisting in the Army, in 1946. Under the G.I. Bill, he went to the Art Center School of Design in Los Angeles, where he found he was color blind. He worked out a simplified palette and color formulas, and he says that today when he "gets a lot of comment about the bright colors, this always tickles me pink." In 1954, he was hired by Walt Disney Studios as an animator specializing in horses. He helped form a new animation company in 1961, won an Emmy, and sold out in 1969.

When his employment contract ended in 1974, he was finally able to paint full time. Now he rarely accepts commissions, "I don't want to bastardize my freedom by hacking out something I'm not really interested in just to turn an extra dollar. When I first started painting up here, I never knew whether people were interested in my work or because I was from Hollywood. Now I'm beginning to get inquiries about giving painting workshops." He was featured in *Art West,* January 1981, and is represented by Gallery Select, Image West, and Ace Powell Art Gallery.

Duke Sundt, TRADING DAYLIGHT FOR DARK, bronze, h 15, w 15

Arthur Sussman, APPRENTICESHIP OF BLUE FATHER, oil, 24 x 18

Hal Sutherland, THE GOOD LIFE, acrylic, 12 x 24

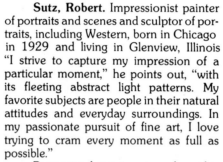

Sutz, Robert. Impressionist painter of portraits and scenes and sculptor of portraits, including Western, born in Chicago in 1929 and living in Glenview, Illinois "I strive to capture my impression of a particular moment," he points out, "with its fleeting abstract light patterns. My favorite subjects are people in their natural attitudes and everyday surroundings. In my passionate pursuit of fine art, I love trying to cram every moment as full as possible."

Determined at sixteen to make art his life's work, he studied art from 1946 to 1951, attending the Chicago Academy of Art and winning scholarships to the Chicago Art Institute and the American Academy of Art. He served in the military from 1951 to 1953 as artist/illustrator and photographer in the Psychological Warfare Detachment, then returned to Chicago to work as a free-lance illustrator. In 1958 he joined the Leo Burnett Advertising Agency where he became executive art director.

While working, he continued to paint. He carried index cards in his pocket and sketched the passengers on his commuter trains and the cityscape out the window. At lunch, he sketched in the park. When the Mongerson Gallery accepted his work, he was on his way. In 1969, he was elected a member of the American Watercolor Society and in 1974 he started on trips to the Southwest, sketching and making life masks of Zuni, Apache, and Navajo Indians. There was a Sutz retrospective in 1975, and in 1980 he left Burnett to open his own studio/gallery to do human interest subjects as fine art and to paint portraits or to make life masks in bronze or in oil over plaster. His work is in the National Cowboy Hall of Fame and he is represented by Fowler's Gallery.

Swanson, Gary R. Realist painter of North American and African wildlife in oil and watercolor, born north of Alcester, South Dakota in 1941 and living in Prescott, Arizona. "My father," he recalls, "gave me a sort of perspective of my place in the world. He never really came out and said, 'Hey, look: you're just a fly in the ointment,' but I got the message. This awareness that he gave me has helped to make me the artist that I am. He also took the time to teach me to handle a gun, and to trap and live in the wild."

After apprenticeship to a taxidermist in Sioux Falls, Swanson was employed as a taxidermist in Seattle and in Anchorage before setting up his own studio in southern California. "I look over the thirteen years that I spent as a taxidermist," he points out, "and I realize that the knowledge of animal anatomy that I received was priceless. In fact, I think that you'll rarely find a taxidermist who could not make it in the art world, particularly in sculpture.

"To begin my art career, I studied under my brother, Ray, and turned professional in 1971. Ray taught me about colors —how to mix them, how to go after them, how to use them. Without Ray, I couldn't have done it. As I progressed, my style became my own. I woke up one morning and literally said to myself, 'Swanson, you're an artist.' Everything I had learned about art came together all of a sudden." He adds that "I can't explain it, but an artist is judged by the way the public accepts his work. If an artist is selling, then he or she must be doing something right. I have received many honors and awards including six gold medals and a 1974 contract with Franklin Mint. Collectors Covey publishes my prints." He was written up in *Southwest Art,* January 1980.

Gary Swanson, UNTITLED, oil, 24 x 36

Robert Sutz, SIOUX WOMAN, pastel, 20 x 16

J·N·Swanson —

Ray Swanson

[signature: Szabo]

Swanson, J.N. Realist and traditional painter and sculptor of the West, born in Duluth, Minnesota in 1927 and living in Carmel Valley, California. "I stress knowing your subject matter thoroughly," he says, "and preferably getting firsthand knowledge to really have the feel of what you're putting down on canvas. Although I realize that a great percentage of buyers of Western art might not see or understand much of what I put into a painting, I paint for those who do, and for myself."

Raised in California, Jack Swanson was doing a man's work breaking horses when he was fourteen. He served in the Navy for two years during World War II and then went to Oregon, to work on ranches his father owned. While attending the College of Arts and Crafts in Oakland under the G.I. Bill, he "seemed to be not getting along with modern-type art teachers who didn't think horses were worth painting but pots were" so he left school to race horses. When his "stud" pulled up lame, he tried the Carmel Art Institute and also had advice from Donald Teague.

"Having a working horse ranch, and training some of the finest stock horses, takes quite a bit of my time from the studio but my love of good horseflesh is almost equal to painting them. The high deserts of Oregon and Nevada are my favorite stomping grounds, and I will be running wild horses in East Oregon with professional mustangers, hoping to record this in paintings. I was honored by having President Reagan take one of my large vaquero paintings to the White House." Swanson is a member of the Cowboy Artists of America, is listed in *Who's Who in American Art*, was written up in Ainsworth's *The Cowboy in Art* and Hassrick's *Western Painting Today*, and is represented by Who's Who in Art and Copenhagen Galleri.

Swanson, Ray. Wholly self-taught realist painter of Navajo and Hopi Indians, born in Alcester, South Dakota in 1937 and living in Prescott, Arizona since 1972. "The most exciting paintings I do," he says, "are portraits of the older Navajo folk. The lines in their faces show the peace within. The real challenge for me is capturing the emotions reflected in their faces."

Born on a farm, Swanson studied for eight years in a one-room schoolhouse. When his father was killed in an accident, the family sold out and moved to California. While he was studying aeronautical engineering at Northrop Institute, his grandfather who had painted as a hobby left Swanson his paint box. Swanson "figured if they were oil paints, they probably should go on oil cloth," but he persevered. After he graduated in 1960 and worked as a civil engineer, he painted farm subjects in the evenings and on weekends. With his brother Gary, he opened a diorama and gift shop where he also hung his paintings priced from $25 to $75.

Swanson bought Indian merchandise for resale in the shop, became involved in studying the Indian civilization, and moved to Prescott because of the established art colony and because it was only a two hour drive from the reservations. He had become a full-time artist, "permanently under the spell of the Southwestern landscape and the effect of light on it." In 1978, *Artists of the Rockies* did a feature article on Swanson, and both *Art West* and *Southwest Art* followed in 1981. He is listed in *Who's Who in American Art*, his prints are published by Mill Pond Press, and his gallery is Husberg Fine Arts.

Szabo, Zoltan. Landscape painter in transparent watercolor, teacher, and writer, born in Hungary in 1929 and living in Tempe, Arizona since 1979. "I price each painting differently," he states. "I usually don't go by size. I just judge how successful it is aesthetically. If you put a really high price on it, as a deterrent, that's the first one people will buy because they think you think so much of it it's got to be the best. If I don't want to part with a painting, I give it to my wife. Then it's protected."

At seventeen, after World War II, Szabo enrolled in the National Academy of Industrial Art in Budapest. When he heard he would be arrested as an anti-Communist, he escaped to West Germany where he was in a displaced persons camp in 1948. After a year, he was accepted into Canada and has been a Canadian citizen since 1957. A commercial artist, he began painting full time in 1966 and has written five books on how to paint in watercolor. He also conducts workshops and in six years appeared in 48 states, before 11,000 painters.

"When I paint," he continues, "I have only one thing in mind; to express my feelings, my emotions, my ideas, to try and see if I can capture and transfer that feeling to the viewer. That takes up my total concentration. The whole world is turned off while it's happening. I honestly never think of money. When I am finished, then I think of putting a value on it because if I don't, who will?" In his workshops, he "sees the country through painters' eyes, the painters who take me right to the best places to paint, just the spots I would go to paint if I knew them." Szabo is represented by El Prado Gallery of Art and Pivan Gallery.

Zoltan Szabo, UNTITLED, watercolor, 22 x 15

Ray Swanson, NAVAJOS AT CASTLE BUTTE
oil, 48 x 36

J.N. Swanson, DAYLIGHT, oil, 32 x 48

Paul Todlock

R. Tanenbaum

TAVLOS

Tadlock, Paul. Traditional sculptor of North American wildlife, figures, and domestic animals, born in Houston, Texas in 1935 and living in New Braunfels, Texas in 1982. "Most people want to know," he says, "how I bring my idea to life in bronze. My answer is, I don't know. When I'm working, I'm amazed I can do this. Many times I get the feeling it's not me doing it. There will be times when I'll be engrossed with a piece, hung up on a detail, and all of a sudden—there it is."

After high school in Dallas, he enrolled at the University of Texas. Working part time for a manufacturing company, he transferred to Arlington State College and North Texas State University before graduating in 1957 with a degree in advertising arts. The manufacturing company hired him and in 1960 promoted him into management. In 1973 at a dinner party, he talked to a dentist who sculpted as a hobby, bought the materials, and started modeling. Two months later, he showed a wax antelope to painter Guy Coheleach and was told to "have it cast." He sold castings, started on an elk and quit his job four months after starting to sculpt.

He set a goal of modeling twenty of the major big game animals of North America, and by 1982 had finished forty pieces including seventeen of the twenty. On the hunt, he searches for a near-perfect specimen of the specific animal he seeks, then measures it extensively, taking sixteen dimensions of the head alone. He starts the sculpture with actual size drawings, frontal and profile. In building the anatomy, he uses calipers to check each waxed-in section of bone and muscle against his sketches and measurements. Written up in *Southwest Art,* September 1978, he has shown at Troy's and The Hanging Tree Galleries.

Tanenbaum, Robert. Realist painter of the American Indian and the cowboy of the new and Old West in oil and casein, born in Chillicothe, Missouri in 1936 and living in Tarzana, California since 1964. "I want to help preserve the heritage of the West in my paintings," he says, "and to that end I try to make my subjects so lifelike that they will seem about to speak."

When he was three, his parents moved back to their hometown of St. Louis, Missouri. He began drawing at six and took a few art classes while attending high school. His formal training began at the Washington University Art School in St. Louis where he won two portrait contests before graduating with a BFA degree in 1959. After a six-month stint in the Army, he worked in St. Louis for four years as a commercial artist before moving to the Los Angeles area where he has been an illustrator and portrait painter for seventeen years.

Among his credits was the commission for a life-size portrait of Howard Hughes and a double portrait of the historians Will and Ariel Durant. For the title treatment of the first segment of Alex Haley's *Roots,* he did a one-and-a-half by eight foot painting of the major stars, and for both the book cover and the TV series on James Michener's *Centennial,* he did a painting that included twenty portraits. In recent years, he has completed 22 paintings of Levi Girls for national ads, as well as posters for the major movie producers. For the commercial art, he has won awards from the Society of Illustrators, and for his easel paintings he was elected to membership in the National Watercolor Society in 1970. He is represented by El Prado Gallery of Art.

Tavlos, (Dennis). Modern artist working in cut-out paintings, watercolor, lithography, and serigraphy, born in Alton, Illinois in 1944 and living in Santa Fe, New Mexico. "He has been referred to as 'the Peter Max of the Southwest,' although he doesn't believe he has been influenced by Max. He does feel influenced by Matisse and relates strongly to Matisse's statement 'keep it simple' which he heard as a young artist."

Of Greek descent, he studied art at the University of Illinois and received his BFA in graphic design in 1968. After college, he was drafted into the Army and served in Fort Bliss and in Alaska. He started out in architecture but "was always design oriented." While visiting a friend in Santa Fe he fell in love with the town and the landscape, sensing a kinship to the foreignness and the magic. After six months of traveling the area and absorbing the atmosphere, he started to paint and print Southwestern images.

In the beginning, he painted non-objective fantasies but changed to hard-edged images in bold colors. He may make from fifteen to twenty drawings of the images that are in his mind before he achieves the greatest simplification that is consistent with a strong "feel." He uses an airbrush to accomplish the blend of color, painting the rest by hand. In his cut-outs, he "translates non-rectangular shapes into three dimensional images to suit his designs and colors." He believes that multiples as such are becoming less popular so he is employing different shades of color to change the appearance and to create a different mood for each multiple. He has exhibited in 33 shows beginning in 1971 and is represented by Los Llanos and Printer's Galleries.

Robert Tanenbaum, SHADOW OF THE BUFFALO
oil & casein, 26 x 26

Dennis Tavlos, THE BLESSING OF THE WALPI BY THE RAINBOW SPIRIT
watercolor, 28½ x 31

Paul Tadlock, ON A DIME, bronze, h 8, w 14½, Edition 50

J.H. TAYLOR

Terpning

Taylor, James H. Representational watercolorist of Utah landscapes and sculptor of waterfowl in bronze statuettes, born in Washington, D.C. in 1946 and living in Orem, Utah. "My paintings," he emphasizes, "are naturalistic landscapes of the Utah Valley and Wasatch Mountain regions. The most common denominator is snow. I've lived in snow country all my life and have grown to love it. I'm constantly challenged and fascinated by the many faces of the snowscape in winter.

"Immediately following graduation from Brigham Young University in 1972 with a Master's degree in art, I accepted a position as high school art instructor in Heber City, Utah. After two years of feeling stifled, I opted to enter the art world as a full time professional artist, specializing in watercolor/acrylic landscapes on sheets ranging in size from 10 by 15 inches to 30 by 40 inches. The larger sheets generally present special problems and are not always successful.

"The rustic buildings, wildlife, and Indian life that I choose as subjects are an integral but subordinate part of the overall landscape paintings. Sometimes these subjects are added only as minor accents to give life and animation to the dominant and encompassing landscape. The Indian life I paint portrays the Crow and Blackfoot tribes of Montana, Idaho, and Wyoming. The waterfowl consists of ducks, quail, and geese. Several years ago, I started sculpting these birds in plastalina clay to better understand their form and structure. This study has now developed to the point where I am casting the waterfowl I sculpt." Taylor is represented by Miner's Gallery Americana and Voris Gallery.

Terpning, Howard. Realist painter of the historical Plains Indians, born in Oak Park, Illinois near Chicago in 1927 and living in Tucson, Arizona since 1975. "So far," he says, "what we've seen from modern Western artists is the cavalry and Indians, trappers and mountain men," the figures in action. "But we're already moving toward art that shows Western *life* the way it was back then, the actual day-to-day living experiences of all the people, and I feel this broadening will attract even greater interest in Western art.

"I wasn't what you'd call a 'child prodigy.' I was educated in public schools," and after graduation enlisted in the Marine Corps late in World War II. "When I got back, I managed to get into the Chicago Academy of Fine Art on the G.I. Bill. Then I moved over to the American School of Art for six months. That was the extent of my formal training." He was hired as an apprentice at a Chicago studio and after eight years moved to New York City. In the early 1960s, he began to free lance.

Despite commercial success including movie posters and national magazine covers, he says that "art directors kept telling me I should be doing gallery paintings. The first few years in the fine art field were pretty lean," but in 1979 he was elected to both the National Academy of Western Art and the Cowboy Artists of America. The following year he won the gold medal at NAWA and two silver medals at CAA. More than 400 potential buyers filed intent to purchase cards on one painting. At the 1981 silent auction at Settlers West Galleries, the minimum bid for a Terpning oil was $35,000. He has been featured in *Saturday Review, Southwest Art, Art West,* and *Prints,* and was in the Peking, China exhibition.

James H. Taylor, WINTER LIGHT, acrylic & watercolor, 10 x 15

Howard Terpning, DUST OF MANY PONY SOLDIERS, oil, 36 x 56

Theroux, Carol. Painter of contemporary Indian children, born in Cardwell, Missouri in 1930 and living in Bellflower, California. "One of the greatest regrets that I have," she recalls, "is that I happened to be born when it was just not 'ladylike' to yearn to attend the Art Center or any other creative place of endeavor for a girl of eighteen. My parents had little patience with a girl who had 'wasted her education' scribbling pictures."

Of German-Otoe-Cherokee descent, she received art awards at the age of six and a scholarship to the Art Center at eighteen, but she was led into "a decent job in a store" where she "earned 23 cents an hour, learning how to do lettering for signs while stumbling around behind a man dressing the manikins, wearing stockings over my shoes." She married, and after seven years she began to copy calendar covers and magazine photographs. She then attended painting classes until 1970 when her teachers "conspired to kick me out of class, to get 'out there' and try out what I had been learning." She had also been involved in Scouting, particularly in helping her children create authentic costumes, so "the Indian theme crept into my work.

"I really feel happiest," she declares, "when using the water-based mediums. Acrylic paints supply the lovely soft flowing quality on paper, but if used on canvas they work as an oil." She is also accredited as an instructor, and "learned more about myself by teaching others." After a late start, her paintings are now advertised nationally, sell in six galleries including Kessler Art, are shown in invitational exhibitions nationally, and are reproduced by International Art Connection.

Thomas, Bernard Preston. Realist muralist and painter of the life of the West, born near Sheridan, Wyoming in 1918 and living in Boynton Beach, Florida since 1953. "Some of my happiest years," he declares, "were also the ones most beneficial to my artwork. I slept on the ground alongside the outfit's top hands. I heard their stories of wilder days, and I'm the one who believes the artist who has lived 'it' is the one who can put the right feel in his work. Nothing gripes me more than a Western illustration done by an Eastern illustrator who doesn't know straight up about the West."

Born to homesteaders, he went to a one-room schoolhouse and was an all-state football player in high school. He "lived near Bill Gollings the cowboy artist. Just watching him in his little studio was all a kid needed, and I determined that some day I too would be a cowboy artist." After receiving a BS in art from Woodbury College in Los Angeles, he served as a sergeant in the Third Army in World War II and was sent by General Patton to the Ecole de Beaux Arts in Paris where he learned mural painting.

Thomas painted the 10 by 200-foot Cyclorama mural in the Rapid City, South Dakota Fine Arts Center, a task that took 455 days, as well as an 80-foot Western mural in a Rapid City bank and the "Autorama" in Florida that was the largest three-dimensional mural painted by one artist. He is a member of the National Society of Mural Painters, was profiled in Ainsworth's *The Cowboy in Art* and Hassrick's *Western Painting Today,* was illustrated in *Western Horseman Magazine,* and is exhibited in Grand Central Art Galleries in New York City and Gallery G Fine Arts.

Thomas, (James Michael) Jim. Traditional sculptor of the lifestyle of the modern cowboy and documenter "of 150 years of Texas history," born in Miami, Florida in 1936 and living in Leander, Texas since 1982. "The cowboys," he insists, "represent the real man versus the plastic man, a real lifestyle versus a hypocritical lifestyle. The cowboy is an international folk hero. He is a clean, simple, easy-to-identify person who represents sincerity, manliness, and positive cultural characteristics — honesty, dependability, resourcefulness."

A forestry major in college, Thomas moved to Texas after his release from the Air Force in 1960. Self-taught in art, he had painted as a hobby before he began sculpting with artist friends who worked in Thomas' Amarillo advertising agency in 1964. Thomas says that Western art was just beginning to gain recognition then, so he did a five-state market survey among museum curators, artists, and gallery owners. The prediction was that Western art "would be the coming rage," leading Thomas to pursue sculpture seriously. An expert photographer, he rode with working cowboys to record authentic scenes to model.

Sculpture "looked interesting, so I decided to dig into it," he explains. "I got to sneaking off from our business to do artwork, and I went full time into art in '68. Now, I plan to concentrate more on historical art, and I expect to incorporate Impressionistic elements at the expense of the total realism that marked my previous work." He is also preserving the style of the state's historic buildings by reproducing the architectural artifacts. A member of the Texas Cowboy Artists Association, he is represented by The Galleries and by his own studio.

Carol Theroux, LITTLE FAWN, acrylic, 30 x 15

Jim Thomas, CHUCKWAGON, bronze, h 12, w 24

Bernard Thomas, TROUBLE AHEAD, oil, 24 x 48

Thomas, Lynn. Realist/Impressionist painter of contemporary and historical Western subjects in oil, watercolor, and pencil, born in Los Angeles in 1939 and living in Las Vegas, Nevada. "I love the mountains," she declares, "and intend to spend a lot of time in the high country without the work involved in the outfitting business we sold. Now, I always have a few colts coming along that I work with. All this has given me unending ideas and material for my painting. It seems that all I do leads back to my art."

Of German, English, and Indian heritage, her ancestors crossed the Plains in covered wagons and her great-grandfather was a blacksmith on the Oregon Trail. When she was five, she moved with her family "to the desert of southern Nevada. I went to a three-room schoolhouse. I've been drawing as long as I can remember, and always loved drawing animals. I went to work one summer in a hunting and fishing lodge in Wyoming, and never went back to my secretarial job. I ran the place on my own for fourteen years and have been a licensed outfitter and guide.

"I'm essentially a self-taught artist with no formal training except for a few good workshops. I never had the opportunity to go to college because my parents couldn't afford it. I don't feel this has been a detriment. My subject matter includes the working cowboy, Western scenery, packing in the mountains, sheep and cattle ranching, wildlife, the fur trade era, Western migration, Indians, animals, and horses, horses, horses. I've won over fifty ribbons in shows, six sweepstakes, and six best of shows. Galleries showing my work include Burk Gal'ry and Pa-Jo's." She is a member of the Women Artists of the American West.

Thomas, Richard D. Representational oil painter of ranch scenes and portraits, born near Coalinga, California about 1935 and living near Florissant, Colorado. "Certainly fantasy has helped me with my Western art," he observes. "I can fantasize about being a cowboy, even though I'm a long way from being a real one. I own horses and I help with roundups —that satisfies the cowboy in me. I'm an artist whose work is portraying Western subjects at this period in my career.

"My dad felt that an artist would never make any money. I wound up attending Arizona State, where I earned a BS in economics." After four and a half years in the Marines, including a year in Vietnam, he was employed by an electronics firm but "began to experience a general unhappiness and decided to buy some canvas and paints. I painted in my spare time for three or four years and started taking paintings to weekend art shows. Then the company moved its operations to Mississippi and I went on the road doing art shows across the country for nearly three years."

In 1976, he settled in Colorado, as "a people painter. When I stand before a white canvas, I know exactly what the subject will be. I have no need to work out the details. I don't like to take too much time on a painting. I don't believe in laboring over a work. Labored art is painting that doesn't flow freely, and it usually shows. I never start out with a predetermined technique. The painting dictates where it is going. You must remain open at all times to the directions that come from your work. If you don't, you're leading yourself to a dead end." Thomas is represented by The Breckenridge Gallery and Kansas Gallery of Fine Arts.

Thompson, Carol J. Realist painter of the northern Pacific Coast, born in Medford, Wisconsin in 1941 and living in Olympia, Washington since 1969. "When I first saw the ocean," she recalls, "I ran in up to my knees and tasted it to see if it was salty—it really is! Having got my 'feet wet' (so to speak) I knew this constantly moving, ever changing, yet always the same, subject would be my master. The challenge is to paint the movement of the water with such believability that if you looked away, the wave would have crashed and been gone.

"I have always wanted to be an 'artist' since I was a little girl, studying because 'someday I'm going to paint that.' " She has taken art classes at Olympic Community College since 1971, has been in workshops with Western master painters like Sergei Bongart and William Reese, and has participated in juried shows in the Northwest since 1971.

"I want to convey the color and quality of light on the moving water, to show on a two dimensional surface the feeling of depth and distance. I paint as realistically as I can, using a variety of strokes and tools, from smooth brushwork in the sky to heavy palette knife on the rocks. Using light, middle, and dark values in the translucency, and blending with a soft brush, gives the effect of light shining through the waves. I use light versus dark, warm versus cool, and soft and hard edges to heighten the dramatic effect." She exhibits at Lincoln Art and Ilona Rittler Gallery.

Richard D. Thomas, NEW STOCK, oil, 24 x 36

Carol Thompson, EAGLE ROCK, oil, 18 x 24

Lyn Thomas, WAITIN', oil, 22 x 28

Thompson, Richard Earl. Impressionist painter of Wisconsin landscapes, born in Oak Park, Illinois in 1914 and living in Hayward at Big Round Lake, Wisconsin since 1974. "The world of light," he emphasizes, "is endless. It'll go on for millions of years after this, as long as the earth is here, and only an infinitesimal part of it has ever been painted. Look at the 10,000 paintings Monet left behind. He only scratched the surface, and I haven't even scratched it.

"I started painting when I was eight. My father was a lay-out man in the advertising business who painted on the side. I used to go down to the Chicago Art Institute when they had the American show there, and every year, I'd see less and less of the paintings that I was affected by until finally I just quit going." A prodigy at fifteen, he enrolled at the Chicago Academy of Fine Art and subsequently attended the American Academy of Art and the School of the Art Institute.

"The contemporary style came in around that time, in the 30s, and then the New York scene came in. The market wasn't there for Impressionists." Due also to the Depression, he worked at commercial art, helping create Coca-cola ads. When commercial photography made inroads on illustration, he turned back to fine art in 1959, regretting "the twenty years as an illustrator. I wish I could take them back. In the beginning, the price range for paintings was just unbelievable. We couldn't exist on it," but this time he was soon able to support his family as a painter. He moved his home and studio to the woods of Wisconsin and established a winter home on the Florida Keys. He publishes his own prints and operates his own gallery in San Francisco. On the opening night of his fall 1981 exhibition, eighteen paintings were sold for $310,000.

Richard Thompson, SUMMERTIME, oil, 40 x 60

Thompson, S. Mark. Realist painter of character studies and landscapes in egg tempera, born in Lakewood, Colorado in 1947 and living in Golden, Colorado since 1972. "I work in three-hour stretches," he explains, "then get up and run or something. I can't sit there and concentrate without taking a break for exercise. There's great release this way. Without breaks, you soon find you're hurrying a part of the painting that you don't want to hurry."

The third generation in Colorado, he did not set out to be an artist. After finishing a year of veterinary medicine at Colorado State University, he took a drawing course and "was drawing all the time when I finished studying for my other classes, and what was worse, sometimes I drew before I finished studying." After earning a BA in illustration in 1970, he worked as a commercial artist in Chicago for a year, but "always hated the town. One day, I decided that even if I had to work in a gas station, I could still do art, so I went back to Colorado, got a job in a gas station and later tended bar until I found a job teaching drawing in high school where I stayed for nine years."

In 1972, he began working with egg tempera where egg yolk is the binder, water is the vehicle, and dry powder is the pigment. "I'd never seen any egg tempera," he recalls, "and there were no books on tempera. I knew Andrew Wyeth had worked with it, but that was all. For a realist, it was a logical thing to use. One reason why I stay with it is that very few people work in it. I don't like being crowded." In choosing subjects, he wants "somebody who has the West or a ranch written in his face." He is represented by Carson's Gallery of Western American Art.

Thorsten, Lloyd. Traditional oil painter specializing in aspen scenes of the Rocky Mountains, born in Ford, near Lake Coeur d'Alene, in northern Idaho about 1930 and living in Englewood, Colorado. He recalls being intrigued as a child by drawings in comic strips and by realizing that he could draw better than his brothers and sisters. He practiced, he says, until he could draw such characters as Wash Tubbs, Dick Tracy, and Boots as well as their originators. "When I was fourteen," he recalls, "my teacher told me I would be the only one in the class to go on and pursue art through life—and so I was."

While in military service in Germany in the late 1940s, he studied European painting techniques at the Holzinger School of Fine Art in Wiesbaden, and visited galleries in Germany and France. "Perhaps nothing of the great masters rubbed off on me," he states, "but the fact that I was able to see and study such revered and priceless works was inspiration enough to guarantee my eternal interest in art and 'doing it myself.' " Back in the United States, he enrolled in a course in commercial art in 1952, but realized it "just wasn't his bag" although he was short of money and holding several jobs at once.

When he moved to Spokane, he took two art courses at Washington State University, and then studied privately with Vesta Robbins, whom he credits with inspiring his "ability to portray on canvas the splendor of Western and Rocky Mountain America from Canada to Mexico." He also painted Pacific seascapes, portraits, and scenes of the Southwest. Written up in *Artists of the Rockies,* fall 1975, he is published by Salt Creek Graphics, shows at Trailside Galleries and is resident artist of Aspen Tree Gallery.

Timmerman, Gerrit. Traditional Western sculptor, born in Salt Lake City in 1942 and still living there. "My progenitors," he says, "participated in the trek of the 1850s, pulling handcarts along the Mormon Trail. The natural talents of my family greatly stimulated my own sensibilities for art. Drawing paper, watercolors, crayons, and modeling clay were part of my Christmases and birthdays. By the time I was ten years old, my watercolors were earning blue ribbons.

"In 1960, I entered the University of Utah, enrolling in the sciences, and in 1961 I began a two and a half year ministry for the Mormon church in West Germany. When I returned to the University, I continued with studies in science and dentistry and sought a degree in German. I graduated in 1969 and found work doing renderings of interior designs for a furniture studio, then began learning dental laboratory technology. For nearly ten years, I was contented working on sculptures in miniature in dental ceramics where each crown and bridge was refined in every detail.

"One of the sculptors who awakened my interest in sculpture was Edward J. Fraughton. Visits to his studio and foundry between 1974 and 1980 provided the necessary impetus. My first sculpture to be cast into bronze was a Lincoln portrait. Showing the clay in 1979 led to the sale of the entire edition to a single investor. That one experience dispelled the 'starving artist' syndrome for me and I knew I was capable of creating sculpture that was beautiful. In 1980 I received a contract from Western Art Classics and my bronze sculptures are currently on exhibition at L.K. Moss and Associates and Main Trail Galleries."

Gerrit Timmerman, LITTLE LADY, h 24, w 22

Mark Thompson, TRAPPER TOM
egg tempera/panel, 18 x 16

Lloyd Thorsten, PINEY CREEK, oil, 22½ x 30

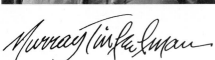

Tinkelman, Murray. Illustrator and painter of Western subjects in black and white and colored pen and ink, born in Brooklyn, New York in 1933 and living in Peekskill, New York. "There are no outlines," he points out, "in any of these recent drawings. I like my work to grow from the inside out. It's a form of Impressionism. Then too, my abstract expressionist background is very strong, even in my realism. I am trying to be realistic, yet the cross-hatching technique cannot be fully so. It's a contradictory method that I happen to love."

At sixteen, he rode a horse for the first time and took odd jobs until he could buy his own horse. He attended the High School of Art and Design in New York City, enlisted in the Army in 1952, went to Cooper Union Art School for two years, and received a scholarship during two years at the Brooklyn Museum School. Until 1964, he worked in a commercial art studio, and then free-lanced, winning more than 150 professional awards, including seventy from the Society of Illustrators. He has also taught illustration and visual communication since 1963.

In 1978, he was commissioned to do fifty Zane Grey paperback book covers that have returned him to horses. "Searching for Zane Grey references," he adds, "I went to a rodeo. I felt like an artist-reporter recording something real and immediate. The rodeo becomes a metaphor and a vehicle. When I'm in the arena, I feel like a fish in kelp. There's no self-consciousness and I really belong." There are books on his illustrations and his Western art and now two on rodeos. He has been featured in *American Artist, North Light,* and *Southwest Art* and has exhibited in Webb and Meinhard Galleries.

Toddy, Marvin. Representational painter of the people and the landscape of the Navajo Reservation in oil, watercolor, and pencil, born in Pine Springs, Arizona and living on the Reservation today. "I have never had any formal art training," he points out, "but I come from a family of overwhelming talent. I am the son of the famous Beatin Yazz (Jimmy Toddy), and although I never knew my father while I was growing up, I feel that I inherited his talent. I also have two brothers, Irving and Calvin, who are recognized in the art world.

"I attended school in Winslow, Arizona, where I took art classes. I have been painting since I was nine, and I was teaching the teacher and the other children. I would paint three paintings a week, and my grandma who realized I had talent drove them into Gallup, New Mexico, where she sold them. I work from photographs I have taken on the Reservation, and also by painting my own family members. My favorite subject is people. They fascinate me.

"At one time, I painted only for the money end of it. Then I met Joe Tanner who influenced me greatly. Now I paint because there is meaning to my paintings that depict the Navajo people, their oneness with Mother Earth, their way of life, culture, and living conditions." His family on both sides numbered silversmiths, rug weavers, and sandpainters. Called one of the most important young Navajo artists, he has placed first in many exhibitions including the New Mexico State Fair, Tanner's Invitational, and at the Heard Museum. His interests include running fifteen to twenty miles a day. He is published by Gallart Reproductions and represented by Tanners Gallery.

Tomlin, Floyd S. Traditional sculptor of "cowboys at work and play, Indians, and Western animals" in bronze statuettes and woodcarvings born in Rifle, Colorado in 1910 and living in Prescott, Arizona since 1971. "I spent my childhood on the family homestead in western Colorado, attended grammar school in the high Rockies at Salida and high school in La Junta and Rocky Ford west of Bent's Fort. During my school years, I was interested in drawing but peer pressure under the mining and ranching influence made art a poor bet.

"As a child, I did do a bit of wood whittlin' and in high school, I ditched art classes and substituted woodworking classes. When I attended the 'Colorado Aggies' in Fort Collins in 1930 and 1931, I did a bit of carving in alabaster. While I was stationed in New York City during World War II, one of my carvings was in the All-Army Art Show in 1944 and hung in the Metropolitan Museum of Art. After my discharge, I moved to California and worked as finish foreman for home building.

"In Santa Barbara, I took advantage of adult education classes to study drawing, woodcarving, and sculpture during the early 1960s. While construction superintendent in Prescott, I became acquainted with the owner of the House of Bronze foundry and was encouraged to work in wax." Tomlin's bronzes and woodcarvings were winning awards by 1974. Most of his work is of Western ranch and Indian scenes because "this is what I know best." While exhibiting at the first Phippen Memorial Show, he was invited to become the first sculptor member of the American Indian and Cowboy Artist Society and has participated in the AICA and Death Valley shows for six years. He does not sell through galleries.

Murray Tinkelman, BRONC RIDER (1980)
pen & ink, 19 x 12

Floyd S. Tomlin, EAGLE DANCER
bronze, h 12, w 15

Marvin Toddy, GRANDPA'S STORIES, oil, 18 x 24

Tommey, Bob. Representational painter and sculptor of the West and its wildlife, born in Ozan, Arkansas in 1928 and living in Carthage, Missouri since 1981. He says that there is sufficient inspiration for him in Missouri, because "after all, this was the West before Arizona. This area is where Western history started. Independence was the main jumping off point. There is a tremendous mountain man, wagon trail, Civil War, and bandit heritage here that people need to be more aware of.

"As a little kid, I was always drawing horses and Indians. I wore cowboy clothes and the other kids teased me and called me 'Tex.' I always wanted to play the cowboy in the skits." At sixteen, he enlisted in the Navy, but his age was discovered and it was another two years before the Army accepted him. He studied commercial art briefly at the University of Maryland, then moved to Dallas where he tried illustrating, did pastel portraits, and had his own television show, interviewing and drawing guests.

In the mid 1960s, he observes, there was no call for Western art. He believes he may have held the first contemporary Western art show where he "sold sixteen paintings and had to go home and get more." When he moved to Liberty Lake, Washington, as a resort designer in the late 60s, he painted and sculpted scenes of the historical Northwest. He also helped to establish the art shows in Spokane and Ellensburg, where he won Best of Show and Viewers' Choice awards. "Buyers down in the Southwest," he pointed out, "go too much by so-called art authorities. In the Northwest, people come out to look for themselves. In that way, every man's his own authority. Quality is still the governing factor at shows here." A member of the Texas Cowboy Artists Association, he is a partner in the Flatlander Gallery.

Toscano, Dee. Pastellist of realistic portraits specializing in Indians, raised near Fort Worth, Texas and living in Wheatridge, Colorado a suburb of Denver. At 24, she was married with children in diapers and no art training when she "saw a 'draw me' type of ad offering $100 for second prize. I sat down at the kitchen table," she recalls, "and drew the picture. I will never forget how disappointed I was when I won first prize—a scholarship for a correspondence course in art. I needed the $100."

Her father was part Cherokee Indian, a trader in Arizona. Her parents separated when she was a child. She says that "I have always drawn and painted. It seems like everyone has someone who spots your talent, but it didn't happen that way with me. In those days there was never any thought of whether you should go to art school or whether you would like to do anything other than just get married when you were very young." After she won the scholarship, she "tried to keep up the studies but it just became too frustrating." She persevered on her own, working with "a 25 cent box of watercolors in a long can, like the children use." Five years later, "some brave soul asked if I would show my work in his gallery." She started exhibiting in Denver in 1968 and by 1976 was winning national awards.

"Art is not a life and death situation," she declares. "My life is based on the realization of who I am. I recognize that I have been given a gift and I'm using it, but I have to be free." She is a member of the Pastel Society of America and was featured in *Southwest Art,* November 1974. Her gallery is Trailside.

Tossey, Vernon. Realist painter of "gentle" Western people, born in Detroit, Michigan in 1920 and living in Portland, Oregon since 1972. He declares that "what I strive for is to show the real people of the West—Indians, ranchers, farmers—men and women with deep roots. I paint a particular person, not some imaginative character. I have these people do something that is natural to them, chopping wood, making bread, etc. At the slightest excuse, I work a horse into the picture."

As a teenager, Verne Tossey was employed in commercial art in Detroit. During World War II he was stationed in Wyoming, where he found his spiritual home. After his discharge, he returned to commercial art in New York City, received a degree in history from Columbia, and studied with Frank Reilly at the Art Students League for four years before teaching at the Reilly School. A book and magazine illustrator for 25 years, he painted over 300 Western covers and pages.

"I find realism based on abstract principles of design the method that best expresses my concept of man and nature," he states. "Over the years I've developed a way of working. First is the trips around the West. I use the camera liberally and make enlargements in black and white for I like to plan my own color. After the photos I make 'thumbnail' sketches, project the best one to 4" x 5", and carry this out in five simple values. I proceed with a color sketch next, make the finished drawings to trace on to the gesso panel, color underpaint, and then I stay with the final painting stage until it's complete." Tossey is a founding member of the Northwest Rendezvous Group, was featured in *Art West,* and is represented by Husberg Fine Arts Gallery.

Bob Tommey, MAMA, oil, 12 x 16

Dee Toscano, CEREMONIAL BLANKET
pastel, 26½ x 20

Vernon Tossey, TALLYING THE HERD, oil, 24 x 36

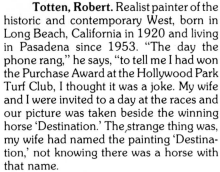

Totten, Robert. Realist painter of the historic and contemporary West, born in Long Beach, California in 1920 and living in Pasadena since 1953. "The day the phone rang," he says, "to tell me I had won the Purchase Award at the Hollywood Park Turf Club, I thought it was a joke. My wife and I were invited to a day at the races and our picture was taken beside the winning horse 'Destination.' The strange thing was, my wife had named the painting 'Destination,' not knowing there was a horse with that name.

"Since four, I liked to draw, although my early schooling was in a one-room class. I kept drawing, and worked as a cartoonist for Screen Gems Studio. When World War II broke out, I drew technical illustrations and in 1943 enlisted in the Coast Guard. After receiving a discharge in 1945, I went full time to art school at the Art Center, Chouinard, and Jepson, then started working in a small studio in Hollywood, where I did whatever commercial artwork came along. In 1953, I found a home down the quiet tree-shaded street from the last home of Charles M. Russell in Pasadena."

He worked on advertising campaigns, billboards, children's book illustrations, Christmas cards, record covers, movie illustrations, television sketches, and in 1961 did documentary paintings for the Air Force. In 1965, he entered the fine arts competitions for the first time, winning national awards. It is said that "he throws himself into his sketching and painting as though there is no tomorrow. In his studio, the floor and walls are sometimes covered with pencil sketches of an idea that is taking place in his mind." He is represented by the Biltmore Galleries and by Trailside Galleries which offered his painting at $10,000 in its 1981-1982 catalog.

Trevor, Jean-Pierre. Super-realist painter of acrylic landscapes, born in London in 1948 and living in Scottsdale, Arizona. "A painting is a combination of what I get" from a photograph, he says, "and what I've absorbed into my life. That's where the passion comes into play. Sometimes people tell me that they have psychic reactions to my paintings, such as seeing an aura around one in a gallery. Well, who knows?"

In 1962, his father who is a novelist founded the Centre d'Art Mediterranee in Vallauris, France that Trevor attended. In five years, he was exhibiting in Nice and Cannes, and winning awards. "I played the role of the mad artist," he confesses, "thrashing about and throwing brushes. I painted in oils in a surreal style with absolutely no reference to the outside world" until "I finally decided to take a different direction." In 1972, Trevor went to Hollywood, where he was hired by Walt Disney Studios as a matte artist, painting small glass panel backgrounds for the separately filmed live action. The key to the matte painting was to look for patterns, "to decode the essence" so as "to represent the object with an added dimension."

Trevor's current landscape paintings are a result of the Disney training, painting real scenes with an attention to detail, a concern for light, and an added dimension of emotion that makes them super-real. "If there is an emotional reason to my work, this may be due to the emotion I feel when I'm painting. I want to make the viewer react, but when I start to work each morning, I don't wait for inspiration. I just start and that's it." Trevor is represented by Miner's Gallery Americana and Trailside Galleries.

Troiani, Don. Painter of historic Western and Civil War scenes, born in New York City in 1949 and living in Stamford, Connecticut. "Some artists think that detail destroys the overall feeling," he says. "I believe that accurate detail adds a completeness." He paints a cavalry charge, for example, with each of the scores of faces drawn from a photograph of the time.

"I've been a collector for twenty years," Troiani declares, "collecting military artifacts before I was an artist. I know every detail, inside and out." He attended the Pennsylvania Academy of Fine Arts and the Art Students League, adopting the French soldier artist Edouard Detaille as his favorite. "I am not an illustrator turned historical artist," he states. "I have painted nothing but historical scenes since the beginning." He claims that "the cavalry was active in protecting settlers in the West before the Civil War, with exciting stories an everyday occurrence."

The walls of Troiani's studio are hung with hundreds of his martial props including an elaborate display of Civil War uniforms. His paintings are in museums such as the U.S. Cavalry Museum, the Custer Battlefield National Monument, the West Point Museum, and the Smithsonian Institution. He is a member of the Society of American Historical Artists and his expertise gives him the credibility to show unexpected details like an 1850s cavalry officer wearing a straw hat in the field. The oils have a luminescence appropriate to the subjects because his technique follows the 19th century European historical painters. He is represented by The May Gallery.

Robert Totten, THE PRO, oil, 24 x 30

Jean-Pierre Trevor, CLOUDS, mixed media, 24 x 30

Don Troiani, REDSKINS OR BLUECOATS, oil, 20 x 30

Valerie Trozelle

Ron Tunison

PHIL TYLER NWS

Trozelle, Valerie. Representational painter of animals and Western scenes, born in Roseburg, Oregon in 1952 and living in Bermuda Dunes, California. "Horses! I love horses," she exclaims. "I have three horses, one I have owned for seventeen years. Most of my Westerns have a horse in there somewhere. I feel really comfortable and natural when I paint them running or grazing or just standing in the shade of a cottonwood. There is something deep-rooted about early American life and horses that fits a Western painting."

At six months, she became profoundly deaf following a virus infection. When she was five, she started training to enable her to lip read and communicate so that she was able to enter public schools in the sixth grade. In 1967, she was elected rodeo queen and two years later began winning horsemanship awards. She entered the College of the Desert to study art, and one of the "riding students asked if I would paint her dog. At eighteen, that seemed an easier way to make a living than breaking horses, so I made up business cards, stuck an ad on the stable bulletin board, and started painting pet portraits. The subsequent sales gave me the confidence to enter the profession." By 1975, she was winning exhibition awards.

"Deafness," she claims, "does have its advantages. Sometimes I get so involved while I'm painting that even if I could hear, I wouldn't. I was so very young when I lost my hearing that I can't honestly tell if I could concentrate any more or any less without my handicap. I train horses and give riding lessons as well as paint. Having children has slowed down the horse training and increased my painting time." She is featured at the Limited Editions Gallery and her art prints are distributed nationally.

Tunison, Ron. Realist sculptor of American military figures from before the turn of the century in Vinagel model compound, born in Brooklyn, New York in 1946 and living near Cairo, New York since 1982. "My great interest," he points out, "lies in the American past between the 1830s and 1880s. I have often thought how much I would have liked to live during that time, but the more I research that period, the more I become aware of the hardship, pain, and suffering our ancestors went through.

"I studied commercial art, painting, sculpting, and photography at the School of Visual Arts in New York from 1965 to 1969 and was awarded a scholarship to study sculpting and anatomy at the National Academy of Design in 1971." For three years, he worked for CBS Television doing photographic sequences for Bicentennial specials. While involved in the Revolutionary War reenactments, he says, "I learned about a Civil War unit which was doing the same thing. Being a member of these different historical groups has been a great help to me in sculpting my figures.

"Unlike bronzes, my sculptures are one of a kind. They are far too detailed to try to make a bronze casting from them. I build a wire skeleton and build up the figure using the man made clay. Once fired, the figure becomes practically indestructable. I make the accoutrements and weapons and the figure is then painted with oils. It takes me a good month and a half from start to finish, but when I complete a figure, I have something totally unique. Many people have said that my figures look as if the real man has been shrunk down to a twelve inch height. A founding member of the Society of American Historical Artists, my galleries are The Soldier Shop and The Grizzly Tree Gallery."

Tyler, Phil. (signs with Rolling-T-Ranch brand). Watercolorist and photographer born in Alabama in 1914 and living in Hood River Valley, Oregon since 1941. Concerned with recording the surviving features of the Old West, he declares that "after Russell, we are left with only a remnant of the West. We cannot experience his West except as historians, but the remnant we do have is essential to our West and our children's West." As his specific interest, he says that "mountains are more Western to me than cowboys or ranch life. I feel affinity with the cowboy, but I gather strength from mountains."

Where he grew up in the Indiana flatlands, Tyler listened to his grandfather's stories about going West with a wagon train. He was an art major at San Mateo Junior College and took the Famous Artists course. When he was eighteen, the sketches he sent to the Art Center School in Los Angeles, won him a three-year scholarship, and after two years in an art agency he quit to build adobes in Mexico and dredge for gold in Alaska, before returning to Oregon, to ranch, build, teach, paint, do mountain rescues, and breed horses.

He says that "you don't decide to paint Western paintings because you want to, but because you have a background in it." Moreover, he believes that "too many Western artists allow realism to dominate the creative process." Once he has visualized the composition and values, he goes directly to colors because "preliminary sketches can come between the experience and the painting." He finishes thirty watercolors a month. Tyler is a member of the National Watercolor Society and the Northwest Rendezvous Group, and is represented by Trails End Gallery.

Ron Tunison, ANOTHER CAMPAIGN (1982)
mixed media, h 12

Phil Tyler, JEREMIAH, watercolor, 27 x 20

Valerie Trozelle, WHERE'S BUTCH??, opaque watercolor, 30 x 40

Ullberg, Kent. Romantic-realist sculptor of wildlife in bronze, born in Gothenburg, Sweden in 1945 and living in Corpus Christi, Texas since 1975. "Good animal sculpture," he stresses, "necessitates distilling the essential forms without losing the specific characteristics. It is possible to render the human figure very abstractly and still have it read as a human form. Each animal, however, has its own characteristics. Therefore, the animal sculptor is more likely to verge on the academic than the modeler of human figures."

The son of a landscape artist, Ullberg has been surrounded by art all his life. As a child, he worked at the local museum and knew then he would be an animal sculptor. After high school, he studied at the Swedish State School of Art and at the museum for animal anatomy. At twenty, he became disenchanted with modernist teachings and went to Paris. Two years later, he traveled to Africa, remaining in Botswana for seven years as a curator.

In 1974, Ullberg was hired as curator of the African Hall at the Denver Museum of Natural History. He soon received an award from the National Academy of Design that let him move to Texas as a full time sculptor. "A wildlife artist," he points out, "chooses animals because it's something that turns him on, not because he's unable to handle other subjects." With work in 25 public collections around the world, listed in *Who's Who in American Art,* and featured twice in *Southwest Art,* Ullberg is an Associate of the National Academy of Design and a member of the National Sculpture Society as well as the National Academy of Western Art. He is represented by Sportsman's Edge and Trailside Galleries.

Utz, Thornton. Impressionist painter of portraits, children, nudes, and animals in motion in mixed media and sculptor, born in Memphis, Tennessee in 1915 and living in Sarasota, Florida since 1949. "How long does it take to do a painting?" he is asked. "My stock answer is 67 years. Next year I'll insist it's 68. In reality, I don't know how long it takes. Works are spread all over the studio and often I paint on many in a week.

"My father claimed Kansas City as West, and our family he insisted were frontiersmen. He believed that Marshall, Missouri where he grew up was where the West began. Certainly from the tall Western tales, I believed I wasn't exactly Southern." Utz (pronounced "ootz") studied for a year at the American Academy of Art in Chicago but quit because he would "never learn art in an art school." He became a free-lance illustrator for national magazines, including more than fifty covers for *The Saturday Evening Post.*

"Starting out in Chicago," he adds, "the way to work and eat was to have many techniques. We were asked to do a 'Norman Rockwell' or any popular artist. Our artwork was done on request. As a result, I am a problem solver." In 1946, he moved to Westport, Connecticut and three years later to Florida. When the illustration market diminished, he began painting portraits in his own style, merging the sitter into a total design and using the sitter as a model only for a photo session. "Next," he says, "I hope to do more animals, mainly animals in motion." There is a long list of Utz paintings and sculptures in public collections. Written up in *Southwest Art,* July 1981, his prints are published by Mill Pond Press and he is represented by Conacher and Brubaker Galleries.

Thornton Utz, UNTITLED, mixed media, 57 x 20

Kent Ullberg, LINCOLN CENTER EAGLE
polished stainless steel, 9½ ft , 14 ft base

Vandehey

C. L. Vander Lans

Gordon F. Van Wert
GVW ★
·82·

Vandehey, Roberta. Traditional oil painter of the Oregon coastline, born in Portland, Oregon in 1944 and living near Spray, Oregon. "I will spend a long time looking at the ocean," she points out, "and when I see what I want, I'll catch it just as it's happening. Later, I can close my eyes and get the image back. I can repeatedly recall a setting. And this is odd. Before I start to paint, I think I see the picture already on canvas. 'You're there,' I say, 'show yourself.' "

Raised on a ketch at San Diego, she did not have a land-based home until she started school in Banks, Oregon. Following high school, she attended Lewis and Clark College, spent a year in Peru, and finished at Portland State University, majoring in anthropology and German while skipping art which stressed the modern. She took "twelve years of ballet lessons. Dancing was to be my career." Summers she was a fire watcher, then she married and had a child and moved into the Oregon mountains with her family.

"It sounds weird, I know, but one day in 1975 we were going to Prineville," she recalls, "and as we drove, 'so pretty,' I thought, 'wouldn't it be fun to paint. I wish!' I went into a stationery store and bought a little starter kit. I really got addicted to painting the water. Only the ocean. I go up on a rocky cliff somewhere and just absorb it, slurp it up. I respect the ocean. In fact, I am really scared of it. I probably could absorb even closer impressions of it, but I don't get my feet wet if I can avoid it. You just pour something out of yourself into a picture and at the end of the day feel so totally satisfied." Written up in *Art West,* September 1980, she is represented by Blue Mountain Art Gallery.

Vander Lans, Christopher. Representational painter of the contemporary West, born in Palo Alto, California in 1954 and living in Cameron, Montana. "I got into Western art through the back door," he explains, "that is to say the Western came before the art. I've always been interested in anything to do with cowboys. From childhood, all I wanted to be was a cowboy. At sixteen, I got my chance, and spent the next six years cowboying. I wouldn't trade the years I spent as a cowboy, but I wasn't satisfied to remain a $350-a-month ranch hand.

"When I met the painter Gary Carter, and saw firsthand the life of a Western artist, I began to make plans for a new occupation. Unlike many artists, I had little or no art training before applying to the Art Center. Enrollment at the Center began three years of the hardest work I had ever done. Whenever I hear anyone say how lucky I am to have been 'given' the ability to paint, I remember the long days and nights I spent learning what I know, studying with Dan McCaw and Don Putman.

"What I'm trying to accomplish is to produce a good painting that happens to be of a Western subject. I try to do this by putting emphasis on design. If the design is strong, there is less need for photographic detail. I also try to capture the effect of sunlight. Most of my paintings have a subtle theme. There isn't a lot of action in them, as there isn't a lot of action in the day of a working cowboy. Though I want the most interesting picture possible, bucking horses and stampedes are by far more the exception than the rule. I try to show the beauty in the commonplace events, the relationships of men, land, and animals." He is represented by the Hole in the Wall Gallery.

Van Wert, Gordon. Contemporary sculptor of Southwestern animals and Chippewa Indian designs in alabaster, born on the reservation at Redlake, Minnesota in 1952 and living in Santa Fe, New Mexico since 1981. When he was an apprentice in Santa Fe, "at one time Earl Biss, Kevin Red Star, Doug Hyde, and the late T.C. Cannon were all working in the same building at the same time, sharing jokes, works, food, and having all kinds of wild adventures. And all of them were really nice to a bunch of us newer, unknown artists.

"My family does not have a tradition of producing artists and they gave me no art education at the reservation, so my early interest in forms and colors was a bit unusual. I really was lucky to enter the Institute of American Indian Arts in Santa Fe at fifteen. Allen Houser and Charles Loloma are just about the most original and famous of all Indian artists. Houser was a good teacher for me." In 1969, Van Wert went back to Redlake to complete his high school education, then served in the Army for two years before returning to the Institute.

"I did so well that I was selected to attend the Rhode Island School of Design. Houser taught me technique, they gave me ideas of designs, and I then became an apprentice of Doug Hyde. I badly needed the experience of the everyday work life of a sculptor and I got that by working with Hyde. My 'professional career' really started in 1974 when I had a two-man show with Hyde." To seek his own style, he "spent three years in Arizona. I worked steadily on my own works and began to sell well." He sold every work he created in 1980 and was forced to turn down orders in 1981. Listed in *Who's Who in American Art,* he shows at Sanders and Linda McAdoo Galleries.

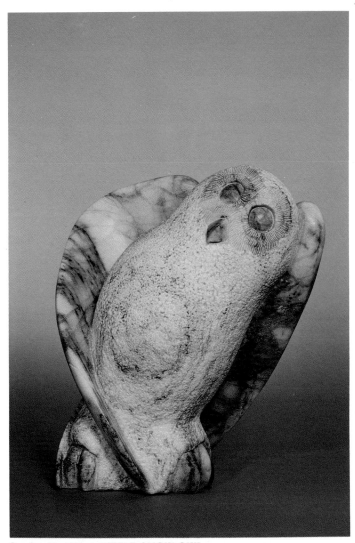

Gordon Van Wert, LITTLE SNOW OWL
New York alabaster, h 11, w 9, d 8

Roberta Vandehey, A SUMMER MORNING FOG, oil, 24 x 20

Chris Vander Lans, THE BUCKSKIN, oil, 15 x 30

Vaupel, Barbara. Realist oil painter of contemporary Western subjects and of horse portraits, born in San Diego, California in 1939 and living near Henryetta, Oklahoma since 1968. "There is much mediocre art being produced and offered to the public at ridiculous prices which some people automatically assume means quality," she says. "If there's an easy way to produce a good painting, I haven't yet found it. I don't mean this to sound like an artist must have a sweatshop atmosphere in which to turn out acceptable work, but I am talking about strong self-discipline. It takes plenty of that."

Raised in southern California, she took the Art Instruction correspondence course when she was sixteen, but had no subsequent art education. After one year as a commercial artist for a furniture chain and three years for the San Diego *Union-Tribune*, she started her professional career as a horse portrait painter. In 1970, she moved her studio to an Oklahoma rodeo-stock ranch so she could live with and paint from real Western subjects, usually in a peaceful setting, with tranquility not violence her theme. She considers herself to be "a rather private person."

"I love painting for a living," she states, "but many people still confuse enjoying what you do with needing to put forth little effort. Painting is WORK!" She spends eight hours painting, five to six days a week, with six or more paintings going at a time, averaging 25 paintings a year. "Every morning I pray for a productive day. This means I need the inspiration and energy flow to last the entire day. As long as the inspiration level stays high, I feel satisfied the painting is going well." Her painting that won the 1981 Harness Tracks of America competition was auctioned for $3,700. Written up in Oklahoma Art Gallery magazine, winter 1981, she is represented by Troy's Gallery.

Vela, Alberto. Realist painter of the historic American West, especially the Indian, born in Mexico City, Mexico in 1920 and living in Los Angeles since 1959. "When I was a young artist in Mexico City," Vela says, "I was encouraged by a magazine publisher to continue my studies at the Academy of Fine Arts. The publisher purchased all of the drawings of cathedrals, plazas, and vaqueros on horseback that I had in my portfolio and a year later when I was twenty, I was working for the publisher as an illustrator for the magazine *La Lydia.*"

Among Vela's teachers had been Jose Clemente Orozco, and he later studied mural painting with Diego Rivera. While working as a magazine illustrator, Vela also did commercial artwork for an advertising agency, designed posters, and was a newspaper cartoonist. By 1950, horses were a specialty and he was official artist for the bullfights. In 1954, he moved to Florida to paint portraits and hotel murals. While illustrating in New York City the following year, he became interested in the American Indian and devoted himself to Indian research while painting hotel murals in Chicago and Mexico.

In 1959, Vela settled in Los Angeles and did the last of his hotel murals, working in San Diego and Tucson. He then returned to painting the Indian, influenced by Russell and Farny, but these early Western subjects were not exhibited because he felt they were derivative. Vela kept them as reference material while he displayed a variety of other subjects in oil, acrylic, and casein. By 1974, he felt that his "soundness of draftsmanship, careful observance of fact, and strong compositional sense" made his Indian paintings convincing, and he began to show them. He is represented by Lesli Art.

Alberto Vela, NO EASY MEAL, oil, 30 x 36

Barbara Vaupel, REFLECTIONS, oil, 22 x 28

Venditti, Jerry. Painter of realistic Western and Southwestern subjects and trompe l'oeil, born in San Francisco, California in 1942 and living in Sebastopol, California. "I was influenced to paint by a friend whom I hadn't seen for years," he observes. "He was having an art show in a town nearby and asked me to come to it. His paintings left an impression on me and after several years, I decided to fly down to New Mexico to see him. I spent a short time watching him paint, and when I returned home, decided that's what I wanted to do too. I began drawing and painting fourteen hours a day and took lessons from well-known teachers, as well as doing voluminous reading and research on my own.

"I had attended college at San Jose State and San Francisco State where I also attended law school. My wife and I moved to the country where our lives began to change. I live life to its fullest, getting up at 4 a.m. six days a week and putting in at least ten hours of painting before doing outside chores. I have been painting for seven years now. One of my specialties, trompe l'oeil art, is a French term meaning 'fool the eye.' People are constantly going up to my paintings and trying to remove something, or they might even try to look behind an object I have painted.

"Some of my paintings are symbolic in that they denote historical statements and cultural events. I perceive Western and Southwestern art as serving as a window to view things out of the past, in an era that is fast coming to a close and yet existed only a short time ago. It is an integral aspect of our culture which is part of our heritage. Painting to me is spiritual. I am represented by Shriver Gallery and Copenhagen Galleri."

Vetter, Bernard. Realist painter of New Mexico and Arizona in transparent watercolor, born in El Paso, Texas in 1940 and still living there. "Growing up in Texas," he points out, "was filled with experiences that have served me well as an artist. On weekends, I often accompanied my parents on outings to Indian ruins in nearby New Mexico where I searched for artifacts—arrowheads, effigies, and pottery shards—often successfully." He also gained knowledge of and appreciation for the Indian cultures of the area.

As a boy, Vetter participated in local rodeo events, particularly calf roping. After graduating from Texas Western College in El Paso with a minor in art in 1965, he taught art and Texas history in the El Paso schools for eight years. Meanwhile, he painted as a hobby, considering himself to be self-taught. When he began making more money from the sales of art than from teaching, he quit school to paint full time. He traces his interest in the American cowboy to the early contact with other rodeo contestants and with New Mexico ranchers.

Vetter says that he is never "off duty. There is no such thing as a day off because even in his leisure time, he is unable to halt the 'creative process,' that subconscious sensitivity to his surroundings that characterizes all artists." He also owns the Percha Bank Building in Kingston, New Mexico, a ghost town from silver mining days. Vetter shows in New Mexico, Arizona, and Texas, and won the gold medal for watercolor at the Littleton, Colorado sale. He is represented by Galeria D'Oros and Troy's Gallery.

Vianello, Franco. Impressionist sculptor of Western figures in bronze statuettes and statues, born in Venice, Italy in 1937 and living in Napa, California. "There will be no more Michelangelos," he points out. "Life is too damn complex. All he did was work. He didn't marry. He slept next to his work. Now, you're forced to go to school and learn geometry you'll never use in your work. Creativity goes to the dogs after awhile."

There have been sculptors and founders in his family for over a century. He began working in a foundry at nine, but "hated to be a sculptor. You work with people who are crazy, making cartwheels on the floor, pulling their hair out." When he was eleven, he was accepted as a sculptor's apprentice, and eventually he earned a Master's degree from the Institute of Arts in Venice. He came to the United States in 1959. One of his first jobs was an 18-foot bronze monument for the 1962 World's Fair in Seattle. He says that "you don't know how great this country is until you come from another country."

In 1962, he was drafted and assigned as a paratrooper to El Paso where he became a Special Services Artist, doing dioramas of Indian villages, Texas cowboys, and the cavalry. The day after he was discharged, he moved to California to set up a studio and foundry. "It was hard in the beginning," he recalls. "The gallery would say, 'We like the piece, but the name, Vianello, you know. Recognition is like a trophy. You get into the better collections and you get next to the big names, you are somebody.'" In 1981, he created the heroic replica of Remington's "Coming Through the Rye" for the Cowboy Hall of Fame. He is represented by Hunter and Meinhard Galleries.

F. Vianello, FIGHTING STALLIONS, bronze, h 17½ x 23½

Jerry Venditti, 40 MILES TO FREEDOM—LOST!
oil/linen, 26 x 22

Bernard Vetter, LONG TIME AGO, watercolor, 9½ x 24½

Russ Vickers

Vickers, Russ. Traditional painter of Western figures from the period of the Civil War to the turn of the century, born in Paris, Texas in 1923 and living in Tempe, Arizona since 1973. "I'm not painting Western because everyone's going for a killing at it," he points out, "but because it's what I want to do. All those cowboys quittin' to paint, all these artists who go live in wigwams, goes a long ways toward explaining why the cattle industry and the Indians both are in such bad shape."

Son of a horse trader, he stresses that "I've known horses since I was four years old, when my father put me up on Big Red, the largest mount in the family compound." He served in the Marines in World War II and as a combat artist in Korea. Without much formal schooling, Vickers spent almost twenty years as a technical illustrator for the aerospace industry in Los Angeles, painting Westerns in his spare time. He took the correspondence course of the Famous Artists School and in 1970, began showing paintings in Sedona, Arizona.

In 1973, Vickers quit illustration and moved to Arizona to paint full time. "You do what you gotta do," he observes. "Then you do what you wanta do. It's good to be able to paint what I wanta paint, instead of working with a bunch of blueprints." Despite his long experience, he emphasizes that he "never paints a horse without a whole series of references to refresh my memory. It's like trying to remember a phone number. If you don't look it up, you're likely to get one of the digits wrong." He was featured in *Southwest Art*, summer 1975, is published by Mill Pond Press, and is represented by Overland Trail Galleries.

Russ Vickers, ANCIENT RIGHT OF WAY, oil, 15½ x 25

Vigil, Veloy Joseph. Abstract-expressionist painter of American Indian figures in watercolor and acrylic, born in Denver, Colorado in 1931 and living in Anaheim, California since 1966. After he was discharged from the Marines, he says, "I had no direction. In fact, I thought I was going to become a farmer. But when I asked myself what I really wanted to do, it was to draw and paint and create art. I then looked up an art school."

Descended from a great-grandmother who was a Pueblo Indian and a great-grandfather who was Spanish, Veloy was raised in Colorado ranch country. After high school, he tried the rodeos, joined the Marines, and then went to Colorado Institute of Art by day and Denver Art Academy at night. In 1958, he was employed as a commercial artist in Cleveland, in 1964 he moved to Colorado Springs as an illustrator, and in 1966 moved to California as an art director. Meanwhile, he was developing his watercolor technique and exhibiting in shows including the National Watercolor Society.

From commercial design where "there was no place for a guy like myself who wanted to do art," he was finally able to paint full time, "a natural transition because I had been working on it for years." His approach to watercolor is to "think masses from the time I grab the sponge and wet down the paper. I begin to break up the shapes and masses in my mind when I'm laying the color down. I develop the negative and positive shapes, and I frequently paint to music." Vigil is listed in *Who's Who in American Art* and was featured in *Artists of the Rockies*, spring 1976 and *Southwest Art*, January 1977. He is published by Richard Henkin Inc. and is represented by Suzanne Brown Gallery.

Villasenor, David V. Painter of "tapestries in sand," born in Jalisco, Mexico in 1913 and living in Glendora, California since 1966. "It took twenty years to develop my 'tapestries in sand' technique," he explains. "These are sandpaintings that roll like a tapestry. I have lectured and demonstrated extensively using my sandpaintings and tapestries as props. The intrinsic value of my work is in helping to preserve the native American heritage. Therefore, my work has appeared more often in museums than in galleries.

"My mother was Huichol and Mexican and my father was Otomi and Spanish. As a child of the Revolution, I was educated from six to sixteen in an Indian boarding school in Hermosillo. I came to this country with no knowledge of English, and lived among the Indians of the Southwest. I was part of the first Native Market in Santa Fe and was 'discovered' by the artist-naturalist Ernest Thompson Seton, founder of youth movements incorporating Indian lore. Years of youth work followed.

"By joining the Army in 1942, I gained U.S. citizenship. In Los Altos, California in 1948 I developed the first successful permanent sandpainting, a new medium as an art expression of the Greater Southwest Indians. In 1951, I prepared my first one-man show of permanent sandpaintings for the American Museum of Natural History in New York, followed by numerous others. My wife and I collaborated on *How To Do Nature Printing, Tapestries in Sand,* and *How To Do Permanent Sandpainting.* A dream of many years was fulfilled with my 12-foot diameter reproduction of the Aztec Calendar stone in the Los Angeles County Museum. I am a member of the American Indian and Cowboy Artists and two documentary films have been made of me."

Vinella, Raimondo J. Painter and sculptor of the land and people of New Mexico, born in Bari, Italy in 1933 and living in Taos, New Mexico since 1968. "My escape from the Lower East Side of New York City," Ray Vinella discloses, "was to join the Air Force in the middle of the Korean War in 1952. It turned out to be the best thing I have ever done. Instead of being sent to Korea, I went to Europe, and I guess I matured in Europe. It was a great education. It was in Europe that I decided to become serious about art.

"My family had arrived in the city in 1935 but I disliked it. I had graduated high school with awards in art, had studied the Art Instruction course, and took the Famous Artist course while stationed in Germany, but it wasn't enough. So when I was discharged in 1955, I enrolled in the Art Center School in Los Angeles where I received my BFA in 1958. The following ten years as an illustrator was all very different and exciting, but not for me, so I moved to Taos where an artist I admired lived, Nicolai Fechin. There I started to do easel painting.

"Most artists today produce pictures and put big prices on them and sell to an uneducated public. I have been fortunate to be able to work at my art, to earn a living doing what I love. The real artists that I have met are professionals. They do not dress or try to act like clowns. They do their work and forge ahead. It is relatively easy to learn to paint, but enormously difficult to put in that air, light, mood, and context." Vinella has been Dean of the Taos School of Fine Art, is a member of the Taos Six, exhibits at Shriver Gallery, and was represented in the exhibition of American Western art in Peking, China in 1981.

David Villasenor, PUEBLO SUN DANCE, sandpainting, 18 x 24

Veloy Vigil, CABALLO DEL MONTE, acrylic/canvas, 60 x 72

Ray Vinella, TAOS LIGHT, egg tempera, 24 x 36

JOE WAANO GANO

(signature)

Robert B. Wagoner (signature)

Waano-Gano, Joe. Cherokee painter and sculptor in "the grand manner of the Masters" as well as in "the Indian style of symbolic painting and design," born in Salt Lake City, Utah in 1906 and living in Los Angeles. He says that "as soon as anyone in my family was old enough to get about, they had to help earn a living as existence was precarious. When a small boy, I created little pottery animals that I sold to tourists. Years later, I was holding an exhibition and one of a group of Norwegians who entered the gallery let out a war whoop! She had remembered my name and said the small clay souvenirs she had purchased so long ago were still treasures in her heart."

After graduating from high school in Los Angeles in 1922, he studied at Von Schneidau School of Art from 1924 to 1928, took extension courses, and studied privately before working as a commercial artist until 1941. He also acted in radio adaptations of Indian legends. During World War II, he served in the Air Force for three years and then was decor designer for Western Air Lines. In 1946 he won his first important purchase prize, and by 1952 he was consistently winning special honors.

When the Los Angeles County Museum devoted three large galleries to his work, including 121 paintings up to 8 by 10 feet, the show broke attendance records. His show of paintings at Houdini's "House of Mystery" raised funds for a youth center in 1949. Over 400,000 attended the 1957 Flower Show where he won Best of Show. He has had more than 130 one-person shows, painted 27 murals, and won more than 100 top awards. Listed in *Who's Who in American Art* and in Snodgrass' *American Indian Painters,* he was written up in *Desert Magazine,* March 1977 and has had his own gallery.

Wagner, Rory. Realist painter of the contemporary cowboy in acrylic, born in St. Petersburg, Florida in 1950 and living in Taos, New Mexico. "I paint big," he explains. "I always have. The only time I create a small canvas is when part of a larger one doesn't work and I cut off those portions of it and restretch it. I want a big image. I guess I like the drama. People are often awestruck when they are faced with the sheer size of my paintings.

"You get bored as a little kid and I filled books and books with drawings until I was twenty years old. It never occurred to me to do anything with them. I went to college for five years and studied everything except art. I got my first inkling when an art professor came up, looked at my work, and said it was very good. He also said I should begin drawing ears, noses, feet, and hands until I could do them from memory. That I did, and when I was drafted into the Army I continued to draw appendages. After I was released, I started drawing full time and I just never bothered to stop."

After selling large paintings for "peanuts" in Baltimore for five years, he "arrived in New Mexico almost broke." When he called on a gallery in Taos, he "found this man in a headband. He took a look at what I had with me and said, 'write out a consignment.' One painting sold the first day, another the second, and so it went. The man was R.C. Gorman. I owe him more than I can ever say. I'm luckier than the devil to be here in the Southwest because there's no doubt this is where it's happening. We're all cowboys under the skin." Written up in *Southwest Art,* October 1981 and the subject of the 1982 book *Rory Wagner,* he is represented by Quail Hollow Galleries.

Wagoner, Robert B. Representational painter of cowboy and cattle subjects, born in Marion, Ohio in 1928 and living in Bishop, California since 1970. When Wagoner wrote the nostalgic popular song "High Country" before he became a full time painter, he was expressing his own lifelong yearning for a ranch of his own. As a professional entertainer, he was able to promote the song on radio and television, and in 1967 he acquired his cattle spread.

He was raised in Long Beach, California and became interested in art at thirteen. After graduation from high school, he joined the Marine Corps, then studied forestry in college until he had the opportunity to travel with a band for several years, playing the electric guitar. When he returned to college, he switched his major to business administration and joined his father's construction business as manager of heavy equipment. Painting was reserved for nights and weekends. He was self-taught except for the advice of Olaf Wieghorst and Burt Procter.

By 1960 when he began painting seriously, Wagoner had owned horses, followed rodeos, prospected in three states, owned and worked a mine, flown sailplanes, written poetry as well as music, and acted in movies. He started painting full time in 1970, won first awards beginning in 1972, and is still singing with the "Reinsmen," recording "Songs of the Trail." In *Preview '81,* his oil "Mountain Way Station" brought $6,800. He is listed in *Who's Who in American Art,* was written up in Ainsworth's *The Cowboy in Art,* won a gold medal at the American Indian and Cowboy Artist show, and is represented by Trailside and Texas Art Galleries.

Joe Waano-Gano, CONFLICT (1972), oil, 6 ft x 5 ft

Rory Wagner, CAT AMONG THE PIGEONS, acrylic, 66 x 70

Robert Wagoner, PRAIRIE MAIL, oil, 24 x 36

Wahlbeck, Carlo. "Romantic surrealist" painter, sculptor, and designer depicting "the American saga," born in Stockholm, Sweden in 1933 and living in Los Angeles. "I was introduced to the arts at an early age by my mother who was born in Italy and raised in an environment of music and visual arts, and by my father, born in Sweden, also involved in visual arts and business as well as being an inventor.

"I began formal studies at the Stockholm School of Art at fourteen. This involved sculpting as well as drawing. The strongest influence was Swedish sculptors Carl and Agnes Milles. At seventeen, I visited the United States and spent one year studying and sculpting. During the years that followed, I traveled to southern Europe to study sculpting and painting in the great museums. The ones that influenced me the most were the museums in Italy, in the Vatican and in Florence. I began to study jewelry design and started work in this field, continuing for many years. In 1957, I relocated to Canada as a jeweler and studied at the Winnipeg School of Art.

"In 1960, I moved to the United States where I began painting and sculpting full time. The following years were filled with work and travel throughout the continent, with many visits to Indian tribes in Canada, the United States, and Mexico. My art depicted the American saga in both sculpture and painting." Wahlbeck has exhibited in Europe and Mexico as well as in the United States. His collectors include King Gustav V of Sweden and Richard M. Nixon, Frank Sinatra and Barry Goldwater, plus public collections in the United States and Israel. He is represented by Lesli Art.

Walker, Edward D. "Rusty." Realist painter of the Southwest, Europe, and North Africa in watercolor and oil, born in Danville, Illinois in 1946 and living in Richmond, California. "An artist," he believes, "has only his work to leave as a hopeful contribution to the world, so it is my responsibility as an artist to paint my unique images of the world. My images happen to be somewhat optimistic. On occasion, I have been called a 'people painter,' but I paint all aspects of life that cross my path.

"I grew up in the Southwest and have a degree from the Queensland Institute of Technology, Australia. During the last fifteen years, the most significant change in my work has been a gradual trend toward heightened realism. I've always considered myself a realistic painter, but because my work for the first ten years was entirely on location, it had a broader effect with less detail. In recent years, I have worked more and more in the studio, preferring a more studied approach but still striving for a spontaneous feel.

"Attention to detail for the sake of detail deadens a painting, so what I'm looking for in approach is a sweeping kind of realism that is sensitive to the elements that can't be seen. This business of art is a 24 hour business. Painting for a living is not relaxing. It is not fun; however, it is enjoyable work. Rather than painting more paintings every year, I paint less and spend more time composing and planning each one. I am a member of the National Watercolor Society, listed in *Who's Who in American Art,* and represented by O'Brien's Art Emporium and John Pence Gallery." He was written up in *Southwest Art,* June 1980 and *American Artist,* October 1980.

Carlo Wahlbeck, TRIBAL DAWN, oil, 20 x 16

Edward D. "Rusty" Walker, NAVAJO AND FRIENDS, watercolor, 22 x 30

Ralph Wall Jr

Kent R. Wallis

Jim Walston

Wall, Ralph Alan. Historical painter of the Southern Plains Indians, born in Hobart, Indiana in 1932 and living in New Braunfels, Texas since 1978. Wall is a student of the period "before the white man came," when "lives were more complex than ours. The Plains Indians were buffalo hunters, demanding courage from the brave and his steed. Other tribes were more sedentary."

Wall grew up in Ardmore, Oklahoma where blanket Indians still walked the streets. He graduated from Oklahoma City University with a marketing degree and quit art school because the fundamentals were not being taught. His art education came through reading, looking, and talking. In 1957, he moved to Houston as a commercial artist, and ten years later when he was commissioned to illustrate Custer's stand, the lack of information on the Indians led him to "try to discover how things were." In 1969, he became a fine arts painter, starting his collection of artifacts and of research books that fill his library walls.

As "a practicing Christian," Wall says that "I communicate with the Holy Spirit who guides me in all that I do. A really good painting has more than me in it—there is something miraculous." He declares that "part of my job as an artist is to read. Something will speak to me. An important part of creativity is meditation, contacting your spiritual side." He paints in acrylic for the spontaneity. "I can't work on more than one painting at a time. I become absorbed in it and must work it through to finish." Featured in *Southwest Art,* October 1981, Wall shows at Quail Hollow Galleries. He documents the story of each painting that is sold.

Wallis, Kent R. Traditional landscape painter of the Utah forests and rivers, born in Ogden, Utah in 1945 and living in Logan since 1975. "I was raised in an economic environment where money was to be spent on bread and butter and the necessities of life," he says. "Art was not considered a necessity, but a luxury only the wealthy could afford or appreciate. To expose the shallowness of that philosophy has been one of my major endeavors. Art, in its capacity to inspire, to communicate the highest of spiritual thought and emotion, must be considered a necessity in life, not a luxury."

While watching Ralph Knaggy draw on Saturday morning television, Wallis decided on art as a career but his confidence was shaken when a teacher told him he'd better stick to sports because he didn't have the patience to make it in art. After graduating from Utah State University with a Master's degree in business administration, he worked for the B.F. Goodrich Company in marketing for six years. When he bought oil paints to use as a hobby in Akron, Ohio, he quit his job and returned to Utah to paint full time.

Self-taught, he feels that his landscapes blend romantic realism with Impressionism. His influences ranged from Rembrandt to Monet. He believes that "real art lifts, enlightens. So much of today's pseudo art degrades, darkens and debases human feelings. The world is beautiful, alive, growing, and endeavoring to improve. Art must communicate that. I try in my paintings to cause others to feel that uplifting side of life." Wallis is represented by Husberg Fine Arts Gallery.

Walston, Jim. Realist carbon pencil delineator of Indians, ranch life, children, and old people, born in Sioux City, Iowa in 1920 and living in Albuquerque, New Mexico since 1955. "Before one can paint," Walston points out, "one has to be able to draw well. The drawing process gives a sense of perspective and good draftsmanship. The success of a pencil drawing depends on the use of a rich tonal quality and a pencil line that is fluid, yet deliberate. However, if the artist is unable to instill life in the subject matter, nothing can make the drawing a success."

After graduating from high school in 1938, Walston attended classes in Morningside College in Sioux City until he enlisted in the Navy in 1943. He returned to Sioux City to work as a commercial artist for ten years, then he was an illustrator in Wichita, Kansas for three years before being employed in graphic design by Sandia National Laboratories, a Department of Energy facility in Albuquerque where he has remained since 1955. Walston's graphics for Sandia have won international awards, including first place at the National Association of Industrial Artists.

In 1968, Walston began drawing as fine art. "I'll see a face that fascinates me," he explains, "and I am challenged to put it on paper. Sometimes it's a situation that I find amusing—like the delightful Indian rodeo in Gallup where the kids run for watermelons. Drawing is an honest medium. I want my drawings to be good, not only for my personal satisfaction but for the interchange with others." Walston has lectured, taught, and held a workshop in Alaska. Featured in *Southwest Art,* August 1980, he is represented by Galeria Del Sol.

Jim Walston, NATIVE AMERICAN WOMAN,
carbon pencil & pastel, 14 x 11

Kent Wallis, ANGELA, oil, 33 x 20

Ralph Wall, SONG OF THE DRAGONFLY, acrylic, 20 x 30

Curt Walters

Wanlass

Jim Ward

Walters, Curt. Realist oil painter of the Southwestern landscape, born in Las Cruces, New Mexico in 1950 and living in Sedona, Arizona since 1979. "My move to Sedona was due, in part, to its proximity to my favorites, the Grand Canyon and the Canyon de Chelly. The area is filled with many fine artists willing to share their ideas with others. Sedona itself has proved to be a wonderland of color and subjects. I would recommend it to any artist as a great place to live and work.

"I grew up in a farming community where the arts had little significance, but my father's walls were hung with many fine paintings. Dad wanted me to follow him in dentistry, but never failed to support my desire to be an artist. In 1960, the family moved to a farm in the La Plata Valley. It was here that I began to develop my love of the majestic Southwestern landscape. In 1969, I started at the San Juan branch of New Mexico State University. Most of my tuition was paid by the sale of my paintings.

"In 1971, I struck out on my own as full time artist while still attending college. Deciding that practice was the best teacher, I did not return to classes that fall. My first big break came in 1972 when I began exhibiting at a gallery in Taos, and I moved to Taos in 1975. My main subject matter is landscape because I am comfortable with the solidity of nature and have a great reverence for its beauty. I consider myself to be a naturalist, painting subjects as my eyes perceive them and rearranging them to suit my compositional needs. To me, Western landscape is so massive and complicated that I feel it requires a large canvas to do it justice." Written up in *American Artist* and *Arizona Highways,* Walters is represented by Trailside Galleries and Baker Gallery of Fine Art.

Wanlass, Stanley Glen. Figure painter and sculptor of bronze statuettes and monuments of the Northwest, born in American Fork, Utah in 1941 and living in Astoria, Oregon since 1971. Asked about his experience in Paris, Wanlass replied that "Europe lives art. Art is part of their everyday life, not something special to be taken out on occasion and admired. I found that the farther I got from Utah Valley the more respectable it was to be an artist.

"I grew up in an atmosphere of support," he recalls. "My parents always encouraged me to work with paints and clay." At Brigham Young University, he was taking pre-med courses and painting in his spare time but when the courses required quitting art, he changed his major. He earned his MA in 1968 while he was an instructor, fulfilled a LDS mission in the Northwest, and taught in France and Canada until he was appointed Professor of Art at Clatsop College in 1971. His commissioned statuary is in Utah, Oregon, and Washington, including a 32-ton work for Everett, Washington and a heroic bronze of Lewis and Clark for Fort Clatsop National Memorial.

On the place of the artist in society, Wanlass comments that "an artist has already fulfilled some of his obligation to the community by creating. His art enriches the lives of everyone." Sensitive to the Indians as "people who were wronged, with every agreement and treaty broken," Wanlass has symbolized such incidents in bronze. Listed in *Who's Who in American Art* and represented by Grand Central Art Galleries in New York City, his statuettes have sold for $3,800 to $5,000.

Ward, Jim. Realist painter and sculptor of Texas ranch life, born in Fort Worth, Texas in 1931 and living in Canyon, Texas since 1965. "There's still enough of the West around today that you never run out of subject matter," he declares. "You can go and watch those old boys on the ranches still draggin' the calves, branding and everything. These cowboys might get in their pickups and drive home for supper every night, but when it gets down to riding horses and working cattle, there's a whole lot that's still the same as it's always been."

Growing up in Austin as the third generation in the Southwest, Ward broke horses when he was in his teens. He earned his way through school as a rodeo clown but quit in his senior year at Oklahoma State University to join the Army as a lieutenant. After he received a medical discharge because of a football knee, he returned to college for his 1953 degree in animal husbandry. For another year he played the rodeo circuit, then worked as an agricultural instructor, ranch manager, and land appraiser. His only art training was the Famous Artists correspondence course where he took five years to complete the three year program. It took another three years as a commercial artist before he was financially able to paint full time.

By 1973, Ward was a charter member of the Texas Cowboy Artists Association. "One problem I have," he confesses, "is that my deep love is the outdoors. I'm forcing an unnatural situation on myself when I paint. I can live with it, but I'd rather be out foolin' around with horses." Ward has been profiled in *The Quarter Horse Journal* and *Paint Horse Journal.* He is represented by The Galleries.

Stanley Wanlass, BROKEN TRUST
bronze, h 24

Curt Walters, SUMMER SHADOWS—
GRAND CANYON, oil/canvas

Jim Ward, TRAIL BOSS (1976), oil, 24 x 30

Mel Warren

Warren, Melvin Charles. "Quiet" painter of modern Western life in "sharp focus realism," born in Los Angeles, in 1920 and living in Clifton, Texas, since 1961. "Because I'm a quiet fellow," he declares, "I just want to paint quiet things. Nowadays my life is not made up of a lot of violence. I don't know how to paint that kind of stuff. I paint what I know, what I experience."

Warren's father was a ranch hand in West Texas, and their home changed frequently. Warren began drawing early in life and earned $200 for a correspondence course in art when he was in high school in Seymour, Texas. He served in the Air Force in World War II, then worked in construction until 1949 when he enrolled in Texas Christian University where he spent five years. After working in commercial art and painting at night, he was able to begin painting full time in 1961.

"I don't like to paint from memory," he says. "Paintings done this way look like they were painted from memory. I have to see it and have a record of it before I paint it. I used to do sketches first but you lose the spontaneity so I just take my charcoal and sketch right on the canvas. A lot of my drawings on canvas look like a finished charcoal." He adds that "when I started out in commercial art, it was my dream to paint what I wanted. I put in a lot of sweat but now I'm doing what I want." In 1967, Warren's first bronze was cast. He sold 26 works to President Lyndon Johnson that are in the Johnson Library, was featured in *Southwest Art*, summer 1981, and is a member of the Cowboy Artists of America. At the 1981 Western Heritage Sale, a Warren oil brought $105,000. His gallery is Reminisce.

Mel Warren, **NIGHT IN CHIMAYO**, oil, **24 x 36**

Melvin C. Warren 1981

Warren, Patricia. Traditional sculptor and painter of contemporary Southwestern Indian women, born in Columbus, Mississippi in 1945 and living in Fort Worth, Texas. As a sculptor without a degree, she says that "everyone is put on this planet to learn all one can. One has merely to call upon Michelangelo, Rodin, Borglum, and MacNeil for existing knowledge. Also, a young aspiring artist today has the advantage of easy accessibility to many good museums, galleries, and fine books. One would have to be foolish not to use all available sources."

While she was growing up, her father Melvin Warren, who is now a leading Western artist, was coping with a daytime job as a commercial artist. When she graduated from Fort Worth High School in 1963, she had already studied at the Art Museum on a scholarship but fine art did not look like a practical career. Instead, she started toward medicine at the University of Texas in 1963, then switched to business courses. In 1965, she quit college and studied art privately.

Her bronzes are big, generally one-third to one-half life size, taking from four to eight months to model, and she usually limits editions to twenty. Ordering bronze castings from the foundry, she points out, "takes a great deal of confidence in what you have done. If you didn't have it, you would never have anything cast!" She also paints in oil and pastel and carves in stone that she calls "a strong disciplinarian. It frees a sculptor from becoming obsessed with modeling and gets him back to basics in sculpture—line and form." She was in five major exhibitions in 1979, six in 1980, and five in 1981. Written up in *Southwest Art,* April 1981, she is represented by her family's Reminisce Gallery and by Shidoni Gallery and Foundry.

Weaver, John Barney. Classic sculptor of Western figures in bronze monuments and statuettes, born in Anaconda, Montana in 1920 and living in Hope, British Columbia, Canada. "I believe that art as a creative, imaginative means of communication should be in an understandable form," he emphasizes. "If an expert has to explain the meaning, then the viewer is being steamrolled into an artificial situation. Art is a way of life. It is a profession which should serve people, not an ivory retreat of self-fulfillment."

Son and grandson of Montana artists, Weaver was his father's pupil until 1941 when he won a scholarship to the Art Institute of Chicago. His first commission came while he was in school, to model a heroic soldier figure for Butte. After five years in Milwaukee, teaching at Layton Art School and modeling commissions, he was awarded a commission in Helena and was appointed curator and sculptor at the Montana Historical Society. In 1961, he went to the Smithsonian Institution in Washington, D.C. where he did portrait sculpture of notables including Presidents and First Ladies.

Weaver emigrated to Canada in 1966 to incorporate his sculpture into the architectural design of the Provincial Museum in Edmonton. After two years, he began working from his home studio there, filling commissions from the United States and Canada and producing statuettes, primarily of Indians. He has done more than eight monuments, eleven reliefs, and 25 portraits, and his work is in ten museums. He is listed in *Who's Who in American Art,* is a member of the National Sculpture Society and of the Northwest Rendezvous Group, and was featured in *Art West,* summer 1978. He prefers to free lance.

Weddle, Joy. Sculptor of bronze statuettes and miniatures, particularly of Indian women and children, born in Wheaton, Illinois in 1933 and living in Dewey, Arizona. "We moved to Arizona in 1934," she recalls, "and lived on a ranch in the desert. Our Daddy taught us to draw. We would sit around our big oak table, each with a stack of typing paper and draw for hours. I never thought my work was very good, and I am still surprised when someone actually buys my bronzes.

"When I was eight, we moved to Horse Mesa Dam on the Salt River. When I wasn't swimming or climbing, I was drawing and painting pictures of the mountains. After I graduated from high school, I took a correspondence course on oil painting with Famous Artists in 1958. People began wanting to buy my paintings. They were going to automate that Dam, so we moved to Coolidge Dam on the San Carlos Indian Reservation. I began drawing and painting the Indian children and the Crown Dancers. I also took a class in clay and ceramics offered at the Indian School, started making clay sculptures, and people wanted to buy them.

"When we moved to Parker Dam, I made and sold lots of clay sculptures. Then I got into bronzes. You can do more detail and make editions and still have one to keep. Because of the expense, I learned to do most of the work myself. After eight years, we moved here. I have been asked by friends how you go about becoming a professional artist. I really can't tell them much. My life just seemed to have provided the ideal settings to inspire me, but mostly I have just always created things for the joy of it, not struggling to become anything. My bronzes are currently displayed at El Prado Gallery of Art and Burk Gal'ry."

John Weaver, PLENTY COUPS, bronze, h 2 ft, Edition 30

Joy Weddle, BUFFALO DANCER, bronze, h 12

Patricia Warren, SHE WAITS HIS RETURN, bronze, h 18, Edition 20

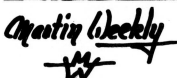

Weekly, Martin. "Somewhat impressionistic" oil painter of the life of the contemporary cowboy, born in Exeter, California in 1936 and living in Folsom, California. "The paintings that require the least amount of time are usually my best," he explains. "If it takes a long time, it is usually because there are problems I have difficulty recognizing and they will invariably show in the end product. I liken the process to that of a baseball pitcher. When he is hot, he can 'mow down' the batters in short order. If he is not, he can be out on the mound a long time.

"In childhood, I found great enjoyment trudging through the fields near my father's farm, alone with a sketch pad. After I received my degree in art from Sacramento State College, I embarked on a high school teaching career. I continued to paint and finally approached a gallery in Carmel. Much to my surprise, my work was accepted! As my paintings began to sell, I terminated my teaching in 1970.

"Frequently, I hear comments about a painting looking 'just like a photograph.' This is intended to be a compliment, but I have been in galleries where magnifying glasses were provided in order for the viewer to scrutinize the detail. If I receive such 'praise' about my work, I realize it is time to get a large brush and 'mess it up a bit.' I like to romanticize the life of the contemporary cowboy. When I paint something from the past, I feel a little uncomfortable about it. The reason for this is that I like to observe my subject matter firsthand. As much as possible, painting 'on location' is extremely important to me. It forces me to include only the essence. My paintings are displayed mainly at the Biltmore and Texas Art Galleries."

Weeks, Garland A. Sculptor of the West in bronze statuettes, born in Amarillo, Texas in 1942 and living in the Grape Creek Community near San Angelo, Texas since 1981. "Initially, I looked at sculpting as my answer to a hobby," he says. "With no formal art education in the beginning, I started out on a tough round of trial and error, looking and listening, asking questions, seeking answers, and in the process earning my credentials in the school of hard knocks.

"I grew up in Wichita Falls, and elected to seek my college education at Texas Tech University in Lubbock. I gave no thought to the art department and earned my BS in agricultural economics while winning athletic letters on the collegiate rodeo team. After college, I rodeoed professionally, served a two-year hitch in the Army, and began to utilize my education by becoming actively engaged in the cattle feeding industry where I did everything from cleaning feed bunks to buying and selling feeders and fat cattle and trading commodity futures.

"My interest in art began to emerge and in 1971 I started modeling in wax at the urging of friends." After trying the school of hard knocks, "I realized the need of formal training and was accepted at the Mustafa Naguib School of Sculpture in Chicago where I concentrated on the study of traditional anatomy, portrait sculpture, and relief sculpture. I am now serving as president of the Texas Cowboy Artists Association. I was commissioned in 1981 to create limited edition bronzes for the National Cattlemen's Association and for other national corporations. My sculpture is in the permanent collection of Buckingham Palace in London and I display regularly in shows." Weeks is represented by The Galleries.

Wells, Justin. Painter in watercolor and pen and ink of "the people, animals, and landscapes associated with the contemporary horse culture of the American West," born in Elk City, Oklahoma in 1941 and living in Amarillo, Texas since 1976. "All my pictures," he states, "are of things I have seen and done or would like to have seen and done. Cattle people are still a unique class of human being. They are distinctly recognizable apart from any other group of men who make their living outdoors."

Raised in Texas and California before returning to Oklahoma in 1950, Wells was a graduate of Putnam City High School and attended Central State University in Edmond, Oklahoma. Next to painting a picture of a good colt, he says, he would rather work with one, and he has bred and trained registered quarter horses. One activity helps the other, he believes. Knowing by personal experience how a horse moves enables the artist to communicate reality more effectively. Wells calls that his philosophy of art, that one should paint what he knows.

Interested in all periods of the American frontier, Wells also draws trail herds of longhorns and the American Indian. For the *Westerner* magazine, he has illustrated stories about subjects "from Comanches to camels, Paiutes to preachers, and bandits to brush-poppers." He points out that "the idea of making one's living on horseback has always been attractive in a romantic way, although the reality of such a life has as much sweat and cruelty as any other occupation." In 1976, Wells was inducted into the Texas Cowboy Artists Association. He won the group's gold medal for drawing in 1977 and 1978 and for watercolor in 1981.

Garland A. Weeks, SCHOOL JUST TOOK UP
bronze, h 8½, Edition 10

Martin Weekly, AFTER THE STORM, oil, 30 x 48

12/450

Justin Wells, BACHELOR'S CLUB, ink, 24 x 36

Helen West (signature)

Rygh Westby (signature)

Eileen Monaghan Whitaker (signature)

West, Helen. Realist painter of "the moods of birds and nature," born in Melbourne, Australia of American parents in 1926 and living in Billings, Montana. "I'm easier to live with when I paint," she points out. "Certain people have to paint. It's an obsession, an uncontrollable impulse and drive. Some people have more talent than others, but 99.9 percent of the success is hard work and experience. You have to work at it. If you do, you can do anything."

After returning to the United States in 1931, she was brought up in the East but spent summers on Wyoming ranches and was an art major at Montana State University. She took additional courses at the Minneapolis Institute in 1948 and the Chicago Academy of Fine Arts in 1950, as well as private study. When she married the Game Supervisor of the Big Horn Basin, she was able to spend days in the field and to quit teaching school in order to paint full time. She says that she "paints in a realistic style as the best way to relate impressions."

She "gets up, eats, puts on classical music, and paints the day away." Mood and weather do not affect her style. She begins by making black and white thumbnail sketches in the field. Back in her studio, she notes colors with the aid of slides, adding a day of composing to the day of sketching before painting. If the medium is watercolor, she may do three or four finished paintings of the subject before choosing one to frame and throwing out the others. "You gamble every time you put a brush to paper," she acknowledges. She has been winning Best of Show awards since 1963, has had a dozen one-person shows, has given dozens of workshops, and has been the featured painter at Ducks Unlimited. She has exhibited in Gallery 85 and in the Wild Goose Gallery.

Westby, Rygh. Traditional oil painter of the contemporary Plains cowboy, born in Oak Park, Illinois in 1949 and living in Sheridan, Wyoming since 1977. "To be perfectly frank," he points out, "I probably would not have decided to try to make a living at painting were it not for the fact that I began to be aware that others had done so. My first love is cowboying, not art. I hope that this will not discourage any collectors, but good ranch jobs are scarce and bouncing around can be rough on your family, so I decided to try art while I was young enough."

A science major at Colorado State University, he became an English major and then an art major at Elgin Community College in Illinois, but says "I am primarily self-taught. My 'art major' consisted of one semester of drawing and one of jewelry and sculpture." When he was twenty, he quit school and went to work for a small outfit in Colorado and then moved up to bigger outfits throughout the West.

"I don't exhibit in shows that emphasize competition," he emphasizes, "and I tend to keep a low profile. If my work is good enough, it will sell, but any 'hype' beyond informing the buyer what kind of product he is getting and what kind of guy made it is not my cup of tea. I don't go in for violence other than what might be unavoidable in the course of a day's work. If I paint a cowboy, I want the viewer to *know* that it *is* a cowboy, not just somebody who looks like one. There never were a whole lot of cowboys, and there aren't now. If cowboying is really any good, it will last. So far, it has been around for a long time." Written up in *Art West*, November 1980, Westby exhibits with Carson Gallery of Western American Art and Riata Gallery.

Whitaker, Eileen Monaghan. Representational transparent watercolorist of figures and animals, born in Holyoke, Massachusetts in 1911 and living in La Jolla, California since 1965. "To me," she says, "painting isn't fun. It's usually hard work. It's a challenge to pull off a painting that really satisfies me. It's something close to agony, but delicious agony. I go over and over paintings, changing and hopefully improving. To me, a finished watercolor is not a spontaneous sketch.

"All I ever wanted to do was paint. I have had this terrific urge to paint since I was a child. I studied four years at the Massachusetts School of Art and worked for more than fifteen years in commercial art. I used to do fashion design, making quick sketches of clothing and figures and window displays. Technique is something that must be learned by any watercolor student, but concentration on it stifles creativity. An artist must know the basics, but that's secondary to composing a painting that works.

"I have no great message for the world. What I paint is simply an interpretation of my observations." In 1943, she met and later married Frederic Whitaker who was called "Mr. Watercolor" before he died in 1980. She became a full time painter in 1947 and has won more than eighty major awards. In 1978, she was elected a National Academician in transparent watercolor, only the second woman named in 153 years. She is listed in *Who's Who in America*, is a member of the American Watercolor Society, and was featured in *Southwest Art*, December 1975 and *Artists of the Rockies*, winter 1982. Her watercolor at Trailside Galleries was listed at $2,000 in 1981. She is represented by Baker Gallery of Fine Art.

Eileen Whitaker, MAYAN GIRLS AT THE TEMPLE
watercolor, 30 x 22

Rygh Westby, COWBOY'S HELPER, oil, 12 x 14

Helen West, FIRST TOUCH OF SPRING, oil, 20 x 30

W. Whitaker.

Whitaker, William. Traditional oil painter of Western figures, particularly young women, born in Chicago in 1943 and living in West Provo, Utah. "After a point," he says, "school does more damage than good because the students must find themselves through isolated, hard work. To become a top-notch artist, talent is not really enough. You must have 'stick-to-itiveness,' the idiocy just to continue. Actually, to become a top quality artist, you've got to train with more intensity than a brain surgeon and for a lot less reward."

As the son of an artist, Whitaker learned the technical background when he was in his teens. A graduate of the University of Utah who also studied at Otis Art Institute, he thinks that the old apprenticeship way of learning was better than current methods, and that "those of us who stand up for so-called realistic painting can't deliver a product as good as our predecessors did." He also objects to art "competition that smacks of a horse race. Judging one work of art against another is like racing a horse, a rabbit, and a dog together. Each work of art is a complete individual.

"Often the more sensitive an artist is, the more difficult it is for him to cope with the art marketplace. An artist must understand that the economics of art are not dirty, not abnormal, not wrong, but something that you can live with. Artists are very stable, very solid, about as responsible as they can be, but we're terrible buyers. We don't know how to get things wholesale." Whitaker was featured in *Artists of the Rockies*, spring 1980, and was in the 1981 Peking, China, exhibition. He is a member of the National Academy of Western Art and is represented by Trailside Galleries.

William Whitaker, PEPPER WALK, oil/panel, 15 x 12

White, Fritz. Sculptor of Indian and other Western figures in bronze, born on the banks of the Little Ohio River in 1930 and living in Denver since 1956. "Western art is not just a scapegoat for bad artistry," he says. "There are too damn many of us who are good, but there are also too damn many of us who are bad. So, a lot of people who are not in Western art say, 'Well, the only reason you're in Western art is because you've got a kind of protected territory.' That's ridiculous."

At twelve, White was enrolled in an art class and at thirteen advanced to life drawing. After high school, he went to Miami University of Ohio on a football scholarship but quit to serve in the Marine Corps for three and a half years. He then started in commercial art in Cincinnati, joined a publisher and became Rocky Mountain Manager in Denver, and quit to return to commercial art. Finding marble cliffs in Colorado led him to sculpture in 1962, and fellow artist Ned Jacob asked him, "Why don't you get into Western art? You've heard of Charlie Russell? That's Western art." White replied, "You mean people buy that stuff?" and he started in.

"In the beginning," White recalls, "I was so poor, I could only afford to cast one or two pieces at a time. I would get the guy who already owned one to let me sell his bronze and then I could afford to cast another to replace his. I went through an issue of 25 like that." He was elected a member of the Cowboy Artists of America in 1972, but until then had not ridden a horse. He had been featured in *Southwest Art*, May 1974, and in *Artists of the Rockies*, summer 1977, and is represented by Altermann Art and Artists Union Galleries.

Fritz White, THE CROW AND THE BEAR, bronze, h 36, l 19½

Olaf Wieghorst, ROCKY MOUNTAIN TRAIL, oil, 24 x 30

Wieghorst, Olaf. Traditional oil painter of the West, born in Viborg, Denmark, in 1899 and living in El Cajon, California, since 1944. "The horse has been my greatest teacher," he says. "Horses have been my companions under nearly all possible conditions. I have frozen with them at night, ridden across the desert in the hottest days on record, starved with them and hunted water with them longer than I care to remember. I have nailed shoes onto hundreds of them, been kicked, bitten, squeezed, bucked off, stepped on by them, and have fallen from them; but in spite of all the broken bones, I have no regret."

Son of a Danish photographer and film animator, Wieghorst performed as a featured acrobat at nine and traveled with the circus as a trick rider. While in his teens, he also began painting, selling oils for as little as 45 cents. His interest was the American West, personified by Remington magazine articles translated into Danish and Wild West Shows touring Europe. Unable to obtain a passport, he signed on as cabin boy on a Danish steamer and jumped ship in New York Harbor in 1918.

From 1919 to 1922, he was a member of the U.S. Cavalry, patrolling the Mexican border during the Pancho Villa campaign. He then worked as a cowboy in Arizona and New Mexico before returning to New York City in 1924 as a mounted policeman. In his spare time, Wieghorst painted. When he retired in 1944, it was in order to become a painter, and ten years later he enjoyed a successful one-man show that was the start of countless honors. He received the first retrospective for a living artist at the Cowboy Hall of Fame, and his oils have sold for as much as $200,000. Limited edition prints are published by The Wooden Bird.

JIM WILCOX

Katheryn Williams .B

hollis williford

Wilcox, Jim. Representational landscape painter of the Grand Tetons in oil, born in Salt Lake City, Utah in 1941 and living in Jackson, Wyoming since 1969. "As a kid," he recalls, "I always wanted to be an Indian when we played, even though I ended up getting shot. I loved the feathers and buckskin. I still love Indians, but I'd hesitate to put Indians or a teepee in a painting because it would look like I'm hopping on a bandwagon."

Brought up in the Mormon Church, he spent his early years in Colorado and returned to Utah to study art at Brigham Young University. To support his painting, he worked as a bellman in a Salt Lake City motel and as a high school art teacher in Seattle, Washington for two years. When he moved to Jackson Hole to paint full time, he operated a small art gallery. After eight years, he built a home out of town where he has his studio and also a gallery to show his paintings. "I know what sells," he emphasizes, "water, a moose, blue sky, white clouds, the mountains, and flowers and trees in the foreground.

"My paintings are about light, the light singing across a meadow or the time after a storm when there are little holes in the clouds that the light pokes through." He never gets tired of painting the mountains. "They're a spectacular subject. The Grand Tetons are to mountains what the Grand Canyon is to other holes in the ground." He paints everyday, starting a sketch in the field by showing the elements of the scene and where the light is coming from, then completing the details in the studio. Wilcox has exhibited with the National Academy of Western Art and the Northwest Rendezvous Group and in the Western Heritage Show. He is represented by the Moran Gallery and Troy's Gallery.

Williams, Katheryn. Realist painter of characteristic adobe dwellings of New Mexico, born in Clovis, New Mexico in 1924 and living in Santa Fe since 1971. Because she thoroughly researches each structural landmark, she says that "I then know what I'm painting, and the act of painting it becomes more meaningful. I am careful to present it correctly, accurately, because that is my purpose: to record it against the day when it may no longer be there."

She began painting in 1952 but did not work seriously for ten years. Then, encouraged by her teacher at Eastern New Mexico University in Portales, she went to Mexico to study with the Academician John Pellew at the Instituto de Allende in San Miguel. After her husband died in 1971, she started painting full time. As her declaration of purpose, she states that "to me, the world in its totality is too overwhelming to tackle, so I personally offer to others the parts that are around me," the adobe landmarks, old missions, churches, and sanctuaries.

Subject matter is thus most important to her, and technique is "whatever best fits the exigencies of the moment." She paints in oil or acrylic, on canvas or panel, signing "Williams - B" as a reference to her second husband. A device she uses is to provide "pockets of beauty" in her work, small areas like trees in the background that are as detailed as if close up. "I like the viewer to find small treasures," she explains. "The overall effect of the painting may be pleasing, but I like to give more, something not first noticed in the totality of a picture." She was featured in *Southwest Art,* October 1976 and is represented by Santa Fe and Sagebrush Galleries.

Williford, Hollis. Traditional sculptor of Plains Indians and painter of Indians and Western landscapes, born in Waco, Texas in 1940 and living in Denver, Colorado since 1970. "Like my grandfather would say," Williford points out, "I'm working from 'can to cain't.' That's an old cotton-country expression used when farmers are trying to get their crops in and they're racing with the elements from sunup to sundown."

The son of sharecroppers, Williford worked as a farmer before a high school teacher noticed his talent. His environment had not prepared him for college but he spent three years at the University of Texas until his family's reverses required him to drop out in order to take on two jobs at the local granary. He then worked as a graphic artist in aerospace, and only after eight years was he finally able to apply to the Art Center College of Design to complete his studies. Los Angeles was difficult for "a country boy," and when he graduated in 1970 he moved to Denver to open his own studio.

In Denver, Williford took skeletal anatomy and it all came together. Sculpture is his forte, but he also draws, paints, and etches. "I'm trying to divide my time between the media. I set quotas of paintings to do by natural light and on location, and do some 120 field sketches a year. In sculpture, I have set a quota of fifteen pieces a year, but only twenty percent of these will actually be produced." Williford has been featured in *Art West, Artists of the Rockies,* and *Southwest Art,* exhibited in the 1981 Peking, China show, is a member of the Northwest Rendezvous Group, and in 1980 won the Prix de West at the National Academy of Western Artists exhibition. His gallery is Carson Gallery of Western American Art.

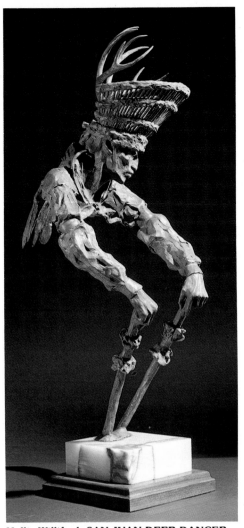

Jim Wilcox, GRAND CANYON STORM, oil, 24 x 36

Hollis Williford, SAN JUAN DEER DANCER
bronze, h 28

Katheryn Williams, A CHANGE OF SEASONS, oil, 15 x 30

577

Loren Willis

Dale Wilson

Willis, Loren. Stylized oil painter of the Indian of yesterday, born in Mesa, Arizona in 1931 and still living there. "I feel deeply about the Indians," he points out. "They were a people essentially free and very spiritual. They sought visions. They could prophesy. I don't feel that you must be Indian to paint Indians anymore than you need to be Chinese to paint Chinese people."

One grandfather was an Indian fighter, the other came West in a covered wagon and was killed by Indians, but Willis' father taught art in Arizona in the 30s. Willis earned his degree in art education from Arizona State University in 1959 and then did graduate work before becoming an art instructor in the Mesa schools where he has remained for 22 years. In his spare time, he "had been painting desert landscapes for years in a semi-abstract manner. When I began this series of Indian figures, they were very large and rather abstract, but with new paintings, I eventually gravitated to a more realistic, descriptive style.

"As I read about Indians, they spark my imagination and I try to portray them as they were—free and wild, without the constraints and problems of the white man. Yes, I intensify and dramatize the real thing to create a personal expression with color and movement. My view of the Indian is certainly a romantic one, but it is my vision nonetheless. The Indians have lost their desire to continue on since the advent of the white man and the loss of their lands. The white man felt little remorse for the displaced Indian. He treated him as subhuman and took what he could." Written up in *Southwest Art,* September 1981, he is represented by Whitney and Enthios Galleries.

Wilson, Dale. Traditional painter of Western scenes, born in Arcadia, Nebraska in 1917 and living in Cibolo, Texas since 1980. He was a commercial artist in Chicago when Vincent Price saw a Wilson exhibition in 1965 and asked that a selection of pictures be brought to his apartment. The actor offered to buy all thirty canvases but Wilson refused to sell more than 24 because "it would have wiped me out."

Growing up in Nebraska, Wilson's uncle let him ride a cow pony until the horse and he went back into the barn "with the top half of the door closed." During World War II, Wilson was in France as a photographer in the Army Engineers and attended classes at the Ecole des Beaux Arts in Marseilles. After the war, he studied with William Mosby at the American Academy of Art in Chicago and then worked in commercial art and as a designer until 1960 "when my 'Sunday painting' avocation turned to professional full time fine art painting.

"Before 1970," Wilson says, "my paintings were mostly Midwestern scenes in oils and watercolors. As we returned to the West on painting trips, my paintings reflected my early heritage. I paint my oils on masonite, prepared with three coats of gesso, unsanded. I like the details of this. Sometimes it takes two or three days to develop a painting, but once I have this in my mind's eye I am enthusiastic and stay with the painting until it is done. It is not easy to portray something out of the past, but it is rewarding to see a fast running horse with dust flying emerge on the white panel." Wilson is represented by the Dagen Bela Galeria and by the Country Store Gallery.

Loren Willis, RAVEN OWNER, oil, 40 x 40

Dale Wilson, IN PURSUIT, oil, 24 x 36

579

Wilson, Douglas Fenn. Modern painter of "constructed" landscapes and seascapes in pastel, watercolor, and acrylic, born in Orinda, California in 1953 and living in San Francisco since 1975. "The technique," he explains, "involves integrating a realistic drawing or watercolor with up to six different levels of balsa wood or foamcore. The levels go deep into the surface of the painting as well as protrude above the surface. My final goal is to marry realistic landscape with geometric abstraction with geometric relief.

"My grandfather was an American Impressionist who painted in the St. Louis area and held a professorship in art and architecture. I had the advantage of being encouraged to appreciate fine painting at an early age, and was entertained by painting in watercolor since my early teens. I was twenty before I seriously considered making a living as a professional painter and I undertook to become a technically deft realist before thinking of developing my point of view into a style that was unique.

"My interest in architecture was always the passion that interrupted my devotion to good painting so I began to work out a way that I could integrate my interest in geometric and architectural forms into realist landscape painting. The solution has evolved over the past six years into 'constructed' paintings. As for the direction of my work, all I can guarantee is that it will become more diverse and more polished. The biggest joy of being an artist is to grapple with inspirations, distill them into solid ideas, execute them in a medium, and finally to refine the result." Written up in *Southwest Art*, June 1980, his current representation includes John Pence and Janus Galleries.

Wilson, Mortimer Jr. Oil painter of historical Western genre scenes and of still-lifes, born in Lincoln, Nebraska in 1906 and living in Tubac, Arizona since 1956. "You can't turn out pictures quickly," he stresses. "Yes, there is money to be made, but how much is enough. You can get to where nothing satisfies you but a five million dollar home. Yes, and to achieve that risks losing the greater pleasure of painting as best as I am able."

Son of a symphony conductor, Wilson went to summer classes at the Art Students League when he was fifteen and full time when he finished high school, although he considers the Old Masters his only real teachers. His spare time was spent at the Metropolitan Museum to copy Hals, Velasquez, Degas, and Sargent. After graduation, he painted portraits but heeded Norman Rockwell's advice to give up easel painting for illustration. Within five years, he was completing "two paintings every ten days" when "the average price was one thousand dollars for a job."

At 39, however, "my eye just blacked out one day. I couldn't paint," and he later moved to Arizona to save money. After thirty years, his vision returned and he began to paint again. Sensitivity to the sun precludes landscapes so his subjects are from his imagination. He works slowly and produces few paintings in a year but he was given a one-person show at O'Brien's Art Emporium where half the paintings sold the first night. His heroes are still the Old Masters. Music is also important to him, as is literature. He was featured in *Artists of the Rockies,* summer 1978 and *Southwest Art*, July 1981. He exhibited in the Peking, China show and is a member of the National Academy of Western Art.

Wilson, Nicholas Jon. Realist painter of wildlife in opaque watercolor on board, born in Seattle, Washington in 1947 and living in Payson, Arizona. "Since I was three," he recalls, "I've been fascinated with every aspect of nature. Shells, insects, and birds became imprinted on my mind after I drew pictures of them. After high school, I copied Michelangelo's sculpture from books.

"I finally settled down to doing portraits of pets on scratchboard, gave lessons, and published my own animal prints. Such efforts fell short of supporting me, so I worked as a picture framer and ski instructor." Illustrations of the Chukar partridge he did in his spare time for the Nevada Game and Fish Department led to a job as staff artist at the Desert Museum in 1970. "Here I was literally surrounded with the things that thrilled me most," he adds, "live animals, insect collections, a nature library, and knowledgeable people.

"This forced my development as an animal artist much like an art school would have, causing me to resign my position after just a few years in order to follow my original ambition as a wildlife artist. Now, I work in a controlled, opaque watercolor technique where hair is rendered by first scratching through the darkened surface, then tinting it with transparent washes." He describes his work as "semi-still-life" because he will not do action paintings. "I want to show a different view of the animals, their casual, passive times." A member of the Society of Animal Artists and written up in *Southwest Art,* April 1974, he is published by Mill Pond Press and is represented by Trailside Galleries and by Settlers West Galleries which required a minimum bid of $3,250 for his painting in its 1981 silent auction.

Mortimer Wilson, Jr., WINE AND ROSES, oil/canvas, 22 x 26

D.F. Wilson, DESCENDING SEACLIFFS, acrylic, 52½ x 37

Nick Wilson, TREASURES OF LA PLATA, gouache, 15¼ x 24

Dalhart Windberg, WOODLAND REFLECTION, oil, 12 x 16

Windberg™

Windberg, Dalhart. "Old Master" oil painter of Texas landscapes, born in Goliad, Texas, in 1933 and living in Austin, Texas. "Develop a theme," he advises, "and then get off it. The copyists are right behind you. It doesn't bother me too much because by the time the copies appear, I've gone off in another direction. I do look at what others are doing and try not to do something they are working on. If a hundred artists are painting quail, there's no point in your doing a quail too."

At fourteen, he attended an art class in a nearby convent and after two years joined the local art guild classes. "None of us," he recalls, "actually knew anyone who made a living as a painter." In 1953, he was drafted as a sign painter in the Seventh Army in Europe where he "visited all of the museums I could. I was impressed with the extreme smoothness the paintings had. I knew that was what I really wanted to do." In 1955, he was back in the art guild, working as a sign painter and eventually teaching art in the evenings. To teach and paint, he quit the sign business, and by 1967 he had given up teaching.

At his first art show, he "took blank canvases with me and while I waited for people to come, I painted. I sold more paintings than I had taken with me. I'll always wonder how people got a wet painting all the way home." By 1970, he felt that the had achieved the smoothness he wanted, and in 1972 he started publishing prints. Since 1979, his prints have been published by his own Windberg Enterprises, and at the end of 1980 he had fourteen employees. What he looks for is "recognition. But recognized by whom? If the public buys my paintings as fast as I can produce them, am I recognized? For me, that's recognition." He was written up in *Southwest Art*, April 1974.

Witherspoon, Kay E. Representational oil painter of Western landscapes, born in Billings, Montana in 1949 and living in Englewood, Colorado. "I want to say something about the West," she emphasizes, "the way it is now, in my generation. There is a West apart, beyond the cowboys and Indians. It is a West that is relevant to the people who grew up in the Vietnam era. My art is about the splendor of the Western wilderness, but there is a danger of it vanishing, being swept away by developers or others in the name of 'progress.'"

Encouraged by her parents, she was painting watercolors and oils by the time she was twelve. At the University of Montana, however, the art program "was so liberal it was stifling." She switched majors and graduated with a degree in history and art. In 1971, she joined the Forest Service, with six months working in the woods and the winter months living in snowbound cabins where she studied Old Master techniques. In 1973, she became a high school teacher of history and art but after two years moved to Colorado to paint.

To get started, she "decided to work long enough to build a nest egg large enough to carry me six months, then start painting professionally. My friend was in the real estate business, and through him I got a job in his office. I was making $3,000 a month and owned my own home where I had set up a studio. Part of me liked dressing up and going out as a competent businesswoman. Part of me liked the quiet, contemplative, personal and intense involvement of painting." When she started painting full time, she opened her own gallery, Colorado Art, that also publishes her prints. She was written up in *Southwest Art,* August 1979.

Wolf, Bob. Sculptor in bronze of birds in flight, born in Lincoln, Nebraska in 1937 and living in La Porte, Colorado since 1951. Wolf calls his bronzes "Wildlife Moments" because they "depict his thoughts, experiences, and dreams." He says that he "tries to capture the spirit or mood of an event—a reflection—a fleeting glimpse—of a moment to be remembered that I may never see again."

In 1966, Wolf was a cross-country ski instructor in Colorado and Wyoming, and he had been a mountaineering guide, river runner, and wilderness survival instructor. By 1970, he was painting watercolors and oils and beginning to experiment with sculpture because it was "something to do simply because I'd never done it before. I enjoy seeing a project being born, grow, and fade, and a new one started. I like to conceive new ideas. I've been doing this for years." In 1973, he started to work full time at wildlife sculpture, with waterfowl heading the list of subjects.

Asked why he specializes in birds, Wolf replies that "I get along with birds. I can talk to them and they understand and listen. Birds fly, and they are an art form when they do fly. My goal is to do the best art form possible along with preserving wildlife for future generations." While the waxes for all bronzes in a series are cast from the same mold, Wolf consciously models differences into the bronzes because "it gives a personal touch to each piece. It helps me identify with the owner and helps the owner appreciate the piece a little more." He also supplies instructions on "The Care and Feeding of a Wolf Bronze." He has exhibited with the Northwest Rendezvous Group and is represented by The May Gallery and Altermann Art Gallery.

Wolfe, Wayne E. Representational landscape painter of Western mountains, born in 1945 and living in Santa Fe, New Mexico since 1976. "When you paint from nature," he points out, "you find about a million things to depict—more than you could ever invent in the studio. Mother Nature does 90 percent of the work for you. All you have to do is move a little real estate in designing pictures and you come up with some crackerjacks."

The son of Byron Wolfe, a member of the Cowboy Artists of America who died in 1973, Wayne Wolfe began painting in December of that year to create Christmas gifts. He had graduated from college, served in the Army, and worked as sales manager for a radio station. While painting part time, he was employed as account executive for an advertising agency until 1975 when he asked his father's friend Bob Lougheed how best to become a full time artist. The advice was "to learn to paint landscapes from life, and figures and animals from models." Wolfe painted more than 100 landscapes on location during the first year.

"Paint about a thousand sketches outdoors, and you'll begin to get the idea," he adds. "When you start out and you haven't done number one yet, that's depressing. But once you get past ten, twenty or fifty sketches, gosh, the world becomes a beautiful place! If I can see a natural design, that's what I like to paint. Light against dark. Something in the background in shadow against something in the foreground in light. Or vice versa." Written up in *Southwest Art,* April 1982, Wolfe has exhibited at the National Academy of Western Art and the Western Heritage Show and has shown at Trailside Galleries and Settlers West Galleries.

Bob Wolf, WHISPERING WINGS
bronze, h 27, w 27, Edition 15

Kay E. Witherspoon, EPITAPH TO BRANDY, oil, 20 x 24

Wayne Wolfe, CROSSSING THE CHAMISH FIELD, oil, 30 x 40

Karl E. Wood (signature)

Francis L. Woodahl (signature)

Lloyd Woodbury (signature)

Wood, Karl E. Representational oil painter of the Canadian Rockies, born in Winnipeg, Manitoba in 1944 and living in Westbank near Kelowna, British Columbia, Canada. "My paintings are not just pictures," he emphasizes, "they are a part of me. If it is not a part of your life, the painting becomes mere illustration. I never paint from memory as paintings done this way usually lack authenticity. Only by observing and painting landscapes under whatever conditions prevail can I accurately interpret these moods and conditions on canvas. Then, when I return to my studio ready to finish a large canvas, my work will have that most important ingredient of all—heart."

Although he considers himself to be mainly a self-taught artist, his early inspiration was his father, Robert E. Wood, who was a painting instructor in the Art League of Victoria where Wood enrolled in 1962. Called "enthusiastic, eagerly looking forward to learning his craft, quiet, even shy," he began painting full time in 1965, after working with the British Columbia Hydro and Power Authority.

"My life," he says, "has been built on capturing the mood of the West and primarily our magnificent Canadian Rockies. I believe that you cannot learn except through experiencing the events and moods of nature. I paint what I am in contact with, where I am, and what I believe in. I like to paint something that *is*. I like nature, its soft colors, the seasons, and everything that's different about each season. I paint outside whenever I can." He refers to his painting as a chess game. Before each stroke is applied, there is a lot of forethought because every move affects all of the moves to follow. He is represented by Gainsborough and Collectors Galleries.

Woodahl, Francis L. Realist oil painter of characterizations of Western scenes and people, born in Baltimore, Maryland in 1938 and living in Garden Grove, California. "The thing that fascinates me about the paintings I choose to do," he points out, "are the various textures such as worn buckskin and denim, the fur and beadwork, adobe and earth. I try to capture the various textures optically rather than physically. The surface of my work is uniformly smooth, regardless of the subject."

He took art courses in high school where he "had to study art at the girls' school. They didn't have courses at the boys' high school. Very strange." After going to the Maryland Institute of Art on a scholarship, he served in the Navy as a draftsman, illustrating brochures, and his later fine art began with seascapes. He changed to portraits of children and then to old men before moving to Western subjects in 1977. "I am not a historian or a chronicler of today's or yesterday's West," he emphasizes. "I attempt to set an atmosphere.

"I paint realistically, but I am not a super-realist. I am not against super-realism. It's just not for me. I take license to compose the painting, adding elements which I feel will work together. I want to express certain feelings I have for the West, inspired by the people. All my people are real and living. I find most satisfaction in what I am doing now. I'm comfortable and continually challenged, but who knows what I will concentrate on next. I don't." Written up in *Southwest Art*, May 1978, he is a member of American Indian and Cowboy Artists and of Western Artists of America and is represented by The Brush Gallery and Gallerie Marguerite.

Woodbury, Lloyd. Traditional sculptor of bronze statuettes of horses, cowboys, cattle, and wildlife of the West today and yesterday, born on a ranch in Baggs, Wyoming in 1917 and living in Center Point, Texas. "Eyeballing the dimensions of a model may be fine," he observes, "but it is not always accurate. It is too easy to unconsciously lengthen or shorten a leg or arm without realizing what you have done. Besides, I have too many customers who would spot a mistake in a hurry."

Growing up in southern Wyoming, Woodbury cowboyed like the other ranch youths but he was also modeling clay dug from the riverbank. In his teens, he began mounting small birds and animals. After service in the Navy in World War II, he found a railroad job in Seattle, Washington where he was introduced to a New York City sculptor who created mounted animal groups for museums. Woodbury worked in New York City for eight years, starting with scale models of the groups in completing commissions for museums around the world.

When he tired of New York, he returned to Wyoming and opened a taxidermy shop where he mounted game animals on forms he cast. He modeled figurines in his spare time. After he moved to Texas in retirement, he established a taxidermy shop again and ran it until his final retirement in 1974. Soon, he returned to his old hobby, modeling animals. Visitors wanted copies so he went to bronze casting, adding Western scenes of the cowboys, hunters, and packers he had known. He also began a series of rodeo subjects, creating the models, pouring the molds, making the wax figures, having them cast, and then assembling and finishing the bronzes himself. He was written up in *Paint Horse Journal*, January 1982 and is represented by Shidoni Gallery and Foundry.

Lloyd Woodbury, THE ROUGH STRING RIDER
bronze, h 18, w 13

Francis Woodahl, PESKY SCALP CRITTERS, oil, 12 x 16

Karl Wood, LATE FALL—CAMPBELL RANGE, B.C., oil, 30 x 48

Woods, Jack D. Traditional sculptor and painter of the Old West, born in Tucumcari, New Mexico in 1930 and living in Taos since 1970. "When I was just a little kid," he recalls, "I was sitting around in the old saloons, drinking coke and eating pretzels, devouring all the yarns about the Old West that my father and his cronies could spiel out. I'll always be grateful to them for sharing their experiences with a young and impressionable boy.

"I had an early ambition to become an artist, but early plans got sidetracked and I was forty years old before I entered the field full time. As a kid, I used to draw and make figures by carving from soap or wood before we moved from New Mexico to a stock farm in Arkansas. After high school, I planned on attending the Kansas City Art Institute, but I was a member of the Arkansas National Guard and went to Korea instead. After my discharge, I obtained a drafting job and studied engineering at night. We had a small place outside of Tulsa where I continued on with my artwork.

"In 1970, we made the decision to give up the job, move to Taos, establish the Western Art Gallery, and go into art full time. It was rough the first couple of years, but it turned out to be the best move I ever made. I have known my roots and never denied them. They gave me joy as a child, strength and tenacity as a growing man, and I am now reaping the rewards doing what I know best. I tell my family story everyday I work. For those who have never ridden a horse in open country, Western art gives everyone a chance to feel some saddle sores." Woods is represented by In The Spirit Gallery and Son Silver West and was written up in *Southwest Art,* June 1978.

Woolschlager, Laura. Painter in acrylics of mystical images of Western American Indians and coyotes, born in Dallas, Texas in 1932 and living in Omak, Washington. According to her, "I have heard remarks at shows ranging from 'Jeez, this is weird stuff' to 'Delightfully refreshing' or simply 'I really like it.' I have learned not to be put down by the former or ego-inflated by the latter. Some of the most marvelous responses are from children, because their reactions are spontaneous and honest and they could care less if you are listening."

After starting art lessons at seven in an Evanston, Illinois studio, she received her BA with honors in painting and design from Syracuse University and then took four months in Europe to tour the museums and galleries. For the next fourteen years, she "free lanced, doing everything from poster designs, logos, letterheads, and illustrations for ads to window displays." Her first one-person show was in Oregon in 1966. Although she is not of Indian descent, she was artist-in-residence at the Museum of Native American Culture in Spokane during 1979.

She paints Indians not with historical accuracy in mind but for "the commonality of all basic human needs. I am not a romantic historian attempting to depict life as it was in an era in which I did not live. For the past 25 years, though, I have lived adjacent to three different reservations and have found friends among people of Native American heritage. I hope my paintings will promote understanding without contributing to the over-worked image of the Indian as the 'noble savage.' " She was written up in *Art West,* January 1980, was in the 1980 Western Experience auction, and is represented by Gallery Select and Loudenbergh Galleries.

J.D. Woods, SWAPPIN' LIES, h 19, w 22

Laura Woolschlager, SUNFLOWER SONG, acrylic, 18 x 22

Reagan Word

T. Wounded Face

David Wright

Word, Reagan. Realist painter of wildlife and nature in dry brush watercolor, born in San Antonio, Texas in 1944 and living in Sedona, Arizona since 1979. "I would like my paintings to do more than just accurately portray the physical structure of an animal and please the eye," Word emphasizes. "There is a oneness in all of life. There is as much delight in watching a bumblebee obtain nectar from a flower as there is in observing the affairs of some of nature's more magnificent creatures."

Raised in Fort Worth, Word graduated from the University of Texas in 1967 with a degree in architecture. He practiced architecture for seven years and feels that his experience was an asset in his development as an artist. The first paintings he made when he launched his art career in 1974 were nostalgic scenes of old Texas farmhouses and windmills. He also painted contemporary Western scenes and character studies. As soon as he began painting animals, he found his niche. Gray Stone Press published his "Snowy Owl" and Husberg Fine Arts Gallery represented him for original paintings.

"Nature is my inspiration," Word states. "I see expressions of an inner power at work everywhere, yielding incredible balance and richness." Word starts with a detailed pencil drawing, refining it until he is satisfied. Dry brush watercolor is the final medium. Some of the smaller animals with highly developed camouflage may barely be discernable in their settings. A member of the Society of Animal Artists, Word stresses that "it would be of great satisfaction to me to know that through my paintings the viewers were inspired to feel a reverence for life and a sense of oneness with all of God's creation."

Wounded Face, Tex. Modernist sculptor of Indian symbolism in alabaster and bronze, born in Watford City west of the Fort Berthold Reservation in North Dakota in 1955 and living in Owyhee, Nevada. As the final project in his high school welding class, he submitted a welded bust of a Mandan Indian along with the dustpans and tool boxes of his classmates. The teacher who did not know that the sculpture had been in process in the back of the room for six months stopped dead when he saw it, hesitated, then gave the piece an A.

Of Hidatsa-Mandan descent, Wounded Face's early talent was recognized by the Institute of American Indian Arts when he was accepted in 1971 for study under the important Apache sculptor Allan Houser. With Houser's encouragement, Wounded Face was exhibiting and selling sculpture that same year. He has continued exhibiting and winning awards while studying at Arizona State University in 1977–78, Boise State University in 1979–80, and San Francisco Art Institute in 1980–81.

"I have often felt," he says, that "the general public is unaware of contemporary native art and what we native artists are about. I feel the need to bring about a certain awareness of our country's most natural resource, the indigenous people and their art. In the past, native art has been viewed as 'utilitarian,' then native art was exploited for tourism, then our art became 'trinkets.' The curio stores helped make them commercialized. Today, we artists have transcended to a higher plane of thought, where our pieces are portraying a moment of emotion or of symbolic gesture. In my sculpture, I utilize symbolism a great deal." His works have sold at exhibitions and associated craft centers.

Wright, David. Realist painter of landscapes and mountain men in casein and gouache, born near Horse Branch, Kentucky in 1942 and living in Cross Plains, Tennessee. "Prints are big business now," he emphasizes, "and any artist who denies it is just kidding himself. Landscapes, country scenes, and barns are strong right now. I've found that people are going to buy what they like whether the print was pulled by hand or manufactured."

Raised where he could trap beaver in his backyard, he "grew up on a farm taking care of animals, but I'd been drawing pictures at home since who knows when." After two years of art school and study in Italy, he served in the Army during the Vietnam war and then worked in illustration and design, saying that "I've never regretted that I went into commercial art first. I know it will help with the prints and I think I can better determine what attracts the public. We never print more than 3,000 of my paintings, but the public doesn't care. They want something they like. That's really what art is all about, isn't it?

"Why is it everybody always wants to compare your work to someone else's? It really burns me up. I don't *fashion* my work after anyone's. We all absorb certain things from the people we like, no matter what their profession. I admire Sargent and Wyeth. I also like Michael Coleman—but that's as far as it goes. I guess I regress to my childhood sometimes. All my work actually parallels some part of my youth or centers around my life on the farm. I wonder what a psychiatrist would say about that?" Written up in *Southwest Art,* September 1979, he is published by Gray Stone Press and represented by Altermann Art.

Tex Wounded Face, GRANDFATHER'S PRAYER
alabaster, h 17

Reagan Word, REDROCK CROSSING, watercolor, 13 x 17

David Wright, UP THE SOUTH SLOPE, casein, 26 x 36

joan wright   BOB WYGANT

Wright, Joan. Traditional oil painter "of the American West as it was or might have been, as well as what we have today of what once was," born in Dayton, Ohio in 1933 and living in Sylmar, California. "Women had a very important role in the development of the West," she points out, "but that role was not acknowledged as glamorously as the men of the Old West. To some extent, I carry this on, as I find I can do more with a male character, I suppose because essentially men had the 'freedom' to the heroic, the outrageous, and so on.

"Ever since I could remember, almost like a reincarnation, the West has fascinated me. Moving to California when I was twelve, I spent countless hours watching Westerns when I wasn't out exploring the countryside or gathering a great collection of books on the West. I now follow the 'present day' cowboys, gunslingers, mountain men, soldiers, fallen doves, etc. There are, all over this country, people who have a great affinity for the Old West. They have formed clubs, regiments, encampments, and they hold rendezvous.

"I spend much time at these events, getting to know these people, taking thousands of photographs. The time spent with history gives me the 'feeling' of being in the Old West as I, too, get lost in my fantasy. These things I put together, in conjunction with my personal research and studies, to compose a painting or drawing. I have won over 100 principal awards in exhibitions all over the country. My major publisher besides Keefner & Wright is Ira Roberts. My galleries include Casa Dolores and Files'." Written up in *Southwest Art*, May 1977, she is a member of Women Artists of the American West.

Wygant, Charles Robert, Jr. Traditional painter of Texas landscapes, scenes, and still-lifes in acrylic, born in Houston, Texas in 1927 and still living there. As Bob Wygant paints, questions challenge him: Who walked here? What was it like? What would I have been doing if I had lived in this place 100 years ago? What strangers have passed here? Who owned this cabin, drank from the stream?

His father, an amateur artist, was manager of the Heights Movie Theater and gave Wygant movie posters to copy, while his grandfather took him hunting and fishing. At eight, he was reading about art and at thirteen he received his first set of paints after he learned the basic rules in school. When he graduated from high school in 1945, he had a choice of twenty art scholarships but he volunteered as a staff artist in the Marines. Home by 1947, he entered the University of Texas and majored in art until his benefits under the G.I. Bill ran out.

He was soon commissioned by Humble Oil to do three paintings. Creole Petroleum then contracted for a series requiring trips to South America over a period of two years, and that was followed by four other industrial commissions. In 1960, he was appointed an art instructor at the University of Houston and after eleven years became a full time Assistant Professor. Personal commissions continued in his spare time and by 1976 the demand for this paintings left him no time for teaching. His work appeared in *Fortune*, the *Saturday Evening Post*, and *True West*. Limited edition prints were issued and his largest collector began reprinting his paintings as calendars. In 1981, he won Best in Show at the Texas Ranger Hall of Fame. He is represented by American Masters Foundation.

Joan Wright, ACOMA TREASURE, oil, 18 x 24

Bob Wygant, DOUBLE BEAUTY, acrylic, 30 x 40

Lidabelle Wylie W.A.O.A.W.

Paul Wylie

Webb Young

Wylie, Lidabelle. Sculptor and painter of Western scenes and subjects, particularly the cowboy and the pack mule, born in a lumber camp in Kopiah, Washington in 1915 and living on a ranch near Three Rivers, California since 1946. "In 1919," she recalls, "we moved to a homestead in the California mountains where we camped under a huge pine tree. My first artistic urge showed up when instead of making mud pies like my sister, I fashioned 'people' and horses to dry in the sun.

"Throughout my whole life, I have painted, carved, decorated, and created. As I grew and improved, I was always in demand and soon discovered that people would actually pay for my artwork. I have always been eager to learn and in high school took every art course possible. At graduation, I was all signed up to attend college on an art scholarship, but that is when the Depression caught up with me. I eventually married and worked side by side with my husband. We dry-land farmed and raised cattle.

"It was not until our children were grown that I could get completely involved in my artwork. I am a slow painter and everything must be right in my head before I start, still I have won many honors in watercolor and oil. I did not work in bronze until 1975. Like everything else in my life, I just decided to do it, and did. Winning the 1981 Judges' Trophy for best sculpture with more than fifty artists participating, including CAA, AICA, and WA artists, men and women, boosted my confidence. I was accepted into the Women Artists of the American West in 1977 and have participated in their shows all over the West." She exhibits in her own Canyon Gifts shop.

Wylie, Paul. Realist sculptor and painter of contemporary cowboy life in the Southwest, born in Lubbock County, Texas in 1933 and living in Lubbock. "Only a handful of men," Wylie observes, "now remain who lived in the freedom of the cowboy way of life as Will James described it. He captured the open range cowboy in as good a way as it can be. I hope that my work will describe where his left off, for future generations to look at and enjoy."

Earning a working cowboy's wages at twelve, Wylie worked alongside his father until he was 21, then moved on to other West Texas and New Mexico ranches as hand or as manager for eighteen years. In 1970, he decided to try painting as a hobby and was encouraged to take a beginner's oil painting class at South Plains College. After one year, he had his first one-person show and then continued in college for two more semesters. The instructor gave Wylie a slab of wax to try modeling, but it was not until 1974 that Wylie had the money to pay for bronze castings.

In 1976, Wylie was elected to membership in the Texas Cowboy Artists Association, and from 1978 to 1981, he won two gold awards, one silver, Texas Cowboy Artist of the Year, and Most Popular work. "I try to keep everything realistic," he stresses. "In one bronze, I have a cowboy sailing over the head of a bucking horse, an actual happening. We kidded the man about what a pretty arch he made, and he remarked, 'Well, at least I looked him eye to eye.' In the bronze, he is looking the horse eye to eye as he goes over." Wyle exhibits with the Texas Cowboy Artist Association, is represented exclusively by International Galleries, and shows his work at the gallery in his home.

Young, Webb. Realist painter of the customs and people of today's Southwest, born in Covington, Kentucky in 1913 and living in Phoenix, Arizona since 1976. "I am a colorist," Young says, "having had this drummed into me as a student of the famous Southwestern painter Gerald Cassidy in New Mexico from 1925 to 1928. I still use Cassidy's palette of colors. Perhaps what makes my work different is the 'idea' put into each painting—realistic, story-telling, but more: a certain slant on the subject having grown out of knowing by personal experience everything I paint."

Raised in Winnetka, Illinois, Young started his career at eleven with Saturday classes at the Chicago Art Institute. At twelve, he was with Cassidy and in 1927 he studied in Vienna. He took additional training at the Chicago Art Institute in 1933 and moved to Santa Fe in 1934 where he continued working as a commercial artist, painting covers for *New Mexico Magazine* and for the National Park Service. He also took a refresher course with the Famous Artists School and recently studied at the Instituto de Allende in Mexico.

Young's book on how to paint watercolors emphasizes his practice of not holding to any one style or technique, although he says that "people seem to be able to recognize a work of mine as distinctively a Webb Young. I love scenery. I like people—the Spanish, the Indian, the cowboy as they are now. I enjoy the super-realism of still-life subjects. So realistic are my watercolor still-lifes that people think they are acrylic or oil." Young has been featured in the Ford *Times* and the Denver *Post*, and he is represented by Fowler's Gallery.

Paul Wylie, TRACKS ALREADY—
DAM' WATERCOLOR GAP. bronze. h 24. w 10

Webb Young, COCHITI SCARECROW, oil, 36 x 24

Lidabelle Wylie, JOURNEY'S END, oil, 16 x 20

Zemsky, Jessica. Painter of past and present Montana ranch life, particularly of women and children, born in New York City in 1923 and living in Big Timber, Montana since 1975. "There were people in those wagons, you know," she points out, "the ones we only see depicted from the outside. People trying to stay healthy and unafraid; mothers being doctor, nurse, Sunday school teacher, and backbone of the family—waiting for the man who did the riding and hunting."

Raised in New York City and a graduate of Pratt Institute Art School in Brooklyn, she became an advertising and editorial illustrator, a world traveler, and an authority on the Old Masters. Her introduction to the West was a 1965 pack trip to the Bob Marshall Wilderness in Montana. She met Jack Hines in New York City when they shared commercial art assignments. After Hines went to Montana in 1972 to manage a ranch and then began working as a fine artist in Big Timber in 1974, she moved West in 1975 to marry him and paint full time.

"Too many misunderstood the Indian whose wife walked behind," she explains. "This was an expression of protection. Those were dangerous times. In truth, the Indian's family life and his love for his children were extremely strong." Hines adds that "while my own art tends entirely toward the masculine, she does a sensitive and perceptive treatment of the softer side of the early days." They share a one-room studio, working only a few feet apart, and both are members of the Northwest Rendezvous Group. She was featured in *Southwest Art*, February 1980, is published by Mill Pond Press, and her gouache was listed at $4,000 by Trailside Galleries in 1982.

Zesch, Gene. Caricaturist of the modern cowboy in wood and bronze, born in Mason, Texas in 1932 and living there in 1982. "I have chosen caricature to record the hard times faced by working ranchers of the past forty years," Zesch explains, "something I am very familiar with. These folks are still out here. They don't have oil wells, a medical practice, or anything else to supplement a miserable ranch income. They're not ranching for tax purposes—their losses are real. There is no logical reason for their existence, but they keep hanging on."

Born into a family that settled the ranch country in the 19th century, Zesch rode his horse four miles to school. After graduating from Texas A&M in 1953 with a degree in animal husbandry, he was an Army pilot from 1954 to 1957. When he saw woodcarvings for sale in Santa Fe in 1954, he said that he could "carve that well," and without training he started in. By the early 1960s, he was carving full time.

"Some people don't consider woodcarving a fine art," he points out. "When I started, I'd sell a figure for $25. Now it costs $1,000 to $6,000." He adds that "wood is the best medium for caricature. My painted bronzes are cast directly from the woodcarvings." Most of his work is about "the aging, hard-luck modern cowboy in southwestern rural America," and "all are Zesch's neighbors." He is prouder that famous Western artists buy his work than he is that a President and other public figures are his collectors. He has been featured in *Artists of the Rockies*, winter 1977, *Texas Highways*, August 1975, *Art West*, spring 1979, and other publications, and is represented by Trailside Galleries and Overland Trail Galleries.

Jessica Zemsky, THE FAMILY, gouache, 28 x 22

Gene Zesch, I SEE BY YOUR OUTFIT THAT YOU ARE A COWBOY
painted bronze, h 12, w 9

GALLERIES

The following is a list of galleries artists within this book identified as their primary gallery representation.

ABERBACH FINE ART
  New York, New York
ACA GALLERY
  New York, New York
ACE POWELL ART GALLERY
  Kalispell, Montana
ACKERMANNS GALLERY
  London, England
ADAGIO GALLERIES
  Palm Springs, California
ADAMS-MIDDLETON GALLERY
  Dallas, Texas
A. HUNEY GALLERY
  San Diego, California
ALDRIDGE FINE ART GALLERY, INC.
  Albuquerque, New Mexico
ALTERMANN ART GALLERY
  Dallas, Texas
AMERICAN ART GALLERY
  Seattle, Washington
AMERICAN FINE ARTS GALLERY
  Irving, Texas
AMERICAN LEGACY GALLERY
  Kansas City, Missouri
AMERICAN WEST GALLERIES
  Loveland, Colorado
THE AMERICAN WESTERN COLLECTION
  Bozeman, Montana
ANASAZI GALLERY OF ART
  Flagstaff, Arizona
  Sedona, Arizona
ANDRAUD STUDIO
  Los Angeles, California
ANKRUM GALLERY
  Los Angeles, California
ANNE MAGEE GALLERY
  Scottsdale, Arizona
ARENA GALLERY
  Houston, Texas
ART BARN
  Farmington, New Mexico
A.R.T./BEASLEY GALLERY
  San Diego, California
ART ECLECTIC
  Billings, Montana
ART ENTERPRISES
  La Porte, Colorado
ART GALLERIES AT BAHIA MAR RESORT
  South Padre Island, Texas
THE ART GALLERY
  Cheyenne, Wyoming

THE ART MARKET
  Tulsa, Oklahoma
ART OF THE WEST GALLERY
  Scottsdale, Arizona
ART RESOURCES
  Denver, Colorado
ART STREAM GALLERY
  Grand Junction, Colorado
ARTHUR ACKERMANN & SONS
  New York, New York
ARTHUR SUSSMAN GALLERY
  Albuquerque, New Mexico
ARTIQUE, LTD.
  Anchorage, Alaska
THE ARTISAN'S SHOP & GALLERY
  Ruidoso, New Mexico
THE ARTIST'S GALLERY
  Lancaster, California
ARTISTIC GALLERY
  Scottsdale, Arizona
ARTISTS CO-OP GALLERY
  Reno, Nevada
THE ARTISTS' UNION GALLERY
  Bozeman, Montana
ASPEN TREE GALLERY
  Aspen, Colorado
ATLAS GALLERY
  Chicago, Illinois
AUSTIN GALLERY
  Scottsdale, Arizona
AUSTIN-BROWN GALLERY
  Irving, Texas
BAKER GALLERY OF FINE ART
  Lubbock, Texas
THE BARN GALLERY
  Shawnee Mission, Kansas
BECKETT GALLERY
  Hamilton, Ontario, Canada
BENT TREE GALLERY
  Dallas, Texas
BERNHART FINE ARTS GALLERY
  Kansas City, Missouri
BIG BEND ART GALLERY
  Alpine, Texas
BIG HORN GALLERY
  Cody, Wyoming
BILL COUSINS' TOWNHOUSE GALLERIES
  New Orleans, Louisiana
BILTMORE GALLERIES
  Los Angeles, California

BISHOP GALLERY
Scottsdale, Arizona
BLEICH GALLERIES
Carmel, California
East Gloucester, Massachusetts
BLUE MOUNTAIN GALLERY
Fossil, Oregon
(BOB HIGGINS') TRAILS WEST GALLERY
Laguna Beach, California
BOUTWELL GALLERY LIMITED
Austin, Texas
BRANDYWINE GALLERIES LTD.
Albuquerque, New Mexico
BRECKENRIDGE GALLERIES
Breckenridge, Colorado
BRIDGER FOUNDRY & GALLERY
Bozeman, Montana
BRUBAKER GALLERY
Sarasota, Florida
BRUSH GALLERY
Houston, Texas
BUCK SAUNDERS TRADING POST AND GALLERY
Scottsdale, Arizona
THE BURK GAL'RY
Boulder City, Nevada
CALIFORNIA FINE ARTS GALLERY
Pasadena, California
CANYON GIFTS
Three Rivers, California
CARLIN GALLERIES
Fort Worth, Texas
CARR GALLERY
Fort Worth, Texas
CARSON GALLERY OF WESTERN AMERICAN ART
Denver, Colorado
CASA DOLORES ART GALLERY
Carmel-By-The-Sea, California
CENTER ART GALLERIES
Honolulu, Hawaii
C.G. REIN GALLERIES
Edina, Minnesota
Denver, Colorado
Houston, Texas
Santa Fe, New Mexico
Scottsdale, Arizona
CHAMPIONS ART GALLERY
Houston, Texas
CHRISMAN TRADE WIND GALLERIES
Dexter, Missouri
CIA BELLAS ARTES
Albuquerque, New Mexico

CIRCLE GALLERIES
New York, New York
CJS GALLERY
Denver, Colorado
CLOSSON GALLERY
Cincinnati, Ohio
CODY GALLERY
Los Olivos, California
COLLECTORS COVEY
Dallas, Texas
THE COLLECTORS GALLERY
Kelowna, British Columbia, Canada
THE COLLECTORS GALLERY OF FINE ART
Taos, New Mexico
COLORADO ART GALLERY
Englewood, Colorado
CONACHER GALLERIES
Venice, Florida
CONCHO GALLERY, INC.
San Angelo, Texas
COPENHAGEN GALLERI
Solvang, California
CORNELL NORBY
Fullerton, California
CORPUS CHRISTI ART GALLERY
Corpus Christi, Texas
COSMOPOLITAN FINE ART GALLERY
Denver, Colorado
COTTONWOOD GALLERY
Kalispell, Montana
COUNTRY ART GALLERY
Locust Valley, New York
THE COUNTRY FRAMER
Lubbock, Texas
COUNTRY STORE GALLERY
Austin, Texas
COWHAND COLLECTIONS
Claresholm, Alberta, Canada
CR GALLERY
Williston, North Dakota
CROSS GALLERIES
Fort Worth, Texas
DEGENBELA GALERIA
San Antonio, Texas
DASSIN GALLERY
Los Angeles, California
DAVIS • McLAIN GALLERIES
Houston, Texas
DE COLORES ART GALLERY
Denver, Colorado

DE GALLERY
Bozeman, Montana
DeGRAZIA GALLERY IN THE SUN
Tucson, Arizona
DEWEY-KOFRON GALLERY
Santa Fe, New Mexico
DOUBLE CHECK WESTERN GALLERY
Morro Bay, California
DOUBLE T RANCH GALLERY
Lubbock, Texas
DRISCOL GALLERY
Denver, Colorado
DUBOSE GALLERY
Houston, Texas
EAGLE ART GALLERY, INC.
La Jolla, California
EDDIE BAUER STORE
Seattle, Washington
EL MUNDO MAGICO GALLERY
Sedona, Arizona
EL TALLER
Austin, Texas
ELAINE HORWITCH GALLERIES
Scottsdale, Arizona
Santa Fe, New Mexico
ENCHANTED MESA
Albuquerque, New Mexico
ENTHIOS GALLERY
Santa Fe, New Mexico
ESCONDIDO GALLERY
Rockport, Texas
FAVELL MUSEUM OF ART & ARTIFACTS
Klamath Falls, Oregon
FENN GALLERIES LTD.
Santa Fe, New Mexico
FILES' GALLERY OF FINE ARTS
Big Bear Lake, California
FINLEY POINT GALLERY
Polson Bay Side, Montana
FLATHEAD LAKE GALLERIES
Bigfork, Montana
FLATLANDER GALLERY
Carthage, Missouri
FLUSCHE FINE ART GALLERY
Tulsa, Oklahoma
FOLGER RANCH GALLERY
Midland, Texas
FOSTER/WHITE GALLERY
Seattle, Washington
FOUR SEASONS GALLERY
Jackson, Wyoming
FREEMAN GALLERIES
Peachland, British Columbia, Canada

FRIGHTENED OWL
Santa Fe, New Mexico
FROST GULLY GALLERY
Portland, Maine
GAINSBOROUGH GALLERY
Calgary, Alberta, Canada
GALERIA CAPISTRANO
San Juan Capistrano, California
GALERIA D'OROS
Ruidoso, New Mexico
GALERIA DEL SOL
Old Town, Albuquerque, New Mexico
GALERIA SIGALA
Taos, New Mexico
THE GALLERIA
Norman, Oklahoma
GALLERIE MARGUERITE
Durango, Colorado
THE GALLERIES
San Angelo, Texas
GALLERY A
Taos, New Mexico
GALLERY AMERICANA
Santa Fe, New Mexico
GALLERY AT SHOAL CREEK
Austin, Texas
GALLERY BRONZE
Mapleton, Utah
GALLERY 85
Billings, Montana
GALLERY G FINE ARTS
Wichita, Kansas
GALLERY-McGOFFIN
Phoenix, Arizona
GALLERY OF THE SOUTHWEST
Houston, Texas
GALLERY SELECT
Seattle, Washington
GALLERY 10
Scottsdale, Arizona
Aspen, Colorado
GALLERY 3
Phoenix, Arizona
GALLERY 203
Taos, New Mexico
THE GALLERY WALL
Scottsdale, Arizona
GALLERY WEST
Portland, Oregon
GALLERY WEST & FRAME PLANT
Laramie, Wyoming
Cheyenne, Wyoming
GARDEN OF THE GODS ART GALLERY
Colorado Springs, Colorado

GASPARD HOUSE AND MUSEUM
  Taos, New Mexico
GATEWAY ART GALLERIES
  Palm Beach, Florida
GEMINI GALLERY
  Palm Beach, Florida
GENE MAKO GALLERIES
  Los Angeles, California
GIORDANO ART LTD.
  Douglaston, New York
THE GLORY HOLE
  Lake City, Colorado
GOLDEN WILLOW GALLERY
  Taos, New Mexico
GRAND CENTRAL ART GALLERIES
  New York, New York
GRENDE LA FORD WESTERN ART STUDIO
  Clarkson, Washington
GRIZZLY TREE GALLERY
  Gunnison, Colorado
GRYCNER GALLERY
  Taos, New Mexico
HADLER/RODRIGUEZ GALLERIES
  Houston, Texas
HAGGENMAKER GALLERIES
  Laguna Beach, California
HAMBURG ART GALLERY
  Sedona, Arizona
HAMMER GALLERIES
  New York, New York
HANG UPS
  Orange, California
HANGING TREE GALLERY
  Midland, Texas
THE HARRISON GALLERY
  Vancouver, British Columbia, Canada
HERRMANN GALLERY
  Estes Park, Colorado
HEYDT-BAIR GALLERY
  Santa Fe, New Mexico
HILL'S ART CENTER
  Denver, Colorado
HOBE SOUND GALLERY
  Hobe Sound, Florida
HOLDEN'S WESTERN GALLERY
  Blue River, Oregon
THE HOLE IN THE WALL GALLERY
  Ennis, Montana
HOUSE OF BRONZE FINE ARTS
  Prescott, Arizona
HOUSHANG'S GALLERY
  Dallas, Texas
HOWARD BOBBS' GALLERY
  Santa Fe, New Mexico

HUBBELL'S GALLERY
  Weaverville, California
HUNTER GALLERY
  San Francisco, California
HUSBERG FINE ARTS GALLERY
  Sedona, Arizona
ILONA RITTLER GALLERY
  Bellevue, Washington
IMAGE WEST
  San Mateo, California
IMAGES GALLERY
  Minneapolis, Minnesota
IN THE SPIRIT GALLERY
  Kansas City, Kansas
INDIAN PAINTBRUSH GALLERY, INC.
  Siloam Springs, Arkansas
INTERNATIONAL ACADEMY OF
WESTERN ART & SCULPTURES LTD.
  Calgary, Alberta, Canada
INTERNATIONAL FINE ART GALLERY
  San Bruno, California
INTERNATIONAL GALLERIES
  Ruidoso, New Mexico
INTERNATIONAL GALLERY
  Vancouver, Washington
INVESTORS GALLERY LTD.
  Lake Oswego, Oregon
IVORY/KIMPTON GALLERY
  San Francisco, California
JAMES M. HANEY GALLERY
  Amarillo, Texas
JAMES PETER COST GALLERY
  Carmel, California
JAMISON GALLERIES
  Santa Fe, New Mexico
JANUS GALLERY
  Santa Fe, New Mexico
J. HARKEN AND ASSOCIATES FINE ART GALLERY
  Spokane, Washington
JIM FOWLER'S PERIOD GALLERY WEST
  Scottsdale, Arizona
JIM THOMAS BRONZE FOUNDRY & GALLERY
  Leander, Texas
JINX GALLERY
  El Paso, Texas
JOAN CAWLEY GALLERY
  Wichita, Kansas
JOE WADE FINE ARTS
  Santa Fe, New Mexico
JOHN PENCE GALLERY
  San Francisco, California
JOHNSON GALLERY
  Bisbee, Arizona

JONES GALLERY
La Jolla, California
JOY TASH GALLERY
Scottsdale, Arizona
JUDITH STERN GALLERY
Minneapolis, Minnesota
KACHINA GALLERY
Santa Fe, New Mexico
KANSAS GALLERY OF FINE ARTS
Topeka, Kansas
KEESE-SOUTHWEST GALLERY
Kerrville, Texas
KENNEDY GALLERIES, INC.
New York, New York
KERN COLLECTIBLES
Stillwater, Minnesota
KESLER ART GALLERY
San Diego, California
LA CASA GALLERY
Abilene, Texas
LA GALLERIA
Kerrville, Texas
LA PORTA ART GALLERY
Englewood, Colorado
LAST STRAW GALLERY
Old Town, Albuquerque, New Mexico
LAUGHING HORSE GALLERY
Salt Lake City, Utah
LAURA POLLAK GALLERIES
San Diego, California
LESLI ART INC.
Sherman Oaks, California
LESLIE B. DeMILLE GALLERY
Laguna Beach, California
LIDO GALLERY
Provo, Utah
LIMITED EDITIONS GALLERY
Palm Desert, California
LINCOLN ART GALLERY
Lincoln City, Oregon
LINCOLN FOX STUDIO & GALLERY
Alto, New Mexico
LINDA McADOO GALLERIES
Santa Fe, New Mexico
LINE CAMP GALLERY
Story, Wyoming
LIVE OAK COLLECTIONS LTD.
San Dimas, California
LOS LLANOS GALLERY
Santa Fe, New Mexico
THE LOST DUTCHMAN GALLERY
Tahoe City, California
LOUDENBERGH GALLERIES
Anchorage, Alaska

LUNDEEN GALLERY
Las Cruces, New Mexico
MAGIC MOUNTAIN GALLERY
Taos, New Mexico
MAIN TRAIL GALLERIES
Jackson Hole, Wyoming
Scottsdale, Arizona
MAMMEN GALLERY II
Scottsdale, Arizona
MANITOU GALLERY
Cheyenne, Wyoming
MANY HORSES GALLERY
Los Angeles, California
MARILYN BUTLER FINE ART
Scottsdale, Arizona
MARJORIE KAUFFMAN GALLERIES
Houston, Texas
MARTIN G GALLERY
Scottsdale, Arizona
MATTSON GALLERY
Denver, Colorado
MAXWELL GALLERY
San Francisco, California
THE MAY GALLERY
Scottsdale, Arizona
Jackson, Wyoming
McCORMICK ART GALLERY
Midland, Texas
McCULLEY FINE ARTS GALLERY, INC.
Dallas, Texas
MEINERS GALLERY
Yreka, California
MEINHARD GALLERIES
Houston, Texas
MEREDITH LONG & CO.
Houston, Texas
MERRILL CHASE GALLERY
Chicago, Illinois
MERRILL'S GALLERY
Taos, New Mexico
MIKAEL REDMAN STUDIO
Scottsdale, Arizona
MILLER STUDIO
DeBorgia, Montana
MINER'S GALLERY AMERICANA
Carmel-By-The-Sea, California
MINNESOTA WILDLIFE INC.
Minneapolis, Minnesota
MONAC GALLERY
Spokane, Washington
MONTANA GALLERY AND BOOK SHOPPE
Helena, Montana
MOODY GALLERY
Houston, Texas

MORAN GALLERY
Tulsa, Oklahoma
MORGAN GALLERIES
Austin, Texas
MORRIS FINE ARTS
Scottsdale, Arizona
MOULTON GALLERIES
Fort Smith, Arkansas
MOUNTAIN ROAD GALLERIES
Albuquerque, New Mexico
MUNSON GALLERY
Santa Fe, New Mexico
MYER'S GALLERY
Park City, Utah
MYLES GALLERY
Scottsdale, Arizona
NANCY HOFFMAN GALLERY
New York, New York
NAVAJO GALLERY
Taos, New Mexico
Albuquerque, New Mexico
NELDA LEE INC.
Odessa, Texas
NEVADA ARTS, INC.
Las Vegas, Nevada
NEWSOM'S GALLERY
Las Vegas, Nevada
O'BRIEN'S ART EMPORIUM
Scottsdale, Arizona
OLD TOWN ART GALLERY
Oak Harbor, Washington
THE OLD WORLD
Dallas, Texas
ONE MAIN GALLERY
Dallas, Texas
OUT OF THE WILD ART GALLERY
Janesville, Wisconsin
OVERLAND TRAIL GALLERIES
Scottsdale, Arizona
Jackson Hole, Wyoming
PA-JO'S GALLERY
Pinedale, Wyoming
PACIFIC WESTERN TRADERS
Folsom, California
PALMCREST ART GALLERY
Long Beach, California
PARK FIFTH AVENUE GALLERY
Scottsdale, Arizona
PARKCREST GALLERY
Austin, Texas
PARKE GALLERY
Vail, Colorado
PAUL METCALF GALLERY
Pasadena, California

THE PEACOCK GALLERIES LTD.
Jackson, Wyoming
Scottsdale, Arizona
PELHAM GALLERY
Santa Fe, New Mexico
PEPPERTREE FINE ART, INC.
Calabasas, California
PETERSEN GALLERIES
Beverly Hills, California
PETERSON GALLERY
Bellevue, Washington
THE PINON TREE
Old Town, Albuquerque, New Mexico
PIVAN GALLERY
Boulder, Colorado
PONDEROSA GALLERY
Kalispell, Montana
PRAIRIE HOUSE GALLERY
Abilene, Texas
THE PRINTER'S GALLERY
Austin, Texas
PRUITT PLACE GALLERIES
Fort Worth, Texas
PUTNEY GALLERY
Aspen, Colorado
QUAIL HOLLOW GALLERIES
Oklahoma City, Oklahoma
RAGLAND'S WOODLAND GALLERY
Running Springs, California
RAINONE GALLERIES INC.
Arlington, Texas
REGAL GALLERY
Paris, Texas
REMINISCE GALLERY
Fort Worth, Texas
RENDEZVOUS GALLERY
Anchorage, Alaska
RIATA GALLERY
Virginia City, Nevada
RICHARD HENKIN, INC.
Beverly Hills, California
RICHARD THOMPSON GALLERY
San Francisco, California
RIVOLI GALLERY
Salt Lake City, Utah
ROBIARD GALLERIES
Colorado Springs, Colorado
ROCKY MOUNTAIN GALLERY
Houston, Texas
ROSEMARY'S GALLERIES
Boise, Idaho
ROSENSTOCK GALLERY
Denver, Colorado

ROSEQUIST GALLERIES
Tucson, Arizona
RUSSELL A. FINK
Lorton, Virginia
RUSTIC REFLECTIONS GALLERY
Greybull, Wyoming
R.V. GREEVES ART GALLERY
Fort Washakie, Wyoming
SADDLEBACK WESTERN ART GALLERY
Santa Ana, California
SAGEBRUSH GALLERIES
Amarillo, Texas
SAGEBRUSH GALLERY
Medicine Lodge, Kansas
SAGEBRUSH GALLERY
Cody, Wyoming
SAKS GALLERY
Denver, Colorado
SALT CREEK GALLERIES
Casper, Wyoming
SANDERS GALLERIES
Tucson, Arizona
SANDRA WILSON GALLERIES
Denver, Colorado
SANTA FE EAST
Santa Fe, New Mexico
SANTA FE GALLERY
Santa Fe, New Mexico
SAVAGE GALLERIES
Santa Fe, New Mexico
SAXON MOUNTAIN GALLERY
Georgetown, Colorado
SCHMULAND AND HASTINGS
Portland, Oregon
SCRIVER STUDIO
Browning, Montana
SCULPTURED ARTS GALLERY
Sedona, Arizona
THE SELECTIVE EYE
Phoenix, Arizona
SERGI BONGART SCHOOL OF ART
Santa Monica, California
SETH'S CANYON ROAD ART GALLERY
Santa Fe, New Mexico
SETTING SUN GALLERY OF FINE ART
Amarillo, Texas
SETTLERS WEST GALLERIES, INC.
Tucson, Arizona
SHELTON GALLERIES
Wichita, Kansas
SHERWOOD GALLERY
Great Falls, Montana
SHIDONI GALLERY AND FOUNDRY
Tesuque, New Mexico

SHIRLEY MEYER'S GALLERY
Laguna Beach, California
SHORR GOODWIN GALLERY
Phoenix, Arizona
SHRIVER GALLERY
Taos, New Mexico
SIERRA GALLERIES
Orinda, California
SIGNATURE GALLERY
Scottsdale, Arizona
SIGOLOFF GALLERIES
San Antonio, Texas
SILO GALLERY
New Milford, Connecticut
SINGLETREE GALLERY OF WESTERN ART
Torrance, California
SLOAN-McKINNEY GALLERIES
Tulsa, Oklahoma
SMITH GALLERY
New York, New York
THE SOLDIER SHOP
New York, New York
SON SILVER WEST
Sedona, Arizona
SONG OF THE WIND GALLERY
Arroyo Seco, New Mexico
SOUTHWEST GALLERIES
Houston, Texas
SPARLING GALLERY
Bakersfield, California
SPORTSMAN'S EDGE LTD.
New York, New York
SPORTSMAN'S GALLERY
Houston, Texas
THE SQUASH BLOSSOM
Aspen, Colorado
STIHA GALLERY WESTERN ART
Santa Fe, New Mexico
STREMMEL GALLERIES LTD.
Reno, Nevada
STUDIO III GALLERY
Hyrum, Utah
SUMMER GALLERY
Santa Fe, New Mexico
SUZANNE BROWN GALLERY
Scottsdale, Arizona
SWANSON ART GALLERIES
San Francisco, California
THE TAGGART TRUST
Las Vegas, Nevada
TALISMAN GALLERY
Bartlesville, Oklahoma
TANNER'S INDIAN ARTS
Scottsdale, Arizona

TAOS ART GALLERY INC.
Taos, New Mexico
TAYLOR GALLERY
Houston, Texas
TEXAS ART GALLERY
Dallas, Texas
TEXAS T. GALLERY
Arlington, Texas
TEXAS TRAILS GALLERY
San Antonio, Texas
THOMPSON GALLERY
Stephenville, Texas
THOR'S ROYAL DANISH
RESTAURANT AND GALLERY
Fort Lauderdale, Florida
THUNDER BOW GALLERY
Taos, New Mexico
TIBOR de NAGY GALLERY
Houston, Texas
TIVOLI GALLERIES
Salt Lake City, Utah
TOM BAHTI INDIAN ART SHOP
Tucson, Arizona
TOM G. PHILLIPS AND ASSOCIATES
Los Angeles, California
TOUCH OF LOVE GALLERY, LTD.
Santa Fe, New Mexico
TRAIL'S END GALLERY
Portland, Oregon
TRAILS END GALLERY OF FINE ART
Ketchum, Idaho
TRAILSIDE GALLERIES
Scottsdale, Arizona
TRAMMELL'S FLYING T GALLERY
Azel, Texas
TROY ANDERSON STUDIO
Siloam Springs, Arkansas
TROY'S GALLERY
Scottsdale, Arizona
TWO GREY HILLS
Jackson, Wyoming
VALHALLA GALLERY
Wichita, Kansas
THE VARIANT GALLERY
Taos, New Mexico
VON GRABILLS GALLERY
Paradise Valley, Arizona
VORIS GALLERY
Salt Lake City, Utah
WADLE GALLERY
Santa Fe, New Mexico
WAGNER GALLERY
Austin, Texas
WAY WEST GALLERY
Scottsdale, Arizona

WEBB GALLERY
Amarillo, Texas
WESTERN ART ASSOCIATION
Ellensburg, Washington
WESTERN ART CLASSICS
Heber City, Utah
WESTERN ART INVESTMENTS
Kalispell, Montana
WESTERN FLYWAY LTD.
Seattle, Washington
WESTERN IMAGES
Cortez, Colorado
WESTSIDE GALLERY
El Paso, Texas
WESTWOOD GALLERIES
Portland, Oregon
WHITAKER GALLERY
Taos, New Mexico
WHITE BUFFALO GALLERY
Wichita, Kansas
THE WHITE GALLERY
West Lake Village, California
WHITNEY GALLERY
Taos, New Mexico
THE WICKENBURG GALLERY
Wickenburg, Arizona
WILD GOOSE GALLERY
Cheyenne, Wyoming
WILDLIFE OF AMERICA
Minneapolis, Minnesota
WILDLIFE WORLD ART MUSEUM
Monument, Colorado
WILLIAM V. DeLIND FINE ART
Milwaukee, Wisconsin
WILSON GALLERY
Fresno, California
WINDBERG ENTERPRISES, INC.
Austin, Texas
WINDSONG GALLERY
Tubac, Arizona
THE WINTERS GALLERY
Carmel, California
WOLDS LOFT
Portland, Oregon
WOOD RIVER GALLERY
Sun Valley, Idaho
WOODROW WILSON FINE ARTS
Santa Fe, New Mexico
WOUNDED KNEE GALLERY
Santa Monica, California
WYOMING FOUNDRY STUDIOS INC.
Cody, Wyoming
ZANTMAN ART GALLERIES LTD.
Palm Desert, California
Carmel, California

PUBLISHERS

The following is a list of print publishers artists
in this book identified as their primary print publishers.

AMERICAN MASTERS FOUNDATION
  Houston, Texas
ANNESLEY & ASSOCIATES, INC.
  Missouri City, Texas
ART FIRST, LTD.
  Cincinnati, Ohio
ART FRAME GALLERY
  Dayton, Ohio
  Scottsdale, Arizona
ARTS LIMITED INC.
  San Antonio, Texas
BACKTRAIL GALLERY
  Atlanta, Georgia
BLOOMFIELD COLLECTIONS
  Los Altos, California
CANYONLAND GRAPHICS
  Santa Fe, New Mexico
CIRCLE ART CORP.
  Chicago, Illinois
COLLECTORS COVEY
  Dallas, Texas
CONNOISSEURS' GALLERY OF ART, LTD.
  Schaumberg, Illinois
CORNHUSKER PRESS
  Hastings, Nebraska
DALLAS PRINTS
  Newburgh, New York
DEER CREEK PUBLISHING
  Colorado Springs, Colorado
DITA ADAM
  Albuquerque, New Mexico

EDWARD WESTON GRAPHICS
  Northridge, California
FRAME HOUSE GALLERY
  Louisville, Kentucky
FRONTIER PUBLISHING CO.
  Eugene, Oregon
FROST FINE ART CO.
  Austin, Texas
GALLART REPRODUCTIONS
  Gallup, New Mexico
GRAY STONE PRESS
  Nashville, Tennessee
GREENWICH WORKSHOP
  Trumbull, Connecticut
GUILDHALL, INC.
  Fort Worth, Texas
HARRISON GALLERIES
  Vancouver, British Columbia, Canada
INTERNATIONAL ARTS CONNECTION
  Anaheim Hills, California
IRA ROBERTS
  Beverly Hills, California
JACKIE FINE ARTS INC.
  New York, New York
LUTISHA PRESS
  Kirkland, Washington
MASTER ART RENDITIONS
  La Grange, Illinois
MASTERPIECE MOLDING AND FINE ART COMPANY
  Morganton, North Carolina

MILL POND PRESS INC.
  Venice, Florida
NATIONAL PRINT GALLERIES
  Scottsdale, Arizona
NEW MASTERS PUBLISHING CO., INC.
  Gulfport, Mississippi
OXMOOR HOUSE
  Birmingham, Alabama
PINE MOUNTAIN PUBLICATIONS
  Whittier, California
RANDOM PRESS
  Houston, Texas
REGENCY HOUSE ART INC.
  Plainview, New York
RICHARD HENKIN, INC.
  Beverly Hills, California
RIVERSHORE LTD.
  Caledonia, Michigan
ROBERT ANDRAUD INC.
  Los Angeles, California
SAGE PUBLISHING
  Cody, Wyoming
SALT CREEK GRAPHICS
  Casper, Wyoming
SCAFA TORNABENE ART PUBLISHING CO.
  White Plains, New York
SEABOURN STUDIO
  Oklahoma City, Oklahoma
SETTE PUBLISHING CO.
  Tempe, Arizona

SOARING WINGS
  Salem, Oregon
SOMERSET HOUSE
STARLINE PRINTING
  Albuquerque, New Mexico
THE STERLING PORTFOLIO, INC.
  New York, New York
THE STUART COLLECTION
TAMARIND
  Albuquerque, New Mexico
TEXAS ART PRESS
  Dallas, Texas
TRITON PRESS
  New York, New York
VOYAGEUR ART
  Minneapolis, Minnesota
WESTERN GRAPHICS WORKSHOP
  Albuquerque, New Mexico
WESTERN PROFILES PUBLISHING CO.
  Denver, Colorado
WILD WINGS INC.
  Lake City, Minnesota
WOLF CHIEF GRAPHICS
  Great Falls, Montana
WOLF CREEK PUBLISHING CO.
  Denton, Texas
THE WOODEN BIRD FACTORY
  St. Bonifacius, Minnesota